D0365042

Why They Don't Hate Us

Anti-Capitalism: A Beginner's Guide, Simon Tormey, ISBN
1–85168–342–9

Democracy: A Beginner's Guide, David Beetham, ISBN 1–85168–363–1

Global Outrage, Peter N. Stearns, ISBN 1–85168–364–X

Global Terrorism: A Beginner's Guide, Leonard Weinberg, ISBN
1–85168–358–5

NATO: A Beginner's Guide, Jennifer Medcalf, ISBN 1–85168–353–4

The Palestine–Israeli Conflict: A Beginner's Guide, Dan Cohn-Sherbok
and Dawoud El-Alami, ISBN 1–85168–332–1

Political Philosophy: A Historical Introduction, Michael J. White, ISBN
1–85168–328–3

Why They Don't Hate Us

Lifting the Veil on the Axis of Evil

Mark LeVine

ONEWORLD

OXFORD

WHY THEY DON'T HATE US

Oneworld Publications Limited
(Sales and Editorial)
185 Banbury Road
Oxford OX2 7AR
England
www.oneworld-publications.com

© Mark LeVine 2005

ISBN-13: 978–1–85168–365–9
ISBN-10: 1–85168–365–8

Cover design by Mungo Designs
Typeset by Saxon Graphics Ltd, Derby
Printed and bound in the USA by McNaughton & Gunn

Cover photographs © Corbis/Cadmium
Photograph on p. 275 courtesy of Andrew Stern

For Lola, Alessandro and Francesca
With love and hope

Contents

List of Illustrations

Preface

As I write these lines nuclear experts are betting that Muslim terrorists will detonate a thermonuclear bomb in a major American city before the end of this decade. George W. Bush polls lower than Osama bin Laden in much of the world, especially in the so-called Global South (what used to be referred to as the "Third World" or "Developing World"). Despite relatively successful elections and subsequent pro-democracy protests across the region, the US occupation of Iraq and the Israeli Occupation of Palestinian territories, which most of the world believes the US sanctions, have eroded America's global standing to an all-time low. A "clash of fundamentalisms" dominates the world stage, while a still inchoate global Left struggles to carve out space between the two extremes. As I'm digesting the news of impending Armageddon, the BBC News shows images of 30,000 protesters – including a couple of Chilean secret service agents – vociferously denouncing President Bush's policies at the annual APEC summit in that country.

Pages more of examples could be provided from yesterday's or tomorrow's news, but the story they'd tell would differ only in detail, not in substance or theme. The reality is that much if not most of the population of the world is angry at the United States and its economic, cultural, and geostrategic policies. It has got to the point that a book entitled *Why Do People Hate America* has become an "international bestseller" (or so its cover claims). Although I have not seen much evidence of it in my regular trips to Europe and the Muslim world, people tell me that they've never seen these regions as rife with anti-American sentiment as they are today.

Given the seeming endless supply of anger and even hatred across the globe – which, depending on whom you read, is either sometimes, often, or exclusively directed at the United States – it might seem strange to title a book *Why They Don't Hate Us*; but that is just what this book will argue. Indeed, not only am I firmly convinced that most of "them" don't hate most of "us," I'm equally convinced that the very idea that there is an "us" and a "them" is part of the problem that leads people to think that we and they can't get along. At least in the Middle East, North Africa, and Europe, the parts of the world I know best, the number of ways people define themselves, their cultural identities and attitudes, are too complex and varied to be subsumed under any one "they." (And if the pundits' take on the 2004 US Presidential election is to be believed, there are at least two "wes" populating the United States, and most likely a whole lot more.)

Moreover, I have rarely witnessed most of the various theys of the Muslim world (or "old Europe" for that matter) irrationally hating or uncritically denouncing the United States. Instead, as I will show in the pages that follow, the vast majority of the world's Muslims have a fairly accurate understanding of the political, economic, and cultural impact of American/"Western" policies that today fall under the rubric of "globalization." Certainly, the average Muslim is better informed about the United States or Europe than the average American is about Arab/Muslim, or even European, cultures and societies. To the extent that Muslims are critical of the United States or the larger West (which today would more appropriately be called the "Global North"), their reasons are as often as not quite rational – as the Pentagon's Defense Science Board put it, "they do not hate our freedom, they hate our policies" – and depending on the issue are likely to be shared by Americans on the Left or Right.

Yet despite the extent and often severity of the criticism, we should not be surprised that most Muslims want to engage with American and Western/Northern cultures – where, after all, millions of them live – as long as they can do so with some measure of cultural confidence and autonomy, and can at the same time participate in the globalized economy on terms that enhance rather than harm their economic well-being and life chances. In these sentiments they are joined by the vast majority of Europeans (old and new), South Americans, Africans, and other citizens of the so-called "Rest" of the world, who, as I show throughout this book, have many good reasons to be extremely upset about the policies of the United States and its allies, and the world they are creating.

Because of these sentiments, most Muslims have as little use or sympathy for terrorists as does the average American. Whether in Cairo or Karachi, Jakarta or Jenin, most citizens of the Muslim world, like their counterparts across the Global South, would much rather find ways to work with the citizens of the Global North to change these dynamics than struggle against them in some zero-sum contest for world supremacy – or worse, survival.

These comments should not be taken to suggest that all's well with the rest of the world, and the Muslim world specifically. There is overwhelming evidence that the majority of Muslim countries are poorer, less democratic, and more riven by internal and external conflicts than almost any other world region besides sub-Saharan Africa. Crucially, however, the sources of these problems don't lie in "what went wrong" with Islam, or in its supposed isolation from the unfolding of freedom, democracy, and Enlightenment of the last four centuries (as claimed by "experts" as diverse as Bernard Lewis and Irshad Manji). Rather, they will be found in the economic, political, and cultural structures of the world system as it evolved during the modern era, a system that has produced dysfunctional societies across the globe, and for whose problems the West bears at least as much responsibility as does Islam.

Indeed, as I show throughout this book, almost every pathology we can find in the Muslim world – from hate-filled ultra-conservative religious beliefs, to a glorification of violence, to faith-based, passive and depoliticized consumerism – has its counterpart in the Global North, and particularly in the United States. The difference is that while "we" are rich and powerful enough to binge, bully or bomb our way through the crises caused by our various disorders, "they" rarely have the luxury of such responses.

But Muslims are no longer willing to suffer in silence. In fact, they haven't been for quite some time, but it has only been with the spread of advanced technologies and the ever-increasing flows of people, money, and ideas that constitute globalization that Muslims have gained the power to make "us" stop and listen whether we want to or not. Of course, Europeans and Americans have long accused Muslims of being irrational, emotional, and childish; of having the bad taste to "cry and suffer out loud like children" (for which an American observer castigated Moroccan soldiers during the World War I battle of Claires-Chêsnes). In fact they've most often been described in stereotypically feminine terms: as passive objects of our benevolence, incapable of thinking, planning, and acting towards their own liberation without our help. Such a condition is, of course, the prerequisite for our "lifting off their veils" and liberating them; a task which somehow never quite works out as planned, in large measure because of the supposedly unchangeable and unreformable nature of Muslim religion and culture.

As I write, the United States has once again joined the noble crusade to liberate Muslim women; this time by killing them and their husbands, sons, brothers, and fathers to the tune of over 100,000 in Afghanistan and Iraq. To make this liberation possible, as I'll explain later on in this book, we've had to generate so much chaos and confusion that it becomes impossible for most of us to understand what's really happening "over there." Instead, we're left to fret over a clash of civilizations between an enlightened and democratic United States and an "Axis of Evil" that is seemingly as dangerous to everything "we" stand for as the German–Italian–Japanese "Axis" was in its day.

But as we'll see in the first two parts of this book, there could be no Axis of Evil without an "Axis of Arrogance and Ignorance" to lay the foundation for its successful penetration into American political culture. Indeed, the Axis of Evil is a ludicrous but very useful fiction, one that helped the Bush Administration strike just enough fear into the hearts of Americans to justify spending hundreds of billions of dollars invading Iraq and preparing for the war-without-end necessary to achieve "full spectrum dominance" of the world's politics, economies, and cultures. Or at least to dominate that part of the world that's home to the vast majority of its remaining easily recoverable petroleum reserves.

This dynamic is a major irony of post-September 11 American relations with the countries of the Muslim world: their liberation necessitates our dominance; but since the vast majority of the world's Muslims, including women, do not want our help to liberate them (not a strange sentiment, considering how deeply we've been involved in their oppression), we cover their cultures with a blanket of war, violence, and anger. In so doing we make the living cultures and societies underneath increasingly impenetrable to all but the most "expert" among us.

But if we can't penetrate, we must engage them if there is to be any chance of bringing a sane conclusion to the imbroglio enveloping both sides of the civilizational divide. We – and here I mean a much bigger "we" than one defined by the narrow bounds of "American," "Western" or "Muslim" cultures in isolation from each other – must lift the veil that has been placed over Muslim, and especially Middle East and North African, societies by those who claim to be their liberators. To do so we must engage in the long and arduous job of providing the information and encouragement to the people most susceptible to the Axis of Evil and clash of civilizations, in *both* Muslim and American (and, to a lesser extent, European) societies to gain a more accurate understanding of who "we" and "they" are, of what the dynamics are that have made the current world system possible, and of the specific histories of the various cultures struggling to achieve a measure of autonomy and genuine political and economic development within it, against great odds.

In this context, one of the main arguments of *Why They Don't Hate Us* is that bringing together the people who are both most interested and most capable of lifting the veil – from our own eyes even more than from Muslim societies – is the sine qua non for achieving any measure of truly holistic and positive social change in Muslim and American/Western cultures alike. This is in fact among the most important tasks before the scholars, activists, artists, and other members of what I call the global peace and justice movement in the post-September 11, post-Iraq world. And it is to help in this endeavor that I have written this book, and focus specifically on the politics, economies, and cultures of the Middle East in the age of globalization. Culture is a focus, because the task of holistic social changes is going to be achieved first and foremost through culture and cultural interaction – what I call culture jamming – rather than through political machinations, upheavals, violence, or revolutionary economic transformation.

As I will argue in the pages that follow, the slow process of achieving cultural maturity worldwide is, in the age of globalization, the primary means of transcending the neoliberal world system and creating a new international order based on real peace, freedom, democracy, and sustainable development. This book provides the knowledge and tools to make a difficult and often painful process a bit easier, and perhaps even enjoyable.

The journey that has led me to the conclusions in the following pages has spanned the majority of my life, from the first time I heard the Middle Eastern-tinged music of bands like Led Zeppelin as a young child, to my most recent trip to the Middle East in spring 2005. Too many people have made it possible to list them all here, but without any one of them my life trajectory might have changed beyond recognition; certainly this book would have never come to be.

For the intellectual and musical grounding that allowed me begin this journey: Fr. Charles Bradley; Albert Collins; Johnny Copeland; Ted Dunbar; Kevin Eubanks; Dr. John; Murray Lichtenstein; Ron Long; Russell Martone; Rabbi David Panitz; Barbara Sproul; Gail Tirana; and John Vitale. For comments, research help, priceless discussions, and musical experiences during the course of my research: Barbara Abrash; Sami Abu-Shehada; Amer al-Adhadh; Sara

Alexander; Stefano Allievi; Paul Amar; Soren Ambrose; Arjun Appadurai; Ala al-Azzeh; Raymond Baker; Filiz Baskan; Taieb Belghazi; Medea Benjamin; Besh o Drum; Homi Bhabha; Mariana Botey; Farouk Bouasse; Lori Brandt; Breyten Bretyenbach, Myriam Cattuse; Vinayak Chaturvedi; Sami Shalom Chetrit; Alev Çinar; Jim Cohen; Juan Cole; Chuck D; the Culic family; Davey D; Lara Deeb; Herbert Docena; Moez Doraid; D'Tripp; Jean Dupré; Vincent Eirene; Tom Engelhardt; John Esposito; Jodie Evans; Basem Ezbidi; Pat Farmer; Rev. James Forbes; Thomas Frank; Michael Franti; Peter Gabel; Paola Gasparoli; Negar Ghodstinat; David Theo Goldberg; the Guidotti family; Hassan Hakmoun; Rema Hammami; Dyala Hamzah; Amr Hamzawy; Hassan Hanafi; the Hertel family; Jason Hill; Jim Holston; Arianna Huffington; Amir Hussein; May Jayyusi; Deborah Kapchan; Ambassador Rich Kazlaurich; Geoffrey Kelly; Shawana Kemp; Eman Ahmed Khammas; Mark Kingwell; Naomi Klein; Lina Kreidie; KRS-1; Dominick LaCapra; Karen Lawrence; the LeVine family; Zachary Lockman; Cecelia Lynch; Peter Mandaville; Brinkley Messick; Ziba Mir-Hosseini; Tim Mitchell; Jacopo Moroni; Viggo Mortensen; Abdellatif Mouhibi; Fred Neuhauser; Jørgen Nielsen; Jonathan Nitzan; Bruce Novak; Ozomatli; David Patel; Pilar Perez; the Perniciaro family; Geoff Porter; Anton Pukshansky; Isam Qasim; Ghidian Qaymari; Jerry Quickley; Dan Rabinowitz; Jesse Rabinowitz; Tariq Ramadan; Oday Rashid; T-Ray; Vernon Reid; Anthony Richter; Nancy Ries; Jakob Rigi; Fidel Rodriguez; Jaime Rodriguez; Nir Rosen; Anant Sanchetee; Saskia Sassen; Nanette Schorr; Daniel Schroeter; Jillian Schwedler; Stefano Sensi; Shannon Service; Gershon Shafir; Jonathan Shannon; Adam Shapiro; Walid Shomaly; John Smith; Paolo Soares; Izzat Soubra; DJ Spooky; Georg Stauth; Bo Strath; Sandy Sufian; Salim Tamari; Rudy Torres; Simona Torretta; Rick Ulfik; Dmitri Vietze; Peter Wagner; Maher al-Wahhash; Rev. Jim Wallis; Keith Wattenpaugh; Charles Wheeler; Jon Wiener; Rev. Ron Winley; Nadia Yassine; Hakan Yavuz; Reda Zine; and Layla al-Zubaidi.

Funding for the research for this book was provided by grants from the Foundation for Ethics and Meaning; the Fulbright-Hayes Committee; the Social Science Research Council; the Stuttgart Seminar on Cultural Studies; the International Institute for Advanced Studies and the Department of Middle Eastern Studies at New York University; the Society for the Humanities at Cornell University; the Robert Schuman Centre for Advanced Studies at the European University Institute; the Global Peace and Conflict Studies Program; the Humanities Research Institute and Humanities Center of the

University of California, Irvine; the Open Society Institute; *TIKKUN* magazine; We, The World; and the US Institute of Peace.

Finally, incredible thanks for their insightful comments, critiques, and editing of various drafts of this book to Valerie Amiraux; Joel Beinin; Carl Bromley; Rebecca Clare; Helen Coward; Mike Davis; Novin Doostdar; Steve Heidemann; Mark Hopwood; Judith Kearns; Rabbi Michael Lerner; Yves Mény; Keith Nelson; Ken Pomeranz; Deirdre Prinsen; Victoria Roddam; Omid Safi; Armando Salvatore; Samer Shehata; Mary Starkey; Chris Toensing; Steven Topik; and Oren Yiftachel. To the extent the final product does not live up to the high expectations of the many people listed here, it is the fault of the author and not the many friends and colleagues who so generously gave of their time to this project.

Figure 1   Just doing it: Musicians jamming in the Jma al-Fnaa in Marrakesh (2002) and a student-painted wall at the al-Nahrain (formerly Saddam) University cafeteria in Baghdad (2004) reveal how American brand icons are translated into the identities and life-goals of Muslims.

Introduction: They Are Us

The world, it seems, is a very cruel place. If there's one thing that the wanton destruction of the last century has taught us, it's that people need little incentive to hate and murder each other, by the millions when possible.

So it's no wonder that within days of the horrific terrorist attacks of September 11, 2001 – which I had watched unfold, dumbfounded, with my infant son across the East River in Queens – newspapers and magazines began running headlines asking or explaining "Why They Hate Us." A logical question, albeit a day late (to say the least). There's just one problem: there's no "They" or "Us" to be the subject and predicate of what as far as I can tell is a meaningless sentence. Meaningless because having spent the last dozen years living, studying, working, performing, and struggling in the Middle East and North Africa (from now on, MENA),[1] I have met few Arabs or Muslims who fit the role of a mythical They whose irrational hatred of the United States caused the carnage of September 11, the subsequent war on terror, and the invasions and occupations of Afghanistan and Iraq.

What I have found instead are exiled Islamist parliamentarians railing against the lack of democracy in their home countries and radical punks accused of being Satanists. I've met Islamist feminists who hate the word feminism and young men who spend hours at the neighborhood internet café surfing the web for the best US colleges and French porn sites. I've seen musicians who were too big to crawl through "security walls" erected in the middle of their towns by occupying armies (and so can't get to their next gig), and religious lawyers teaching in secular universities; six-year-olds singing songs about love, eight-year-olds dancing to songs about hand grenades. I've jammed with metalheads willing to face arrest and torture to

1

play their interpretation of Black Sabbath, met Sufi singers who wanted me to convert to the "beautiful religion"; sat on panels with fiercely independent coeds whose attire would lead the average American to assume they're horribly "oppressed," and with progressive Muslim intellectuals barred from speaking at progressive conferences by progressive Europeans who can't imagine there's such a thing as a progressive Muslim. I've danced with nouveau riche ravers on fake coffins in open-roofed discos next to the sites of real-life massacres, and interviewed terrorist intellectuals who admitted the futility of suicidal violence but were clueless as to how to stop it, and young activists in refugee camps whose bookshelves are lined with Subcommandante Marcos and the latest in Western critical theory. And so on and so on.

Of course, I could have spent my time in the region as a covert CIA operative. That seems to be what the US Government wants people like me to do these days – "stop criticizing American foreign policy and help America win the war on terror" – but I never quite figured out how a long-haired Jewish guitar player was supposed to move covertly through the Middle East.[2] On the other hand, if I'd become a spy, maybe I would have met more representatives of what the *9/11 Commission Report* labels the "Islamist terrorist menace." But what good would that have done? Didn't the CIA train Osama bin Laden? Familiarity clearly doesn't always breed insight.

Even so, from the CIA analysts I've met (I don't think I know any covert operatives, but how can one be sure?) there seems to be a general consensus that the citizens of the Arab/Muslim world, and the MENA in particular, are pretty much like us. Not just because their experiences, personalities or tastes are the same as ours, whoever we are, but because behind the seeming monolithic "Arab" or "Muslim" identities lies an enormous variety of cultures, attitudes, beliefs, and practices – some laudable, some disturbing, some just plain wrong – about which it is impossible to make broad generalizations.

Without the crutch of such simplistic identities it becomes impossible to offer the kind of sweeping questions or conclusions found in the writings of best-selling authors like Thomas Friedman, Samuel Huntington, Richard Perle, Bernard Lewis, or Niall Ferguson, whose books speak of civilizations clashing, gone wrong, forced to choose between cars and trees, needing a good dose of enlightened Anglo-Saxon imperialism, or mired in unredeemable evil. So instead I have brought together the insights of the thousands of people I've come across from all walks of life during my many travels in the region, thrown them together with an equal number of documents, books, articles, videos, CDs, pamphlets, manifestos, and other sources, and after endless sifting have written what I am fairly confident is the most accurate possible assessment of the assortment of concepts, ideologies, practices, and phenomena commonly referred to as "globalization" as it's been experienced in the MENA region.

According to *Webster*'s online dictionary globalization means "to make global, *especially*: to make worldwide in scope or application."[3] The term was coined in the 1980s as a verbal noun to refer to the expansion of multinational corporations into new markets in untapped regions of the world. Ever since then globalization has evoked equal parts of delirium and fear: for its supporters it seems the natural evolution, even highest imaginable stage, of human economic relations, providing the engine for unlimited growth and wealth for the world. For its opponents – whether Seattle's Turtle People, Tehran's turbaned morality squads, Africa's undersold farmers or Najaf's imams – it has proven the greatest threat to economic, cultural, political, and ecological well-being since the heyday of European colonialism, to which it is often compared.

Whatever it is, and however you feel about it, offering yet another in a seemingly endless supply of books about globalization may not seem like such an urgent task. After all, last time I checked amazon.com I could buy 14,581 books about globalization, and this doesn't include all the books dealing with the war on terror and the Middle East more specifically since the terrorist disaster of September 11, 2001. As we'll see in the course of this book, however, the problem with most of them is that they're either wildly inaccurate, deal primarily with economic globalization, or barely touch most of the countries of the MENA in a systematic way.

What has yet to be written is an in-depth analysis of globalization in the MENA region that explores its cultural and economic dynamics equally, and ties them to worldwide experiences and trends – whether studying the various levels of chaos that are challenging societies across the developing world or working as an activist, artist, scholar, or policy-maker in the still-maturing "global peace and justice movement," a term I use to recognize the coalescing of the anti-corporate globalization and anti-war movements in the wake of September 11 and the war on terrorism. Without this kind of information, the breaking down of barriers and building of bridges and coalitions between the world's still-divided cultures, which are surely among the most urgent tasks facing humanity today, will be frustrated by the power of a "neoliberal globalization" gone wild – gone wild precisely because neoliberalism and the chaos it creates makes a true globalization of human relations, economies, and cultures impossible.

Critics of globalization have used "neoliberal globalization" as a catch-all phrase to signify a largely corporate-controlled agenda of global economic integration which, in their opinion, has wreaked economic and cultural havoc on developing societies. While I share this critique in many respects, I use the term to represent the dominant ideology of the major industrial powers and international financial institutions (both "public" institutions such as the World Bank and IMF and "private" institutions such as international banks) that govern the international economy. More specifically, I take neoliberal globalization to signify the process of global economic integration based on principles of supposedly "free" trade and markets, low tariffs and taxes, free exchange rates, and the privatization and liberalization of national economies. In the developing world, such policies are usually accomplished by the use of structural adjustment programs administered by the World Bank and IMF whose goal is to "open" countries to private, usually Western corporate, interests. As we will see in Chapters Two and Three, historically such policies have not led to greater global integration, distribution of wealth and/or resources, or more open migration policies. Instead they have led to greater concentration of wealth, inequality, and conflict.

If terms such as the "global peace and justice movement" or "neoliberal globalization" are difficult to pin down, it is equally hard to generalize about the countries of the MENA, never mind across the "cultures" or "civilizations" that many writers use to represent the supposed antagonists of the post-Cold War – and now, post-September 11 – era. And so the majority of the sources, stories, and reminiscences in this book will be drawn from individuals and movements (usually below our media and political radar screen) whose experiences of and responses to the "West" and the United States are much more complex than most of us would imagine.

Of course, I'll spend quite a bit of time exploring important issues such as al-Qa'eda, the wars on terrorism and Iraq, the imperial dreams of the Bush Administration, and the reasons for the widespread dictatorship and corruption in the region. But while they are important subjects, exploring them is not the primary reason I wrote this book. For me it was more important to use these issues as the entrée to exploring why voices across the so-called civilizational divide have yet to come together in a critical mass for dialogue, peace, and democracy, and how such activities can be nurtured.

Empathy and Culture Jamming in the Global Middle East

The idea to write a book about globalization and culture in the Middle East first came to me in the middle of a culture jam I was hosting at the Patriotic Hall in Los Angeles. As I have imagined it, a culture jam is a combination of "roundtable" and performance bringing together an international (or at least multicultural) group of artists, scholars, and activists who don't normally have the chance to be in dialogue with each other, let alone an audience. Some readers might feel that a Westerner calling for Middle Easterners to adopt "culture jamming" – a concept that usually is meant to describe progressive artists in North America "jamming" advertisements with images that contradict the idea or product the ad is supposed sell – is just one more example of cultural imperialism, this time from the post-Seattle Left. But to do so would be to miss the musical core of the concept, which envisions the meeting of cultures as a true collaborative effort in which, like a great jam session, all the participants contribute uniquely yet equally to the cultural product being created.

In fact, as we'll see in Chapters Six through Nine, such culture jamming is already occurring regularly in the MENA in ways Westerners don't easily recognize. One goal of this book is to help increase the mutual awareness by scholars, activists, and other concerned people about promising developments that are rarely covered, studied or accounted for in the mainstream press, academia, and policy-making. What makes this task so important is that, without a broader understanding of the ways in which cultural interconnections can and do occur today across the MENA, attempts to bring scholars, activists or policy-makers together will be more likely to include a narrow, and often problematic, group of participants who together are not capable of creating new cultures of peace, justice or democratic development based on positive, inclusive yet self-critical identities.

The particular culture jam that inspired this book was taking place in the middle of the 2000 Democratic Convention, for me the Shadow Conventions, and my boss Arianna Huffington was understandably worried as she watched a dozen or more masked anarchists descend to the hall's basement café (no doubt looking to hide from the not too friendly forces of LA law and order). I wasn't too thrilled either, as they had literally run me over a couple of hours earlier charging into battle with the police at a free concert by Rage Against the Machine and Ozomatli.

But here they were, and what could we do but welcome them – in peace – and continue the jam, which had begun earlier that day with

KRS-One, Ozomatli, Vernon Reid and the Doors' John Densmore. In the space of ten minutes, as DJ Fidel of the collective Seditious Beats spun some old NWA, Muslim preacher and activist Minister Conrad Muhammad delivered an impassioned sermon on the need for large-scale grass-roots activism, San Francisco's Company of Prophets hiphop collective threw down some powerful rhymes excoriating the duplicity of Democrats and Republicans alike, and several anarchists took to the stage to report on their activities.

The audience was simultaneously spellbound and literally jumping to join in the performance. It was then, in the midst of moderating a heated discussion between militant anarchists and pacifists over the post-Clinton World Order, that it occurred to me that the same kind of conversations between artists, scholars, activists, and a politically aware audience that were taking place here could, and should, take place elsewhere. Especially in and around the Middle East.

Why are culture jams so important to this endeavor? Because from my experience in the worlds of art, academia, and activism, culture jamming is the best – and even only – way to grasp and work through the unprecedented complexity of globalization and the problems it has generated, which demand the kind of radical strategies that only can emerge collectively – by bringing artists, activists, writers, and scholars to work, perform and struggle together; not in the recording or TV studio, not in closed conferences or on unapproachable stages, but in close dialogue with the very public whose views and attitudes they have great power to shape.

The idea of bringing culture jamming to the MENA might seem a bit naïve considering the seeming hostility towards the US in the region. But what the discussions throughout *Why They Don't Hate Us* will show is that, contrary to official Government and media rhetoric in the US (and to a lesser extent in Europe), most of the people of the Middle East do not "hate us" or long for jihad against Western culture and imperialism: this despite being justifiably appalled by decades of Western support for the most repressive and corrupt regimes imaginable, not to mention the overthrow of regimes "we" don't like, and even invasion and occupation of countries when it suited "our" interests. In fact, culture jamming is the best way to overcome the marginalization of Middle Eastern voices from the coalition of forces and movements opposed to neoliberal globalization.

Indeed, when Seattle's anti-WTO protests of late 1999 shook the world, I hoped, and even assumed, that the Muslim world would soon join the worldwide grass-roots movement against globalization; especially since many of the earliest protests against neoliberalism occurred in the Middle East. I knew that the time was ripe for such a coalition to emerge since I was in the middle of a project examining Arab and Muslim experiences of and responses to globalization, and had found numerous similarities between the perspectives of heavy metal rockers, world musicians, and their more well-known "radical Islamist" counterparts, and those of activists and intellectuals in the West.

But I was surprised and angry at the lukewarm response I received from leading organizations in the movement, none of whom understood the implications of the long history of European and US imperialism on globalization in the region, or even considered the MENA part of the globalized world. As important, none seemed interested in including the voices of Arabs and Muslims in their teach-ins, literature or collective mobilizations until September 11 woke them up to a common enemy in the Bush Administration (but sadly, for most, not in Saddam Hussein).

Since September 11 Middle Eastern voices have thankfully become less marginalized in the global peace and justice movement, or at least in the anti-war movement. Yet this hasn't signaled a drastic improvement in rhetoric or strategy, as the anti-corporate globalization and now anti-war coalitions seem much more interested in and capable of explaining what they're against, or critiquing specific countries (usually the US and/or Israel), than in offering a comprehensive system-wide critique of neoliberal globalization. But as the chapters that follow will show, such a holistic critique is the necessary first step in developing a positive vision of how to build another, more just and peaceful, world. Without it, how can the global peace and justice movement attract and mobilize the tens, even hundreds, of millions, of people it will take to turn the dream into reality?

What's more, even with the coming together of Arab/Muslim and Western anti-war voices, the level of ignorance of and sometimes hostility to Islam and its cultures within the progressive movement, among leaders and the grass roots membership, remains high. And when these voices do converge (as they did in December 2002 in Cairo to condemn the war then still to come, and then in Beirut in October 2004 to strategize about future collaborations between Middle Eastern and Western activists) they generally offer platitudes about Zionist and American imperialism, refuse to take on the issue of violence within their movements, and can find nothing worse to say about regimes like Saddam Hussein's in Iraq than that they suffer from "challenges to democratic development."[4]

These dynamics have helped create the situation in which I'm writing these words: the Bush Administration and its "coalition of the willing" is engaged in a brutal, chaotic, yet extremely profitable and successful occupation of Iraq, one made possible by victories over both Saddam Hussein and the strongest anti-war movement in history. This situation has convinced me that what the forces of peace and justice are fighting against is not just an "axis of evil" concocted by the US Government, but an equally dangerous axis of arrogance and ignorance that in various proportions has infected the American Left, Middle, and Right. To overcome the violent synergy produced by the intersection of these two axes, the global peace and justice movement needs to create an "Axis of Empathy" which, as the French philosopher Emanuel Levinas taught us, is the foundation for building true solidarity across cultures, nations, and religions. It is to help foster such an enterprise that I have written this book.

The Dangers of Google History

Empathy is not easy to come by these days, especially in the middle of so much war, and especially on the part of conservatives (however compassionate some may claim to be). And the warriors of the Right will use every method at their disposal to win their arguments – even, as President Bush's Yale yearbook bragged about him, deliver an "illegal but gratifying right hook" to opponents.[5] This includes avoiding unpleasant facts or detailed analyses of core issues (as the *9/11 Commission Report* did by defining terrorism as simply the irrational "tactic to kill and destroy" while "praising" the US occupation of Afghanistan; lauding Pakistan's coup-leader President Musharif for his "enlightened moderation"); or, on a more personal level, conservative talk-show hosts using Google searches to erroneously call honest professors liars on national radio.

I experienced the latter tactic when I claimed during a debate with a right-wing radio-show host named Dennis Prager that I'd witnessed a Palestinian demonstration against Hamas-sponsored suicide bombings while living in Israel and the Occupied Territories. But when he couldn't find evidence of such a demonstration on Google.com he called me a liar.

As a historian, journalist, musician, and activist I use Google dozens of times a day; but I was stunned by Prager's accusation, especially the idea that a 1.3-second internet search would provide sufficient evidence to pass judgment on a historical claim, let alone a person's moral and professional character. But in today's post-modern, depthless and confrontational culture, speed and stridency have become more valuable than accuracy and deliberation. Those who search for historical and moral complexity are too often shouted down and dismissed as liars or as supporters of the enemy – al-Qa'eda, or American imperialism, or both.

As absurd as Prager's argument might seem, it had the intended effect on his listeners, who expressed disgust at my "looseness with the truth" (as one caller described it). This exchange taught me how dangerous what I call a "Google standard of history" is for rational and well-reasoned public debate of crucial issues facing a society. Indeed, it's a perfect example of the kind of shabby research done by so-called scholars and pundits, which (among other things) often seems to assume that if something hasn't made it onto the web, it never happened.[6] Google history also ignores the fact that quite a few important events occurred *before* the birth of the web. Did the Revolutionary War not happen because it's not cached by Google or in the New York *Times*' online archive?[7]

It took me several days of searching on and off the web, as well as a helpful email from a journalist friend, but I found the "evidence" of the Palestinian demonstration that, according to Google, never happened. It took place on March 5, 1996, and was covered by the *Los Angeles Times* and other major newspapers. But for some reason, it never made it onto the web, or at least Google's web server. Or maybe Prager didn't enter the right key words in his search.

The ancient Greeks long ago realized that history is crucial to democracy. Especially in wartime, we Googleize it at our peril. But it's not Google or the web more broadly that's the main problem here. Instead, it's the way these sites are used by commentators and even educators as a substitute for the hard work of providing the public or students with the detailed and accurate information they need to become good citizens.

And so as the US was preparing to invade Iraq I was invited to lecture to Orange County, California history and social studies teachers about the crisis. To better prepare my lecture I asked to see the materials given to teachers to design lessons about Iraq and the Middle East. I was shocked and frustrated by what I read; or, more accurately, by what I didn't read in them, as several of the most important episodes and dynamics of the country's short history – which would have direct bearing on the soon to be US–UK led "administration" of the country – were completely erased from the history they present.

The missing history surrounded British colonial rule in Iraq and its impact on the country. What will be clear by the time we've finished Part One of this book is that we can no more write colonialism out of Iraq's history than write slavery out of America's, for if we want to know "why they hate us," or how the Ba'athist regime could commit such atrocities on Kurds, Iranians, Kuwaitis, and Iraqis, we must first understand what it is like to be colonized. Without the colonial context we have no way of understanding the roots of the country's more recent history, including the dynamics of US rule, which, not surprisingly, have mirrored the British period in many ways.[8]

Moreover, the United States has long acted in a similar fashion when it came to Iraq. Indeed, copying its earlier success of overthrowing the Iranian Prime Minister Mossadeqh in 1953 (the details of which *are* available to Google users if they type in the coup's code word, "TPAJAX"),[9] the CIA helped stage two coups in Iraq, in 1963 and 1968, for almost identical reasons as the 1953 Iran operation; both times it helped the Ba'ath party secure power in its wake.[10] The history of US foreign policy in Iran or Iraq should be required reading for all high school students and teachers precisely because it teaches us how the most enlightened democracies repeatedly violate their professed ideals.[11]

A New Agenda for Understanding "Them" and "Us"

In the face of the Axes of Arrogance and Ignorance, Google history, and the realities of our educational systems and larger cultures, how can we accomplish the goals of exploring neoliberal globalization, its impact in the MENA, and the development of the global peace and justice movement in response to it? By engaging in three levels of discussion, each of which moves from the general to the particular: from world history to the history of the MENA, from globalization in general to its experience in the region, and from the history of the anti-corporate globalization and now global peace and justice movements to their impact on activism and politics in the Muslim world. Why is this strategy necessary? Because without a strong grasp of the major historical processes that have shaped the modern world and through it, the MENA, we can't understand the fundamental dynamics of contemporary globalization, how they have been experienced in the MENA, and how the responses to them in the region compare with those around the world.

To accomplish this goal I have divided the chapters that follow into three groups: Part One blends my personal odyssey through the Middle East with an exploration of the modern history of the region.

In Chapter One I present several vignettes from my travels through the region and experiences of the divides between "Them" and "Us." I then use these stories as the foundation to explore how the Axis of Evil can be overcome by a broad-based, sophisticated, and self-critical "Axis of Empathy." Chapter Two explores key themes in the history of modernity, imperialism/colonialism,[12] capitalism, and nationalism in order to build a foundation for exploring the history and development of five Muslim societies. Here I'll introduce some of the key themes and processes that are crucial to understanding the Middle East's problems, including longstanding European and US domination of the region, the denial of peace, democracy, and development such power has long required, and the inability of citizens in the region to develop positive, democratic responses to this situation.

Part Two examines contemporary globalization in terms of its worldwide development and unique trajectory in the Middle East. This part includes the book's most detailed discussions of the economic dynamics of globalization, both broadly and in the MENA specifically. With this foundation I bring various Arab/Muslim voices into dialogue about globalization's crucial but underappreciated cultural impact, and then add voices from other cultures (especially Europe and the United States) to broaden the discussion. In particular, Chapters Three and Four provide a detailed critique of the economic focus of mainstream analyses of economic globalization, while Chapters Five and Six explore how Muslim scholars and activists, from religious extremists to rock musicians, experience and respond to what I believe to be its more important cultural impact on their societies.

Part Three moves the discussion outside the Arab/Muslim world to explore the history of the "movement of movements" that stormed the world stage with dozens of major protests against neoliberal globalization during the 1990s, epitomized by the Battle in Seattle of late November 1999. The experiences and insights of these movements are then brought to the MENA to see whether they are relevant for understanding the region's recent history and possible futures. Some readers doubt the possibility of significant similarities existing between such seemingly different movements and contexts. But as we'll see in the chapters that follow, there are compelling similarities in the nature of the struggles and the challenges facing the participants to make such a comparison worthwhile, especially in the era of globalization.

Chapter Seven explores the history of the anti-corporate globalization movement beginning with the once-famous American and European protests of 1968, and explores how progressive movements evolved between them and their post-Seattle and September 11 incarnations. With this historical background Chapter Eight offers a more detailed discussion of three of the most important strategies and movements that have emerged in the last decade Zapatismo, anarchism, and the world social forums – to determine how they might impact Middle Eastern struggles for peace, justice, and democracy. Here my research and personal relationships with younger scholars, activists, and artists from the Middle East provide important insights into the perspectives of the generation that will lead the region in the coming years. At the same time my experiences with leading activists and intellectuals in the global peace and justice movement help me offer a unique perspective on the similarities between the arguments of the "movement" and those of their Arab/Muslim counterparts, and as important, on the stereotypes and prejudices – anti-Semitism in its broadest sense, really – that frustrate the cooperation such sympathy should encourage. Only by overcoming these prejudices can dialogue and collective efforts for real peace and justice be undertaken.

With this goal in mind, the Conclusion tests the arguments developed in this book against the realities of occupied Iraq, which has become ground zero for contemporary globalization – a place where chaos, violence, corruption, profits, and various extremist ideologies have combined to create a powerful portrait of the future for those who can't, or won't, join the crusade for a neoliberal world order. I end by arguing that only a truly positive and proactive culture jamming – one of which I caught precious glimpses of in war-torn Iraq – can support the kind of cross-cultural, transnational communication, coordination, and solidarity necessary to turn the tide against neoliberal globalization and its unending war for empire. The first step in such a process must be a "truce" called by the United States, as the leading protagonist of the war on terrorism, with the Muslim world. If coupled with a serious attempt to accept at least a measure of responsibility for the lack of democracy, peace or development in the Middle East and a few targeted changes in American (and Western) foreign policy, such an action would provide the space for peoples and governments alike on both sides of the so-called civilizational divide to reflect on their share of responsibility in creating this mess, and on what kind of paradigm shifts in their most basic social, political, and economic mores and institutions are necessary to begin the hard task of healing their cultures, and the world at large.

A note about style. Readers may find this book a bit schizophrenic in its style and presentation of information. Sometimes it will have the feel of a travelogue or memoir; other times it will be knee-deep in statistics or theoretical debates. For some readers the detailed analysis of arguments surrounding economic globalization will be laborious, others might find the discussions of artists and protests uninteresting or beside the point and the first-person tone of the narrative frivolous or egocentric.

My response to these quite understandable feelings would be that if there's one thing I have learned in the last decade of working on the issues covered in this book, it's that globalization encompasses and impacts every sphere of life and can only be understood holistically – that is, when all its facets are examined in their relationship to each other. I firmly believe that to understand how globalization is actually experienced on the ground in the Middle East, or anywhere for that matter, you need to have a firm grasp on the major academic theories, data, and debates, while at the same time having direct experience of the innumerable ways people come together to respond to globalization, whether in mosques or boardrooms, protests or dance clubs.

Ultimately, my experiences taught me that art, activism, and academia can never exist apart from one another; attempts to separate them only weaken discussions of any of them. In fact, the ideas and arguments in this book emerged precisely because I spent much of my time in the region at archives in the morning, protests in the afternoon, and clubs in the evening. So perhaps a good strategy for reading the book is to read the more detailed economic discussion at work or school and the more descriptive and culturally focused sections at the beach, or on the way home after a long night out.

To the extent that such a strategy fails, it's the fault of the writer and not of the individuals and cultures we'll encounter in the pages that follow.

PART 1

Who Are They, Where'd They Come From, and Why They Don't Hate Us – Yet?

Figure 2   The poor in Morocco consume the images, if not the products, of globalization, July 2002

1 From Evil to Empathy: The Orient Beats Back the Axis of Arrogance

Introduction: Four Scenes
Scene One: The Marrakesh Express

Riding the air-conditioned train back to Rabat from Marrakesh on a hot July day it's hard to understand what the authors of the recently released, widely acclaimed *Arab Human Development Report* (*AHDR*) were thinking. The much celebrated 2002 report is the latest in decades – indeed centuries – of reports, dossiers, books, and exposés aiming to understand why the Arab and larger Muslim worlds have not attained levels of democracy and development similar to those of their neighbors to the West. And along with the *9/11 Commission Report* of two years later, the *AHDR* has become a foundational text for understanding why they seem to hate us for their failures.

This being rush hour the passengers are largely well-dressed young women chatting on cell phones; the lead story in today's paper is the Spanish military occupation of the tiny disputed Island of Leila (just 100m off the Moroccan coast), which has led Moroccans to wonder which of the two is the modern, civilized, and peace-loving European country. The newly purchased books in my backpack offer various takes on how globalization is impacting the Middle East and what Arabs and Muslims can do about it. The landscape alternates between beautiful country and urban slums, both similarly dotted with countless satellite dishes.

Together the scene challenges the central argument of the report and untold predecessors (and indeed the entire history of US and Western policy towards the Arab and Muslim worlds): that it is Arabs and Muslims themselves, their institutions, structures, and cultures, who are primarily responsible for the innumerable problems plaguing their societies, and that only a combination of Western tutelage, reforms, and even intervention can reverse this sad state of affairs. As I leaf through a Sufi magazine on the train I'm reminded once again of just how far removed mainstream policy-making, news coverage, and scholarship is from the realities of life in the Middle East and North Africa. Especially since September 11, 2001.

Scene Two: Nablus, Palestine or Freetown, Sierra Leone?

I'm sitting at a new hotel café in the casbah (old city) of Nablus with a colleague of mine and his best student, assessing the role of violence in the three years of the second intifada. My colleague, a British-educated Palestinian sociologist, and his student, a twenty-year-old woman dressed in conservative Muslim attire who's hoping to go to the United States or Europe for graduate school, are explaining how the Palestinian experience of both globalization *and* occupation has produced a unique situation, one which has had an as yet underappreciated impact on the dynamics of the conflict. As if on cue, as we delved deeper into this subject and finished off another plate of hummus (Palestinian hummus is by far the best in the world) four Palestinian youngsters, aged between twelve and seventeen years old, burst into the restaurant brandishing a Kalashnikov and other weapons, screaming at the manager to close and at the customers to leave in honor of the previous night's "martyr" at the hands of the Israeli Defense Forces.

I have seen plenty of Palestinians with guns in my travels in the Occupied Territories, but never anyone as young as these without any supervision or control by an adult, or at least a trained militant. I have rarely felt unsafe in Palestine, even as an American Jew, because I speak Arabic, and have friends in most of the places I visit and enough experience to avoid – and where necessary, talk my way out of – potentially dangerous situations. But this was different, not just because of the look the young man with the gun gave me and the fact that his finger was literally on the trigger (not to the side as anyone with a minimum of military training would do), but because of the feeling of anarchy that enveloped me during this brief incident, a sensation I'd never experienced in the Occupied Territories before.

As the group moved on and we got up to leave, the youngest boy, about twelve, and carrying nothing more threatening than a belt, ran back in and said sheepishly to the manager, "*Shukran!* (thank you)," before disappearing into the street. Once in the street we saw them again and quickly hopped in a taxi as they wandered around the old city looking for anyone not obeying their orders.

I recount this little incident, so minor in comparison with the level of violence Palestinians and Israelis live with daily, because it – indeed, the Occupied Territories as a whole – represents everything that's dangerous about globalization, especially after September 11: the gradual disintegration of social authority and the unmooring of communal identities in countries unable to keep up with "turbo-capitalism"; the whirlpool of desperation and nihilism that is slowly tearing apart "failed" states and societies across the "Global South";[1] and the unilateral power of the United States to engage in, support or ignore oppressive policies and even brutal occupations against the will of the world community. In short, Palestine could soon resemble Sierra Leone, with a state that has been effectively dismantled by external and internal political forces; a workforce that has seen jobs and wages decimated by regional and global economic processes;[2] and a "weapons–petrodollar coalition" that manipulates the conflict to ensure a more or less permanent state of manageable hostilities, from which seemingly endless profits can be siphoned.

Scene Three: Independence Day in Baghdad

It's half a year later, and I'm in Baghdad. March 19, 2004 to be exact: the one-year anniversary of the US-led invasion and occupation of the country. I had traveled to Iraq specifically on this date not just to do research on the situation in the country one year after the invasion, but also to experience an anti-occupation demonstration where the occupation actually is taking place, rather than NY or LA, where the moribund anti-war movement seems incapable of organizing much more than politically tired demonstrations that have little impact on the larger public. In fact, I was supposed to be in the middle of a hundred or more European activists who had organized a "caravan" to Iraq in solidarity with Iraqis. What I got instead was about two thousand extremely religious and angry Iraqi men, chanting "Oh Jews, remember the battle of Khaybar [the battle where Muhammad defeated the Jews as recounted in the Qur'an]; Muhammad's army is returning!" And that was the nicest thing they chanted. Needless to say, I stayed on the sidelines, actually on the roof of a building overlooking the street.

The caravan, sadly, was canceled due to the chaos enveloping the country. While 100,000 New Yorkers marched against the occupation, only one-fiftieth that number were willing to risk their lives, Sunnis and Shi'a together (to march) in Baghdad. And with good reason. Only two weeks before over sixty Shi'ites were killed in a suicide

Figure 3   Marching to anti-US and anti-Jewish chants, Baghdad, March 19, 2004

bombing at the Qadhamiyya mosque where this march started. Two nights before, a hotel around the block from mine was blasted out of existence with such force it blew out all the windows on my hotel's first three floors. Within a few weeks of the anniversary most international peace activists had fled Iraq, as even Iraqi religious leaders who supported their presence couldn't guarantee their safety.

What I didn't realize in Nablus but had become clear by the time I left Baghdad was that the chaos in both cities, in both countries, was not just a by-product of the occupations suffered by Palestinians and Iraqis. Rather, chaos has become crucial to the success of the occupations and the strategic goals motivating them, in good measure because of the profits and repression it facilitates and even enables.

Scene Four: Indonesia Comes to Irvine

There are only a few days left to go before the start of "Operation Shock and Awe" and I have just spoken at yet another anti-war rally against Iraq at my university, UC Irvine. Perhaps two hundred students sat on the steps in front of the Administration Building and heard their fellow students denounce the war, and me, the resident all-things-Middle Eastern professor, try to explain why just opposing war on Iraq is not going to solve anything. I explained that even in the decade of "peace" after the first Gulf War at least five thousand Iraqis have died every month – that's 500,000 mostly children and old people. And they would continue to die each month even if "we" managed to stop President Bush's drive to finish his father's war.

My aim was to get students to face the moral quandary at the center of the anti-war movement: in a political context where there seem to be only two alternative policies, ineffective yet never-ending sanctions that kill thousands of innocent people each month (not to mention the untold number killed by Hussein), or a US-sponsored invasion that could kill tens of thousands immediately – but, I thought, might put an end to the mass deaths from starvation and disease – which is the more moral choice? What I could not imagine then, and was incensed to learn when I traveled through Iraq, is that the numbers did not improve after the war. In fact they were so bad that the US-run Ministry of Health stopped publishing most health statistics. How could I know, as the chief resident anesthesiologist of Qadamiyyah Hospital would tell me fifty-four weeks later in utter exasperation, that trying to convince the American-controlled Coalition Provisional Authority to do something about the dire health situation in Iraq would be like "banging your head against a wall"?[3]

While many of the students seemed to understand my point, I wasn't prepared for the young Indonesian student who came up to me (and the female Muslim students standing next to me) after my talk to disagree politely but powerfully with the demonstration. She introduced herself by explaining that she was a Christian whose mother was blown up in her church by Muslim terrorists, and whose father and uncle were forced to convert to Islam or be killed. Making matters worse was the fact that once converted, her uncle took advantage of his new religion by taking a second wife, and now beats her aunt – his first wife – every day. Turning to the Muslim students she described her recent visit home, where people are "wearing Osama shirts and laughing for every non-Muslim they killed ... In Indonesia nowadays, jihad is everywhere. When the US was there everything was better. There where jobs, we could walk the streets at night, we could practice our religion."

"Yes, the US has done bad things, but it isn't to blame for everything bad in the world. Now you are not in Indonesia but they are still killing each other, even worse. The US is kind to many countries. It never invaded other countries in an extent that the Japanese did. The only thing the US did was capitalism ... Do you think that if the Arab/Muslim countries had the same power as the US they wouldn't invade here and kill all the Christians?" she added in a follow-up email to our conversation. "I would ask the Muslim students, would you rather be a Christian living in a Muslim country or a Muslim living in the US?"

I have quoted her words at length because I think they highlight serious problems in the discourse and strategy of the anti-war movement, and with the progressive movement more generally. Yes, the student has forgotten some very important facts – that the previous regime killed half a million East Timorese Christians with the full support of the US, that the US has invaded dozens of countries in the last century, that "doing capitalism" has done quite enough damage to the world, succeeding in large part because it involved doing colonialism at the same time.

But against the force and tragedy of her life experience what point would there be to explain the links between the US and the violence she experienced or witnessed? Indeed, even if "we" are partly, or even largely, responsible for planting the seeds of the horrific violence that is threatening the soul of Islam today (and ours, as well), what does this have to do with the fanatics that killed her mother, or the local imams who sanctioned her uncle's new marriage and wife-beating?

The issues her poignant plea raises for the global peace and justice movement are profound. Particularly for the "progressive" wing of the movement, to focus so much on the sins of America without addressing the crimes committed by countries and cultures not allied with the US, or even those of countries we've victimized, leaves out too many people who have been victims of all three. As important, such a narrow focus generates a perception within mainstream society that the global peace and justice movement is less interested in pursuing justice, human rights, and peace in Iraq or Palestine than in bashing the United States government.

After all, if we were interested in justice for all, wouldn't there have been as large a coalition against the deadly sanctions regime during the last decade as against the war? Wouldn't Muslim students at my university spend at least a few minutes a year raising consciousness about genocide and slavery in the southern Sudan, never mind the plight of Muslims in Chechnya, Kashmir, China, or the Philippines, even as they organize week long teach-ins on "55 Years of Israeli Terror"? Wouldn't we be raising our voices against the authoritarian regimes in control of almost every country in the MENA and not just against Bush, Blair, and Sharon?

This attitude was revealed more strongly in the pre-war protests, where the "Cairo Declaration" of December 2002, mentioned in the

Introduction, could find nothing worse to say about Saddam Hussein than that there were currently "restrictions on democratic development in Iraq." (My Iraqi Kurdish Arabic professor would certainly have an interesting perspective on the meaning of "restricted" democracy in Iraq when under Hussein male members of Kurdish families were singled out for gendercide and the women for sexual slavery or worse.)

But the saddest part of my brief conversation with the Indonesian student was the complete inability of her fellow students – young head-scarf-wearing Muslim activists-students who themselves come from countries where men need little encouragement from the US to oppress and engage in violence against all sorts of "Others" – to acknowledge or respond to the incredible tragedy that has befallen her family and her country, one in which the "West" and "Islam" (if we can make such gross generalizations) both share tremendous responsibility. Sadly it seems that for too many people at all levels of the progressive movement, if it's not a US crime, it's not worth their time.

As problematic as the positions of the progressive wing of the anti-war movement might be, the more mainstream groups, especially Win Without War and even United For Peace and Justice (in its pre-war rhetoric), were far more so. Their main arguments for opposing war had little to do with bringing justice to Iraqis, but were almost entirely focused on the potential for the war to make the United States less safe. The problems with both wings' rhetoric didn't start after September 11 and the war on terrorism, and it's not just about Muslims. Indeed, Muslims were largely marginalized from the movement until the lead-up to the invasion of Iraq. For example, in September 2000 I spoke at the Prague "S26 Countersummit" against the World Bank meeting taking place in the city at the same time. While discussing Muslim responses to globalization it occurred to me to ask the assembled crowd and speakers to raise their hands if they were Arab or Muslim. To my surprise, the only hand that went up was a cameraman's from German television. And in the US the situation is not very different, as in the four years since the seminal events of November 1999 in Seattle the major US organizations have rebuffed repeated attempts to bring a Middle Eastern presence and/or perspectives to their literature or public forums.

While there has been some incorporation of Arab/Muslim voices into the current anti-war coalition, there has been little discussion or dialogue on issues other than Iraq and Palestine, which leaves conflicts from Sudan to Kashmir outside of the dialogue. In so doing the movement disregards the millions of Muslim victims of terror sponsored by states who don't happen to be US clients or allies, even though the conflicts involved are often far more bloody than the worst-case scenarios for the two most well-known occupations in the region. It is this combination of unparalleled and unprincipled American dominance in the Middle East, widespread ignorance and misinformation in the mainstream press, academia, and public, and the inability of the global peace and justice movement to develop a holistic, critical yet positive alternative paradigm for the region that has led me to write this book.

These problems are no doubt tied to the fact that most people concerned about globalization and the New World Order don't actually know what globalization is (with good reason, as we'll see in Chapters Two through Six). However powerful and threatening, today's globalization is not a recent phenomenon. Instead, it's the latest of at least three phases of global integration during the modern period, with the Age of Imperialism and the post-World War II era of integration its predecessors.

Given globalization's deep historical roots, any examination, especially one focusing on the centuries-old relationship between Islam and the West, must account for the mutual impact of long-term processes such as capitalism, colonialism nationalism, and modernity itself on this relationship. As I explore in greater detail in Chapter Two, the relationships between these four processes can be usefully summarized by the idea of a "modernity matrix." Certainly Arab and Muslim critics of globalization, like their predecessors for well over a century, view the West and the US in particular through the prism of these complex historical processes. This has led one Arab critic to lament the imposition of an "inhuman globalism" on a region that has yet to develop a "human nationalism."[4]

And indeed, US policies toward the region draw from the same civilizing mission as European imperialism and colonialism before them. Even Bush Administration Secretary of State Condoleeza Rice admitted that America is an imperial power, albeit in her view a benign and non-imperialist one. Other officials and their allies in the corporate media are more blunt in describing the goals of the war between "our God" and "their idols," as a US military intelligence chief described his battles with Muslims in Somalia. As serious, despite decades of compelling failures, the rhetoric of "modernization," "development," and making the world safe for global corporations remains the justification for myriad policies of Western governments (especially the United States) and the international financial institutions they control.

Emphasizing globalization's imperial past should not suggest that it is an inevitable or direct continuation of past imbalances of power. Just the opposite is at least potentially the case; globalization has opened new spaces for resistance and dialogue by individuals and communities across cultures, particularly those committed to a democratic future based on mutual recognition, genuine peace, and social and environmental justice. In contrast to the common wisdom of *Newsweek*, *Commentary* or the Defense Department, "They" don't hate "Us" – at least not most of Them. As I've already argued, however convenient it may be to condense one billion people down to a single "they," the fact is that there is no one Muslim or Arab "they" out there, let alone one point of view, to support the all-too-familiar Us versus Them rhetoric. Nor are "Jihad" or "McWorld" the only two choices facing either of Us. Instead, there is a startling plurality of cultures, approaches to, and reflections on the problems behind today's headlines.

Our goal, then, must be to make sense of this pluralism, which means first and foremost that we can't underestimate the importance of cultural issues in exploring globalization. This is because in the global era, more than any time previously, political and economic processes "are globalized to the extent that they are culturalized"; that is, expressed through cultural mechanisms and/or symbols. This fact is why, as Baghdad's best blues guitarist and leading film maker Oday Rasheed explained to me, "Only building bridges between cultures can provide the chance to overcome both occupation and the violence it breeds." His point, and mine now, is that exploring and utilizing culture in the process of imagining an alternative collective future must be the foundation for a sorely needed dialogue of civilizations.

Understanding the Axis of Arrogance and Ignorance

Building bridges across cultures is a lot harder done than said, especially when we consider how the "problem" of Islam and the unending Middle Eastern conflict are framed by American image- and policy-makers. When President Bush rhetorically asked "Why do they hate us?" in the aftermath of the horrific destruction of September 11, 2001, his answer was that they "hate freedom and democracy," and that only a "crusade" by America against the largely Muslim "Axis of Evil" could counter this existential threat.[5] The Administration's rhetoric quickly grew more sophisticated – dropping the inflammatory "crusade" rhetoric and adding North Korea to the list of evildoers – yet behind the photo-ops with local imams and platitudes that "Islam means peace," US policy toward the Middle East during the last decade has been grounded in the belief that (1) History is over, (2) We have won, and (3) They either must catch up, get out of the way, or end up, literally, road-kill of the globalization express. As the New York *Times* explained not long before September 11, in the global era you either "dominate or die."[6]

The ideological basis for this belief retains a strong dose of late-nineteenth-century Protestant jingoism, one reminiscent of the Evangelical preacher and social Darwinist Josiah Strong's argument that Americans would conquer the world in the twentieth century. While such rhetoric was secularized and sanitized in the intervening decades, the sentiment and conclusions have not changed all that much. In fact, they remain in evidence in three well-known books that have shaped the mainstream discussions and debates on globalization: Francis Fukuyama's *The End of History*, Thomas Friedman's *The Lexus and the Olive Tree*, and Samuel Huntington's *The Clash of Civilizations*.

Together these books exhibit an ideological passion that strongly resembles the religious fervor of the evangelists of American ascendance a century ago. If the Protestant theologian Paul Tillich defined religion as any belief or activity that is of "ultimate concern" to a person or group, neoliberal globalization can be rightly described as a religion (or at least a very successful cult); and Fukuyama's, Friedman's, and Huntington's books are clearly among its sacred texts. Not surprisingly then, they are often cited by Arab and Muslim critics, with much consternation, as the foundational texts of US foreign policy in the global era.

All three books have justifiably been criticized by leading historians, economists, and political scientists for factual and historical inaccuracies, methodological inconsistencies, and unstated but clear political agendas. And none of the authors have made much of an effort to defend their main arguments against these critiques.

But despite the sometimes trenchant criticism they have received *The End of History*, *The Lexus and the Olive Tree*, and *The Clash of Civilizations* not only reflect the dominant beliefs of America's political and economic elite, but have had a profound influence on (or at least reflect a profound influence of the ideas they represent on) the shaping of American policy in the post-Cold War period. Moreover, they are intrinsically linked to the work of leading right-wing "Orientalists" like Bernard Lewis, the so-called "sheikh of Islamic studies,"[7] whose *What*

Went Wrong argues – wrongly – that European imperialism/colonialism was a "comparatively brief interlude, and ended half a century ago; that Islam's change for the worse began long before and continued unabated afterward" and "[was] a consequence, not a cause, of the inner weakness of Middle Eastern states and societies."[8]

In this context one of the main arguments of this book is that the message of neoliberal globalization's holy texts, elaborated and disseminated by numerous apostles and comrades, is the foundation of an Axis of Arrogance and Ignorance that guides the work of its devotees and "Bolsheviks" worldwide,[9] whether at the IMF, Pentagon or investment banks. This axis is the overlooked but indispensable companion, even the foundation, of the "Axis of Evil" that drives US foreign and even domestic policy in the global era.

How so? If we start with Fukuyama, his primary argument is that the collapse of Soviet Communism and the end of the Cold War signify the "end of history" in the sense that humankind has arrived at the highest level of political and economic organization with the kind of neoliberal, market-based capitalist democracy (or as he more simply puts it, "liberal democracy") epitomized by the United States and, to a lesser extent, Western Europe and Japan. Thus any attempt to imagine alternative forms of social, political or economic organization, or to arrive at "freedom" or "democracy" through indigenous traditions, concepts or practices, can only be "outside" of history and therefore illegitimate.

Indeed, Fukuyama has in his post-September 11 writings labeled "Islam" as inherently incapable of adapting to the "modern," let alone global, world (a dominant theme in the writings of other Neoconservatives such as Michael Ledeen, Richard Perle, David Frum and others).[10] Because of the power of his arguments, which seemed to make so much sense in the wake of the collapse of Soviet Communism and the end of the Cold War, *The End of History* has had an enduring impact on debates and policy-making in the US and in the Middle East, achieving a life of its own regardless of recent changes in Fukuyama's perspectives on these issues.

Thomas Friedman takes Fukuyama's argument global with his "explanation" of (better, paean to) globalization in *The Lexus and the Olive Tree: Explaining Globalization*. The thrust of Friedman's argument is that you can't live off olive-picking – his metaphor for low-tech, labor-intensive old-world industrial production – and expect to get your Lexus too in the era of globalization. Instead, to live large in the global era you need to get web-savvy, a code-word for the entire World Bank/IMF, Washington Consensus set of political and economic reforms that today are recognized even by their proponents as having brought significant (and often avoidable) hardship to hundreds of millions of people.

Yet for Friedman the "www," *the* symbol of globalization, is accessible only via the rough road of structural adjustment liberalization and privatization of the economy, greater "transparency" and independence of financial markets, the "rule of law" – that is supposed to lead to democracy and wealth for everyone. Needless to say, these days Friedman would have a hard time selling his theory of web-based global prosperity to my wife's many colleagues who've seen lucrative web careers end up on the unemployment line (or even the local Walmart). Never mind trying to convince the millions of Iraqis experiencing America's latest – and purist – version of neoliberal structural adjustment, or the 95 percent of the Arab world's 415 million people who don't even own a phone (let alone a PC), how they can and why they should buy into America's digital paradise.

But as important, underlying Friedman's argument is his belief that the world's poor "just want to go to Disneyland" if given a chance.[11] Yes, the foreign affairs columnist of the world's most important newspaper actually believes that the greatest desire of the billions of people living on $2 a day is to shell out the equivalent of a month's salary (if they're lucky) to take the family to an overrated amusement park.[12] And if they're prevented from doing so, Friedman warns us (and we can assume, tree-hugging environmentalists in particular), they'll tear down the rainforests, tree by tree. In other words, neoliberal globalization is the only hope for the rainforest, and thus for life on earth.

Friedman's main point in *The Lexus and the Olive Tree* is that there is only one way that globalization can proceed, and so any alternative model or trajectory is doomed to fail. Such neoliberal fundamentalism leads directly to Samuel Huntington's *Clash of Civilizations* because to the extent that a "civilization" either fails or refuses to adapt to the American-dominated world order (the latter because it sees its own traditions or cultures, such as Islam, as offering a viable alternative) it will enter into a permanent state of conflict with the West, and the United States in particular. What makes such conflict particularly virulent in the era of globalization is that it is not based on modern political "ideologies" or politics (as was Communism or fascism) but rather on much more "dangerous" and "irrational" motivations such as religion and culture. With this endpoint of perpetual and irremediable conflict the road to the World Trade Center, Afghanistan and Iraq is opened before us. As economist Jeffrey Sachs explains, when these beliefs are translated into action, "the combination of ignorance and arrogance in [US] foreign policy has proved especially lethal."[13]

What's the Matter with Muslims? What's the Matter with Us?

European and now American intellectuals like Friedman, Huntington or Fukuyama have long played a central role in disseminating and legitimizing the kind of Orientalist – that is, institutionally biased and politicized – analyses that purport to show why Muslims are not like us, need our help in order to become like us, but are in fact too irrevocably different ever really to be like us. With the end of the Cold War and the "creative destruction" unleashed by neoliberal globalization (creative destruction, a term originally used by sociologists to describe the destructive power of capitalism as it created new social and economic relations, is now used by supporters of corporate-dominated globalization to celebrate the violence involved in its spread across the globe),[14] a whole new generation of authors began to ponder these questions; the most successful among them being the axis of arrogance and ignorance authors we've discussed.

As we've seen, most of these authors seek to explain "what's the matter with Muslims," "why they hate us," and how we can win the war on terror. Irshad Manji, a Ugandan-Canadian Muslim who has become something of a darling of American conservatives (despite describing herself as a lesbian-feminist Muslim) even titled her book *The Trouble with Islam*. She argues, without citing a single book written by a Muslim feminist scholar – in fact, any serious research on Islam – that what her religion needs is "reform" in its basic theology and attitude toward women in particular (as if these topics haven't been among the chief points of debate within the Muslim world for years, or are possible without a simultaneous transformation in the policies of the West, and US in particular, toward the Muslim world).[15]

One of the primary reasons I wrote this book was to demonstrate the analytical, empirical, and moral problems with these various arguments. And so I began by arguing that a more accurate comparison between the average Muslim and American reveals many more similarities than differences. To quote the Introduction, Muslims are "pretty much like us." But in the course of writing this book I have come to realize that tens of millions of Muslims (at the least) are *really just like us*, especially if the "us" we're talking about is "middle America" as epitomized by a state like Kansas.

In his recent book, *What's the Matter with Kansas*, Thomas Frank offers a powerful analysis of how pro-business conservatives have turned class warfare into culture war in order to redirect public anger away from their policies and toward a so-called "liberal elite."[16] Given the centrality of culture to contemporary globalization, it shouldn't surprise us to see how similar the phenomena he studied are to those operating in the MENA.[17] In places like Kansas, Frank explains, "values matter most" as cultural issues outweigh economics as a chief matter of public concern.[18] And so, for tens of millions of lower- and middle-class – largely white and Christian – Americans, the social hierarchy in which they live is accepted as both natural and just, despite being strongly and increasingly skewed against them.

Why do they actively support a system that threatens their economic interests and even financial solvency? Because their focus is on "social" rather than "economic" issues. And what keeps their attention focused away from economic issues during a time of economic distress? Their class antagonism has been deftly turned away from the economic actors whose policies negatively impact them and towards a demonized (and largely mythological) liberal elite that is defined as the very moral and political antithesis of "normal Americans."

Why do so many Kansans hate liberals? According to Frank, Kansans and others who think as they do believe that "authenticity" and "humility" define their character as decent, hard-working Americans (and that of the politicians whom they support). These goals are believed to be the opposite of the "snobbery" and "selfishness" of the liberal establishment that is believed to run the country, or at least its culture, and supposedly wants nothing less than the destruction of everything that makes the United States a sacred, even "pure," nation.[19] But if Kansans and their compatriots across America feel morally superior to a Godless, foreign-food-eating liberal elite, they also feel powerless and victimized by their immoral enemy.

Central to the functioning of this populist backlash ideology is "its airtight explanation of reality, its ability to make sense to the average person's disgruntlement." However divorced from reality, such arguments are made to seem natural, in good measure through the spread of conspiracy theories and "lurid fantasies of victimhood."[20] And in response to the constant attacks from enemies foreign and domestic only "God, guts and guns" will make American great again.[21]

We'll come back to the subject of guns and violence and their role in contemporary culture in later chapters. What is important for our purposes now is how reminiscent Frank's account of "middle

America backlash" syndrome is of the worldview and psychological perspectives of millions of Muslims, who believe very similar things to middle Americans, and who also see God, guts and guns as central to returning Islam to its golden age. If Kansans – and by extension, the half of the United States that votes Republican – are so easily guided into directing their feelings of victimization and marginalization against a largely imaginary "elite" that is believed to run the United States against their interests, can we expect Muslims to feel very differently toward the real global elite when the majority of them (especially in the MENA) live under autocratic regimes at third world levels of social development, with the memories and impact of colonialism still fresh in their collective consciousness, and the United States *actually* playing a crucial role in their victimization and marginalization?

Conservative Muslims have long believed that they possess traits of modesty and authenticity that have been lost in their larger societies' slavish desire to ape Western consumerist culture. And both conservative Americans and conservative Muslims also see culture as a primary tool of their oppression, while believing their societies to be living in a state of "cultural decline,"[22] creating bogeymen – the "culture industry" and "liberal entertainment elite" for conservative Americans, the "American cultural invasion" for conservative Muslims – that simply "must exist" for their worldviews to make sense.[23]

As important, the members of both communities who seek political power are willing to work far harder than most of their more moderate neighbors to organize people at the grass-roots level. Why? Because both believe, in the words of one Kansas politician, that "we have an agenda – the Kingdom of God." Given this priority, "material goals just don't seem to matter."[24]

Finally, in both societies people who were once radical, whether Arab socialists or Kansas progressive populists, have become increasingly reactionary during the last thirty years. And with this transformation the once great goals of Enlightenment modernity – increasing democracy, social justice, and cultural tolerance – have been replaced by a desire among both groups to be "the grave digger of modernism." As Frank warns about his countrymen and women, "With a little more effort, the backlash may well repeal the entire twentieth century."[25]

This desire to kill modernity, which for its victims is not a strange wish, can only be accomplished by "setting up a conflict so unresolvable that everyone … would eventually have to choose up sides and join the fight."[26] If this is how Frank describes the world we are becoming as viewed through the looking glass of Kansas, it is a world that much of the Middle East has already become. This is one reason why people living there are even angrier than the average denizen of the Midwest.[27]

"After Jihad," and Other Liberal Fantasies that Keep People Clueless as to What's Really the Matter with the Middle East, or Kansas

The dynamics of the populist backlash help us understand the popularity of the conservative books with titles such as *Taking America Back, Why We Fight*, or *A Heart, a Cross, and a Flag*. And then there's the *pièce de résistance, An End to Evil: How to Win the War on Terror*, David Frum and Richard Perle's violently racist book that calls for perpetual, unremitting battle against America's enemies while resisting any attempts at "appeasement and defeatism" at home.[28] Extending the culture war to a general war of the worlds, *An End to Evil* conveys the sense that America is at war with Islam itself around the world, with Muslim societies viewed as little more than cauldrons of hate, murder, obscurantism, and deceit.[29] We will explore the impact of such a crusader worldview on Muslims' perception of globalization in Chapters Four through Seven.

Perhaps more important than the right-wing screeds are the seemingly objective and even sympathetic writings of so-called "liberal" scholars, a good example of which is the book *After Jihad* by the Oxford-, Harvard- and Yale-educated law professor Noah Feldman. Despite its title and its author's impressive-sounding credentials, this book misuses crucial religious texts, cites only four Arabic sources in the entire book, and is ultimately unable to present a convincing argument why "doing the right thing" means supporting the spread of democracy in the Muslim world but not calling for a democratization of American foreign policy as well.[30]

On top of everything, Feldman, a professor of law, decided to work for the American occupation authorities to draft an Iraqi constitution, no doubt based on his gospel of a post-jihad liberal Islam premised on a benign American foreign policy. I'm not sure why, but it never occurred to him, or so many other academics – such as another Harvard Ph.D. who, with nothing better going on at home, went to Iraq and wound up being appointed the de facto Education Minister, or an Oxford Ph.D. serving as a US army counter-insurgency expert – that they could have come to Iraq as private citizens and offered their help directly to the Iraqi people without the imprimatur of the world's greatest imperial power behind them. (Perhaps they never studied Iraq's modern history and the impact of British colonialism on the country. Then again, I'm sure many an idealistic young Brit set their sights on Iraq in the early 1920s full of dreams of helping the once great Mesopotamia reclaim her glory.)

Instead, Feldman and his colleagues became part of an occupation regime whose rationale for dealing with Iraqis, in the words of another ex-academic who became one of Coalition Provisional Authority Administrator Bremer's intelligence chiefs, was: "If you starve a dog he'll follow you anywhere."[31] Of course, this has always been the reality of empire, whether in generations past or today. (And as an Iraqi friend reminded me when I mentioned this expression to him, it was also used by Saddam Hussein to describe how he ruled the country.) But to acknowledge the realities of how colonies are actually administered would undermine the intellectual and moral foundation for imperialism, yesterday or today.

So instead each generation, even decade, produces a new crop of neoliberal and/or conservative apologists for empire. Just in time for the invasion of Iraq, a new member of this club emerged into the media spotlight, the British Tory economist Niall Ferguson, to argue for the US to relish the role of world imperial leader and follow Britain's example by benignly shepherding the Global South towards development and perhaps, if they're lucky, democracy.[32] For Ferguson, Feldman or Frum – and no doubt in good measure through their efforts, the *9/11 Commission Report*[33] – the problems that ail the Muslim world are believed to be all the fault of Muslims themselves.

The only solution is for us to help them become more like us, and the only way to achieve this is, however painful for all concerned, more violence and foreign domination. As for decades of Arab/Muslim frustration and anger at US policies in the MENA and the corrosive impact of its hyperconsumerist culture, or accepting the possibility that it might be helpful to understand and address the issues that breed hatred and radicalism as part of the war on terror (as John Esposito has thoughtfully implored the policy-making establishment), such ideas can only be the concern of appeasers, self-hating Americans. These are today's "squeamish" counterparts to British colonial officials who questioned Winston Churchill's decision to gas and carpet bomb Iraqi villages after the British conquest of the country – and people who just don't have the stomach to lead the world into the twenty-first century.[34]

Changing Our Orientation

Fukuyama, Friedman, and Huntington provide a good foundation for understanding how We see Them. Yet we still need to examine how the thought-processes produced by the "Axes of Arrogance and Ignorance" are reflected in seemingly objective analyses by leading experts, and what possible alternatives exist for exploring the region, its peoples, and their relationship with other cultures, especially the West.

Such an exploration would be based on a paradigm of dialogue and empathy rather than conflict and empire. It would appreciate the differences *and* common threads running through the slums of West Beirut and its chic open-roof BO-18 disco downtown; through the sounds of Alabina on West Jerusalem's Allenby Street and of an "oriental" remix of Michael Jackson on Salahhadin Street on the city's occupied East side; and through the innumerable cell-phone stores or internet cafés in "traditional" Fes or funky Marrakesh, war-torn Baghdad or closeted Tehran.

To help build this much-needed Axis of Empathy let's return to the comfort of the Rabat train and the *Arab Human Development Report*, where this chapter began. Across from me, next to the women on their *portables*, sits a young Moroccan man named Abderrahmane. Wearing a T-shirt emblazoned with a big US flag, Abderrahmane is putting the moves, in fairly commendable English, on an American girl via his sleek, Italian-designed Nokia cell phone. While I'm eavesdropping on his attempt at cultural hybridity (not bad, but not likely to get him into either promised land) my ostensible work on the train is to edit a piece I was commissioned to write for the journal *Middle East Report* on the AHDR.[35] What made the eavesdropping so relevant was the great fanfare and evident satisfaction greeting the release of this report, which has quickly become a new benchmark in discussing the contemporary Middle East and its problems.

The accolades in large part were due to the fact that it was specifically researched and written by "a team of *Arab* scholars and policy-makers with an advisory committee of well-known Arabs in international public life." They might have been well known, but from reading the report they don't seem very well knowing, at least of the primary subject of the report: young people like Abderrahmane who represent the amalgam of youth, integration, and communications technology that constitute the heart of the authors' agenda. Yet despite its numerous problems, commentators, whether in the *Washington Post*, *Le Monde* or the New York *Times* (the latter of which featured an article, an editorial, and the inevitable Thomas Friedman column) applauded the *AHDR*'s "bluntness" and "brutal honesty" in analyzing what to the *Times* remains the only "substantially unchanged" region of the world in the global era.[36]

No doubt many members of the Arab elite would be unfriendly to reforms that actually benefited the bulk of their populations. But the *AHDR* stunningly (although perhaps in the present climate, not surprisingly) avoided two fundamental issues – namely, money and power – without discussing which of its analyses or conclusions are ultimately irrelevant to achieving its stated goal of inspiring a "new social contract in which a synergy is generated between a revitalized and efficient government, a dynamic and socially responsible private sector, and a powerful and truly grassroots civil society."[37]

Such a vision is certainly laudable, but under present circumstances it can hardly be realized in the US or France, let alone Syria or Morocco – where, as I write, the US has just changed the focus of its "Forum for the Future" from supporting democracy to business. Rather, it is the lack of historical context for the data compiled by the *AHDR* team that made their analyses so removed from the socio-political and economic realities of the global era. Employing an argument similar to that of Thomas Friedman in *The Lexus and the Olive Tree*, the authors of the *AHDR* take their data to indicate that "while most of the rest of the world is coming together in larger groupings, Arab countries continue to face the outside world, and the challenges posed by the region itself, individually and alone." This may be true; but how does this make the region unique? Who can the average American count on for solidarity and support as s/he faces the "dominate or die" global order? Certainly not the US Government. So who is the average Syrian supposed to trust? President Bashir al-Asad? The WTO?

A Few Minor Questions

Undisturbed by such a Herculean political, economic, and moral/societal task, the *AHDR* calls for a "holistic development" strategy that can achieve the "new social contract" necessary to overcome the isolation of the Arab world. This is certainly a good prescription; and it should be mentioned that the call for holistic, or balanced, development is a centerpiece of the growing critiques of market-oriented neoliberal development policies advocated by the World Bank, IMF, and their supporters in academia and the media.

Yet such holistic development is not as holistic as imagined by many of its proponents. First, these analyses lack a discussion of how Arab states can secure the massive amounts of money needed to pay for all of the programs and policies they advocate (think of the money the US had to spend to begin to rebuild Iraq and multiply by two dozen countries). How, for example, can the Arab world increase its per capita spending on health care by the recommended 2 percent of GDP when GDP growth for the industrial countries stood only slightly more than 1 percent in 2004, with the developing world (aside from China) not far ahead?[38] What's more, how can countries such as Egypt, Libya, Morocco, Syria, and even Kuwait and Saudi Arabia, pursue more balanced food production (and thereby increase nutritional health) when the United States simultaneously increases subsidies for its own farmers, floods their markets with below-market-price US grains, and through USAID and other international programs attempts to transform agricultural production from crops devoted to local human consumption to animal feed and export-oriented textile crops?[39]

And how can these countries increase spending for pre-school when their military budgets are three times greater, in per capita GDP, than the world average? Or when the Bush Administration increases military aid to Colombia and spends $100 billion per year in Iraq while claiming poverty when faced with requests for *maintaining* already low levels of foreign aid to the Global South? Or when Bush and Company talk of democratizing the Middle East while engaging in their own brutal occupation, and their top aides and confidants publicly inform us that "too much democracy" wouldn't be such a good thing (no doubt as much for us as for them)? Or when this argument is supported by leading members of the press corps, such as Fareed Zakaria, whose October 15, 2001 *Newsweek* cover story was titled "Why Do They Hate Us" and was followed by a book that argued that "liberal autocracies" like Morocco and Jordan are a better bet for the MENA than democracy in the near future? (According to him, this is because they respect citizens' rights, heed the rule of law, and "provide a better environment for life, liberty and happiness" than illiberal democracies like Venezuela, Russia or Ghana.)[40]

I'm not sure which Morocco or Jordan Zakaria has visited lately, as neither country's government seems respectful of their citizens' rights or laws whenever I'm there. What is important to recognize now is that none of these reports or analyses offer scenarios for Arab grassroots forces to attain the political power that could produce governments and development policies which are "of, by, and for the people." It is inarguably true, as the *AHDR* states when calling for large increases in spending on education and information technology, that "modern knowledge is power." Yet precisely for that reason, most Arab regimes – and increasingly the US Government – share knowledge only selectively, if at all, since they have little desire to encourage the kind of bottom-up democracy that policies advocated by the *AHDR* would engender.

And so the advice of the follow-up 2003 *AHDR* that "Arab societies close a growing knowledge gap by investing heavily in education and promoting open intellectual inquiry" falls on deaf ears with the US sitting squarely in the middle of the Arab world on top of all that oil. Indeed, beyond the clear need at least to mention the impact of external influences *on the Arab world*, is not political transformation *in the West* surely a prerequisite for achieving real democracy there? How could any developing country radically reduce spending on strategically crucial US/Western products, whether surplus grains or high-tech weaponry, unless developed countries had themselves radically restructured their political economies so that retaining favorable balances of trade based on exports of wheat or F-16s, or through imposed liberalization of markets, was no longer among the most important strategic considerations for the political and economic elites?

And how can Arabs or citizens of other developing countries, whether in Russia, Indonesia, or Latin America, successfully challenge corrupt and autocratic regimes when Western countries, particularly in the context of the war on terrorism, turn a blind eye to – in some cases, encourage – large-scale abuses of human, civil, and political rights by client or friendly regimes, and even competitors or supposed enemies like the Sudan or China? And what, short of a historic change in American political culture and ideology, will be required before our Government would actually pursue "freedom and democracy" in the developing world?

The Soul of Development, or The Orient Beats Back

How can we transcend the Axis of Arrogance and Ignorance that plagues mainstream analyses, policy-making, and commentary on the so-called Axis of Evil and the MENA more broadly? In my opinion, a culturally and popularly informed undertaking is crucial. None other than Samuel Huntington argues this in the title of one of his recent books, *Culture Matters*. Even the first *AHDR* described culture as "the soul of development," although it devoted only one out of 178 pages of the report to the subject.

Much of the progressive literature on globalization discusses cultural issues, and there is even a whole field of intellectual inquiry, "cultural studies," devoted to this task (although its famously infuriating jargon has rendered its insights unavailable even to most academics). Thankfully, younger writers like Naomi Klein, Thomas Frank, Greg Tate, and Jason Hill have been opening the field in important and innovative ways. And they are being joined by veteran critics like Tariq Ali, who brilliantly demonstrates that Huntington's clash is not one of civilizations, but rather of fundamentalisms – neoliberal against Islamist.[41]

But most of these important contributions either focus largely on the United States or parts of the world other than the MENA region, and don't engage the important (if overly complicated) academic literature, or else harbor a clear bias against religious activists as partners in progressive dialogue and social change.[42] But the people who are the objects of the Axis of Arrogance and Ignorance, the scholars who spend years studying and interacting with their cultures, and the religious personalities who are important culture shapers, must be included in the global conversation on how to build alternatives to the existing system. The good news is that there are voices trying to be heard.

Indeed, the Axes of Evil, Arrogance, and Ignorance might support the status quo among Western and Arab elites alike, but on the level of popular culture in the MENA today we can say that the "The Orient Beats Back." This is the title of a popular dance and electronica CD in Morocco featuring Arab-style remixes and re-imaginings of Western dance hits. The adoption, translation, and transformation of other languages and technologies demonstrated by this and hundreds of offerings at kiosks throughout Morocco constitute the productive creativity advocated, albeit largely ignored, by the *AHDR* (probably because most of the authors of the report are of a different class and generation than the producers and consumers of this music).[43]

When considered with the avaricious acquisition of so-called Western technologies and languages (i.e., computers and the internet, French and increasingly English) by an ever-expanding section of young urban citizens of the Arab world, there is clearly a sizeable (if still too small) minority of young people who are finding ways to embrace the ethic of cultural creativity and thirst for "modern" knowledge that the *AHDR* and other reports feel are urgent to the task of reform in the MENA. Moreover, they are doing so on their own terms, many refusing to embrace the secular–religious dichotomy that defines Western culture, and in ways that move beyond the problematic criticisms of the *AHDR*, the self-celebratory writings of

Friedman or Fukuyama, or the false dichotomies of Samuel Huntington and George W. Bush.

"The Orient Beats Back" represents the essence of this process, which for me is one of culture jamming. This is a good point to explore the history of culture jamming in a bit more detail. Although the practice goes back to the 1930s, culture jamming originated in the mid-1980s contemporary techno-rock scene and quickly became identified with the practice of parodying advertisements and hijacking billboards by drastically altering their messages to critique the depicted product or activity. Over the past decade jams have become sophisticated "interceptions" – counter-messages that hack into a corporation's own method of communication to send a message starkly at odds with the one intended.

But while a glance at the culture jams and the "alternative" communities that often imagine and execute them testifies to their originality and creativity, I argue that ultimately they represent individual or isolated acts of cultural resistance. Their power is limited in comparison with the power of contemporary globalization to homogenize and defang minority, third world, "resistance" and "bohemian" cultures even as their diversity, hipness, and originality are celebrated.

Corporate culture has in fact been coopting and even conquering critical cultures for at least two generations. In the early 1970s advertisers realized the need to meet the growing anti-capitalism of the youth movement head on; today business gurus like John Kao and Richard Foster are writing best-sellers with titles like *Jamming* and *Creative Destruction* (a term used by scholars to describe the impact of capitalist modernity), while Bloomingdales' advertisements exclaim, "Welcome to the Culture Bash" – which for them means cute guys, Hawaiian shirts, and a secluded beach.

This situation is why Naomi Klein asks in *No Logo*, "Did all our protests and subversive theory only serve to provide great content for the culture industries? Moreover, why were our ideas about political rebellion so deeply non-threatening? And how did diversity become the mantra of global capital?"[44] Perhaps because the corporatization of cool strengthened the Axes of Arrogance and Ignorance during the last generation, so that when it was connected to the Axis of Evil after September 11, 2001 a seemingly impregnable ideological cage was erected that has trapped American society within the neoliberal paradigm, which appears natural and devoid of viable alternatives but is in fact radically constructed and opposable from many sides.

My belief is that if we can jam in the musical sense of the word – that is, bring together diverse and even dissonant voices to compose a truly world music – we can break down ("deconstruct," as some philosophers might say) the "iron cage" of neoliberalism by widening conversations, shedding outmoded stereotypes and paradigms, and developing greater compassion for both the victims and beneficiaries of globalization. In this sense, "The Orient Beats Back" and similar projects, with their disregard of Euro-American notions of copyright and musical protocol, are not just a jam *at* the corporatization of music in the West (especially world music), but also a step *towards* the kind of truly global cultural production that made world music so ground-breaking and appealing in the first place. As I will demonstrate in the following chapters, such cultural performances help develop the shared language, strategies, and vision to transform critics and protesters into prophets of a true globalization in the new millennium.

Conclusion: "Arabica 2002"

There are some things you would only think of while watching the Muslim Broadcast Channel with a hotel clerk in Marrakesh. One of them is that Robert Plant stole his famous repertoire of stage moves from the Lebanese diva Najwa Karam.

What is the logic behind the strange assertion that the stage presence of "Liz Plin's" frontman (to transliterate the Arabic spelling of Led Zeppelin on the cover of a recent CD of Robert Plant and the Gnawa master Mualem Brahim) is drawn from a singer who, like me, was in grade school during the band's glory years? The insight occurred while I was watching a live performance of Ms. Karam on the MBC (a Saudi-owned satellite channel broadcast from London) in a hotel in Marrakesh after a night of wandering through the Jmaa el-Fna, the open-air market famed for its magicians, snake-charmers, palm-readers, boxers, acrobats, and dozens of open-air restaurants.[45]

But how could Karam's body language of 2002 have influenced Plant's circa 1973? Perhaps Plant, who has frequented the Arab world since the late 1960s, was influenced by the same artists – especially the seminal 'Um Kalthoum – as Najwa Karam (that was his take on the situation when I asked him). Of course, Karam could have stolen the moves from Plant; but since Led Zeppelin never toured in Lebanon and never produced music videos, that would have meant she saw the group's concert film *The Song Remains the Same* on Lebanese TV, which is highly unlikely. And Karam agreed that it was probably through mutual influence when I enquired. In this context the Plant–Karam axis is a useful example of our larger discussion because its revelations of cross-cultural, gender, and generational conversation directly challenges the nexus of the Axes of Evil and Arrogance that are determining how entire civilizations interact in the newest global age.

Such interaction represents the generally unheralded side of globalization. In my travels in search of this elusive globalization I have noticed that there are three kinds of reactions by peoples of the so-called "developing" or "third" world to its promises and perils: The first is the wholesale adoption of things American, which is the goal of the great commercial Culture Bash but rarely occurs except within a very small and wealthy elite. The second is its antithesis, the one epitomized by Osama bin Laden, al-Qa'eda, and the violence and hatred they represent.[46]

The third response is represented by "The Orient Beats Back." Its adaptations and remixes of Western (inspired) dance and trance music by leading Arab DJs represent not a postmodern continuation of some sort of hegemonic Euro-trash dance music, but rather a true "anti" modern response to the sins of modernity matrix in a process of superimposition and blatant theft that defies convention and copyright at the same time. How so? Because by adapting and transforming Western styles and technologies into something new, rather than a supposedly "postmodern" collage of already existing styles and sounds, the music of "The Orient Beats Back" challenges the very premises of modernity that are at the heart of the Axis of Arrogance and Ignorance: that the Rest can only copy the West, never transform and even improve it.[47]

Along with numerous other musical collaborations, such as the "Arabica" series (yearly compilations of Arab remixes of well-known Western songs), this genre offers a most tantalizing clue to how we can move beyond the rhetoric of mutual suspicion and recrimination to a true jamming of cultures whose force can match the monotonous, Soviet-style drumming of the neoliberal apparatchiks. Consider my finds the morning I was leaving Marrakesh for Rabat: Arab DJ remixes of Santana, Missy Elliot, even Pink Floyd's "Us and Them." And the original version of the Missy Elliot was itself built around an Arabic-music sample, making this "Arab" remix particularly flush with cultural and musical significance.

Allow me to explore this line of reasoning further. As I write this particular paragraph I'm sitting in a Rabat internet café. Behind me is a young, stylishly dressed young man blasting Busta Rhymes' "Pass the Courvoisier" out of his computer speakers (computers at almost every internet café in the Middle East, from Morocco to Iraq, seem to be fully multi-media), followed by Snoop Dogg and the North African-

French actor-singer Jamel Debousse doing a French–English language duet, "Mission Cleopatra." As he bops his head he's typing away to his chat-room buddies in French, peppered with knowing Englishisms. It seems that everyone – and everyone here is largely young, college-age men (although between a quarter and a third of the customers in the internet cafés seem to be women) – is chatting, or judging from the URL history list of the computers I've been using, checking out the latest Billboard charts, or the French porn sites I mentioned earlier.

Even many university professors use these cafés for their email, as the price – less than a dollar an hour – makes them a good substitute for more expensive and slower home connections. And everyone is typing in English or French, though one can now do email in Arabic, which is supposed to be the primary language in Morocco after two decades of an "Arabization" program whose goal was to "decolonize" the heads of Moroccans from their former French rulers. Moreover, the customers at the cafés are by and large not the elite of Morocco. If they were they'd be at home surfing on brand new P5 computers hooked up to wanadoo.ma, or even wanadoo.fr if they're particularly francophone. Instead, these are the very people that Tom Friedman and the authors of the *AHDR* are looking for but can't seem to find (perhaps because they don't listen to enough hiphop, or need to spend more time frequenting neighborhood internet cafés).[48]

Of course, there is more to globalization in Morocco, or anywhere else in the Arab and Muslim worlds for that matter, than hybrid hiphop, French porn, and Berber carpets of varying quality. As I sat in my hotel room contemplating the origin of Robert Plant's stage repertoire, the sounds of the Gnawa streamed into my room from the Jmaa el-Fna. Gnawa music is itself a form of globalization, as it emerged from the blending of religious traditions and musical styles of West African (former) slaves, Berber and Arab cultures, and now rock and funk. And the exoticized, orientalized landscape of the Jmaa el-Fna, which seems to come out of some nineteenth-century British travel book, in fact caters mostly to Moroccans themselves – another case of cultural (re)appropriation in which the formerly colonized now enjoy the cultural fantasies of their former rulers.

What this suggests is that today's globalization is not a new phenomenon. It's just that it's been so distorted by its association with neoliberalism that forms of cultural, political or economic integration that don't involve the same scale of (primarily Western) money and power are considered outside of "our" globalization. Yet as the French Muslim thinker and activist Tariq Ramadan explains, whatever the power of and problems stemming from the dominant model of globalization, it is ultimately "not the 'West' but rather some governments, some institutions and important multinationals … There are very active movements of resistance in the West that are very important for the future. It is absolutely necessary that, in the Muslim world, we don't fall into the too simplistic reading of the Huntington thesis, which is fundamentally misleading."[49] We need to take Ramadan's point seriously if we are going to move beyond the present "inhuman globalism" to a shared, just future. And that is why unpacking the relationships between power, knowledge, and culture is central to the project of understanding Why They Don't Hate Us, as we will explore in the pages that follow.

2 Overcoming the Matrix, Re-Imagining Middle Eastern History

The Numbing Power of Colonialism

On the following page is a table showing the dates of occupation and the occupying countries for over thirty nations. The list is numbing as it is long, and it is the modern history of the Middle East and larger Muslim world. Every single Muslim majority country in the world, with the exception of parts of the Arabian Peninsula, was conquered by Europe by the end of World War I. Where are the dates of independence? For many Muslims, especially those opposed to globalization, their countries have yet to become truly independent, so I have not included these dates to reflect this widespread sentiment.

The situation is not much better today. As the first *AHDR* informed us, per-capita growth in the twenty-two Arab countries surveyed is lower than anywhere except in sub-Saharan Africa. It will take the average Arab citizen 140 years to double his or her income while people in other parts of the world will do it in fewer than ten years. Of the 280 million Arabs in the region, 65 million are illiterate; two-thirds of them women. The GDP of all these Arab states combined is less than that of Spain; one out of every five Arabs lives on less than $2 a day.

How are we to respond to this history and present reality? More important, how must it feel to be part of the culture on the losing end of the last 500 years of history, especially in light of the events of the past three years? What must it feel like to be a Muslim? To know that there is practically no part of the *ummah*, or Muslim nation, that hasn't been ruled by others, and today still remains, to a greater or lesser degree, under the influence, or even occupation, of the West and its allies?

To understand these questions we first need to understand the dynamics through which Europeans were able to conquer or

Table 1: Occupations of Muslim Majority Countries 1511–2001

Country	Date(s) of Occupation	Occupying Country/Countries
Malaysia	1511, 1641, 1785, 1941, 1945	Portugal, Netherlands, Britain, Japan, Britain
Ghana	1600s	Britain
India/Pakistan	1757	Britain
Egypt	1798, 1882, 1940, 1942, 1956, 1967	France, Italy, Germany, Britain, Israel
Palestine	1799, 1831, 1917, 1948, 1967	France, Egypt, Britain, Israel, Egypt, Jordan
Syria	1799, 1917, 1941, 1967	France, "Allied Powers," Israel
Bahrain	1816	Britain
Algeria	1830	France
Indonesia	1830	Netherlands
Yemen	1839	Britain
Somalia	1836, 1889, 1940	Britain, Italy
Persia/Iran	1851, 1907, 1941	Divided into British/Russian "spheres of influence," United States and Britain
Mauritania	1850s	France
Mali	1871	France
Ottoman Empire	Dismantled 1876–1920	Concert of Europe/Allied Powers
Tunisia	1881	France
Trucial States (UAE)	1882	Britain
Sudan	1883	Britain and Egypt
Nigeria	1886	Britain
Chad	1890s	France
Niger	1890s	France
Kenya	1895	Britain
Kuwait	1899, 1990	Britain, Iraq
Morocco	1912	France
Libya	1913, 1941	Italy, Germany, Britain, Australia
Qatar	1916	Britain
Jordan	1917	Britain
Lebanon	1917	France
Iraq	1917, 2003	Britain, United States
Ethiopia	1936	Italy
Afghanistan	1979, 2001	Soviet Union, United States

otherwise control most of the world during the modern era. And to do this I would like to begin by discussing one of the most popular movie series of the last decade, the *Matrix* trilogy. The plot of *The Matrix* revolves around the idea that the world people think they inhabit is really a simulation of reality generated by computers. What is the reality underneath? That human beings are slaves – batteries, really – to machines, who through an elaborate computer program connected directly to their brains have convinced humans that they are actually living in the world they imagine. As Laurence Fishburne's character Morpheus explains to Keanu Reeves' Neo:

> What is the Matrix? Control. The Matrix is a computer generated dream world built to keep us under control in order to change a human being into [a battery] ... The Matrix is everywhere. It is all around us, even now in this very room. [It has made] you a slave, born into bondage. As long as the Matrix exists the human race will never be free.

This being the case, the only way to get "unplugged" from the matrix was to be disconnected from the system and flushed into its gigantic sewer, at which point a strange-looking craft might scoop you up and bring you to Zion, the one place in the world where people live free and in full possession of their faculties (this would certainly be news to most Palestinians and Israelis I know, but that's another story).

If only the right color pill and a few fashionably dressed phantasms were all it took to escape the real matrix, learn kung fu, and fight for humanity's freedom. Even more, if only machines, not humans, were responsible for the mess we're in. At least then, with a common enemy, we'd all be on the same side instead of hopelessly divided.

Yet, like the members of the "resistance" in *The Matrix*, millions of people around the world feel that there is something fundamentally wrong with the world even as they participate in the existing system. And this fact points, for me, to an interesting possibility: that however fanciful the plot of *The Matrix* seems, there is in fact a real matrix, every bit as powerful as the screen version, which has also been around for hundreds of years. But the real matrix is made and run by humans, not machines, and it's a lot more complex and harder to escape than the one terminated by Keanu Reeves.

For some people the dissonance caused by the matrix between their experiences of everyday life and their ideals and dreams becomes "like a splinter in your mind driving you mad," as Morpheus explains to Neo. The depths of the madness produced by the matrix became clear to the world on September 11, 2001; but we have yet to understand the real matrix that made such terror inevitable, not to mention the centuries of oppression and exploitation, death and destruction leading up to it. So let's explore how the real matrix has shaped the way millions of Arabs and Muslims experience globalization today and, because of this, how they understand and feel about the United States and its role in the world.

What is the real matrix? It's not a computer program; instead it is a combination of historical processes, identities, and power relations whose roots go back at least six centuries to the dawn of the modern era. More specifically, as I alluded to in Chapter One, the matrix has four components, or "coefficients," as they're technically known:[1] modernity, imperialism/colonialism, capitalism, and nationalism. Over the centuries these four processes evolved together into a densely woven economic, political, and cultural fabric that has shaped the way people have experienced, understood, and responded to the world around them. The power and pervasiveness of this matrix is such that, like the humans still plugged into the movie Matrix, most of us consent to a system that has consistently delivered the opposite of the freedom, unity, and progress it heralded. This is clearly one reason why the movie struck such a cord among audiences.

The Modernity Matrix

Both the matrix as a whole and each of the coefficients have shaped the history of the Middle East in ways that have a direct bearing on how contemporary globalization is experienced, understood, and responded to in Muslim societies. By exploring each component we will have the basis to understand both how colonialism worked and how and why Muslim critics of the West and modernity at large have reacted in the manner they have.

Let's begin with modernity, one of the most misunderstood, even abused, concepts in common usage. We all know we live in the modern world – even if it's "post"-modern or "globalized" it's still modern. We also know that the more modern something is the more advanced and useful it's supposed to be; this means that modern societies and cultures, especially in the so-called "West," are fundamentally different from and superior to those that came before them. But what does modernity really mean? Essentially, it involves three distinct but interrelated concepts: a historical era; an aesthetic, moral, and political project; and an ideology that operates under various names, such as modernism and modernization. Each process has long been used to justify far-reaching changes in the politics, economies, and cultures of various societies, but needless to say, each is problematic.

When did the modern era begin, and when did or will it end? Are the laudable aims of the "project of modernity," such as increasing freedom, unity, enlightenment, progress, and democracy around the world, realizable? Does modernization really mean the "secular-ization," "progress," and "rationalization" of previously "traditional," "backward," and "primitive" societies? One thing is for sure: modernity is the most unique and intensely experienced period of human history because for the first time people have been conscious that they were living in a new historical period that was both discon-nected from the very recent past and, if you bought into the ideology, was leading to an inescapably brighter future.[2]

Perhaps the most well-known description of the experience of modernity was that penned by the French poet Charles Baudelaire around 1860, when he described modernity as "the fleeting, the tran-sitory and the arbitrary." This combination of sensations occurred in large part because the process of becoming modern (that is, modern-ization) was accompanied by a *drive* to be "modern," which at the most basic level was a drive to be new and up-to-date, but gradually meant no longer being bound to the "traditional" world.

Baudelaire realized that the experience of modernity is felt most immediately as a new and accelerated mode of existence. The indus-trial revolution, the increased circulation and consumption of goods from around the world, the speed at which these new goods, and information as well, circulated because of improved means of travel and communication (steamships and trains, telegraphs and tele-phones), all increased the pace of life more than all the inventions in human history before them. As important, it seemed that as quickly as new things were invented or arrived in the new department stores of London or Paris, they went out of style or were replaced by even newer and supposedly better items.

This led him to focus on the "ephemeral" nature of modernity, which made modernity very difficult to grasp hold of and master. Moreover, it was becoming increasingly clear that modernity's speed and ephemeral nature made the process of becoming modern incredibly violent and filled with misery for millions of people in order to achieve its goals. No wonder then that the great early-twentieth-century German philosopher Walter Benjamin argued that modernity was filled with both beauty and "the savagery that lurks in the midst of civilization."[3]

On top of the violence involved in becoming modern, modernity has long been tied to a belief that there was only one road for a "culture" or "civilization" to become modern. This narrative of modernity imagined it starting in Western/Northern Europe, specifically because of cultural advances that occurred only there, such as the Enlightenment, the Reformation, rational thinking, science, secularism, democratic forms of government, and, of course, capitalism. If these ideas and processes were to spread to other regions and peoples of the world, it would be the initiative, power, and good graces of "the West" that would bring them there.

The flip-side of the privileging of the West/Europe as the source of modernity was the belief in the long decline and/or stagnation of the "East" along with its separation and isolation from the rapidly modernizing West. As one economic historian wrote of the Middle East, "the fact of Arabs decline itself stands plain."[4] The drive to stem that decline and "help" the Middle East and other non-European peoples reach the promised land of modernity has, it should be remembered, subjugated, enslaved, and killed tens of millions of people. And it's apparently not over yet.

The main tools that allowed modernity to conquer the world were colonialism and capitalism, on the one hand, and the nation-state with its "imagined communities" and real boundaries through which colonialism and capitalism were nurtured and directed outward, on the other. Together they made the original "globalization" of modernity possible. The link between colonialism and capitalism is clear. As the historian Samir Amin describes it, capitalism as a potential world system did not exist until there existed a consciousness of its "conquering power."[5] That is, it was precisely when Europeans, flush with the gold, silver, and blood of the new world, realized that their civilization could literally conquer the whole world, that modernity begins in earnest. And not just the genocide of native Americans and the enslavement of Africans, but the death camps of Hitler and the gulag of Stalin; all are the products of this conquering spirit.

Moreover, imperialism/colonialism was also the context that shaped capitalism and nationalism. There is no America without the thirteen "colonies"; many of the concepts and technologies of industrial capitalism were born in Europe's overseas colonies, while its ideologies gestated closer to home in places like Ireland and Scotland. And the nationalism that was produced through the interrelationship of these forces created an imagined community of citizens whose identity was largely defined by opposing the national "self" against all possible "others."[6] When all these dynamics came together, the project of modernity at large became the "point of departure for the conquest of the world."[7]

Capitalism and the Costs of Colonialism

Needless to say the costs of colonialism and colonially derived capitalism are incalculable. How do you calculate the socio-economic impact of thirty million Africans kidnapped from their homelands, or tens of millions more massacred by the British, French, Belgians, and Germans in the name of progress and enlightenment, or the almost successful genocide of the Amerindians? And the political, cultural, and even psychological costs were as expensive as the economic and physical consequences. As the economist Karl Polanyi observed, "social calamities are primarily a cultural, not economic phenomenon that can be measured by income figures or populations statistics."[8] That is, more than economic exploitation, it was the disintegration of the cultural environment of conquered societies that was the greatest cause of their seemingly insoluble problems – a point that the great anti-colonial writers such as Frantz Fanon, Aimé Césaire, and Albert Memmi well understood.[9]

But the colonialism was not just practiced on "others," it was also practiced on the emerging working class of Europe. As far back as the eighteenth century, European thinkers accepted that poverty was inseparable from capitalism and progress. English and Italian economists commented that the greatest number of poor people lived in the richest and most "civilized" nations and that the market economy would create "great and permanent evils."[10] We can even say that capitalism would not have been possible without the "satanic mills" – that is, the factories – of the industrial revolution, which prospered only by bringing millions of Europeans and "natives" close to starvation in order to produce a steady supply of cheap labor willing to put up with the hellish conditions of modern industrial capitalism.

The destructive impact of modernity around the world was not just the result of the greed of individual capitalists, but of the structure of the modernity matrix and the world system that emerged with it. Given this, it's no wonder that the components of the modernity matrix have been generating harsh critiques among Muslim thinkers since the Egyptian chronicler al-Jabarti first lambasted the French for their crass materialism and lack of morality when Napoleon invaded Egypt in 1798. And if Karl Marx firmly believed that the "iron laws" of history would lead to a workers' paradise, his Muslim contemporaries had no such illusions about their future under modernity's iron rule.

What historian Mike Davis calls the late Victorian holocausts, along with the Jewish Holocaust, the Cambodian, Bosnian, Rwandan,

and now Sudanese genocides, all have deep roots in the four coefficients of the modernity matrix, which extend deep into the colonial
period. Whether Africans or Jews, existing social and cultural institutions had to be destroyed to secure colonial conquest or purify Europe
in order to realize modernity's grandest visions. Yet even in this
context it is hard to plot the full costs of colonialism. As the President
of Nigeria, Olusegun Obasanjo, tellingly described it, "It is virtually
impossible to estimate the full social costs of colonialism, from its
inception, through its exploitative existence, to the huge human and
material resources that went into dislodging it from our continent."[11]
Indeed, Africa is perhaps the seminal example of the absolute
exploitation, rape even, of a continent by European imperial powers,
from slave raiding in the 1500s to strip mining today.[12]

If we take one of the most powerful economies the world has ever
known, that of the pre-colonial Indian subcontinent, we can see the
impact of the modernity matrix: in 1750 India/Pakistan had about
25 percent of the world's manufacturing output, yet in 1980 the
subcontinent's share was 2.3 percent (and this while being home to
around one-fifth of the world's people).[13] Traditional "Eurocentric" or
Orientalist history would explain the roots of this problem by first
ignoring the fact that India was ever one of the world's most powerful
economies, and then claiming that inherent backwardness and
cultural inferiority were the reason for its subsequent problems.

A more accurate assessment would point to the imperial policies of
Britain and local elites: the combination of violent destruction of the
existing economy and alliances with local elites who were guaranteed
wealth and power in return for helping the British exploit the masses
of their populations in new ways and for unprecedented profits. For
reasons I'll discuss in Chapter Four, the contemporary Middle East
has largely avoided the absolute poverty and immiseration suffered by
Africa, but it too has been marginalized within the modern world
economic system.

If Europe was the original home of modernity, modernity's will to
conquer found a welcome home in the United States near the end of
the nineteenth century, when it began its rise to world dominance.
The "manifest destiny" of the United States to rule the world was most
clearly and forthrightly described by the preacher and moralist Josiah
Strong, the Secretary of the Evangelical Alliance of the United States
and a friend of Teddy Roosevelt. Strong's writings greatly influenced
the political culture of the United States as it entered the "American
century"; using language that mirrors those of European colonial officials such as Lord Cromer (whom I quote at length below), he argued

that the "all conquering" American people had a unique "genius for colonizing." As he wrote in his 1885 *Our Country*:

> There are no more new worlds. The unoccupied arable lands of the earth are limited, and will soon be taken. The time is coming when … the world will enter upon a new stage of its history – *the final competition of races, for which the Anglo-Saxon is being schooled.* Then this race of unequaled energy, with all the majesty of numbers and the might of wealth behind it – the representative, let us hope, of the largest liberty, the purest Christianity, the highest civilization – having developed peculiarly aggressive traits calculated to impress its institutions upon mankind, will spread itself over the earth. If I read not amiss, this powerful race will move down upon Mexico, down upon Central and South America, out upon the islands of the sea, over upon Africa and beyond. And can any one doubt that the result of this competition of races will be the "survival of the fittest?" Nothing can save the inferior race but a ready and pliant assimilation. The contest is not one of arms, but of vitality and of civilization.[14]

There are many ways to look at this statement, but for me its most disturbing aspect is the resonance of Strong's comments to those of his twenty-first-century counterparts on the religious right. Like them, Strong justified American imperialism with the argument that the US was doing God's work by fighting greed, selfishness, and tyranny; at the same time, taking the fight abroad would maintain the order that would otherwise be threatened at home – an opinion that clearly inspired George W. Bush (consciously or not) as he "misarticulated" his reasons for invading and occupying Iraq. What's more, Strong's belief in a "final competition" for scarce resources, in which the US is morally justified to do whatever it deems necessary to win, coincides exactly with the public opinions of the US security establishment, whether articulated by scholars like Samuel Huntington or by documents such as the Strategic Space Command's "Vision 2020," which clearly states that globalization is producing a zero-sum game of winners and losers and the US needs to be prepared to do whatever it takes to win.

To quote US Space Command: "Widespread communications will highlight disparities in resources and quality of life – contributing to unrest in developing countries. The gap between have and have-not nations will widen – creating regional unrest."[15] And as I write these words, the newly appointed Undersecretary of Defense for Intelligence, William Boykin, has been quoted in strikingly similar terms to Strong: "We in the army of God, in the house of God, kingdom of God have been raised for such a time as this ..."[16] If he didn't say this after having read Strong, it's only because the sentiments are so ingrained in our culture he didn't have to. Indeed, Boykin also admitted that "George Bush was not elected by a majority of the voters in the United States ... He was appointed by God," and that "the battle that we're in is a spiritual battle ... While other countries have lost their morals, lost their values, America is still a Christian nation."

The meaning of Strong's – or Boykin's – words, their honest chauvinism and even delight at the prospects for assimilating, if not destroying, other cultures, is clear. And the fact that some of the main proponents of this unadulterated imperialist ideology were missionaries and preachers like Strong or General Boykin cannot be ignored. But these religious figures, interestingly, were not diametrically opposed to science, at least when it could be put to the service of the emerging empire. As Strong continues, quoting Charles Darwin (normally not a friend of evangelical preachers): "'At the present day,' says Mr Darwin, 'civilized nations are everywhere supplanting barbarous nations, excepting where the climate opposes a deadly barrier; and they succeed mainly, though not exclusively, through their arts, which are the products of the intellect.' Whether the extinction of inferior races before the advancing Anglo-Saxon seems to the reader sad or otherwise, it certainly appears probable ... On this continent God is preparing mankind to receive our impress."

Strong's words offer a clarity and honesty of vision and intention that few advocates of today's American empire would dare to match – but that doesn't mean they don't share his worldview and goals. And his focus on culture as being central to empire is a crucial argument that can help us understand why today, in the global era, those opposed to American-dominated, corporate-led, and consumer-driven globalization focus as much if not more attention on culture as on its economic, political, and/or military impact. What's more, if we take Strong at his word about the effects colonialism has on colonized societies – assimilate or die – we see that it anticipates the mantra of the Axis of Arrogance and Ignorance luminaries such as Friedman or Fukuyama. But today, however, we know that assimilation is really not an option; as the New York *Times* describes the survival of the fittest environment of the global era, it's "dominate or die."[17] And so whether yesterday or today we see how colonialism robs entire societies of their historical line of development, to a degree that cannot be compensated for, even after decades of formal independence or billions in foreign aid and international loans.

Moreover, given the motivations driving it, we can understand why modern colonial powers (unlike previous world empires like Rome which were much more "multicultural") made few, if any, cultural compromises or concessions to the societies they colonized. Instead, the history and cultural development, if not the peoples themselves, had to be "erased" in order for colonialism to succeed (that they never were is one of the reasons colonialism always failed in the end, but only after untold bloodshed and pillaged resources).

Finally, if we put together the economic and cultural aspects of the modernity matrix we can understand the roots of what the historian André Gunder Frank famously termed the "development of underdevelopment." That is, the penetration of colonial capitalism and then nationalism in these countries radically changed their social and economic structures so that autonomous capitalist economic development became impossible. Yet such was – and remains – the power of the modernist ideology behind colonialism that the resulting backwardness and stagnation were understood as natural, as if they existed before the West arrived to implement what the World Bank has euphemistically described (referring specifically to the MENA) as a "shake down period to clear out the accumulated structural problems" and bring the region into the global age.[18]

Re-imagining the Modern History of the Middle East

Hopefully, our discussion of the impact of the four-fold modernity matrix on the history of the Middle East has helped us understand the roots of many of the deepest fears of Muslims (and third world peoples more generally) about contemporary globalization. Globalization at the same time expands and amplifies the powers of modernity, colonialism, and capitalism, while weakening the bonds generated by modern nationalism that until recently could act as a buffer (however problematic) to the complete "assimilation" or destruction of non-Western societies. These dynamics well sum up the dilemmas facing Arab/Muslim societies under the conditions of contemporary globalization. They also help explain why many Muslims cling to the powerful combination of national and religious identities (as we've seen most recently in Iraq) in the face of an imposed neoliberal globalization that has yet to prove it can bring either democracy or freedom.

Specifically, on the one hand, the most destructive – to be more accurate, "creatively destructive" – processes of modernity are left intact or even strengthened by neoliberal policies. On the other hand, we are told that globalization celebrates hybridity and openness to the world, which in the previous period of modernity were kept in check by the supposedly "pure," territorially and ethnically bounded identities of the nation-state.[19] While this process can be liberating and exhilarating for those with the tools (money, connections, education) to take advantage of it, experiences of hybridity and openness lift people out of – or as scholars often describe it, "disembed" from or "deterritorialize" – their established identities, leaving them floating between their more rooted national and/or religious identities and a more plural and hybrid global identity defined primarily through what people can consume.

Since most citizens of the Arab/Muslim world can't afford to consume the vast majority of Western products they're exposed to, most can't hope to buy into and benefit from globalization. In such a situation "extreme" religious or nationalist identities, politics, and of course cultures, become one of the few available means to give people a renewed sense of place, to feel at home and re-rooted in the world again. And through this process we can understand how culture, which was so central to the power of colonialism, has become perhaps the primary means of experiencing globalization.

It should be clear now that the reality of modernity's rise and spread is very different from the traditional story. European history and development were never as "pure" and separate from the history of other cultures and societies as Europeans imagined them to be. Even the ancient Greeks, heralded as the fountain of Western, democratic civilization, owed much of their mythology (and through it, their philosophy) to the traveling cultures that moved west from Mesopotamia across the fertile crescent almost two thousand years before Homer. And let's not forget that the Judeo-Christian culture, supposedly the defining and unique possession of Western civilization, also emerged in the East.

During the last two decades there has been a revolution in scholarship on the worldwide evolution of modernity that has challenged previously dominant conceptions about the centrality and uniqueness of Europe in this narrative. Broadly put, we now know that the roots of modernity and capitalism extend both further into the past and wider across the globe than used to be imagined by historians. We also know, however, that the time of the European Renaissance and Enlightenment – 1400–1800 – was the very period of Asia's greatest strength compared with the rest of the Old World. Europeans of the time readily admitted that Asia represented the "richest trade in the world"; that's why they wanted to conquer it.

Indeed, it was because of the power of the major Asian empires (Ottoman, Mughal, and especially Chinese) that the emerging European nation-states sought, first, a direct route to Asia that would bypass the Ottomans and other competitors, and then, with the "discovery" of the Americas, overseas colonies that would act as a substitute for overly regulated trade between European countries and largely impenetrable Asian markets. With those new colonies Europe could use the money it pulled out of the ground in the Americas (i.e., silver) to buy its way into Asia's markets, establish more equal trade with and ultimately dominate or conquer most Asian societies.[20]

What's more, thanks to the new scholarship on world history, we now understand that there was an extensive and complex system of (old) world trade linking China to Europe, and everything else in between, that reached its peak in the century between 1250 and 1350. This is the period which saw most of the main ingredients for what economists would later define as "capitalism" – money, credit, mass production of goods, rationalization and bureaucratization of government, long-distance trade, private property, etc. – emerge in urban centers throughout the Old World in surprisingly similar forms. In fact, many of these processes (including credit and banking) arrived in Europe through the contacts of Italian cities and merchants with their Arab/Muslim counterparts.

If we look at the dynamics behind the explosion of worldwide trade in the fourteenth to sixteenth centuries the role of the four-fold modernity matrix becomes even clearer. During this period, particularly in the fifteenth century, Europe still lagged far behind China and much of Asia more broadly in terms of wealth. At the same time the Ottoman Empire – the great Muslim empire that at its peak stretched from Morocco to the borders of Iran[21] – strode aggressively across the land routes to Asia. This situation meant that Europeans had to pay high tariffs to the Ottomans for goods shipped overland by the famed caravan route or via the Mediterranean Sea, the eastern part of which the Ottomans largely controlled.

Clearly, Europeans had to find a new way to reach Asia, which first led the Portuguese – who were best equipped to build new kinds of ships that could reach Asia since they had experience sailing the open Atlantic – to make their way around the African continent between the 1440s and 1497, when Vasco da Gama led the first European ships ever to penetrate the Indian Ocean. At the same time, the ravages of the Mongol invasion and the Black Death in the thirteenth and fourteenth centuries had stripped Europe of much of its wealth, and led to a shortage of gold and silver, the only commodities the Chinese (then as today the West's great untapped market) wanted from Europe.

In the process of making their way south on the West African coast the Portuguese "discovered" gold and, as important, the islands of São Tomé, Cape Verde, and Madeira, which became the first European sugar-plantation colonies (Arabs had developed sugar plantations centuries earlier) and the entrepôts for launching voyages to the New World.[22] Both to mine the gold and farm the plantations the Portuguese required labor, which was increasingly provided by African slaves.

And so by the first decades of the sixteenth century two crucial triangles emerge that together created the first era of true, if unequal, global integration. The first was the Asia–Africa–Europe triangle, where Portuguese and then other Europeans used African slave labor and alliances with local African elites in the interior of the continent to extract and produce raw commodities that were traded with the East.[23] (And from what we now know, the Africans were very picky consumers of the finished products the Europeans tried to sell them, often rejecting Indian textiles if they weren't convinced they represented the latest styles and fashions.) The second triangle was the Europe–Africa–Americas triangle, which saw Europeans similarly, but on an exponentially larger scale,[24] use African slave labor as the basis for extracting precious metals and establishing plantation agriculture. If we can picture the slightly crooked latitudinal line connecting Asia to the Americas through Africa, the demarcation between what would eventually be termed the "Global South" and "Global North" emerges, with the South being structured into the world system as both the location for producing/extracting raw materials and a primary importer of finished products from Europe.

Merchants and Modernity

More than economic necessity drove this system; as important were philosophy and politics, which intersected in the form of mercantilism, the dominant system for the expansion of European-dominated trade beginning in the fifteenth century. Mercantilism is important to our discussion because it was based on a belief that there was a fixed amount of wealth in the world, that all peoples were in a zero-sum conflict to obtain it, and that the best way to succeed in this game was to have powerful, "absolutist" monarchies with strong economic elites that would create an economy based on manufacturing and exporting finished commodities while importing only needed raw materials, and not finished products.

Mercantilism helped structure the world economic system along its present lines through its focus on shifting primary production outside Europe to its colonies of the "periphery." It also led to the building up of strong European monarchies that were the core of the emerging nation-state identities and structures that helped solidify the drive to acquire overseas colonies. As mercantilism became the dominant mode of worldwide economic integration in the sixteenth century the seams of the modernity matrix were sewn together, with untold blood, lives, and wealth squeezed from the peoples of the South (and the indigenous peoples of North America as well) ever since.

And this history reminds us of a basic principle of biology: it takes a wound a lot longer to heal than to inflict. How many centuries should the West expect it will take for the societies of the Global South to "get over" colonialism and/or slavery and achieve the modernity and development demanded of them? Especially when new wounds (wars, AIDS, structural adjustment programs) are being inflicted before the old ones have had time to heal. We can begin to understand the immense toll of this centuries-long process by looking at the numbers given in Table 2.

How do we comprehend the vastness of the toll European colonialism and imperialism had on the rest of the world? In 1900 the world's population was about 1 billion, so we can make the following comparison: imagine approximately 13–20 percent of the world's population at that time being killed directly or indirectly as a result of European "expansion." Or imagine the destruction it would take to kill 27–41 million Americans; then imagine that a dozen or so more powerful countries do everything possible to profit from that destruction at the expense of the United States, and to prevent a severely weakened America from ever recovering its former economic resources, population or strength. Then go read Niall Ferguson's celebration of imperialism, *Colossus*, which mentions none of these statistics or even attempts to account for the impact (for a reality check, compare his argument to Mike Davis's depressingly riveting *Late Victorian Holocausts*), and you'll have a good idea of the ideology guiding the people who have managed the world's affairs for the last two hundred years.

Re-orienting and Decolonizing History

Mercantilism might have dominated Europe for much of the 1300–1750 period, but as we've already seen, the dominant economic region in the world was still the Far East, and especially China, which

Table 2: Impact of European Expansion, 1492–1900: Some Examples[25]

Number of indigenous peoples killed throughout the Americas by European disease and war, 1492–1900	70 million, 50 million from disease, 20 million from wars
Total production of silver and gold in Americas shipped to Europe, 1493–1810	102,000 metric tonnes of silver and 2,490 metric tonnes of gold
Total value of gold, silver, pearls, emeralds, and other precious stones exported from Americas to Europe during this period	£1.8 billion sterling, £166 billion in 2002 prices, or approximately $297 billion in dollars (2004)
Total value of exports to Spain from Spanish America, 1501–1800	£1.106 billion sterling, £102 billion in 2002, $183 billion in dollars (2004)
Total value of Brazilian exports to Portugal, 1601–1820	£570 million sterling, £53 billion in 2002, $95 billion in dollars (2005)
Total value of exports from British and French America, c. 1660–1796	£43 million sterling, £3.97 billion, $7.1 billion in dollars (2004)
Number of African slaves transported to the New World, 1451–1870	10–13 million (of whom half didn't survive the voyage)
Number of Africans killed by Europeans through colonial wars	Number too high to establish accurate total
Wealth extracted, expropriated or earned through European-controlled trade in Africa, 15th–20th centuries	Number too high to establish accurate total
Number of Chinese dead from famine, floods, and rebellions associated with British and other foreign imperialism, 1854–1895	33.7–61 million
Number of Chinese addicted to opium sold by Britain at time of Opium Wars, 1839	10 million
Number of Indians killed during British imperial rule in India (disease and war), 1776–1947	Number too high to establish accurately with available data
Amount of wealth extracted/expropriated from India by British, 18th–20th centuries	Number too high to establish accurately with available data
Number of Southeast Asians (Vietnam, Laos, Cambodia) killed by French and American forces, 1946–1975	3–4 million

grew faster than and maintained economic superiority over Europe until the end of this period. This is despite the European conquest of the New World and extraction of its resources, and the slave trade. Most important, Europe needed to use an incredible amount of energy and land to catch up with and surpass Asia and the rest of the world. This led to an ideology of constant growth and consumption whose costs are still evident today. In this context, the conquest and exploitation of Southern countries was crucial to the ability of many a European state to "consume beyond its means and invest beyond its savings,"[26] and in so doing gradually achieve world dominance. Indeed, as many Muslim commentators on globalization point out, this dynamic is the root of the "consume and conquer" policies of the United States today, which is why so many Muslims and others – Hindus, Native Americans, or Africans – see globalization as a new form of imperialism.

The recent advances in our understanding of the history of the MENA point to the importance of decolonizing the histories, as much as the lands and peoples, of the region.[27] By decolonizing this history it becomes clearer, on the one hand, how the sixteenth to eighteenth centuries were not a period of decline, but rather saw the emergence and spread of capitalism, and of modern political processes and social relations throughout Eurasia, in the East as well as West. And so it's inaccurate to conceive of the Ottoman Empire as somehow fundamentally different from or backward compared to European states. At the same time, we see how through colonialism Europeans were able to force other people to extract the resources that were used to increase trade with Asia, and also to sell European finished products back to the colonies that couldn't compete with Asian products in a truly open or "free" market.

Most importantly, decolonizing history means moving beyond the narrative of Europe as the prime historical player in the modern period and everyone else as responding to its advances, in favor of one that helps us understand the dynamics of a multi-centered world with long-standing interconnections and no single dominant center until the nineteenth century. It was only then that a combination of luck; closeness to the New World and sailing expertise to reach it (which non-Atlantic sailing powers such as the Ottomans did not develop); zero-sum competition between numerous relatively small states and the constant innovation in warfare it necessitated; and an abundant supply of the coal needed to fuel industrialization all combined with the ideologies of modernity to enable a transformation from mercantilist to imperialist capitalism that only the major European states were positioned to make.

The Ottoman Empire in the Context of Modern World History

Viewed with this background, we cannot assume that the increasing power of European states like England and France signaled an absolute "decline" of the East, and especially the Ottoman Empire (otherwise known as "the sick man of Europe"). In fact, the eighteenth and nineteenth centuries were a period of significant state modernization and centralization efforts by the empire (the main territorial equivalent to the major European states). Despite occurring under conditions of European inter-imperialist rivalry, this process allowed the Ottomans to maintain a fair degree of autonomy and initiative despite losing significant territory as the period continued.[28]

If we want to understand how and why the Ottoman Empire was ultimately unable to keep up with Europe and maintain its independence, even survival, the answer lies in the intimate relationship between colonialism and capitalism. Put simply, colonialism made modern European capitalism both possible and sustainable: from the provision of raw materials and "free" or cheap labor, to the stabilization of currencies and other prerequisites for the kind of "free market" that, once imposed, seems to have arisen naturally and without any external intervention. In other words, the free market "could not exist for any length of time without annihilating the human and natural substance of society."[29]

But why was the Ottoman Empire able to maintain a tenuous parity with the majority of European states until the nineteenth century, even in the face of the destructive power of colonial, capitalist modernity? Because it was only then that cotton and coffee, two of its major cash crops from which the state drew important revenues, were replaced by competing American-produced crops. And here we see another way that European colonization of the New World, along with the slave trade, had a profound impact on the economic dynamics in the Middle East. In fact, it's an early example of the negative impact of Western-directed "globalization of trade" on countries outside Northern and Western Europe.

During this period Europeans would go further and largely destroy outright much of the Ottoman textile industry, while preventing the establishment of a new competitive center in Egypt (about which I will say more below). This process was similar to Britain's actions in India and related to the rationale behind the Opium Wars with China as well (which were launched because the British had little besides opium that the Chinese were interested in buying, a situation which drained England's currency reserves and therefore couldn't be tolerated, even if it meant addicting millions of people to heroin). At the same time, the increasing military power of the major European states led the Ottomans to undertake significant political and administrative reforms (known as the Tanzimat, or "Reorganization," which began officially in 1839) and to spend huge sums to modernize their own military. Not only was this effort supervised in large part by European officers, it led to greater levels of debt to Europe, which then increased the weakness and dependency they were seeking to overcome through modernizing their military in the first place. Ultimately, by the time the Ottoman state announced a modern constitution, the empire was bankrupt.

But despite these events our story is not one of absolute decline and/or stagnation. As we've already mentioned, during the 1830s and 1840s, at the same time as Europeans like Jeremy Bentham argued for the importance of private property to the wealth of the British nation, the capitalization of land (that is, transforming state-owned land to private property) increased significantly in the Ottoman Empire. In fact, both European powers and the Ottoman elite sought to "modernize" and "centralize," and in so doing strengthen, their states. The policies they enacted to achieve their goals helped states across Eurasia become more powerful, rationalized, specialized, and capable of imposing their will on their subjects than before.

But we shouldn't understand this continent-wide modernization process as one where the Ottomans merely copied the "best practices" of Europe. Instead, what one could call an Ottoman modernity involved a process of mediation and translation that made possible the adaptation of new ideas arriving from London and Paris (from new concepts of property rights to new fashion dictates) through the prism of Ottoman-Islamic culture and perceived geostrategic interests. In fact, many of the most important reforms of the Tanzimat era had roots as deep in Islamic law and theology as in European concepts.[30]

And so "modern" did not have to mean European to Ottomans; in fact, it often meant just plain "new." Yet it is also true that if the reforms undertaken by the Ottoman state were inspired as much if not more by Islam than by France or England, as the nineteenth century wore on Ottoman governments increasingly imagined and portrayed the empire in much more specifically European terms, especially as they lost ground to England and France, and suffered military defeats and territorial losses to their Hapsburg and Russian neighbors.

The dynamics of the nineteenth century hint at two important points. First, had the Ottoman state not ultimately felt it necessary to copy, and wasn't ultimately dismantled by, its European competitors, its modernization efforts could have supported a "Levantine modernity" in the Middle East. Such a system, based on a combination of Muslim, local, and Western laws, technologies, and cultural traditions, could have created a non-colonial capitalism. And ironically, it was precisely the weakness of the state in the outlying provinces that encouraged one to emerge, at least in some of the major port cities like Jaffa or Beirut, at the turn of the twentieth century. These "world cities" were meeting places for European and Levantine economies and cultures that were free of the most pernicious effects of colonialism, nationalism, and even capitalism, in large part because no one system or political authority had absolute control. Because of this, they nurtured, however briefly, a kind of non-colonial, cosmopolitan modernity where various subcultures and communities lived side by side, and which created a sense of hybridity and newness that have always defined modernity as it hoped to be. It is communities just like these that the world needs to nurture today.

Second, such was the power of European modernity that as the Ottoman state became weaker it increasingly portrayed itself as a "modern member of the civilized community of nations," the "committed advocate of reform in the Orient,"[31] and even a colonial power seeking possessions in the "dark continent" – not surprisingly, Africa. This transformation of Ottoman modernity towards a colonial framework suggests, as I argue below, that it is ultimately impossible to have a modernity that is not ultimately a colonial modernity. Once it set out to become modern, the Ottoman state absorbed the inherently hierarchical, exclusivist, and colonialist paradigms that were at the heart of European modernity. This fact would ultimately facilitate the imposition of European power and control over the empire and its territories; in good measure because these colonial paradigms supported the development of ethnically exclusive rather than cosmopolitan nationalisms throughout the empire.[32]

As important, the process of privatizing or capitalizing land, which was a central component of Ottoman reforms, pushed increasing numbers of peasants off their land. This violated one of the most important obligations of the Ottoman state which was to maintain the peasantry on the land. And here we see how the needs of modern, colonial capitalism forced the empire into a catch-22 from which it was unable to extricate itself – in striving to become as modern as Europe, the Ottoman state became just another European imperial power, albeit an unsuccessful one, spreading a modernity that was defined by the separation of and hierarchy between peoples and increased exploitation of the poor.

Colonialism and Modernity in Five MENA Societies

The modern history of the Ottoman Empire is vitally important for understanding the experience of and responses to globalization in the MENA. Let's look briefly at five of the twenty-five countries of the Middle East and North Africa, which can serve as examples of the larger impact of the processes we've been discussing: Egypt, Palestine, Iraq, Algeria, and Iran.[33]

Egypt: From almost the moment Islam arrived in Egypt in 641 C.E. the country has been at the center of the Arab and Muslim world, with only Baghdad and later Istanbul rivaling it for intellectual and political dominance. In the early Islamic period, a line of rulers called the Fatimids took control of Egypt based on their descent from the family of Ali, the Prophet's cousin, whose family Shi'i Muslims believe to be the rightful heir to the "caliphate," or political leadership of the *ummah*.

In the Middle Ages Egypt fell under the rule of the so-called Mamluks, or "slave soldiers" (in reality they were "slaves" – meaning they owed allegiance only to the Caliph) who rose to prominence as the caliphs became weaker. Even after the Ottomans conquered the country in 1517, Egypt maintained a significant amount of de facto independence from Ottoman rule, in good measure because of its wealth of resources, especially its fertile soil which was the breadbasket of North Africa and the Mediterranean for thousands of years.

This tension came to a head at the turn of the nineteenth century. In 1798 Napoleon invaded Egypt, and was forced out in 1801 by a combined English–Ottoman force. After four years of struggle between the Ottomans and Mamluks, an Ottoman officer, Muhammad Ali, who succeeded in rallying crucial popular support to rout the Mamluks, was appointed Governor by Istanbul, and quickly set about creating his own mini-empire in Egypt while serving as the main enforcer for the Ottoman state against revolts such as the first Wahhabi/Sa'udi takeover of Arabia (which he defeated in 1819).

Flushed with increasing power and income from cotton production and industrialization, Muhammad Ali invaded Palestine and Syria in 1831 and threatened the very existence of the Ottoman state with his sweeping military victories and challenge to Ottoman sovereignty. There are two consequences of Muhammad Ali's rule that are most important for our story. The first arises from his attempt at autonomous modernization (and especially industrialization) of the country, which given its resource base could well have led to Egypt becoming a major world power within a generation (and likely more powerful than his nominal Ottoman masters in Istanbul). In fact, Muhammad Ali's rapid "modernization" of Egypt attempted to develop it to levels comparable with Europe. His wholesale reinvention of the Egyptian state involved the military, educational, health, industrial, and other crucial sectors of society, and had as one of its important goals the direct collection of taxes by the Government, which helped pay for the reforms.

Muhammad Ali's modernization program was by no means pretty or painless (modernization never is); in fact, by the 1830s it had showed clear signs of failing, in large part because the rudimentary system of administration could not handle the rapid development of the economy. As important, the land seized by the Government wound up being assigned to senior officers and members of the royal family instead of being put into "productive" use as happened in England during the previous two centuries.

But while Egypt's modernization program began to flounder by the 1830s, its economic potential was recognized by both European powers and the Ottoman state, who came together in 1840 to force Muhammad Ali and his family to relinquish the territories they had conquered over the last decade and give up any dreams of creating their own empire in return for a hereditary position in the country. This action not only thwarted the one viable Arab/Muslim competitor to the Ottoman state, in so doing it stopped perhaps the one possible chance a MENA society had to chart an independent and autonomous path towards modernity and capitalist development – something that needless to say Europe, and especially Britain and its textile industry (which needed Egypt's raw cotton, not a competitor in producing finished textiles), would not allow.

And so by the 1850s European financial capital was financing modernization projects that the new Khedive, Ismail,[34] believed were necessary to achieve his grandfather's dream of modernization and de facto independence. In reality, however, they led to increased dependence on Europe that in turn led the Egyptian Government toward bankruptcy. The second consequence relates more to the steep price paid by the Ottomans for British help: beyond the Tanzimat reforms, which on the face of it were neutral, a series of treaties and agreements opened the Ottoman economy to increased foreign penetration and control that bankrupted the state by 1875. Not surprisingly, Egypt followed the same path, and was increasingly opened to foreign competition and control of agricultural production (which was increasingly concentrated into fewer and fewer large-scale landowners, and also bankrupted the Egyptian economy by the same year).

But while Istanbul could maintain at least de facto independence after bankruptcy, Egypt, whose strategic importance to Britain only increased with the opening of the Suez Canal (which made shipping to and from India much cheaper), could not. When Egyptians attempted to reassert autonomy from European economic pressure and restore "Egyptian" control of the military (in an episode known as the 'Urabi Revolt) the British invaded the country, remaining in de facto control (despite formal independence in 1922) until the Free Officers' Revolution of 1952, which brought Gemal Abdel Nasser to power.

In the intervening decades the British utilized the full force of colonialism to control and exploit Egypt to its maximum strategic and economic advantage. In so doing the British cemented a social system where a few major landowning families controlled the bulk of the country's agricultural land, and thus wealth. This made it very difficult for any kind of autonomous social, economic or political modernization – that is, one that would have benefited the majority of the population – to occur. Most interesting in this process was the ideological justification for British rule, which was succinctly and evocatively summarized by Viceroy Lord Cromer, effective ruler of Egypt for twenty-four years, in his *Modern Egypt*.

After explaining that "the European is a close reasoner ... a natural logician," Cromer explained that "the mind of the Oriental, on the other hand, is eminently wanting in symmetry. His reasoning is of the most slipshod description ... [The Oriental's] descendants are singularly deficient in the logical faculty ... and wanting in lucidity." But under the bright light of British colonial supervision Cromer believed that

> Egypt may now almost be said to form part of Europe ... But it may be doubted whether any instance can be quoted of a sudden transfer of power in any civilized or semi-civilized community to a class so ignorant as the pure Egyptians, such as they were in the year 1882. These latter have, for centuries past, been a subject race ... we have to go back to the doubtful and obscure precedents of Pharaonic times to find an epoch when, possibly, Egypt was ruled by Egyptians. Neither, for the present, do they appear to possess the qualities which would render it desirable, either in their own interests, or in those of the civilized world in general, to raise them at a bound to the category of autonomous ruler with full rights of internal sovereignty.[35]

And finally, as if anticipating the arguments of George W. Bush as he invaded Iraq, Cromer argued that "a great nation cannot throw off the responsibilities which its past history and its position in the world have imposed upon it. English history affords other examples of the government and people of England drifting by accident into doing what was not only right, but was also most in accordance with British interests." That British (and later American) interests have never had the slightest correspondence to the interests of most Egyptians, or Iraqis, hasn't stopped generations of viceroys from claiming so.

While the socialist-inspired policies of Gemal Nasser attempted to redistribute land and wealth to poorer Egyptians, most of the gains of his rule were undermined by the autocratic nature of the regime and its inability to fundamentally challenge the existing socio-economic structure. This reality is what helped the Muslim Brotherhood, the most important religious oppositional group in the country (and perhaps the Muslim world), established in the 1920s, to expand and become more radicalized under the leadership of the (in)famous Sayyid Qutb, who as we'll see in Chapter Five, offered a much harsher and culturally centered critique of the West than had been developed until then.

Ultimately, the policies of Nasser's successor, Anwar Sadat, destroyed any possibility of autonomous development or democracy through his rapprochement with the United States and Egypt's *infitah*, or economic "opening," to Western capital. The re-entry of Western corporations into the Egyptian economy permanently oriented it toward servicing the economic and military-strategic needs of the United States. Today, "America's Egypt" (as one leading political scientist has described it) is more dependent on American aid – more precisely, the increasingly autocratic Mubarak regime is more dependent – than at any time since the re-establishment of relations in 1973. The over $2 billion Egypt receives every year in US aid (the second largest amount in the world after Israel), ties the Government umbilically to Washington (and because of this, we can imagine what tens of billions of dollars in "reconstruction aid" will do to Iraq). Most important, Egypt plays a crucial role in maintaining the arms–petrodollar system in the Middle East intact, of which the main beneficiaries are the US corporations in these two sectors and the Egyptian military and agricultural elites whose power is tied to this system.

Israel/Palestine: Palestine/Israel is one of the most tragic examples of the intersection of the four coefficients of the modernity matrix. In fact, much of the discussion in this chapter was drawn initially from my work on the history of modern Palestine/Israel.

Why is Palestine such a seminal example of the way modernity has unfolded in the Middle East? There are several reasons, the most obvious of which is that the indigenous Palestinian Arab population was forced to contend with both British imperialism and Zionist colonization of the country, a double blow that few societies could have withstood. The Zionist part of the equation in particular allows us to see in great detail how modernity, colonialism, capitalism, and nationalism come together in a powerful and almost unstoppable manner.

A good example of their intersection comes from Supreme Court Justice Felix Frankfurter's 1931 explanation for the intensification of hostilities between Jewish immigrants and Palestinians: "We who love the simple Oriental life in its beautiful setting may be pardoned if we regard with a sigh its pulverization beneath the wheels of progress. Change is inevitable. It is a mere accident that the Jews should happen to be its agents ... Palestine is inexorably part of the modern world. No *cordon sanitaire* can protect her against the penetration of the forces behind Western ideas and technology."[36]

As we can see, Zionism always saw itself as the epitome of a modern nationalist movement and as a modern colonial enterprise, and because of both, as the agent of change and progress in a backward and stagnant Middle East. Many early Zionist leaders had extensive experience working in European colonies in North and sub-Saharan Africa, and clearly defined their movement along these terms (thus the major organization promoting Jewish settlement was the "Jewish Colonization Association").[37] At the same time, Zionism defined itself as a quintessentially "modern" nationalist movement. This modern self-definition was reflected both in how Zionist leaders described non-Jewish Palestine – not surprisingly as either sparsely settled and/or backward and stagnant – and in how they justified their colonization of the country: it would bring modernity, development, and prosperity to the land and its "native" population.[38]

Needless to say, what Zionism actually brought to Palestine, at least from the perspective of the non-Jewish indigenous population, was exactly what colonial modernity always brings: eviction from much of the best land; increased factionalization of the society; greater unemployment of a population no longer able to maintain itself on the land; and ultimately civil war and dispossession of a significant part of the colonized society. As we've seen, what makes the case of Palestine so interesting is the synergy that was quickly achieved between Zionism and British colonial rule in Palestine.[39] This allowed Zionist leaders to convince the highest levels of the British Government (the British on the ground in Palestine were more skeptical, seeing the impact of Zionism up close) that, like British colonialism, Zionism was a beacon of light and progress for Palestinian Arabs, and whose activities, far from hurting them, were the prerequisite for the advancement of the country as a whole.[40] But before we blame it all on Europe we need to remember that the Europeanization of Ottoman modernization laid the foundation for Zionism that was so well cultivated under British protection.[41]

In defining itself so explicitly as a modern nationalist movement the Zionist enterprise has provided us with a seminal example of the intimate connection between modernity, colonialism, and nationalism (although not in the manner in which its leaders likely envisioned it). Moreover, we also know that much of the reason Zionism became what Israeli sociologist Gershon Shafir calls a "militant nationalist movement" well before World War I was because of the economic competition faced by Jewish immigrants from cheaper and better-skilled Palestinian Arab workers. This largely zero-sum competition led socialist Zionist leaders (who also felt they did not come all the way from Russia to be bourgeois "exploiters" of the local population) to invent the strategies of the Conquest of Labor and then the Conquest of Land between 1904 and 1909. The goals of both conquests were to create exclusively Jewish spaces within Palestine where no Palestinian Arabs could live or work, and so would not be a source of competition for or exploitation by the Jewish immigrants.[42]

If we stopped here, however, the story of Palestine would only be about the negative impact of Zionism on the country. But we also need to understand how the country was developing before Zionism permanently altered the trajectory of the country's history. While it is impossible to describe the conditions in the whole country in a uniform way, what is clear is that as far back as the eighteenth century, and certainly by the closing decades of Ottoman rule, much of Palestine, especially cities such as Jaffa and Nablus, experienced significant economic growth through the expansion of local industries such as citrus and soap and increasing exports both to other Middle Eastern lands and Europe.[43] We also know that land in Palestine had been undergoing a process of privatization and capitalization for much of the nineteenth century.[44] Finally, it is clear that the combination of a weakened Ottoman state and increased local wealth and contact with cultures as far away as Afghanistan created the basis for a cosmopolitan culture – the Levantine modernity I mentioned earlier –

in the major cities of the country (especially Jaffa). But this culture was slowly suffocated once the main cultural determinant was the conflict between Zionism and Palestinian nationalisms instead of the continual interaction between people arriving from far and wide.[45]

The post-1948 relationship between Israelis and Palestinians was clearly rooted in the dynamics established over the previous five decades: the conquest and settlement of land; intercommunal violence; the forced flight of civilian populations; semi-colonial rule over Palestinian citizens of Israel and the unvarnished colonial rule over the West Bank and Palestine; and the marginalized incorporation of and then closure against Palestinian workers. All are a direct outgrowth of the colonial nature of the Zionist enterprise and its impact on Palestinian society. What is only now becoming clear, however, is how these dynamics shaped Israeli society.

On the one hand, the Orientalist attitudes towards Arabs by the European/Ashkenazi Jews who led the Zionist movement resulted in similar feelings toward the over one million Jewish immigrants who arrived in Israel in the 1950s from Arab and other Muslim countries. These immigrants were sent to "development towns" that were established in "frontier" regions of the new state specifically to isolate them from the European majority while simultaneously asserting Jewish presence in formerly Palestinian Arab regions, creating a situation of intra-Jewish racism that has profoundly shaped Israeli Jewish society to this day. In the society more broadly, under the rubric of a socialist-style economy, leading Israeli capitalists gradually established an unassailable position in the economy, through which they led the drive towards privatization once Israel entered a period of neoliberal adjustment in the 1980s (sponsored by the same economists who designed the British, American, and Chilean neoliberal transformations). This dynamic could not have developed were it not for the colonial roots of the Israeli state and society.

Internationally, since 1967 Israel has played a crucial role in US economic and military strategies that are at the heart of the current global system. The hypermilitarization of the Israeli economy (and society as well), in the context of half a century of conflict between it and the other major countries in the MENA, has been central to the functioning of the famous but easily misunderstood "arms–petrodollar cycle," through which billions of dollars have circulated back and forth among despotic Middle Eastern (and other) regimes and US oil and arms companies.

Indeed, we now know that there is a direct relationship between war and profits of the major US arms and oil companies, and that the

Israeli–Palestinian conflict is one of its most important facilitators.[46] The occupation of Palestine, by keeping the whole region at a constant level of tension and necessitating massive arms purchases by various countries to meet the threats of their opponents, is the engine for the whole process. This dynamic is why most Arabs/Muslims were frightened rather than enthused by the first President Bush's New World Order, Shimon Peres' vision of a "New Middle East" with Israel as its economic and cultural engine, or the second President Bush's supposed democratization of the Middle East in a context where real peace and justice were nowhere on the horizon. It is also why the focus on Israel as being the root cause of the Arab–Israeli conflict is misplaced, as for all its culpability in the conflict's origin and continuation, Israel has been used by the "weapondollar–petrodollar coalition" as much as other Middle Eastern countries.

Iraq: As we saw in the Introduction, Iraq also is a particularly telling example of the impact of colonial modernity on the Middle East. The three Ottoman provinces that became "Iraq" had been the scene of continual fighting between rival ethnic and religious groups (Arabs and Kurds, Sunnis and Shi'a) for centuries before the onset of Ottoman rule in the sixteenth century.[47] Though not as strong as in other Arab provinces, the Ottoman presence brought a measure of stability through a reorganization of local administration and an increase in trade, which improved the economic and living conditions of many inhabitants, especially in the towns. However, the tenuous position of Ottoman control meant that the state constantly struggled to assert its authority over local interests, and by the time it was able to reimpose direct rule in the nineteenth-century Tanzimat period it was in direct competition with British and other European interests.

As occurred in Istanbul and Cairo, the local Governor of Iraq began to import large numbers of European weapons and advisors to improve his military, communications, and trade, with Britain leading the way.[48] In fact, it was the Ottomans' awarding of railway concessions and mineral rights to Germany that led to British plans to invade once the war broke out in 1914. As in Palestine, before the British conquest the three Iraqi provinces of Mosul, Baghdad, and Basra were by no means autonomous; however, the specific borders of the country were shaped by the British after the war in order to secure various geostrategic interests in the Middle East (chief among them control of the increasingly important oil resources). And just to make sure they alienated the newly formed "Iraqi" nation even more, the country was given a king from a hostile neighboring tribe (the

Hashemites from Arabia), and ruled with an iron fist by Britain and its local allies until a nationalist coup in 1958.

How can we assess the impact of British rule in Iraq? Described briefly, rather than build on a long process of Ottoman modernization (however uneven and painful), the British strengthened the position of the country's most conservative and venal forces (landowners, tribal and religious elites that were no longer directly responsible to the people for their positions) – civilizing rhetoric aside – in the name of political expediency and economic "efficiency." Naturally, this system led to increasing concentration of wealth and poverty in the ensuing decades.

As in other colonial settings, the British used Iraq as a laboratory for testing out the newest theories and weapons of war and pacifying hostile native populations while promoting their presence as a necessary and ultimately benign affair. And so British administration could only be secured through extreme violence and autocratic rule, including the repeated use of poison gas – Winston Churchill explained to a subordinate about Iraq, "I am strongly in favour of using poison gas against uncivilised tribes"[49] – and large-scale aerial bombings of civilian targets that have made Saddam Hussein infamous, and which according to a recent biography of Hussein, "administered a shock to the country's social system from which it has never recovered. It was the British conquest of Iraq which set the stage for what is happening today."[50]

In other words, the large-scale violence of the colonial era so distorted the collective Iraqi psyche that any chance of a democratic evolution, let alone revolution, remained almost inconceivable until the present day.[51] The contrast between the rhetoric of a "civilizing mission" and the brutality, corruption, and sheer incompetence that characterized colonial rule on the ground in Iraq is not the exception but the rule for imperialism and colonialism across the globe, especially in the Middle East, from France's Algeria in the mid-1800s to the US's Iraq in 2004.[52]

This is why it's not surprising that if we move forward to the post-World War II political scene,[53] when the US replaced Britain as the main actor in the Middle East, both countries used the nationalist coup in 1958 (after which Iraq withdrew from the British-sponsored "Baghdad Pact")[54] as an excuse to interfere in Iraqi politics in a similar manner to the CIA-supported coup against Iranian Prime Minister Mossadeq, five years before (about which more below). In fact, the CIA, which had plans for invading Iraq as early as 1958, helped stage two coups in the country, in 1963 and 1968, in order to put the friendly and anti-Communist Ba'ath party in power. In the first coup, the CIA literally broadcast the names of suspected communists from a clandestine radio station in Kuwait, thousands of whom were summarily murdered by the new regime. The second coup brought to the center of power a young, ruthless, and power hungry Saddam Hussein.[55]

The history of US support for the Ba'ath party is crucial to help us understand why it did such good business with Hussein while he routinely gassed Kurds and invaded Iran, and why it was only when he overplayed his hand vis-à-vis older and more important clients[56] that the US went to war – not to oust him, but rather to restore the "status quo ante" in which the surrounding regimes would in fact be more dependent on the US for their survival. And once the war on terrorism generated by the terrorist attacks of September 11 made another invasion of Iraq possible – in fact, inevitable – the vast US military industrial complex planned and executed a war that has resulted in perhaps the greatest theft, in the course of only one year, of a country's resources and US tax-payer dollars (hundreds of billions of dollars to date and counting) in the history of the world.

Algeria: Algeria, one of the longest-colonized countries in the world, has an extensive history of integration with the larger Mediterranean region, and south into sub-Saharan Africa. As in Iraq, the Ottomans took nominal control of the main districts of what would become post-independence Algeria in the sixteenth century; yet their power never extended beyond the major cities in the north of the country.

Piracy was crucial to the Algerian economy in the sixteenth to eighteenth centuries. In response, European powers, especially the British and French, engaged in periodic military campaigns to stem the privateering out of Algeria's port cities. When the French invaded Algeria in 1830, however, it wasn't to stop piracy. Instead it was to conquer and colonize the country, in good measure to compensate for the loss of New World colonies to the British in the previous decades. After much violence, in 1847 the country was "pacified" and large-scale European colonization began.

A year later the country was declared French territory, and by 1880 upwards of 400,000 Europeans had settled in Algeria – more than fifteen percent of the total population. They controlled most of the good farmland, and pursued a policy of large-scale economic expansion and modernization – roads, railroads, schools, hospitals, urbanization, etc. – that left "native" Algerians with little political or economic power and almost no legal rights.

The official goal of French policy in Algeria was the "assimilation" of Muslims into modern French culture as preparation for full citizenship.

In practice, however, the two communities were kept largely separate and the situation resembled in some ways that in the Occupied Palestinian Territories today, as there was virtually no mixing between the European and Muslim populations. The conditions of life for most Arab Algerians are what led gradually to movements of protest and for independence after World War I. As reforms promised in the wake of World War II failed to materialize a guerrilla war slowly enveloped the country, led by the National Liberation Front (FLN). In 1962 Algeria achieved independence after a bloody eight-year civil war which killed at least 100,000 Algerians and tens of thousands of French soldiers, and led to the evacuation of most of the country's European population.

However significant Algeria's formal independence, in reality the FLN was tied umbilically to France, and the French maintained a level of economic and political power in the country, strengthened by the hundreds of thousands of Algerians living in France, that prevented any possibility of true economic and/or political independence. The situation led to a steady increase in corruption and authoritarianism in the country, as occurred in most post-independence Arab states (similar to their socialist counterparts in the Soviet Bloc).

These dynamics intersected with the rise of neoliberal economic policies by the world financial community in the 1980s, which imposed structural adjustment programs on the Algerian Government that led to cuts in subsidies of staple items, higher unemployment, and quite naturally, to significant unrest in the country. Because the FLN-dominated political system was – rhetorical nods to Islam aside – militantly secular (in the sense that the army, which basically controlled the country, was not going to allow Islam, the main potential competing ideology, a space in the political culture), religion became the most important outlet for political frustration. And it is this process that led to the Islamic Salvation Front (FIS), the party established in 1988 by lay Muslim intellectuals and activists. In fact, in line with the growing power of youth throughout the MENA region, the party was derided by older religious figures as "not an elite of religious scholars, [but rather] a bunch of kids."[57] Nevertheless, they swept into power locally, and then nationally, in the general elections of 1992.

The cancellation of the second round of national elections after it became clear that FIS would win conveniently led to a ten-year civil war between the Government and Islamist insurgents. What made the violence so intense was not just that the Government canceled the elections but, as important, the fact that the international community let the Government *get away* with canceling the elections. With international

Communism no longer challenging the world domination of capitalism, the Western powers were not about to let a militant Islamist movement they didn't sponsor (like the Saudis and Gulf monarchies) take control of one of the major oil- and gas-producing countries in the world.

Culture also played a prominent role in the rise of the Islamic Salvation Front, much more so than economic issues, despite the grave economic problems plaguing Algeria.[58] In fact, the civil war can be understood as a "war of identity" in comparison with the war of independence against France, one where the Islamist forces specifically sought to destroy any "illusion of French Algeria." Because of this dynamic, the FIS focused not on offering a detailed economic program, but instead on the kinds of cultural issues that were becoming increasingly important in the country in the 1980s as satellite television and other international media technologies and television networks became more broadly available in Algerian society. And this dynamic is an important reason why religion became so violently politicized in the ensuing civil war, as the army shut out all other vehicles for political protest, let alone taking control of the state.

Iran: Iran's modern history is inseparable from the great political games of the major nineteenth-century imperial powers, especially Britain and Russia. The famous "great game in Asia" essentially concerned the British–Russian competition to control the territory and/or politics of Afghanistan and Iran, whose strategic position vis-à-vis India (for Britain) and as a warm-water port (for Russia) made the region among the most important and contested zones of imperial competition in the modern world.

In fact, the British had been working to install puppet regimes in Afghanistan since almost the turn of the nineteenth century, precisely because of the region's historic location on the main route for invading India. For its part, Russia feared a permanent British presence right on her borders, and the resulting competition was made easier in Iran because the ruling Qajar dynasty, established in 1794, was fairly weak, having little control of the incredibly mountainous countryside, and no real allegiance from the religious establishment.

And so by the 1850s Persia was divided into Russian and British spheres of influence; by the 1870s the Qajar rulers were using Russian-trained Cossack brigades to regain and/or expand their authority. However, the constant need to manipulate rivalries between various tribal chiefs prevented the efficient collection of taxes necessary to modernize the state. To get revenue in this situation Nasir Shah, who ruled from 1848 to 1896, awarded many concessions to both the

British and Russians, especially oil and tobacco. This process mirrored the increasing penetration of European economic interests in the Ottoman Empire and North Africa during the nineteenth century. Indeed, it was the awarding of a concession to grow, produce, and sell tobacco to a single British citizen that sparked the first "revolt" (the Tobacco Revolt) in modern Iranian history, in 1891. This process led fifteen years later to the Constitutional Revolution of 1905–09, perhaps the most democratic moment in Persian history till that time. The "Revolution" (which I put in quotes because in reality there was no permanent change in the basic structure of politics of the state, nor was there a takeover by a previously oppressed class was caused by the greater European penetration of the economy allowed by Shah Muzaffir, which was epitomized by his granting of an oil concession to another British firm. However, the Constitutional Revolution petered out by 1909, at which point both the British and Russians sent in troops to secure "their" areas of the country.

Ultimately the Cossack-trained soldier Reza Pahlavi succeeded in seizing power and naming himself the new Shah in 1925. He soon embarked on a massive modernization program modeled in large part on that undertaken by his Turkish contemporary, Ataturk. But while Ataturk succeeded, despite his personally autocratic style, in laying the foundations for a functioning (if often troubled and sometimes suspended) parliamentary system, Reza Shah was interested primarily in cementing his power and ensuring the survival of his new dynasty, and so no framework for democratic politics was laid.

Besides the lack of any consideration for democracy, what is crucial about Reza Shah's modernization program was not just the rapid expansion of the state bureaucracy and the military, but his imposition of an adamantly secular civil code in 1928 and equally self-consciously "modern" codes of dress that prohibited "traditional" Muslim fashion symbols. Together these reforms threatened the social and legal power of Islamic law (Shar'ia) and the larger Muslim culture. And unlike the modernization program directed by Ataturk in Turkey, Reza Shah's economic policies made upwards of 95–98 percent of Iranians landless and did little to improve the lives of urban Iranians either.

When Hitler invaded the Soviet Union in 1941 the Soviets and the British invaded Iran (which had leaned toward supporting the Nazis) in order to secure supply lines from the Persian Gulf to the Soviet Union. With the invasion Reza Shah abdicated in favor of his son, Muhammad Reza, and the country spent the rest of the war under British, Soviet, and American occupation. Under the rule of the new Shah Iran became a central player in the US Cold War doctrine in the post-war period. When this position was threatened in 1953 by the oil nationalization policy of the elected nationalist Prime Minister Mohammad Mossadeqh, the joint US–British "TPAJAX" operation described in the Introduction overthrew his Government in one of the most important imperial maneuvers of the second half of the twentieth century.

A recently declassified review of the operation written by senior CIA personnel candidly discusses the reasons behind the coup: the Iranian Government's supposed support for Communism and desire to gain control of the oil industry. The coup led the US to solidify its position as the major imperial power in the Middle East, although it should not be forgotten that the US honed its imperial skills for more than half a century in the Philippines, Mexico, Central America, Haiti, and other countries of the Western hemisphere.[59]

Once the Shah was restored to power Iran became a major hub in the US drive to dominate the Middle East militarily and economically. What made the country especially important was that unlike Egypt or Israel, which had to obtain US weapons through grants and loans, Iran was "blessed" (from an American perspective) with both the oil wealth to buy its own weapons and a megalomaniacal leader who wanted Iran to become a world, not just regional, military power. To achieve this the Shah copied his father by attempting to modernize the country from above while delegitimizing the country's religious heritage and maintaining his family's, and regime's, dominance of the economy.

It was the arrogance, greed, extreme oppression, and literally wanton Westernization of the Shah (much of which had roots in the dynamics of imperial rivalry over and control of Iran in the previous century and a half) that created the conditions for the Islamic Revolution of 1978–79. Sadly, while much of the impetus for the revolution lay with workers and especially students and their energy and "insane" desire[60] to rid the country of well over a century of foreign dominance, the revolution was hijacked by Ayatollah Khomeini and his brand of puritanical yet quite modern Islam once his plane touched down in Tehran on February 1, 1979.

Conclusion: A Way Forward?

From the discussion in this chapter it should be clear that modernity, imperialism/colonialism, capitalism, and nationalism are inextricably bound together, and that the resulting matrix profoundly (and for the peoples of the Middle East, largely negatively) shaped the history of the world during the last half millennium. Of these four processes, I hope it is clear why, for Muslims, it has been imperialism/colonialism that was the driving force shaping the character of the other three. And apparently, the Bush administration agrees. As Bob Woodward details in *Plan of Attack* (his insider's account of the planning for the invasion of Iraq), the structure of the invasion was based around a "63-box matrix" that became the foundation of the US occupation of the country. Similarly, a "72-point matrix for stress and duress" was standard operating procedure for "inducing" Iraqi prisoners to provide information to interrogators.[61] And one of the men primarily responsible for the stress and duress matrix in Iraq, General William Boykin, has been described by his own colleagues in the military high command (no doubt in part because of his anti-Muslim speeches) as a dangerous combination of "arrogance" and "ignorance," providing yet another link between the modernity matrix and the Axes of Evil, Arrogance, and Ignorance.[62]

But of course, we can't really separate imperialism from capitalism. And so, as Arianna Huffington informs us in a section of her book *Pigs at the Trough* titled "The Matrix," none other than Enron developed its own computer software, called "the Matrix," whose job it was to determine whether a particular Government regulation would cost Enron money:

> Over the course of its now infamous life, the energy company turned the art of lobbying into a science. Enron did this through an ingenious piece of computer software it called "the Matrix." Like the one in the movie Enron's matrix sought to control other people – you know, members of Congress and presidential candidates – with a simple computer program. Every time a potential change in federal regulations loomed on the legislative horizon, a team of Enron statisticians, programmers and public affairs officers … would input the relevant data into the Matrix. After some high-tech number crunching the Matrix would put a price tag on the cost of that change to Enron. If the number was not to Enron's liking, the company's Washington team of lobbyists and well-funded legislators would swoop in like marauding Huns.[63]

What is crucial about Enron's matrix is that it was inseparable from what Huffington labels a "modernization madness" that infects the financial industry at large, where "modernization" actually means demolishing rules and regulations that separated investment and commercial banking – that is the existing structure of the system (whether in eighteenth-century India or twenty-first-century

America). And this process has been sadly facilitated after "the pigs turned into vultures" in the wake of September 11, when the scent of billions in profits from manipulating the hot war on terror filled the air above Alexandria, Virginia, and Lower Manhattan.[64] It's hard to imagine Keanu Reeves and his Zionist rebels (remember, in the Matrix's mythology the name of the only free region on earth was Zion) having a much harder time destroying their matrix than the global peace and justice movement will have dismantling the one currently enveloping the world.

Indeed, the historical and continuing power of the modernity matrix points to the difficulties faced by the Middle East and the "Rest" of the world in confronting a system whose functioning for centuries has been geared toward their oppression, exploitation, and marginalization. What the history we've discussed in this chapter suggests is that the world did not evolve along only one path over the last five hundred years, that the dominance of the West was not pre-ordained or due to its peculiarly modern culture, and that the world is not divided today between those who are advancing toward some mythical "end of history" and the rest who are headed either backwards, towards becoming just like us, or to a final competition with the forces of good. As the French philosopher Henri Lefebvre reminded us half a century ago, in studying other cultures, we are confronted "not by one social space but by many ... the worldwide does not abolish the local."[65] In Part Two we'll explore how and why the global and local have struggled against each other in the most recent phase of globalization.

PART 2

Branding Islam in the Global Era

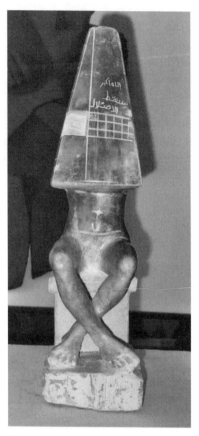

Figure 4 Art – and God – are against the US Occupation at a Baghdad Gallery, March 2004. In a joining of ancient Mesopotamian art with modern Muslim politics, the Arabic writing etched on this sculpture reads: "God is greater ... He [will] defeat the occupation"

3 Grounding the Globalization Concorde

Now that we have a basic understanding of the historical processes that produced globalization we can explore its contemporary dynamics. But defining globalization today is in fact a lot easier said than done, in large part because most people don't realize how the history we discussed in the last chapter has shaped it. Examining contemporary globalization's economic dynamics is especially difficult, and is certainly not as fun as discussing Moroccan heavy-metal bands or radical Islamist feminists, as I do beginning in Chapter Five. But for those readers who are more comfortable with cultural and political discussions than statistics and economic arguments I ask you to bear with me for the next two chapters, because it's impossible to understand the cultural dynamics of globalization and how people experience them without understanding its economic impact as well.

As important, a discussion of the economic implications of neoliberal globalization is crucial to piercing through the scientific veneer of the kind of economic analyses we'll be looking at in order to understand the ideologies governing them. For two centuries these same arguments have been used by Europeans, Americans, Japanese, and other empires to convince "natives" worldwide of the need to follow their liberalizing and/or modernizing prescriptions for development. And for just as long the policies they represent have produced similar kinds of resistance among the colonized everywhere once they experienced its negative results on the ground. We'll talk about these responses beginning in Chapter Four.

Defining Globalization: What? When? and Where?

Globalization today is both more complicated and less broad than most of its devotees or critics assume. Perhaps the two most important pieces of evidence of this reality for our purposes come from the facts that (1) the MENA region, which is so central to the various facets of globalization (sometimes by its absence or marginalization vis-à-vis certain key processes, as we'll see below), is more often than not left out of mainstream analyses of the phenomena associated with it; and (2) culture rather than economics is ultimately the main driver of global integration and interaction today.

The world has seen roughly five periods of "globalization," which can more accurately be described as significantly increased economic, cultural, and/or political integration. We can organize these periods into "preglobal," "protoglobal," and "global" eras, as in table 3. The pre-Columbian "old" and "new" worlds had long-distance trade routes and economic systems that stretched across continents and back thousands of years. However, few members of these societies other than people engaged in long-distance trade, war or religious study and/or pilgrimage ever came into direct contact with other cultures. The most important types of identity were either very broad (religious) or very local (family, clan, village). Because of this dynamic we can consider world history until 1492 as the "pre-global" (in the fullest sense of the word "global") era. The primary regional exception to the more closed cultural identities arose in the Indian Ocean and Southeast Asian regions, which because of their island/peninsular geography and the paramount importance of long-distance trade, saw much greater contact and influence between cultures on a daily level than most other regions of the world.

The post-Columbian world system that emerged after 1492 was the driving force behind unprecedented global integration. Its engine was the emerging and increasingly powerful modernity matrix – both at the level of material development, through the impact of capitalism and the rise of nation-state and imperial/colonial systems, and through the accompanying ideologies associated with colonial modernity. These justified the large-scale dislocation (if not destruction) of existing social systems and societies for the good of the modern nation or empire. Yet in many ways this was still a "proto-global" system, because neither the level of economic integration nor that of nationalist political development was close to what they would become by the nineteenth century.

The "global" era in its most meaningful sense can be said to have begun with the Napoleonic invasions of Africa and the Middle East, although its roots reach deep into the industrial revolution that spread across Western Europe and its colonies in the six decades leading up to Napoleon's coronation. Also giving impetus to this new period of imperial expansion and global integration were the American, French, and Haitian revolutions, and the spread of the steam engine, railroads, large-scale industrialization, and instantaneous communications technologies. This period can be subdivided to highlight three sub-periods: the unparalleled power of Great Britain and its "Pax Britannica" in the first two-thirds of the nineteenth century; the "Great Depression" of 1873 to 1896; and the era of "high imperialism" proper (epitomized by the "scramble for Africa") that ended with the outbreak of World War I in 1914.

If the Pax Britannica sub-period saw Britain rule the world's oceans and dominate the increasingly globalized circuits of trade, the depression was characterized by price deflation, low growth, and the promotion of national industries at the expense of free trade, all of which signaled a relative decline in British economic power vis-à-vis other imperial states. At the same time, the depression laid the groundwork for the emergence of a "new imperialism" following the 1878 Congress of Berlin – which is also where the major European powers agreed on the slow dismantlement of the Ottoman Empire – as Britain and its competitors sought to extend their colonial possessions, in good measure to acquire new colonies that would provide raw materials *and*, as important, export markets free of foreign competition.

By the mid-nineteenth century these processes helped cement the era of high European imperialism, perhaps the most truly "globalized" era of human history. This unprecedented level of global economic integration occurred for two reasons: a much higher proportion of world capital was invested in the third world;[1] and a much greater percentage of the world's peoples were migrating freely across the globe. Imperialism played a crucial role in all these developments, in comparison to which modern globalization seems hardly global at all.[2]

Global Era phase 1 is particularly important to our story because in many ways it parallels what happened to the world economy beginning in 1973: the previous regime of state-guided capital accumulation exhausted its capacities, which led to enhanced international aggressiveness of the leading powers of the day. If this late-nineteenth-century aggressiveness culminated in World War I, in the contemporary era it produced a series of smaller interventions that have led up to an increasingly militarized economy, politics, and culture in the US epitomized by its invasion of Iraq.[3]

The era of nineteenth-century high imperialism ended with World War I. The devastation of that war, the rise of Soviet Communism, the global spread of Henry Ford's system of mass production and Frederick Taylor's system of "scientific management," the Depression and World

Table 3: Periods of Globalization

Period	Characteristics
Pre-1492 *Preglobal*	• Extensive trade networks within old and new worlds, but aside from major port cities and the Indian Ocean and Southeast Asian worlds there is little contact between and/or awareness by the average person of other cultures. • Beginnings of mercantilist capitalism that would foster the Age of Exploration and processes associated with modernity.
1492–1797 *Protoglobal*	• Modernity, capitalism, imperialism/colonialism, and the nation-state take root at various speeds and intensities around the world. • Age of Exploration. Mercantilist, and at the end of this period, imperial capitalisms based on zero-sum competition between emerging nation states. • New types of long-distance credit, financing, insurance, and other financial technologies become central to economic growth and development. • American, French, and Haitian revolutions shock the international system in distinct but related ways by offering radically democratic and republican ideologies. • People around the world, especially outside of Europe, are profoundly affected by the dynamics of an emerging world economic and political system, especially by European colonial capitalism/imperialism, transatlantic slavery, emerging technologies of factory production, and later the steam engine.
1798–1914 *Global phase 1*	• Full development of the industrial revolution – through *laissez faire* policies in England's textile-based economy; through greater state intervention and centralization in France and Prussia/Germany.
Three sub-periods: 1. 1798–1873 2. Global Depression: 1873–1896 3. 1896–1914	• Era of high or "new" imperialism and capitalist industrialization. Vast majority of the world falls under European domination producing the most fully integrated economic system in world history. • Large-scale investment in colonies, financial integration (through long-distance credit and financing), innovations in transportation (steamships, locomotives, automobiles) and communications (photographs, telegraph, telephone, phonographs). • People around the world become truly conscious of the impact of events far away on their lives, in particular because of the speed of new communications technologies and mass migration of tens of millions of people.

- Intensified circulation of people and goods radically changes the way in which identities are constructed and experienced.

1914–1944
Depression and World Wars

- Processes of global integration slow and even reverse as worldwide trend is towards Fordist industrialization within countries. Depression, collapse of gold standard, and World War II significantly hamper global integration at all levels. But at least until the late 1930s, from India eastward, internal trade (India to Japan, China to Java) is rapidly increasing even as trade with the rest of the world declines.

1945–1973
Global phase 2

- Era of post-war globalization. World divided into competing capitalist and communist systems. Worldwide capitalist economy run largely on Fordist-Taylorist and Keynesian principles coordinated through the Bretton Woods system of macroeconomic regulation.[4]
- Significant expansion of trade within developed countries, but limited mobility of capital and labor.
- Birth of official international banking system (World Bank, IMF). Towards end of the period, floating of exchange rates and surplus dollars begin to destabilize system.

1973–present
Global phase 3

- Era of contemporary, post-Fordist globalization, characterized by increasing transfer of labor-intensive manufacturing from old centers in Europe and the US to the Global South, unprecedented innovations in technologies of production and communication, and transformation of previously state-managed macroeconomic systems to more "flexible" consumption-driven model.
- Rise of neoliberal structural adjustment, based on liberalization of markets and exchange rates and privatization of state industries, as dominant mode of adapting political-economic systems to new global economic ideologies and environments.
- Large-scale rise in "illegal" migration of workers from the Global South to "world cities" of the North.
- Cultural globalization becomes an important, perhaps primary, avenue of contemporary global integration.

War II – all these contributed to the development of specifically national models of economic organization and development that reversed the levels of economic, political, and cultural integration (however unevenly distributed) of the previous era. They also, crucially, helped cement the positive aspects of modernity – falling infant mortality, greater equality, rising democracy – precisely because states were more politically and ideologically responsible to the people (from the New Deal, civil rights and War on Poverty in the US to the "social welfare states" of Europe and Japan, to the self-defined socialist bloc).

Even in the colonies, the deprivations brought on by the Depression, coupled with the need for more progressive European administration to check rising nationalist sentiments, led to education and health policies that could be described as "social imperialism," at least until World War II shifted European priorities to (in the minds of European leaders) much more pressing needs.[5]

It also needs to be remembered that while worldwide integration certainly slowed significantly during the inter-war period, in Asia integration and trade increased significantly. This occurred as Japan sought to create an "East-Asian Co-Prosperity Sphere" whose primary goals included checking if not eliminating Western power in the region, and whose dynamics – however disrupted by World War II – laid a foundation for the post-war prosperity in East Asia. The immediate post-World War II era did, however, experience a quick return to a more integrated world system; more precisely, two systems: the Soviet-dominated Warsaw Pact and the US-administered "Free World." In the framework of the superpower rivalry, the construction of the UN system, and through it of global economic institutions such as the World Bank and IMF, and the Bretton Woods/GATT system of managed international trade directed by the United States, defined the world political economy for the next five decades.

"Globalization" in the sense that most people use the word emerged in the early 1970s as a response to the changing dynamics of world capitalism. There were two important factors in this transformation. The first was that the economy was increasingly driven by trends and demands related to consumption as opposed to production, which had been the driving force in the previous "Fordist" or "Keynesian" era.[6] The second was a new cycle of rapid technological innovations in production and communication that has been labeled by scholars "post-Fordist, flexible accumulation."[7]

What this term means is that the most successful transnational corporations were able to use new technologies to make rapid changes to manufacturing techniques and production lines in order to adjust to the most minute changes in consumer preferences. At the same time they learned how to move money and factories in and out of countries at relatively small expense, and to "work" the world's financial systems to reap unheard-of profits, often at the expense of workers *and* shareholders (as the Enron, WorldCom, and numerous other financial scandals remind us). The meaning of this transformation from a production to consumer-driven economy, coupled with the increasing mobility of manufacturing, can be summed up by the following historical comparison: whereas almost a century ago Henry Ford paid his workers extra so that they could afford to buy his Model Ts, today Walmart pays its workers (and by extension, all the workers who make its discounted products or drive the trucks that deliver them, and so on across the production process) so little they *can't afford to shop anywhere but Walmart and similar discount megastores.*

This emerging system has also produced new divisions among workers, with those who have the "knowledge" and skills to manage and even drive the system seeing their incomes (if not job security) skyrocket, while those who don't acquire the necessary skills are forced to work at increasingly lower paying service or manufacturing jobs that are constantly threatened by the "race to the bottom" of wages, tax revenues, and environmental regulations around the world.

As I explain in more detail in the next chapter, while neoliberal globalization understood as the "Washington Consensus"[8] model of economic development has received most of the attention from activists (at least until the US invasion of Iraq), we should bear in mind that the globalization of warfare in the twentieth century – and especially of the business of war – has played a leading role in this larger process. That is, defense establishments, and in some cases an "arms–petrodollar complex," have earned great profits and achieved increasing power within the national economies of many states, making it impossible to establish truly liberal and free systems of international trade, capital flows, and migration.[9] This dynamic is a major reason why contemporary globalization doesn't live up to its billing. Another – competing – system, based on violence, war, and the economies tied to them (President Eisenhower's "military industrial complex") is shaping the world's politics and economies in profoundly negative ways, even if they don't dominate the world economy in terms of share of GDP or profits.[10] As Chalmers Johnson puts it, "From the Korean War to the first years of the twenty-first century, the institutionalization of these huge defense expenditures fundamentally altered the political economy of the US. Defense spending at staggering levels became a normal feature of 'civilian' life."[11]

We can find evidence for the power of the war-economy in the decline in all forms of international assistance other than military aid since 1980, or the shifting of debates around poverty within and between countries toward blaming the "victims" of neoliberal policies for their failures to reform and/or improve themselves or their countries. At the same time, governments, most notably in the US, have militarized their police forces and built a huge prison system to deal with those who didn't fit into the new game plan.[12]

Given these dynamics it's no wonder that contemporary globalization is as inseparable from war and empire as it was in the last era of significant global integration, although we wouldn't learn this from reading most discussions or histories of it. But as the eminent sociologist David Harvey argues, "globalization represents the 'new imperialism,'" in which corporations and governments have found it as easy (if not easier) to "accumulate by dispossession" (that is, by controlling a country's resources, land, and labor) as through expanded but sustainable production.[13]

What Globalization Is Not

With the invasion and occupation of Iraq it no longer is far-fetched to claim that globalization, especially since September 11, is intimately linked to war and the power of petroleum, military and related sectors of the economy. But such a realization is only the first step toward arriving at a common understanding of what globalization is and is not. Even from a narrow economic perspective scholars and activists *on either side* of the debate have largely failed to explain the "costs of globalization" concisely and with reliable empirical data, or in a clear and easily understandable manner. Instead, both sides use various types of statistics (some going back hundreds of years) to buttress arguments about globalization's positive, benign or negative impact on countries, cultures, and the world more generally.

Let's analyze a few examples of how globalization is discussed in various settings so we can get a feel for what we're up against in trying to bring clarity to the situation. My examples are not special in any way, just a few of the hundreds of scholarly projects by economists and critics seeking to understand what globalization is about and does and does not do. Yet the way issues are framed and the language used reveals exactly how mainstream economists in particular distort statistics and history to justify an argument that globalization is ultimately a positive force, when the data largely suggest the opposite.

The first article is "Does Globalization Make the World More Unequal?" by economists Peter Lindert and Jeffrey Williamson. It is from a recent book on globalization, titled *Globalization in Historical Perspective*, that emerged out of a 2001 conference sponsored by the National Bureau of Economic Research.[14] The title of the book suggests a broad discussion of all the facets of globalization during the last few hundred years, although a glance at the introduction or the chapter titles reveals that the authors are interested only in its economic aspect, and only in specific factors related to monetary policy and trade at that. We'll discuss the impact of this narrow focus later.

One of the many arguments made by Lindert and Williamson is that "globalization favors all participants who liberalize." More specifically, "The nations that gained the most from globalization have been those poor ones that changed their policies to exploit it, while the ones that gained the least did not, or were too isolated to do so." This is an astonishing claim, given the overwhelming evidence to the contrary – no less than World Bank President James Wolfensohn admitted as much when he explained that the economic policies of communist Cuba were more appropriate for developing countries to follow than the Washington Consensus.[15]

Perhaps an even more important aspect of Lindert and Williamson's argument is the way they frame it: the authors never define who's a participant in the much-heralded liberalization – the country, the elite of the country, the whole population or just major corporations. And if, as it appears, it's the "country" they're referring to (more precisely, the national economy), can we safely assume that when a country or economy "benefits" from something called globalization the majority of its citizens are seeing an improvement in their incomes and/or standard of living?

What's more, when the authors argue that "those who gain the least from globalization are the non-participants," they don't explain how or why a "non-participant" – again, is this a country, class, ethnic group, culture, gender? – is not participating. The clear implication is that it's somehow their (clearly irrational) choice, not an imposed marginalization, or even a rational response to a set of policy options that can't possibly benefit the majority of the members of the society.[16]

Most important, Lindert and Williamson refuse to compare the roots of inequality within and between countries because, they argue, they have different causes and solutions. But if globalization is to mean anything, how can we understand one without the other? And for similar reasons imperialism is left out of their list of factors influencing the history of globalization. They even claim that "globalization in the past has been driven mostly by forces unrelated to policy," as if imperialism was a force of nature, not a policy that had some role in establishing the "core" and "poor periphery" they refer to several times.

The absence of any account of imperialism is not limited to this book; it is the rule in almost every international discussion between policy-making elites and academics. This conscious avoidance of any discussion of imperialism is especially galling when it comes to regions such as Africa or the Middle East, in which entire swaths of the earth were largely under European control for decades, if not more than a century. But this is exactly what happens in mainstream accounts (including the much publicized *Arab Human Development Report* discussed in Chapter One).

In the few instances when imperialism is raised, such as in an August 2000 IMF report titled "Factors Driving Global Integration," it is used purely in the past tense, as in discussions of "the end of empire," or arguments that the twentieth century was "bad for imperialism."[17] Could it be that the IMF has never heard of the Evil Empire, or its slicker alter ego on the other side of the Iron Curtain?

I have spent a fair amount of time on *Globalization in Historical Perspective* because it is a major new book by leading scholars published by a top academic press that claims to provide a historical context for this complicated phenomenon. Yet despite its enviable pedigree the book is a perfect example of how arguments are made by economists as if they were objective facts needing no supporting evidence (I suppose because they are self-evident to them), but which in reality are problematic at best, and dead wrong at worst.

The impact of such an attitude is evident in the remarks by commentators on Lindert and Williamson's chapter at the conference held to announce the book. One participant expressed his hope that the arguments of the authors would help overcome public "sympathy with the erroneous belief that globalization raises poverty in the Third World." We'll explore this claim later in the chapter; for now it's worth noting that a few months after this book hit the stores a groundbreaking report by UNICEF demonstrated that global trade keeps more than a billion children in poverty.[18] Another commentator, Harvard University economist Lant Pritchett, asked, "If the Seattle/Quebec protester crowd were to read and understand this report would they stop their anti-globalization agitation? In part it depends on what you think the protesters are on about. I approach this question with a pinch of Dylan 'gentlemen, Congressmen throughout the land, don't criticize what you don't understand.' I don't really understand what it is that gets the protesters on the streets."

Let's look at the language here. Beliefs are labeled "erroneous" without supporting evidence for this accusation; the protesters are a "crowd," and so like all crowds, are irrational (as crowds have been considered by governments from the French Revolution to the occupation of Iraq); a bit of Dylan is thrown in to show that Pritchett is not an out-of-touch IMF bureaucrat or ivory tower professor, and then the author admits he doesn't really understand what all the fuss is about. Perhaps if he and his colleagues spent a few months in the working-class neighborhoods of Cairo, the crumbling middle-class neighborhoods of Buenos Aires, almost anywhere in sub-Saharan Africa or Iraq, or just read one of the hundreds of books and articles detailing the negative impact of the economic policies of neoliberal globalization, they would gain a better understanding of what's behind the worldwide uproar against it.

But none of these experiences have to count, however, because globalization is limited to explanations of numbers derived from neoliberal economic models that may or may not bear any resemblance to reality. It's much easier to write that "the source of inequality is poor government and non-democracy, not globalization" than to explain how the two are intimately related. That's how the men and women at the IMF justify one billion malnourished children.

But for all their sophisticated mathematical models, they can't see the obvious: that inequality is entrenched within the existing international order and that the policies behind neoliberal globalization are making it worse, not better. It is no wonder then, as the editors of a recent book, *Inequality, Globalization, and World Politics*, point out, that arguments against inequality have virtually disappeared from the agenda of world politics in the so-called global era, just when inequality is reaching unprecedented levels worldwide.[19]

This dynamic leads me to believe that what we're dealing with here is fundamentally a question of perspective: either power, imperialism, and the destructive impact of centuries of imperial domination are an essential part of the globalization equation or they're not, in which case you get ludicrous arguments by people smart enough to know better. Indeed, we have to turn deeper into the UN system – far beyond the glare of the IMF and World Bank – to find a publication that has a simple yet honest assessment, such as was recently offered in the UN's Economic Commission for Latin America and the Caribbean 2002 Report, *Globalization and Development*: "The dynamics of the globalization process are shaped, to a large extent, by the fact that the actors involved are on an unequal footing. Developed-country governments, together with transnational corporations, exert the strongest influence, while developing-country governments and civil society organizations hold much less sway."[20]

Is Globalization Economic? Political? Cultural?

We shouldn't assume that the inaccurate views of globalization I've recounted so far are largely the fantasies of corporate executives, international financiers or mainstream economists. And it's not just the Right or neoliberals who suffer from such a narrow understanding. While critical of the economic impact of neoliberal globalization, most progressive/Left authors still focus primarily on globalization as at base an economic phenomenon.

As the leading socialist journal *Monthly Review* describes it, globalization is an "extreme" form of capitalism that is essentially "the spread of self-regulating markets to every niche and cranny of the globe."[21] This definition is fixated almost entirely on the economic aspects of globalization, which the editors wrongly assume is a smooth process, when in fact it can expand and contract over time and in different countries, and even thrives on chaos in places like the former Soviet Union and Iraq.

So it seems that it is as hard to define globalization from the Left as it is from the Right. Let's take a very different perspective, one that by the end of Chapter Six will hopefully be understood to be a more accurate, and perhaps even more interesting, barometer of globalization's real impact than any number of IMF reports or their critiques. The view is that of a Turkish Islamist activist, who is writing about the problem of "Islamic fashion" in his country and the impossibility for even believing Muslims to resist the "magic of the market." I will explore the interesting phenomenon of Islam in Turkey in Chapter Five, when I discuss "Islamist Republicans," but for now, his perspective offers a rich source for information on what globalization is and how we need to examine it in all its complexity.

As he argues:

> Turkey, as part of capitalist world, entered the atmosphere [of globalization]. Whatever their religion may be, people are unable to keep from adapting to the rules of capitalism. So-called Islamic fashion shows were approved by Muslims who submitted to the hegemony of capitalist relations of business ... And they show that we have been defeated in front of the reality that one cannot be a Muslim without being a capitalist.

What is the solution? There is no solution to this. Because the lifestyle which befits a Muslim – one which emphasizes abstention from worldly pleasures – would paralyze all markets, if you were to remove the consumerist practices of fashion shows, the capitalist structure would be destroyed. We are either, once and for all, going to remain under this wreck or we are going to, as long as we live, be entrapped in imperialism's vicious circles of debt in continuing to sell Islam to one another.[22]

While we can criticize this essentialist view of Islam as having only one proper lifestyle, the critique is still one of the most powerful and poignant assessments of the problems plaguing the developing world I have come across; its implications need to be fleshed out precisely because we can substitute almost any culture or country for Islam here and get a similarly valid assessment.[23]

To begin with, capitalist globalization has become the "atmosphere," or air that we breathe; and so to escape from it means to suffocate in our freedom (which is why he's resigned to living with it). Second, we see that even attempts to "Islamize" capitalism – that is, globalization – wind up enhancing capitalism rather than strengthening Islam. Such a scenario can only end up as a "defeat" for Islam, because today one can't be a Muslim without being a capitalist, yet in many ways – as many leading Muslim critiques of capitalism have been saying for two centuries (and as I explore in detail in the next chapter) – Islam and capitalism are incompatible in their approaches towards life and society. Finally, we see a slippage between capitalism and imperialism which reflects the "vicious circle" created by the modernity matrix we discussed in Chapter Two.[24]

Let's compare this critique – which reflects the attitudes of the majority of Muslim writers and activists towards globalization (although, as we'll see in Chapter Five, not all Turks) with what is perhaps the most well-known defense of neoliberal globalization yet written: Thomas Friedman's *The Lexus and the Olive Tree*. Since I have already labeled Friedman's work part of the Axis of Arrogance and Ignorance, his definition of globalization is a good basis of comparison. Not surprisingly, Friedman defines globalization as the world integration of finance markets, nation-states, and technologies within a free-market capitalism on such a scale as to create a single global market and, to some degree, a global village.

As he describes it in *The Lexus and the Olive Tree*, globalization is

the inexorable integration of markets, nation-states and technologies … in a way that enables individuals, corporations and nation-states to reach around the world farther, faster and deeper and cheaper than ever before ... Any country that wants to thrive economically today must constantly be trying to build a better Lexus and driving it out into the world; but no one should have any illusions that merely participating in this global economy will make a society healthy. A country without healthy olive trees will never feel rooted or secure enough to open up fully into the world.[25]

This is a nice sentiment, although it's clearly impossible for enough wealth to be created so that anything approaching the majority of people in a country, let alone the world, could afford to drive a Lexus, never mind do so and still have time to work in the family olive grove. Moreover, in describing the various stages of globalization, Friedman doesn't mention imperialism in his discussion of what drove the process during the very era of high imperialism in which they occurred. Instead he describes how important foreign investment into emerging markets has become in the global era, without telling us, when he surely knows, that foreign direct investment in developing countries constitutes a small percentage of the total world trade, most of which continues to be between developed nations.

Friedman also claims that because today's globalization is largely technology driven, "these new technologies are able to weave the world together even tighter. These technologies mean that developing countries don't just have to trade their raw materials to the West and get finished products in return; they mean that developing countries can become big-time producers as well."[26] Would that this were true! In fact, companies can do this, but "countries" – well, that would mean state-led or managed development, the antithesis of neoliberal globalization.

If Friedman's description of globalization is problematic in many ways, where can we find a more suitable one? As we've already seen, there is little agreement on either globalization's economic impact or even how to define it economically. Writing around the same time as Friedman – that is, the pre-Seattle neoliberal honeymoon – economist Peter Martin not surprisingly singled out integration as its most important characteristic, explaining that the (supposedly) "accelerated integration of previously marginalized societies is the best thing that has happened" since the end of World War II.[27] For him there is no doubt that globalization is leading to "an irreversible shift of power away from the developed countries to the rest of the world." Let's see if he's right.

Global Politics?

There are two ways to approach the question of what impact global-ization has had on the world's currently dominant political structure, the nation-state. On the one hand, in the 1980s and 1990s both supporters and critics believed that increased international economic integration (through trade and agreements like NAFTA and the WTO), coupled with the fluidity of currency and investment flows, would have important, even profound effects on politics. It wasn't just the relations between states that were supposed to be changing; state-centered political processes, even the very structure and identity of the nation-state, were all supposed to be "fading away" with the pene-trating power of economic and cultural globalization.

On the other hand, many assumed that the enlargement and close integration of members of the European Union (and to a lesser extent, other regional groupings such as ASEAN (Association of South-East Asian Nations)), would work in tandem with a (hoped for or feared, depending on one's politics) robust international role for the United Nations to create a truly global web of governance that would increas-ingly shape the lives of citizens around the world.

The EU has certainly grown and become an increasingly powerful figure on the world stage as well as in the lives of its citizens. It is perhaps the only example in the global era of a significant body of states actually ceding political, economic, and cultural sovereignty to a supra-state institution based on a common, over-arching, and supra-national ideological goal. But aside from the unique circumstances of the EU, it's clear that most states are not about to fade away, come together in EU-like groupings, or cede significant sovereignty to inter-national bodies or organizations any time soon.

Part of the reason for this is certainly the demise of socialism and strong union movements as checks on (if not alternatives to) the complete "capture of the state" by corporate elites (who know a good milking cow when they see one and rightly believe governments will more freely hand over the public's money than the public would). And so neoliberal globalization has proven successful for its sponsors precisely *because* states are managing their economies and populations in ways that promote the agendas of corporate elites, not because they've become so much weaker or disappeared. Indeed, the reality is that the revenues and expenditures of most states have grown dramatically during the last forty years; in the US (which by the summer of 2004 had spent itself into record deficits) as else-where the real issue is what these expenditures have been utilized for:

building an infrastructure for sustainable socio-economic development, or for enrichment of the local and international elite and the control of the majority of the population.

At an even deeper level, the complex relationships between states and corporations challenge the notion of firm boundaries existing between them. When senior public officials in the United States are hired almost immediately after retiring from public service as executives or lobbyists for the companies whose industries they regulate, then return to public service, and back and forth over the course of decades, who's to say where the state ends and the corporation begins? Or China or Egypt, where the armed forces are behind much of the so-called "privatization" efforts. On the other hand, in the Middle East (not to mention China) states and public sectors continue to possess great power in directing their countries' development; a reality that conflicts with new global norms that demand a contraction of the role of the state. This situation might seem paradoxical, but only until we realize that these states remain "bloated" in good measure to ensure stability and basic level of welfare *in place* of an integration process in which they can't participate fully because of the structure of the larger system.

While states remain the most important institutions mediating between individual people and the international economic system, not all can manage their countries' integration into the globalized world economy with equal success. In fact, "weak states" without sufficient revenue, legitimacy, or independence from one of the major economic powers will necessarily have a harder time than members of the G-8 in adapting to changing global economic realities. But however weak, the structures and institutions of the states themselves are not about to disappear, at least not for most countries (Somalia, Sierra Leone, Liberia, Iraq, Palestine are exceptions that at least for now prove the rule). Nor is the EU or the UN going to make the nation-state redundant in the foreseeable future. But what is increasingly clear from the experience of the post-Cold War era is that a global agenda of democratization, peace, and self-determination on the one hand, and neoliberal liberalization on the other, are incompatible. Humanity can have neoliberalism as its governing system or it can achieve peace, democratization, and truly global integration. But not both.

It's the Economy, Stupid?

If political globalization is not a major force at the present time, what about economic globalization? We might imagine that the economic dynamics of globalization have fundamentally transformed the world economy. We'd be wrong. If contemporary globalization is defined by its proponents as the (supposedly) greater integration of the world economy and distribution of wealth, resources, technologies, and commodities, the reality is that these processes are not occurring today to a degree that would approach the levels attained during the nineteenth-century phase. But there's an even more basic problem in defining our terms: like globalization, the word "economy" as it is commonly used is both a recently invented term and as hard to define as globalization. In fact, the very idea that there's such a thing called "the economy" that can be statistically analyzed and managed by states, corporate and international financial elites, and "grown" to the benefit of society as a whole, is a new phenomenon in the history of economic thought and practice.[28]

If the economy as a commonly understood concept is both a relatively recent invention and describable in contradictory ways, it becomes clear that the term "economic globalization" is a combination of two relatively new and ambiguous terms merged into one confusing and unmanageable meta-idea – not exactly the best way to achieve clarity. In fact, we can ask how it is possible to use either term with any accuracy; as the economic historian Neil Fligstein rightly asked after demonstrating how little economic convergence is actually occurring in the real world, "If there is so much globalization, why isn't there more convergence?"[29]

In order to answer this question we need to understand what exactly it is that mainstream accounts describe as economic globalization. Friedman's quote above provides a few clues when he mentions "the inexorable integration of markets, nation-states and technologies." Almost every book or article on economic globalization highlights several processes, with perhaps the characteristics most commonly attributed to it being (1) the growth in the world economy, (2) the changing relations between first and third world countries resulting from the use of information technologies to reorganize production, (3) the integration of world financial markets, and (4) the greater openness of domestic economies to world trade. For the IMF, the growth in world trade and migration are also crucial to globalization – although the figures regarding both of these phenomena are much more problematic than the IMF lets on. Other accounts add the phenomenon of the Asian Tigers and the simultaneous deregulation and integration of advanced economies into regional blocs such as the EU and NAFTA as the defining features of the new system.

There are many problems with using parameters associated primarily with economic liberalization to define economic globalization. First of all, it confuses globalization as an inevitable process of technological advance and cultural interpenetration – the ability for someone in New York to speak instantly to a friend in Jakarta through her computer's videophone – with a set of economic policies (what I refer in this book to as "neoliberal globalization" or just "neoliberalism") that are neither universally applied nor approved of. Indeed, during the last three hundred years the most successfully "globalizing" countries in the world, from the US to Britain, to Japan and many former colonies, have achieved their success precisely by pursuing policies that were the opposite of those (neo)liberals say are necessary to achieve such results.[30]

In fact, it was specifically economic growth resulting from protected industrialization that fueled the expansion of international trade in the last two centuries, and not vice versa. As a 2002 World Bank report concludes, "The idea that free trade was the primary engine of world economic growth between the mid-nineteenth century and the First World War is one of the great myths of history."[31] And the same situation prevailed in the twentieth century, as it is well known that large-scale public investment in industrialization in East Asia was a primary reason for the "East Asian miracle," while the prohibition against such policies in other regions, such as Latin America, prevented them from growing to their potential in a long-term and sustainable manner.

Not only that, there seems to be great confusion between the undeniably phenomenal growth in financial transactions during the last generation and a less distinguished growth in world trade more broadly. The reality is that financial transactions are now five times the value of world trade. This is important because while financial transactions can sometimes involve trade – when dollars are converted to Euros in order to buy European products, for example – financial transactions more frequently involve "playing the currency markets" in order to profit from slight fluctuations in exchange rates.

Such transactions are not productive to world growth, and have the added negative of tying the hands of national governments who see the value of their currencies shift rapidly and dramatically, which makes it very difficult to manage their economies in the interests of their citizens.[32] And there are even problems with the supposed importance of financial integration to development in the global era. As a recent IMF report admits, there is a "sobering but, in many ways, informative" discovery: "It is difficult to establish a robust causal relationship between the degree of financial integration and output growth performance."[33]

By now we might suspect that many of the claims by neoliberal and/or mainstream economists and policy-makers as to the level or quality of global integration, or the success of various policies associated with "structural adjustment" in the developing world, are at best questionable. But the problems are actually deeper than this. If we can argue that much of the developing world (and a good part of the populations of Western countries too, it turns out) haven't reaped the benefits of globalization, the case can also be made that the larger process of economic globalization is much less widespread than is assumed by both proponents and critics alike.

Research by scholars like Neil Fligstein and Paul Pierson demonstrates that the three core processes of economic globalization – the growth in the world economy, the transformation of production by new communications technologies, and the integration of world financial markets – are in fact *not* occurring to the extent described in the mainstream literature, if at all.[34] If the single defining dynamic of globalization is the integration of the world economy, why is it, as the chief economist of the Organization of Economic Cooperation and Development put it, that "most global markets are far less integrated than their domestic counterparts, even though OECD economies have become increasingly open to international trade?"[35]

So perhaps the most accurate argument to be made is that globalization is less about either the fading away of states or a clear increase in world economic "integration" – whatever that really means – than it is about what happens "when corporations rule the world," as the economist David Korten titled one of the most important books ever written on globalization.[36] By this he means that when transnational corporations with no ties or sense of obligation to the countries in which they operate join together with local political and economic elites they form a powerful "international managerial elite." And when this elite has the power to influence the most important economic and political processes of a country, the result is more often than not an increase in poverty, inequality, and other negative economic indicators at the same time that the managers of the economy and their allies around the world either celebrate its "growth," "efficiency," and "integration" into the world economy or blame the people or their corrupt and uncooperative government for failing to do so.[37]

Growing Pains

Here we need to stress a very important point: what we're talking about is not just some evil cabal of financiers happily starving the world to their profit. A primary reason for corporations engaging in such damaging practices, and why they need neoliberal policies to help them succeed, lies with the individual consumer living in Kansas City, Glasgow, Paris, Jakarta, Moscow, and every other part of the world. That is, neoliberal economic structures have spread like wildfire during the last quarter century because hyper-consumerist culture has become the dominant worldview for hundreds of millions of people around the world.[38] While the policies of Western governments and their allies on Madison Avenue (or Tokyo's Ginza district) are responsible for much of this trend, it is also true that much of the reason for its spread has been the failure of secular and largely socialist nationalist regimes across the Global South, and especially in the MENA, to deliver their end of an "authoritarian bargain" that promised social and economic development in exchange for consent by the people for undemocratic regimes. And because of this, people who once had other ways to make their working lives meaningful – it was contributing to the good of "Egypt" or "China" – now have no reason to work other than to take care of their own personal needs (and, if they're lucky, wants) as defined by the dominant international culture.

The system produced by a hyper-consumerist culture puts incredible pressure on businesses continually to innovate in design, upgrade equipment, and lower prices, creating a dynamic that is driving the world towards the precipice of global ecological disaster. As with so much in life, the blame ultimately lies with us. But the one good thing about a consumer-driven economy, however, is that we the consumers have the power to change it. We *can* get off the neoliberal "globalization Concorde" (as the head of the Islamic movement in Israel described it to me not long after the fateful crash that grounded the Concorde), and even ground it altogether. The bad news is that this would mean radically changing not just "what makes America America,"[39] but increasingly what makes humans human; the key ingredient of which seems increasingly to be "growth" – in the size of our economies, TVs, cars, houses, sexual organs (if the spam in my inbox each morning is any indication), executive salaries, defense establishments, and, of course, waistlines. In order to stop or at least slow down and redistribute gains from this growth, we need to understand how the world economy is or is not really growing.

The debates over how to define and judge economic growth are extremely complicated, yet they are crucial for understanding what's at stake in the larger globalization debates, especially in the MENA. In fact, there are significant "problems with growth" and other concepts such as "inequality" and "poverty."[40] The first problem is one of defi-

REPONSE PAYEE
GRANDE-BRETAGNE

Oneworld Publications
185 Banbury Road
OXFORD
GREAT BRITAIN
OX2 7BR

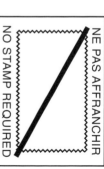

NE PAS AFFRANCHIR

NO STAMP REQUIRED

IF YOU WISH TO BE PLACED ON OUR MAILING LIST, PLEASE RETURN THIS CARD

NAME: _____

ADDRESS: _____

ZIP/POSTAL CODE: _____ COUNTRY (IF OUTSIDE UK): _____

EMAIL: _____

O N E W O R L D
O X F O R D

To ensure we send you the correct information, please could you answer the following questions:

In which book/catalogue did you find this card? _____

If in a book, where did you purchase it? _____

Which of these best describes your interest in our books? Please tick as appropriate:

You use them for personal use or as gifts ☐

You work in book retail ☐

You are a student and our book(s) are recommended ☐

Other reason? _____

You are an academic ☐

If so, do you have responsibility for selecting
books for course adoption? Yes/No

If yes, for what course? _____

PLEASE INDICATE ANY AREAS OF PARTICULAR INTEREST

☐ Comparative Religion

World Religions:

☐ *Hinduism*   ☐ *Buddhism*   ☐ *Bahá'í Faith*

☐ *Judaism*   ☐ *Christianity*   ☐ *Other* (specify)

☐ *Islam*   ☐ *Sufism*   _____

☐ *Mysticism*   ☐ *Inspirational*

☐ Middle East

☐ Politics

☐ History

☐ Philosophy

☐ Popular Science

☐ Psychology and/or Self-help

☐ Other (please specify)

_____

For further information, please e-mail us at info@oneworld-publications.com *or visit our website at*
http://www.oneworld-publications.com

nition: even in the most recent economic text books and larger academic literature it is impossible to find a coherent definition of the term or a discussion of how economic growth relates to actual growth in individual incomes and standards of living. Related to this is the fact that the very measures of "growth" used by mainstream economists – GDP or GNP – only measure the increase in the market value of economic production and the rate at which resources are converted into commodities that can be sold. But these are lousy ways to measure growth if you're concerned about justice, democracy, equality, and the health of the planet, because considered this way the hundreds of billions of dollars spent on the war on Iraq, on rebuilding the World Trade Center, or on stockpiling nuclear weapons all contribute to a "growing" economy. As would the conversion of all the world's resources into commodities, even though it would destroy life on Earth.

The second problem is that while advocates of neoliberal globalization stress the relationship between growth and openness to the world economy, the strongest arguments mainstream economists seem able to make about this relationship is that the existing literature "leaves open the direction of causality between growth and openness."[41] Third, most of the growth models used by economists are also based on some sort of "freedom of choice" by individual consumer-citizens. But such a hypothetical model is hard enough to sustain in the reality of contemporary America or Europe, let alone the Global South or MENA.

Fourth, making the focus on growth even more unrealistic is that so-called emerging market economies can only "catch up" to individual Western countries if their growth is rapid, sustained, and internally generated. Indeed, the growth prescriptions of the international financial community are often set to levels that are much higher than the world GDP growth, making them impossible – and even if they were possible, probably undesirable – to meet. Finally, the speed of growth depends in large part on the size of a country's internal markets and its geographic location, which are largely unchangeable. This is an important reason why, even in the EU, for every Ireland that beats growth expectations, there is a Greece that sees its income eroding compared with the rest of the EU.

Deciding for Ourselves if Growth is Good

If globalization has become inseparable from confusing and some-times dangerous "growth" strategies, how can we define it? Let's decide for ourselves what are the most important indicators that can help us determine whether the global system as it has evolved during the last fifty years has benefited or hurt the majority of the inhabitants of the world. Just think for a minute: what would be the most important indicators for you to determine whether your country was better off today than last year, or the last decade?

For me the most important measurements would be the absolute number of people in poverty, and share or percentage of the population living in poverty, the Human Development Index (which includes not only economic parameters but also health, education, environment, and political factors as well), the level of unemployment, participation in global trade, and the concentration of wealth in a country compared to the increase or decrease of its GDP.

Based on this clearly incomplete – but hopefully for the reader, comprehensive enough – list of important factors, we can look at the data collected by bodies such as the UN and the World Bank and judge for ourselves how well the countries of the Global South have done since 1960. For the majority of the countries of the Global South, it's not a pretty picture. If poverty, inequality, and concentration of wealth have all fluctuated in the last three decades,[42] the situation is much more distressing in the developing world. If only four countries saw the HDI score go down in the 1980s, twenty-one saw a decline in the supposedly booming 1990s. The "distribution of population and wealth" in the world has grown more unequal in the last fifteen years.[43] According to the 2003 *Human Development Report*, fifty-nine developing countries are in danger of not meeting the "Millennium Development Goals" set for 2015 unless wealthy countries raise their development aid very significantly, coupled with a fairer trade environment and meaningful debt relief.

We'll explore the specific data related to the MENA region in Chapter Four. What is clear from examining the picture worldwide is that for most of the countries and regions making up the Global South contemporary globalization has brought increased inequality and poverty (in absolute numbers almost everywhere, even if in some places – here China, with its one billion people, looms large – the percentage of the population living in poverty has apparently declined).[44] On the other hand, it's undeniable that there has been progress in some areas of social and economic development. For example, there has been a sevenfold increase in global wealth in the last fifty years and a dramatic increase in global trade (the hallmarks of neoliberalism although largely confined to the developed world), and perhaps more importantly, an increase in life expectancy, literacy and primary education, access to basic health care, and a lowering of infant mortality.

These are very important advances, and should be celebrated. But as the UN declared already in the mid-1990s, "we recognize that far too many people, particularly women and children, are vulnerable to stress and deprivation. The insecurity that many people, in particular vulnerable people, face about the future – their own and their children's – is intensifying."[45] In a place like Africa, where AIDS, the first disease of the globalized era, is ravaging the continent, the improvements in other areas are largely irrelevant. And in fact, the rapid spread of AIDS is rooted in the economic dynamics and consequences of widespread poverty. AIDS doesn't just increase poverty; as important, its spread to humans and growth into a pandemic is a structural result of the poverty and inequality produced by a century of modernization and war.[46]

Let's look in a bit more detail at poverty levels, particularly for children (see Table 4). Here the numbers are quite grim, especially in light of the incredible wealth that exists in the world, only a very tiny percentage of which, if redistributed through any means – voluntarily or through taxes – would erase children's poverty and all the problems that come with it. As the UNICEF report mentioned above explains (the position of the Middle East in this area will be discussed in the next chapter), "globalized trade and cuts to aid budgets are creating an ever-greater chasm between the richest and poorest countries ... More than half the children in the developing world living in severe deprivation, 674 million in absolute poverty, one third of all children live in dwellings with more than five people to a room and only a mud floor. A similar proportion has no toilet facilities, only one in five had access to safe drinking water, 10 percent have never been to school, and one in seven severely malnourished."

In looking at poverty levels, what the new data are teaching us is that the requirements of neoliberal structural adjustment programs increasingly force countries to choose between training more bankers and accountants in order to meet the standards of financial liberalization, or using these resources to hire more secondary-school teachers or boost spending levels for the primary education of girls. So even if the policies do lead to something called "greater integration into the world market," the costs of that integration when it occurs – fragmented safety nets, lowering of health services and other social services – is steep and largely unsustainable.

Indeed, a spokeswoman for the international charity Christian Aid explained about the findings of the 2003 UNICEF report: "We have to look at how globalization has affected these countries. There is a real link between that and poverty levels. They are put under enormous pressure to liberalize their markets, then they lose their indigenous trade to subsidized markets in the EU and the US; and the poorest people, such as subsistence farmers, are left with absolutely nothing."[48]

As bad as this situation may be, is it in fact related to growth? A July 2001 study comparing the 1980–2000 period of globalization with the 1960–1980 period of "pre-globalization" suggests it might not be, since growth rates actually fell significantly for the poorest and middle income groups during the second period. So did life expectancy, while progress in reducing infant mortality rates and increasing education "slowed considerably."[49] And so after noting the fact that today world trade and foreign direct investment is even more concentrated in the developed world than a generation ago, the study's authors conclude that "globalization has been associated with diminishing progress" during the last generation.[50] Another study was even more blunt: "Trade openness (liberalization) increased poverty and inequality … Those countries liberalizing most rapidly fared worst [in both areas]."[51] And these arguments highlight a major point of our discussion: the policies are disastrous, even though – or perhaps because – they are often not producing the advertised results. But even when they do, they're still problematic, as we'll see when we discuss China and India below.

Finally, we should bear in mind that these terrible costs are being felt in the heart of the West as well as the more often discussed third world. As a report on poverty in Britain explains, "The UK vividly illustrates the consequences" of neoliberal policies made famous by Thatcher and continued largely undisturbed by Tony Blair's "new" Labour government.[52] So it should be no surprise that in the UK two decades of Thatcherism have produced a situation where today inequality of income in the UK is "exceptional compared with international trends," while child poverty rates were "found to be the third highest of 25 nations for whom information was available."

But such is the nature of neoliberal economics and politics, and the race to the bottom they produce, that these policies have slowly but inexorably spread throughout the Continent. And so the report concludes that "although the UK is the extreme case, other European countries in the last two decades show that a majority of [EU] member states and of intending member states have experienced a growth of inequality of living standards and of poverty, as measured by incomes relative to average income per household."[53] Of course, from Prime Minister Blair's perspective such a leveling of the playing field might improve Britain's ranking, but few others would be happy about it.

Table 4: Percentage of Children Living in Absolute Poverty and Severe Deprivation, by Region, 2003[47]

Region	Percent Absolute Poverty (2+ severe deprivations)	Percent Severely Deprived (1+ severe deprivations)	Percent Severely Shelter Deprived	Percent Severely Sanitation Deprived	Percent Severely Information Deprived	Percent Severely Water Deprived	Percent Severely Food Deprived (U5 pop)	Percent Severely Health Deprived	Percent Severely Education Deprived
Sub-Saharan Africa	65	83	62	38	39	53	19	27	30
South Asia	59	82	45	61	40	18	27	23	19
Middle East & North Africa	40	65	45	26	23	24	12	14	23
Latin America & Caribbean	17	35	23	17	10	7	5	7	3
East Asia & Pacific	7	23	8	5	7	10	5	3	1
Developing World	37	56	34	31	24	21	15	15	13

The situation in the US is sadly similar, as the number of people living in poverty has increased in the new decade, with the general level at 12.4 percent in 2002 and child poverty rate increasing to 17.2 percent the same year. That's 34.7 million poverty-stricken people in the richest country in the history of the known universe (12.1 million of them children). And this is when poverty is defined at the ridiculously low measure of less than $18,000 a year in income for a family of four (another 12.5 million people lived just above the official poverty line).[54]

It must be pointed out that the international community has long been aware of the realities of neoliberal fantasies made reality. Already in the mid-1970s the Brandt Report, authored by leading European social scientists, recommended an immediate "large-scale transfer of resources to developing countries," as well as an international energy strategy, global food program, and reforms of the international economic system. The UN's Economic Commission for Latin America and the Caribbean (ECLAC) put it more bluntly twenty-five years later, in 2001:

> In the past three decades it has become clear – and has been scientifically documented – that the planet is facing an unprecedented situation as a result of the increasing scale and cumulative effect of human activity. The impacts are worldwide and include global warming, the thinning of the ozone layer, the decline in biodiversity and the spread of desertification and drought, which have taken on the perverse dimension of "global public ills." This has highlighted the increasing ecological interdependence among countries, which has made the current moment in history unique. The need to reverse these processes has given rise to new imperatives and opportunities for international cooperation, and the threat they pose to the sustainability of economic growth has been debated widely and at length. The responses that have been developed thus far, however, are clearly inadequate given the magnitude of these problems.[55]

Concentrating Wealth and Power

We may not yet know what "globalization" is, but I think it's safe to say that neoliberalism will never achieve the goals set by its proponents, let alone deal with the immediate needs of literally billions of people who are on the losing end of the existing world system. Perhaps the most important reason for this is that the liberalized world economy has led to an unprecedented concentration of wealth in the hands of the world's richest people and countries, whether we're talking about the richest 1, 5 or 20 percent of the world's population.

We know, for example, that the gap in incomes between the richest and poorest countries increased from a ratio of 30:1 to 74:1 between 1960 and 1997. Not surprising, we also know that "high-income" countries were the only group of countries to increase their group share of global GDP (that is, compared with the categories of middle- and low-income countries, and even China and India) during this period[56] (Chart 1).

And while it might be a cliché when referring to the United States to say that the "rich have been getting richer and the poor poorer," it's true just the same – in spades.[57] Clearly something needs to be done about this situation, right? Apparently not. As mainstream economist and Brookings Institution fellow Nancy Birdsall calmly argued in the journal *Foreign Policy*, "The simple and painful truth is that inequality is nobody's fault and cannot be fixed in our lifetimes."[58] In other words: If you're on the losing end of the restructuring of the world economy during the last generation, too bad (or more bluntly, which is how one Iraqi professor described his experience being at the wrong end of

Chart 1: Average Yearly Change in Real Per Capita GDP

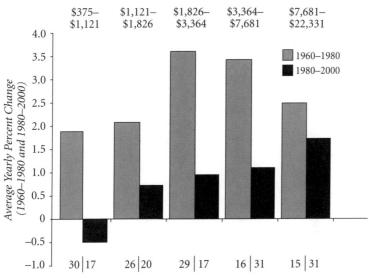

Per Capita GDP at Start of Period (1960–1980 and 1980–2000) in Constant 2000 US Dollars

Number of Countries in Each Group (1960–1980 and 1980–2000)

Sources: Penn World Table, International Monetary Fund

neoliberal globalization: "Tough Shit"). To paraphrase Supreme Justice Frankfurter's wistful remarks about Palestine from Chapter Two, "No *cordon sanitaire* can protect you from being pulverized."

So there's no point complaining. If you do it will just make your life worse (all the sweatshops that in fact pay higher wages than the local factories will just pick up and move to a country not filled with whiners). But if you behave and keep doing what we tell you, maybe your grandchildren will have a decent middle-class life, assuming global warming, deforestation, war, increased pollution, and the poisoning of the environment don't make a decent life almost impossible for most of the world by the end of the twenty-first century.[59]

But whether we complain or not, the reality is that the world has become a lot more unequal in the last forty years, as shown by Table 5:

Table 5: The Composition of the Four Worlds in 1960 and 1998 (Number of Countries):

	Rich	*Contenders*	*Third World*	*Fourth World*
1960	41	22	39	25
1998	29	11	19	78

Of course, more unequal isn't necessarily bad if average incomes are rising and most people are better off than before (even if the rich have become a lot richer than the poor or middle class). But this does not seem to be the case much if not most of the time. Rather, what seems increasingly clear is that if a country is already rich, or at least an advanced "transitional economy" (such as the Czech Republic), "openness is good for equality." But if a country has a GDP similar to the average of Latin America or the MENA, the impact of neoliberal policies will most often be negative. This is not just the case within countries; in fact, the disparities *between* the regions of the world increased by at least 15 percent from 1960 to 1998.[60]

But it's not just inequalities between countries that's worsening; new research on inequality trends in seventy-three countries finds that over the last two decades inequality rose *within* two-thirds of them, a process that was accompanied by a slowdown in growth and stagnation in poverty rates.[61] In fact, the poorest 5 percent of the world population lost one-fourth of their real income during this period, which, according to scholars, is due to the adoption of neoliberal policies that "remain a major impediment to growth and poverty alleviation."[62]

More generally, as George Monbiot incisively describes it:

We are living off the political capital accumulated by previous generations, and this capital is almost spent. The massive redistribution
which raised the living standards of the working class after the New
Deal and the second world war is over. Inequality is rising almost
everywhere, and the result is a global resource grab by the rich. The
entire land mass of Britain, Europe and the United States is being re-
engineered to accommodate the upper middle classes. They are
buying second and third homes where others have none. Playing fields
are being replaced with health clubs, public transport budgets with
subsidies for roads and airports. Inequality of outcome, in other
words, leads inexorably to inequality of opportunity.[63]

We should be fair to the World Bank and IMF economists and try to
imagine how they'd respond to these figures. Most likely they'd argue,
as does a recent study, that "income inequality tends to increase at
early stages of economic development [but] fall at later stages."[64] This
is all well and good, we could reply, but *only if* a country actually
reaches a "later stage" of economic development, which the MENA
region has yet to do even after decades of "modernization" of various
kinds. What we need to ask is: can the MENA ever reach the "later
stages of development" in the present configuration of the world
economic system?[65]

Regardless of how we want to define or judge growth, inequality,
and poverty, or whom we want to blame, the contemporary world
system, which for the last generation has been increasingly administered under neoliberal principles commonly understood as "globalization," has produced the following situation:[66]

- 1.2 billion people live on less than US$ 1 per day;
- 800 million people are suffering from chronic malnutrition, mean
  life expectancy in developing countries (62 years) is much lower
  than in most industrialised countries;
- 40% of the world's population is affected by communicable
  diseases such as malaria, and in Africa alone 2 million people die of
  AIDS each year;
- more than 80% of global consumption is accounted for by 20% of
  the world's population;
- the income of the richest 20% has risen from being 30 times to 82
  times that of the poorest 20%;
- the global population is predicted to increase by about 2.5 billion
  between 1990 and 2020, with almost 90% of this increase taking
  place in the developing countries;

- even conservative scholars admit that "in the twenty-first century … major and pervasive health setbacks will be a characteristic feature of the global population profile. These steep increases in mortality do not seem to be transitory, but will probably continue for decades";[67]
- 60% of the poorest people live in ecologically fragile areas;
- 33% of the world's poorest people are currently experiencing a shortage of water resources and this situation is worsening, such that almost 60% of the poorest populations will be affected by 2025;
- there are 900 million illiterate people today, with 130 million children never attending school and a further 150 million having had to leave before they achieve literacy.

Whatever you want to call the system that has produced these statistics, it's a disaster. Arguing whether something called "globalization" is the cause is perhaps ultimately a waste of energy because by the time we settle the argument over how to define globalization – without which we can't figure out if it's to blame – millions of people will be sick or dead of starvation, disease, and war, or increasingly marginalized from the system's centers of power and wealth. Better to spend our time figuring out whether and how to redress this sad state of affairs, and whatever the best way is, call that globalization.

Don't China and India Count?

Even if the statistics and arguments we've been discussing are valid, mainstream economists would surely remind us that we haven't mentioned either China or India in our discussions, even though they are home to nearly 40 percent of the world's 6.25 billion people. And these critics would point out that both countries have seen unprecedented growth and poverty alleviation which, they might add, is probably why we haven't included them.

It is true that both China and India have enjoyed historically unprecedented growth rates between 1980 and 2000, of around 10 percent and 6 percent of GDP growth per year respectively. It is also clear that in both China and India poverty has been reduced in the last two decades of the twentieth century, precisely when both were experiencing this accelerated growth.[68]

But there are several problems with the Bank's claims about poverty reduction in China and India. Specifically, the measurements used by the World Bank rely on something called "Purchasing Power

Parity" (PPP) adjustments to compare across countries. This means they compare what amount of currency in various countries is required to buy the same "basket of goods" in each of them, which allows economists to compare incomes across countries. But this method understates poverty in poor countries, especially rural poverty, because it evaluates the incomes of people by the relative cost of a complete "market basket" of goods *and* services in rich and poor countries – the basket includes almost every imaginable service and good available on the market, including those that poor people wouldn't or can't afford to buy.

That is, even "normal" services like haircuts, maids, or taxis, might be vastly cheaper in China than in the United States, but poor people in China don't use them, making them irrelevant when figuring out poverty or standards of living. What is relevant are the prices of the things that poor people do buy – especially food – which, while cheaper in China than the US, are much less so than the prices of a haircut or taxi (maybe one-third or one-fourth the price rather than one-twentieth for services). On the other hand, a product such as computer software, which could be considered a cultural good or services, can also be profoundly economic, as when a Bangladeshi woman wants to learn to be a graphic designer but can't afford legally to buy the PageMaker tutorial program necessary to learn this skill.

And so if we narrowed the basket from all goods to a "basket of basic necessities" as some economists do, we would come up with a more accurate measurement of poverty, but one that would mean there are a lot more poor Chinese than we imagined. However, this is only half the problem with the current way poverty is determined, in China or anywhere else. Not surprisingly, the other major issue involves how growth is defined. That is, a lot of the economic "growth" of China is attributable to the fact that activities which previously went unaccounted for now involve money. For example, communes used to provide services to members – everything from child, elderly, and health care to the burial of the dead – that are now commercialized, adding new sources of income to purchase food and other products. And as markets have been established for housing, prices have sky-rocketed even though the actual physical structure hasn't improved (so the same apartment that went for $1 a month would be worth thousands). In this situation, both the salaries and the buying of food or increase in housing prices raise the GDP and register an enormous growth in income, even though total production or the standard of living haven't risen.[69]

Most importantly, as China historian Ken Pomeranz (author of the award-winning *The Great Divergence*) argues, and as the Bank and IMF grudgingly admit when pushed far enough,

> In the Chinese case, while the pre-1978 years did not produce very impressive gains in income, they did produce huge advances in life expectancy, literacy and school attendance rates, public health, and in infrastructure creation. These gains were in fact the pre-conditions for the successes since then.[70] And even as many state-owned enterprises are gradually privatized there are still a huge number of enterprises owned by village and township governments, which have been one of the principal engines of the country's growth. Taken together, the growth strategies pursued by China during the last two decades are a combination of old-fashioned "Keynesian demand stimulus" managed by the government, various institutional measures to prevent inequality from getting too extreme, *slow* deregulation of things like food prices, and the important fact that China is so big that it has been able to negotiate the terms of openness to the world economy in a way that's much more difficult for smaller and less strategically important countries.[71]

So even *the* supposed success story of globalization, China, is not as clear-cut a case study as the neoliberals would like us to believe. And that's if we take the numbers that the World Bank provides us about China (or other countries) at face value. But what if the numbers themselves are problematic? In fact, much of the economic data used to celebrate the successes of China and India are based on guesswork and out-of-date data, which has led some younger economists to offer a "scathing" critique of the way the World Bank defines and counts poverty.[72]

As the authors of one important study explain, "Most readers, including many economists, take these [World Bank] figures as clear-cut facts. But the method used to calculate them has serious flaws, which render the resulting estimates untrustworthy."[73] The authors of this study, Thomas Pogge and Sanjay Reddy, argue that if the Bank used baselines that better reflected the actual needs of poor people (whether in China or the US) their official poverty line would have to be much higher, and so a lot more people would be considered as living under it.[74]

Even if we accept that China and India have seen decreased poverty (which in the case of China can't be attributed to the country becoming "capitalist" since so many of its economic practices are still socialist in various ways), World Bank economist Martin Ravallion reminds us not only that such reductions have been uneven, but that *"the growth rate needed to achieve this trend decline has been rising over time."*[75] This sentence is absolutely crucial to understanding the problem of growth, inequality, and poverty. What it means is that in order to continue lowering poverty, growth levels in China will have to keep rising (in other words, growth rates have to keep growing). But this is both unsustainable environmentally and also tends to increase inequality and the concentration of wealth, which increases relative poverty even if the absolute number of poor people doesn't change.

Finally, and here is where culture barrels into a seemingly economic discussion, in exploring issues like poverty, the culture and ideology of consumption as driving forces behind neoliberal globalization becomes crucial. That is, even though the new formulas used by the World Bank to calculate poverty have lowered the official levels in India or China, what is really happening is that the Bank is "telling poor Indians that their opportunity to buy services very cheaply has become more valuable." But valuable to whom? Since citizens of wealthier countries spend more on services relative to basic necessities than they used to, should poor people in the Global South do the same? At least in India, "the poor can plausibly reply that the international shift toward consumption of services is quite irrelevant to them," because they have to spend all their income on basic necessities like food, shelter, and healthcare just to survive.[76]

The Heart of the Matter: The Cultural Foundations of Contemporary Globalization

Here we have arrived at the heart of the matter. In the era of contemporary globalization the changing cultural preferences and economic trends of the world's richest countries profoundly shape expectations among policy-makers and citizens alike in the Global South. Changes in what and how people consume in wealthier countries don't just influence the tastes and desires of people in poorer ones, they help shape an international economic agenda in which poor people are told that they should be consuming services or other essentially cultural products they don't necessarily need and can't really afford in order for their economies to "grow." And because they "should" be able to afford them, they are no longer considered as poor as before.

However we design the statistics and however much we'd like the world's poor to take more taxis, have more pedicures, or buy more legitimate – that is, ridiculously overpriced – software, DVDs or CDs (and not the pirated versions available on the sidewalks of almost every major city of the world), the reality is that political and economic globalization are not occurring in the manner and to the extent generally assumed. And to the extent they are occurring, they're dividing rather than integrating the peoples of the world, within as much as between countries.

Given these dynamics, how can we define globalization? Let's remind ourselves of what we know. First, there is great confusion about how to define and measure its economic dynamics. Second, to the extent that we can agree on a definition of economic globalization, it turns out that the current period is not nearly as globalized as we might imagine. Third, we know that since neoliberalism has become the dominant mode of globalization the world economy statistics on poverty and other major indicators have either deteriorated or barely managed to hold their own in most of the countries of the developing world. Where they've done better (on paper), as in China or India, it's been because leaders did *not* follow the Washington Consensus model. Finally, we know that true global integration will not occur as long as the world is being managed according to a model that concentrates wealth, necessitates a militarization of economies, politics, and cultures, frustrates democracy, and makes sustainable development and truly free trade impossible to achieve.[77]

The data we've been discussing suggest that if there is such a thing as an "anti-globalization" movement, it has been fighting a straw man. Activists and scholars working for global peace and justice have long been aware of this, which is why many describe themselves as an "alternative global" (in Europe, "alter-global") or true globalization movement and focus their strategies on addressing the actual economic consequences of the existing world economic system, rather than some fictional globalization bogeyman the neoliberals accuse them of fighting. This has not stopped neoliberals like the New York *Times'* Thomas Friedman or the *Wall Street Journal* from writing articles explaining (more like celebrating) how and why the "anti-globalization movement is losing steam."[78]

Friedman even uses India as an example of the supposed petering out of the movement, completely ignoring the over one hundred thousand people who participated in the 2004 Mumbai World Social Forum, never mind the incredible levels of poverty that continue to exist in the country. As important, he conveniently ignores the transformation of the anti-corporate globalization movement into a global peace and justice movement that has had to focus most of its attention on the invasion and occupation of Iraq while facing ever more severe "security" restrictions.[79] The transformation from "lite" to "heavy" globalization is a major reason why leaders of the movement began focusing more on organizing their own events – such as the World and European Social Forums – rather than following the G-8, WTO, and IMF around with little chance of disrupting meetings or getting favorable press coverage.

We can dismiss the writings of Friedman as those of someone who can't or won't admit how little he actually knows about globalization and the movements he spends so much time glibly belittling. But even more serious scholars, activists, and policy-makers have yet to understand fully the meaning of the dynamics we've described so far: that in the absence of economic globalization it is culture that is the most powerful vehicle for globalization. This claim, that culture is the most important foundation for contemporary globalization as it is experienced by people around the world, is one of the most important arguments of this book. If accurate, it suggests that policies toward and activism in the MENA have focused far too much on economic and political issues and not enough on the cultural issues that often drive them.[80] Yet the problem with focusing on cultural globalization is that it's not much easier to pin down or measure objectively than economic globalization.[81]

As the great literary critic Raymond Williams once put it, "culture is one of the two or three most complicated words in the English language." We can imagine it's not so very different in most other languages either.[82] Whether in English, French or German, since the sixteenth century culture has been tied to the idea of "civilization," a meaning that is still favored by conservative scholars like Samuel Huntington. That's why when Huntington opens his famous "Clash of Civilizations" article with the words, "It is my hypothesis that the fundamental source of conflict in this new world will not be primarily ideological or primarily economic. The great divisions among humankind and the dominating source of conflict will be cultural," and then goes on to divide the world's culture into seven "civilizations," he's clearly imagining culture in civilizational terms.[83] By this I mean that he is conceiving of it as a vast collection of customs, traditions, laws, books, and "high" art produced by a society which by definition makes culture rigid and slow to change. In fact, this property is precisely what makes a culture identifiable as belonging to one particular society and no other.[84]

Clearly this kind of definition of culture, which the Ugandan anthropologist Mahmood Mamdani refers to as "Culture Talk" because of its obsessive focus on negative stereotyping and talking *about* – rather than *with* – other cultures, is highly problematic. The person most responsible for it in the context of the Middle East is none other than Bernard Lewis, who actually coined the term "clash of civilizations" later made famous by Huntington specifically to refer to the seemingly intractable conflict between "Islam and the West." What Mamdani shows us is that Culture Talk is tied directly to the modernity matrix through its roots in the ideologies and strategies of imperialism/colonialism, capitalism, and nationalism going back to the birth of political modernity in 1492.

This date simultaneously represents a crucial moment in the emergence of the European Renaissance (and so modernity as an idea and ideal) and "two related endeavors, one the unification of the nation, the other the conquest of the world."[85] That is, there could be no political modernity, no national unity, and no European capitalism without the European conquest of much of the rest of the world. In Chapter Two we discussed the importance of "New World" silver and then slave economies (and the genocides they necessitated) to the modernization of European economies in the next several hundred years. Equally important for our discussion is to recall who was the source of much of the knowledge that fueled the Renaissance, who was the Other against which Europeans increasingly tried to unite themselves, and who was ultimately a major object of European conquest and control: the Muslim world. In short, there would be no modern Europe without Islam and the Muslim world.

Clearly then, Muslim cultures, even "civilizations," have long played a crucial role in the development of something called "the West."[86] We'll focus specifically on them in the next chapter. Here we still have to figure out what we mean when we talk about culture more broadly. By now it should be clear that there's no such thing as *a* or *the* culture of a society sitting there waiting to be learned and passed on like a good book or folk dance; but such a realization isn't exactly new. In fact, as early as 1784 the German philosopher Johann Gottfried von Herder understood that the "civilizational idea" of culture today favored by Huntington and his comrades was in fact a mask for "imperial conquest." To avoid chaining culture to imperialism he described culture as existing always in flux and "in the plural."[87]

Two centuries later scholars talk about culture existing in its "performance" by the people who define themselves as part of it; that is, people "acting out" – living really – with the knowledge that others are watching and judging their "performance."[88] So culture only exists as it is expressed by ordinary people (since most people in a society are ordinary) in their everyday lives. It's not a static identity, but rather a site for the invention, intervention, and performance of many different and often conflicting identities with which, depending on the situation, they can reinforce, or resist, larger nationalist or globalizing projects.

What is especially important about this understanding of culture is that it becomes the one space where citizens of the MENA, and everywhere else, can become active producers, and not just passive consumers in the global era. Or as one critic describes it, using a musical analogy that is crucial for the notion of culture jamming utilized in this book, culture must be both understood and experienced as operating "in the line between conception and execution, between … composition and performance" in order for people to feel they have a stake in it.[89] But of course, this kind of positive understanding and performance of culture only occurs if people understand that culture can be like this; that it doesn't have to be the kind of heavy, unchanging mirror of a society's greatest fears and dreams that has to be uncritically worshiped and passed on, generation after generation. Few leaders, whether states, insurgencies, or terrorist groups, have much interest in a positive, open, and changeable experience of culture.

In order to account for the reality of culture as moving, changing, and "performing" all the time (that's why we can speak of culture jamming in a real and not just metaphorical sense), the British sociologist John Tomlinson describes cultural globalization as a "complex connectivity" among states, societies, corporations, and ecosystems. What makes these connections global rather than just complex is that people reshape their cultures through the feedback generated by their interaction with other peoples *and* products located all over the world.[90] For our discussion, the most important thing about this dynamic is that the more people define themselves and their sense of self-worth through what they buy and own (which is reinforced by the unprecedented number of relationships they have with other people who also define themselves this way), the easier it is for corporations and the international financial systems they work through to gain power over them.

Equally important is the way corporations and politicians alike – and in fact together – use marketing, polling, and niche production (whether of products or political ideas) to integrate changes in cultural or political preferences into the style or function of products, or even the larger management and functioning of markets and political systems. In fact, the sheer power of the commodification and even militarization of culture has become one of the most important processes driving contemporary capitalism,[91] because it has turned cultural practices that were previously not part of the money economy (or were part of it in a very different way) into symbols or activities that can be bought and sold.

There are literally millions of examples of this dynamic. On the one hand, there is the increasing popularity of "reality TV" and talk shows, where the most intimate aspects and practices of peoples' lives become the vehicles for selling advertisements to viewers; on the other hand, there is the simultaneous globalization of tourism and labor migration, which has seen an explosion of the manufacture, performance, marketing, and sale of "authentic" third world cultural products like music, clothing, art or handicrafts. What's most important about this dynamic is that the feedback between producers and consumers has become so rapid that companies can not only stay on top of the latest shift in thirteen-year-olds' sneaker preferences, but critical cultural production – music, fashion, art – can be coopted and used to market a product as cool or cutting edge before the original, perhaps critical message has a chance to become part of the public debate.

Needless to say, this makes it very difficult to maintain a sustained critique of the system, let alone transcend it, especially when the circulation of cultural – that is, largely symbolic – commodities (movies, music, DVDs, CDs, software, books, computer coding systems) increasingly takes place through networks that corporations either control and make money from, sponsor, in the case of high-profile but largely non-commercial art (museums, classical music), or, in the case of intellectual or "piracy" or politicized culture, heavily police.

Is Cultural Globalization Good or Bad?

For many of its critics, especially in the 1980s and 1990s, globalization was feared to be creating a homogenized world culture, where all difference would be erased by processes like "Cocacolonization," "Disneylandification," "McDonaldization," or just plain "Americanization." Everyone was supposed to become "just like Mike" – that is, just like the US, whether they wanted to or not.

Without underestimating the fear of Americanization, we know now that it has been largely unrealized. But despite its inaccuracy, the belief in a US steamroller crushing all other forms of culture continues to define the way many people experience the "threat" of globalization around the world. There are clear problems with this belief. First, it ignores the fact that other peoples and cultures have the power and agency both to resist and, more often, selectively adopt and adapt to American and other cultures.[92] Moreover, it assumes that there are no other "global" cultures that can compete against American products.

But in fact we know that in much of the third world American cultural products face stiff competition from those of other cultures, whether it's Latin American telenovelas or Indian cinema. Of course, soap operas and movies were originally American forms of cultural production, but they are no more so today than spaghetti is Chinese. And while non-American culture has a harder time widely penetrating the US market, everything from sushi to reggae and surf guitar – invented by Lebanese American Dick Dale (which is why his solos use the same techniques and scales used by 'oud players) – have had a big impact in the US, and an even larger impact in other societies.

So clearly the United States should not be confused with the larger global marketplace. But more important is the fact that however much some Muslims might complain about the "invasion" of Western culture in the Middle East and larger Muslim majority world, the main cultural threat in the MENA is internal: a well-funded ultraconservative Wahhabi movement which has been engaged in a twenty-year jihad against more open and tolerant forms of Islam throughout the Muslim world, and now in London, Paris, and New York as well.

The idea that everyone and everything is becoming homogenized, let alone Americanized, should also raise certain questions. On the one hand, it is true that globalization reaches into the most remote locations in the world.[93] But can we really place al-Qa'eda members in Lahore and gangsta rappers in LA within "one network of social relations between whose different regions move flows of meanings, peoples and goods," as one famous definition of globalization describes it?[94]

Well, maybe. In fact we know that the critiques of mainstream American culture and politics by gangsta rappers and radical Muslims are quite similar; precisely because one of the main political inspirations for the political hiphop of Public Enemy or NWA (Niggaz With Attitude) was the ideology of the Nation of Islam, which for all its heretical religious views (from an orthodox Muslim perspective) closely followed the political and cultural critique of the West offered by leading "radical" Muslim thinkers like Sayyid Qutb, about whom we'll talk in Chapter Five.[95]

But while globalization doesn't have to produce anger and resistance within a culture, it's also true that it disturbs existing relationships in new and powerful ways. The resistance that this process produces in cultures around the world has led authors like Samuel Huntington to argue for the clash between, and now within, cultures. Benjamin Barber similarly describes this conflict as one between a "McWorld" whose very power leads to the kind of visceral reactions described by him under the rubric of "jihad." What Barber is arguing here is that the "commodifying logic" of globalization brings together a historically unprecedented number of sites and spectacles of consumption (shopping malls, 20-screen movie theaters, theme parks, spectator sports, fast foods) "into a single, vast enterprise that on the way to maximizing its profits, transforms human beings."[96]

We've already discussed the problems with Huntington's worldview; there are also problems with Barber's McWorld versus Jihad scenario, not the least of which is his essentialization of the globalized world into two monolithic blocs. As I'll demonstrate in the following chapters, it's incorrect to assume that the only opposition to hyper-consumerist globalization is jihad, since the rise of the global peace and justice movement demonstrates that the most radical opponents of globalization can define themselves in positive and open, rather than negative and closed, terms. But Barber's symbolism does constitute an advance over Huntington's because the members of either new tribe aren't restricted to particular cultures the way Huntington separates them. It's not the West versus the Rest, but peoples within all societies who either choose or are forced into one of the competing sides.[97]

Which side you choose is often determined by whether you experience globalization in a positive way or as the "tearing of space away from place." This slightly jargony-sounding phrase means that the long-distance relationships I mentioned above "tear" (if you're lucky, just lift) people out of their ties to the places in which they've always lived.[98] The question then, is how and where globalization puts (or throws) them down.

As I have already argued, such a process can produce feelings of exhilaration and/or freedom for those who no longer wanted to be tied to their place of origin or who have the means to move freely about the globe – whether immigrants to Europe or the US from oppressive Southern regimes, "travelers" through the worldwide rave, drug, and/or sex circuits, "masters of the universe" who jet around the world making deals for millions – sometimes billions – of dollars, or scholars traveling just as extensively (but much more cheaply) on their quests to discover what globalization is all about. In contrast, cultural globalization can produce dread and confusion for those whose horizons are more limited, or who realize they don't have the money, skills or desire to float around the world trying to find a new job, home or cultural identity. And if you are one of the millions of people either cleansed from their lands or forced to migrate across continents each year to search for work, the "deterritorialization" is all too concrete.

Borders, Oceans, and Plural Globalizations

As we've seen, culture drives economic globalization in large part because symbolic and cultural exchanges are the fastest and most efficient way for commodities (or at least their images) to be distributed to the widest possible audience.[99] This dynamic has resulted in an uncountable number of products and (less so) people in constant motion throughout the world. And because of this, most people today – even if like my father-in-law in Queens, New York, they rarely leave the neighborhood – are all living "on the border" of other cultures (that he, or a resident of Falluja, remains within his home culture or rejects that of his "neighbors" does not move the border farther away). To use a Persian/Arabic term from the Qur'an which I'll explore in the next two chapters, we're all moving back and forth across the *barzakh*, or barrier, that divides us.

And here we arrive at one of the crucial arguments of this book: if all cultures are plural, then globalization itself can only be considered in the plural too. Not only is it not a homogenous or homogenizing phenomenon, it's not even one phenomenon to begin with. Instead, it is a group of processes that have the structural power to open up the boundaries erected by modern institutions and identities, and produce what Tomlinson calls "an age of boundary crossing ... not erasure."[100]

The only problem with this description is that, to the extent that you're being pushed across a boundary you don't want to cross by the impact of neoliberal economic politics, globalization will in fact feel like "an erosion rather than globalization of cultures ... which is further reinforced by colonialism," even if in fact your culture or state isn't fading away. And one of the main responses to this situation will be an "increase in cultures of resistance" by those excluded from or trying to break free of the dominant economic and cultural system.[101]

This is a good description of the dynamics of resistance in much of the MENA region to neoliberal globalization, especially those coming from religious or nationalist motivations. But as I've already hinted, if a culture stops with resistance it is doomed. Instead, cultural hybridity and difference must be recognized and encouraged in order to achieve "creative cultural diversity." If traditional neoliberal economic theory believes that when cultural attitudes and institutions hamper economic growth "they are to be eradicated," today we must embrace a framework that builds cultural insights into broader development strategies, that can use cultural freedom as a basis for economic and political freedom as well.[102]

Conclusion: Problems with Culture

While they don't deal with the MENA or Islam, two books, one by Naomi Klein and the other by Thomas Frank, are perhaps the most important critical interpretations of globalization and its relationship to culture to be produced in or outside of the so-called "academy." Klein's book, the seminal *No Logo*, is crucial for our discussion because of the way she discusses the cultural and spatial impacts of the economic processes associated with neoliberal policies. Thus for her the cultural power of multinational corporations has increased significantly over the last two decades thanks to a unique innovation in the history of capitalism: the new emphasis on primarily producing "brands" or "brand names" instead of the products themselves, which means that instead of making things the focus has moved to marketing, while production is shifted to third world countries that offer the cheapest possible labor and laxest regulations.

For Klein this corporate takeover of society has been one in which the deregulation and privatization policies of the last three decades are intimately related to an assault on the three social pillars of civic space, civil liberties, and employment. Our civic spaces and cultures have been surrendered to marketers, our civil liberties have become prey to franchises and mergers that reduced cultural choices, and the corporate assault on employment has seen multinationals break free of any social contract with employees – and even of the need to have employees.

As important for our purposes is the centrality of advertising in this process, as the need to find ever more powerful ways of penetrating consumers' consciousness has led to ever more intrusive advertising (in classrooms, libraries, phone calls, etc.). What is interesting about Klein's argument is that, as Thomas Frank's equally seminal *The Conquest of Cool* also informs us, advertising had already achieved such a conquest of public space, consciousness, and even identities, by the 1960s. It was then that big business assimilated and re-sold hippy culture to a nation hungry to be "new," "hip," "rebellious," and "countercultural," at least when they looked in the mirror or got in the car.

What both Frank and Klein remind us, each in their own period (the hippy 1960s and the Gen-X 1990s), is that big business, indeed capitalism itself, is as much about non-conformity, individuality, and rebelliousness as the most devoted slackers or countercultural activists. In fact, at the very moment that hippies were realizing the importance of rebelling against the social conformity of their parents, young business and advertising leaders were realizing the importance of rebelling against the same "organizational men," and the slow, monolithic business culture they represented, that created the social world against which hippies rebelled. So far from being on opposite sides, business and counterculture had the same revelations and fed off the same disgust with the status quo.

That's what made it so hard, impossible really, for the hippies to transform, let alone "overcome," the dominant culture, which shifted to embrace their cultural style – as opposed to ideals – while largely maintaining the economic and power balance in place. And the fact, which Frank reminds us, that hippies were as brand conscious and willing to spend indiscriminately to maintain their stylistic edge as their bourgeois counterparts, points to a crucial fact that will determine the discussions of the remainder of the book. It is almost impossible to break free of the modernity matrix as long as you're operating within any of its guiding paradigms. Hippies, like today's Generation X, thought their cultural and political activism could destroy the existing system, but because they didn't focus on the fundamental economic and cultural dynamics of capitalist culture they wound up strengthening the very system they were trying to topple. As we've seen, this was precisely because the same critical insights and self-awareness that produced "cool" also produced a system of advertising and business planning that worked through the commodification of culture to "construct consumer consciousness" – their parents', theirs, and today their children's – with unprecedented power and success.

The manner in which cool was conquered shows both the limitations of dissent and suggests that a binary understanding of some "counterculture" – whether hippy or Christian – as the positive moral opposite of a bad or evil mass society is both analytically wrong and strategically counterproductive. Yet today we see a similar attitude within the culture that is attempting to counter the neoliberal global order; one that will likely fall into the same trap of feeding the system it seeks to dismantle unless a way can be found to break free of the modernity matrix that has entrapped the most bohemian and rebellious children of modernity for centuries.

As one friend asked me after reading a draft of this book, "How can the culture jamming you advocate step far enough outside the dominant paradigm to critique and move beyond it and not be coopted like hippy or hiphop culture before it?"[103] For me the answer is that it has to involve enough people from outside any one culture or paradigm so that the methods used by capital's culture warriors to coopt, diffuse or expel them don't work. In the next three chapters we'll explore what lessons can be learned from the experiences and strategies of citizens of the Middle East as they have attempted to critique and resist the modernity matrix, and today globalization.

4 New Logo: Rebranding the Middle East in the Global Era

It's Your Own Damn Fault! Growing Pains of the MENA Region in the Global Era

In the last two chapters we explored the worldwide dynamics of globalization in its various stages during the last half millennium. This chapter will specifically examine how the processes of neoliberal global economic restructuring have been both justified by policymakers and experienced by citizens of the MENA. Such a discussion is important because it provides a rational, reasoned basis for so many Muslims to oppose globalization, for which they've normally been labeled as crankpots or worse. Moreover, the economic discussion provides the basis for investigating how citizens of the Middle East and North Africa have experienced and are responding to these processes from a cultural perspective.

In order to explore the economic impact of neoliberal globalization in the MENA we need to answer three questions: What do the data for the region in terms of "growth," trade, liberalization, and other relevant indicators tell us about the degree to which the MENA is participating in what mainstream economists consider "economic" globalization? What are the possible reasons for the numbers that we find? Finally, what other ways might the region be tied into the globalized world economy that are not considered by mainstream accounts, but which in fact help us understand why the region is not "globalizing" at a satisfactory rate?

But, as important as the statistics, we'll explore how changes in the world economy have necessitated what I would describe as a "rebranding" of the Middle East into a leading world source of terror, chaos – indeed, evil (and an axis, to boot) – in a way that both

Figure 5   It starts young: a birthday present for my 3-year-old son from his cousin, an Air Force sergeant

reconfirms its traditional image as an exotic, irrational, and dangerous Other and adds a new focus on its role as the source of an especially powerful, "virulent," "nihilistic," and even "apocalyptic" kind of terrorism that threatens the West.[1]

The militarization of America's politics, culture, and economy[2] makes this rebranding that much more crucial, since a militarized society needs a constant supply of new enemies to fight and, I would argue, creates the dynamics through which they emerge – in this case through the policies of neoliberal globalization.[3] As we saw in the last chapter in our discussion of the work of Klein and Frank, the culture of branding is central to the administration and functioning of a liberalized global economy, which is why the Middle East has been positioned by the global economic and political powers (the US and Europe, the World Bank and IMF, the petroleum, defense, and now heavy engineering industries) as the object of military, financial, and social restructuring. In fact, with the occupation of Iraq all three processes have efficiently been brought into a single location, at great profit for those with connections to the center of empire along Pennsylvania Avenue.

Where's Globalization?

From the discussions of the last chapter we know that economic glob-alization is not occurring to the extent normally assumed. Yet this reality should not suggest that the Middle East hasn't been impacted significantly by the restructuring of the world economy along neoliberal lines. In fact, the region saw some of the world's first anti-World Bank and IMF riots in the late 1970s; and while the MENA is close to the bottom of the rung for GDP growth, trade, integration, liberalization, and internet usage, this is more a result of its structural position within the global economy than a self-imposed isolation from it.

We'll examine the numbers in detail below; but first let's explore how they get deployed by institutions such as the World Bank and IMF, especially when they deal with the MENA. In a 2001 IMF paper titled "Globalization: Facts and Figures,"[4] the economist Paul Masson argues the following:

> This paper aims to give a concise summary of the economic dimen-sions of globalization, while leaving to one side other aspects – such as cultural, environmental or political ones – that are beyond the scope of the IMF … The IMF helps to ensure economic gains from global-ization by encouraging trade liberalization, reducing countries' vulnerability to crises, lending to them when they are in difficulty, and assisting them in helping to put in place structural reforms that reduce poverty.

Let's begin with the first sentence, which is clearly based on an assumption that cultural, environmental, and political aspects of glob-alization don't have to be considered in relation to its economic dynamics (otherwise the authors would have to deal with it).[5] At this point in our discussion it should be clear how problematic a claim like this is; yet by making it right at the start the author – and the IMF – can "leave aside" many of the nasty consequences of neoliberal global-ization that are caused by the economic policies of the IMF, the major economic powers, and transnational corporations by labeling them as "cultural." How convenient! Except that, as we'll see below, what winds up happening is that everyone from government to business specifi-cally confuses the two, making culture the culprit for the problems of development.

Let's move to the second sentence: the claim is that increased globalization leads to "generally rising standards of living." While this has been true of East Asia, it is not true for most of the rest of the developing world. For most developing countries, especially in the Middle East, we can't assume that countries that open up to trade see an increase in their total wealth (GDP) – in fact, the data we'll discuss below show the reverse to be the case. Nor can we assume that increased wealth is distributed fairly or evenly throughout a country (another reason why, as we saw in the last chapter, mainstream economists don't like to discuss inequality *within* and *between* countries in the same breath). Most of the new wealth could go to the richest 5 or 10 percent of the population, and because liberalization programs almost always permit the rapid repatriation of profits, most of the profits generated by foreign direct investment in an "opened" country often wind up in corporate bank accounts outside the reach of local or Western treasuries.

So when Masson argues in the next sentence that the IMF "tries to ensure economic gains from globalization" we can see that this is a meaningless claim, as the issue is not whether there are "gains" – i.e., increased wealth produced – but who's getting that increase (local businesses and working people or international banks and corporations) and whether they are generated at the expense of the increased impoverishment of a large section of the population.

Finally, Masson's claim that the IMF assists countries "in helping to put in place structural reforms that reduce poverty" would be laughable if it wasn't so tragic. The overwhelming evidence, at least for the MENA, suggests that structural adjustment programs increase poverty and inequality, precisely because these programs cater to the needs of international banks looking to recoup and/or "open" new markets for loans rather than developing new industries on a solid economic footing.[6] Perhaps if we consider that the rich of the country under discussion are poor relative to the rich in other countries, it relieves poverty, but for most people the economic, environmental, political, and cultural impact of structural adjustment programs are largely negative.

This is all very well, you might be thinking, but what does it have to do with our story? Well, Masson's arithmetic problems also extend to geography: his analysis simply leaves out the entire Middle East! For reasons that are not explained, an article that is supposed to be providing readers with facts and figures surrounding globalization examines Korea, China, Ghana, Mexico, sub-Saharan Africa, East Asia and the Pacific, and Latin America, but not the Middle East and North Africa. No Egypt, Turkey, Iran, Tunisia, Israel, or any other of the two dozen countries of the region.

And this is not the only large-scale study simply to leave the region out of the picture of globalization it constructs. A 1999 study titled

Inequality, Globalization and World Politics[7] and published by the venerable Oxford University Press also manages to avoid dealing with the region. And it's not just the mainstream economists of the Bank who often avoid discussing the region; several recent progressive analyses of globalization don't mention it either.[8]

What's going on here? Is there something about the Middle East that so disrupts or challenges otherwise neat formulas and analyses that scholars and policy-makers would rather leave it out than adjust their theories and prescriptions to account for it? Let's look at the numbers and see for ourselves.

What's Wrong with the Middle East? The Economic Dimensions of Globalization in the MENA Region

According to a famous phrase from the first *Arab Human Development Report*, the Arab world is "richer than it is developed." What this slogan suggests is that the region has the money to confront its problems and achieve adequate levels of development if only the right combination of skills and political will could be brought together. What's also implied, and is seconded by other reports and commentary (such as the *9/11 Commission Report*), is that many if not most of the region's problems (such as political freedom or gender equality) are due to internal flaws in human/social development, and not to the basic structures of the world economic system and their impact on the region's economy and politics.

When the World Bank compiled statistics on the relationship between poverty, liberalization, and growth in the MENA region (both compared with other developing regions, and specifically focusing on the "early reformers") the data were telling.[9] In terms of poverty levels for both $1 and $2 per day, the MENA had the lowest in the developing world by far; not only that, the ratio of inequality in the region decreased far more than any other developing region in the world (only South Asia showed even a slight decrease; East Asia saw the largest increase). Quite naturally, in terms of the share of the national income going to the poorest 5 percent of the population, the MENA was the only region to show a significant increase in distribution, and thus equality.

Yet if we look at measures of trade and integration, the Bank is correct in arguing that the MENA has seen the lowest growth – more precisely, the largest decrease – in its ratio of real trade, among the lowest growth in exports of goods and services, the lowest speed of integration, and the lowest rate of decreasing tariffs. What we have is a situation where billions of people remain mired in poverty under the rule of neoliberal globalization, and the MENA region is able to keep from joining them only because most countries do not implement the Washington Consensus policies advocated by the international financial community.

A similar picture can be painted of the unemployment problems in the MENA. For the past decade the World Bank has argued that the region could achieve levels of growth capable of providing "productive employment" for the ever-increasing numbers of young people of working age – but only if there was sufficient regional cooperation, domestic policy reform, and external financial support.[10] Of course, the realization of any of these conditions would depend on a radical change in the external and internal politics of the region that, sadly, show no signs of occurring any time soon despite recent elections and protests. What has happened is that governments have had to lower budgets for education and job creation and training programs, leaving young people with fewer skills and lower prospects for succeeding in the "new" economy.[11]

But even if they acquired the proper skills, how useful would they be for the low-wage factory jobs that constitute the majority of new employment in the Global South? And what good will the Bank's advocacy of a "true system of collective bargaining" be when companies today go to great lengths to avoid countries with effective collective bargaining systems? Similar problems can be found with arguments about integration and its relationship to growth, as the Bank or the IMF expects MENA countries to increase spending on health or education far in excess of the expected total world GDP growth, without mentioning the need to cut disproportionately high military budgets.[12]

And even if Arab governments wanted radically to reduce spending on strategic US and Western products such as surplus grains or high-tech weaponry, it's hard to see how they could do so without losing their strategic importance for the US and Western political and economic establishments. Could Middle Eastern governments do so and survive? Not unless they initiated a truly democratic transformation along the way. But that would mean most leaders relinquishing power to someone other than their sons or political heirs. And how can Muslim citizens successfully transform corrupt and autocratic regimes whose large-scale abuses of human, civil and political rights are tolerated and even encouraged by their Western patrons? Here's an even more profound question: can grass-roots political power in the MENA succeed in democratizing the region without a grass-roots political transformation in the West?

Ultimately, the data on economic globalization in the MENA are confusing and contradictory, which is probably due to the fact that there are so many statistics to choose from and, as we saw in the last chapter, problems with accuracy. Two recent descriptions of the region provide a glimpse at how varying and often-conflicting assessments can be drawn from using the innumerable available statistics. The first comes from a 2003 World Bank report on employment prospects in the MENA region. In describing the situation, the report explains that the historical social contract in the region generated "unprecedented levels of economic growth and social development. Between 1965 and 1985 MENA's economic growth rates were among the highest in the world."[13] To be sure, this was achieved in significant part because of the oil boom as well as an "authoritarian bargain" with leaders like Nasser, Asad, and even Saddam Hussein. But it was real nonetheless (it also helps us understand why the MENA is so often left out of discussions of globalization, since the oil boom and authoritarian bargain between postcolonial states and citizens together created a unique situation in the region).[14]

The commitments of MENA states, during the 1960s through 1980s period, to some form of redistribution of wealth and investment in social infrastructure was a primary reason for the region's seeing primary school enrolment rise by ten percentage points since 1980, youth literacy climb twenty percentage points, infant mortality cut by two-thirds, and immunization rates approaching 100 percent in the subsequent generation. What's more, "Many countries have adopted comprehensive social safety net programs, including food and utility subsidies and unemployment insurance. Despite tremendous water scarcity, the region now provides access to improved water to nearly 90 percent of city dwellers and 70 percent of those living in rural areas. Similar progress can be noted for infrastructure services such as roads, and especially for mobile phones, but also telephone land lines, which doubled in the 20 years since 1980."[15]

The region has among the most equal income distributions and lowest levels of absolute poverty in the world (especially when the impact of the decade of sanctions on Iraq is accounted for). This feat has been made possible both by remittances from Arabs working abroad and by a "strong and cohesive system of social responsibility" within Arab society. From such assessments it would seem that the MENA region is one that other developing regions might want to emulate, or at least not run away from. But what then of this next assessment, from an October 2003 speech by the Palestinian Finance Minister, Salaam Fayad? In introducing his argument for major structural reforms of the Palestinian economy Fayad argued that in the MENA as a whole "living standards declined substantially [during the same period]. Over the period 1980–2002, real GDP growth in the MENA region averaged about 3 percent per annum, and the region's per capita GDP declined by about 1.5 percent annually. This compares with an annual growth rate of about 5 percent and per capita GDP growth of about 3 percent for developing countries."[16]

And if this isn't bad enough, foreign direct investment also remains weak and concentrated in a few countries, in good measure due to perhaps the most "restrictive trade regime" in the world. Finally, because the region's governments are large by international standards, a substantial portion of their expenditures are allocated to nonproductive uses such as the military (which in the MENA region runs at about twice the average for developing countries). Overall, "the MENA does worse than most of the world's regions on issues of poor governance … and is dead last on some, such as accountability."[17]

Whose vision of the Middle East is correct? If they both are, then how can we assess the region's position and possibilities? In the opinion of the IMF, the World Bank, UNDP, and other institutions, the main problem is that financial liberalization has not occurred to the necessary degree, and the reason for this is the "poor quality of domestic institutions."[18] As the Bank describes it, "over the last three decades, a striking feature of the MENA region is how little the region's economies have increased their integration with the rest of the world."[19] The equation underlying this argument is that integration leads to growth, which leads to poverty reduction, but whether this in fact occurs "depends heavily on the set of *domestic policies pursued by individual governments.*"[20]

Of course, it *is* hard to exaggerate how corrupt, incompetent, and authoritarian most MENA governments are; and certainly the region's political leaders deserve the utter contempt with which most of their citizens view them. As one of the authors of the first *AHDR* explained to me, it was precisely this fact that led the UNDP team behind the report to focus exclusively on the Arab world's internal problems, even though they understood full well how important external forces have been in causing and continuing the region's problems.[21] (But the scuttling of the third report by the US and Egyptian governments in response to its criticism of their policies demonstrated the impossibility of making such a separation.)

Can we assume that internal problems, however severe, are the most important cause of the region's lack of integration into the world economy? We know from the last chapter that the percentage of world trade between developed countries has continued to dominate total world trade during the last thirty years. We also know that the Middle East's share of world trade decreased significantly – in large part because of falling oil prices in the 1980s and 1990s (which has been reversed since September 11). As Table 6 demonstrates:[22]

Table 6: Percentage of World Trade by Region

Region	1980	1985	1990	1995	2000
North America					
Exports	14.4	16.0	15.4	15.9	16.9
Imports	15.5	21.7	16.4	18.7	23.1
Western Europe					
Exports	40.2	40.1	48.3	44.8	40.0
Imports	44.8	39.6	44.7	43.5	40.1
Middle East					
Exports	10.6	5.3	4.0	2.9	4.3
Imports	5.0	4.5	2.8	2.6	2.4
Latin America					
Exports	5.4	5.6	4.3	4.6	5.8
Imports	5.9	4.2	3.6	4.9	4.9
Asia					
Exports	9.2	11.78	13.3	17.5	26.4
Imports	9.9	12.3	14.5	18.3	22.8

And so the MENA, unlike regions that have successfully been "integrated" into the world market, "is in danger of becoming marginal to the world economy," a situation made worse by the fact that the level of public accountability and good governance in the region is so low.[23] And the reason for this situation is clearly believed to be rooted in internal, cultural problems.

For example, the leading international business consulting firm Dun and Bradstreet announced the *AHDR* this way: "D&B Special Report: MIDDLE EAST – September 2002. Cultural impediments to development."[24] Now, D&B describes itself as "the world's leading provider of business information." Let's assume that this is true. What does it mean when it simplifies an almost-400-page report that devoted only a single page to culture into the notion that "cultural impediments" are the single biggest obstacle to development? Especially when the report doesn't say that culture is the biggest obstacle? What the D&B report tells us is that by focusing exclusively on the internal aspects of the problems affecting the Middle East, the *AHDR* played into a centuries-long discourse about the Middle East that since Napoleon has seen Europeans, Americans, and now "leading Arabs themselves" lay the blame squarely on some mythical Arab/Muslim "culture."[25]

If the issue is finally cultural, then it's not surprising that the Bank concludes that the "MENA needs a new social contract ... [one] that takes into account the social needs of workers and ensures that economic outcomes are socially acceptable among MENA's citizens."[26] As we'll see below, this is an excellent prescription, but in reality it is the opposite of the environment sought by the corporations who are crucial in the Bank/IMF's prescription to creating growth and jobs in a country.[27]

What's Wrong with This Picture? Or, Can Development Be Human?

A fall 2003 IMF report on the effects of financial globalization on developing countries provides a rare glimpse of honesty within the Fund or Bank, as it actually admits to the distorting reality of neoliberal reforms on developing countries. Specifically, the authors offer a "sobering" but informative conclusion: "There is little evidence that financial integration has helped developing countries to better stabilize fluctuations in consumption growth. While there is no proof in the data that financial globalization has benefited growth, there is evidence that some countries may have experienced greater consumption volatility as a result."[28]

Yet if the Washington Consensus structural adjustment model is finally being criticized inside the Bank for reducing the ability of international institutions to develop policies outside the box of the Washington Consensus, the Bank still endorses a boxed-in growth-pushing dynamic for the countries in the MENA. In fact, policymakers argue that "to improve the standard of living and create the necessary jobs, most Arab economies need to grow by at least six percent of GDP."[29]

But how can the MENA achieve such a high level of growth when world GDP growth averaged between 3 and 4 percent during the late 1990s and early 2000, and rose at best to around 5 percent in 2003 worldwide and in the developing world?[30] And even if it occurred, the push for "growth" could well have serious and detrimental effects on millions of citizens of the MENA.[31]

We have already discussed the problems with the "growth discourse" of the World Bank, IMF, and other international financial institutions. We know that the World Bank claims that growth is the primary instrument against poverty.[32] Yet in the MENA there is clear evidence that it could well be the *lack of growth* in the region that has been an important, if not primary, reason for the relative lack of poverty. This actually was the view of two senior World Bank economists who, in a preliminary study for the 2002 *World Development Report*, argued that there is a demonstrable correlation between the evolution of growth and *in*equality in the developing world.[33] However, their conclusions were omitted from the final version, which led the chief editor to resign in protest and to significant criticism of the report's accuracy and integrity.[34]

What can account for these seeming contradictions and/or disparities between the official Bank discourse vis-à-vis globalization in the MENA region and the work of more critical scholars? This is an important question for which we still don't know the answer. One answer is clearly that the "official" and mainstream analyses have a habit of reducing complex often contradictory and open processes into simplistic and more ideologically driven standardized formulas.[35] At best, we would seem to be in a situation where the World Bank and its critics (including those inside the Bank) are marshaling different sets of statistics which seem to support their contentions. This raises the question of how we can judge these competing claims based on different data that are nevertheless from the same source (i.e., the World Bank's statistical compilations). What is clear from the available data is that the "seemingly anomalous pattern of rapid poverty reduction with lackluster economic growth" in the MENA is most likely *not* anomalous, because "the MENA recorded the largest improvement in income distribution of all regions of the developing world between 1970s and 1999," precisely at the time that economic growth slowed down significantly.[36]

It would seem that we have arrived at another paradox. During the last thirty years the region has simultaneously decreased its levels of poverty while losing ground in terms of integration into the world economy.[37] But this isn't really contradictory when we realize that the pro-trade and pro-growth structural adjustment strategies preferred by Western governments and financial/aid institutions, based on the "more trade equals more growth and thus less poverty" equation, could well worsen the situation for lower-middle-class and poor citizens of the region.[38]

What about the Countries that Played the Game, the So-called "Early Reformers"?

Perhaps we're not being fair to the World Bank and mainstream economists when we look at the MENA as a whole, since only a few of the countries of the region have actually followed through with the prescriptions it and its sister institutions have proposed (some would say, imposed). What story emerges if we look only at the countries which the international financial institutions themselves say have made a good-faith effort to "reform" their economic systems?

Let's examine several countries which since the late 1970s have enacted significant structural adjustment and liberalization programs: Morocco, Tunisia, Egypt, and Jordan, all of whose regimes have close ties to the United States (we'll discuss Israel later in the chapter).[39] While policy-makers claim that the "structural reforms" undertaken by these countries have paved the way for renewed growth,[40] we are once again not told what that means if a country is integrating into a "Walmartized" regional or even world economy.[41] What does the race to the bottom mean for people in Egypt, Mauritania or Morocco? Is it really worth trying to be competitive in this kind of game, one where "improving efficiency" equals lowering wages and relaxing labor, environmental, and related laws? Do Middle Eastern workers want the rapidly increasing rates of cancer and work-related injuries, very low wages, overtime with no pay, and repressive labor policies and police that are necessary to enforce such a system? That's because together these conditions define the environment for workers in China, the most recent country to be touted as the model for the rest of the developing world to copy? How much is China's "spectacular" growth worth to the tens of millions of workers whose bodies are being deformed and spirits crushed by the new economy?[42]

Indeed, if we look at those countries of the region that have most fully participated in neoliberal reforms, the World Bank's own data tell us that

> the pay-offs in terms of accelerated growth in the region are seen to have been elusive. Even in the earlier reform countries such as Egypt, Jordan and Morocco, there wasn't the desired growth; and the diversification of the economy (which was described as "the aim of reform efforts") still left most of the early reformers with a slow or gradual rating.[43] So it is not surprising that the Bank reports that the four leading liberalizers in the region are still "in the bottom two-thirds of countries in terms of cumulative liberalization since 1985."[44]

Moreover, even as countries such as Egypt, Jordan, Lebanon, Morocco, and Tunisia are described as "relatively advanced in the broad direction of reforms," they are still urged to "move on to a new round of more decisive and credible trade liberalization. There is little reason for gradualism."[45] The urge for swift reforms is a common refrain, but it is one that has often brought negative results in the developing world.[46] For the MENA region it's enough to remember the "riots" of the 1980s in many countries when the first IMF "shock treatments" were administered, to know how ill-informed such policies can be. In fact, Egypt experienced riots as early as 1977 in response to the deteriorating economic situation produced by President Sadat's "economic opening" (*infitah*), which itself was a response to the changing world economy.

These riots should not be conceived of as the kind of "blue–green" alliance bringing together union workers and radical middle-class young people that is symbolized today by Seattle. Rather, they were composed heavily of the working class, and were sparked by the failure of governments to live up to their end of the authoritarian–social-development bargain. Moreover, the combination of (periodically) greater attention to social development and harsher techniques of political repression over the last twenty years has meant (as opposed to Southeast Asia, where the assault on the working class was more recent and activists more engaged) that there was no pool of activists at the ready to join the post-Seattle upsurge in international activism.[47]

If we want to understand the roots of the riots that spread throughout the region in the 1980s, the statistics on growth, poverty, and related issues among the early reformers show that the countries that reformed most saw increases in *both* growth and poverty, while spending on key social services fell, along with wages.[48] In fact, if we look at Syria, one of the most controlled economies in the region, it witnessed the greatest growth of the MENA countries in the 1990s, while liberalizing countries like Jordan, Egypt, and Morocco saw struggling private investment growth.

Clearly the model is in some way seriously flawed, especially if in countries such as Syria or China the state has, at various times, been as capable of directing the economy towards positive development as the private sector.[49]

Be Like Latin America! Or, Imperialism Still Matters

Perhaps the early reformers didn't reform enough. In this context, the majority of the reports and analyses of the MENA compare the region unfavorably to Latin America, the world region seemingly most similar to it in terms of income and development levels. For the IMF especially Latin America has been a major success story for its ideology of structural adjustment, and so implicit in comparisons between the two regions is the argument that the MENA should copy Latin America's openness to liberalization and related reforms.

But what happens if we look at the actual statistics for Latin America during the last two decades to explore how the MENA might learn from the experiences of this region? The fact that in the last few years countries like Brazil, Bolivia, Venezuela, and Peru have all elected governments that are antagonistic to neoliberal ideology would seem to suggest that neoliberalism isn't working as well as advertised in Latin America. And indeed, according to World Bank statistics, in the decade of peace and NAFTA, between 1980 and 1999 the number of people living in poverty in Latin America and the Caribbean grew from 136 million to 211 million. The region's GDP per capita grew only 6 percent from 1980 to 1998, while it grew by 75 percent from 1960 to 1980. Eighteen countries in the region have lower per capita incomes than ten years ago, and this figure doesn't include the economic debacles in Argentina and Bolivia of the early 2000s.[50]

If we look specifically at the effects of economic liberalization in the Americas, it is true that imports to and exports from the region have jumped over 500 percent during the last twenty years, while the region's share of world trade has increased by at least 15 percent.[51] But at the same time there has been a decline in real growth and wages (both in absolute terms and in comparison with the US). And while productivity has increased significantly in countries such as Mexico, much of the boost has been due to an increase in the number of hours worked rather than increased efficiency – a situation that is also behind much of the supposedly "miraculous" increase in US productivity as well.[52]

And so if we want to know whether the MENA region can achieve significant growth and maintain these low levels of poverty, Latin America's numbers suggest the answer is no. And if this is the case, we have to ask, which is better: growth at the cost of significantly increased poverty and inequality, or continued low (relatively) levels of poverty and inequality at the expense of growth? Few developing countries outside of East Asia have eaten their cake and been able to have it too, and the MENA will most likely not be an exception to this rule.

But Latin America reminds us of another important part of the story of globalization in the Middle East: imperialism. In fact, Latin America has perhaps the earliest, and in some ways the longest, history of colonial and imperial domination of any region in the world. More recently, the invasions of Grenada and Panama were clear tune-ups for a reinvigorated US military posture, which a few years later would bring us the first Iraq war, and now Afghanistan and Iraq II. When we recall these and literally dozens of previous invasions by the United States of other countries in the hemisphere, along with the active US support of incredibly repressive regimes and opposition movements during the twentieth century, the crucial role of imperialism in the region's (and through it, globalization's) history and dynamics becomes impossible to ignore. Yet while globalization and imperialism/colonialism have been equally bound together in the MENA, we have to move outside the universe of the Bank, IMF, UNDP or "liberal" think tanks and consulting firms to read that "Globalization [is] today's equivalent to yesterday's imperialism ... The drama of globalization is a continuation of the colonial dialectic played out by earlier generations of indigenous elites ... with Islamists playing the role of erstwhile nationalists."[53]

So What's Really Happening in the MENA? Sorting Through the Numbers

The arguments over economic development, especially in the MENA, are so vague, complicated, and ideologically charged that we shouldn't feel bad if our heads are spinning at this point. Let's step back from all the analyses and look at some of the raw data so we can decide for ourselves what's going on in the region. According to the World Bank, as of 2002 the MENA region as a whole had a population of 306 million people, with a per capita Gross National Income of US$2,070, a total Gross National Income of US$670 billion, a population growth of 2.7 percent per year, and a labor growth of 2.9 percent (both of which were well over the developing world average of 1 percent and 1.2 percent respectively).[54] Moreover, we know that the Human Development Index – perhaps the key statistic for measuring the overall economic, social, and political quality of life of a country – has risen by varying degrees throughout the region during the last three decades, to levels that are on average a bit lower than the average for medium income countries, and a bit worse measured against either Latin America or the world average.[55]

We also know that in terms of the kind of revolution in communications and production that is generally believed to be the hallmark of globalization, the Middle East is doing quite badly. In terms of PC and internet usage, and "IT" issues more generally, other than Israel, Turkey, and the wealthy Gulf emirates, the MENA's statistics are "dismal" – one-seventh of the international average and significantly below other developing regions for computers, and over twenty times less than the international average for internet usage, with its rate of increase even less than that of sub-Saharan Africa, at least as of 2002.[56] Basically, not more than approximately 3 percent of the residents of the MENA have regular access to the internet – that's only nine million out of 306 million people.

For a more detailed picture, let's look at Tables 7 and 8, which detail some of the most important statistics regarding the economic dynamics in the region.

What can we say about all these statistics? First, it would seem to be almost meaningless to make generalizations about a region as big and diverse as the MENA. Despite this, if we want to try to tease out some trends, at the broadest level we see that it is within the lower middle-income range for developing countries in terms of the most basic indicators related to growth and income, but with statistics for health and education that are higher than its income would suggest. This should not be surprising from our discussion of the relationship between poverty and growth in this chapter, which makes sense of the simultaneous slow growth and lack of poverty compared to the rest of the developing world.

But there are some interesting paradoxes when we look at growth statistics, since most of the countries of the region apparently saw their best year of GDP growth near or at the turn of the new century, precisely in the period when growth is supposed to have been at its lowest ebb. On the other hand, growth spurts among the "early reformers" still left them at the low end of the middle-income countries on the HDI index, despite at least two decades of reform that was supposed to improve these figures. What did increase or remained sky-high was debt – which shouldn't surprise if we recall how Europeans used debt politics to ensnare the Ottoman Empire and Egypt a century and a half ago – even though countries like Egypt benefited from large-scale post-Gulf War I debt-forgiveness packages.

Table 8 is useful because it focuses specifically on how trends have developed over the last two decades.

The Early Reformers: If we look at the "early reformer" countries we see, first of all, a mixed situation in terms of GDP growth, with Morocco and Egypt decreasing and Jordan and Tunisia seeing increased growth. Yet these numbers don't correspond with increased exports, since Egypt saw decreased growth and increased exports, while the others saw growth and exports move in the same direction. Nor did the ratio of industry to services move in the same manner for all countries; and while all the early reformers saw increased exports and imports, their share as a percentage of GDP decreased for all countries except Egypt.

The only numbers that moved across the board in the same direction were decreases in government consumption and inflation – both prescribed by structural adjustment reforms. But this was accompanied by a significant increase in external debt (as much as 250 percent). So even if the early reformers have moved statistically in the direction of what the World Bank or IMF would call "successful globalizers," we need to wonder what this actually means for the almost 100 million people living there.

Major Oil Producers: If we look at the large oil producers, their GDP growth was mixed, with Saudi Arabia's and Kuwait's declining significantly while Iran's and Algeria's rose by around 300 percent. These numbers are very important, because they suggest one reason why al-Qa'eda sprouted in the southern Gulf. While at first it might seem strange that a relatively wealthy society like Saudi Arabia would breed such anti-regime violence, sociologists since Emile Durkheim a century ago have understood that relatively quick and steep downturns in indicators such as income, standards of living or political and/or cultural horizons, more than levels of absolute poverty, can lead to the kind of social "anomie" that breeds violence and criminal behavior. From this perspective we can see the oil crash of the early 1980s, from which Saudi Arabia never really recovered financially, as marking the beginning of a period of economic stagnation which, coupled with the near-permanent positioning of American soldiers so close to Islam's holiest shrines, inevitably produced the kind of violent ideologies and activities epitomized by al-Qa'eda.

Others: Finally, let's look at the figures for the "other" category – those countries that neither were the teachers' pets of the IMF nor had enough oil income to resist the Washington Consensus. This group is in fact quite interesting. First of all, with the exception of Palestine, Yemen, the Sudan, and Mauritania – all countries in the middle of ongoing severe military or political crises – most of the countries have a national income that is above the developing-world average. Most have seen their GDP rise in the last two decades, reaching a peak in the late 1990s, and most have seen the percentage of exports-to-GDP ratio

Table 7: Economic Indicators for Countries of the Middle East and North Africa

"Early Reformers"

	Morocco	Tunisia	Egypt	Jordan	Israel
Population (millions) 2002	29.6	9.8	66.4	5.2	6.5
Human Development Index Rank and Value (2001)	126/.606/ medium	91/.740/ medium	120/.648/ medium	90/.743/ medium	22/.905/ high
GNI per capita 2002 (US$)	1,190	2,000	1,470	1,760	NA
GNI total 2002 (US$ billions)	35.3	19.6	97.6	9.1	NA
Avge population growth 1996–2002 (%)	1.6	1.2	1.9	3.0	2.2
Avge labor force growth 1996–2002	2.5	2.4	2.9	4.0	3.0
GDP in US$ billions	15.4/28.5/	8.1/15.5/	25.6/41.9/	4.8/5.4/	24.6/
1982/1992/2002	37.3	21.2	83.7	9.3	65.8/NA
Year of highest GDP (as of 2001)	2001	2001	2001	1986	2000
Exports of goods and services as % GDP 1982/1992/2002	19.2/25.1/ 29.9	36.9/39.5/ 44.3	27.0/29.0/ 16.2	39.4/49.9/ 45.1	38.l/30.6/ NA
Total debt as % GDP 1982/1992/2002	80.4/79.7/ 49.94	46.4/55.1/ 57.3	106.8/74.4/ 32.1 (2001 figure)	54.9/148.5/ 87.1	NA
Poverty as percentage of population	19	NA	17	12	NA
Urban population as percentage of total	57	67	43	79	92
Life expectancy	68	73	69	72	79
Infant mortality (per 1,000 live births)	39	24	35	25	5
Child malnutrition (% children under 5)	NA	4	4	5	NA
Illiteracy (% pop. over 15 years)	49	27	43	9	5
Military expenditure as % GDP 1990/2001	4.1/4.1	2.0/1.6	3.9/2.6	9.9/8.6	12.2/7.7

Major Oil Producers" *...di Arabia*	*Kuwait*	*Qatar*	*UAE*	*Bahrain*	*Iran*	*Iraq*	*Algeria*	*Libya*	*Developing World Avge*
	2.1	.61	3.0	.67	65.5	24.2	31.3	5.5	2,411 million total
.769/ dium	46/.820/ high	44/.826/ high	48/.816/ high	37/.839/ high	106/.719/ medium		107/.704/ medium	61/.783/ medium	.655
50	NA	NA	24,860	11,860	1,720	1,090	1,710	NA	1,390
5.8	NA	NA	75.8	8.0	112.4	26.4	53.8	NA	3,352
	3.6	2.8	3.6	1.9	1.5	2.2	1.5	2.2	1.0
	5.4	1.9	3.3	2.1	4.8	2.9	3.3	2.3	1.2
4.1/	21.6/19.9/	7.6/7.6/	30.8/35.9	3.6/4.8/	124.8/93.1/	NA/4.7/	45.2/48.0/	29.3/33.5/	
8.5	35.3	16.6 (2001)		71.4	8.4	107.5	26.1	55.9	NA
80	1979	NA	NA	2000	1976		1985	NA	
.8/45.1/ 8	54.5/40.5/ 48.3	NA/NA/ 67.8 (2001)	63.3/67.3 73.1	119/84.4/ 81.3	16.4/15.2/ 26.8	27.3/13.0/ NA	30.9/25.3/ 35.9	52.7/30.6/ NA	
A	NA	NA	NA	NA	6.6/17.3/ 6.8	NA/448.2/ 344.1	39.0/57.0/ 40.8	NA	
A	NA	NA	NA	NA	21	NA	NA	NA	
	96	93	88	93	65	68	58	88	
	77	75	75	73	71	63	71	72	69
	10	11	8	13	30	107	38	17	30
A	2	NA	7	NA	11	NA	6	NA	11
	17	18	23	12	15	60	31	18	13
.8/11.3	48.5/11.3	NA	4.7/2.5	4.0/1.8	2.7/4.8		1.5/3.5	NA	

Table 7: (Continued)

"Other/Lower-Middle Income MENA Countries"

	Turkey	Palestine	Lebanon	Syria	Yemen	Oman	Sudan	Mauritania	Developing World Avge
Population (millions) 2002	69.6	3.2	4.4	17	18.6	2.5	32.4	2.8	2,411 million total
Human Development Index Rank and Value (2001)	96/.734/ medium	98/.731/ medium	83/.752/ medium	110/ .685/ medium	148/ .470/ low	79/.755	138/ .503/ medium	154/ .454/ low	.655
GNI per capita 2002 (US $)	2,500	1,110	3,990	1,130	490	NA	390	340	1,390
GNI total 2002 (US$ billions)	174	3.6	17.7	19.2	9.1	NA	12.5	0.96	3,352
Avge population growth 1996–2002 (%)	1.7	4.2	1.4	2.5	2.9	2.6	2.0	3.1	1.0
Avge labor force growth 1996–2002	2.2	NA	2.6	4.0	3.0	2.4	2.6	3.3	1.2
GDP in US$ billions 1982/ 1992/2002	64.4/ 158.9/ 182.8	NA/ NA/ 3.4	NA/ 5.5/ 17.3	16.3/ 13.3/ 21.9	NA/ 5.8/ 9.7	7.6/ 11.3/ 20.3	10.7/ 13.7/ 13.5	0.75/ 1.2/ 0.98	
Year of highest GDP (as of 2001)	1998	NA	1998	1998	2001	NA	2001	1976	
Exports of goods and services as % GDP 1982/ 1992/2002	11.9/ 14.4/ 28.8	NA/ NA/ 12.3	NA/ 11.4/ 13.9	14.2/ 26.3/ 35.6	NA/ 21.5/ 33.9	58.5/ 49.7/ 56.9	10.1/ 4.5/ 14.3	40.1/ 37.6/ 36.8	
Total debt as % GDP 1982/ 1992/2002	30.6/ 35.6/ 71.9	NA	NA/ 32.6/ 98.7	37.9/ 145.0/ 98.1	NA/ 114.2/ 54.7	12.7/ 25.2/ 28.2	67.2/ 113.1/ 105.4	151.5/ 176.8/ 252.2	
Poverty as percentage of population	NA	59	NA	NA	42	NA	NA	46	
Urban population as percentage of total	67	NA	90	52	25	77	38	60	
Life expectancy	70	73	71	70	57	74	58	51	69
Infant mortality (per 1,000 live births)	33	20	26	23	78	12	66	108	30
Child malnutrition (% children under 5)	8	NA	3	NA	46	NA	11	32	11
Illiteracy (% pop over 15 years)	14	NA	13	24	51	26	40	59	13
Military expenditure as % GDP 1990/2001	3.5/ 4.9	NA	2.4/ 1.7	6.9/ 6.2	8.5/ 6.1	18.3/ 12.2	3.6/ 3.0	3.9/ 2.1	

increase also during this period, although this hasn't stopped more than half the remaining countries from having social indicators (life expectancy, infant mortality, illiteracy, etc.) below the developing-world average.

On the other hand, Turkey, which is by far the richest, most developed, diverse, and "integrated" economy of the "other" countries, was the only one that saw decreased GDP growth during the last twenty years, although in per capita terms it increased slightly during this period. And the only consistency across the board was the increase in exports for all the countries in this section of the table, which is exactly what the World Bank and IMF would want.

Clearly, the economic data are not just hard to pin down, they are often confusing and downright contradictory. Not to mention that if I chose different tables from other World Bank reports claiming to examine the same issues, I'd have found different statistics. What this complex situation tells us is that we must be very careful generalizing across countries, and certainly across four thousand miles or more of uninterruped territory from Morocco to the Iran–Pakistan border. At the very least, we can wonder exactly how the institutions and reports we've looked at in this chapter can make "regional" generalizations, or separate the "Arab" from the rest of the MENA countries.

The Post-Iraq Invasion Discourse of the World Bank and Sister Institutions

In the aftermath of the epochal US invasion and occupation of Iraq it is worth examining how the World Bank and other institutions have accounted for the military and political developments on the ground in their analyses. Since April 2003 the World Bank has published reports on good governance and how to enhance the business environment and create jobs in the region. Together, they can help us understand what lessons, if any, the Bank has drawn from the events from September 11 to the occupation of Iraq.[57]

Broadly speaking, the reports' recommendations are certainly worthwhile: "empower[ing] poor people" and reshaping global priorities through a focus on maternal and child health, supporting trade and integration, improving both governance and the business environment (which if the US is any indication, don't usually go together).[58] The problem is that "on an index of public accountability ... virtually every MENA country ranks behind, typically far behind

Table 8: Development Indicators for the MENA, 1982 to Present

	Avge % GDP Growth 1982–1992 1992–2002 2002–2006	Avge % GDP Growth per capita 1982–1992 1992–2002 2002–2006	Exports of Goods and Services as % GDP 1982–1992 1992–2002 2002–2006	Agriculture as % GDP 1982 1992 2002	Industry as % GDP 1982 1992 2002
"Early Reformers"					
Morocco	4.2/3.0/3.4	2.0/1.3/1.7	7.8/4.8/5.1	15.3/15.4/16.1	31.9/32.3/3
Tunisia	3.7/4.7/4.7	1.3/3.2/3.7	7.2/5.6/5.5	13.2/16.1/10.4	31.1/28.5/2
Egypt	4.5/4.7/3.0 (2002 only)	2.0/2.8/1.1 (2002 only)	7.5/2.1/–10.4	19.6/16.5/16.8	32.4/33.3/3
Jordan	1.3/3.7/5.8	–3.0/0.4/3.2	5.0/2.4/5.9	6.1/7.8/2.0	30.3/27.1/2
Israel	4.2/4.6/NA	1.9/2.1/NA	5.3/9.9/NA	NA	NA
"Major Oil Producers"					
Saudi Arabia	2.8/29.2/1.0 (2002 only)	–2.1/25.8/–2.2 (2002 only)	NA	NA/NA/5.2	NA/NA/51.
Kuwait	2.2/2.9/–1.0 (2001)	1.5/–1.5/–3.9 (2001)	1.6/3.4/–4.8 (2001)	NA/0.3/0.4	NA/41.6/50
Qatar	NA/9.8/7.2 (2001)	NA/6.5/4.9 (2001)	NA	NA/NA/0.4 (2001)	NA/NA/68. (2001)
UAE	0.7/8.7/1.9 (2002)	–4.6/4.5/–0.6	4.0/NA/1.2	1.0/2.1/3.6	67.2/59.5/5(
Bahrain	4.3/2.5/5.1 (2002)	0.9/–0.1/1.9 (2002)	NA/4.9/5.6 (2002)	1.1/NA/0.7	55.3/NA/42
Iran	1.8/3.5/5.8	–1.2/2.0/5.8	5.1/–0.7/4.7	20.23/23.9/15.2	37.1/29.2/38
Iraq	–17.6/26.1/NA	–20.2/23.2/NA	–14.0/104.8/NA	NA/36.6/24.6 (2002 figure)	NA/NA/13.((2001 figure
Algeria	1.5/2.7/4.4	–1.3/0.9/2.4	3.3/4.0/4.5	8.4/12.1/10.0	56.1/49.7/52
Libya	–.67/NA/NA	–10.3/NA/NA	NA	2.6/NA/NA	65.7/NA/N
"Other/Lower-Middle Income MENA Countries"					
Turkey	5.1/2.8/4.7	2.7/1.0/3.6	5.5/11.4/4.9	22.7/15.3/13.0	25.1/29.9/25
Palestine	NA/–0.8/5.8	NA/–5.0/1.3	NA/–3.2/10.2	NA/NA/6.3	NA/NA/13.
Lebanon	NA/3.3/2.8	NA/1.7/1.6	NA/9.4/10.5	NA/NA/11.7	NA/NA/21.(
Syria	2.5/3.5/3.5	–0.7/0.7/1.1	10.6/10.1/2.9	20.0/31.7/23.1	23.4/17.4/27
Yemen	NA/5.6/3.1 (2002 only)	NA/2.6/0.0 (2002 only)	NA/7.5/–6.2	NA/23.0/15.2	NA/22.7/46.
Oman	6.4/8.3/2.0 (2002 only)	2.3/5.5/–0.4 (2002 only)	NA/8.1/37.2 (2001 only)	NA/NA/2.1	NA/NA/53.7
Sudan	3.5/5.9/9.4	1.2/3.6/6.9	–8.7/18.1/–2.6	35.1/39.7/39.2	15.1/11.1/18
Mauritania	2.1/4.3/3.3 (2001 only)	–0.4/1.2/0.4 (2001 only)	–1.6/4.7/14.2	33.1/28.0/21.4	23.4/29.2/31

(Sources: World Bank, IMF, UNDP tables for the periods under review)

rvices % DP 82 92 02	Government Consumption as % GDP 1982 1992 2002	Inflation (% change from previous year) 1982 1992 2002	Total Exports in US$ millions 1982 1992 2002	Total Imports in US$ billions 1982 1992 2002	External Debt in US$ millions 1982 1992 2002
.8/52.3/52.8	18.3/16.8/16.0	10.5/5.7/0.6	2,065/5,045/7,663	4,315/8,113/12,083	12,401/22,674/18,601
.8/55.4/60.5	16.5/16.0/16.3	NA/5.8/2.8	1,980/4,014/6,857	3,389/6,432/9,503	3,772/8,543/12,100
.0/50.1/50.2	17.8/10.4/10.3	NA/21.1/2.7	NA/3,880/6,643	NA/10,054/14,644	27,332/31,129/29,234 (2001 figure)
.7/65.1/74.6	28.1/21.7/25.1	7.5/4.0/3.5	750/1,220/2,522	3,241/3,257/5,296	2,648/7,967/8,094
A	38.3/28.8/NA	120.4/11.9/5.6	5,255/13,119/29,465	9,655/20,261	35,240
A/NA/42.9	NA	NA/NA/−.5	NA/NA/67,270	NA/NA/30,952	NA
A/58.1/48.6	19.3/55.5/26.4	NA/NA/1.4	NA/NA/16,098	NA/NA/8,234	NA
A/NA/31.4 (2001)	NA/NA/24.2 (2001)	NA/NA/1.4	NA/NA/11,222 (2001)	NA/NA/6,301 (2001)	NA
.8/38.4/45.5	19.4/17.3/16.9	NA/NA/2.0	NA/NA/45,968	NA/NA/37,320	NA
.6/NA/53.6	17.0/23.9/17.9	NA/NA/−1.2 (2001)	NA/NA/5,786	NA/NA/3,956	NA
.7/46.9/45.8	−3.7/3.3/5.0	18.2/25.8/15.0	20,452/19,868/25,761	12,552/23,274/26,450	8,236/16,084/7,345
A/NA/61,9	NA/15.5/14.9	NA/NA/70.0	10,033/609/13,300	21,134/603/8,000	5,971/20,917/89,800
.5/38.2/37.3	16.2/16.0/15.3	6.6/31.6/1.4	13,509/11,510/18,700	10,735/9,085/11,300	4,564/9,331/4,166
.7/NA/NA	34.6/28.9/NA	NA	NA	NA	NA
.2/54.7/61.6	9.8/12.9/14.0	NA/70.1/40.8	5,890/14,891/39,827	8,843/22,871/51,270	19,716/56,554/131,407
A/NA/80.4	NA/NA/51.7	NA/NA/5.7	391/299/410	729/1,232/1,406	NA
A/NA/67.3	NA/14.8/13.6	NA/120/4.3	NA/NA/894	3,947/NA/6,182	721/1,806/17,077
.6/50.9/49.4	22.0/10.9/12.2	14.3/11.0/3.0	2,030/3,090/6,300	4,030/3,490/4,664	6,184/19,215/21,466
A/54.3/38.5	NA/19.4/14.2	NA/−85.7/15.8	NA/1,073/3,052	NA/1,935/2,829	2,403/6,571/5,290
A/NA/44.2	26.1/31.4/22.4 (2001)	NA/NA/−0.7	NA/NA/11,168	NA/NA/5,997	957/2,855/5,716
.9/49.2.42.5	9.2/5.9/NA	28.3/125.3/8.3	NA/NA/1,839	NA/1,068/1,503	7,169/15,450/14,224
.5/42.9/47.6	32.1/16.4/18.4	NA/10.1/4.0	NA/400/321	NA/459/388	1,137/2,105/2,479

almost all comparator countries … In fact, the richer the MENA country, the worse the gap with its worldwide peers."

This shouldn't be a surprise, as the richest countries in the region are specifically the oil-producing countries, many of whose ruling elites wouldn't last in power – literally – one minute without massive US support (although this is slowly changing in the interesting cases of the smaller and less oil-rich Gulf sheikhdoms such as the UAE, Qatar or Bahrain, which are both diversifying their economies and opening up their political processes). And so it is shocking, really (but not, as we've seen, surprising), when one report concludes that *"The next steps are in the hands of the countries in the MENA region … The people and their governments must publicly commit to bring the quality of their governance up to par with the best in the world, and to formulate and implement their programs to do so in a participatory process that guarantees inclusiveness and accountability."*[59] The emphasis is in the original report, but what's not emphasized is the dominating role of external powers, and especially the US and the arms–oil industrial complex, in frustrating any commitments peoples or governments might dare to make. In fact, the occupation of Iraq proves just how difficult it is to achieve these goals, as the US-administered Coalition Provisional Authority was riddled with the same problems of corruption and lack of accountability that these reports condemn in Middle Eastern governments.

Is it all the fault of the American people and their culture that the US Government has engaged in such a disastrous invasion and occupation of Iraq? Actually, this isn't far off the mark. The difference between the US and the MENA is that American citizens are ultimately in control of the system – or if they're not, it's because they've chosen to abdicate their responsibility. They aren't ruled by authoritarian regimes supported by the most powerful countries in the world – *they are* the most powerful country in the world.

Late Nights at the Amman Safeway and the Mecca Mall

I remember walking into a huge Safeway supermarket in Amman, Jordan my first time there and feeling like I had just walked into a piece of America in the Middle East. Even the cash registers and receipts were in English. But the reality then, as now, was that the majority of Jordanians couldn't afford to shop there. And the kiosks full of religious books right outside the store – which I think had more shoppers than the store did – showed that many Jordanians saw their way to safety along a very different path.

Seven years later, on my way home from Baghdad, I decided to stop by the Safeway to see how it had changed; but instead I wound up across town at the upscale new "Mecca Mall." With an array of shops, boutiques, cinemas, chic bowling alleys, high-powered air conditioners and ads for *Sex and the City* on Arabic Showtime, the assault on one's senses, especially after war-torn Baghdad, was almost too much to bear. Mecca Street itself reminded me more of an Arab Rodeo Drive than the Amman I knew as a graduate student only half a decade earlier.

One thing's for sure, there's been a lot of growth and wealth creation in Jordan, at least for some Jordanians. Yet according to the World Bank in the last decade Jordan (like the rest of the MENA) saw "disappointing … results on the ground. The 1990s were marked by stagnant or declining trade and private investment – MENA was the only region in the world to experience a reversal."[60] In response to this situation, the Bank suggests Jordan, like everyone else, needs to shift "from oil to non-oil sectors; from public, state-dominated to private, market-oriented activities; and from protected, import-substitution to competitive, export-oriented activities." Clearly Jordan has attempted to do this; yet if we look at the numbers above, it would appear that most of the people crowding into the Mecca Mall are window shoppers, as $1,706 (the average yearly income in Jordan) doesn't leave a lot of disposable income to do much more than window shop at the Mecca Mall. In this situation, why should leaders, as the Bank puts it, "favor policies to make the needed transition from safety and comfort of the old model to the uncertainty of gains from a new model"?[61]

And why should we assume that, with what we can call the "Walmartization" of the world economy, international companies looking to invest in Middle Eastern countries won't do so on terms that will hurt, rather than help, most workers in the region (especially with China and Southeast Asia competing for the same jobs)? After all, that's exactly what's happened in Jordan, Egypt, the Occupied Territories, and other places that have undergone "successful" structural adjustment, not to mention in Latin America – and, of course, the United States as well.[62]

Even in the region's most advanced economy, Israel, neoliberal policies have led to a tripling of the number of families living below the poverty line since 1988 (including 30 percent of the country's children), a decline in wages of over 9 percent since 2000. And since the mid/late-1970s the move to liberalization turned what was formerly one of the most egalitarian societies on earth into one of the most unequal in the "West."[63] If the average Israeli is losing ground, can we expect the average Jordanian or Egyptian to fare better?

The Arms–Petrodollar Cycle: A Major Cause of the MENA's Problems Strangely Unaccounted For

I have already mentioned the negative impact of the massive levels of military spending in the MENA on the ability of its countries to reach adequate levels of sustainable development. What we need to explore is how spending by the region on arms relates to oil sales, and through it, links the region to the world economy. We can take one obvious example to understand how this dynamic works: the US–Saudi arms and oil relationship. Since the 1940s, when the Roosevelt Administration first guaranteed the survival of the Saudi monarchy in return for access to a steady supply of oil through US companies, the Saudi–American strategic alliance has been the foundation of US Middle Eastern policy. The first direct evidence of just how important this alliance was, and how much power US oil companies had to shape US policy to the region, came when the Saudi Government demanded a much larger royalty payment from Aramco in 1950.[64] With the help of the US State and Treasury departments, Aramco and the Saudi Government set up an accounting scheme that allowed profit-sharing between the company and the Saudi Government to be written off as foreign income taxes. Because of this, the "taxes" paid to the Saudi Government canceled out income taxes that would have had to be paid to the US Government. This scheme meant tens of billions of dollars in extra profits for both the oil companies and the Saudi Government.

This is just the oil half of the equation. If we look at the arms-purchasing side, the numbers tell an incredible story. From 1950 through 1999, the US sold Saudi Arabia $107.9 billion worth of arms.[65] Not surprisingly, these figures were largely responsible for the build-up of almost $100 billion in debt by the regime (a replay of the situation faced by that old arch-nemesis of the House of Sa'ud, the Ottoman Empire, over a century ago).

The amount of money the Saudis have spent on weapons during the last two decades compared with their total budget is extraordinary: State Department estimates put the numbers between 15 and

30 percent of GDP, a greater share than any other country in the region (and perhaps the world), including Israel. As important a measure is that Saudi military expenditures have averaged around 40 percent of all central government expenditures in the 1980s, and after peaking as high as 70 percent at the height of hostilities with Iraq, still remained up to 40 percent of all Central Government expenditures, and 12.9 percent of the GNP in 2000. The developing-world average remains well below 5 percent outside the MENA.

These are startling numbers. ABC News military analyst and Saudi specialist Anthony Cordesman argues that the Saudis have long bought far more arms than they could possibly integrate into or use effectively in their small armed forces. If we want to understand how Osama bin Laden was able to recruit fifteen well-educated Saudis to turn commercial jets into cruise missiles, think of all the projects these billions of dollars could have funded within Saudi society, what kind of culture they could have helped to foster, and what kind of culture they *did* actually foster, and you begin to get the picture.[66] Especially when we consider that the MENA region saw the biggest drop in its GDP of any region in the world during the 1980s and early 1990s, and Saudi Arabia the biggest drop in real income of any country of the region, just at the time when the men who commandeered the planes were becoming adults.[67]

But it's not just Saudi Arabia; the region as a whole spends disproportionately more than any other in the world on military expenditures. To give just an inkling of the disparity in expenditures, China spent only 2.3 percent of its GDP on its military in 2001; even the United States, by far the biggest spender in the world, allocated only 3.1 percent of its GDP to defense spending.[68] The Middle East average was 6.3 percent of GDP for 2001, which constituted by far the largest current percentage *and* increase in military spending over the last decade of any region in the world.

It is clear, then, that arms sales and transfers to the MENA, which remain a cornerstone of US policy to the region, have been crucial to building political alliances, placing US-made systems on the ground when war – as in Iraq or Afghanistan – does occur, and keeping the defense industry production levels up during years of lower domestic military budgets.[69] In fact, for many years US arms sales to Saudi Arabia have come close to equaling oil sales to the US, which means that billions of dollars paid to the Saudis for oil are funneled back to the US and in so doing it has helped keep the overall balance of trade largely as favorable to the US as possible. And of course, when we consider the tens of billions of dollars paid to US oil companies by

American consumers, we begin to understand the combined strength of the "weapondollar–petrodollar" coalition in shaping US policy toward the single most important strategic country in the region.[70]

The issue of defense spending by the Saudi and other MENA regimes is clear, but it is almost entirely avoided in mainstream commentary or analyses. This absence means that when the World Bank examines issues of good governance in the MENA it can argue that "the challenge of radical movements" helped create a "revived" and "reinvigorated" national security state in the region, but doesn't have to consider why and how this happened. As it should now be clear, however, the existing system is determined significantly by the relationship between the oil and weapons industries that sit astride the region and connect it so tightly to the power of the US.

This dynamic became even more crucial after 1973, when the so-called oil shock led to record increases in profits to Middle Eastern governments, who couldn't just sit on the money because it would either lose value or lead to inflation. In order to remain useful (and not antagonistic) to the US and cement their hold on power the oil monarchies recycled tens and ultimately hundreds of billions of dollars in oil profits back to the US, UK, and to a lesser extent France and the Soviet Union, in the form of arms purchases. It isn't surprising that this first took off just as the world economy was transforming into its current neoliberal phase.

A recent ground-breaking book by two Israeli economists, Jonathan Nitzan and Shimshon Bichler's *The Global Political Economy of Israel*, provides the level of analysis and insight that until now has been sorely missed in the study of globalization in the MENA. Specifically, the book places the Israeli–Palestinian conflict in the larger world system. This is crucial for our discussion because in doing so it helps us see that narrow attacks by the anti-war movement on the Israeli occupation – however justified on their own terms – aren't very useful if they don't simultaneously address the larger political and economic dynamics of the region that make the occupation not just possible but necessary. Even more important, the authors show how the combined "weapondollar–petrodollar coalition" that depends on the region-wide conflict has gained control of a disproportionate amount of the world's resources and corporate profits, to the extent that they have been able to ensure that their profits remain much higher than their size, relative to the larger economy, would dictate.[71]

Specifically, what Nitzan and Bichler show is that "during the 1970s, there was a growing convergence of interests between the world's leading petroleum and armament corporations … The …

politicization of oil, together with the parallel *commercialization* of arms exports, helped shape an uneasy weapondollar–petrodollar coalition between these companies, making their differential profitability increasingly dependent on Middle East energy conflicts."[72] What is most important here is that in this process, and viewed from within the larger context of neoliberal globalization, "the lines separating state from capital, foreign policy from corporate strategy, and territorial conquest from differential profit, no longer seem very solid."[73] We only have to turn to post-invasion Iraq, where the relationship between oil, violence, and political, economic, and cultural chaos has been so important, to understand their implications.

But what these processes tend to do is to "deepen" the wealth and power of a certain cluster of companies (especially oil, defense, and heavy engineering companies) while often undermining the broader health of the economy (leisure, civilian high tech, and other sectors that did so well during the 1990s "peace dividend").[74] In fact, the political and economic "depth strategy" deployed by the weapondollar–petrodollar coalition – the real "coalition" behind the invasion and occupation of Iraq – has made possible an unprecedented comeback by these sectors of the economy after significant retrenchment in the 1990s.

Most important, because these dynamics have such political and economic synergy with the Walmartization of the economy, when you enlarge the weapondollar–petrodollar complex into the "Walmart-weapons–petrodollar complex," it becomes clear how an unparalleled concentration of wealth and power is reshaping – often brutally – the world in its image.

Conclusion: From the Boardroom to the Oval Office

Given the discussion of this chapter, we might consider it amazing how much effort the World Bank, IMF, the 9/11 Commission, and other institutions expend to explain the obvious: that the countries of the MENA region are by and large undemocratic, authoritarian regimes that need to promote greater political democracy in order to advance out of the political, economic, and even cultural mess that they're in. It's not amazing, but perhaps sad, that they spend so little time explaining the role of the international system in the origin of and solution to these problems. But without addressing the US, European, Japanese role – the G-8 really – in perpetuating this system, there's just no chance that any reform could succeed, even if it could get mass public support. In a real sense, the peoples of the region have to fight two battles simultaneously: against their own despotic and corrupt governments, and against the larger "world" financial system.

What I hope our discussion of neoliberal globalization in the MENA demonstrates is that the political and economic systems of the region are determined in crucial ways by an arms–petrodollar cycle that can only function in an environment devoid of peace, justice, democracy or autonomous development. And this environment is one that was planted and nurtured during the era of high imperialism and colonialism in the MENA. In fact, the economic dynamics and struggles they generate concern many of the same issues as a century or more ago: who controls the region's resources, who gets to set the "development" agenda, how open the region is to trade with the leading capitalist powers, and on whose terms the MENA can integrate further into the realities of the contemporary world economy without standards of living deteriorating greatly for a large percentage of its inhabitants.

And it is in this context that we must understand one of the central dynamics of contemporary globalization in the MENA; namely, that even if "we" (whoever we are) wanted to bring freedom, peace, justice, democracy, and development to the Middle East, the very structure of "our" control of the region's resources, revenues, and politics, and the insatiable yet unsustainably toxic culture of hyper-consumption this system feeds, demands the opposite of all of these laudable goals – ongoing low-level conflict punctuated periodically by war, institutionalized injustice, oppression, and dependency – to survive and prosper. As former international banker John Perkins recently "confessed," if anyone threatens the system in fundamental ways the US government and its corporate allies send in the "economic hit men, and when we fail, the other type of hit men, the CIA-sanctioned jackals [are] always right behind us ..."[75]

This realization must be at the heart of any progressive political response to the current realities of global policy toward the region. It further reminds us that to change the face of globalization we must transform not only the very basis of our foreign-economic policies, but the fundamental structure and ethical framework of American, in fact world, culture. The "rest" of the world increasingly understands this fact, which is a major reason why so many people seem to hate us, and do so in increasing numbers. But the reality of how negatively neoliberal policies have impacted the region (to the extent they are actually being implemented) has yet to be accepted by mainstream exponents of globalization in the Middle East, let alone the policy-makers who continue to advocate the Washington Consensus, and even invasion and occupation, as the best means of solving its problems. In the next chapter we'll explore how and why Muslim/Arab critics have so often seen through the rhetoric of European and now American globalization during the last two centuries, and what kinds of alternative systems might be constructed in its place.

5 Beyond bin Laden: Human Nationalisms versus Inhuman Globalization

The problem in Iran we have right now is that any[thing] Western is cherished. I told my cousins I would give money to my grandma to buy them stuff from [the] bazaar. They were like no we want made in America.

I was like idiots what you buy in America and Iran is all made in china what f**king difference does it make.

Posting to English-language Iranian culture web forum,
"Iransportspress.com," Dec. 26, 2003

Globalization, Culture, and Resistance in the Twenty-first Century

So far in this book I have tried to make several arguments that I hope are now clear. First, the dynamics of the relationship between the so-called "West" and the Arab/Muslim world goes back centuries to the roots of what I have called the modernity matrix, a system in which colonialism, capitalism, and nationalism have all played a vital role. Second, the core ideologies and economic processes impelling the modernity matrix helped create a world system whose structure placed the Middle East – its peoples and its resources – at what we can call the "vital margins of the system."

Third, the processes commonly known as contemporary globalization are in many ways a redux – if by some indicators watered down – of the processes of global integration that marked the period of high European imperialism over a century ago. However, while most commentators on globalization tend to focus on its economic aspects and impact, closer inspection reveals that outside of the major industrial countries key indicators of economic globalization are less robust than suggested by the claims of either its proponents or opponents.

But this doesn't mean that globalization is not occurring: on the one hand, the fact that much of the world is marginalized from the global flows of capital, technology, information and related processes is not an aberration, but rather a crucial part of, the story of contemporary globalization – especially in the Middle East. On the other hand, to the extent that economic globalization is not occurring as advertised, then it is culture that is the driving force behind its spread around the world (especially in the Global South), as well as in the growing resistance to it.

This phenomenon of culture in contemporary globalization is nowhere clearer than in the Middle East and larger Muslim majority world. But it is not culture alone that matters. Ultimately, cultural perceptions and experiences are intimately related to economic conditions; that is, detailed analyses of the cultural attitudes of Muslims reveal that levels and patterns of economic development play a crucial role in determining the shape and contours of culture, which then determine political institutions: "economic development bring[s] cultural changes that are conducive to democracy."[1] What this means, of course, is that if we want to transform culture and politics of MENA countries we must transform their economies first. Ironically, the neocons and neoliberals know this intuitively, which is why they believe that creating "liberal market economies" is the best way to make the Middle East more like us culturally and politically. But as Iraq has laid bare, we're not exactly who we think we are.

We're not yet ready to discuss who "we" are in detail (we'll do that in Part Three); first we need to figure out who Muslims think we are, and how these views are influenced by how they understand the impact of neoliberal globalization on their societies. This chapter will explore these questions; before we begin, however, two things need to be mentioned. First, while I don't have the space to offer a detailed discussion of the perceptions and responses of Israeli Jews (or the region's Christians for that matter) to globalization, Israeli scholars and my own research have demonstrated that ultra-Orthodox European Jews (*haredim*) and their religious Arab/Middle Eastern Jewish compatriots (such as Shas) see globalization very similarly to many of their Muslim Palestinian counterparts, including a strong dislike for the dominant values of "modern" America.[2] Second, while my focus in this and the next chapter is on the way scholars, critics, activists, and artists in the MENA understand globalization's cultural impact on their societies, my travels throughout the MENA region in the last decade suggest that their experiences and sentiments are shared by the larger societies they claim to represent.

Indeed, detailed polling over the last three decades shows that in Muslim countries well over 50 percent of the population consider cultural invasion by the West among the very important problems facing their country. This data shows that citizens of major US allies such as Jordan or Egypt score much higher than supposed enemies like Iran – as many as 85 percent of Jordanians share this sentiment, while supposedly fundamentalist Iran has among the lower numbers of people who fear Western cultural invasion, at 55 percent: "In Iran, where the society has been dominated by a religious fundamentalist regime, the public appears to be less religious, less anti-West, more secular, and [have] more pro-modernist values than the public in either Egypt or Jordan, where the state is secular and decidedly pro-West."[3] This doesn't mean that they wholeheartedly support neoliberal globalization; but it clearly suggests that they are not against globalization per se, and like their Turkish counterparts see market liberalization as a way to obtain increasing freedom from an oppressive state.[4]

Most interesting for me in the process of reading through literally hundreds of books and articles is how the great Muslim critics of the West of the last two centuries have mirrored and, in many cases, anticipated the great critiques of Western modernity offered by the likes of Marx and Thoreau, Walden Bellow and Amartya Sen. Yet as the quote at the beginning of the chapter shows, it's not as simple as oppressed cultures piercing through the veil of modernity and showing the West the truth about its history – although it's partly this. For the modernity matrix, like any asymmetrical system of power relations, also produced its own pathologies and disfunctionalities within Muslim majority societies, with al-Qa'eda, religiously inspired Muslim terrorism, and anti-Jewish conspiracy fantasies being the most obvious symptom.

What leads some young Muslims to gravitate to the most atavistic and extreme forms of their culture, others to respond to oppressive and stifling official cultures by falling in love with everything produced by the Great Satan, and a precious few to see the futility of both responses? This is a crucial set of questions; in the wake of September 11 and the war on terror we need to gain a better understanding of why and how critiques of the West, however severe, cross the line to outright hatred – how the pendulum swings between what we could term a "worldly Islam" that is fully engaged with other cultures and processes from a positive perspective (what the sociologist Manuel Castells terms a "project identity" because it can support the creation of open identities that can build broad yet strong communities), and a "ghetto Islam" that is closed and lacks the ability to do more than resist encroachments and threats from the "outside" (what Castells calls "resistance identities"). With this information we can initiate the much-needed discussion of what all of us, Muslims and their neighbors, can do to build the inter-communal solidarities and cross-cultural bridges to make the drive toward violent resistance less attractive or viable an option.

Much of our discussion in this chapter will center on the idea of a cultural invasion from the West, but this notion is in fact much more complicated than most people imagine. For example, in the Arab/Muslim world the prevalence of American soap operas such as *Dallas*, *Dynasty* or today *Baywatch*, have long been decried by religious and nationalist figures for corrupting the morals and values of supposedly gullible, uneducated, and unsophisticated viewers. Yet when we actually look at who's watching these shows and how they perceive them, it becomes clear that a significant percentage (if not the majority) of the people watching them are middle- or upper-class people who understand English, can read well enough to follow the Arabic subtitles, or even have the luxury of coming home after a long and hard day's work and watching TV instead of cooking, cleaning,

Figure 6   If these walls could talk: anti-Jewish graffiti – in Hebrew, reading "Yafo for Muslims only" – in the once Palestinian, today mixed neigh-borhood of Jaffa, Israel, 2000

and taking care of children. And the poorer, supposedly more gullible, viewers often see through the ludicrous plots and clothing to the stories' focus on mothers' love for their children (a ubiquitous theme in soaps around the world). In other words, we can't read culture that easily and can't take for granted the nature, scope, and dynamics of cultural penetration just because Arab/Muslim writers say there's a dangerous invasion going on.[5]

Moreover, however interesting the focus on American culture, there is an equally important circulation of Latin American, Asian, and especially Indian cultures in the Middle East that has to be considered if we want to understand what globalization truly means in the region. (Indeed, given the level of Hindu–Muslim animosity and violence both between India and Pakistan and within India, we can wonder why Indian cultural production doesn't arouse anything close to the level of suspicion encountered by American culture in the Muslim world.) And while many in the anti-corporate globalization movement focus considerable energy on the problem of sweatshops in the production of goods for fashion industry elsewhere in the Global South, in places like Turkey and Iran an Islamic fashion industry is redefining their cultures, especially for women, allowing them to be both fashionable and in some sense "Western" and "modern" (in its original fashion sense of *au courant*), while holding to what many Muslims believe to be properly modest dress.

Most important, it is undeniable that millions of citizens of the region, especially young people, enjoy Western culture – or at least certain cultural products like pop stars, movies, and even heavy metal and rap acts – and find it neither dangerous nor threatening to their cultural identities (in fact, for some they are essential components). This, of course, is precisely what makes Western culture so threatening to those who feel the need to preserve a so-called "traditional" culture under siege.

But what needs to be stated here, and which I'll discuss more below, is that enjoying Britney Spears, *Finding Nemo* or *The Simpsons* does not mean a (young) person buys into the US or European policies that clearly go against his or her country's or culture's interests. This is precisely the fallacy of the promoters of US-sponsored Arab radio or television networks such as Radio Sawa' (the American-created Arabic language music and news radio network), who believe they're opening the minds of young Arabs by pumping in American pop music laced with supposedly unbiased news programming. It is quite simplistic to imagine that because young Egyptians or Lebanese listen to an American radio station they'll support, or at least forget about, US policies towards Iraq, Israel/Palestine, or the majority of the two-dozen-odd other oppressive regimes in the region. Yet American politicians and their corporate media allies seem to imagine that if only we can get them to like our culture, they'll like our politics. It might surprise them, but most Arab young people don't experience any cognitive dissonance simultaneously liking Justin Timberlake and disliking George Bush.

But it's even more complex than this, as there can also be multiple levels of cultural interaction, which can mask each other in potentially dangerous ways. As one Saudi doctor explains, "My daughter is for bin Laden. When I go to wake her up, I see pictures of Palestinian girl martyrs on her wall. It scares me to death. If we go into her room at night, she'll be listening to Britney Spears, but as soon as we close the door she's listening to martyr songs."[6] This kind of cultural schizophrenia is also globalization, and not a very comfortable one at that – in fact it's awfully depressing (an astonishing number of Saudis are, it seems, clinically depressed).

But we can't limit our analysis of culture to the most violently negative responses to globalization by the likes of bin Laden. For every Saudi or Egyptian who sympathizes with al-Qa'eda there are dozens or even hundreds searching for ways to adapt to and work with the dominant cultural and economic trends, however difficult this may be. And since Muslim societies are so increasingly young, by examining the culture of young people, and particularly (but not only) the music they listen to and in some cases perform, we can find precisely the bridges between cultures where the possibility of positive transformation of both Muslim and Western culture is possible. But such a transformation would require the active participation of people on both sides; much like a jamming musically, the culture jamming I advocated at the start of this book will require great ears, a sensitivity to the various "styles" (cultures) being brought to the stage – that is, the global public sphere – an unwillingness to tolerate amateurism (bigotry), and the courage continually to expand the repertoire to include new voices, strategies, and styles.[7]

Beyond the Clash of Civilizations: Arab/Muslim Perspectives on Globalization and Dialogue

We can understand how teenage girls and young Muslims more generally draw selectively from the vast repertoire of symbols and practices circulating in the global village (or mall). But how does this relate to the perspective of the (usually older and largely male) Muslim critics and activists on what one recent book calls the "specter of globalization"? In reading through the major writings on the subject we see, not surprisingly, that the works of Samuel Huntington, Francis Fukuyama, and Thomas Friedman – all charter members of the Axis of Arrogance and Ignorance – are felt to be fundamental in understanding how the US and West more generally understands the project of globalization. Indeed, a constant theme in contemporary Arab discourses on globalization is the "clash of civilizations" discourse of Samuel Huntington, and the globalizing American foreign policy system it is believed to represent. The choice offered by America is understood to be stark: a "civilization" (or culture or country) either joins the New World Order (and in doing so, repudiates the essence of that civilization) or faces conflict with and likely exile from it.[8]

Such a system is contrasted with what many critics would hope to be a "true democracy," whose most basic components would be justice, tolerance, and "the right to be different."[9] The focus on the right to cultural difference is crucial, because globalization is understood to create not a "multicultural" difference that is celebrated and encourages mutual respect and cooperation, but rather a forced difference that deepens poverty and inequality both within and between countries.[10]

This emphasis on democracy should not surprise us. As sociologists Ronald Inglehart and Pippa Norris discovered in their extensive review of polling data on attitudes towards democracy in the Muslim world,

> Huntington is mistaken in assuming that the core clash between the West and Islamic worlds concerns democracy. The evidence suggests striking similarities in the political values held in these societies ... the Huntington thesis fails to identify the most basic cultural fault line between the West and Islam, which concerns the issues of gender equality and sexual liberalization. The cultural gulf separating Islam from the West involves Eros far more than Demos ... as contrary to Huntington's thesis, compared with Western societies, support for democracy was marginally slightly *stronger* (not weaker) among those living in Islamic societies.[11]

We can criticize this quote for overly generalizing between what are ultimately fictional entities such as "Islam" or the "West." Nevertheless, the argument they put forth is very important: ultimately it's not questions of democracy, but of power relations between men and women that are the major fault lines within Muslim majority societies. However, what the authors don't take into account is that Muslim cultural norms regarding gender and sexual relations and equality are much more complex than their black-and-white portrayal. For it is clear that the more conservative the society, the more sexually obsessed are the men; the large black market for pornography throughout the Muslim world and the constant complaints about pornography by women in letters to religious advice columns (the Muslim equivalents of Dear Abby) shows that Muslim men are no different from men anywhere else. And in the chaos of post-occupation Iraq (perhaps because of the chaos) Shi'i "entrepreneurs" started bringing in Iranian prostitutes and setting them up in hotels to serve as "temporary wives" for Iraqi Shi'i men to "marry" for a few hours (a legitimate practice under Shi'i religious law).

So the issue is first of all more about sexual power than a larger cultural view of "women" as a gender category. Second, without diminishing the oppression of women in Muslim history (or European or any other societies' histories for that matter), the so-called "traditional" view of women in the MENA region – as having few rights, especially economic ones – emerged in good measure in response to European colonialism, precisely because Europeans justified colonialism largely through a rhetoric of "liberating" "oppressed" Muslim women.[12] And because of this, to assume that the position and treatment of Muslim women vis-à-vis Muslim men is the fault line between civilizations is to forget how European imperialism's insistence on "liberating" Muslim women helped shape the conservative positions of so many Muslim men in response.[13]

What's more, however, it's not "Islam" that has a traditional view of women and gender equality, but rather one half of Islam; that is, Muslim men. And then it's not all Muslim men who have such views (and of course some Muslim women accept the conservative view of their role in society while many men reject it); so perhaps it's about one-third of the total Muslim ummah, or community, that actively support what from a "Western" perspective would be a more traditional role for women.[14]

For all its importance and focus by Western commentators, women are not the primary focus of Arab/Muslim writings on globalization (although their importance shouldn't be underestimated). Rather, the more structural dynamics are a concern of almost every commentator. As one Arab critic, Musa al-Darir, argues, "end of the twentieth century globalization, even more so than its counterpart at the end of the nineteenth century, is about the substitution of a penetration of culture for an ideological struggle …" that is, of the type that characterized capitalism and Marxism during the Cold War.[15] I will return to the theme of penetration shortly; but it needs to be remembered how this combination of enforced difference and lack of tolerance promoted by Huntington's thesis is seen as inevitable in a "new global order where all culture is diffused into one global village."[16]

Not surprisingly, the importance of focusing on culture has not been lost on scholars in the MENA; within this context globalization has become one of the most salient issues in contemporary Arab political writing.[17] From numerous conferences, books, and articles in leading Arab publications debating its various ramifications, three main responses to globalization are apparent: outright rejection, enthusiastic support, and cautious engagement.[18]

It would seem that the consensus of Arab scholars is not that different from their critical European and American counterparts: globalization is neither a new phenomenon nor just another stage in the development of capitalism. Rather it marks a continuation of the basic dynamic of the relationship between the West and Orient dating back hundreds of years, the hallmark of which is a Western desire for global hegemony which in earlier eras was represented by imperialism and colonialism.[19] The most prominent feature of the new system – which is essentially a more powerful version of the old system – is the attempt by the United States, the main instigator of globalization, to overthrow existing political, economic, and cultural norms.[20]

This focus on culture is tied to the mainstream US rhetoric that America and neoliberalism are the only tickets to a better future for the citizens of the MENA. As one Arab commentator argues, "America is attempting to utilize globalization to realize its interests in many countries around the world and especially in the Middle East ... The belief that the new world order will be an order of peace, and countries freed from backwardness, stagnation and subjugation, is [pure] fantasy."[21] This is because with neoliberal economics and the ideology of the market the driving forces of globalization, poorer countries in the Arab world in particular are left on the margins of the supposedly unified world.[22] Multinational corporations are central actors in this drama because of their unique ability to "leap over" existing distinctions between "inside/outside" the territorial and administrative boundaries of the state.[23] Yet here too it is not just the economic aspects of globalization that are important, since cultural exchange always follows on the heels of "free trade" – an exchange which in reality is "the negation of culture."[24]

Most important, globalization's cultural/ideological foundations provide it with the "fine power" to realize its imperialist aims without causing classic revolutionary reactions to it, as did Western imperialism before it. These characteristics in turn make it an even more dangerous form of imperialism, one with the uncanny ability to undermine the sovereignty of Arab nations. Against such a powerful force, the question arises, "How can we become part of this global village without losing the particularity of the place in which we live?"[25]

Muslim Responses to Globalization in Historical Perspective

In the aftermath of the September 11 attacks, scholars and intelligence analysts finally began to investigate Muslim writings on globalization in some detail. In doing so they discovered that the writings of many Muslim critics were not that different from Left critiques of the capitalist world system (which is perhaps why neoconservatives consider France as much "our" enemy as Islam[26]). This is not a surprise – in fact, such similarities are what motivated me to write this book. Muslim critics themselves, including the leading thinkers behind "radical Islam" such as Mawlana Mawdudi, Sayyid Qutb, Ali Shariati or the Ayatollah Khomeini, have all addressed Marxist/socialist critiques and alternatives to the dominant capitalist order, agreeing with many of the polemics while criticizing the materialism and lack of spiritual attention in the Marxist/socialist alternative.

Yet if some of the more honest mainstream commentators will admit that radical Islam is "both a symptom and an agent of globalization," it is wrong to argue, as does the French scholar Olivier Roy, that "bin Laden is taking up the anti-American protest that, up until now, was the privilege of ultraleftists in the West and supporters of the Third World elsewhere."[27] Indeed, an important argument of this book is that Arab/Muslim critiques of the West and its modernity have a long pedigree in Muslim political thought. And it is from this historical perspective that Muslim critics today argue that the politicians and economists who buy into neoliberal ideology and "celebrate" the new freedoms it heralds are as "gravely deluded" as their counterparts a century ago.[28]

Then as now, the development and advance of globalization and the liberalization and privatization programs it sponsors are "at expense of the state and people":[29] "Privatization, free trade and competition are in fact ideologies for separation, marginalization and the demobilization of workers under the principle of 'greater profits, lower wages."[30] What is most important about this argument is that it is based on a belief that globalization today is really global imperialism dressed in the new clothes of privatization, freedom of initiative and competition, and a "culture of excess or penetration."[31] This focus on penetration is important, because it links globalization to earlier processes of imperialism and colonialism, which were never just about military and political conquest and control but involved the "penetration" of new systems of ordering societies and administering power over them.[32] In fact, as the infamous pictures of Iraqi prisoners at Abu Ghraib prison show, this penetration is always highly sexualized, as the verb itself suggests.

For two centuries, then, the penetrating power of capitalism and other discourses of modernity have brought strong reactions from Arab/Muslim intellectuals and activists. The roots of the Arab/Muslim critique of globalization go back to nineteenth-century critiques of European imperialism. Interestingly, one of the earliest Muslim commentators, the Egyptian al-Jabarti, had an ambivalent and complex reaction to the arrival of Napoleon's army of soldiers and scholars in Egypt in 1799. He declared his admiration of the French love of knowledge but criticized both their desire to "rob" and "despoil" Egypt and their being "*dahhriyuun*," or materialists.[33]

As the nineteenth century progressed there were debates throughout the Middle East over whether Western liberal ideas would bring freedom or rather "lead men astray to go for wealth" (as a leading Persian critic of constitutionalism argued at the turn of the century). Sometimes the same thinker, like Jamal al-Din al-Afghani (the father of twentieth-century Islamic reformism), could hold potentially contradictory views. Specifically, he advocated adopting the political and technological advances of the West, yet at the same time believed that following it culturally would lead to "retrogression" rather than progress. Not surprisingly, "materialists" within the Muslim world were rending the social order specifically by aping Western ways and encouraging the growth of "egoism."[34]

Accusations of materialism were a frequently repeated theme as the twentieth century wore on. In the 1920s Hassan al-Banna, the founder of the Egyptian Muslim Brotherhood, also preached against "the tyranny of materialism" in Muslim society and its direct role in Western economic and military hegemony over the Middle East.[35] As the Arab/Muslim world achieved formal independence from European colonial rule and began the "nationalist period" of the 1950s–1970s, thinkers like Muhammad Iqbal, Mawlana Mawdudi, and Sayyid Qutb critiqued nationalism, the nation-state, and capitalism together,[36] and specifically focused on the "gratification, consumerism and hedonism" increasingly associated with middle-class/bourgeois lifestyles (and even more so today).[37]

In the Iran of the 1950s and 1960s a similar critique was evolving, which is not surprising since the progenitor of modern Islamic political thought, al-Afghani, was himself Persian born. Thinkers like Jalal al-e Ahmad, Mehdi Barzagan, Morteza Motahhari, and the Ayatollah Khomeini all deployed – consciously or not – Marxist critiques of capitalism as centerpieces of their analyses. Ahmad's notion of "Westoxification" (or "Westruckness" (*gharbzagedi*)) is perhaps the most well-known example of this critique, as it focuses on the infatuation and blind following of the West within Iran, which Ahmad argues resulted from the country's dependent relationship on the United States.[38]

The most powerful Sunni Islamist voice of the second half of the twentieth century has been Sayyid Qutb, the leader of the Egyptian Muslim Brotherhood who was executed by the Nasser Government in 1966. Qutb's writings span the gamut from Qur'anic commentary to social critique; perhaps the most relevant for our discussion is his *The Battle between Islam and Capitalism* (*Ma'araka al-Islam wa-al-Rasma'liyyah*), which constitutes a seminal Muslim critique of capitalist, materialist, consumerist modernity and its cultures.[39]

Qutb spent several years in the United States in the 1950s, and his experience of endemic racism, poverty amidst affluence, and non-segregated gender relations cemented an abhorrence of the West, and the United States in particular, that had predated his sojourn there. But there is no doubt that his time in the United States hardened Qutb's belief that capitalism and democracy were inseparable from each other – an understanding of this relationship in which both ideologies used culture to divide the world.[40] At the same time, he criticized American society not because it was a Christian society (as later extremists would do with a more intensive and essentialized focus on "Crusader" Christianity), but rather because America had abandoned its religious values for a culture of hedonism and materialism.

For Qutb, American culture ultimately suffered from a "hideous schizophrenia," which "through colonialism was spread throughout the colonized world." This situation made the Muslim experience of modernity a "doubly painful" one of alienation combined with subjugation and humiliation.[41] What is interesting to note here is that Qutb arrives at a similar insight to the great French post-structuralist critics Gilles Deleuze and Felix Guattari, who wrote two grand volumes precisely on the subject of how capitalist modernity produces schizophrenia, and how that schizophrenia could be the source of liberating people from capitalism.[42] (Of course, if not handled right, it can also be the source of our collective self-destruction.)

Needless to say, for Qutb Islam was the one system that could heal the rifts that humanity's humanistic hubris had created and bring "complete social justice" to society. In order to achieve this goal "exploitative capitalism" would have to be divested of its ownership of political and economic power, while the Islam that would replace it would have to be more than "merely a veil for inciting the masses" (this was Qutb's evaluation of socialism, a system that he felt was unable to resolve the conflict between the individual and society).[43] Only an Islamic system, one in which sovereignty belonged not to man but to God (*hakimiyyah*), would realize the best ideals of both socialism and Christianity, which he felt had become locked inside the church and far removed from daily life.[44]

If Qutb was the father of contemporary Islamist radicalism as a negative and violent phenomenon, today, however, the pendulum between moderate (once called "modernist") and extremist Muslims has changed dramatically; while al-Qa'eda gets most of the attention from the Western media and policy-makers because of its terrorist activities, the vast majority of the literature produced by Arab/Muslim critics of globalization shows that few Islamist critics of capitalism equate the two and conceive of democracy negatively. But for Qutb, rejecting democracy in favor of the "sovereignty of God" was the only possible way to confront capitalism by moving the focus away from humanity and material needs and towards worship of God.

This is a crucial perception because once someone turns away from humanity as a reference point for social change it becomes much easier to justify all kinds of violence, including "jihad," to change it. If we look at Osama bin Laden's view of globalization, this becomes clear. Yet we should also bear in mind that taking the focus off humanity and our lust for power and possessions is also an important prescription of liberation theology, the environmental movement, and progressive and non-violent politics more generally. It's not Qutb's insights and critiques that are completely off the mark, but rather the myopic and destructive way he sought to address the problems faced by his and our societies.

Indeed, what is important for us to see in Muslim critiques is how many of the issues they focus on have become cornerstones of progressive thinking, especially in the environmental and progressive religious movements.[45] It is in this sense that I mean that the Muslim critics of the last two centuries have anticipated many of the issues at the core of the debate over globalization – from the fading away of the state (which was variously celebrated and lamented until people figured out it wasn't happening any time soon) to the centrality of culture, to the relationship between globalization and imperialism – that "Western" critics have developed fully much more recently. And it also needs to be pointed out that, however much the Western press might celebrate the *Arab Human Development Reports* as ground-breaking works of self-criticism by Arabs, the history of modern Islamic political thought can be understood as one long analysis and critique of the failures of their own societies to engage successfully with modernity. (This should not, however, lead people to assume that groups such as the Muslim Brotherhood naturally supported the working class against the bourgeoisie. In fact, in Egypt the Brotherhood had a history of breaking strikes for the greater good of the Egyptian "nation," which is yet another demonstration of the complex interconnections of the coefficients of the modernity matrix and how one will work against the tendencies of another.)

Jamal al-Din al-Afghani powerfully described the problem this way over a century ago: "In reality [European] usurpation, aggression and conquest have not come from the French or the English. Rather it is science that everywhere manifests its greatness and power."[46] More recently, scholars like Samir Amin, along with less-well-known professors from Beirut to Rabat, have provided us with important new research on the realities, problems, and prospects of integrating Muslim societies into the larger world system.[47] Several recent studies by Arab scholars in particular are breaking new ground on the relationship between culture and development ideologies in the MENA.

One recent Moroccan study explained that during the last decade Arab scholars have increasingly recognized the importance of culture at precisely the moment that globalization has brought on the cultur-alization of politics. Because of this, contemporary Arab/Muslim writings have moved beyond using culture in lieu of (prohibited) discussions of politics, and have allowed more honest discussions related to the future development of the region to emerge: "Something radically different is happening when [culture] signifies the perception of new dimensions of social conflict, of the formation of new identities and new forms of resistance. [Today] the field of culture refers us not only to the past, but to the present in all its conflict and creativity."[48]

Writings such as these show that Arabs and Muslims have not just come to the idea of self-criticism lately, but instead have long looked at themselves and the world around them with a critical eye. But their self-critiques have always been inseparable from their critiques of the West, which makes them unappealing to Western commentators even when they're not compromised by the bigotry of a Qutb or Khomeini.

The Ideology of al-Qa'eda and the Blowback of Globalization

In an interview a little over a week after the World Trade Center and Pentagon attacks Noam Chomsky argued that bin Laden, al-Qa'eda, and the WTC attacks are not related to globalization and US cultural hegemony. For Chomsky, such an explanation

> is an extremely convenient belief for Western intellectuals. It absolves them of responsibility for the actions that actually do lie behind the choice of the WTC. Was it bombed in 1993 because of concern over globalization and cultural hegemony? A few days ago the *Wall Street Journal* reported attitudes of rich and privileged Egyptians at a McDonald's restaurant wearing stylish American clothes, etc., and bitterly critical of the US for objective reasons of policy, which are well-known to those who wish to know: they had a report a few days earlier on attitudes of bankers, professionals, businessmen in the region, all pro-American, and harshly critical of US policies. Is that concern over "globalization," McDonald's, and jeans? Attitudes in the street are similar, but far more intense, and have nothing at all to do with these fashionable excuses ... What happened on September 11 has virtually nothing to do with economic globalization, in my opinion.

On the one hand, it's clear that what Chomsky is referring to is precisely the hazy "specter" of globalization that becomes the all-purpose scapegoat to explain behavior by the victims of US and European policies who choose to use violence to strike back at them. But to argue that the economic and cultural dynamics and consequences of globalization have nothing to do with the ideologies and activities of Muslim extremists and/or terrorist groups is to fail to appreciate how the cultural and economic aspects of globalization are tied together. On the other hand, the US was attacked by al-Qa'eda because of its relationship to the Saudi regime, an economic and political relationship that, as we saw in the last chapter, is very much related to globalization. Moreover, the implantation of US troops on Saudi soil is continually described as a matter of "honor" for Arabs and Muslims, and a symbol of their subjugation, humiliation, and further marginalization in an era of supposed global integration. Finally, if bin Laden wasn't specifically responding to cultural globalization, the fact that he has such a strong following throughout the Arab world, which in turn generates more funds and ability to gain recruits, is certainly tied into global flows of culture and the political, military, and economic hierarchies to which they are bound.[49]

According to one of bin Laden's deputies, al-Qa'eda is in fact focusing significant effort on youth, who "are looking for advice on how to remove the Americans from this land ... Young Muslims today refuse to bow [their] heads to the Arab regimes' open conspiracy against the Islamic nation."[50] Similarly, at the Pakistani madrasas (religious schools) that remain fertile ground for recruiting new members among poor and otherwise illiterate people, Taliban teachers tell their young students that "Americans are killing Muslims in Afghanistan and Iraq, and they are busy trying to poison Muslim minds everywhere with films, music and television."[51]

Clearly, culture is crucial to the universe of al-Qa'eda and is closely linked to a critique of US military power and economic and foreign policies. As the Pakistan newspaper *Jang* argues, "the biggest tragedy of the Americans growing up in the vulgar culture is that they believe in the magic of money and incorrectly believe that money is the strongest and most decisive power in history." Instead, it is culture that drives bin Laden and others like him.[52]

It is impossible to separate the cultural from the economic dynamics; certainly bin Laden and his colleagues and deputies don't.[53] As a CIA analyst who's spent years tracking bin Laden frankly admitted, the United States' "imperial hubris," coupled with its reliance on so-called experts who have little knowledge of the current realities and dynamics in the Muslim world and Americans' "focus on making a buck" and "insular eagerness to get on with life and pursue personal and local interests" have together left Americans "singularly unprepared to really hear what Osama bin Laden has been saying ..."[54]

If we look at his 1996 "Declaration of War Against the Americans Occupying the Land of the Two Holy Places" we see it combines an extended attack on the mismanagement of the Saudi economy (which resonates widely in a country whose incredible oil wealth goes mostly to service the debauchery of its rulers and its massive debt burden while more and more well-educated Saudi men have no prospects of ever finding a job in the kingdom), at the same time it offers a cultural attack on the "Jews and Crusaders" believed to be subjugating Islam.[55] We can even understand bin Laden as playing a classic revolutionary's role in the form – but certainly not content – of Gandhi, Che Guevara or Subcommandante Marcos precisely because he brands himself as a figure who, unlike most others in his society, has the courage to take on a system of which he is very much a product, and in many ways, a beneficiary.[56] (The problem, of course, lies in the way in which he's chosen to attack the system that has oppressed so many people as opposed to other "revolutionary" heroes.)

Indeed, the situation in Saudi Arabia demonstrates clearly the fundamental link between culture and development. We know that many Muslims who are drawn to extremist politics and even violence come from backgrounds of poverty and feel a lack of alternatives to violence; on the other hand, the nineteen hijackers who flew into the World Trade Center were not poor, and their time in the West in fact allowed them opportunities many Saudis only dream of. Most likely, the anomie described earlier that inhabited their psyches only made the situation worse. Yet the hijackers could have returned to the kingdom with truly radical ideas – radically progressive ideas based on the growing global peace and justice movement that could have formed the groundwork for challenging one of the most oppressive regimes on earth. Of course such views could easily have landed them in jail if not the executioner's block, while those of bin Laden were subsidized by the elite of their society. But did they suffer any less or get any closer to Paradise dying in a jet-turned-cruise missile rather than as a *mujahid*, or soldier, for human rights and social justice?

Why did the hijackers choose the terrible path that led them to the skies above lower Manhattan rather than taking the struggle back home in innumerable creative but non-violent ways? Perhaps, like Sayyid Qutb, they were radicalized by their experiences of living in the West. Perhaps for them Europe and/or America represented a culture that they knew their societies couldn't attain, yet couldn't resist either. And it is because of this reality that it's ludicrous to argue, as do Thomas Friedman and lesser pundits, that these Lexuses or McDonald's are "the best weapon against terrorism."[57] Seeing purple-haired, motorcycle-cruising Kuwaiti punkers wearing bin Laden T-shirts – one poll showed that most likely a majority of Kuwaitis think bin Laden is an "Arab hero and an Islamic Jihad" warrior – should give one cause to think about just how far the US has alienated itself in the hearts and minds of even the one people who owe it their very national existence. And when we consider that 82.7 percent of respondents to a 2001 al-Jazeera internet poll agreed with this sentiment – and remember that only the richest 2 percent of the Arab world even has access to the internet – we can imagine how the poorer and less educated Arabs and Muslims feel.[58]

Beyond just the Muslim world, it is increasingly clear that in much of the Global South bin Laden is perceived as a latter-day Che Guevara; in fact, one of his associates in Lebanon made just this comparison on a call-in show on al-Jazeera, while an al-Qa'eda official described bin Laden as "the symbol that the nation has been seeking for a long time."[59] Even in a primarily Hindu neighborhood of Calcutta, India, where centuries of Muslim rule and the current conflict over Kashmir have left Hindu–Muslim relations tense under the best of circumstances, the most popular street play (or Jatia) is a reenactment of September 11 where the audience cheers the destruction of the towers, and boos and throws food at the representation of the US.[60] Bin Laden has, in this globalized era, become a cultural symbol, even cipher, par excellence, of the anxieties, fears, and suffering of all those left behind or out of neoliberal globalization.

And so for Muslims especially, but also for others who feel victimized by the New World Order (or whatever their order happens to be, new or old), al-Qa'eda has become the response of those whose imagination is limited to the creation of "resistance identities" that only know how to fight back against, rather than overcome or transcend, the status quo. The question that I will raise later on, and which is, I believe, absolutely crucial for the global peace and justice movement to pay attention to, is how other models, Muslim and not, can compete with bin Laden. Might Subcommandante Marcos inspire disaffected Muslims as much as he has inspired Latin Americans and their supporters worldwide?

Maybe. According to a young Palestinian activist, 'Ala al-Azzeh, who lives and works in a Bethlehem refugee camp, the Zapatistas represent an important and as yet untried model for resisting Israeli occupation. And a few brave Iranians have actually spent quite a bit of time with the Zapatistas in Chiapas, translating their writings into Persian, and trying to bring their philosophy to the student union in Iran – which might account for their relative success compared with their Arab counterparts who, to my knowledge, have yet to spend a summer in Chiapas. But with Muslim moderates in places like Indonesia desperately trying to liberate the "lush Islam" of the archipelago from the arid "Arabism of bin Laden's Islam," perhaps the "mountains of the Mexican East" (Chiapas) where Marcos lives can provide some much-needed inspiration. We'll discuss this possibility in the last two chapters.

Al-Qa'eda as a Symptom of the Modernity Matrix

While ideologically bin Laden and his followers are certainly self-described enemies of the West – indeed, of anyone, even Muslims, who don't share their violent vision of world revolution – we must be careful not to assume that al-Qa'eda and similar groups are somehow "unmodern" or "traditionalist." Notwithstanding its 1996 "declaration of war" on the United States, its "bitter hostility" to modern nation-states (and especially corrupt Muslim regimes), its labeling of Muslims who don't support it as "infidels," and its desire to spread its version of a "true Islam" that is starkly at odds with the existing world system, al-Qa'eda is a quintessentially modern and even globalizational phenomenon.

And I don't mean just the cliché that al-Qa'eda's intricate system of worldwide financing and decentralized operations represent a quintessentially modern, even global, phenomenon. As John Gray writes in his recent book *Al Qaeda and What it Means to be Modern*, "the ideology of Al Qaeda is both Western and modern. Itself a byproduct of globalization's transnational capital flows and open borders, al-Qaeda's utopian zeal to remake the world descends from the same Enlightenment creed that informed both the disastrous Soviet experiment and the neoliberal dream of a global free market."[61] Indeed, the same dynamics are at play in all "fundamentalist" religious movements, including American Protestant ones, and are deeply tied to the similar impetus at the heart of both capitalism and colonialism.[62]

On the ideological level, its extremist utopian and revolutionary ideology shares many parallels with the classic "Jacobin" (that is, republican-nationalist) ideologies that have terrorized citizens around the world since the original terrorists of the French post-Revolutionary Jacobin regime, to Marxist/Maoist states, and more recently, to secular guerrilla-terror groups of the 1970s. More deeply, even their desire for "America to stop interfering between us and the tyrannical governments which rule Muslims and for us to set up an Islamic caliphate (state)" (as one al-Qa'eda proclamation after the multiple bombings in Istanbul in November 2003 put it) does not represent a "traditional" or atavistic notion. This is because by their very existence all contemporary religious states no matter what their ideology or how they see themselves, cannot be anything but fully modern: the very concept and structure of the institution of the "modern nation-state" makes it impossible for them to be anything else.

Even al-Qa'eda's desire to kill as many civilians as possible is not an aberration, for the widespread use of mass killing perfected by Stalin, Hitler, and their counterparts has been shown to be a peculiarly modern phenomenon that is shared by the leaders of the Khmer Rouge, Rwandan Hutus, Bosnian Serbs, and other ruthless and/or puritanical (in the widest sense of the term) political movements. In fact, as we saw in Chapter Two the need to "purify" is one of the hallmarks of being modern. And so we must see Osama bin Laden as a "thoroughly modern Muslim" – certainly no less so than more moderate Islamist forces, despite their profound ideological differences: both seek to modernize their societies and politics, recast tradition from a modern viewpoint, believe that there is more than one way to be modern, and both try to ally themselves with the still more numerous "traditionalist" sectors of Muslim societies, who are generally less educated, believing in mystical and personal authority and skeptical of modern social forms, even as they are harshly critical of traditional religious authorities and beliefs. And since contemporary modernity is global modernity, al-Qa'eda is clearly a creature of globalization too: "global, decentralized, and ruthless," as innumerable websites describe it.

But what even the most insightful critics of modernity generally don't take into account is that al-Qa'eda – or at least the radically utopian and egalitarian (for Muslim men, that is) vision that the movement is said to represent – is also *anti*-modern in the sense that it rejects many of the core ideological components of the modern project. Not just democracy and so-called secularism, but the entire psychological infrastructure inherited from colonialism and capitalist exploitation. In short, they've given up on the possibility of modernity delivering on its promises, even as they make good use of the most modern technologies, communications media, budgeting or bureaucratization techniques. This is what makes deciphering al-Qa'eda and Islamic radicalism more broadly so difficult, never mind building a set of counter-arguments that would appeal to millions of young Arabs and Muslims.[63] Yet al-Qa'eda's rejection of much of the ideology of modernity does provide hints of what kind of ideology progressives need to develop to attract its constituency.

In perhaps the most original and important analysis of al-Qa'eda I've seen, Georgetown University professor John Voll explains how recruitment videos made by bin Laden

> emphasize a significant dimension of global conflicts and interactions that the religio-cultural models often ignore: the importance of raw physical, military power in shaping the contemporary "world order." Many of the most powerful images in the film are those of military force. The repetition of pictures of large tanks in battle formation and of soldiers ... pushing and beating children and Islamically-dressed women emphasize the military and force dimensions of the situation ... The words of the songs and the exhortations as well as the visual images of the film emphasize that the conflict in which bin Laden and those associated with the film are involved is, in many important ways, an issue of power. The constant reference to the Quranic message and the mission of Islam provides a religious framing for the presentation, but the subject of the presentation is power and how the

power of the forces that have suppressed and exploited Muslims can be countered and defeated.[64]

This is a crucial analysis, because it shows, against the view of Chomsky recounted above, that power and culture are inseparable, especially in the global era with the way images are constructed and deployed around the world instantaneously and help shape people's experience of the world. The Egyptians sitting in McDonald's mentioned above by Chomsky may be economically well off, but that does not mean that culturally they don't feel under assault – not by McDonald's, Coke or Disney per se (and certainly not as isolated phenomena), but rather by the entirety and enormity of the inundation of foreign products and the lifestyles they represent into all aspects of their lives. Voll continues, "There are virtually no images of McWorld as the enemy in this recruitment video. Instead, the enemy is defined in terms of the military power of the 'Crusaders.' It is important in this regard to note that the film concentrates on the *military* occupation of the Arabian Islamic holy land … The conflict is presented not as a clash of cultures and lifestyles, or even of civilizations. It is presented as a conflict between righteous but weak peoples who are oppressed and subjugated by the tremendous physical power of an unbelieving enemy."[65]

What Voll does not mention, however, is the psychological impact of being constantly inundated with the message that to be modern you need to wear clothes and eat food – that is, surrounding your body with and literally ingesting products – that are not just "foreign" to your cultural heritage, but are made by (or at least symbolically represent or signify)[66] the nation who is oppressing you. On top of this, we need to recall the mental ledger of Europe's and America's imperial exploits (at the beginning of Chapter Two) that remains in the mind of almost every Arab or Muslim.

Together, this cultural universe accounts for the desire of many Muslims to wear "traditional" clothing which if not locally made at least has a Muslim "logo"; or to drink the recently invented "Mecca Cola" rather than its Crusader counterpart, or even to shop at the Mecca Mall.[67] And because of this, we can't separate the way culture is deployed by al-Qa'eda from issues of power. Voll is right that "'modernity' is not so much an issue as is the power that modernity has given to people who are viewed as unbelievers," but the reason bin Laden is able to mobilize the weak and the powerless is because he offers a simple, coherent, and appealing cultural program that starts with attacking the financial and military foundations of global modernity (with the World Trade Center and Pentagon attacks, quite literally).[68]

Beyond bin Laden: Contemporary Arab and Muslim Understandings of Globalization

Since September 11 bin Laden and his kind of rhetoric and terrorist actions have dominated the news and mainstream discussions of the MENA and Islam more generally. This is natural; certainly scholars – and while we're at it, the CIA and MI6 – should be devoting greater attention to understanding the ideologies and dynamics of al-Qa'eda and similar movements. What is wrong, however, are the increasingly harsh attacks on scholars for devoting their energy to investigating the reality of how duplicitous, counter-productive, and just plain immoral US policies towards the region have long been, not to mention the assumption by conservatives that the function of scholars is to figure out what makes al-Qa'eda tick so "we" can defeat "them" (isn't that the job of the intelligence community?).

Indeed, anyone who truly wants to understand why "they" are so angry at "us" would do well to consider the sordid history of colonization and support for authoritarian regimes by Europeans and now the US in the MENA. With this background could we blame most Arab critics for viewing globalization in a uniformly negative light – definitely not as violently hostile as al-Qa'eda, but certainly with little support for its goals and impact? Not really, but the reality is that they don't view it this way. If we move beyond the blaring headlights of al-Qa'eda and the strident language of the kind of extremist interpretations of Islam derived from certain cultural traditions within the religion (such as the Hanbali legal school, Ibn Taymiyya, Saudi-inspired Wahhabism, and some very conservative Shi'i scholars) a much more critical, in the sense of well-reasoned, understanding of globalization and the contemporary world more broadly emerges.

As we've already seen, a review of the recent literature on globalization reveals that while most scholars are critical of American-dominated globalization they nevertheless believe that it is a natural process – "neither Hell nor Heaven" – from which the Arab/Muslim world cannot opt out.[69] Instead, the main issue is how to profit from it (both economically and in terms of incorporating universal norms such as human rights and educational reform) without losing too much of one's culture, hurting the poorest members of society, and allowing it to "hollow us out from the inside and domesticate our ... identity."[70]

Since culture in this context is so important from a global perspective the main question is whether globalization will lead to the building of a world civilization based on peace between peoples, or merely to an entrenchment of cultural (as well as political, military, and economic) Americanization.[71] In exploring this issue the majority of Arab and Muslim critics (other than economists such as Samir Amin) are more concerned about cultural issues: about the potential of the "globalization wave" to sabotage and perhaps even destroy the "Islamic Personality" if not neutralized by an Arab/Muslim cultural and economic resurgence.

If a Muslim personality is not rebuilt, the "poisoned idols" of capitalism and now globalization will continue to infect the people. This will lead to a "planned exchange" with true Muslims that will make it impossible for a Muslim personality to develop that can stand its ground.[72] It is interesting to note that such sentiments are as prevalent in Iraq in 2005 as they've been in Cairo, Algiers or Beirut during the past decade.[73]

One of the main reasons Arab/Muslim critics fear globalization is that the consumer/materialist culture feared to be at its heart will tear down the more traditional borders and identities erected and maintained by their religion and more recently nation-states.[74] And here that "symbol of globalization, the www" (as Thomas Friedman argues) plays an important but ambivalent role in their thinking. For many critics the internet and other global means of communication are of little help in responding to the threats to their identities, as the cybercommunities of the internet age are like "new nations ... unconnected to geography or history"; they do not foster freedom but rather destroy the meaning of citizenship by substituting the "right" merely to shop and communicate on the web for the right to participate in the real politics of the body politic.[75]

Perhaps the most eye-catching depiction of this perceived dynamic is the cover of one popular book on globalization that depicts (in the fashion of an old dime-store novel) the American cowboy lassoing the world (another book shows an American octopus with tentacles spread over the world (a symbol that is also used by anti-globalization activists to criticize the WTO).[76] Once the cowboy ropes the Muslim societies into the globalized world order it will enable a "conquest by the infidels of Muslims' capabilities" by establishing an alternative leading social class that would introduce, as we've already seen, "materialist culture."[77]

So once again we see the strong link between the "assault" against the "deep cultural roots" of Arab/Muslim identity by cultural globalization and the struggle over "the world's purse strings" in which it is imbedded.[78] In both cases people are led (if not forced) by the United States to withdraw loyalty from their "cultural national identity." This in turn fractures the already unstable state in which the people's collective identity resides, and ultimately causes the extinction of independent cultural assertions such as Arab nationalist thought.[79]

Despite the harsh criticism of globalization by secular and religious critics alike – much of which, we should bear in mind, is now shared around the world – most Arab/Muslim critics are more concerned with surviving in and even profiting from, rather than opting out of, what is viewed ultimately as a natural process.[80] But for this to occur, issues of human rights, education, and especially democracy are crucial. As one writer evocatively describes the relationship between democracy and development, they are "like the wings of a plane – you can't fly with one wing."[81]

Such sentiments are also shared by self-professed "moderate Islamists" (in Arabic, known collectively as the "*wasatiyya* movement"), whose leaders have explicitly criticized the more extreme views of bin Laden and of more pedestrian conservative/orthodox Muslim theologians and politicians, for doing inestimable damage to Islam and Muslims. Thinkers such as Egypt's Yusuf al-Qaradawi, Tunisia's Rachid Ghannouchi, Morocco's Abdesalam Yassine, and their younger counterparts in the Arab – and indeed, all the Muslim – world (whom I discuss in more detail below) have all gone to great lengths to deal with the "chaos" of the emerging global era and reformulate key aspects of their faith to re-establish Islam in the most holistic manner possible. And this includes, by the way, issues related to gender equality, which as we saw above are supposedly the fault line between Islam and the West.

If we read the texts of these writers it becomes clear that while they're not about to join the Age of Aquarius, they are trying to reconcile the need for women to have the real freedom to live and grow fully as human beings with equal rights to men with a cultural and religious heritage that, like Judaism and Christianity, has for millennia been hostile to such an idea. Yet while the majority of Muslim intellectuals and social activists are opposed to neoliberal globalization, a new breed of Muslim "televangelists" increasingly preach the values of personal success, self-awareness, and getting rich – what some have labeled an "air-conditioned Islam" that is as at home in the Mecca Mall as in the mosque.[82] For some commentators this trend actually signals both a "depoliticization of Islam" and an "Islamization of neoliberalism"; but it would be wrong to see the newer generation (in Arabic known as *al-jil al-jadid*) of moderate Islamists and their televangelists merely as founders or exponents of the sort of "liberal Islam" for which Western scholars and policymakers have been searching for decades.

Indeed, at the same time that religious figures young and old call for Muslims to see that the West can be *dar al-Islam* (that is, a land of peace), that democracy and (something quite approaching) "Western" notions of gender equality are Islamically sanctioned (and even required), or that Muslims should fully engage in dialogue with other cultures, they remain quite critical of the policies of Western governments and the ideologies behind them. We can actually see the *wasatiyya* Islamists as being as critical of and opposed to modernity as their more extreme colleagues. For example, the Moroccan Sheikh Yassine rails against "armed capitalist modernity," using a phrase that echoes the description by the philosopher George Sorel of the inherent similarity between "the capitalist type and the warrior type." His view arose from the recognition that modernity has never lived up to its billing as the herald of freedom, justice, and democracy. More broadly, Yassine urges all people to "address modernity with questions it has no interest in, and which its citizens haven't the time to ask … [because] two way communication is beyond reach with a modernity that is comfortably installed in a way of life hardly troubled" by the misery it produces.[83]

What we learn from the writings of so-called moderate figures like Sheikh Yassine is the desire for "concluding a pact of mutual aid among humankind that crosses the boundaries of state structures and goes above the heads of official institutions. [For Islam] this is our ideal of beneficence strictly bound to our ideal of spiritual perfection. This plan for a worldwide humanitarian coalition responds to the utopian dream and the actuality of the flagrant imbalance that rages between north and south." Subcommandante Insurgente Marcos would find much to appreciate in this, although I doubt Osama bin Laden or George W. Bush would agree. In the Conclusion we'll see just how hard it is to achieve such a goal in what as I write is the chaotic epicenter of militarized neoliberal globalization, Iraq.

The younger generation of religious intellectuals and activists can be even harsher with their criticism of both the West and Islam. And so Sheikh Yassine's daughter, Nadia, who is one of the most powerful Muslim women political figures in the world, argues that in many ways Islam was hijacked by men – that is, literally, men, not men and women – after the era of the first four rulers (the "Rightly Guided Caliphs"), who distorted its message of tolerance and equality (including between the sexes) in favor of a vision based on power and patriarchy.[84]

What is most important, given our discussion of the importance of power above, she continues by arguing that "Lord Acton said: 'Power corrupts, and absolute power corrupts absolutely.' So where to seek vaccination against those deadly viruses of lust of power, intolerance, violence etc. ...? Here spirituality and morality come to center-stage. So long as all the social groups within a society do not partake in the formulation of a consensus-and-conciliation oriented communal project, room will be left to extremists who will fish the troubled waters to thwart any attempts to interpret Islam in a different manner."

This is a crucial vision, one shared by leading European Muslim intellectual and activist Tariq Ramadan, who argues that "During the Prophet's life he came with a liberating process but after he died the message was hijacked by people, jurists and scholars more interested in the power and the discrimination against women. What this means is that we had a religion originally coming with universal values, which allows/allowed us to take everything that wasn't against our principles as Muslims."

The attempts recounted above by moderate and progressive religious Muslims, young and older, to find new readings of sacred texts of religious law that support full freedom and democracy for *all* Muslims is sympathetic with the work of more secular Muslim thinkers, such as the Moroccan cultural studies professor Taieb Belghazi.[85] Viewing the situation from an understandably Mediterranean vantage point, his insight is to stop attempting to build one unitary Mediterranean sphere (which has been the goal of the so-called "Barcelona Process" since the mid-1990s)[86] and instead accept the existence of – and in so doing, help to foster – "plural Mediterraneans." Though not an Islamist thinker, his inspiration for accomplishing this is to recognize the Mediterranean Sea as what the Qur'an terms a "*barzakh*," which in the Qur'an and in Sufism means the isthmus or peninsula of land that separates the bitter and sweet oceans representing Heaven and the material world, but which Belghazi uses to mean a limit or barrier between different experiences which can't be simply transcended.[87]

For Sufis the peninsula symbolizes the "perfect Muslim," for Belghazi the *barzakh* represents a "liminal" or in-between space, where differences are not homogenized à la neoliberal globalization, but instead are allowed to remain heterogeneous and at the surface, defining people's consciousness at the same time they allow a space for new, hybrid identities to develop.[88] (And indeed, Indonesia, where there is a huge struggle between militantly extremist and liberal-moderate Islam, is also the home to the Barzakh Foundation, which bills itself as a "non-profit Islamic organization which was founded by a group of young Moslem intellectuals" who seek to focus on developing Sufi approaches to dealing with poverty, education and even HIV/AIDS.)[89] The focus on hybridity – of what we will recall one Arab commentator described when thinking of democracy as "the right to be different" – is crucial because it allows for the creation of and respect for identities that are plural, rather than trying to break down and suppress some in favor of others as neoliberal globalization is feared to do.

Turkey and the Rise of Sufi Republicans

The views we've been discussing until now have been primarily from the Arab world. Yet Turkey and Iran present perhaps the most interesting cases in the MENA region of how the experiences of and responses to globalization continuously change within societies. The first time I visited Turkey I checked into my hotel just a block off the Bosphorus and went out for a walk through what is surely one of the greatest cities of the world, Istanbul. But what surprised me more than the sights of the city was Turkish television. I don't mean the imported stations from Germany or other European countries, but rather Turkish TV.

And it wasn't ads for phone sex; rather it was the videos on the local Turkish equivalent of MTV. The scantily dressed singers were a bit unexpected in an ostensibly Muslim country, to be sure. But most important for me was the mix of musical styles – flamenco, rock, and traditional Turkish Arabesque music mixed together in the same song to produce music with energy and originality that was downright infectious. I ran right out to the local bazaar and bought as many Turkish pop music cassettes as I could afford, and I wasn't disappointed.

We know from Chapter Two how Turkey, and the Ottoman Empire before it, have been a bridge between Europe and Asia for much of the last millennium. For two centuries at least Ottoman and then Turkish elites have identified themselves increasingly as part of Europe – to the point of seeking African "colonies" and viewing Arabs as "backward" – even as they've been (and to a certain extent, remain) the foil against which the identity of "Europe" has been defined.[90] With Ataturk and the founders of the post-Ottoman Turkish state in 1921 there was no longer any question of where Turkey's loyalties should lie; it was to be a "reformist, republican (militantly), secular, nationalist, populist, and statist country." In short, fully modern and equal to Europe while fully retaining its independence.

To make sure citizens of the new republic got the point Ataturk outlawed supposedly "traditional" clothing like the fez (which was, ironically, the symbol of the formerly dominant Ottoman self-perception as a modern nation, the call to prayer in Arabic), and other symbols of the old regime and its failed attempts to modernize. And by joining NATO after World War II, and more recently establishing strong relations with Israel, the Turkish state has attempted permanently to cement its status as a country firmly of, and even in, the West.

But just because Turkish leaders have sought to become fully Western doesn't mean that the majority of the population ever bought into this philosophy. Indeed, there has long been and remains significant tension between the state and millions of its citizens who don't agree with the way the state has framed a "Western," "secular," and "modern" future (whatever these terms actually mean). Instead, while desiring to develop and progress like their counterparts to the West, the majority of Turks outside of the elite have fought to retain their cultural and religious traditions, and despite state control of religious institutions, religion has since the birth of the Republic remained one of the few areas of life where people could retain an identity and set of values not dictated from above.

And so it's no surprise that after decades of a military-dominated statist political system Turks turned to Islamist parties in the 1980s and 1990s as the political system opened slightly. Two major religious parties, Refah (Welfare) and Fazilet (Virtue), were established and subsequently closed by the military in the 1990s; their strong public base of support was due precisely to their simultaneous focus on preserving the country's Muslim identity while criticizing the corruption and lack of democracy of the state.[91] Both parties and the larger movements they represented were at the forefront of a process of "re-Islamization" of Turkey that was both a product and enabler of globalization.[92] Their views were ultimately suspicious of, if not hostile to, the West and Europe in particular, but such sentiments did not emerge out of an ideological predisposition against the West or Europe. Instead they were largely reactions to the continued hostility of European governments and publics to integrating Turkey fully into the EU during the 1980s and early 1990s.

The views of the more outspoken and critical Turkish Islamists are perhaps best symbolized by the writings of the one-time Leftist turned Islamist social critic Ali Bulaç. Bulaç has long seen modernity as being based on "colonial fundamentals" that "make people more and more dependent to the West ... create a monolithic world and thus destroy customs and traditions all over the world." For him the replacement of the "unity" of religion with the "affluence" of capitalism has "led to chaos, and what is occurring in the modern world currently is this state of chaos." This chaos, which is also the way that *wasatiyya* Arab thinkers like Qaradawi view globalization, requires that Muslims replace the "world view of the modernity" with the "Islamic ideal."[93] As we'll see in the Conclusion, similar views are emerging out of the chaos of Iraq, and reveal crucial but as yet unappreciated insights about the core dynamics of contemporary globalization.

In fact, for Bulaç the challenge facing the Muslim world in the era of globalization is symbolized by the US invasion of Iraq. As he wrote in criticizing the devotion of Turks and Muslims more generally to the Eurovision Song contest,

> Turkey is at the stage of being "a model country" on this matter. We have become a pornographic society but we don't even realize it – and we are not even perturbed by it. Our most important export products are our pop and arabesque music artists. To be willing to send Ibrahim Tatlises, Hulya Avsar, Sibel Can to Iraq – and in future Petek Dincoz and Nez might also join them – is part of this regional plan. If one day Nez finds the opportunity to give a concert, where she will be able to display all her femininity in Baghdad, there won't be anything left to resist. Because she will tell them, "Don't! Don't resist, Watch me!" And meanwhile of course, the dollars from Iraq's crude will go into the pockets of others and the West and Israel will settle in the region even more.[94]

Not surprisingly, I would disagree with his moral criticism of popular Turkish music. But what's clear is the importance of the cultural dimension in analyzing globalization, even in the context of the military occupation of Iraq. As he continues: "The unpronounced aim of those who want to bring democracy to the whole region starting with Iraq in the frame of social engineering is to shelve Islam's claim that hasn't been completed yet and to integrate the whole region into the global system."[95]

What is most important about the writings of Bulaç and his colleagues[96] is that because the points of view they represent have a stake – however tenuous – in a semi-democratic political system, they have not been as opposed to engagement with Europe as they might otherwise have been. Indeed, ultimately it's been hard for this line of thought to retain significant influence in Turkish society, even when (as of early 2004) Turkey has a fairly stable Islamist government. A primary reason for this can be described in one word: Europe. For most Turks the single most important economic, political, and cultural objective in the recent past and near future is to join the European Union. Indeed, while the Refah Party and its intellectual allies often voiced negative views on the issue of joining the EU, today there is widespread support even among Islamist figures for joining it.[97]

What makes Turkey so interesting vis-à-vis contemporary globalization is that, unlike Arab countries where Islamist thinkers and politicians have been largely critical of neoliberal globalization, in Turkey new Islamist movements have emerged to challenge the heavy and often stifling hand of the state; they represent a resurgent Turkish bourgeoisie class of merchants and businesspeople whose progress has been stifled by it. And so they see privatization and other liberalizing reforms as a way to strengthen their power and economic opportunities.[98]

As important, since the late 1990s the most important proponents of the growing Islamist resurgence in Turkey have been Sufi orders, especially the movement led by Fetullah Gülen, which rapidly spread to become one of the most important Sufi movements in the world (certainly in Turkey).[99] Gülen's movement, which has evolved out of the Nurcu Sufi order (whose founder, Said Nursi, advocated the compatibility of Islam and science), has long focused its message on self-help, civic participation, education, and industry. It resembles 1950s bootstrap Republicanism in the US – particularly in the subordinate role offered to women in his movement – as much as it does liberal Islam.

Working through the main Turkish association of religiously oriented small and medium-sized businesses (MUSIAD),[100] the Gülen movement demonstrates that for many religiously oriented Turks succeeding in business becomes an important ideological, indeed, religious, goal (much like the "Protestant Ethic"), to which other political or social goals become subservient.[101] This dynamic has had a profound impact on the political scene in Turkey, and in 2003 helped elect as Prime Minister an Islamist-leaning former mayor of Istanbul, Recep Erdogan,[102] whose Justice and Development Party is made up largely of younger and pragmatic "modern Islamists" that "increasingly challenge the antimodern, dogmatic policies of the former [Islamist] prime minister."[103]

And so today in Turkey we see an approach to globalization, fundamentally driven by the need and desire to integrate fully with Europe, which has led even Turkish Islamist politics to advocate a European-parliamentary-style "Muslim democracy" loosely patterned on the Christian democratic parties of its neighbors to the West. Even when they criticize neoliberal globalization for a "lack of sensitivity needed to build and maintain peace" and "inequalities on the behalf of developed countries and feeds political instability," they feel that Turkey, "with its historical heritage and with its identity blending Western and Eastern civilizations," is uniquely qualified to act as a guide and facilitator of a new global civilization.[104]

Conclusion: Iran and the Importance of Young People Leading the Dialogue

Iran is a very interesting case, because it is clear that until quite recently, and even still today, there is much less debate over "globalization" than there is in either the Arab world or in Turkey. Although this has changed in the last few years, the relative lack of interest is probably because of the strength of the ideology governing the Islamic Republic which, even though it is becoming weaker by the day, is still powerful enough to set the terms of the debate. This is not to say that many of the same issues taken up by Arab writers haven't been addressed by Iranians. It is clear that the "Western cultural invasion" has been a primary topic for Iranian critics at least since the time of Jalal al-e Ahmed. But in Iran such a discourse was specifically put forth not by opposition figures, but rather by the Khomeinist state.

If during Khomeini's rule the West was vilified and demonized, today it's likely that a majority of the ruling elite understands that the cultural effects of the emerging globalization are not predetermined. Even for more conservative religious figures cultural globalization has "some attractive things," while the problems it causes are not unique to Iran or Islam.[105] As one conservative Ayatollah explained, "The problem of cultural invasion is not just with Iran. China, Malaysia, Japan, South Korea and France have already allocated parts of their budgets to efforts to contain the invasion of American culture."[106] At the same time, however, "the western cultural invasion reveals the will of certain powers to put their cultural dominance on the world." And through satellites, which were banned in Iran (officially, although in practice they flourished), the West has succeeded in creating a "Western cultural occupation" of people's most private spaces – the home.

For conservatives such an assault has necessitated the regime to propagate a "culture of abnegation and sacrifice," especially with the beginning of the war with Iraq. But such a culture holds little attraction to young people, and so in Iran, with one of the youngest populations in the world, this created a situation in which the younger generation, already suffering by the end of the war "from a lack of hope," saw its situation exacerbated by the impact of structural adjustment programs, whose economic impact only served as the pretext for the Government to use the "cultural invasion" discourse as an excuse to arrest critics.[107]

In the last half decade the situation changed greatly. Iranian President Khatemi exerted considerable energy on his "dialogue among civilizations" project, which he pushed everywhere from UN speeches to articles in Russian encyclopedias. Although suppressed somewhat after the conservative election-coup of 2004, the space opened by the wide public support for Khatemi's attempts to reform the country's political and religious system allowed younger religious figures, even up to the level of Ayatollah, to reform the laws of the Islamic Republic – and in so doing, Islamic law more broadly – to provide for greater gender equality and more freedom, democracy, and individual rights for all citizens.[108]

In fact, while we can criticize Khatemi's uncritical acceptance of the supposed reality of two separate civilizations (how else could they come together to dialogue as distinct units?), it is undeniable that he is tapping into progressive themes when he advocates a dialogue of civilization as a "means of humanizing the process of globalization ... Globalization should not be utilized to open greater markets for a few or to assimilate national cultures into a uniform global one." But like most commentators on globalization from the Global South, Khatemi criticizes the "misuses" of globalization and the belief by the US that "all the world must move to the tune of a superior power as the nucleus of the world" (which he believes is caused by those with science, wealth, and technology using it to increase their power).[109]

It would seem that Khatemi's dialogue of civilizations project is specifically designed to counter claims that Iran is part of the Axis of Evil, or that there is a "clash of civilizations" that puts it on the other side of an unbridgeable East–West divide.[110] And in this framework even more conservative leaders like former Foreign Minister Ali-Akbar Velayati argue that globalization is inevitable and Iran should "clear its way" by gaining necessary information on its global dimension. What is interesting about this sentiment is that it has opened space for criticism of the still heavily state-centered economy and the economic inefficiency it generates.[111]

These sentiments are a far cry from Khomeini's original vision of Islamic revolution.[112] Yet we must remember that while Khatemi advocates a "coalition for peace as the key to uprooting terrorism," the Iranian state remains an incredibly repressive regime that has sponsored, supported or given refuge to a range of terrorist groups worldwide and is likely on the way to developing nuclear weapons.[113] Moreover, the democratic setback of the 2004 Iranian parliamentary elections reminds us not to overestimate the power of Khatemi's discourse of dialogue.[114] For in fact the inability of the Khatemi Government to translate progressive-sounding rhetoric into concrete political reforms (particularly curtailing the power of the much more conservative Council of Guardians) has led to a situation where dialogue is becoming more difficult among competing social forces.[115]

Indeed, on the level of what we can call Iran's "street politics,"[116] Iranians are losing faith in the Government and are increasingly creating a parallel society where the Government doesn't factor in it at all. For the poor this might mean the gray or black markets, for the more wealthy it means wearing designer clothes under chadors, paying off the religious/morality police, or holding big "charity balls" in Western embassies (the British Embassy being the most popular) where people can party all night without fear that the Komités will crash the festivities, as embassies are legally extraterritorial spaces.

But there is also good news in Iran, in which the globalization of issues such as gender equality and democracy have played an important part. A younger generation of religious scholars has emerged in Iran that is willing to challenge the existing conservative and patriarchal understandings of Islamic law with a "dynamic jurisprudence" that combines the insights of religion, science, and history in order to foster legal interpretations that support gender equality.[117] For example, Abdelkarim Soroush, who like Tariq Ramadan has been called a Muslim "Luther," sees interreligious dialogue and a search for common truths based on "reason and freedom" as crucial to engaging globalization in a positive manner.[118]

While the younger generation of religious figures gets most of the press, the reality is that the younger generation at large – especially the millions of Iranian Gen-Xers and their Gen-Y brothers and sisters – is pushing the boundaries of Iranian identity ever further outwards toward its one-time enemies in the West, with music, fashion, and culture more broadly perhaps the primary arena in the struggle for Iran's soul. In this framework it is the student movement that has become the embodiment of the thrust for change in Iran, just as it was a generation ago when students helped bring down the Shah's regime. But this time, having learned the lessons of Khomeini's hijacking of their revolution, the movement is explicitly stating that "although we have differing views for a post theocracy Iran, we are united based on our shared beliefs in non-violent resistance, secularism, peace, democracy and free markets."[119]

The questions remain whether a push for secularism will alienate progressive religious thinkers, and whether peace and democracy can be achieved if "free markets" means the same thing as it does elsewhere in the Global South. In the next chapter we'll explore these struggles and what they tell us about the future of globalization and global solidarity in the MENA.

6 Facing the Music: Rock and Resistance in the Middle East and North Africa

Ozzy Vs. Osama

Ali Bulaç and Ayatollah Khomeini might not approve, but the reality is that the listening habits and in some cases "performance" styles of young people are crucial locations for exploring the complicated nature of cultural globalization in the MENA. This is because more than most segments of society, popular youth culture has the social space – and even expectation – to be intolerant of the hypocrisies and injustices of the dominant culture. (When the bulk of youth cultural production fails to question and even celebrates the dominant cultural paradigms we can assume there is either significant repression in a country or an abnormal level of deference to the ideologies and policies of the dominant group.) And so, as we'll explore at the end of the chapter, the stories underlying the arrests and trials of rock musicians and their fans in Morocco or Iran offer important clues about the subcultures at the forefront of resisting repressive regimes, and through them, about the society as a whole.

I first understood this point as a kid hanging out with my best friend, Dennis, who was from Yugoslavia. Dennis's older brother, Emil, was a metalhead. Rainbow, Deep Purple, Nazareth, especially Judas Priest and Black Sabbath – he worshiped them the way I loved Led Zeppelin or Santana. I couldn't understand why someone from behind the "Iron Curtain" could or would be so into hardcore heavy metal, especially when it was (at that time) somewhat marginal in the US. While I liked the music, I didn't understand what made these groups, with their dark personalities and in-your-face attitude, so particularly appealing to Emil and his peers on their small fishing island off the Croatian coast.

When I asked him to explain it, he told me the story of how rock music was banned in Eastern Bloc countries, and had to be smuggled in and sold on the black market along with Levi jeans. He and his friends would save up for months to get the latest Sabbath album and have clandestine parties to listen to it. Dressing in black leather, growing their hair long, listening to supposedly "obnoxious" music that according to their country's leaders "threatened" the morals and stability of their societies was for Emil and his friends a powerful means of resisting an oppressive political and cultural system that no longer spoke to them, except through repression and demands for conformity, and whose days, in their view, were numbered.

Why is this story relevant to our discussion? Once upon a time Ozzy Osbourne might have offended parents across America (before he became an icon of family values, however warped), but he really pissed off the Politburos of the Warsaw Pact. And so Muslim autocrats would do well to remember that in the end, Black Sabbath beat (or at least outlasted) Stalinism and its milder cousins in Yugoslavia and Czechoslovakia; there's no reason to imagine Ozzy or his musical heirs won't triumph over the oppressive regimes of the MENA as well.

Of course, as al-Jazeera reporter Omar al-Issawi once explained, when he was a Beirut radio DJ in civil-war-torn Beirut everyone's favorite music was heavy metal too. American tank soldiers interviewed in Michael Moore's *Fahrenheit 9/11* similarly showed off their heavy metal mix tapes that were blasted inside the tank when they went into battle. But however rock-'n'-roll is used in other settings, in the globalized MENA there's no reason to think that oppressive regimes in Casablanca or Tehran will ultimately fare any better against Ozzy, Rob Halford, or even Chuck D and Nas, than their aging, close-minded, and patriarchal counterparts did in the former Eastern Bloc. We can only hope that the revolutions to come will be more velvet than steel, whatever their soundtrack. I'll return to the more nefarious uses of heavy metal later in this chapter.

At this point in our discussion it might be useful to introduce you to a Moroccan musician named Reda Zine. Reda and I first "met" (I put this in quotes, because in fact all our meetings have been online or on the phone) in early 2004 when I was trying to find some Moroccan heavy-metal fans or musicians to explore the role of the music in the larger social struggles between young people and the state (upwards of two dozen fans and artists were jailed in early 2003 for "Satanism" and defaming Islam because they wore black T-shirts and listened to heavy metal). I finally found a website, which was in French, and sent an email in my bastardized French, to which Reda responded (naturally, in flawless French), explaining that he was in Italy and giving me a number to call him there to talk.

I wrote back explaining that my spoken Arabic was probably better than my French these days, so he sent the next email in an English transliteration of Arabic, to which I responded likewise (although using a very different transliteration, which confused both of us). Then when I called him, we started to speak Arabic, and then realized that we both know Italian. So the conversation quickly became quatra-lingual: mainly Arabic, but with bits of French, Italian, and when desperate, English words thrown in to fill in the gaps in our vocabularies. Finally we decided it was best to communicate in Italian via email because I don't have an Arabic email program, and we've been having fascinating discussions about the political role of heavy metal in Morocco and the aesthetic qualities of world music more broadly ever since then. If all goes well one day soon we'll be writing songs together and recording them by swapping digital files over the web (that is, if I can ever figure out how to use this software).

When I first contacted Reda I didn't expect to get much from the conversation. After all, in the US or Europe metalheads aren't exactly known for their intelligence, never mind social activism (the biggest heavy metal group in the world, Metallica, joined forces with the recording industry against Napster and free internet sharing of music). But it turns out that most of the musicians and fans are quite intelligent and socially active. Reda for one is finishing his Ph.D. at the Sorbonne on semiotics and aesthetics – which in France is as complex and rarefied a subject of study as quantum mechanics or artificial intelligence in the US. As Reda put, we clearly hit it off because we have "la même biographie" – musician-activist-academics.

My point in offering this little particular, virtual vignette of my wanderings through the MENA is to counter one of the more prominent and powerful arguments of the *Arab Human Development Report* and similar publications: that a major sign of the backwardness and stagnation of the Arab world is that so few foreign books are translated into Arabic. Apparently, more books are translated into Spanish each year in Spain than have been translated into Arabic in the whole Muslim world in recorded history. This is clearly a sad commentary on the Arab publishing industry, and on the larger societies as well, which haven't had the wherewithal to devote greater resources to translating crucial knowledge from abroad to their culture.

But it's only one indicator of cultural development, and perhaps not the best one at that. This is because, unlike Spanish-speaking countries, where the overwhelming percentage of citizens speak only Spanish, the MENA's history of colonization and migration have meant that an unusually large percentage of the literate population knows one major Western language (mostly French or English, but German as well, and even Italian). In fact, the average educated Arab is far more likely to know a foreign language than the average educated American. And so, at least from my own evidence traveling through the region, when many educated Arabs – and remember, Arabs have among the highest education levels of any developing region – want to read a foreign book, they'll likely read it in the original language.

Moreover, if you visit a college bookstore in the Arab world, you will quickly notice several things: first, that many science and business textbooks are sold in the original language; second, many of them are actually (and, I would assume, "illegally") photocopied versions of the books, since very few Arab students can afford US\$40–80 per text book; third, there are also (most likely unauthorized) translations of books available. So in reality the statistics on book translations, while important and even troubling, needs to be contextualized within a whole set of other factors – as much economic as they are cultural.

We can also mention that while the Arab and larger Muslim worlds are not big importers of foreign books, they are big exporters of their own culture. If you're reading this book, chances are you've seen or at least heard of the numerous Iranian films that win accolades and awards at film festivals worldwide. And throughout Europe and increasingly the United States, dancing to the latest fusion house track composed of Turkish Arabesque and the latest electronica music is de rigueur. And millions of Americans have at least heard of, if not actually read, at least one volume of Naguib Mahfouz's *Cairo Trilogy* (although as one academic friend pointed out to me, how many Americans can name another Egyptian novelist besides Mahfouz? Probably not a greater percentage than Egyptians can name two American novelists).

In fact, the Arab and larger Muslim world has produced some of the most exciting and ground-breaking musical artists and styles of the last two decades, with artists such as Rachid Taha or Cheb Mammi reaching millions through their own albums – which blend together Rai and hiphop and rock in innovative ways – and their work with leading Western artists like Santana or Sting. And then there's artists like Natacha Atlas or Alabina, who come from Jewish-Arab backgrounds but have embraced Muslim culture. And as I write this, the second Festival in the Desert is going on in Mali, where the best local and Western artists will be performing for several days before a sold-out crowd of several hundred Bedouins, just for the chance of hanging out and creating new music together.

Indeed, if one thinks in terms of artists and music, it's not clear that one can even speak of a "Middle East" versus a "West." Take the Iranian pop music scene for example. We've all heard about how young Iranians subvert the oppressive morals and culture of the conservative regime and wear tight jeans, drink Johnny Walker, and play rock music at parties – always with their head-scarves ready in case the morality police crash the party (although the squads are often paid off by their peers to move on to the next party).

But this underground, seemingly Westernized culture doesn't mean that young Iranians (or anyone else for that matter) uncritically accept everything Western, although, as the quote at the beginning of Chapter Five demonstrates, many do. The larger cultural dynamics is much more complex; for the web bulletin board where I found the posting at the start of Chapter Five is one that has Iranian participants living in Iran and in the US and Europe as well. And the music people dance to in Iran is often "Tehrangeles pop music," that is, music produced by Iranian artists based in Los Angeles. And because it's illegal to write explicitly sexual lyrics, classic Iranian poets like Omar Khayyam and Rumi are used for lyrics (which are rapped as well as sung), since they can't be censored, even though their poetry is often extremely suggestive. And now, perhaps in response to the threat of the "corruption" of foreign rock, the Iranian Government actually sponsors its own "pop festivals" with specifically non-political goals such as "bringing together different styles in music and lyricism with contrastive features."

What all this activity tells us, if one actually hangs out with musicians in the Arab and larger Muslim worlds (which I try to do as often as possible), is that there is an incredible cultural transmission going on via music and art more broadly – and it goes far beyond Sting and Cheb Mammi doing commercials for Jaguar, or Eddie Veder and the late, great Pakistani Qawali singer Nusrat Fateh Ali Khan recording together, or more recently John Mellencamp and various Iraqi musicians or Ozomatli and Hassan Hakmoun. As important, it's not just one way, as happens when a book is translated into Arabic from English or French. And we should bear in mind that while scholars and religious jurists write about globalization, artists and musicians live and literally embody globalization, making them a powerful source for understanding its dynamics and impact on the so-called "Arab/Muslim street." We would do well to follow the musicians as much as we follow the terrorists.

Indeed, as Iraqi film maker and guitarist Oday Rasheed chastised me, "I know all your artists and cultural figures – Jimi Hendrix, John Coltrane, F. Scott Fitzgerald. But I also know my culture – 'Um Kalthoum, Farid al-Atrash and Adonis. But how many Americans even want to know my culture, let alone take the time to do so?" Along with this question, we can also ask, when can we expect Christian or Jewish writers to quote Muslim artists or historical-religious figures the way Muslim scholars like Omid Safi or Amir Hussein quote Bob Dylan or Bob Marley to support their calls for justice?[1]

Rasheed's point is well taken; but we can't just assume that all Iraqis who listen to Hendrix or Coltrane or read Western authors do so in the same way, and that these works of art only have one meaning (or that a significant number of Westerners are becoming similarly familiar with Iraq's most famous singer, Kazim al-Sahir). Take Rai music, for example. In a detailed study of how young Algerian men listen to Rai, the anthropologist Marc Schade-Poulsen shows how this style of music, whose roots lie in working-class Algerian culture (especially in the port city of Oran) but which first gained international popularity after being "modernized" in the Parisian club scene, is a seminal example of the dynamic of globalization.[2] More important, however, is who is listening to the music. While conservative and extremist religious forces condemn Rai as un-Islamic and have even killed prominent Rai artists, many religious people love to listen to Rai. They may not listen to it at home, or with their parents (that would be "an insult," as one young man described it), but they listen to it when they're alone or with their friends and engaging in activities which they later admit aren't exactly sanctioned by Islam. And sometimes the whole family dances to it at weddings – but only at weddings, where the strong sexual atmosphere is allowed (in Morocco, even conservative families will often have "*sheikhat*" – female singers who have a reputation (sometimes well earned) for being prostitutes – perform for their mixed-gender audience).

If the way popular music is performed and experienced in the MENA were just about aesthetics, it would be interesting enough, as Arab artists have been "sampling" Western music for decades to create original hybrid styles. But as the musicologist Philip Hoffman explains, all music, especially hybrid styles such as world music, are experienced through a process of "aesthetic imbeddedness," a vitally important concept for understanding globalization which explains that all cultural (that is, aesthetic) experience and production, music included, is "imbedded" within the larger social, economic, and political processes of the society in which it is produced.

Aesthetic imbeddedness helps explain why Iranian film makers have the freedom to express in film what is forbidden to be expressed in more directly political ways. It helps us understand the roots of what my friend Reda calls the "metal intifada" in Morocco, or why Rai or punk are such powerful musical forms (both arose in a context of neo-liberal structural adjustment and political oppression, and a resulting working-class sense of alienation and despair). And so it is no surprise that artists such as the Algerian Rai star Rachid Taha are explicitly political in their music, and often blend punk, hard rock, and hiphop motifs into their songs.

It is crucial to highlight the political nature of Rai, or heavy metal, in the Arab world, especially since in the West styles like hiphop, which in the days of Public Enemy was so political,[3] has now become so commodified and politically emasculated (or at least irrelevant). Moreover, when the Western press sends people to write about "cool" or "hot" examples of Arab/Muslim culture, they'll usually write about the great dance or gay scene in Beirut, or some other aesthetic phenomenon, without exploring either their political implications or more overtly political styles of cultural performance through music.

Just as important as hot dance scenes, however, are the struggles of less fashionable musicians and their fans for freedom of expression and resistance against the oppressive status quo. In Morocco, as I've already mentioned, this struggle actually landed fourteen heavy-metal musicians and fans in jail (although most for only a few weeks). While this case might seem trivial compared with the hunt for Osama bin Laden, in fact it reflects an incredible array of forces and ideas that are coalescing and clashing through the processes of cultural global-ization as it's unfolding in the MENA region, especially as one of the protagonists is Egyptian, and many of the supporters are European.[4]

The nine musicians and five fans were jailed after being convicted of being "satanists who recruited for an international cult of devil-worship," of "infringing upon public morals," "undermining the faith of a Muslim," and even "attempting to convert a Muslim to another faith" – as if rock-'n'-roll were a religion on the same par as Islam (well, that depends on whom you ask …).[5] Apparently it was para-phernalia such as an ashtray in the form of a skull, heavy-metal CDs, and black T-shirts worn by the accused, along with the fact that some groups wrote in English rather than Arabic or French, that got them into trouble.

Similar raids have occurred against heavy-metal-listening "devil worshipers" in Lebanon and Egypt in the last few years (in Egypt 97 young fans were jailed in the 1997 satanic rock hysteria); most of the time those arrested were from relatively well-to-do families with good educations. Perhaps these sweeps are the governments' ways of reminding them to toe the cultural – and through it, political – line. If so, however, the strategy is backfiring, as hundreds of people showed up for a metal concert outside the Parliament building in Rabat a week after the Moroccans were sentenced. And it invigorated human rights campaigners and youth groups in Morocco – including the quickly formed Comité de soutien de ces jeunes amateurs du hard rock (Committee for Support of These Young Enthusiasts of Hard Rock) – as well as liberal members of the Moroccan and French press.

Indeed, the satanic metal affair only added to the growing dissent in a country where authorities are "losing touch with the country's youth." What is frightening about this fact, however, is that al-Qa'eda, if we'll recall our discussion above, understands this all too well. But while Middle Eastern governments spend precious resources on fighting against hard rock, they do little to address the root social and economic problems that lead less musically adventurous peers of the Moroccan metalheads to cross over to the real dark side – al-Qa'eda.

Perhaps some of those young people became the suicide bombers who ripped through Casablanca in the spring of 2003 – not long after the satanic rock affair occurred. What is clear is that it pushed other young Moroccans into positive social activism. As one Moroccan human rights group, Jeunesse des democrates marocains à l'étranger, argued, "In this time where doubt floats through the Moroccan sky to the level occupied by alarming problems that Morocco suffers from today – poverty, unemployment, impunity, etc., and the widening of the field of liberties that had been torn from us by our elders, the Government has invented a new way to intimidate the Moroccan people in general and young people in particular."[6]

In fact, the drama over the jailed rockers actually provided the Young Moroccan Democrats with the opportunity to fulfill their self-described social function of "promoting a culture of citizenship," which for the thousands of signers of a petition against the jailing clearly includes the right to "express themselves in their own way and through their music." As important, it has led to a wonderful burst of subversive-artistic creativity and solidarity, as signs at the sit-ins for the rockers read "Rockers, Dockers, même Combat!" (with Dockers signifying yuppies wearing Dockers jeans …), while cartoons on the wonderfully titled website Marock sans frontiers included one with a picture of Satan in the judge's chair with a red pentagram – which is, after all, part of the Moroccan flag – handing down a *verdict satanique*," and another one featuring the English caption "there's no life, no where" under a drawing of Jimi Hendrix singing (in French) "Hey Joe, I've been to Morocco, I ain't going back there again."[7]

Even more astonishing, the Marock sans frontiers website (Morocco Without Frontiers – let us recall the imagery of the *barzakh* here) actually printed an open letter to the King of Morocco, asking him if the thugs who arrested and jailed them "acted on your orders." In a text whose boldness is reckless, considering the penalties for insulting the King, they continued, "We want to believe with all our force, No. But in this case, one can't escape this fact: some among your subordinates escaped your control. That you have reasons not to clamp down [on them] (balance of forces, etc.), is, to a point, under-standable. But to let the psychosis take hold isn't. The 'new era', I repeat, is in danger of losing all credibility, and Moroccans are in danger of losing all hope … Justice is rendered in your name, Your Majesty. This isn't nothing … If it is, God knows what sort of [disease] it could induce. Your uncontrollable subordinates have a joyous heart and we are entering a vicious circle which could lead our country into the fire."[8]

As for Reda, from Paris he wrote a piece called *Blood for the Vampires* (*Du sangs pour les vampires*), where he argued that the arrest of the rockers will mark the spirit of Moroccans like the example of the Dreyfus Affair. More provocatively, if the Moroccan Crown was supposed to guarantee "a moderate Islam on the same image of Moroccans," after September 11, with the hatred everywhere and the need for harmony and tolerance,

> our musicians are the mirror of society, who try to reconcile the old and the new, and accusing the youth (the majority) in our society so is an admission of failure, of generational uncoupling … Who are we? The Prosecutor might see the hand of the Devil or Zionism, the tribunal becomes the antechamber where the exorcism will take place, of a civilization with no power, where fear wins out over reason, because this sacrifice, because offering these young people to this monster who is trapped [se trappe] and draped in the coat of morality of true Islam, Algeria is not far from us, the barbaric and bearded vampires always require more blood, without concession![9]

Reda's strategy for defeating the vampires of intolerance and super-stition is: "Trust each other, brandish our tolerance against these hideous visages of regression of all kinds." But as he explained to me in one of our conversations, the "each other" he's talking about is much larger than just Morocco. The "we" that needs to trust itself can only come about through a globalization of solidarity and sympathy – an

Axis of Empathy, to recall our discussion in the Introduction. As I'll explore in more detail in the Conclusion, his sentiments are shared by Iraqi artists who are facing a much more profound and deadly struggle than Reda.

Clearly then, the affair of the satanic Moroccan rockers has deep political implications – at least the musicians and fans clearly believe so. And so they wear their long hair proudly, arguing that "if the devil lives in our guitars," it is because "if you are a musician, you have long hair and a black T-shirt, you play hard rock, you are an amply resplendent figure and a profile that is quite sought after at the moment by the Moroccan police, and this is certainly an invitation to play in one of their police stations, the high decibels risk to shake their consciences … Before anything else, we note that hard rock music is completely neglected by our judicial system."[10]

However positive the outcome of the satanic metal affair might be from an activist perspective, on the negative side the incident has pitted two forces who could and should be working together precisely because they recognize the same disease in Moroccan society: rock-'n'-rollers and Islamists, as it appears that some of the main forces behind the hysteria were members of the very movements spawned by *wasatiyya* figures like Sheikh Yassine. What even some moderate Islamists have yet to realize is that if "justice and spirituality" (the name of Yassine's movement) doesn't apply to Moroccans with long hair, black shirts – the color doesn't seem to bother religious author-ities when women cover their bodies with it in 120-degree heat – and culturally strange musical tastes, it will never be achieved for Morocco as a whole. And it seems they are getting the picture, for as a younger leader of the movement admitted to me, "The Government used this issue to trap the Justice and Spirituality Party and label it as an intol-erant movement. Unfortunately, we fell into the trap and made a great fuss about young people who had done nothing serious. Love of music is not something condemnable. Instead of tackling the main issues befalling the country, the JSP engaged in futilities, and that's what the *makhzen* [i.e., the Government] wanted."[11] Such insights demonstrate the importance of younger activists taking on greater leadership roles in progressively oriented Islamist movements.

But Let's Put the Satanic Metal Affair in Perspective

As interesting as the dire situation of Moroccan rockers is the much more upbeat situation of heavy metal on the other side of the MENA, in Iran. Perhaps surprisingly, considering the Western imagination of

Iran, the situation for rock-'n'-rollers in the Islamic Republic is far less dangerous these days than in Morocco or elsewhere in the Arab world. As one Iranian website devoted to rock music described it: "Heavy metal and rock musicians are becoming more popular in Iran today ... In all that they say there is a sparkle of hope. They think globally and see no geographical boundaries for their work ... In East and West, the language of rock-'n'-roll is one of rebellion and pushing the limits. And in the Islamic Republic of Iran, these musicians are creating a parallel reality that could not be further removed from Friday prayers and routine calls for revolutionary sacrifice and waging war against the West."[12]

Just to put the whole uproar of heavy metal and Satanism into some perspective, it turns out that in occupied Iraq American soldiers and intelligence officials from the Psychological Operations Company (Psy Ops) are exposing uncooperative Iraqi prisoners for "prolonged periods to tracks by rock group Metallica and music from children's TV programmes *Sesame Street* and *Barney*" in the hope of making them talk and "breaking their resistance through sleep deprivation and playing music that was culturally offensive to them ... These people haven't heard heavy metal," Sergeant Mark Hadsell of Psy Ops told *Newsweek* magazine.[13]

Of course, with the revelations in Spring 2004 of systematic torture of Iraqi prisoners by US military intelligence agents, we can perhaps assume that *Barney* and Metallica didn't have the desired impact. Maybe that's because, hard as it might be to believe, Iraq had its own heavy-metal groups (if not quite a scene), and so the music wasn't as strange to Iraqi ears as we might imagine (about *Barney* there's not much to say). At any rate, human rights organizations haven't determined if the forced listening to metal or *Barney* was a violation of the Geneva Conventions, but for the Psy Ops operative the effects of songs like "Bodies" from the soundtrack of the film *XXX* and Metallica's "Enter Sandman" were obvious, at least during the occupation's first few months: "They can't take it. If you play it for 24 hours, your brain and body functions start to slide, your train of thought slows down and your will is broken. That's when we come in and talk to them."

Conclusion: Creating a Real Culture Jam

Over the course of the last two chapters I have tried to bring to life many of the major cultural processes that are impacting the way Muslims in the Muslim majority world experience and respond to globalization. What is clear, I hope, is that Arabs and Muslims are developing their own cultural responses to globalization – some through the introduction of a re-energized Islam into the modern arenas of social life, others through "Morock-'n'-roll." Such cultural politics are generating new Muslim lifestyles and identities in the global era that are able to engage – and demand to be engaged by – their counterparts in Europe and the United States.[14]

For the religiously motivated Muslims who most worry policy-makers and pundits, what motivates their attitudes is the belief that in a global era there can be no alternative for the Arab world except unity and loyalty to its original culture.[15] But how to remain loyal? More cosmopolitan citizens might choose their homegrown hiphop or metal as the best vehicle, but for most Muslims a "cultural revival" built on a "firmly rooted infrastructure," Islam, is the only force that can unify, rather than divide, humanity.[16] Indeed, scholars and activists around the world consider such "revival" and "protection" to be the foundation for successful "cultures of resistance" against the negative effects of globalization.[17] Yet more broadly, a new "universalism" is advocated, one which would "open up to the world," enriching rather than diluting or even erasing local identities.[18]

The younger "radicals – but in a positive sense" such as Nadia Yassine, Tariq Ramadan, or dozens of other brave voices from across the Muslim majority world – call for concerted dialogue and solidarity with international forces, including those in the United States, who are fighting for true peace and social and economic justice around the world. What would a self-confident and re-invigorated Islam bring to such a dialogue? According to American Sufi leader Kabir Helminski, "The dialogue that is necessary today is not primarily between Islam and the West, in which Islam represents *Iman* or faith and the West represents *Kufr*, unbelief. Rather it is between those who stand on the side of true human-ness, *insaniyyah*, and those who are the true *jahiliyyah* or ignorance of today."[19] In a key insight that moves beyond Sayyid Qutb's much more violent and exclusivist notion of *jahiliyyah* as demanding violent revolt, Helminski explains that

> the major *jahiliyyah* [for all cultures, Western and Islamic alike] is the belief that violence solves problems, whether through the bullying tactics of national power or the tactics of terror that justify the killing of non-combatants … Today's *jahiliyyah* puts money values over human values. It promotes a commercialized way of life. It is the rush to accumulate, *takatthur*, which disperses the human soul, rather than *tassawuf*, self-purification, and *tawhid*, the recognition of the one-

ness of being. This rush toward materialism is taking place in the East and the Middle East. Only it has not been as successful as it has already been in the West.

Most importantly,

> The greatest threat to world peace and the natural environment is not Western values. The West may have traveled a little further down the road of consumerism, materialism, and a pop culture that caters to the lowest drives of human beings, but Eastern and Middle Eastern societies are quickly falling prey to the same disease and seem to have even less immunity to the disease than a certain percentage of the population in Europe and North America who have become disillusioned with what the consumer culture can offer.

We can compare the vision of Islam described here with that of one of my favorite authors, Salman Rushdie. In a fascinating Op/Ed written in 2002 where he catalogued the oppression and violence being visited by Muslims on Muslims the world over, Rushdie cried out, "Where, after all, is the Muslim outrage at these events? As their ancient, deeply civilized culture of love, art and philosophical reflection is hijacked by paranoiacs, racists, liars, male supremacists, tyrants, fanatics and violence junkies, why are they not screaming?" He further wonders, "If the moderate voices of Islam cannot or will not insist on the modernization of their culture – and of their faith as well – then it may be these so-called 'Rushdies' who have to do it for them. For every such individual who is vilified and oppressed, two more, ten more, a thousand more will spring up. As long as the majority remains silent, this will be a tough war to win. But in the end, or so we must hope, someone will kick down that prison door."[20]

We can sympathize with Rushdie's desire for comrades in arms against the fanaticism of too many of his coreligionists; but it's shocking that the man who wrote *The Satanic Verses*[21] has now completely bought into the notion that the Muslim world's jailors are all Muslim. Perhaps he's not listening closely enough to find voices of support, or forgot that soon after Khomeini's fatwa a group of leading Arab and Muslim activists and scholars wrote a wonderful and courageous defense of him titled *For Rushdie*.

Clearly, there is a lot of blame to go around, but most of the main structural constraints on achieving the freedom and prosperity Rushdie hopes for have been put in place by European and later US policies during the last two centuries; Muslim elites have largely played the roles assigned them all too well, taking whatever opportunities came to enrich themselves at the expense of their "fellow citizens." And it is because the blame is so widely shared that breaking the Muslim world free of its many prisons (military, political, economic, cultural) will take a concerted effort of people of good faith (literally) from many cultures and countries, not just Muslim Rushdies, however numerous they may become.

Hitting the Bandstand, but it Better not be Amateur Night

What it will take, as I've argued repeatedly, is a true jamming of cultures. When I was just starting out as a professional guitarist I had the great fortune of playing with the late great bluesman Johnny Copeland. One night while we were rehearsing in his Harlem apartment and his daughter Shemekia (now a star in her own right but then only a twelve-year-old with the thirty-year-old's voice) sat braiding my hair, a friend of his from the building came in, and after sitting down for a minute began spewing out an anti-Jewish diatribe that sounded as if it came right out of Louis Farrakhan's playbook. This man didn't know I was Jewish, and I'm not even sure Johnny did, but after a minute or two of listening Johnny cut him off and started berating him, that the kind of stereotypes and lies he was throwing around were ridiculous and going to get black people nowhere. The man left a few minutes later and that was the last I saw of him.

It was the same with other great artists with whom I have worked, such as jazz great Dr. John or blues legend Albert Collins. If you wanted to hang with them musically or otherwise you had to be operating at their level. Unjustified ego, envy, and tired clichés (racial, cultural or musical) had no place in their universe – on or off the bandstand. Albert Collins even showed me a bat he kept in the back of the driver's seat of his tour bus just in case any "fools started talking stupid." Very few people dared to talk stupid around him.

And it wasn't only bluesmen who were utterly intolerant of foolishness. At Woodstock 1994 I was lucky enough to spend some time with Carlos Santana between my group's show and his once-again legendary set. The man is as gentle as a lamb, he literally has a halo – or so I thought until I wound up standing on the stage for his show right next to keyboardist Chester Thompson and the percussion section. There was a fairly young guitarist from a then up-and-coming R&B group who asked Santana if he could sit in with him (a show of hubris that made me incredibly angry and jealous since I was too nervous to ask him the same question – an act of cowardice for which I'll never forgive myself). But only a few bars after Santana signaled him to take a solo he cut him off with a dismissive glance – a surprising response from as seemingly quiet and forgiving a person as Carlos Santana.

I realized then that if you aren't taking the music higher, for someone like Santana you're dragging it down – quite unacceptable for someone in his position. And that's when I realized that while from the audience Santana always looked and sounded like the ultimate free jam band, up on the bandstand I could see Carlos directing the band with the ferocity and uncompromising character of James Brown. In order to be loose and free, you had to be perfectly tight first. You had to know every angle of every song and be prepared to roll with the slightest shift in tempo, cadence or rhythm. In the words of Led Zeppelin guitarist Jimmy Page, you had to be "tight but loose." Otherwise get off the bandstand.

What does this discussion of what we could call "musical etiquette" have to do with our story? Everything. As I was finishing this chapter I received an email inviting me to fly to Washington, DC and join two other (senior) professors in a workshop for government officials about Islam, Europe, and globalization. While we were in the middle of an intense discussion about how progressive figures like Tariq Ramadan are vehemently attacked by conservative American commentators for being "wolves in sheep's clothing," one of the Government participants asked an unusually pointed, and very important, question: "Clearly Ramadan is the real deal," he said. "But it is also clear that there are people out there who speak one way to Western audiences in Western languages and another way to Muslim audiences in Arabic or Farsi. How can we tell who's honest and who's being duplicitous?"

I had to think for a minute, and then I realized that the issue that separates not just Muslims, but "progressives" who are truly interested in dialogue and solidarity towards peace and justice from those whose vision is ultimately exclusivist and myopic is that of anti-Semitism; more precisely, anti-Jewishness. The history of anti-Jewish attitudes among Muslim activists or the European and American Left is a long and complicated story that I can't delve into here. But what is important to bear in mind is that, because of the history of anti-Semitism in Europe, and also in the American Left after the 1960s, and specifically the well-worn notion of Jewish conspiracies to control the world's finances, it has been very easy, and all too common, for the anti-globalization and now anti-war movements to slip into anti-Jewish rhetoric as a simple way to vent frustration at the dominant system and stoke the emotions of core constituencies. Similarly, in the Muslim world a combination of fifty-plus years of the Palestine

Problem coupled with the fact that there are no longer sizable Jewish communities to protest, let alone counterbalance, blatant anti-Jewish sentiments has made anti-Jewish rhetoric a mainstay of critiques of the West and the US in particular.

I'm not talking about criticizing Israel or even anti-Zionism, which are both legitimate positions as far as I'm concerned. Nor am I talking about the kind of rabid and easily dismissed anti-Jewish rants that one can find in the writings of Sayyid Qutb or the speeches of bin Laden. Rather I'm talking about the (sadly) more respectable rehashing of the Protocols of the Elders of Zion (which are easily available in most bookstores in the Arab world), the substitution of "Judaism" for "Israel" in critiques of Israeli policies (as if Egypt and Islam were identical terms), the legitimization of Palestinian suicide bombings by jurists like Yusuf Qaradawi who condemn all other forms of terrorism, the use of rhetoric about Jews controlling the media or the banks (as even Sheikh Yassine wrote in his latest book), or the argument that Israel wants to colonize the whole Middle East (as we saw Ali Bulaç argue above). And of course, almost identical sentiments are once again becoming common among the European and American Left.

From a moral standpoint this kind of prejudice is bad enough; what's ultimately more dangerous is that it reflects an intellectual and strategic laziness and sloppiness that will make it impossible to build the kind of program that can unite millions of people to struggle together to overcome the overwhelming odds that exist when pursuing global peace and justice against a hypermilitarized global system (which is itself based on racism and religious stereotypes). Moreover, such easy bigotry cheapens the oppression of Muslims elsewhere – not to mention the oppression and violence by Muslims on others – and overlooks equally (and from a Muslim standpoint, more) damaging anti-Arab and Muslim sentiments and stereotypes that are still harbored by the European Left, which have prevented Muslims and Christian Europeans (never mind Jews) from working more closely together against their common foe in neoliberal globalization and the American-led world system that demands its implementation.

My point is that just as Carlos Santana or Johnny Copeland would never tolerate someone on their stage who played or behaved sloppily or uncreatively, or would never start a jam without a mental map of how they were going reach their musical *barzakh*, so leaders of the global peace and justice movement and the global culture they strive to produce need to be relentlessly, and sometimes brutally, critical of themselves and anyone else who wants to join the dialogue of cultures. Moreover, they need to be just as strategically proactive in developing a vision and roadmap for achieving it. It's the only way to translate the cultural *barzakh* advocated by Taieb Belghazi from an in-between space where different cultures interact but retain their individuality to a threshold at which the culture jam, as in a great Santana or Nusrat Fateh Ali Khan solo, or Page and Plant performing with an Egyptian orchestra, becomes truly sublime and opens up possibilities for cultural and even societal transformation we haven't yet imagined.

From this perspective, as I will discuss in the following chapters, I would take issue with many leaders of the global peace and justice movement who argue that the movement's anarchy is one of their greatest strengths. The downside of anarchy (which I explore in greater detail in the next chapter) is that unless you're the Miles Davis Quintet or Led Zeppelin, without "band leaders" or "musical directors" to establish the harmony, even the tiniest mistakes in tempo or pitch can feed back upon themselves until communication – musical or cultural – breaks down into an unpleasant, and in real life dangerous, chaos (as we'll see in Iraq or Palestine in Chapter Nine).

From my experience with the rising generation of Muslim intellectuals and activists, there are plenty of honest and self-critical personalities to lead the Muslim side. The more interesting question is, who will lead the younger generation of Western intellectuals and activists? We'll look at this question in more detail in the next three chapters.

PART 3

We're Jammin': Global Solidarity in the Post-9/11 World

Figure 7   Globalization's seductive allure: Prague kiosk advertisement near site of S26 anti-IMF demonstration, September 2000

7 Paris '68–Baghdad '04: The Evolution of a Movement of Movements

Introduction

With Part Two we have completed two of the most important goals of the book: first to explore the history and contemporary dynamics of globalization worldwide, and then to use this discussion to understand how the peoples of the MENA have experienced and responded to it. We are now ready to return to the world at large and explore the histories, strategies, and activities of the global peace and justice movement and its struggle against neoliberal globalization. In doing so we need to remind ourselves, however, that what we're talking about isn't really true economic, political or cultural integration on a worldwide scale – that is, globalization as most people imagine it – but rather the globalization of neoliberalism as an ideology and set of economic policies and political strategy.

We might wonder why we need to spend so much time exploring the history of the broader anti-corporate globalization and anti-war movements in a book about globalization in the MENA region. The fact is that we can't understand the difficulties involved in developing progressive social movements (never mind real democracy) in the MENA, or how its citizens can join the struggle for global peace and justice as equal partners, unless we first have a grasp of the history, problems, and successes of the movement worldwide. Moreover, many policy-makers and commentators on world affairs consider building grass-roots progressive activism in the MENA region as unrealistic or even undesirable. They'd rather focus on how the "international community" can, in the words of President Bush, bring "peace" and "democracy" to the region through the formal political process; or how, according to best-selling author Noah Feldman, "liberal" Muslims can create a post-jihad religious reformation and in

213

so doing free themselves of the shackles of authoritarianism and religious violence.

Chapters Three through Five demonstrated the structural difficulty of the Bush Administration, or any outside power, bringing real peace and democracy to the region – assuming they actually wanted to – as long as neoliberalism is the dominant economic and cultural force in the world and especially American politics. Put simply, it's "impossible to have neoliberalism at home and enlightened foreign policy Abroad."[1] In practical terms, it's hard to push democracy on countries you regularly use to "interrogate" – read: torture – "ghost detainees" of the war on terror. As for the idea that "liberal" Muslims can or want to radically transform their societies, we need to remember that liberal politics faded in the West precisely because it was no match for its twin – or better, doppleganger[2] – neoliberalism, and the conservative politics and culture that both have encouraged, whether by reaction or design.

1968: The Year the Dream Died?

It is hard to see how a merely "liberal Islam"[3] – rather than a radically progressive Islam – can overcome neoliberalism in the oppressive political culture of most Muslim majority countries. European and American activists began to realize liberalism's false promise in the late 1960s, which is at least part of the reason for the turn toward a more radical politics during this period. In particular, the events of the summer of 1968 and afterwards reveal important parallels in the student movements in the first, second, and third worlds that anticipated the more organized and permanent solidarities of the 1990s.[4] What we need to understand is what happened to the unprecedented political power of youth culture epitomized by "1968" that led to its corporate conquest within a few years, and why it re-emerged with such a vengeance seemingly out of the blue three decades later.[5]

Thanks to the ground-breaking work of Thomas Frank discussed in previous chapters we have a fairly good idea of why the impetus toward peace and justice around the world in the 1960s, and especially in the US, was easily "conquered" or coopted by corporate culture. This shouldn't suggest, however, that the protests of 1968 in Paris or Chicago (and let's not forget the Monterrey Pop Festival of the previous year) didn't have a lasting effect on American and European progressive movements. But what 1968 didn't produce was a generation of movements and leaders with the vision, or a large enough base of support, to build a progressive social order in their societies.[6]

Once defanged and coopted, the moderate (in tone and tactics) peace movement of the mid-1970s through 1980s – especially in the US – posed little significant threat to the policies of the Western governments. Whether under Reagan or Clinton, Thatcher or Blair, Kohl or Schroeder, Mitterand or Chirac, the strategy of building "mass" movements for peace based on the Vietnam protest model have been largely unsuccessful. Most European and North American citizens have remained "notable by their absence" in the peace movements, a problem that continues to plague the movements today even as millions of people march periodically against the US war on and occupation of Iraq.[7]

Why did things turn out this way? If we look at the way French scholars have recently discussed May 1968, it appears (apart from higher tuition fees for college students, which was the immediate cause) that the protests were a reaction against two things: first, the clear pacification of French society by the post-War "republican" establishment; and second, against the movement of French society towards "une société à l'américaine."[8] However important the cause, the movement didn't have much of a lasting effect on the larger French or European societies. In reality, May 1968 was not what most people thought it was, didn't achieve its larger, revolutionary goals, and can't be repeated today.[9]

And so, to discover the democratic passion that symbolized that era we must "undertake a critique, rather than mythmaking of May 68."[10] From the US perspective, the assassinations of Malcolm X and Martin Luther King, Jr. in 1965 and 1968, and the rise of Black Power, Weather Underground and other "radical" movements soon after, coupled with the growing militancy of the anti-war movement in the early 1970s, alienated the New Left from mainstream America (as witnessed by a string of conservative presidential victories from Nixon to Bush II), even as it laid the groundwork for much of the organizing by the anti-nuclear and Central American peace movements in the 1980s.

Can we compare the late 1990s generation of protests with important turning points of the previous generation? In some ways, there is a fairly direct line between the two events: first, the attack on labor unions and the welfare state that began after 1968 can be seen as delayed responses to (what from the state's and corporate elite's perspectives was) a dangerous mixture of students, women and environmentalists, third worldists, indigenous peoples and minorities –

not just Martin Luther King, but Ceasar Chavez too – all coming together to assert a compelling competing vision both to American capitalism or Soviet Communism.[11] Second, in pushing back the progressive movements that emerged in the late 1960s, European and especially American elites forced the mainstream political Left to "evacuate" the economic and social content of its political agendas: "Already in 1968 we see the beginnings of the collusion between the ideology of the left and political and financial power."[12]

There were two primary reasons this occurred: first, political elites deployed a strategy of refusing to negotiate or compromise with progressives and instead chose to "demonize their adversaries."[13] This put the Left on the defensive, even though with the successes of the anti-Vietnam war movement it could have moved on the cultural – and as important, economic – offensive. What prevented it from doing so was the second reason for this dynamic: transformation of the world economy to the "post-fordist, flexible accumulation" system championed by neoliberalism, which along with political conservatism, cultural individualism, and consumerism dominated American political culture by the time of President Reagan's election in 1980.

This new ideology succeeded precisely because it pacified the spiritual and economic insecurity of the white middle class (and people of all colors and cultures who shared their values) with what *TIKKUN* magazine editor Michael Lerner has aptly described as an ethic of materialism, "looking out for #1," a worship of money and power, and a religious revivalism – to assuage all the guilty feelings the other sentiments caused. This combination of emotions has been wrapped together in the language of "freedom," "opportunity," and "fairness," and combined with a populist backlash rhetoric that is the very opposite of policies like affirmative action and the welfare state that are the supposed favorites of selfish and naïve liberals.[14]

The Increasing Militarization of American Culture and the Eclipse of Liberalism

How did this happen? As we've already discussed several times, the dynamics of branding are central to the "culturalization" of economic processes as a defining characteristic of contemporary globalization, which in turn has made it much easier for corporate and political elites to manipulate the population at large. Indeed, as I discuss in more detail in the Conclusion, a 2001 study by the ad agency Young & Rubicam "proved" that in the global era branding has become *the* "new religion" in the West and the single most important dynamic of globalized culture.[15]

This idea of branding as a religious phenomenon is not new or that controversial. Department stores and now malls have long been known as "Cathedrals of Consumption" that have an enchanted, even sacred or religious character that through various techniques often "coerce us into consumption."[16] In fact, returning to our discussion of Kansas, we can say that at the very time the worsening economic situation disenchants many Americans vis-à-vis their Government and society, conservative backlash populism uses *both* religion and "hyper-consumption" to re-enchant their lives in a powerful manner. Yet it is precisely the export of the "American means of consumption," rather than just American products, that is so threatening to many people around the world.[17]

If the brands being deified were limited to Nike or Coke things would be bad enough (at least for the workers in Nike's sweatshops and the millions of overweight Coke addicts). But one of the most important American brands is none other than the US military, which has achieved a frightening level of cultural dominance within mainstream American society in good measure because of its successful marketing as a brand, which is in complete synergy with the backlash populism we discussed above.

The successful branding of "the war business" is occurring at the same time that the Republican Party – and through it, the military industrial complex – has cemented a powerful base of tens of millions of conservative Christians[18] who along with their religious beliefs are spreading the gospel of the military as an essentially positive and even righteous institution. And for those not religiously inclined there are the hyper-violent video games (often designed by joint private–Defense Department research and development teams) that indoctrinate tens of millions of teenagers into the art of mass slaughter.[19]

Indeed, the role of the "military entertainment complex" in the larger military industrial complex is crucial today because it successfully indoctrinates millions of young men into the ethos of killing automatically, without pain or remorse, through the "computer simulated immersive environments," such as video games, which have been shown to be excellent trainers of young minds and bodies. And it's not the military leading the corporations anymore; today the Marines license *Doom* to create their own simulated battle game, *Marine Doom*, which has proven especially successful in training soldiers to be killers – "hardwire young people to shoot at humans … they train you to kill every living creature in front of you."[20]

It is clear that since the Carter and especially Reagan administrations the Republican Party and larger Washington establishment has sought increasingly to militarize American society, the majority of whose citizens were no longer compelled to engage in military service.[21] And so today more Americans trust the military's "integrity" and "ability to do the right thing" than any other institution and believe it to be the "last remaining refuge of many democratic values in a society that seems ever more shallow and materialistic." These sentiments are a key reason why these same people support a military budget that surpasses the totaled military spending of the rest of the world.[22]

Why is the phenomenon so important for our discussion? Because consumerism combined with significant levels of religious conservatism, and support for the military, has created an almost impregnable social, political, and economic force to support, however passively for most people, the agenda of corporate elites.[23] Indeed, as Kevin Baker argues in a 2003 *Harper's Magazine* exposé (echoing Thomas Frank's argument), this force has helped the Republican Party turn America into a *Volksrepublik* – a mythologized notion of a pure America with "strong Judeo-Christian values" that liberals corroded away since the 1960s, a situation in which a "culture war" against the "internal" enemies of "America" must be waged in order to reclaim America's "soul."[24]

Through this war the United States is slowly being transformed from a republic rooted in individual rights into a classic "Jacobin republic":[25] one that, like post-Revolutionary France, sees the supreme value placed in the state as the embodiment of the collective will of the people. Of course, the will of the people is increasingly defined by the political and corporate elites, not we, the people; but the populist backlash rhetoric makes this an easy trick to pull off.[26]

The Jacobins possessed a militarist ideology that was shaped in response to the tyranny of the French monarchy, yet led to the establishment of their own, even worse, reign of Terror (with a capital T). In a similar but thankfully less bloody manner, today's turn to "core" American values is terrorizing those who don't fit into the conservative vision of America. All signs of dissent are attacked by the state and its corporate media allies, even if it means sacrificing its own intelligence agents or diplomats or returning to the once discredited practice of using the FBI to intimidate political dissenters.

It is in this context that we need to understand the 2001 Young & Rubicam report, which argued that "brands are the new religion" because (according to Y&R) belief in consumer brands has replaced religious faith as the thing that gives purpose to young people's lives. The report even argued that today's brand builders can be compared to the missionaries who spread Christianity and Islam around the world.[27]

This assessment got it only half right, in fact, for September 11 changed the brand equation significantly: Coke, Apple, and Nike might still be the brand of choice for many, but more and more, as we might expect from the arguments of Baker and Frank, "Christ is replacing Coke as the focus of youthful longing," as young people have "turn[ed] to the latest aggressively-marketed youth fad: Christianity."[28] That is, even as the world's most valuable brands such as Coca-Cola and Microsoft have lost "brand value" since September 11, 2001, Christian merchandise of all kinds have seen theirs sky-rocket as Americans want their brands to become a form of spiritual self-expression.

The problem is, if "Christianity is cool" (and more meaningful and exciting than the drivel of mainstream culture), then like its hippy counterpart of a generation or so ago, it has also been conquered by corporate capital. But not the 1990s lite capital of neoliberal globalization's glory years; instead it's the militarized capital of post-September 11 capital with a vengeance. We'll see the results of this marriage of religion and empire in our discussion of Iraq in the Conclusion.

What the jacobinization of US political culture does tell us, as Hannah Arendt and Tariq Ali have both pointed out, is that like all empires before it the United States cannot sustain its imperialism abroad without active repression, even tyranny, at home.[29] As the founder of modern cultural studies, Stuart Hall, would no doubt remind us, this process entails a lot of "hard work," but the political and economic rewards are huge. What we have now is a kind of "hegemony" – that is, a combination of consent of the majority that has been "educated" to see the interests of the elite (usually wrongly) as their own, backed by coercion (more or less political or violent depending on the situation) against any signs of dissent – that is unprecedented in recent US history.[30]

Within the context of America's brand culture the Middle East and Islam have been branded and marketed in very specific ways during the past twenty years, and especially since September 11. In the most recent campaigns Osama bin Laden has become the perfect brand name for a marketplace driven by militarized hyperconsumption combined with social conservatism (the reality-TV equivalent of the "Iron Sheikh" in the World Wrestling Federation of the 1980s).[31]

Yet as we've seen, while the bin Laden brand and logo signifies certain negative ideas and traits to Americans, for many Muslims, and people throughout the Global South, he signifies something totally different – he's Pepsi to the US's Coke. And so we have a "bin-Laden Generation" that is composed of potentially hundreds of millions of young people who are marginalized from the dominant world political, economic, and cultural system which they see, rightly or wrongly, as being directed by the United States. Not surprisingly, "al-Qa'eda has a promising future as a brand name" through a combination of "franchising, partnership and organized crime"; this combined with the cultural cache of the "company's" founder and name "offers an effective way to maximize the impact of any attack."[32]

Why is this the case? As French novelist and critic Noël Mamère writes in his famous (at least in France) *Non Merci, Oncle Sam!*, "Un Sud ainsi condamné à la pauvreté serait l'otage du plus fort. Et qui est le plus fort aujourd'hui: les États-Unis."[33] The logic is so strong that even if you've forgotten your high school French it's still clear: as long as the US (really, the American corporate elite and their counterparts in other major countries) is "driving" globalization, those held hostage to the current world system will hold the US responsible for their woes.[34]

It would be very unfair to look at the situation today and see only the unfulfilled promises of May 1968 and the inability of the Left to stop the neoliberal onslaught. In fact, the events of the late 1960s and early 1970s had a profoundly positive legacy too. Perhaps their most positive long-term impact was the breaking down of national borders, or the "sans-frontièrisme," of the 1968 generation. Spring 1968 showed activists the importance of interacting with and supporting each other, a realization which clearly influenced new kinds of social activism that developed in the next two decades, particularly the "militant humanitarianism" that would become so important in the 1990s.[35]

Whatever its faults, a similar openness at crucial moments also characterized the American New Left, as it focused on mobilizing African Americans and young people along political–cultural issues such as desegregation and the Vietnam War (a discussion of whose economic bases was largely shunted aside with the assassination of King). But this focus came at a high price: the failure to organize the working and middle classes at precisely the moment that its grand bargain with US corporations and political elites – good wages and working conditions for a then still largely white union membership in return for the support for the Cold War and marginalization of minorities and the poor – was breaking down.[36]

Since the Left didn't reach out to this potentially huge constituency (in fact, in many ways it actively alienated it), conservatives stepped in with the brilliant combination of market and religious fundamentalism that made the rich richer and while giving the middle class peace of mind and soul even as their pockets were being picked for untold billions. This is the political dynamic that has been governing America for the last two decades uninterruptedly.[37] Luckily, much of the rest of the world is no longer so easily manipulated.

The South Rises

Indeed, the situation evolved differently in the Global South, as the period of socialist or at least state-led development in the 1950s through early 1970s, coupled with autocratic (and often military-dominated) regimes, stifled similar levels of protests to those in Europe and the US. The unprecedented levels of growth achieved by state-led development strategies also pacified many citizens of the MENA and Global South more broadly (especially in the third, as opposed to fourth – or truly poor – world). Around the third world, as long as capitalism was producing state-led development that brought a measure of growth and improvement in major indicators of social welfare, struggles remained on the local level, against specific policies. But "beginning in the late 1970s people in Latin America, and throughout the Global South, faced the same struggles – against Western multinationals like Monsanto, whose practices were literally threatening their survival."[38]

With the imposition of structural adjustment programs in the second half of the 1970s poverty and inequality began to increase. Mass food riots erupted in communist Poland and autocratic Peru in 1976, followed by riots in several Egyptian cities in 1977 after the Government raised food and gas prices in response to IMF austerity demands.[39] By the 1980s there were significant protests throughout the MENA region, including Algeria, Morocco, and Egypt, against the raising of basic food prices demanded by the IMF and its accountants. Not surprisingly, this was also the period that "radical" or "fundamentalist" Muslim groups began an increasingly violent conflict with MENA states.[40] As we discussed in Chapter Two, there is a strong link between the imposition of neoliberal policies and civil violence, even civil war, around the MENA.

Since the world capitalist system has historically been most oppressive and exploitative in the Global South, it should not be surprising, as Arab economist and theorist Samir Amin once wrote, that Southern protest (in his language, revolutionary) movements have long held the key to "upsetting the world system."[41] Perhaps because Southern activists faced issues of sheer survival while many of their comrades in the North "grew up" and moved onto Wall Street and other profitable careers, the worldwide progressive activism that began in the 1970s was in many respects led by Southern activists and scholars, who produced innovative theories and popular practices to resist and even transcend global capitalism (and even modernity). As important, these struggles brought together secular and religious forces in a manner that is a model for European, American, and now, more than ever, MENA movements for global peace and justice.

The combination of the experiences of Euro–North American and Southern movements laid the groundwork for the unique organizational style and strategies of the contemporary global peace and justice movement. The South provided the focus and strategies of specific policy protests (around issues such as the impact of IMF and related SAPs [structural adjustment programs]), while the North saw protests focused on larger issues such as "peace," the "environment," and nuclear war. In the 1990s connections between activists across the equatorial divide grew increasingly strong.[42]

The various global experiences of mobilization and activism converged on January 1, 1994 when the Ejército Zapatista de Liberación Nacional, or EZLN, attacked Mexican army units stationed in Chiapas in response to the NAFTA agreements, which became effective that very day. I'll discuss the Zapatistas in more detail in the next chapter; what made their battle cry of "Enough is enough" so important was that it was an explicit response to the imposition of neoliberalism on their communities through the NAFTA accords signed the year before. The Zapatista response to the neoliberal onslaught became the inspiration for many of the most successful European movements of the second half of the 1990s.

Two years after the revolt, and one year after the founding of the WTO in 1995, a historic *encuentro* (meeting) was held under Zapatista auspices. Titled the "Intercontinental Meeting Against Neoliberalism and for Humanity," it was attended by 3,000 activists from Mexico, Latin America, and indeed the world at large (including Iran, Turkey, and Mauritania). The *encuentro* was important for two reasons: it was one of the first international meetings where a truly global collection of activists came together to strategize about how to resist neoliberalism on the grass-roots level in their home countries; and at the same time there was a significant focus on building international solidarity networks as a fundamental part of this struggle.

In 1997 a second *encuentro* was held in Andalusia, Spain, this one attended by four thousand international activists. It was here that more militant groups such as People's Global Action (PGA) began to coalesce around the call for a "very clear rejection of ... all trade agreements, institutions and governments that promote destructive globalization."[43] In fact, PGA, one of the most important worldwide movements, adopted a specifically "confrontational attitude, since we do not think that lobbying can have a major impact on such biased and undemocratic organizations ... a[nd] call to direct action and civil disobedience." That is, it understood four years before the rest of the global peace and justice movement that it was in a war for survival against globalized neoliberal capitalism, one where compromise would only bring defeat that much more rapidly.

1997 was also an important year in the United States as labor rights and the environmental activists were joined by conservatives and libertarian isolationists to block the fast-track presidential trade authority so desired by President Clinton (which would have given him the power to sign economic agreements without congressional scrutiny). By 1998 worldwide protests were occurring regularly against the WTO, IMF, World Bank, and neoliberalism more broadly. In May of that year a "People's Summit" was convened to oppose the G-8 meeting in Birmingham, England. Less than a week later tens of thousands of protesters convened against the WTO summit in Geneva.

This protest was important not just because of its size but for who led it: "hiphop kids" from the city's working-class neighborhoods (the "Council Estates") – that is, the economically and politically marginalized but culturally avant-garde of Swiss society; exactly the people who need to take the lead everywhere else in an era where globalization is more culturally determined than ever before. Things heated up even more in September, when upwards of 75,000 protesters greeted the IMF and World Bank in Berlin; a crowd not matched till Genoa in 2001, Seattle included.

1999 saw continued protests around the world, including the UK, Romania, Argentina, Ecuador, and, in the weeks leading up to the November 30 Seattle protests, in the Netherlands and Turkey (where peasants, environmentalists, and trade unionists marched over 2,000 miles to protest the WTO and global capitalism). Given this building momentum it should be no surprise that the business world expected trouble in Seattle. Months before the protests pro-WTO economists argued that the Seattle meeting "will be very controversial from the start and face very strong opposition. In addition to the usual resistance from business and agriculture groups that benefit from protection . . . there is the new public interest opposition from national, labour and environmental groups that is less obviously based in raw self interest."[44] *The Economist* even warned ominously that Seattle was "only the latest and most visible in a string of recent NGO victories" going back to the 1992 Earth Summit in Rio de Janeiro.[45]

The Battle in Seattle

The seminal Seattle anti-WTO protests of November 30 to December 3 1999 were born of a movement that had clearly "emerged first outside the United States."[46] Taking their cue from the experiences of activists literally around the world, the Seattle protests involved some thirteen hundred civic, social movement, and trade union organizations from over eighty countries. The setting: the annual "WTO Ministerial" held during the final week of November 1999 in Seattle. The response: tens of thousands of people, supported by an equal number worldwide, engaged in the most vocal and important protests ever organized against neoliberal globalization.

Why did Seattle succeed in penetrating the consciences of people around the world, including the normally apathetic United States, which as President Clinton never stopped reminding people was then in the midst of the "longest economic boom in postwar history"? Among the most important dynamics that paved the way for Seattle was the coming together of "localized, regionalized and globalized" resistance as the fundamental starting point for challenging the neoliberal globalization juggernaut.[47] Moreover, the organizers of "N30" had learned many of the lessons of May 1968, turning Seattle into a laboratory for a "new repertoire of flexible and militant direct action tactics."[48]

The role of the "performance" of culture in Seattle and subsequent demonstrations was vitally important: the images of black-clad anarchists and turtle people, of WTO officials blockaded in their hotels or meetings by "roving gangs" of young people, of intifada-like chaos and resistance, sparked the imagination of an American public anaesthetized by the "prosperity" of the Clinton years. Because of these dynamics, the protests forced, if only briefly, a societal-wide recognition of the stakes and problems involved in the emerging global system. But of course, more mundane matters also influenced its success. Despite the supposedly robust American (if not world) economy, the fact was that in 1999 American workers were not doing particularly well, and in fact were on average making less in real dollars than their counterparts a generation earlier. Income inequality had also hit historic heights, leaving most families with less net worth than they had two decades before.[49]

And so as the elite "Green Room" representatives from the US, Canada, EU, and Japan met to figure out how to liberalize trade across the globe, on the streets organized labor, environmentalists, religiously faithful, secular humanists, all "called [Clinton's] bet ... and this time manipulation failed him."[50] In one of the most powerful real-time analyses of the events in Seattle, *Tikkun* magazine editor Michael Lerner compared the protesters' struggle against the WTO to the Jewish story of Hannukhah, which

> was about a massive Greek empire, which had taken over ancient Judea and attempted to subvert the independent right of the Jewish people to shape its own cultural, religious and political life. Today the form of empire has changed: fifty MNCs have gross incomes greater than those of many countries ... As a result, the guerrilla struggle waged by Judah the Maccabee was not just a national liberation struggle, but also a civil war between the accommodators to "reality" and those who believe that there was a Force in the world (they called it God) that made it possible to fight for what was right even against overwhelming odds.[51]

This is a crucial argument for our story, because it demonstrates the essentially spiritual – and because of this, cultural – nature of the enterprise of struggling against neoliberal globalization that was symbolized by Seattle. In fact, Lerner uses an argument similar to the Protestant theologian Paul Tillich's belief that religion is at its core whatever a person or group believes to be his, her, or their "ultimate concern." By this I mean that both understand, crucially, that making money, or saving starving children, or conquering the world, could all be a person's (or group of people's) religion if these activities or goals are what dominates their life. Because of this, the rebels of Seattle can be seen as the avant-garde for the kind of worldwide progressive spiritual resurgence that is vital to any expansion of the global peace and justice movement beyond its traditional young and usually secular base.

In fact, the kind of seemingly impossible victory commemorated by Hannukhah (which was celebrated around the time of the Seattle protests in 1999) "has happened throughout history when people realized that the Spirit is greater than the wealth and power of arrogant elites. It may take many generations here, too, but the demonstrators in Seattle have taken a first step toward the modern miracle that will eventually lead to serious constraints on corporate domination."[52] I'll return to such a religiously inspired metaphor in the Conclusion, but for now what makes this dynamic important is that it opens space – if the larger and largely secular movement doesn't close it – for believing Christians, Muslims, and Jews who have so far remained estranged from the movement to join it without having to leave aside their core identities.

The Meaning and Impact of Seattle

The Seattle protests clearly inspired activists across the globe, revealing a progressive movement that was no longer open to slick manipulation by politicians. Yet at the same time it marked the movement's entrance "into unmapped territory, creating a politics that's not yet been defined."[53] A cottage industry emerged to analyze its impact and chart a way forward, with important books being published in countries as diverse as Sri Lanka, Lebanon, and France.

The best writings about the protests have sought to explore how the "event" of Seattle could become a more lasting "movement."[54] They reveal the coming together of insights, theories, and strategies from around the world, but in the eclectic and non-hierarchical fashion that has become the hallmark of the movement's "anarchism," its spirit of "one no and many yeses." For example, from a Sri Lankan book on the protests the insights of Western authors like David Korten (who has extensive experience in the Global South) were blended with local experiences to complete a circle of experience and knowledge that began in the third world, moved to the first, and now is being reinterpreted by Southern activists. This feedback loop clearly helped support the global peace and justice movement that emerged in the wake of September 11.[55]

For leading French activists, Seattle was nothing short of a "rebellion" against globalization[56] and the birth date of a "Seattle Generation" that is as much a pan-European as an American phenomenon. But this isn't a new generation in the sense of age; it's generation as a verbal noun, as in a new generation of ideas and strategies – the well-developed philosophies of the editors of *Le Monde Diplomatique* brought together with the innovative and in-your-face tactics of younger activists, such as the French-Tunisian activist Leyla Dakhli (founder of the group Aarrg!!, or *Apprentis agitateurs pour un réseau de résistance globale*, [in English, Agitators in Training for a Network of Global Resistance]) who focused on bringing both art and immigrants into the movement.[57]

There have been at least two books written in Arabic on the impact of the Seattle Protests. The one that is most relevant for our comparison is titled *Globalization – Disaster in Seattle: War of the Market and Market of War between the West and the West.*[58] The subtitle of the book makes three crucial points: first, the stakes of Seattle involved a war over whether the "market" would define social relations for the rest of society; second – in an eerie premonition of post-September 11 "heavy" globalization – that the market for war would be one of the most important elements of the larger neoliberal market; and third, that the most important conflict that Seattle pointed to was that between different visions of the future of Western society, not between the West and the Rest.[59] In other words, it's the struggle between neoliberalism and the global peace and justice movement, not Islam and the West, that is crucial today.

These are all crucial issues that since September 11 have become the dominant points of conflict over neoliberal globalization. Not surprisingly, the book depicts Seattle as marking, more than anything else, a transition "from cold war to hot war." This was made clear by the level of chaos at the meeting, which led the author to ask if the "new world order" will be a "system" or a reign of "chaos" made possible because the Global South, and indeed the world at large, has been "stumbling" in the face of the dangers posed by the New World Order.[60] But what he couldn't imagine then, but what is now clear, is that the chaos he feared after Seattle has now become fundamental to the functioning of the system.

After Seattle: Between Marcos' Jungle and bin Laden's caves

The Seattle protests clearly had a profound and positive impact on the global peace and justice movement. Yet for all the giddiness of the protests themselves, and the role they played in checking the cementing of the WTO's worldwide power, the long-term impact of the protests on the neoliberal economic system has been questionable. As Susan George, one of the founders of the French anti-corporate globalization organization ATTAC (Association pour la taxation des transactions finacières pour l'aide aux citoyens)[61] and a leading voice of the anti-corporate globalization movement, reflected in early 2001, "We haven't actually won anything from the world-wide corporate Government ... The same old people with their same old policies are still firmly in place. We have a long way to go before we win."[62] This assessment was written before September 11, and so her point has even more resonance now that it's really the same old people in charge. As important, the message of Seattle that "another world is possible" continues to confront a reality in which the majority of the American people seem happy with, or at least unconcerned or apathetic to, the world we have now.

In fact, a week earlier *Le Monde* exclaimed "Le sommet de Seattle a échoué, mais la mondialisation continue de plus belle"[63] – the WTO summit might have failed, but globalization is still continuing on quite nicely. Certainly the chances of the global peace and justice movement being able to "organize globalization" were still slim, and "without assigning blame, one can ask about the role of the movements of protest."[64] Naomi Klein put it more bluntly: "It's ugly out there ... We have in no way reversed the flow toward more privatization, let alone stopped it."[65]

The unique and perhaps unrepeatable success of Seattle left a legacy, at least temporarily, of optimism and renewed energy that fueled subsequent campaigns against corporate globalization.[66] Nevertheless, in the US subsequent protests in April, July, and August 2000 (in Washington DC, and at the Philadelphia and Los Angeles political conventions) drew smaller crowds. At the same time, police violence and political repression against protesters increased.

In Europe and Latin America, however, the movement continued to gain strength, in good measure because of the awareness and suspicion of American cultural, economic, and political power that naturally was far greater than in the US itself. This led to an increasingly powerful strategy of claiming space "outside the logo-ized, corporatized media-colonized realm" (as the activist and author Starhawk described the impact of Seattle).

Such a goal seemed within reach by the anti-IMF protests in Prague in September 2000, where I was fortunate enough to speak at the "Countersummit" to the IMF's meeting organized by an amazing array of grass-roots activists (whose budget was probably less than the coffee bills of the Seattle organizers). In fact, the "People's Summit" in Prague was more important and concentrated than any previous protest, in particular because it was "the first pan-European anti-capitalist demonstration."[67] What made Prague so important was that it marked the first time that activists and students from the former Soviet system helped shape the agenda and dynamics of the protests against the global capitalist system. With streets of the Czech capital filled with chants of "Prague, Seattle, Continue the Battle," the high level of coordination and positive energy of the organizers and marchers alike overcame a significant level of police violence. Sadly, however, this violence didn't just aim to rule out the possibility of successful non-violent protest, it foreshadowed even worse violence in Genoa ten months later.[68]

Despite the violence, Prague was important because for the first time one could sense a realization by organizers and leaders of the need to develop a vision that would encourage mainstream public opinion to consider new ways of imagining their future. In fact, Bernard Cassen, former editor of *Le Monde Diplomatique* and co-founder of ATTAC, argued that "a big problem is that the Left wants to ask 'what kind of organization do we need' and then 'what kind of ideas do we need,' as if you can ask them in that order."[69] In response to this concern, developing a more mainstreamable (but in no way compromised) vision was increasingly felt – although not universally, as we'll explore below – to be crucial to expanding the movement's base and increasing its likelihood of success. And doing so demanded the coordination of two separate but interrelated tasks: first, supporting and facilitating concrete campaigns with limited objectives; and second, at the same time promoting social alternatives to neoliberalism that could resonate with the majority of Europeans.[70]

In January 2001 the inaugural World Social Forum was held in Porto Alegre, Brazil, bringing together thousands of activists from around the world to discuss the realities of contemporary neoliberal globalization and strategize about how to build a different world. This meeting was followed by protests in Mexico, Buenos Aires, Quebec, Gothenburg, Geneva, Beirut, and Brussels, all carrying the imprint of Porto Alegre by deepening the reflections on solutions and globalizing the hope that "another world is possible."

Despite the increasing attention to thinking through the strategic course of the movement, the Prague and subsequent protests also revealed several problems, not least of which, as I mentioned in the first chapter, was the fact that there was little if any representation from the Muslim majority world, or even the more than 10 million-strong European Muslim communities, at the events.[71] By the massive July 2001 protests against the G-8 meeting in Genoa it was clear that the movement had reached its highest stage of development in its present form and strategic perspective. On the one hand, the sheer size and positive militancy of the protests meant that the belief that another world is possible seemed realizable for the first time. But it was just this fact which led the Berlusconi regime (which controlled a state that was no stranger to using significant violence against Leftist dissent) to deploy the most severe violence yet unleashed against peaceful protesters, leaving one protester dead and many injured.

The violence of the Italian state – here acting as a surrogate for the larger G-8 – was meant precisely to shatter the hope generated by the global peace and justice movement as it began to develop the more sophisticated and unified ideology called for in Porto Alegre. If such a platform could have been developed and spread around the world, it would have put the entire neoliberal system at risk. This was something no G-8 government was going to allow.[72] In fact, the violence used by the Italian state in Genoa led Italian activists, in the words of the title of one book about Genoa, to describe the protests in the city as evidence of a "global civil war" (*guerra civile globale*) that was soon to spread around the world. What is most important about the type of state repression witnessed in Genoa is how it is moving close to the kind of everyday repression deployed by regimes in the MENA.

The Aftermath of September 11, 2001: The Occupation of Iraq and the Limits of the Global Peace and Justice Movement

Coming less than six weeks after the violence of Genoa, the terrorist attacks on the World Trade Center and Pentagon on September 11 were perhaps the biggest gift given to corporate capitalism since the Soviets built the Berlin Wall. With the attacks, the political space that had been pried open by the anti-corporate globalization movement during the last decade was "instantly pulverized"; the disaster was immediately used by the US and other governments as the pretext to repress the movement everywhere in the world.[73] In the context of George W. Bush's "you're either with us or against us" mentality, senior US government officials began labeling anti-corporate globalization protesters as al-Qa'eda sympathizers. The Bush Administration's scare tactics didn't end there; in early 2004 it justified passing the second Patriot Act with warnings about the threat of "anarchists" – as we've seen, one of the most important groups within the anti-corporate globalization movement – to America.

It has been in the context of post-September 11 American culture that the global peace and justice movement has had to

> find a way to articulate that it is for Peace *and* Justice, and against terrorism of all kinds. This is a challenging project, since the anti-globalization movement must now complexify that which appears to

be simple [good Us vs. the evil terrorists] while previously its task was to simplify that which appeared to be complex [the WTO, neoliberalism, issues of growth and inequality, etc.].[74]

Since September 11 the global peace and justice movement has faced its greatest challenge of the last generation: how to continue gaining momentum in a climate of public fear and repression.[75] The enormity of the challenge led the magazine *Utne Reader* to exhort the movement to transform itself into the "ultimate peace movement ... we need to reconnect with the mission of Gandhi and Martin Luther King, Jr ... [as] the ethics of corporate globalization is essentially violent."[76]

In the aftermath of the supposedly "quick victory" by the US upon invading Iraq, the movement's task became both more urgent and difficult, which led to a period of self-evaluation. Despite its inability to prevent the invasion and occupation of Iraq, leaders and/or organizers clearly felt positive about the achievements of the hastily converged global peace and justice movement, especially the movement's unity, global reach, and "constant motion." Similarly, Leslie Cagan, the chair of United for Peace and Justice (UFPJ), explained to me soon after the invasion of Iraq that "millions of people are in motion." Such coordinated motion was, of course, one of the strategic goals of the anti-corporate globalization movement, and what made this possible was the coalescence of anti-war and anti-corporate globalization forces into one larger global peace and justice movement. This combined movement was heralded by the New York *Times* as "the second superpower," the most important unintended consequence of President Bush's drive to war.[77]

As one activist explained, "the fact that we connected with the doubts of millions of Americans in the post-September 11 environment is amazing. We built a strong degree of unity in action against the war while allowing for groups that had substantial differences to work together." Another activist, the Institute for Policy Studies' Phyllis Bennis, added that "the most important aspect of the movement is that it's global."[78]

Once again, however, it was not the US that took the lead. Rather, as Medea Benjamin of the leading anti-corporate globalization movement organization Global Exchange explains, "Outside of the US, there was a quicker realization among globalization folks that these issues were tied together."[79] Continual images of millions of Europeans, and especially Americans, marching against the war had a deep effect on Arabs and Muslims around the world. According to Pakistani scholar Pervez

Hoodhboy, because of strong public opposition in the West, demonstrations in his country featured the sort of signs that were seen in New York or Paris – "No Blood for Oil," "No to War" – rather than the blanket condemnations of America and the Christian/Jewish West or the radical Islamist slogans that one might have expected. The anti-war movement "proved to Muslims that their enemy was the US government, not the American people or the West per se."[80]

In a strange irony, however, the authoritarian regimes in the Middle East were able to use the vibrant anti-war movements in the West to contain their own populations, in part because while the Western anti-war movement was as angry at US policy as Middle Easterners, it refrained from offering sustained indictments of Middle Eastern regimes – even the one in Baghdad. Moreover, the limits of the consciousness of the anti-war movement and the larger global peace and justice movement was revealed in the general absence of sustained focus on the crimes of Saddam Hussein's regime, the need to bring him to justice, or to support a democratic transformation in Iraq.

One reason for this was no doubt that most organizations were concentrating on countering the specific justifications offered by the White House for war – especially the alleged threat of weapons of mass destruction – rather than offering an alternative to George W. Bush's version of "regime change."[81] Perhaps most important, even after the invasion most senior organizers remained opposed to offering a systemic critique of Middle Eastern political economy or an alternative to war to "democratize the Middle East," either because they felt it would dilute the simple "no to war" message, or because their coalitions might not have agreed upon a broader platform.

Whatever the reason, however, not doing so revealed a serious flaw in the reasoning and motivations of most of the main organizers and leaders – and, we can assume, the grass-roots activists as well – of the movement. Indeed, this reluctance brings to light the more general ideological problem of the movement. As Hany Khalil, a senior organizer with three anti-war organizations, including United For Peace and Justice and Racial Justice 9/11, explained, "we should have focused more on Hussein and a more holistic discourse, and in fact, the movement should have done a better job at thinking ideologically to counter Bush. We weren't sophisticated enough." This is an important insight, because it points precisely to a lack of ideological sophistication as a major cause of the movement's failure to mobilize the tens of millions of Americans and Europeans whose active participation would have been necessary to prevent war, or to view more critically the goals of the occupation-as-reconstruction.[82]

But few people in the movement feel that they could have prevented the war. In the words of Sara Flounders, director of the anti-war coalition ANSWER, "This was a war for empire, which is almost impossible to stop at the beginning. In fact, the current in the movement that supported inspections, sanctions, or war with UN authorization, was more ideologically muddled than our direct stand against war. These groups now might not stand firm against occupation, or call for what amounts to a UN fig leaf to replace US troops."

Ideological firmness and clarity are nice goals, but not at the expense of a strong grip on reality. As a past president of the Middle East Studies Association put it to me: "The anti-war coalition, the left and Arab intellectuals have not come to grips with the problem of the lack of democracy and development in the Arab world. Period. They have thus left this issue to Fox and the neo-cons." I'll return to this issue in a moment. But this perspective is clearly reflected by the final communiqué produced by the landmark meeting of American, European, and Arab anti-war activists in Cairo in December 2002, which as I already alluded to in the Introduction, reflects what I believe to be a serious, perhaps fatal, flaw in the strategic thinking of the global peace and justice movement. On the one hand, the communiqué contains perhaps the most concise explanations of the relationship between globalization and US military aggression yet offered by the movement. Yet it could only "admit" to "restrictions on democratic development in Iraq," while the majority of the document focused on Israeli and US crimes.

While attendees ignored the oppressive reality of the Egyptian or other Arab regimes – which angered at least a few organizers and participants – the declaration was, according to one Egyptian academic with ties to the Mubarak regime, used as a propaganda tool in its campaign to deflect public anger. By allowing the conference to proceed, the Government appeared to be criticizing the war only to arrest local activists after the media and foreign activists moved on.[83] Without underestimating the symbolic and networking importance of the gathering, we have to ask how organizers could claim that the event "conceptualized the Iraq problem in a global context" when it refused to address the regional, let alone Egyptian, situation as part of its critique.[84]

"It's America Now"

My reason for this rather detailed critique of the activities of the anti-war movement in the lead-up to the Iraq war is that they reflect larger problems within the global peace and justice movement. The well-known European Muslim activist and intellectual Tariq Ramadan describes them as follows:

> The worryingly deficient and conformist nature of the arguments put forward by the "alter"-globalisers on the question of the Middle East or Islam cannot be emphasized enough. One has to ask what alternative was really being proposed (beyond saying "No to the war") to counter America's unilateral stance and its programme of supervised democracy. Absence of awareness about Islam, as much as the fear cultivated and shared at the heart of the caricaturally constructed West, have led those seeking another kind of globalization to engage in superficial, if not dangerous talk on Islam. Where are the Arab and Muslim alter-globalisers? How can we reach out to the millions of activists in the Middle East, Africa and Asia who could become the new life blood of the movement?[85]

Whether in the US or Europe, most groups (particularly on the left) paid less attention to Hussein because they felt, and continue to feel, that the United States and its current drive to empire constitutes the most important, and even sole, threat to world peace and security. With few exceptions, this sentiment was shared across the board in the anti-war and anti-corporate globalization movements. "We have no option but to demonize the United States," an Italian participant at the Cairo conference declared.[86]

A senior organizer at the International Forum on Globalization explained, "The criticism shouldn't be that we didn't pay enough attention to the Middle East, but that we didn't pay enough attention to the US willingness to use all means to further its agenda …. We must face that it's America now." Yet another senior activist argued that Americans must be educated to understand that their government is "now 'enemy number one' for the peoples of the world."[87]

But there is no precedent in the history of empire for masses of citizens to oppose, let alone transform, a state's imperial policies. Majorities of British and French citizens alike were proud of their countries' world dominance – only the financial and physical losses of large-scale war, and massive indigenous resistance, changed their minds. Few Americans remember the last "Anti-Imperialist League," started in 1899 to oppose the invasion of the Philippines; the Vietnam War became unpopular after heavy American casualties, not because of significant moral disgust with the war.

Today it takes little to inspire new imperial visions at the heart of our political system, while motivating the public *actively* to oppose its results (and not just complain about it to pollsters or vote Bush out of office in favor of a President who wants even more troops in Iraq) is, it seems, beyond the reach even of tens of thousands of deaths, photos of torture, videotaped beheadings, and the theft of a few hundred billions tax-dollars. But beyond its lack of appeal to mainstream America, such a narrow discourse is "replete with dangers. The resurgence of a very limited understanding of empire in left academic circles is disturbing. Powerful and dangerous interests are served by this retrograde focus solely on US empire, because it's not just the US that is imperialist. Argentina is suffering under imperialism, but part of what's made Argentina so vulnerable has been that the main imperial players here are European – Spanish, British, French and Italian companies are the owners of most of the privatized industries, and their interests and modus operandi are little different from the US in the Middle East."[88]

There's also a structural problem with this focus on the United States, even after the occupation of Iraq. As Naomi Klein presciently explained it to me: "It's no longer about the US building empire in a traditional sense, but rather a multinational imperialism. Europe is laughing at the US's empire discourse because it lets them off the hook. European leaders enjoy the idea that they're a counter-power – Chirac playing the hero of the oppressed – when what Europe is doing on the international stage is 90 percent the same as the US. What we need is an analysis of empire that understands that the forces are genuinely transnational. They can't be tied to the nation-state, and the class of global managers within the developing world are part of the same class as their northern counterparts." And it's not just imperialism that takes advantage of this dynamic; capitalism and nationalism are also crucial to its success. So to bet that Americans will respond to anti-imperialist discourse when the power of the modernity matrix has never been stronger in post-September 11 America seems an unwise wager.

Indeed, if the new anti-imperialism is to succeed where earlier incarnations did not, it will be crucial to develop a positive yet viable alternative paradigm that resonates with the concerns and highest ideals of American and European societies. And getting that paradigm to penetrate public consciousness will mean overcoming the Axis of Ignorance and Arrogance that is defended not just by the current occupants of the White House and majority in Congress, but by the vast majority of the Fortune Five Hundred corporations, the entire weapons–petrodollar coalition, Rush Limbaugh and the men who run Clear Channel Communications (the largest radio network in the US, owned by the ultra-conservative Randy Michaels), Disney (whose CEO

Michael Eisner refused to distribute the Michael Moore documentary *Fahrenheit 9/11* because it might jeopardize pending favorable legislation in Congress), most local school boards, Fox News, conservative and so-called liberal "experts" like Daniel Pipes, Bernard Lewis, Samuel Huntington, Tom Friedman or Noah Feldman, David Frum and Richard Perle, and so on. And that's just in the United States.

Anti-Semitism and the Internal Problems of the Global Peace and Justice Movement

The global peace and justice movement clearly has its hands full given the power and ruthlessness of its opponents. But besides the challenges posed by the advisors to empire on the ground in Iraq, the movement is facing problems within its ranks, many of which surround accusations of "anti-Semitism"[89] in the US by some Jewish peace activists who've felt that the focus on Palestine after the Iraq occupation and the vehement and sometimes strident criticism of Israel reflected anti-Jewish sentiments within the movement.[90] Others have argued that the supposedly anti-Israel attitudes by many in the movement reflect a difficulty embracing critical voices from, or avoiding generalizations about, groups like Jews who are perceived to be too implicated in the power structure.[91] (Why this doesn't happen with white Protestant men points to an underlying truth, however exaggerated, in the accusations of anti-Jewish sentiments.)

My sense is that within the North American movement – we'll talk about Europe and the MENA region in the next chapter – there are some anti-Jewish sentiments, but they are marginal. Instead, the debate over anti-Semitism points to other problems.[92] That is, the focus on Palestine or Iraq is not wrong in itself, but in the context of the narrow strategic vision of the movement as a whole it is problematic. This is because by focusing on "Palestine, Afghanistan and Iraq" (as one protest slogan described it), the movement has maintained a narrow vision that can't acknowledge that the forces responsible for the lack of peace, justice, and adequate human development in the Middle East are far more diffuse and numerous than just the US and Israel, however important their roles.

Indeed, the rhetoric on Palestine reveals a one-directional understanding of the situation that is similar to the movement's stand on Iraq: there has been little discussion of the corruption and brutality of Yasser Arafat and the Palestinian Authority, or the crucial debates over non-violence and democracy now taking place among Palestinian activists and intellectuals.[93] Such sentiments continued in the lead-up to the major protests organized by the ANSWER coalition on March 20, 2004 (the one-year anniversary of the US invasion) where Iraq and Palestine were singled out, while places like Chechnya, the Sudan, Tibet, and other occupied lands were relegated to the status of "everywhere else." At my own university, in the middle of intense violence in Iraq (and only days after the beheading of the American Nicholas Berg) a rally in support of "Zionism Awareness Week" featured speakers shouting their "support for the Iraqi and Palestinian resistance against the US and Israel," without any consideration of the political, human, and even moral fallout of the violence they were uncritically defending.

This unwillingness to adopt a critical perspective on the use of violence to resist occupation is not just a post-September 11 phenomenon. In early 2001 I moderated a culture jam in Los Angeles that featured some of the most important political artists in the United States, during which one of them explained to the audience that what was needed was the violent overthrow of the US Government. Having just returned from Israel/Palestine a few weeks before and seen the violence of the then still new intifada first hand, I tried to explain why this kind of discussion of violence hurt more than helped the fight for peace and social justice, but he wouldn't accept it.

Finally, one of the other artists on the panel, who unlike the one advocating violence grew up in the midst of LA's notorious gang culture, interjected exasperatedly: "Man, have you ever been stabbed or shot?" to which the other panelist answered, "No." "Have you ever stabbed, shot or killed anyone, or used any violence against anyone before?" to which he replied, "No." "So then what right do you have to talk like this and advocate violence when you have no idea what it means to inflict or be the victim of it?" I mention this small argument because it reveals how easy it is for many in the global peace and justice movement, who have little knowledge of the realities of violence in their own lives, to advocate or at least condone violence by various sides in the conflicts they're protesting against, even though the cycles of violence they would extend are so crucial to maintaining the status quo throughout the MENA.

But there's an even deeper ideological problem with the focus of US anti-war movements on Iraq and Palestine and the refusal to condemn violence by the victims of oppression. This is the fact that, aside from the descendants of African slaves, virtually no one in the movement in the US isn't him or herself a settler, who isn't directly benefiting from the greatest genocide and largest occupation of other peoples' lands in the history of the world. How many peace activists even know the names of Native American tribes on whose lands, most likely stolen, they're living, working or studying? What right does anyone have to protest the occupation of Iraq or Palestine and not work to improve the lives and even reclaim the lands of the Native American communities in the United States (and we'd assume wrongly if we figured they've all become rich off casinos)?

The near destruction of Native American societies through the establishment and expansion of the United States is every bit as much the result of imperialism as the more recent occupations of Palestine or Iraq. And if we turn to the MENA, most countries in the region are plagued by significant and often violent discrimination against, oppression and even enslavement of minority ethnic, religious and/or cultural groups. As our discussion of the roots and dynamics of globalization in Chapters Four and Five make clear, however good it feels to criticize the US and Israel, their occupations will not be confronted successfully until the "movement of movements" throughout the world becomes a truly holistic vehicle for social transformation, one that is as critical of its own ideologies and practices as it is of the political and economic system it's combating.

Conclusion: Two Superpowers?

Whatever its failings, the global peace and justice movement has scored a major victory in replacing the defunct Soviet Union as the world's "second superpower." But if it doesn't want to wind up with the same fate as the last major challenger to the "free world" it has a lot of ground to cover, especially if it hopes to achieve the kind of unity, global reach, political motion, and ideological coherence possessed by the fundamentalists of neoliberalism or Islam, and with far fewer resources than either of them at its disposal.

Soren Ambrose, a lead activist with the group of the Fifty Years is Enough network, provided a cogent assessment of the task at hand in the wake of the US invasion of Iraq: "What we didn't have was enough structure to take us through and keep unity and organizational identity past the war. That's the crisis we're in now." While some organizers feel there is a strong base on which to build for future activities, Ambrose realized within weeks of the invasion that "there's just not a sense of an ongoing movement for peace in this country, a permanent bulwark against the military side of the empire. Organizations like my own did insufficient work making plain the links between US militarism and the dominance of the world economy. Part of that is lack of knowledge, time and being intimidated by how much we need to know." Antonia Juhasz of the International Forum on Globalization agreed: "If it takes so long to figure out the policies of the World Bank or trade issues, taking on the much larger task of understanding the intricacies and dynamics of a worldwide US empire is even more daunting."

But this process is made more difficult when organizers like ANSWER's Sara Flounders argue that "people are realizing that their real enemy, the enemy that stands against all human progress, is the US and its imperialism."[94] What this accusation omits is that imperialism never succeeded without the active cooperation of crucial sectors in the colonized or "peripheral" countries. Moreover, if the US suddenly retired from the empire business any one of a dozen countries would be happy to take its place. This reality is what led one frustrated participant in the December 2002 Cairo anti-war gathering "furiously" to criticize the tone of the meeting: "The Iraqi people are also suffering because … their regime is as corrupt as all the others. You can only be credible if you don't turn a blind eye to your own failures."[95]

This could be a tall order for a Left that, in many ways, has still to address the problems caused by the infighting and dogmatism of the 1960s and 1970s. Yet it is perhaps the *sine qua non* for the ideological maturity that would make possible a more holistic message by the peace movement, one that would resonate with much wider numbers of Americans.

At the forum of leading Islamist activists I discussed in Chapter Five, Tariq Ramadan and Nadia Yassine forcefully argued that Muslims and Europeans must move beyond facile denunciations of the US. Ramadan explained: "To face this reality, we have to speak of the common risks we are facing – not just the Muslim world but everyone. It's important to find a way to come to universal values and to say this period is a challenge to all of us together. The current security strategy is against all of us as citizens – we are losing our civil rights in Europe, in the US, not just Muslims, but everyone … That's why we have to avoid simplistic and superficial anti-Americanism."

Activists such as Erik Gustafson of the group Education and Peace in Iraq Center (EPIC) consider this type of cosmopolitan thinking and international action to be the core of the necessary transformation of the anti-war movement into a genuine solidarity movement. "[The movement] must become more about human rights, balanced perspective, recognizing just how [the] US has contributed to the Iraqi people's suffering, but also how the Hussein regime, the UN and outside powers contributed too. Only then can we show true solidarity with the Iraqi people."[96]

If the global peace and justice movement is to develop a more sophisticated message and strategy and offer a positive alternative to militarized neoliberal globalization, intercommunal solidarity through dialogue and committed non-violence will be the key mechanisms. If such relationships can be forged between the Arab and Muslim worlds and activists in the West, the global peace and justice movement may yet gain the upper hand in the struggle against global empire. But first we all have to – literally – join hands. In the next chapter we'll explore three strategies for doing just that.

8 Inspiring the Impossible: The Global Peace and Justice Movement Between Old Problems and New Horizons

Which Movement Will Take the Lead?

Now that we have a basic understanding of the history, achievements, and problems of the global peace and justice movement, we can explore the challenges it faces as it seeks to transform itself from a group of "meeting stalkers following the trade bureaucrats around as if they were the Grateful Dead" into a collective of innumerable local movements, fighting the way neoliberal politics are playing out in their communities at the same time as they struggle collectively to develop global strategies and philosophies.[1]

On the one hand, the strategy of localism has been influenced by the experiences of the Zapatistas and the loose coalitions of anarchist-inspired groups whose presence was so important, if also problematic, at the worldwide protests epitomized by Seattle.[2] But localism is only one of several strategies envisioned in the struggle for global peace and justice. Various trends within the movement advocate giving more power to governments to defend their economies and cultures against neoliberalism, or call for an explicit "deglobalization" of the world economy in favor of a more decentralized system so that countries can pursue their own paths towards sustainable development and democracy.[3]

The common thread running through all these strategies is a combined anti-capitalist and anti-imperialist perspective that is trying to break the bonds between militarism and neoliberal "development."[4]

When we add the quintessentially cosmopolitan personalities of many members of the movement – that is, their willingness to put universalistic principles ahead of the narrowly defined "interests" of their countries (in fact, many feel little allegiance to their own countries or even the concept of the nation-state) – we see how the global peace and justice movement is ultimately fighting not just neoliberal globalization but the larger modernity matrix behind it.

But for Muslims or their comrades of other faiths and cultures, the reality is perhaps that choosing between systemic change and spaces of autonomy would be self-defeating, and even unnecessary. In fact, the two are better understood as inseparable rather than as incompatible: clear goals and objectives are necessary to mobilize large numbers of people, acquire social and political power, and in so doing "change the world" at the structural level. Yet it's the essentially "disorganized" nature of the movement of movements and its focus, not on achieving power, but on draining it away from politicians and others currently holding it, that makes it strong. Finding synergy between these two strategies will be central to any successful campaign against empire, in the Muslim world as well as the West. Let's look at three strategies – anarchism, Zapatismo, and the World Social Forum movement – to see what they can teach us about the possibilities of achieving such synergy.

Anarchists: Finding the Limits of Confrontation

Perhaps the most important strategies to emerge in the late 1990s protests were those associated with the various "anarchist" groups who constituted the core of the more militant protesters since that time.[5] It is difficult to nail down a set of core beliefs shared by the majority of people and groups labeled as anarchist. In fact, on the face of it it's hard to understand how a movement whose principal goals are "ideological and tactical unity, collective action and discipline" can be anarchist.[6]

We can even say that viewed broadly, the larger anti-corporate globalization movement is itself essentially anarchic, given the deliberate lack of an over-arching program or strategy. Yet we shouldn't confuse anarchism with a desire for social chaos, which is exactly the opposite of what most anarchists want. If it is possible to generalize about the social and political views of the various anarchist tendencies in the anti-corporate globalization movement, it seems, on the one hand, that they're concerned "less with seizing state power than exposing, delegitimizing and dismantling mechanisms of rule and in so doing winning ever larger spaces of autonomy from it."[7] On the other hand, they want "national governments to be free to exercise their authority without interference from the WTO, and ask for stricter international rules governing labor standards, environmental protection and scientific research."[8] But however much they might want to strengthen the power of governments to protect citizens against corporate power, their most basic political focus is on a re-invention of democratic processes through new forms of "horizontal networks of interaction" as close to the grass-roots level as possible.[9]

Perhaps the most well-known type of anarchist grouping to emerge since Seattle has been based on the "black bloc" strategy of coordinated, militant protest against police forces and symbols of corporate power at the major protests. The black bloc emerged as a natural outgrowth of the loosely organized, self-sufficient support systems known as "affinity groups," which are composed of anywhere between five and fifteen people who come together during the planning of larger protests to pursue a shared philosophy, set of goals or strategies (such as a willingness directly to confront police, focus on a specific issue, or perform various types of "street theater"). By the time of the Seattle protests in late 1999 one of the most prominent types of affinity groups revolved around the "anarchist black bloc" strategy, which called for engaging in various forms of economic disruption such as (in Seattle specifically) the targeted destruction of corporate property like NikeTown, Levi's, Fidelity Investment or other banks.

In reality, then, the black bloc is not a group or "bloc" of people. Instead it's a tactic deployed by collections of anarchists and sympathetic affinity groups to achieve two main goals: first, to provide solidarity in the face of repressive police or government tactics; and second, to offer a specifically anarchist critique of the issues surrounding a protest (depending on the circumstance, we could also add the goal of destroying corporate property around the location of a protest).[10] In the US the anarchist black blocs were organized through the activities of the Direct Action Network (DAN), which was itself a loose coalition of individuals and organizations set up in the months leading up to Seattle.[11]

To accomplish their goals DAN trained hundreds of people in civil disobedience tactics at sites throughout the northwest in preparation for Seattle, a practice which caused alarm in law enforcement and received significant – if biased – media attention.[12] But it wasn't just the militant civil disobedience that made the DANs and black blocs

unique and important; as important was the level of trust and solidarity within their affinity groups. This supported a radically non-
hierarchical decision-making structure that was recognized to be the
complete opposite of the existing authoritarian world system.[13]

This kind of radically democratic structure is important when a
movement – as has happened with the global peace and justice
movement in and since Seattle – has to develop new strategies and
politics. In this situation the tactics of Direct Action and the black
blocs act to define the limits and potential of various methods of
confronting the increasing levels of government repression.[14] Indeed,
in the US particularly, if the political system becomes more closed and
oppressive, and if a significant percentage of Americans actually refuse
to accept this state of affairs (a big if, to be sure), the level of direct
confrontation with the state will likely increase as more traditional
styles of protest lose their effectiveness.[15] This situation would make
the black bloc strategy that much more important; but the question is
clearly whether such confrontations will see increasing violence used
by protesters or move towards the direction of a militant pacifism.[16] As
we'll see below, much of the answer depends on whether these movements can be as holistic and welcoming to different cultures and
politics as they portray themselves as being.

Shades of Grey

I must admit I have a very ambivalent attitude toward the anarchist/
black bloc movements. On the one hand, the more I have examined
the strategic role of the anarchists in the movement the more I have
come to appreciate their courage and thoughtfulness – especially after
spending time in Iraq. I also know from personal experience that the
same ninja-dressed guerrillas who hours earlier were battling police
could speak passionately and perceptively about the problems faced
by the larger movement and the positive role of anarchist tactics in the
struggle. The LA culture jam that I described at the start of this book,
and the time I've spent with European anarchists demonstrate this in
spades.

Moreover, the black bloc and similar affinity groups have helped to
bring in to the movement minorities and communities with histories
of police violence who had no desire to stick to polite middle-class and
often middle-aged protest. Indeed, their actions clearly helped teach
the movement at large what people of color have long known – that
the price of defiance in American or European democracy can be one's
freedom or even one's life.[17] And while to an American eye the mask

that symbolizes the anarchist desire for anonymity brings to mind Hamas more than Subcommandante Marcos, there are good reasons for the movement to avoid public leadership, as any leaders that arose publicly would be immediately targeted for arrest and abuse. For any movement so radically challenging the political system today it's better not to have leaders.

But for all their talk of non-violence towards anything other than property, the reality is that the anarchist blocs have literally barreled me over running to battle the police in LA and Prague. And this isn't just my experience, as there is a documented history of low-level violence within the movement.[18] Of course, even the worst violence by protesters pales in comparison with what governments have deployed against them. Yet I would argue that these actions would seem to be politically and culturally counterproductive; especially when neither the movement nor the public it is "performing" for have the level of sophistication, social support and/or awareness that led a whole village to join with José Bové in dismantling a half-built McDonald's and depositing the pieces in front of their City Hall (as happened in Millau, France in the Year of Seattle).[19]

And so while I understand the reasoning and the potential media and/or attention-getting value of limited property destruction, I remain torn about such tactics, from personal experience. For example, I'm a vegetarian, and while Prague has a couple of the best vegetarian restaurants I've ever eaten in, I could literally find nothing resembling a vegetable in any of the restaurants in the new downtown area when my wife and I took a break from protesting during the September 2000 protests. We wound up with no choice but to go into a McDonald's that hours later would be attacked by the black bloc and order fries (which thankfully in Europe aren't made with "beef flavoring") and salads. If the anarchists – many of whom we had had lunch with earlier in the day at the Hare Krishna restaurant on the other side of town – had beaten us to McDonald's, we would have literally gone to bed hungry.

Of course, we could afford to spend a night without food; certainly it's a fair price to pay in the struggle against neoliberalism. And our particular convergence of the global war against capitalism (protesting in the morning) with the kind of global tourism (ogling at Prague's architectural heritage in the afternoon) that is at the heart of global capitalism today does point to the contradictions inherent in battling neoliberalism on its home turf. My point however is ultimately more serious: if we're talking about creating a truly worldwide movement that would bring Evangelicals in Des Moines, Iowa or

Muslims in Ryadh, Saudi Arabia, into a shared social network that could move forward towards a radically holistic transformation of the world, the question needs to be asked, can the present anarchist model of concerted direct action confronting the state, including the use of limited and largely symbolic violence, work in Cairo? Houston? Gaza? Sioux City? Falluja? Tehran?

I am not competent to answer definitively such an important question from an American perspective, although I suspect the answer is no. If we're talking about the "anarchist" strategy of dressing in black and engaging in violence, even if symbolic or directed only at corporate property, it seems clear that in post-September 11, hyper-patriotic America, let alone the Middle East, the state has so much power and freedom to deploy excessive violence in response to any kind of violence – however symbolic – used by demonstrators, that such violence would seem to be counterproductive. In today's climate, the danger is not just to be arrested, but much worse.

On the other hand, what would have happened if Iraqi insurgents in Falluja or Najaf, or Palestinian militants in the West Bank or Gaza, had used Zapatista and/or black bloc tactics rather than full-scale violence against the forces occupying their countries? Certainly far fewer people would have been killed or injured, and the leaders of the movement would have been in a much better position to command the world stage and demand a full return of Iraqi or Palestinian sovereignty – precisely because the world community would have been more likely to sympathize with such a movement.[20] (Of course, this begs the question of whether Iraqi insurgents care about international public sympathy or even desire to build the kind of democracy that would win international public – as opposed to governments' – support. To the extent they never had this interest, it demonstrates how disastrous the closure of the public sphere and civil society has been to progressive forces in the country.)

Perhaps the answer to the question of the utility of largely symbolic violence depends on which side of the spectrum of violence we look at it from. In a country like the US, where public violence is rare and unacceptable to the majority culture, symbolic violence may shock people but will usually have little positive strategic impact. But in autocratic and/or violence-torn societies, whether in the Middle East or Latin America, black bloc or Zapatista tactics constitute a moral and strategic advance over the violent insurrections pursued by resistance groups.

In fact, there would be many advantages to Middle Eastern movements adopting anarchist strategies such as loosely affiliated, leaderless networks and horizontal, democratic relations between members, with a focus on overcoming patriarchal or racist dynamics in the larger society; or building grass-roots pro-democracy and social and economic justice networks. This is for several reasons. First, because the level of state repression of dissent is such that it makes sense not to have identifiable leaders who would likely be arrested as soon as they achieved some notoriety. Second, because the strength of patriarchal and otherwise intolerant and hierarchical structures within these societies is so strong that a clear attempt to build coalitions around direct action and anarchistic principles would ensure that these tendencies were at least confronted head on rather than pushed beneath the surface (as so often happens in progressive movements around the world). And third, because the "many yesses" and affinity group structure of the Direct Action Networks would allow the space for plural views and strategies to exist side-by-side without directly challenging each other, which is vitally important in the still struggling public spheres of Muslim societies.

In fact, direct action-type activities could have worked well in a space such as US-occupied Iraq – especially if many more internationals were there working with Iraqis – because the US administration didn't (at the time of writing) have complete control of the situation on the ground. And it could perhaps succeed in countries like Jordan or Morocco, which permit some autonomous political space, if actions were extremely well thought out and coordinated. The problem is that anarchism has such a bad name within mainstream Western political consciousness, and has so little traction within Muslim societies, that it would be incredibly difficult to develop a self-consciously anarchistic Arab/Muslim political force. Even more so since "Islam" is portrayed by almost every Muslim religious figure as *the* alternative social order to capitalist modernity or globalization, while historically and even theologically anarchy is considered worse even than oppression. But even if "anarchy" as a name can't travel (and certainly for successfully passing it on to the MENA its symbol looks too much like the pentagram that keeps getting Middle Eastern metalheads into trouble), the strategies and practices of anarchists in the West have a lot to offer activists in the MENA.[21]

Marcos in the Middle East?

If there's one movement that people and groups around the world continuously look to for strategic, ideological, and even spiritual inspiration, it's the Zapatistas. Despite their humility, self-criticism, and renunciation of any claim to be a vanguard force in their society, the Zapatistas have come to embody many of the most important insights of anarchist thinking and strategies.[22] With their focus on fighting for autonomy rather than seeking state power, their desire to use symbolic rather than physical violence whenever possible, their radically democratic decision-making structure, and the prominent role of women in the movement, the Zapatistas have quickly become a model that inspired individuals and movements struggling against neoliberal globalization around the world. It's probably no exaggeration to say that without the Zapatista revolt and their subsequent organizing and intellectual and ideological vanguardism, Seattle would never have happened, nor would the anti-corporate globalization movement have gained such strength in Europe in the late 1990s.

So much has been written on the Zapatistas by movement activists and intellectuals that I won't provide a detailed history or description of their ideology here. What I'm interested in is how the movement helped shape the larger ideologies and strategies of the anti-corporate globalization movement, and how they might assert a positive influence on the evolving progressive movements for social change in the Muslim world.

From this perspective neoliberalism was crucial to the Zapatistas' revolt.[23] Why did the Zapatistas cry "Enough is enough!" as they ran into battle with Mexican troops? "For all intents and purposes we were already dead. We meant absolutely nothing … Enough dying this useless death; it is better to fight for change. If we die now, it will not be with shame but with dignity, like our ancestors."[24] Such sentiments, it isn't hard to realize, are shared almost word for word by tens of millions of Muslims in the MENA region and beyond.

We also know that the Zapatista movement was born out of a desperate need for indigenous rights and autonomy from state and corporate power, a situation that became more urgent with NAFTA and the dumping of Monsanto and other GMO seeds in Mexico. Seizing political power was not the desired end. Instead the goal was a push for sovereignty and autonomy (first to all Mexicans, then to all peoples of the world) as signified by the call to "express Zapatismo." This in turn was part of a strategy of "globalization from below" that would involve the "delinking" and relocalization of the indigenous regional economies of Mexico.[25]

In his Foreword to a collection of Marcos's writings the Brazilian Nobel Prize-winning author José Saramago discusses the French philosopher Montesquieu's 1721 *Persian Letters* in order to argue that "the Zapatistas and the people in Chiapas are the 'Persians of Chiapas.'" For him Zapatistas essentially seek "a world where there is room for many worlds, a world that can be one and diverse ... that for all people and all time declares untouchable the right of everyone to be a 'Persian' any time he or she wants to and without obeying anything but one's own roots."[26]

Perhaps the distance between Tehran and Chiapas isn't as far as we might imagine. And so the Zapatista experience is very important in the context of the post-September 11 global peace and justice movement, not just because of the (at least strategic) humility of Zapatista leaders and their influence on European groups like Ya Basta![27] As important, the movement has been able to construct in Chiapas "an extraordinary apparatus of culture, communication and cooperation," which provided it with the opportunity to express its "distance from Western culture." As Marcos explains, if in Iraq the US occupies a country with its *águilas gritonas*, or "screaming eagles," in SouthEast Mexico the *caracoles* – or snails – have defined new forms of self-governance for the indigenous communities.[28] This is an important argument, because it shows that the Zapatistas have a specific strategy to counter "the rapacity of military power and of a destructive economic system: the metaphor of '*el Llentitud del caracol*' – the slowness of the snail, as only a slow and long process can be able to succeed in the anthropological transformation necessary for reconstructing a world devastated by neoliberal domination."[29]

The phenomenal influence of the Zapatista movement on the worldwide anti-corporate globalization movement shows that the Global North can and must learn from the South.[30] But the Zapatistas can also be of great inspiration for Arab and Muslim activists struggling against their own oppressive social, political, and economic systems. How exactly can this happen? What inspiration can Zapatismo give to Muslims working for progressive change in their societies?

First, in the role of women. If a society as traditionally patriarchal as Mexico's can spawn a movement that can radically recognize the power and influence of women working for revolutionary change, then there's no excuse for a lack of similar maturity in the MENA,[31] a possibility that is strengthened by the increasingly prominent public role of Islamist women throughout the Muslim majority world. Second is the belief that "the seizure of power does not justify the revolutionary organization taking any means that it pleases. We do not believe that the end justifies the means. Ultimately we believe that the means are the end."[32] This perspective is a clear and positive alternative to the use of terror and other forms of violence by Muslims engaged in resisting occupation, or the neoliberal globalization more generally.

Third is the belief that today's globalization is a "pay-per-view globalization," as Marcos described it in *Le Monde Diplomatique*. This is perhaps the perfect description for the out-of-reach globalization as cultural spectacle that constitutes the experience of so many in the Middle East, where the only way of experiencing the United States and its seemingly unquenchable culture is through satellite TV. Ironically, this is a condition which, as Marcos puts it, is leading to "le future passé," where "the dull images can signify [only] this: the reappearance of fascism."[33] If we consider the role played by scholars and experts in shaping and defending neoliberalism in its various facets, Marcos's analysis is cutting:

> In other words, in the hour of globalization, the intellectuals of the right are … "multicartes," gravediggers of critical analysis and of reflection, believing anything they're told of the neoliberal theology, prompters of governments who forget the "script," commentators of the evident, supporters of soldiers and police, arbiters of saying the "true" and the "false" according to their convenience, theoreticians-guards of the corps of the Prince, and presenters of a "new history."[34]

Such a critical focus on the intellectual handmaidens of empire is crucial for the Middle East, but as important is the fundamental role of religion in the birth of the Zapatista movement. Marcos and his comrades could never have developed their "army" if Bishop Samuel Ruiz, a long-time advocate for the indigenous people of the Chiapas region, hadn't prepared the groundwork (which was also made possible by the prominence of liberation theology in Mexico during the 1960s and 1970s). Indeed, one of the reasons that Ruiz became so involved in the plight of his flock was that the growing choice of religious expressions – from various strands of Protestant churches to missionary Islam – were encroaching into a region were the Catholic Church had failed to serve their interests. Here too, the resonances with the important role played by Islamist and other religious forces in any holistic reform of MENA societies has antecedents in the Lacandian jungles.

Whatever the limitations of the Zapatista experience,[35] Marcos's writings reveal wide similarities with the situation in the MENA region, and offer important examples of how a more successful grass-roots movement for democracy and economic justice could emerge there: the Zapatistas emerged "out of the impossibility of struggling peacefully for our elemental rights as human beings. The most valuable of these rights is the right to decide, freely and democratically, what form the government will take."[36] Such a claim is the absolute *sine qua non* for any kind of progressive agenda in the region. Moreover, the Zapatistas set an important example by calling for "*consultas* and revolutionary conventions presided over, freely and voluntarily, by civilians, prestigious public figures, launched by local, state and regional committees."[37]

Finally there is also the Zapatista view of modernity and its links to neoliberalism: For Marcos,

> it is not possible for neoliberalism to become the world's reality without the argument of death served up by institutional and private armies, without the gag served up by prisons, without the blows and assassinations served up by the military and the police. National repression is a necessary premise of the globalization neoliberalism imposes ... on the one side is neoliberalism, with all its repressive power and all its machinery of death; on the other side is the human being.[38]

This argument is clearly sympathetic to the Arab/Muslim sentiment about the conflict between human nationalisms and inhuman globalizations as a defining struggle of the global era.

In fact, Marcos's definition of modernity squarely puts him in the camp of the most vocal critiques of globalization. As he defines it, to achieve modernity,

> carefully combine a technocrat, a repentant oppositionist, a sham businessman, a union bully, a landowner, a builder, an alchemist in computational arts, a "brilliant" intellectual, a television, a radio and an official party. Set this mixture aside in a jar and label it "Modernity." Put the indigenous Mexican in another jar, set it aside and label it "Dispensable." One must not forget to disinfect oneself after this last operation.[39]

Other leading Latin American thinkers, such as Enrique Dussel and Nestor Garcia Canclini, have a similar view of modernity – one developed in my view because Latin America has felt the full brunt of modernity longer and more tragically than any other continent. But if modernity has to go, so do the other three coefficients of the modernity matrix: capitalism, colonialism, and nationalism. And so too must the nation-state as it's currently configured: "By suicide or execution the death of the current Mexican political system is a necessary, although not sufficient, precondition for the transition to democracy in our country ... [it] must have a context of new local, regional and national political relationships – relationships marked by democracy, freedom and justice."[40]

By now it should be clear that the experience and ideology of the Zapatistas are crucial sources of inspiration at many levels of the MENA movements for peace and justice, something which Marcos implicitly recognizes in this universal call to arms: "We will make a collective network of all our particular struggles and resistances, an intercontinental network of resistance against neoliberalism, an inter-continental network of resistance for humanity, recognizing differ-ences and acknowledging similarities, will strive to find itself in other resistances around the world."[41]

What is most amazing about this call to arms is that it comes from a people that has been brutalized far worse during the last five hundred years than anything faced by citizens of the MENA. Perhaps the situ-ation hasn't become bad enough yet to disabuse many Muslims of the kind of violent fantasies of meeting the US/West in holy war that was understood to be a futile option in Chiapas by the 1980s, the very time that a violent Islamist politics was emerging in the MENA.

But Can Zapatismo Work on the Ground in the Midlde East?

While the Zapatista experience and ideology has a lot to offer to activists for progressive change in the MENA, their impact would be limited if the social and larger institutional environments faced by activists in both regions were too different. Luckily, Amory Starr in her important book, *Naming the Enemy*, provides a detailed analysis of how the various types of anti-corporate globalization movements understand and address crucial questions and issues. Among them are the Zapatistas and "religious nationalist" movements (which can be understood as comprising the majority of Islamist movements, even those with transnational networks and agendas).[42]

If we focus just on the Zapatistas and progressive religious move-ments, we learn that both share similar perspectives and strategies on almost every major issue related to globalization. These include their support for both popular and "traditional" cultures as bases for resis-tance against neoliberal globalization, a suspicion of ideologies of progress, a view of multinational corporations as inherently colo-nialist, and a desire to engage in a "transformative dialogue with the enemy."[43] Clearly in theory the ideas and experience of the Zapatistas are relevant to the Middle East, at least as inspiration for building grass-roots social movements in the region. But can the Zapatista ideology and tactics of resistance be applied to occupied settings, such as Iraq or Palestine, where they're needed most?

In the next and final chapter I will explore this question in Iraq. Here let's look at how Zapatismo plays out on the ground in Palestine. I put this question to a young Palestinian activist, 'Ala al-Azzeh, who as I mentioned in a previous chapter runs a grass-roots community center in the Azza refugee camp in Bethlehem. Drinking tea and talking politics in a bedroom riddled by bullet holes from various Israeli shootings, I noticed that he had a copy of Marcos's *Our Word is Our Weapon* on his book shelf. I was immediately struck by the idea of the Zapatistas inspiring new and more creative ways for Palestinians to resist the occupation through building grass-roots networks and symbols in the manner of the Zapatistas. But as we discussed the virtues of Zapatismo in the camp and continued our discussion over the phone and email, it became clear that taking the much celebrated Zapatista way and applying it to Palestine is not as easy as I had first imagined.

Al-Azzeh's comments are extremely insightful and worth looking at carefully. As he explains,

> In principle, we have much in common with the Zapatista experience: the concept of an indigenous community with its land stolen and continuing oppression is the same. But the issue is the objective reality that has taken root on the ground since then. In Palestine a more "romantic" attachment to the land developed, not just because so many people became refugees, but because of the way Israel has relentlessly confiscated more land, pushed out people, and the like. On top of that, it became almost impossible to make a living just by farming, and as people began to work in Israel we went from being peasants to being cheap labor and so we lost the strong direct connection with the land that had been so important in our history.
>
> What this means is that today we need to reconsider, reimagine and reconstruct the Palestinian political discourse ... It's hard to adopt the Zapatista lessons about resistance, and even the way they directly bring neoliberal globalization into their critique, because for us resisting occupation is a practical strategy that must address our objective reality in the occupation rather than some idealized goal such as neoliberal globalization. Look what happened at al-Quds University, when the Israelis were about to build their "separation (apartheid) wall" straight through the athletic field, even though Sari Nusseibah, one of Israel's favorite "moderate" Palestinian leaders, is President of the University. We held vigils, hunger strikes, festivals, all sorts of non-violent protests for weeks and weeks, and in the end, for all that energy, the wall was moved a few meters.[44]

Al-Azzeh also argued that

> ... our starting point of the struggle is completely different than the Zapatistas, which started in response to globalization while we have a long history as a national liberation struggle going back to the anti-colonial period. Because of this, pressing global issues such as civil society or advocating some kind of "autonomy" rather than total independence (as the Zapatistas ask for) is a non-starter in Palestine.

Nevertheless, al-Azzeh did feel that the Zapatista experience was very valuable for Palestine as inspiration for trying to forge similarly global connections with the transnational anti-corporate globalization movement, and now the larger global peace and justice movement. As he explains it,

> The ideas of Marcos are an inspiration, to link myself and the Cultural Center to other actors around the world this is the inspiration of the Zapatistas, their networking with other communities. Even social movements in Europe, like the environmental movement, are inspirational for our long term strategies.
>
> But on the daily level the acceleration of struggle here is so intense you can't even think about new and more creative, even non-violent ways to resist. Just going about daily life is an act of supreme non-violence in the context of the occupation. You're on the defensive. It's very hard. In fact, for normal Palestinians living daily life, they don't care any more if we have a good or bad image in West. They say, "We have to self-exist, whatever we have to do to survive. We have to fight to show the world we're alive."

Of course, I pointed out, this is the same language and reasoning used by the Zapatista leadership to justify their revolt: "We have to fight, to show the world we're alive," as al-Azzeh put it, is very similar to Marcos's belief, "Enough dying this useless death; it is better to fight for change." But while in the heart of the remote Lacandian jungle region of Chiapas this view led to an innovative strategy and larger ideology, in the refugee camps of Palestine or cities of Arab Iraq, with their daily toll of dead and wounded, there is little time for reflection:

> Non-violence and a more developed strategy might be a good long term goal, but people want quick solutions for their situation, and in that way, violence works, even if it is "suicidal," particularly when the Palestinian leadership has totally abandoned them through its corruption and cooperation with Israel.

I believe there is an important lesson in al-Azzeh's critical inspiration from the Zapatista experience, one which supports the notion that the

Figure 8   In a Bethlehem refugee camp teachers preach peace; children prefer dancing in ode to hand grenades

worldwide global peace and justice movement has a long way to go before it arrives at any kind of unifying ideology or set of strategies to achieve the goals that most of its adherents across the globe share. Ideas can travel and inspire people across oceans, but tactics and strategies are much more difficult to transfer from one historical, political, and social context to another. For example, one day when I visited al-Azzeh's community center the children were learning a new dance (the Palestinian national dance, or *dabkah*, is an important means of preserving Palestinian identity). What was troubling me, however, were the lyrics the six- through twelve-year-olds were singing and dancing to, which were in praise of hand grenades. Al-Azzeh was equally troubled by the lyrics, and explained that "we try hard to bring in more positive lyrics that don't involve violence, but the reality of life here is so bad that they make no sense."

Creating Another World: Islam and the World Social Forums

Perhaps a combination of anarchist tactics, the Zapatista philosophy, and the political strategies emerging out of the World Social Forum

(WSF) movement can together provide the kind of positive unity, or "project identities," that Palestinians so desperately need. What's interesting is that before September 11 neoliberals told us that these trends represented little more than a "motley crew [that] comes almost entirely from the rich countries and is overwhelmingly white, largely middle-class, occasionally misinformed, often wittingly dishonest, and so diverse in its professed concerns that it makes the output from a monkey's romp on a keyboard look more coherent," while soon after the global peace and justice movement is referred to as little more than a bunch of anarchists with terrorist sympathies.[45] In both cases the aim of such characterizations was to discredit the movement. But after the amazing success of the World and European Social Forums, and especially the 2004 WSF in Mumbai, such claims have been shown to be as misinformed and wittingly dishonest as the global peace and justice movement is accused of being.

The roots of the WSF movement go back to the struggles against the Multilateral Agreement on Investment in 1998, when the public uproar forced France to withdraw from the secret discussions and led to the founding of organizations like ATTAC (Association pour la taxation des transactions financières pour l'aide aux citoyens). In 2000 ATTAC was approached by several Brazilian NGOs to found the World Social Forum, both to give a collective voice to those challenging neoliberal globalization and to flesh out what the anti-globalisation movement was for, rather than simply what it was against.

As ATTAC's Bernard Cassen puts it, the WSF attempted to create a "Porto Alegre Consensus" to counterpose to the Washington Consensus model of neoliberal globalization. In this sense the model for the gathering represents a transformation of the anti-corporate globalization movement from a culture of no to a culture of yes, as epitomized by its slogan, "another world is possible."[46] Our discussion in Chapter Seven demonstrated that, in order to reach this other world, the first task was to transform the culture of the progressive movement so that it focused on ideas as much as on organizational tactics.[47] To address this problem the WSF was established "not as an entity, but [as] a process."[48]

The website for the 2001 inaugural meeting put it this way (the stilted English is in the original text, obviously written by Brazilian volunteers):

> Economists and other university students against neo-liberalism, they were already making in Europe, with the name of Anti-Davos. What they intended nevertheless was more than that. It was proposed to

arrange another meeting of world scale with participation of all the organizations who were already articulating the mass protests, turn round to the social – the World Social Forum. These meetings would take place to have a symbolic dimension in the beginning of this new period, at the same time that the big of the world would meet themselves in Davos. And Cassen chose Brazil and Porto Alegre because it was capital of a third world state that has become known all over the world because it's democratic experiences and fights against neoliberalism. Cassen launched the challenge back to us again: if we were able to organize a Forum, we would have the support not only of his journal as well as the organizations that around the world are demonstrating against capital domination.[49]

The notion of the WSF constituting a "new culture" in its own right is crucial, and is based on the belief that "there are alternatives, not [one] alternative, as we can no longer invoke a single rigid model which a priori offers the solution to all problems. The alternative to capitalism has to be developed collectively and always in terms of what we might call utopianism, in the best sense of the word."[50] Most important, the WSF would seek to "recreate the possibility of an alliance between radical forces in the periphery and those in the core – a connection sundered by the triumph of neoliberalism and the fall of the USSR."[51]

The first year of the WSF saw 700 movements from 122 countries, and 4,700 delegates and 15,000 participants arrive in Porto Alegre to commence a "joint thinking process."[52] What role did Islam and the Muslim majority world play in the first meeting? There was some Muslim participation on the international steering committee, with organizations from Senegal, Palestine/Israel, Mali, Tunisia, Morocco, Bangladesh, and Malaysia listed as sponsors. But these constituted a total of only seven out of well over 250 organizations coming from the Arab/Muslim world. The only Muslim country represented on the Mobilizing Committee was Bangladesh, while only about four sessions dealt with religion or culture specifically.

The protests of 2001 – Mexico, Buenos Aires, Quebec, Gothenburg, Geneva, Beirut, Brussels, even Genoa – carried the imprint of the first WSF. They deepened the reflections on solutions and globalizing hope that another world is indeed possible (although by Geneva it was clear the states were going to pursue a strategy of criminalizing the so-called "anti-globalizations").[53] The second WSF, held in 2002, was dominated by the fall-out of September 11 "and the tentativeness of certain liberals to present their opposition because ... to be anti-globalization is to be anti-American, and is thus to be complicit in terrorism."[54] As José Bové explained, "military and economic globalization go together after the fall of the [Berlin] Wall and the (second) Gulf War. We need to understand that the one serves the other ... But media environment changes in which to express opposition. And in this context, the second WSF acquires an additional importance [beyond] defining the common goods for humanity ... It will also be the occasion, just five months after 9/11, to put forward a world non subsumed under the law of the strongest."[55]

The WSF moved across the globe to Mumbai for the 2004 meeting in order to bring more Asian voices into the gathering. A glance at the wonderfully long program for this round, attended by 80,000 people (about six times the number attending the first one), reveals a significantly greater emphasis on the Middle East and Muslim world, which is not surprising considering the impact of September 11, the war on terror and the US-led invasion and occupation of Iraq in the ensuing three years, the greater attention to themes related to religion and culture more broadly, and the location itself (so close to the MENA compared with Porto Alegre).[56] Forum panels featured some of the most important thinkers and activists from the region (especially from Palestine).

Along with (then) recent Iranian Nobel Peace Prize winner Shirin Ebadi's stirring speech, Mustafa Barghouti, head of the Palestinian Medical Relief Services, explained at the opening plenary, "Maybe the WSF does not have weapons of mass destruction or power from money. But we get our strength from the people."[57] On the other hand, the Middle East, Islam, religion or culture-related panels totaled about fifteen out of upwards of 1,500 panels. Not a single one dealt explicitly with the problem of violence or terrorism within the Middle East.

While clearly an incredible success in terms of numbers and multicultural participation, by the 2004 WSF the strains between those wanting to "take action" and those satisfied with talking and sharing experiences (a conflict that has plagued even the smallest activist and education groups I've participated in) had come to the surface.[58] As important, given our discussion in these last two chapters, was the criticism that "the movement lacks any strategy for transforming the growing feeling of exasperation and distrust of neoliberal dogma into an alternative policy."[59] If the attendees at the annual WSFs constitute the "second superpower" it seems they share the problems of gridlock and inability to translate policy into concrete action that often plague gatherings of the world's other elite.

Globalization and the European Social Forums: Motivating the World Against War

If the World Social Forum has been the meeting place for the world's activist class, the two European Social Forums held in Florence in 2002 and in Paris in 2003 have been equally important for defining the goals (and, as often, the debates) of the European and worldwide movements. It should not be surprising that Europe (and especially the EU) is central to any discussion of the global peace and justice movement's activities and future. The continent is central to the narrative of globalization – a "laboratoire de la mondialisation" – both because of the presence of sizeable Muslim communities that are reshaping European identities and politics[60] and because the expansion of the EU is also an example of international political unity that reminds residents of the MENA of the promises and failures of both Arab nationalism and transnational Islamic politics.

Yet even as the EU expanded by fifteen new members in the spring of 2004, globalization was dividing Europe (both within and between nations) as much as uniting it, leaving European scholars and policy-makers wondering "what future" there is for a Europe that "had always been the promise of something more; but now is increasingly perceived as the risk of something less."[61] That something less – as opposed to something else, which could be something better – clearly results from the slow strangulation of the social welfare state by governments in London, Berlin, Paris or Madrid through the policies of a "regressive liberalism" that is "tearing" the social fabric and sense of national solidarity in Western Europe.[62]

But whatever Europe's problems, including the increasing threat and (in the case of the horrific attacks in Spain in March 2004) reality of violent Islamist terrorism inside European countries, Muslims worldwide have come to look towards Europe as an alternative model and power center to the United States, in large part because of the growing anger of Europeans against the US. As the New York *Times* reported in 2000, "More vehemently than ever, Europe is scorning the US," in particular because it is "a society ruled by profit – an unchecked force on its way to ruling the world."[63] Even before the invasion of Iraq the United States was seen in Europe as well as the Arab/Muslim world "as a menacing, even dangerous force intent on remaking the world in its image."[64] Such sentiments were once the province of "radical" Islamists and radical European Marxists, today they reflect the mood of not just the European Left and Right, but increasingly its Center.[65]

In Paris as much as Cairo, bookstores filled with titles deploring neoliberal globalization, and the "invasion" of American culture it heralds, attests to the common fears of American political and economic dominance coupled with cultural power that is, as we've already seen, often perceived to be the most dangerous aspect of globalization. And it is precisely the shared attitudes toward the US and neoliberal globalization that brings me to the final reason that Europe is so important to any discussion of globalization, especially in the MENA: because the changing nature of Muslim life in Europe has spawned "an effervescence of thinking and mobilizations in the Muslim world that make possible a South–North synergy."[66] A "critical Islam," perhaps even the "most radical and innovative Islamic thought," is emerging in Europe, and can grow healthy if Muslims living in Europe can successfully "implant" themselves in the economies and cultures of their host countries.[67]

But this, of course, is much easier said than done. In fact, Muslims in Europe have experienced great economic, cultural, and political difficulties in securing a permanent and accepted place in contemporary European societies. Most people are aware of the intense hostility in France generated by the legislation to compel Muslim girls and women to remove their head-scarves in schools and other public places. The situation in the UK is little better; in the aftermath of September 11, the occupation of Iraq and the continued social prejudice against British Muslims produced warnings in the spring of 2004 about the "real anger and threat of riots by young Muslims pitched against the police" if something wasn't done quickly to make Muslims feel more at home and less ostracized in the UK.[68]

Europe Confronting Islam

Despite many political and economic gains there remains among the wider European public a generalized and diffuse anti-Muslim sentiment that has been exacerbated by terrorism, on the one hand, and continuing marginalization, on the other. Long-term discrimination and the cultural differences between the host and immigrant societies have played a crucial role in the shape and influence of Islamist and other communal politics in these countries, and is an important reason why extremist Islamist ideologies and even terrorism have found an exceedingly dangerous, if still small, place in European Muslim societies.

While there isn't space here to go into the rich detail that the subject of European Islam deserves,[69] we can summarize the situation by saying that similar to its predicament in the MENA, Islam in Europe is poised between the formation of a "Euro-Islam" that sees itself as permanently and positively implanted in the space of Europe, and a "Ghetto Islam" that mirrors the continued rejection of Islam by the white/Christian majority cultures. For all the cultural, political, and economic advances by second- and third-generation European Muslims – from world-renowned DJs or artists to the less sexy but more important "Beurgeoisie" (slang for bourgeois Beurs, or successful second-generation Arab-French citizens) or "Yummies" (Young and Upwardly Mobile Muslims) and even members of Parliaments,[70] the fact remains that millions of Muslims living in Europe remain on the margins of their societies.

The primary reason for this has been that Muslim immigrants – like the working class around the world – have borne the brunt of the social costs of the neoliberal agenda that has swept from England to France, Spain, Germany, and other formerly "social-democratic" states beginning with the Thatcherite revolution in late 1970s Britain. This has created problems for European Muslims that mirror those facing their home societies: unemployment, juvenile delinquency, the need to search for new identities, material frustration coupled with the absence of communal spaces to struggle for alternative solutions.[71]

And so by 1990, around the time of the first Gulf War, an "intifada of the cities" in France broke out, waged by "all those who did not take part in the mass workshop of business, the orgies in praise of money"; that is, by the poor who had no other way of expressing their disgust with their economic situation.[72] The economic problems have been exacerbated by political decisions by the Government such as the support for the Algerian state after the cancellation of the 1992 elections and coercive cultural regulations, such as the laws banning headscarves in schools or prayer in the workplace.

It is with this background that we must understand the first two European Social Forums and the role of Muslims and the MENA within it. It's no surprise that the first two ESFs were in Florence, Italy, and Paris, France. These two countries have been home to some of the strongest trade union activity on the continent. Although the French movement was started and is still run by middle-aged (and largely male) activist-intellectuals such as José Bové, Bernard Cassen, Susan George, and their organizations,[73] it doesn't represent the full force of French activism. There are also younger groups, such as "Ponte Per ...," or "Bridge for ...," which has been working to send European volunteers to work in solidarity with Iraqis and other violence-torn societies, or more generally organizations like Aarrg!!, whose credo of "festive radicality" reflects a specifically "transversal" strategy to help minimize hierarchical relations or rigid structures within the movement.

While the older groups have focused more on intellectual and theoretical-strategic discussions,[74] the younger French groups, and especially the Italian movement, with groups such as Ya Basta! and the Disobbedienti (formerly Tute Bianche), have been at the forefront of militant activism, and are clearly inspired by anarchist and Zapatista experiences and strategies. Not surprisingly, then, groups like Aarrg!! or Ya Basta! pursue a "direct action" approach that purposefully straddles various cultures of protest and activism. In fact, Aarrg!!, the organization founded by the French-Tunisian Leyla Dakhli mentioned in the last chapter, was born out of Dakhli's activist experiences in Italy, combined with her participation in the defense of José Bové after his 2000 arrest for the "attack" on the McDonald's.[75]

If Aarrg!! is the prototype of a new generation of more anarchist-inspired French activism against neoliberal globalization, Italian anti-corporate globalization movements have long been much more in debt to anarchism, and Zapatismo in particular. One of the most important Italian "no global" groups, Ya Basta!, even took its name directly from the Zapatista credo.[76] Yet as we discussed at the beginning of this chapter, we should not confuse the seeming anarchy of the movement with a hostility to solidarity on a large scale, as the overall agenda of the Italian groups surround the attempt to create a "united" (*solidale*) civilization precisely through the activities of continuous mediation and debate on globalization that most groups seek to encourage. And while the more militant groups within the movement, such as the "Anarchist Collectives" (Colletivi Anarchici), "Anti-Imperialists" (Anti-imperialisti), and the black bloc advocate a direct assault on the global economic and political order, half if not more of the movement seems to prefer a more moderate ideology and approach, similar to the older French groups that seek to build a "public class of opposition" against policies they don't like.[77]

There are two specific aspects of the Italian anti-corporate globalization movement that are most important for the evolution of the European Social Forum and our discussion more broadly. First, of course, is Ya Basta! and the impact of the Zapatistas on it. Ya Basta! was literally born out of the intense Italian participation – hundreds of representatives – in the Chiapas movement until the Mexican Government expelled most foreigners from the region in 1998. In the spirit of Zapatismo Ya Basta! works to engage in direct non-violent civil disobedience against neoliberalism in Europe using the model of Gandhi.[78]

What has made the Ya Basta! strategy at least partially successful has been that

> with peaceful methods of direct action, the language of violence stays on the side of the police, of governments ... That attracts society's attention, which echoes our protest. Seattle came, and with it the confirmation of a new movement which had regained civil society's participation, even though it didn't have a program yet. We added a new factor, a form of radical confrontation which went beyond classic demonstrations, and which presents us with the possibility of mass participation with secure methods.[79]

The direct "military" confrontation against the state and its police forces pioneered by the "White Overalls" movement ("Tute Bianche," more recently called the "Disobedient" faction ["Disobbedienti"]) was an important development for Ya Basta! because their strategy of wearing heavily padded clothing allowed protesters to withstand physical assaults by the police without responding with violence of their own.[80]

Groups like Ya Basta! might seem militant and secular, but in reality their roots, like the Zapatistas, lie in the well-established Italian left-wing Catholic tradition, with the eco-pacifist and religious wing of the movement probably its most powerful and inspirational part. Using the Gospel as inspiration and example, groups such as Rete Lilliput ("Lilliput Network," an umbrella group of seventy organizations and collectives) believe that human solidarity has to be the basis and the goal of action. Strategically they take their cue from the Jonathan Swift classic *Gulliver's Travels*, in which the tiny Lilliputians capture the giant Gulliver, many times their height, by tying him down with hundreds of threads while he slept. With this inspiration they believe that people can utilize the relatively modest sources of power available to them in a combined form to defeat the globalization giant.[81]

In fact, Rete Lilliput have actually pulled out of the Social Forum movement because they felt there was too much talk and growing hierarchization within the movement, and not enough direct action and horizontal solidarity.[82] I believe that the Rete Lilliput movement holds significant potential for adoption in the Middle East. We'll test this hypothesis in the next chapter. What is important to realize for now is that what makes the various Italian (and in many ways, larger European) movements so resilient is that "differences in practices and forms of militancy have been transformed over time, their original elements modified, forgotten and brought to life again and again in hybrid forms, sometimes to such an extent that they do not reflect their origin anymore."[83] This level of adaptability is exactly what is needed in the MENA.

The European Social Forums in the Context of Activism after September 11

Based on the unprecedented success of the WSF in 2001, the inaugural 2002 ESF was planned as "a new mode of organization for the movements and individuals who are opposed to neoliberal globalization and who are attempting to construct a society based on human development."[84] The most important thing about the ESF has been that from the start the European-wide meeting has built on a base of hundreds of local and regional Social Forums, particularly in Italy and France, but also throughout the EU and even North Africa and beyond.[85]

The ESF has goals as grand within the European context as the WSF has for creating another world, but for our purposes many of the important discussions were missing in the first gathering, in large part because there were few panels dealing with Islam, the MENA or religion in any specific sense other than the then upcoming war.[86] Aside from the avowedly secular Tariq Ali the only Muslim speaker (besides an Amnesty International representative) was Tariq Ramadan, with his invitation causing harsh criticism among some secular members of the movement.[87] The 2003 ESF in Paris was much more sophisticated and developed in the kinds of questions that were addressed, in the themes related to Islam, or religion and culture more broadly, and in the participation by Arabs and/or Muslims. Once again Tariq Ramadan participated, and as I'll discuss below, this time with even more controversy, but he was no longer one of the few Muslims to participate.[88] The increasing Muslim presence demonstrates how far the movement has come since I asked an audience of hundreds in Prague three years earlier how many Muslims were there and only a German TV cameraman raised his hand.

Nevertheless, Middle Eastern themes and participants in the WSF and ESF are still relatively minor considering the importance of the issues they represent. Is this due to an inherent incompatability between the Social Forum and Muslims' ideologies or activists? Definitely not, as attested to by the increasing number of instances where Western and Muslim activists have worked closely against the common threat of neoliberal globalization. But there's a long way to go. Perhaps the best way to understand why the relationships have not been more frequent and deeper through the Social Forum process would be to compare the arguments of two multilingual pamphlets prepared specifically for the 2003 Paris ESF. The first, titled *Common Places: The Global Movement as an Open Space for Politicization*,[89] was written by the editors of the progressive Italian journal *Derive Approdi*; the second, *Globalization: Muslim Resistances*, was written by Tariq Ramadan, also for the fall of 2003.

Common Places was written specifically for the Paris ESF to help build on *Derive Approdi*'s idea for a "network of European journals" that together would engage in new strategizing and joint actions against neoliberal globalization. Its main argument surrounds the need to revitalize a "movement" pacified (however much activists might deny it) by the Bush "victory" in Iraq and prove that the setback doesn't signal the cementing of power in the hands of government and corporate elites. The authors argue that to accept the claim that resistance to neoliberal globalization is futile is to believe an "illusion" that masks "the symptoms of global resistance and … assumes the adversary's viewpoint of the triumph of capitalism and the end of history."[90]

But while it encourages war-weary protesters, *Common Places* warns that if the movement doesn't reflect on its weaknesses as much as its strengths, "we will keep projecting shadows and ghosts from the past onto the future." And so the goal must be to "empower theoretical practice that neither aims at evoking distant futures nor at reviving unproposable pasts, but at interrogating the present in order to change it."[91] To accomplish this, the most important thing is to acknowledge that the movement is no longer operating in an era of classical international solidarity but rather in one where a variety of movements are "inevitably interlinked. They communicate and fuel one another."

From my perspective, perhaps the most important point of the pamphlet is its focus on the "social movement of migrants" as a paradigm for analysis, as their mobile critique put into crisis the international division of labor and national as well as wage borders. "Fleeing and searching for another possible world, they bring their conflicts and tensions to the places they arrive."[92] Needless to say, Muslim migrants are the core of this international movement, and the call by *Common Places* to consider Europe still as "an ambivalent space and possible terrain of experimentation for transformation … for another globalization – a globalization of struggles and resistance" opens crucial space for dialogue with the ten-million-strong Muslim community.[93]

Ramadan's booklet overlaps with many areas touched on by *Common Places*, particularly the importance of immigrants to the future of progressive European politics and the need for "any serious critique of the World Order ... to be based on a meticulous analysis of the economic system."[94] In a passage clearly addressed to his fellow Muslims, Ramadan argues that while the world is changing and in upheaval, "it seems as if the Ulama and Muslim intellectual's thought is stuck, particularly in the field of economics," and so the Islamic world has produced economic or financial institutions that supposedly seek to avoid its pitfalls like the use of interest, but which in reality "strengthen the global system more than they resist it."[95] What makes the situation worse is that it didn't have to be this way, because when the Arab world was flush with petrodollars in the 1970s it could have invested its wealth at much lower interest (as it should have done by Islamic precepts) in the Global South, instead of letting Western banks lend the money to the third world at exorbitant rates that led directly to the crippling debt crises of the last generation.[96]

This leads Ramadan to ask, almost plaintively, "hasn't this *Islamic* participation in the dark machineries of the capitalist economy, been a terrible betrayal, one of the worst ever?"[97] Such a discussion, coming from perhaps the leading Muslim intellectual in Europe, is crucial precisely because Europe is increasingly becoming the world hub of Muslim extremist and terror groups, a reality that will likely cause much suffering and repression for Muslims and all Europeans if not turned around soon.[98]

While this discussion is commendable for its honesty, by itself it breaks little new ground. What is important, in my view, is Ramadan's argument that "in the age of globalization the appropriateness of our principles and code of ethics is no longer defined by the geographic space but rather by the field of activity." What he means here is that while Western democracies clearly provide the space for Muslims to live in peace, "if we observe the neoliberal system as a whole and the logic that underlies it, we are clearly in *'alam al-harb'* (the world of war), or in *dar al-harb* if one wants to use the old terminology."[99]

In other words, neoliberal globalization produces a world at war where no one – neither Muslims nor any other culture – can live in peace. This is a very important argument because while it recognizes the line of Islamist thought (starting from his grandfather, Hassan al-Banna, who founded the Muslim Brotherhood, and culminating in Sayyid Qutb) that argues that Muslim countries are living in a state of ignorance (*jahiliyyah*) and war if they don't govern based on Islamic law, Ramadan extends this to a worldwide argument in which the criteria for judgment is no longer the imposition of laws that violate the Shar'ia but instead the imposition of an inhuman neoliberal globalization. And so he argues, "The picture would indeed be quite dark if there wasn't a general movement of resistance; as regards the Islamic message faced with the neoliberal economy there is no other option than resistance … we must always start from our reference points and in partnership with all those who resist and propose 'something different.'"[100]

Ramadan's vision is clearly sympathetic with the editors of *Derive Approdi*. But as I've explained throughout this book, and has been clear from the battles that Ramadan has himself been forced to fight, the reality is that even in attempts to integrate Muslims into the Left in Europe or the US Muslim activists have found "difficult relations, a dialogue between the deaf, [although] the responsibility is shared."[101] Yet genuine dialogue is crucial to the achievement of a common front of "resistance against human madness, injustice and exploitation."[102] If Muslims are going to play a role, it will be young people, who are "beginning to 'connect' to the world" who are best positioned to lead the struggle into the future.[103]

Yet there are for Ramadan inherent *cultural* problems in the ideologies and practices of the global peace and justice movement that make it difficult for such connections to grow or be sustained:

> The terms of the confrontation are clear … what is nevertheless astonishing is the near total absence of serious consideration of culture and religious diversity, outside the usual conventional talk which reminds us of the so called "duty of tolerance" … Those seeking an alternative to neoliberal globalization, the anti- or "alter"-globalisers, all too often think of cultural, as well as religious diversity as a principle of goodwill to be affirmed but rarely see it as a reality with which it is necessary to engage … from forum to forum one grows accustomed to meeting this new species of activist – a living contradiction of the contemporary Left – economically progressive but culturally so imperialist; ready to fight for social justice but at the same time so confident and sometimes arrogant as to assume the right to dictate a universal set of values for everyone.[104]

It is that arrogance that is perhaps most troubling for the movement and its desire to be as open and democratic as possible.[105] What makes this situation worse is that while the peace movement finds it difficult to bring Muslim youth more actively into its activities it leaves the door open to extremist Muslim religious movements which are doing increasingly well at recruiting young Muslims in the absence of a positive alternative.

Anti-Semitism Again?

We have already discussed anti-Semitism several times in the course of this book. What I have tried to explore is how the conflicts over anti-Semitism point us to areas where much work needs to be done to address issues and heal wounds that if left unresolved will make it that much more difficult for the global peace and justice movement to achieve its goals. In Europe this dynamic has become much more central to the functioning of the movement, for two reasons. First, because of accusations that anti-Semitism in Western Europe has increased sharply since 2000; and second, because of attacks on Muslim leaders, such as Ramadan, by leaders of the European Left in response to criticisms he has made of Israeli policies in the Occupied Territories and the lack of outspoken criticism by leading French Jewish intellectuals against them.

The reappearance of significant levels of anti-Semitism in Western Europe is a serious and even dangerous phenomenon that must be addressed by the Left and Muslims within and between their communities. But there's an equally dangerous "collateral" issue involved in this dynamic, which is the attacks on progressive Muslims like Ramadan by leading European (and especially French) intellectuals during the last two years; specifically, in the months leading up to the 2003 ESF in Paris after Ramadan wrote an article criticizing several French intellectuals (most of them Jewish) for being uncritically supportive of Israel, to an extent that contradicted their progressive stance on other conflicts, such as Bosnia.

What exactly did Ramadan say that so angered the French intellectual elite?[106] The article, titled "Critique of (New) Communitarian Intellectuals" argued that while leading French Jewish intellectuals talk about debating issues based on the universal principles of a "common European tradition," when it comes to Israel they "take a position that reveals a communitarian attitude (*attitude communautariste*) that distorts the terms of the debate in France on subjects such as Palestine and the recent war in Iraq ... One can ask why such justifications: eliminating a dictator (why not earlier?), for democratizing the country (why not Saudi Arabia?), etc."[107]

Ramadan also criticized them for accusing the larger anti-corporate globalization movement of anti-Semitism, and for automatically labeling any attack on their positions as anti-Semitic, "a dynamic which sadly displaces the courageous universalist positions taken by other Jews on the left."[108] What's amazing about this argument is its ordinariness. This type of accusation is made by Jews against other Jews regularly on the Op/Ed pages of the Israeli press, especially liberal papers like *Ha'aretz*. In the US *TIKKUN* editor Michael Lerner made essentially the same argument with his 1994 book *Jewish Renewal*, in which he went so far as to warn about the creation of a "Settler Judaism" – a premonition that has sadly been proven all too accurate – if Jews didn't look honestly at what was being done in their name by Israel in the Occupied Territories. So it's a bit surprising – and very revealing – how European progressives responded to Ramadan's article, especially when Ramadan has been so forthright and outspoken about condemning all forms of anti-Semitism and hatred of and attacks on Jews by Muslims in Europe (a position which won him praise by the Israeli paper *Ha'aretz* in early 2003).[109]

The intellectuals he criticized shot back by accusing Ramadan – as he predicted – of vile anti-Semitism, of being in touch with known terrorists, and of supporting the Islamist scholar-turned-de-facto Sudanese dictator Hassan al-Turabi. All these accusations and rumors are demonstrably false.[110] They also variously claimed that "the true nature of Tariq Ramadan" is dangerous and will cause a "fracture in the European Left,"[111] that he's Hassan al-Banna's grandson (true, but not relevant unless the sins of the grandfathers pass down to the grandsons), and that he hasn't condemned Islam's position against homosexuality.[112]

One of the intellectuals Ramadan criticized, Bernard-Henri Lévi, even went so far as to compare Ramadan's article to the *Protocols of the Elders of Zion*, and demanded that the French Left distance itself from it and its author: "Mr. Ramadan, dear anti-globalizationist friends, is not and cannot be one of yours ... I call on you quickly to distance yourselves from this character who, in crediting the idea of an elitist conspiracy under the control of Zionism, is only inflaming people's thoughts and opening the way to the worst."[113]

But it gets worse, as several leading French socialists wrote an Op/Ed arguing that Ramadan "only pretends to be our friend" (deploying a classic Orientalist stereotype of the duplicitous and untrustworthy Arab) and that in reality, "Monsieur Ramadan is not one of us! ... His presentation of himself as a member of the alterglob-alization family, as a valuable interlocutor in our common debates, is unsupportable ... We are socialists, republicans, alterglobalizationists. And for this reason, M. Ramadan can't be one of us."[114]

Believing that anti-globalizationists must be "republican" and socialist points to the larger problem of the French, and through it, European Left. That is, the history of French "republicanism," from the violence of the Jacobins, to the colonial policies in Algeria or

Indochina, to the ideologies of assimilation and *laïcité*, is so thoroughly modern that republicanism is utterly incompatible with the progressive theories and strategics of the global peace and justice movement. In effect, the socialist critics of Ramadan mentioned on the previous page are disqualifying themselves and their movement from true participation in the creation of "another world," as they clearly remain trapped in the ideologies of the old one.

The fact that none of these accusations bears any resemblance to the text that caused the uproar is what makes it so important, especially given who's making them, to detail them. We might want to take heart that these were largely "establishment" intellectuals who weren't meaningfully part of the "alterglobalizationist" Left. But, surprisingly, many others on the Left agreed that Ramadan's text "had no place" in the European Social Forum community. "It is not relevant to the ESF question," said Bernard Cassen. Only a few members of ESF-sponsoring organizations, such as Peter Khalfa of ATTAC and José Bové, defended his right to express his opinions, although both misread its meaning in various ways.[115]

What is clear from this discussion is that no matter how often and courageously a leading progressive Muslim intellectual like Ramadan criticizes anti-Semitism, it's never enough. Make one criticism of Israel or Jews, and you go from being hailed as a modern-day Muslim "Martin Luther" to a secret supporter of al-Qa'eda. Of course, when progressive Jews and Israelis critique the tendency to put community ahead of human rights and justice, we're called self-hating Jews; I guess it's not a surprise that he'd be called an anti-Semite for the same "crime" (the word used by Vallis and his socialist comrades to describe Ramadan's remarks).

If the attacks on Ramadan by the Left were limited to Europe, we could perhaps treat it as a parochial problem of the European (pseudo) Left and therefore not worthy of the attention I've given it. But the controversy has an equally disturbing international context. On the one hand, in Israel *Ha'aretz*, which celebrated him a year earlier, attacked him because of comments that are no stranger to its own opinion page. On top of this, PRISM, an Israeli on-line think tank which specializes in intelligence, terrorism, and political Islam, published an academic analysis of his writings which purported to show – but clearly didn't if anyone bothered to read it – that he supported fundamentalism and violence despite his public rhetoric to the contrary.[116]

At the same time American "pro-Israel"[117] conservatives like Daniel Pipes went after him for being anti-Semitic and a closet extremist, just as he and other right-wing Jewish "intellectuals" have gone after other Muslim reformist intellectuals (such as Khaled Abou El Fadl of UCLA) when they "dared" to criticize the Israeli Occupation. And by late summer 2004 the attacks on Ramadan by Pipes and others succeeded, most likely beyond the dreams of the attackers, when the Homeland Security Administration revoked a work visa earlier granted to Ramadan after he was awarded a prestigious professorship at Notre Dame University in Indiana (which forced him to resign his position). The reason: precisely the innuendo – made with absolutely no supporting evidence – that "he is engaged in a complex game of appearing as a moderate but has connections to Al Qaeda," as Pipes cleverly puts it.[118]

It is precisely in such a situation, where any Muslim who's as courageous as Ramadan or Abou El Fadl puts themselves at risk to vicious attacks by the Right, that one would imagine the Left would be supportive of them, rather than engaging in their own ill-informed and uncritical attacks. The fact that the opposite has largely happened – with the crucial exception of numerous supporters in academia – shows that despite the clear movement towards bringing Muslims into the progressive conversations on, and struggles against, neoliberal globalization (as seen by the increase in panels devoted to related issues at the WSF and ESF), European progressives and the global peace and justice movement at large have much work to do before they shed centuries of prejudice and stereotypes and can deal with Muslims based on the facts and issues at hand.[119]

Conclusion: Heading Towards a New Stage

The last two chapters have contained much criticism of a movement in which I've spent much of my adult life. Yet I believe such soul-searching is absolutely crucial to any possibility for the movement to attain its radical, even revolutionary, goals. What I hope we've seen in the discussions of Part Three is that the vision of "another world" developed and reflected in the worldwide global peace and justice movement since Seattle (and in fact, since the early 1990s) is one that the vast majority of the world's one billion Muslims would support – that's one-sixth of humanity.

But if "we" keep wanting Muslims to be a bit more like us – speak English or French, discard their "veils," assimilate to the dominant Western culture of the protest movements, in order to be part of the global coalition for peace and justice, such a rapprochement will be long in coming, if it ever arrives. As important, while "we" make demands (however subconsciously) on our Middle Eastern comrades to be more like us, many more of us would do well to learn Arabic, Persian, Turkish or Hebrew and go live in the Middle East, learn the cultures and bring back that knowledge to use for the larger movement.

As we'll see in the next and last chapter, if international support and solidarity was crucial to the success (in fact, the survival) of the Zapatistas in Chiapas a decade ago, such cross-cultural activities are even more crucial today in the MENA, particularly given the need to learn what "we" need to learn and adopt from "them" in order to nurture a truly collaborative effort at creating peace and justice. In fact, that's what culture jamming is really about – using culture to create solidarity and develop new strategies for surviving and ultimately transcending oppressive political, economic, and social systems. But such "performances" need to work both ways in order to produce the difficult but rewarding harmonies (rather than just a bunch of voices that may or may not be in the same key)[120] that can blend together American blue notes, Middle Eastern quarter tones, and European tetrachords into a new and powerful form of music and culture.

Without this, Lilliput will never defeat Gulliver. In the final chapter, we'll explore the work of a small group of international activists in Iraq who've displayed an inspiring degree of courage, creativity, and willingness to cross the wide and turbulent *barzakh* dividing Islam and the West during their sometimes harrowing time in the country. At the same time, we'll meet a young religious figure from Sadr City nicknamed the "elastic sheikh," who throughout the violence of the occupation worked to spread a more progressive and open message of Islam than is normally heard in Moqtada' al-Sadr's home base; and many other Iraqis who are working tirelessly with "internationals," often at risk to their lives, to help build another Iraq, and through it, another world. Their activities, which both confirm and challenge the insights and strategies of the Zapatista, anarchist, and Social Forum movements, offer us a model for the exceedingly difficult but absolutely necessary kinds of struggles that must be waged to overcome the chaos, violence, and outright thievery made inevitable by a neoliberal globalization gone wild, in Iraq and around the world.

9 Conclusion: Chaos and Culture Jamming in the "New Middle East"

There's only so much oil in the ground
Sooner or later there won't be much around …
We just assume that we will not
Exceed the oil supply
But soon enough the world will watch the wells run dry.

Tower of Power, "There's Only So Much Oil in the Ground," Urban Renewal, Warner Bros. Records, 1974

Those who can make you believe absurdities can make you commit atrocities.

Voltaire

Introduction: Three Scenes

Scene One: Ayatollah Baghdadi and his Kalashnikov

The road from Baghdad to Najaf is much longer and more beautiful than the road to Falluja. It goes through the heart of central Iraq's farm country, land that has been under continuous cultivation since the dawn of human civilization. And it looks like it, as the land is incredibly beautiful and the earth is a deeper and richer color than I've ever seen before. But more beautiful than the scenery is the air – it's fresh! The air in Baghdad is so polluted – from a combination of old cars and diesel fumes from the thousands of generators that run most of the day due to constant blackouts – that I felt permanently nauseous after a week there. But as we approached Najaf the smell starts again, made worse by the fear, after driving through Falluja, of being stuck in yet another traffic jam, in a major town, in an intensifying insurrection, surrounded by thousands of young, angry, and armed men.

After negotiating the way for another hour, we arrive at the home of Ahmed Hassan al-Baghdadi, an older mid-level Ayatollah. He's not the scholar we were supposed to meet, but given the chaos in Najaf in those days he was the only one around and willing to talk. In his solemn, book-lined study we all sat whispering, waiting for him to arrive, and staring at the Kalashnikov next to an old computer in the corner (as our driver pointed out to us, it was an original Russian AK-47; very expensive and much more durable than the Iraqi knock-offs).

When he arrived Baghdadi introduced himself with an infectious smile and a quiet voice, shook our hands gently, and informed us that for security reasons he normally doesn't meet people unannounced or at his home. But once he sat down – he wanted us to sit right next to him, with a woman on either side, for the cameras (one of our group was a producer for Free Speech TV) – it was clear that he was dying to talk, and he was especially excited about the possibility of getting on American television.

"Are you filming?" he asked. With a nod yes from Shannon Service, the Free Speech TV producer/camerawoman, Baghdadi transformed before our eyes from a seemingly modest and even frail man of religious introspection into an anti-American, anti-Western, anti-Jewish firebrand, spewing out warnings to the US and threatening to fight America to the "last drop of our blood." He explained with a wagging finger that it was the duty of every Muslim to "fight infidels" until they leave Muslim lands, and that globalization was a Zionist–American plot to take over the world and destroy Muslim culture (with the UN as its terrorist enforcer). He also repeatedly admonished us to put the interview on American TV and to send him a copy of the tape.[1]

When he finally exhausted his rants, he apologized for having to leave immediately for both his own and our security. Before we left, however, he showed us a new video CD he was distributing of his recent public talks. It seemed he had turned the volume to 11, because when the video began his voice (which was already raised in anger) was piercing. And over it was an even louder backing track of the kind of martial music featured in Hamas, Hizbollah or al-Qa'eda recruitment videos. Both the voice and the music had the kind of echo on them that DJs on Spanish-language radio stations are fond of using to grab listeners' attention. Together they produced a disturbingly surreal atmosphere in this quiet study of an elderly "holy man."

It got stranger, however, when I turned around to take a last look at the room before leaving, only to see the Ayatollah facing me, finger on

Figure 9   Najaf's real OG: Ayatollah Baghdadi and his Kalashnikov, March 2004

the trigger of his Russian Kalashnikov, and once again smiling mischievously. I looked at my friend and for a second our faces had what must have been the last expression of the St. Valentine's Day Massacre victims. But then we realized that our photographer was taking pictures of Baghdadi, asking him to pose in various positions which at the time reminded me of the kinds of poses hunters in gun magazines adopt. What's more, it turns out the idea to have him pose was our photographer's, not Baghdadi's (although, as our photographer joked later in the car, Baghdadi was only too happy to oblige).

As we left Baghdadi's home I said to my friend Maher, a Shi'i with family ties to Najaf, that Baghdadi's extreme, almost comical rhetoric, and his pleas for us to put him on TV, suggested he was looking to get arrested, so that his prestige in the community would rise (at his age and level of scholarship, there aren't any other ways left for him to move up the ladder). "No," Maher replied sarcastically, "he wants to be martyred. Then his prestige will really go up."

Scene Two: Essen, Germany, five months later

I'm at a conference in Essen, Germany on the public sphere, Islam and pluralism. One of my colleagues, a fiercely secular, feminist Syrian professor, begins her presentation by showing a montage of video clips from various religious talk shows currently broadcast on Arab satellite channels and available to any Syrian with a satellite dish. Stringing together various clips, from mean-looking ultra-conservative preachers broadcasting from low-budget sets, to hip young "air-conditioned" imams (some speaking in English) whose sets are reminiscent of *Good Morning America* or *Oprah*, her goal was to explore the various techniques used by contemporary Muslim preachers to appeal to the region's main demographic: young people.

She had another motive: to demonstrate the "threat" posed by the spread of this type of religious programming. Her evidence for this threat was that during the past five years the number of head-scarfed students in a French Department that had traditionally been a bastion of Syrian secularism had risen from about 5 to over 60 percent. In speaking to her later, I learned that there was also a more personal reason for her fears: "Two years ago I lost my daughter," she explained.

I offered my condolences, thinking that perhaps the daughter had been caught in the cross-fire of a shoot-out between the Government and religious militants or, more mundanely, had died in a car accident. But seeing my misunderstanding, the professor elaborated that she "lost her" when her daughter started wearing a veil. Now, even though she remains "a very sweet girl, she's become a stranger to us." My Syrian colleague's fear is that a whole generation of smart young women will be similarly lost.[2]

But lost to whom and to what? To modern secular society? That's a highly dubious assumption; even for those attracted to more conservative preachers the modern world is never absent. To the fundamentalists? Perhaps to what she described as "a scary looking imam with the big beard" in another of the clips she showed us? Yet here she didn't think it worth mentioning that the viewer could simultaneously enjoy the preacher's discussions of the nuances of the Shar'ia and check out the latest stock quotes (in Arabic) scrolling beneath his imposing visage. Apparently conservative Muslims like to multi-task as much as the rest of us – who wouldn't want to check their portfolio while getting the latest take on what the Shar'ia says about adultery or jihad?

Along with the scary imam was a clip of a much younger and better-looking preacher, the well-known Egyptian television imam Amr Khaled. Khaled is not really a religious scholar; rather he's a lay preacher with an economics degree from an American university. His sermons mesmerize audiences and even make women cry – just like Elvis, the Beatles, or any one of a number of famous contemporary Arab singers. In fact, as my Syrian colleague pointed out, the similarity of his persona and impact to those of current pop stars was exactly why she included him in her montage: he's become a symbol now that he's on TV; a star who's worshiped like all the other Arab TV, movie or pop stars. "He's a brand and a commodity."

Why is this so important? Because his celebrity gives him access to the burgeoning public sphere in Syria (and the Arab world more broadly) that she, a well-known theater professor and critic for twenty years, can only dream of: "These imams can come and speak anywhere, in mosques, big hotels, etc. But me, as a free thinker, I'm not allowed to speak anywhere; if I did I'd be arrested. We need to realize what this means that they're free to speak and I'm not."

We don't have to be as upset at Khaled's presence in the Syrian public sphere – however virtual, for he hasn't at the time of writing appeared in Syria – as my professor friend is to understand her point: religious personalities who largely stay clear of political rhetoric or criticism of existing regimes are allowed to proliferate in the slowly expanding public spheres of the MENA, while secular critics remain penned into their classrooms where they can do little harm. Clearly, Middle Eastern rulers are as adept at playing the religious populism game as their counterparts in the United States (as we explored in our discussion of Kansas in Chapter One).

Yet Khaled is hardly a reactionary or even an agent (as far as I know) of Egyptian Government propaganda. In fact, he's the kind of "moderate" religious personality that would be familiar to most watchers of mainstream Christian programming in the United States. In fact, on a flight to Lebanon later that year I read a rather flattering profile of him in the French magazine *L'Expansion*, right after reading one on the African American "prosperity preacher" Creflo Dollar in the *New Yorker*.[3] Nor surprisingly, it turns out that both men share working-class backgrounds and a focus on neo-liberalizing their religions through a gospel of wealth that combines age-old religious text and the most modern management theory.[4] All told, Khaled's views are clearly not those of the scary imam with the stock quotes whizzing under him; but for my colleague all religious figures are but shades of the same color – the black of the veil her daughter now wears.

Indeed, while the Western media focuses largely on the Jordanian arch-terrorist Musab al-Zarqawi and the other mini-bin Ladens that have increasingly appeared as al-Qa'eda moves (like all smart corporations) from producing its own products – terrorists – to branding its image, a public feedback mechanism has emerged across the Muslim world that is forcing the majority of Islamist movements to moderate their rhetoric when they go too far. For example, last year a publicity spot was aired on Arab satellite stations that featured a teenage boy working very hard on his computer before bedtime. When his father came into the room, turned off the light, and told him to go to sleep he didn't listen and kept working. Even the muezzin's call to prayer from the local mosque didn't stop him. Suddenly, as clear punishment for not stopping to pray, he keeled over, dead. The next scene showed the family washing the body and then burying him, and the clip ends with the words "Say your prayers before you're judged" flashing on the screen.

The clip scared young people across the region so much that many refused to use a computer after watching it! This led to such a public outcry that a new spot was filmed in which the same young man walks down the street, hears the call to prayer and goes into the nearest mosque to pray. The new clip ends with the slogan "Say your prayers and enjoy life." Millions of Muslims would seem to prefer their religion as upbeat as the rest of us – at least some of the rest of us, as we'll see below.

Scene Three: Night Club, Beirut, Lebanon, October, 2004

It's 2:30am and Beirut's best, and not incidentally largely gay, disco is just getting started. Even if one is familiar with the city's fabled "cosmopolitan" past, it's still hard to process a gay disco operating in full view of the authorities on the eastern shores of the Mediterranean. Well, maybe it could happen 100 miles due south in Tel Aviv; and in fact Beirut in general and this club in particular reminds me of Tel Aviv and its famous dance clubs, right down to the beautiful ocean views and the tight hip-huggers favored by so many young women. But it's not just that it is a gay club; it's a gay and lesbian and straight club. And while I assumed that it must be a *Christian* gay club, an anthropologist friend who's spent a year doing field work in Beirut explained that the patrons are as likely to be Muslim as Christian. So here we are, surrounded by young Muslim and Christian men dancing together and young Muslim and Christian women dancing together (and not like at a wedding, mind you), the same-sex pairs switching seamlessly to more socially acceptable partners whenever one of the half a dozen or so security men approach. These security men – who wear pulsating pins on their T-shirts to alert amorous dancers of their imminent arrival – are trying to keep the situation "normal" enough so that the police don't close down the club.

The idea of scantily clad young Muslim lesbians dancing with their girlfriends (who might well be Christians) to a blend of American hiphop and Arab dance music in gay clubs until the wee hours of the morning would no doubt surprise and even shock many people (including many if not most Muslims). I've described this scene not for its shock value however, but because it raises several crucial issues for understanding the possibility of building truly democratic public spheres in the MENA. Most important among them, Do meeting places such as this have social equivalents in the daytime hours? Can these late-night liaisons foster the kind of "active citizenship" that is fundamental for any social change?

In other words, if in a city and country still licking its wounds from more than a decade of brutal civil war young men and women, Christian, Sunni, and Shi'i Muslim together, are risking arrest or worse to share each others' bodies under the stars, are these same young people meeting together in the light of day to push for greater democracy, government accountability, and social freedom for all Lebanese?

It's too early to tell. As I write these lines Beirut's vibrant and growing progressive NGO culture is at the forefront of unprecedented demonstrations to force Syria to withdraw from Lebanon in the wake of the assassination of former Prime Minister Rafik Hariri. It's hard to know how many clubgoers – many of whose families benefit from a corrupt system of which Syria has been the main protector, enforcer, and beneficiary – will join the challenge to it. Certainly it will take an unprecedented and radical commitment to social critique, justice, and activism, by clubbies and Hizbollah activists *together*, to bring democracy to Lebanon (never mind winning the right to walk down the street openly gay at 3pm).

Indeed, while Lebanese have long had comparatively great freedom to say what they wanted to say publicly and do what they wanted behind closed doors (of their houses or clubs), this state of affairs existed precisely because it never challenged a system in which corruption, the power of Syria, and the country's sectarian divide left the majority of young Lebanese with little hope of encouraging change through political activism until Hariri's murder reopened the abyss of civil war before them. And so dancing the night away with one's partner of whatever sex was, until quite recently, the closest thing to a useful political act available to many young Beirutis. Such an attitude will be that much harder to overcome when, as I explain below, the very activists behind the incipient democracy movement have been ignored by the global peace and justice movement in its discussions of and visits to Lebanon.[5]

But dancing isn't the only mode of coping with the dysfunctional reality of contemporary Lebanon. In the absence of the possibility of meaningful political or economic change, perhaps the majority of young Lebanese men who can leave the country will continue to do so to work in the Gulf (and here we must remember that labor migration is one of the few economic dynamics of globalization in which the MENA participates fully). As for young women, one of the most popular eighteenth birthday presents for Muslims as well as Christians, working as well as upper class, is a breast-enhancement and/or a nose-reduction. Why? In order to be more successful when competing for the limited supply of relatively well-off young men constantly returning home to look for a wife.

We have yet to scratch the surface of how to understand the dynamics of a society that can produce young women who variously dress "like dykes" at 2am and/or have surgically sculpted bodies tucked neatly inside their *abayas* (the black full-length pullover worn by conservative Muslim women) in the daylight hours. Certainly one undeniable conclusion is that young women in Lebanon, or their counterparts in Iran, Saudi Arabia, or any other Muslim country, are as varied and complex as young women in the United States or Europe (at the very least, we can conclude that *Baywatch* has affected the self-image of millions of Middle Eastern women much more than might have been hoped).

One thing is for sure: whether in "cosmopolitan" Beirut, with its hiphop artists, Syrian heavy-metal groups, high-rent downtown, "Che Bars" with drinks Che could never have afforded, minutes from poor, half-bombed out Hizbollah-controlled neighborhoods where the garbage collection and social services rival those in the wealthy al-Hamra quarter; *or* in more sedate Amman, with its Safeways and a luxury "Mecca Mall" filled with ads for *Sex and the City*, a chic bowling alley and first-run multiplex; *or* in overcrowded, smog-filled Tehran, with its shanty towns and embassy parties; *or* in desperate Baghdad (about whose plight more below), life in the MENA defies the kind of simple categorizations favored by the Axis of Arrogance and Ignorance.

Anarchy, Inc.: Iraq, Corporatized Chaos, and the Unending War on Terror

> To thrive "amidst" chaos means to cope or come to grips with it, to succeed in spite of it. But that is too reactive an approach, and misses the point. The true objective is to take the chaos as given and learn to thrive on it. The winners of tomorrow will deal proactively with chaos, will look at the chaos per se as the source of market advantage,

not as a problem to be got around. Chaos and uncertainty are (will be) market opportunities for the wise; capitalizing on fleeting market anomalies will be the successful business's greatest accomplishment.[6]

Tom Peters, *Thriving on Chaos*

We're here to stabilize the economy – I mean country.

US Marine brigade commander, interviewed by author, March 2004, Baghdad

No one knows why you're there but you.

My wife Lola, screaming at me over the phone from New York City after a particularly violent day in Baghdad

Why indeed? Why would someone whose job doesn't require leaving his pregnant wife and two-and-a-half-year-old son to go to a country descending into chaos, if not civil war, even consider doing so? Was it worth having three floors of windows blown out of one's similarly unprotected hotel as a result of a bomb a block away, or to sleep with shoes on, a cellphone in one pocket and a flashlight in the other, clutching a satellite phone, just in case the next hotel to be bombed was mine?

Since I'm still here writing the book, the answer is yes. But whether it's worth it or not, it's undeniable that Iraq has become both the epicenter of, and metaphor for, contemporary globalization in this era of increasing global chaos and the great damage it inflicts on local attempts to forge non-violent, inclusive, and democratic alternatives to the status quo. As such the example of Iraq challenges the popular notion within the global peace and justice movement that "dancing on the edge of chaos" (as one writer celebrated the movement's anar-chistic flair) is a viable strategy against neoliberal globalization, espe-cially once the Pentagon and not just the IMF and WTO got into the chaos business.[7]

From an economic perspective, the chaotic dynamics of post-September 11 globalization should surprise no one. Business leaders predicted such an environment a generation ago. For example, in one of the seminal books on business management in the age of global-ization, 1988's *Thriving on Chaos*, business guru Tom Peters argued that "the times demand flexibility and love of change" in order to thrive on the chaos of the emerging world system. For Peters, embracing change was crucial to taking advantage of the emerging globalized marketplace; for today's neoliberal Government and corporate elite, embracing and even instigating rapid social change is believed to be more crucial to advancing the interests of American foreign policy than during the heyday of "modernization theory" in the 1960s.

Why? Because only such a strategy could meet the challenge of the "coming anarchy" that already a decade ago mainstream and conservative scholars were predicting would soon envelop large swaths of the planet. But it's not just responding to chaos; initiating change and even chaos has been considered a crucial strategy in the context of the war on terror and the need to maintain and even expand an "empire of bases" that costs upwards of five hundred billion dollars per year.[8]

How does this discussion of chaos relate specifically to Iraq? Well, we know that the National Intelligence Council bluntly warned the Bush Administration in January 2003 – two months before the invasion – that "an American-led invasion of Iraq would increase support for political Islam and would result in a deeply divided Iraqi society prone to violent internal conflict," including insurgency against any new government.[9] The Bush Administration and its intellectual confidantes clearly had a strong inkling of what would happen when they ordered the invasion.[10] Except through wilful ignorance they had to know that the country would become the poster child of chaos-driven neoliberal globalization, with all the negative implications that come with it.[11]

Perhaps they felt powerless to stop it; more likely they figured that if chaos was inevitable the US might as well be the one controlling and profiting from it (which could yet turn out to be true). One thing is clear, whether it's Peters writing at the end of the Reagan Presidency or George W. Bush trying to rewrite the map of the Middle East (literally, as we'll see below when we discuss the role of oil in this story), the global era would seem to demand that leaders search for the best way to "face up to the need for revolution" and find "prescriptions for a world turned upside down."[12]

Iraq as the Poster Child of Post-September 11 Globalization

In this context there are several reasons why Iraq can be understood as the epicenter of post-September 11 globalization. First, the decision to invade and topple Hussein, which we now know was made soon after September 11,[13] clearly marks the transformation from the "lite" version of globalization that epitomized the Clinton years, in which wealthy countries increasingly realized that their interests were threatened by chaos, to a heavy globalization in which the US economy is driven to a much greater extent by war, oil, and the economies related to it.[14] For those tied into the new globalization the scale of profits available is awesome. As a senior Wall Street oil analyst said of the profits of the major oil companies (and his words hold also for the major defense companies), "Things could not have been better... In the last three years, they died and went to heaven... They are all sitting on the largest piles of cash in their history."[15]

We also know that profits of the major arms and heavy engineering companies, like Halliburton, Bechtel, ChevronTexaco, and Lockheed Martin, saw revenues rise by as much as 158 percent in 2004 because of "steep profits from their Iraq operations," while profits and stock prices have also increased dramatically (especially since September 11).[16] This situation has led some scholars, like Chalmers Johnson, to look at these post-September 11 dynamics and ask "Whatever happened to globalization?" From Johnson's perspective, "the aftermath of September 11 more or less spelled the end of globalization" because it signaled a change from economic to military imperialism.[17]

But as the first two parts of this book make clear, to assume that militarism and globalization are contradictory processes is to make two mistakes: first, to misunderstand the roots of globalization in classical imperialism, which, as we saw in Chapters Two and Three, was simultaneously economic and military; and second, to assume that militarism is somehow antithetical to globalization, which it clearly is not.

Simultaneously with the transformation to heavy globalization, US foreign policy toward the Middle East changed dramatically from a Cold War-era "obsession with order" to a desire (rhetorically at least) to be the engine of a radical democratic transformation in the region.[18] Such policies would be maintained even if "embracing the revolution" of democracy and free markets created significant "creative destruction" to economies and cultures along the way (about which more below). But the transformation isn't that straightforward, because at the same time the entire intellectual machinery of US foreign policy today argues that one country – the United States – must be the world's dominant singular power precisely to keep it from falling into the kind of chaos or (as Zbigniew Brzezinski terms it) "global anarchy" that such attempts at bold transformations are bound to generate.

And so in Iraq the US presented itself as the only possible guarantor of the social cohesion that the invasion itself violently disrupted. This is why anyone who has got on the wrong side of America's protective might, who stepped (or fell) into the chaos – Iraqi or

Table 9: Net Profits, Major "American" Corporations: New Economy, Oil, and Defense Sectors ($US million/year)

(Note: parenthesis equals negative income/loss)*

New Economy Companies

	Time Warner	Microsoft	Dell	Siebel	Oracle	Sisco	Intel	Sun	Yahoo	IBM
1994	n/a	n/a	n/a	n/a	283.72	n/a	n/a	n/a	n/a	n/a
1995	(33.60)	1453.00	1492.00	441.50	441.50	421.00	2288.00	355.80	(0.60)	6295.00
1996	29.80	2195.00	272.00	603.30	603.50	913.30	3566.00	476.40	(2.30)	5602.00
1997	(499.30)	3454.00	518.00	821.50	821.50	1048.70	5157.00	762.40	(22.90)	5312.00
1998	92.00	4490.00	944.00	813.70	813.70	1350.10	6945.00	762.90	25.60	5001.00
1999	762.00	7785.00	1460.00	1289.80	1289.80	2096.00	6068.00	1031.30	61.10	4992.00
2000	1232.00	9421.00	1666.00	6296.80	6896.80	2668.00	7314.00	1854.00	70.80	6585.00
2001	1152.00	7346.00	2177.00	2561.10	2561.10	(1014.00)	10535.00	927.00	(92.80)	4595.00
2002	(4921.00)	7829.00	1246.00	2224.00	2224.00	1893.00	1291.00	587.00	106.90	4820.00
2003	(98696.00)	9993.00	2122.00	2307.00	2307.00	3578.00	3117.00	3429.00	237.90	4379.00
2004	2639.00	8168.00	2645.00	2681.00	2681.00	4968.00	5641.00	388.00	N/A	4731.00
Average net income per year	(9824.31)	6213.40	1454.20	2003.97	1902.13	1792.21	5192.20	1057.38	42.63	5238.20
Average net income per year (of companies cited)	1092.65									

Defense Companies

	Lockheed Martin Corp.	Boeing Co.	Northrop Grumman Corp.	Raytheon Co.	General Dynamics Corp.
1994	1018.00	856.00	35.00	759.20	238.00
1995	682.00	393.00	252.00	792.50	321.00
1996	1347.00	1095.00	234.00	761.20	270.00
1997	1300.00	(178.00)	407.00	527.00	316.00
1998	1001.00	1120.00	194.00	864.00	364.00
1999	382.00	2309.00	467.00	404.00	880.00
2000	(519.00)	2128.00	608.00	141.00	901.00
2001	(1046.00)	2827.00	427.00	(763.00)	943.00
2002	500.00	492.00	64.00	(640.00)	917.00
2003	1053.00	718.00	866.00	365.00	1004.00
Average net income per year	571.80	1176.00	355.40	321.09	615.40

Oil Companies

	BP	Exxon	Shell	ChevronTexaco	Marathon Oil	Conoco Phillips
1994	2468.00	5100.00	6267.00	1693.00	(88.00)	484.00
1995	1740.20	6470.00	6919.00	930.00	664.00	469.00
1996	4370.30	7510.00	8886.00	2607.00	456.00	1303.00
1997	4079.70	8460.00	7753.00	3256.00	310.00	959.00
1998	3260.00	6370.00	350.00	1339.00	654.00	237.00
1999	4686.00	7910.00	8584.00	3247.00	432.00	609.00
2000	11870.00	17720.00	12719.00	7727.00	157.00	1862.00
2001	8010.00	15320.00	10852.00	3288.00	516.00	1661.00
2002	6845.00	11460.00	9419.00	1132.00	1321.00	(295.00)
2003	10267.00	21510.00	12496.00	7230.00	491.33	4735.00
Average net income per year	5759.62	10783.00	8424.50	3244.90	491.33	1202.40
Average net income per year (of companies cited)	10398.87					

Heavy Engineering

	Bechtel	Halliburton
1994	N/A	177.80
1995	N/A	168.30
1996	N/A	300.40
1997	N/A	454.40
1998	N/A	(14.70)
1999	N/A	438.00
2000	15108.00	501.00
2001	13400.00	809.00
2002	11600.00	(998.00)
2003	16300.00	(820.00)
Average net income per year	14102.00	101.62
Average net income per year (of companies cited)	7101.81	

*Note that "New Economy" companies include representatives from leading computer, information technology, internet, and entertainment companies. Oil companies include major American companies plus foreign-based companies that have major US operations and are among the biggest spenders on lobbying and campaign contributions. Also note that while Halliburton posted major losses in 2002 and 2003, these come from its non-Iraq operations and liabilities, and without the several billion dollars in no-bid contracts received for Iraq the company might well have had to declare bankruptcy.

American – is deemed to have "strayed from the program" (as one Pentagon official put it) so thoughtfully and generously laid out for them by the US Government.[19]

There is another reason why Iraq is a central battleground in the struggle over post-September 11 globalization: because the leading intellectuals, activists, artists, and other members of the global peace and justice movement could – indeed should – have made Iraq (the country itself, not just the debate over the occupation) the epicenter of their resistance to and transcendence of America's imperial chaos. Certainly neoliberals went out of their way to make Iraq the epicenter of their grand strategies; during the first year of occupation the Green Zone was populated by scores of "KPMG accountants, investment bankers, think-tank lifers, and Young Republicans."[20] But the rest of Baghdad, never mind Iraq, was far more scarcely populated by their counterparts in the global peace and justice movement. I'll explore why this was so and what it means later in the chapter, but one reason was clearly the spread of chaos across Iraq as the occupation wore on, which sometimes made it harrowing to work in the country if you weren't safely ensconced in the Green Zone, even if you could afford the large security details that traveled with government employees and contractors.

And Now, A Word from our Sponsors: Chaos Theory in Iraq

Writing in the wake of September 11, the French philosopher Jacques Derrida argued that "globalization is not taking place. It is a simulacrum, a rhetorical artifice or weapon that dissimulates a growing imbalance … a hypermediatized noncommunication and tremendous accumulation of wealth."[21] The language is a bit convoluted, but Derrida's argument is very important. As we've seen in Part II of this book, judged by mainstream economic definitions globalization *is* little more than a "simulacrum" or rhetorical artifice for an exploitative and even violent order. But as we've also seen, once viewed through its cultural – and increasingly militarized – dynamics, globalization is much more than a simulacrum, while the lack of economic globalization, as traditionally defined by mainstream economists, itself has profound consequences in the MENA.

More important is Derrida's larger argument that the growing imbalance and lack of communication between cultures caused by neoliberal globalization is directly tied to a permanent skewing in the balance of wealth in the world (one of the singular accomplishments of neoliberal globalization). The rapid spread of "new" and "hyper-mediated" communication technologies such as satellite television, the internet, and cellphones has increasingly made this imbalance harder to ignore, which is why so many people in the Global South describe their cultures as being "invaded" or "penetrated" by politically and economically more powerful cultures. This dynamic is also why, as we'll discuss below, terrorists are using increasingly spectacular forms of violence – flying airplanes into skyscrapers, sawing off people's heads in front of a worldwide web audience – to make themselves heard in an era where the official lines of communication are closing.

Derrida's description of globalization is quite suggestive in another way as it evokes the widely felt but (as of the time of writing) little understood increase in various levels of chaos across the Global South and Muslim world particularly. There is at least a two-decade-long history to the spread of chaos across the Muslim world, the start of which coincided with the end of the Cold War and the spread of neoliberal structural adjustment policies in the region. The seminal examples of this phenomenon are the Lebanese civil war, followed by the civil war in Algeria, and most recently the slow disintegration of the political and social structures of Palestinian society and now Iraq.[22] In all these cases, potential or genuine democratic processes were aborted by those in power, with the endorsement and even active collaboration of Western powers, precisely because such processes fundamentally challenged the position and power of the governing elites and/or foreign corporations and their government backers.[23]

Let's recall our discussions in Chapters Three and Four where we explored how the MENA region has been structurally marginalized from many of the "official" processes of economic globalization. In this situation it has been a combination of an increasing prevalence of low-wage manufacturing (often textile) jobs, the growth of informal (gray and black) economies, and the full weight of cultural globalization that has defined globalization for a large percentage of the world's Muslims.

What is important is how these processes in the MENA and other developing economies have become a primary generator of the sometimes violent identities and networks struggling against the emerging world order. The chaos has also widened the separation between the "resistance" (closed, often violent) versus "project" (positive, open) identities described earlier in this book, especially with the transformation from a "lite" to a "heavy" form of globalization as a result of

September 11, the expanded war on terrorism, and occupations of Afghanistan and Iraq.

The high levels of social, political, and economic chaos these dynamics have generated in various countries of the Muslim world are also evident in Russia and the Central Asian states of the former Soviet Union; parts of South America; in border zones such as the Indian Ocean/South China Sea; the "Northern Frontier" between Pakistan and Afghanistan; and sub-Saharan Africa. What makes this chaos important for our discussion – as predicted by chaos theory as it's applied in the natural sciences – are the seemingly paradoxical levels of order and systemic logic to it.

What I mean by this is that if we look hard enough we can understand the chaos to be a predictable outcome of the policies pursued by various actors to achieve other identifiable goals. Indeed, the dynamics of globalized chaos are best understood as a kind of "sponsored chaos," as there are almost always outside powers with strategic interests in generating chaos locally, and various local actors who can take advantage of the chaos to advance their own ends. Yet the chaos is also potentially unmanageable, often leading to significant "blowback" against its sponsors precisely because it escapes their control and allows new actors a foothold in the local political and cultural economies. Iraq is the perfect example of this phenomenon. Only time will tell how well the Bush Administration and its allies were able to manage the chaos in Iraq.

Let's take two examples of this process to establish our discussion of chaos in the MENA. The first is Africa. Of course Africa has long been politically and otherwise chaotic. But while the continent has been beleaguered by violence for decades – centuries in fact – there is something "discernibly new" in the forms of political violence plaguing countries like Liberia, Sierra Leone, Sudan, or the Congo.[24] What most scholars believe is that in the last two decades the liberalization of the economies of these countries, coupled with (and in many ways, encouraging) the weakening of their political systems, have produced a state of confusion, uncertainty, and chaos that has led people at all levels of society to seek whatever means possible to survive in or even profit from the growing disorder.[25]

In a climate where both states and societies have become increasingly weak – a combination not accounted for by most political scientists, it should be pointed out – the "business of violence" has been one of the best growth industries on the continent.[26] Why? In large part because of a political and economic environment dominated by IMF-sponsored (more often than not, imposed) reforms, coupled with foreign aid that is increasingly tied to issues related to the war on terrorism or oil wealth.[27] Together these dynamics have nurtured an environment of "disorder" where criminality, corruption, and violence of all sorts thrive by operating in the gaps between the official and gray or black sectors.[28]

Similar to the situation in Iraq or Palestine, political leaders in many African countries use neoliberal policies as a convenient whipping post to distract citizens from their own corruption and oppression, while continuing to enrich themselves and re-entrench the very autocracy and patriarchal cultures the liberalization of their countries' political and economic systems were supposed to challenge.[29] In the absence of any hope for a common future, corruption and chaos are irresistible ways to advance people's most narrowly defined interests.

If chaos is becoming increasingly "instrumentalized" in Africa, in Russia and the former Soviet states of Central Asia a system of "post-Soviet chaos" has come to dominate large sectors of the economies and politics of these societies. Across the post-Soviet landscape *bardok*, the Russian word for chaos, has become a central experience of the post-Cold War order, and one that is increasingly dispossessing people economically, politically, and culturally as a result of "the sudden and brutal emergence of market forces in non-market societ[ies]."[30]

Figure 10   Victory or defeat in Gaza, September 2003

This situation has become so intense that it has created a new experience of political power – the "chaotic mode of domination" – out of the almost total breakdown of existing social compacts between governing elites and the rest of their societies.[31] In this context, there are several defining characteristics of *bardok*/chaos that are particularly important for our discussion: first, the accumulation and concentration of wealth in fewer and fewer hands; second, the increasing scarcity of public funds for core social services; third, the privatization of theft, bribery, and manipulation of credit or aid. This situation is being repeated across the Global South, along what the Pentagon calls the "arc of instability" running from Africa to Indonesia, with Palestine and Iraq as key examples.[32]

Chaos in Iraq and Palestine; or, Searching for the Elastic Sheikh

In Sadr City there lives a young Shi'i preacher, Sheikh Anwar al-Ethari, known as "the Elastic Sheikh." He got his nickname because of his penchant for innovative and even (from a Western perspective) progressive interpretations of the Qur'an and Shar'ia. Indeed, Sheikh Anwar, who runs half a dozen mosques in the same poor Baghdad neighborhoods that are Moqtada al-Sadr's home base, earned one degree in sociology from Baghdad University and another in religious subjects from the "Hawza," or prestigious Shi'i religious seminary. Until the uprising started in earnest in March 2004 he constantly sought to receive training from, and otherwise work with, international peace and related NGO activist organizations. Yet once the violence exploded he seemed to disappear. No one knew if he had gone into hiding, or if he was being secretly held in Abu Ghraib, or if he was dead. What was certain was that an alternative to the violent voice of Moqtada al-Sadr had been silenced when he was needed most, and the chaos enveloping Iraq was the most likely culprit.

A strikingly similar process is happening in Palestine, except that it took thirty-five years for Israel to create a level of chaos that was achieved by the US occupation of Iraq in just one year. As I explained in Chapter One, my personal experience of increasing chaos in Palestine, coupled with my more intense experience in Iraq, has led to my belief that the chaos in both countries was not a by-product of the occupations suffered by Palestinians and Iraqis. Rather, it has become crucial to the success of the occupations, in significant measure because of the profits and repression it facilitates, if not enables.

This is why I argue that neoliberal globalization is the most important frame of reference for understanding how chaos functions in Iraq (especially when we understand the similar experiences of other countries of the MENA, Africa or Central Asia).[33] In fact, we can see that in both Palestine and Iraq chaos, a combination of weakened political systems and societies and a weak or even absent public sphere, have had a disastrously synergistic effect on each other. Each negative trend has strengthened the others, all of them increasing the violence and extremism that in turn nurture each other, leading the societies towards a slow and bloody implosion.

Iraq, sadly, is a perfect laboratory for understanding how neoliberal globalization is tied to this process. As I argued in several articles after visiting Iraq, as of early 2005 there is chaos everywhere in the Arab two-thirds of the country (it oscillates in the Kurdish north depending on the level of violence).[34] It was reflected in everything from the unwillingness of the American and Iraqi officials to publish health statistics or even regularly visit hospitals, to the rampant corruption that was built on the foundations of the previous regime. Billions of dollars budgeted for such things as school or infrastructure rehabilitation disappear into contractors' offshore accounts when they haven't been reallocated to "security concerns," which of course means they wind up in other contractors' bank accounts.[35]

If Iraq in the early spring of 2004 was sliding toward chaos, this was exactly where Iraqis increasingly believed the US wanted them to be. As a prominent Iraqi psychiatrist who worked with the CPA and the US military explained to me, "There is no way the United States can be this incompetent. The chaos here has to be at least partly deliberate." Similarly, as the November 2004 siege of Falluja was winding down, a former head of the town's council similarly explained, "The Americans don't want this place to be quiet... From the beginning they brought chaos and treated people badly."[36] Long before the flattening of Falluja, the main question on most Iraqis' minds was not *if* these assertions were true, but *why*?[37] We'll answer this question below.

Soon after I returned home from Iraq, as the insurrection that had exploded during my time in the country intensified, I called some of my friends who were still in Iraq to see if they were okay. When I reached one of them, an Italian activist named Simona Torretta (who was kidnapped for twenty days in September 2004 by an unknown group – the "*forze oscure*" (obscure or dark forces) that arrived with the chaos[38]) her first words upon recognizing me were "Ah, Mark, è un casino." In Italian, this phrase usually means something like "it's crazy" or "it's overwhelming." Mothers of young children use it a lot when you ask them how they're doing. But it has a darker meaning when said by an Italian in Baghdad in the spring of 2004. In this context, it means something closer to "total chaos and violence," while also evoking images of the prostitution and perversion that accompany the wholesale breakdown of social order.

In fact, *casino* is quite close in meaning to the Russian word *bardok*; both conjure images of extreme chaos, and of moral degeneration as epitomized by the spread of brothels and prostitution in Iraq in the aftermath of the invasion. *Casino* and *bardok* distill into a single word what the violence of "globalization," or as it's called in Iraq "privatization," does to those on the receiving end of the enterprise. Indeed, Iraq was becoming more and more like a "casino" since the day US troops crossed the Kuwaiti border; a reality that made the work of international humanitarian, aid, and peace organizations increasingly difficult in the ensuing year.

Multiple Levels of Chaos and Incompetence ... or Brilliance?

As I've already explained, it's hard to assess how much of the chaos dominating Iraq in 2004 and early 2005 is: (A) just the product of war and occupation generally; (B) the product of Bush Administration ill-planning, arrogance, or as Ted Kennedy described it, "arrogant ideological incompetence)";[39] or (C) planned, or at least welcomed, by elements in the Administration. Most Iraqis I know opt, almost automatically, for option (C). If it's true that at least some of the chaos in Iraq has, to one degree or another, been consciously let loose on the land, the broadest reason is obvious: as Maher, an Iraqi friend who worked for the UN before the suicide bombing that drove the organization out of the country in 2003 explained, "One thing is clear; it is impossible to build a peaceful alternative to the occupation when the chaos reaches its current levels."[40]

As long as the violence continues at a level comparable to 2004, the chance of building a truly democratic, progressive alternative to the status quo is quite low. Indeed, along with the insecurity it brings, the chaos denies civil society the possibility of promoting any alternatives to collaboration with or violent opposition to the occupation.

Watching a similar dynamic at work for over a decade in the Occupied Territories, I had grown increasingly frustrated with Palestinian society for not being able to build a non-violent means of resisting an occupation that only digs in deeper in response to the violent resistance it breeds. But seeing the dynamic evolve before my eyes at hyper-speed in Iraq gave me a better understanding of why it's been so difficult for Palestinians, or Iraqis, to build such a movement. What Nancy Ries calls the "planned chaos" of an occupation, coupled with the "structural adjustment" that is a euphemism for the harsh imposition of a so-called "free market" economy on formerly more "socialist" economies, steamrolls over almost any attempts to resist non-violently in the spirit of Gandhi or King.[41]

Some might argue that the idea that the chaos in Iraq was even partly planned is preposterous: wouldn't the violence and anarchy it unleashed, which clearly called into question the success of Bush's Iraq policy, be too big an electoral risk to unleash? In, fact, as the 2004 election demonstrated, it cost Bush nothing, because Americans largely bought the notion that in some vague way Iraq was tied to al-Qa'eda and that whatever the faults in its execution, the Bush Administration had little choice but to invade and occupy Iraq. Tens of millions (perhaps most) Americans intuitively believe that Arabs and Muslims are half-civilized at best, so who really expected them to seize hold of the wonderful opportunity the United States bestowed upon them by getting rid of the dictator Saddam and build a real democracy? The US might fail, but at least it tried!

Perhaps President Bush and his neoconservative advisors meant well; perhaps they really felt that all America had to do was light the beacon and freedom and democracy would follow. If this is the case, these "true believers" in the fantasy of rapid victory followed by rapid free-market democratization comprise the first of at least three circles of chaos involved in the occupation of Iraq. They would be, as one Washington insider put it to me, literally "that incompetent"; an assessment that perhaps could be made about British and Spanish Prime Ministers Tony Blair and José Maria Aznar and their closest political advisors as well.[42]

As I explain below, perhaps they knew exactly what they were doing. Whichever turns out to be the case, there are two groups within the American governmental system who are definitely not that incompetent: the radical right-wing ideologues in the White House and Pentagon, and their corporate sponsors. And these two groups make up the final two circles of chaos creators in Iraq. The two groups, comprising the chief government and corporate architects of the Iraq war, are not at all distinct, yet are embodied in the personage of former Defense Secretary and Halliburton CEO, Vice President Dick Cheney. On the more directly political level, neoconservative officials and their media allies neither expected the occupation of Iraq to be a "cakewalk" nor cared if it spread chaos to other countries, as long as it furthered their aim to reconfigure the political map of the region and solidified American control over Iraq's oil resources.

In fact, as we've seen in Part Two of this book, for years key American governmental figures and the leaders of institutions such as the World Bank and the International Monetary Fund (IMF) understood that US-led globalization was going to necessitate and generate violence throughout the third world and in the Middle East specifically. And already in the early and mid-1990s hawkish scholars were writing of "the new Cold War" taking shape as Islamic nationalism confronted the region's secular states. As important, the early post-Cold War experiences in Bosnia, Haiti, Rwanda, and other parts of Africa led well-known mainstream and conservative intellectuals, including Robert Kaplan, Samuel Huntington, and even Bush Administration Assistant Defense Secretary Paul Wolfowitz, to publish articles and organize conferences on "Managing Chaos" and the "coming anarchy."[43]

Of course the main points of these analyses – which are being repeated in the country's opinion pages by Kaplan and others literally as I write these lines, as if nothing has been learned in the last decade – is to create what the Middle Eastern scholar Yahya Sadowski argues is a "myth of global chaos."[44] Indeed, the cover of the magazine *L'Expansion* that featured the profile of Amr Khaled included the headline "Spécial Islam: Voyage dans une économie au bord du chaos" (Journey through an economy on the brink of chaos). Needless to say, the artwork consisted of an image of the MENA engulfed by the flames from an oil well.[45]

Such thinking is much easier and more politically useful than reflecting on the actual dynamics on the ground. It is also directly related to the multi-billion-dollar enterprise of fabricating – in all meanings of the word – a myth of global terror.[46] This is accomplished, of course, by describing the chaos as primarily the result of the failure of the peoples and cultures of the region to adapt to the post-Cold War world order (or even "modernity" itself) and build successful democracies. In a "barren region for democracy," the best the US can hope to do is to "manage" a situation not of its own making, while helping those who would accept the offer.

And so in Iraq, as Donald Rumsfeld would explain in October 2004: "Iraqis are free to become vicious killers. And because they're free, they are running around, the terrorists... and former regime elements, cutting people's heads off... blowing up people willy-nilly to try to create chaos." This is just as Robert Kaplan and Samuel

Huntington predicted free Muslims would behave, and echoes the sentiment in the *9/11 Commission Report*'s argument that the US has no culpability for the problems plaguing the Muslim world. As Rumsfeld concludes, "It's going to be Iraqis that decide" whether they allow the terrorists to prevail.[47] The best America can do is hold out a helping hand filled with upwards of 150,000 soldiers risking their lives to make the country safe for democracy.

Sadowski, for one, has been extremely critical of the basic premises and "popularization" of chaos theory, which for him is a dangerous theory precisely because of how easily it had "won converts in the US military, the intelligence community and the foreign service" by the second half of the 1990s.[48] I wouldn't argue with his critique of writers like Kaplan and Huntington (which is strongly supported by the contributors to a new volume, *Why America's Top Pundits Are Wrong*, that also features strong critiques of other members of the Axis of Arrogance and Ignorance like Thomas Friedman and Dinesh D'Souza).[49] But Sadowski is only half right in his analysis: the idea of global chaos *is* a myth if we conceive of it as something unleashed purely by the backwardness and irrationality of the peoples of the Global South (which is what Kaplan and co. argue). Yet it is just as clear that chaos *is* an increasingly troubling reality across the Global South, and that outside powers, including the US and its allies and enemies, are managing – and when useful, initiating or "sponsoring" – it for their advantage.

What evidence do we have to support this claim? First, by the mid-1990s the World Bank had already reported that the Middle East would likely require a "shake-down period" to adapt to the new global economic order coming out of Washington.[50] And in 2000, the US Strategic Space Command (whose mission is to dominate space in order to "protect US interests and investment") produced its *Vision for 2020*, in which it admitted that globalization was producing a zero-sum game of winners and losers and that in such a world Americans needed to be prepared to do whatever it might take to "win."[51]

For the ideologues in the Bush Administration a "shake-down" wasn't enough if the US wanted to "win" Iraq. And so the country, already emaciated by years of war and sanctions, was targeted for the shock-down that came with Operation Shock and Awe. If we take seriously the statements and writings of Ledeen, Perle, Frum, Feith, and Wolfowitz, the invasion and occupation of Iraq was supposed to create a domino effect that would weaken local states (or in their polite words, "democratize" them), open their economies to Western corporations by establishing market economies, and at the same time lead to a much-needed "reformation" or "modernization" of Islam (by producing conservative Muslims who would feel comfortable with the conservative Christians in the White House).

Of course, to accomplish such a "revolution," a significant amount of force would be necessary. This, itself obviously a chaos creator, was not seen by them as a bad thing. As neocon "philosopher" and Bush advisor Michael Ledeen typically argues, the United States is "an awesome revolutionary force"; its "iron will" naturally leads it to engage in the kind of creative destruction – "our middle name," according to him – that has been the hallmark of imperialism, capitalism, and modernity for almost half a millennium.[52]

Ultimately, however randomly chaotic, or beyond America's ability to control or determine, events in Iraq may seem to the casual observer, we need to remember another important comment made by Derrida after September 11: "The word 'anarchy' risks making us abandon too quickly the analysis and interpretation of what indeed *looks like* pure chaos. We must do all that we can to account for this appearance."[53] It is in this context that we need to understand how and why the press suddenly discovered "chaos" in Iraq in the summer of 2004, especially as the Abu Ghraib scandal grabbed the headlines.

As the Abu Ghraib torture scandal spun out of control, the press started reporting that the Pentagon was being "blamed for [the] Abu Ghraib 'Chaos.'"[54] But while even some Iraqi politicians were confused by the chaos gripping Iraq, one could make a strong argument as to why the Pentagon and its corporate allies would not find this situation troubling (if it did, why would the Defense Department have awarded more contracts to firms whose employees were directly implicated in the abuses at Abu Ghraib, even *after* the scandal broke?).[55] After all, the chaos allowed not just hundreds of billions of American tax dollars to be spent in Iraq and on the larger war on terror, but also allowed US corporations like Halliburton to grab upwards of $10 billion in Iraqi assets under control of the CPA during the year of official occupation alone.[56]

The chaos in Iraq can also be understood as something expected and even hoped for if we consider the way the modernity matrix we discussed earlier in the book has evolved in the age of globalization. From this perspective what the Iraqi occupation represents is the full force of a modernism gone wild; a "turbo-modernity" that has injected the other coefficients of the modernity matrix – imperialism/colonialism, capitalism, and (in many ways in response to all three) nationalism – with renewed ferocity.

This turbo-modernity – what could also be called "modernity on meth" in light of the rapidly increasing meta-amphetamine use by overworked Americans[57] – is reflected in the desire of Iraq's American planners to make Iraq a *tabula rasa* for neoliberal globalization. By this I mean "a country of 25 millions would not be rebuilt as it was before the war; it would be *erased, disappeared*. In its place would spring forth a gleaming showroom for *laissez-faire* economics."[58] This act of "disappearing" local economies, cultures, and peoples – the creative destruction we've been describing – has always been at the heart of the modern project, especially under colonial conditions, where it's mixed together with the kind of "imperial hubris" that characterizes contemporary American (and British) foreign policy.[59] And we shouldn't forget that violence is a prime means through which chaos enables the creative destruction *and* creative accounting that together symbolize the occupation of Iraq.

But of course, the program can't be sold this way. Rather, as an army spokesperson explained at a Las Vegas conference for potential American contractors in Iraq, "There are lots of good deeds to be done in Iraq… Iraq is full of 25 million people who are ready to embrace the American Dream… but more than anything, the Iraqi people want to buy things… if it sells in Beaumont it will sell in Basra."[60] Such rhetoric might remind us of Thomas Friedman's dreams of Disney vacations for the world's working poor, but it also raises the question of just what America is selling to the Iraqi people. So far, not much besides a failed reconstruction program and a lot of low-paying and high-risk jobs in the police or National Guard. But it's clear that at least some Americans and Iraqis are doing quite well by the sponsored chaos of Iraq – "It's a question of who's in a position to call the shots," explained a researcher who spent the first year of the occupation in Iraq.[61]

In the United States it's not hard to figure out who called the shots over Iraq, as Vice President Cheney and the Defense Department trumped Secretary of State Colin Powell and his colleagues at the State Department at almost every turn in the lead-up, prosecution, and "rebuilding" efforts in the country. But it's not just at this level that the profits are important. As we've seen, the money train that is Iraq has many stops across America before crossing the ocean on a big jet plane.

Iraqis Respond to American-sponsored Globalization: Religious or Secular, It's Not What They Hoped For

It shouldn't be surprising given the discussion in Chapter Five that among the biggest opponents of globalization in Iraq are radical religious figures such as Ayatollah Baghdadi and his younger and more famous colleague, Moqtada al-Sadr. Opposition to neoliberal globalization, or any kind of global integration that would force a sacrifice of their view of essential Muslim values or open Muslim societies to the "penetration" of Western corporations and culture, did not start on March 20, 2003. In the years leading up to the invasion, figures like Baghdadi were already publishing books with titles like *Irfan* [Mystical Knowledge] *and Jihad* and *The Other Way* – meaning the way of rejecting the emerging US-dominated globalized system.[62] Another popular book is *The End and Destruction of America and Israel*, which predictably blames the Jews for turning the United States into a global Crusader state.[63]

And it's not just Shi'i religious leaders who speak like this. Most Sunni leaders express similar sentiments; none more so than Harigh al-Dhari, the head of the Association of Sunni Religious Scholars and the Imam of the 'Um al-Ma'arak (Mother of Battles Mosque) that was built by Saddam to thank the people of a Baghdad neighborhood where he hid during the 1991 Gulf War. When I interviewed al-Dhari in his mosque office, with dozens of machine-gun-toting bodyguards outside the door, he railed against globalization in language and tone almost identical to Ayatollah Baghdadi's, and focused on Islam's role in fighting its ill effects, even if it meant "not sparing" any infidel.[64]

We could dismiss these statements as just more boilerplate anti-Americanism from radical religious figures, but we'd be wrong to do so. Such views (minus the endorsement of violence) were felt across the board in Iraq as the occupation ground on past its first year. Artists, intellectuals, writers, professors – most people I met – had a similarly negative view of neoliberal globalization and the prospects for any real democratic and sustainable development under such a system, even if they understood that some compromises had to be made to attract foreign investment and retire Iraq's massive foreign debt.[65] Even more moderate figures, such as Sheikh Jawad al-Khalisi, head of the Qadamiyyah mosque in Baghdad, who spoke convincingly to me of the need for Muslims, Christians, and Jews to have a place in the new Iraq, opposed American-sponsored neoliberal globalization.

It should not be any surprise then that when Iraqis were polled on the question, about 85 percent of them said their system of choice was a managed, state-run economy with maximal distribution of the country's oil wealth to health care, education, and other social services. That is clearly not what George W. Bush had in mind on March 18, 2003, however, and thus the post-occupation shake-down – or slap-down – was inevitable the moment the troops crossed the border.

The disaster that is Iraq teaches us that we still don't have the language to describe accurately the dynamics and impact of contemporary globalization, especially after September 11. One could argue that the planners and managers of the occupation knew well enough what they were doing in Iraq and what the impact of what I would call sponsored chaos would be. As an Iraqi friend explained, in a society so brutalized by twenty years of Saddam Hussein and constant war, oppression, and corruption, "the idea of building a coherent, positive resistance cannot fit for the Iraqi mentality. They can easily be driven to any fight and will hand the mess over to the Americans by giving them an excuse to stay here. And the Iraqi intellectuals are doing nothing: they are more worried about their chairs [that is, their possessions and social position] than the country or the people."

We can be more charitable than he is, since the very Iraqis who have the training, skills, and desire to rebuild their country – the engineers, doctors, lawyers, and other professionals – are, like the architect I talked with, either ignored by the CPA, the Allawi regime, and now the post-election Government contractors in favor of more corrupt colleagues, or are themselves targets of assassination just by virtue of the fact they might be imagined as cooperating with the Americans. Either way, with local intellectuals in hiding or dead, and international activists mostly gone, it's no surprise that Iraqis feel very much alone and have little in the way of a positive, forward-thinking leadership.[66]

In this context, the British journalist Jonathan Steele argues that the chaos in Iraq has led the US to "creat[e] its own Gaza."[67] For me, however, chaos-ridden Iraq has created, at the time of writing at least (November 2004), a sad mixture of Gaza and Tel Aviv: on the one hand there's the violence of the resistance against the occupation, which feels like Gaza or Nablus (at least you know who your enemy is and who's shooting at whom). But on top of this is the violence – the suicide bombings, assassinations, and sudden American attacks whose randomness gives one the feeling of living in Tel Aviv. Put the two together and the chaos, tenseness, and violence of daily life in the main cities of Iraq are hard to bear; and as of the time of writing it's been getting worse by the day, making it impossible for civil society to produce an alternative political discourse either to collaboration with or violent religious opposition to the occupation.

When Chaos Works Out Just Fine

All this chaos and violence may ultimately turn out no better for its managers in the Pentagon and White House than Vietnam turned out for their predecessors. But it could also turn out quite well. We can see the results in Afghanistan, where as I write the Bush Administration is celebrating – and being celebrated for – sponsoring the "first democratic elections" in the country's history. Of course, even if the elections aren't discredited by fraud, the winners are almost all warlords or their allies: people whose rule of the country in the 1990s was so bad that Afghanis welcomed the Taliban's rise to power; whose view of women is little different from that of their predecessors, and who've returned the country to its preeminent position as the world's leading opium producer right under the nose of the United States.

It is not hard to envision such a scenario developing in Iraq. As the November 2004 battle for Falluja raged on I wrote an article entitled "Four Times Falluja Equals?" that described four possible outcomes of the invasion.[68] By the time you read this it will be clear which one if any came to pass, but at the time of writing what's clear is that the Bush Administration would break even or come out ahead with three of them. These include what I call the "Hama solution," in which Falluja is flattened and enough insurgents killed to sap the insurgency of its strength and enable an Afghanistan-style election (with President Bush then celebrated for bringing democracy to both these benighted countries); and the "Jenin solution," in which the flattening of Falluja sparks wider violence and chaos across Iraq that, however nasty, either leaves the US in a stronger strategic position when the dust settled (as Jenin did for Israel) or provides the cover for spreading the chaos across the borders to Syria or Iran. In both cases the US would maintain both a military presence in Iraq and a major interest in the management of its petroleum resources.

My final outcome seems, at the time of writing, to be the most unlikely, as the window of opportunity for its realization likely had closed by the end of the occupation's first year, while the US and Allawi Governments seem willing to sacrifice tens of thousands of people to prevent it. It would have encompassed massive protests by local, grass-roots civil society and democratic forces in Iraq, backed by strong pressure from European countries like France and Germany,

UN Secretary General Kofi Annan, and a resurgent peace movement. Together, they would have used the violence, anger, and political chaos unleashed by the invasion of Falluja, and the larger occupation-gone-awry it represented, to push forward a new dynamic of resistance, one based on the kind of inclusive and democratic "project identities" without which any insurgent victory over the occupation, however hard-won, would be an empty one.

As I finish this book the newly elected Iraqi Legislative Assembly is struggling to figure out how to get rid of both the US occupation and the foreign jihadis who have little interest in reaching an accommodation with the country's Shi'i or Kurdish communities. While the violence of the last twenty months has made it nearly impossible to imagine civil society and mass protest defeating violence in the short term, the sparks are there. Perhaps, if as in other developing countries some measure of stability and "democracy" can be achieved in the short term, a progressive opposition to the emerging order can develop in Iraq. Certainly there were glimpses of such a future when Ayatollah Sistani ordered millions of Shi'a to Najaf with explicit instruction, to use non-violence – acts of prayer and pilgrimage – to end the siege. And the small but incredibly brave group of Iraqi and international civil society and NGO activists whom I've discussed throughout this book are the vanguard for any possible progressive change. But Sistani's call for active non-violent opposition to the status quo was noteworthy for its uniqueness (there was no solidarity march to Falluja six months later; even Moqtada al-Sadr mostly held his tongue), while the numbers of local and foreign activists remain, by their own admission, far too small to change the political equation in Iraq.

Considering the importance and difficulty of the task, it's surprising how little energy most "anti-war" activists, artists, and even scholars put into supporting and even joining the struggle on the ground in Iraq. Apparently few people realized the risks involved in losing Iraq to George W. Bush and his weapons–petrodollar coalition of the willing.[69] One thing is certain, however: a Bush "victory" in Iraq will strike a blow from which the global peace and justice movement will find it very hard to recover.

Oil and the Geo-strategic Factor: Does an Axis of Empathy Have a Chance in an Age of Entropy?

If it is true that the Age of Growth is over [then] the Age of Entropy has begun, and if we are to retain any hope of a reasonable quality of life without destroying other people's, then our infrastructure, our settlements, our industries and our lives require total reconstruction.[70]

Why is the Age of Growth over? As *Guardian* columnist George Monbiot explains, because the Age of Oil is over, and with it the basis of the worldwide debt-based financial system that requires unchecked growth to keep the US economy from collapsing. Making the passing of the epoch of cheap oil and unchecked growth more painful is the fact that those whose power and wealth have long depended on both will not let them go easily; rather they'll do whatever they can to preserve the illusion that both can continue as the foundations of Western – indeed, world – society.[71]

Like it or not, however, the slow and often painful transformation of the world economy away from cheap oil and endless growth to something most of us can't even yet imagine is inevitable. Whatever the future may hold, it is increasingly clear that today the world has reached, or within a decade will reach, peak oil production. This means that new discoveries will no longer be of a magnitude large enough to replace the amount of oil pumped out of the earth every day. At the very least, as the *Financial Times* concludes, the world will soon "become more dependent on Mideast oil" no matter how much Russia, Venezuela, or any one of a half-dozen African countries can increase their output in the coming years.[72]

This view is supported by the research of international geologists, the French Petroleum Institute, Colorado School of Mines and Uppsala University and Petroconsultants in Geneva; all believe that "[its] economic and social consequences will be staggering."[73] Indeed, none other than Texas oil tycoon and corporate raider T. Boone Pickens admits that "never again" will the world be able to pump the 82 million barrels it currently pulls out of the ground every day; and oil companies have been overstating their reserves in active oil fields for at least a decade to hide this fact.[74]

Given this dynamic, it shouldn't be surprising that the epicenters of globalized chaos I described above (the MENA, Africa, Asia, Latin America) can be mapped closely to major oil deposits, sources of other crucial resources and to the "resource conflicts" caused by the increasingly zero-sum conflict to control them.[75] As Monbiot points out, without cheap oil and the possibility of limitless growth, the world's countries will soon be fighting like "cats in a sack." And this is why, as Michael Klare argues in his important book, *Resource Wars*, it's *not* the civilizational clashes of Huntington, but rather the struggles over crucial resources like oil, water, gems, and timber, that are becoming the engines of twenty-first-century global conflict.[76]

The US foreign policy establishment has in fact been well aware of the consequences of oil scarcity for at least a decade. It actually produced a major shift in US security policy in the 1990s, which Klare describes as an "econonomization of international security affairs."[77] That is, national security is being impacted more than ever before by economic issues rather than the (supposedly) political or ideologically driven conflicts of the Cold War. This might seem like a rehashing of Samuel Huntington's famous claim about the end of the Cold War signaling the end of "ideological"–political conflicts, but while Klare might support the first half of his argument, he clearly challenges the second, which claims cultures/civilizations as the new antagonists. Instead, Klare argues that economic processes are the roots of the current "clash" between Muslim and Western "civilizations."[78]

Doesn't this focus on economics as the roots of conflict contradict my arguments in the first two parts of the book that culture defines globalization? No, especially if we're talking about post-September 11 globalization. This is because the dynamic that has evolved since September 11 has seen America's Government, corporate, and cultural elites use the culturalization of globalization's economic processes to create the hostile and fear-filled cultural environments that make both a war economy *and* culture possible. And here we should remember that the conservative religious establishment is as much America's cultural elite as Hollywood; in fact it's more powerful when it comes to getting people to do something other than passively consume.

This dynamic might describe America, but what about the Middle East? We know that the Muslim world is to a significant extent excluded from the global flows that define economic globalization. Yet while economic globalization is not a strong presence *in* the MENA, thanks to massive labor migration it in fact has great impact *on* the region, as over thirty million migrant workers send or bring "home" billions of dollars in remittances *and* innumerable "foreign" cultural influences, from American movies to Wahhabi Islam.[79]

Ultimately, as Klare argues, however powerful cultures and ideologies may be they can't hide the fact that the "clash of civilizations" between radical neoliberalism and radical Islam is in reality a sadly predictable outcome of consumer nations, epitomized by the United States, doing what's necessary to preserve their access to and control over the oil that alone can fuel their high-octane economies.[80] What exactly is necessary for the Government–corporate elite to do?

Recently declassified documents from Vice President Cheney's Energy Task Force provide some clues as to what the Bush Administration and its corporate sponsors determined was the best course of action:[81] first, get a secret energy task force chaired by Vice President Cheney to conduct an exhaustive review of Iraq's proven reserves. The review will naturally determine that foreign oil companies – especially the reviled French – have virtually locked the US out of the Iraqi market since the 1991 Gulf War. In this situation, as Germany's Deutsche Bank explained, the major US oil companies will be the "big losers" when UN sanctions end, because foreign rather than American oil companies will develop the largest remaining untapped oil fields in the world.[82]

Next, draw up a new map of Iraq that literally erases all the features of the country other than the location of major oil fields. With such a stark picture of the potential gains and losses involved in who "wins" Iraq, it becomes clear that the US simply *cannot* afford *not* to invade Iraq; the cost of letting anyone else gain control of all that oil would be too great.[83] (If it wasn't clear yet why the US military headed straight for the Oil Ministry while letting Baghdad's cultural heritage burn, it should be now.) Finally, unleash creative destruction experts: the US military, followed by USAID's and the World Bank and IMF's "privatization" and "efficiency" consultants, and sit back and watch the entropy creep across the country as sure as the smog creeps across Baghdad most mornings.[84]

In fact, entropy, as George Monbiot insightfully terms it, is a perfect word to describe the situation in Iraq as of early 2005; the word suggests the disorder and randomness associated with chaos, but also embraces a loss of information (or communication, to use Derrida and Habermas's phrase) that causes unrepairable social fragmentation.[85] It also happens to be a great cover for surreptitiously dividing up the spoils of the war – all that oil – among the US, Britain, and select Iraqi and other clients.

Entropy; chaos; anarchy – whatever we call it, such a scenario demands we ask some hard questions: What will the United States do to protect its privileged position in a world where oil production is approaching and will soon pass its peak? What role would "sponsored chaos" play in its strategy? What countries would benefit or be threatened from such policies, and so would work either with (the UK, Russia) or against (China, Iran) US geostrategic objectives?[86]

It will take years to answer fully these important questions. What is almost certain from the events of 2001 to 2005 is that the United States, especially a Bush Administration whose ties to the oil industry are umbilical, would see its interests centered on securing access to existing major petroleum reserves while controlling and where necessary even limiting direct access to them by allies and rivals (especially China). Some scholars with whom I've discussed this issue believe that the "fungibility" of oil makes its supply nearly impossible to control or limit, and so makes a policy based on these goals impossible to enforce. But as we saw in Chapter Two, US Middle East policy since President Roosevelt met with King Sa'ud sixty years ago would seem to have been based on just this strategic objective, rational or not.[87] It is therefore not far-fetched to assume that the US and "allies" like Russia would consider it preferable from a geostrategic point of view for countries or regions like Iraq, the Sudan (with whom China has recently negotiated oil agreements), or even Iran, to fall into increasing anarchy or chaos, or find themselves in the midst of Western-sponsored regime change. Rather this than to have stable governments that provide China, America's chief economic competitor today, with the fuel it needs to threaten America's dominance of the world economy.[88]

Such logic is even more compelling if we realize that China is no longer content to play the role of the world's chief low-cost manufacturer of American consumer products (assigned to it in the neoliberal division of world labor), but is now seeking to challenge the US as a preeminent technological power too as symbolized by its purchase of IBM's computer business. If it could accomplish this the United States' position as the world's dominant economic power would be lost; we can imagine what a Bush Administration convinced about America's divinely appointed role as world hyper-power would do to meet such a threat.[89]

Spectacular Violence and the Cult of Martyrdom: Religion, Violence, and Globalization in Iraq

As I have already argued, the resource conflicts we have been discussing have to be contextualized in a global environment where world military spending has neared the unprecedented level of $1 trillion per year (compare that with about $50 billion in yearly development aid).[90] Most readers know America's share of this pie – at least 40 percent of world military spending and half of all discretionary domestic spending, *before* September 11, 2001.[91] If we can recall Kevin Baker's belief that Americans are increasingly "in the army now," the roots of this trend lie in the "dangerous dual obsession that has taken hold of Americans, conservatives and liberals alike. It is a marriage of militarism and utopian ideology – of unprecedented military might wed to a blind faith in the universality of so-called American values."[92]

As we saw Thomas Frank explain in earlier chapters, this ideology first emerged at the dawn of the neoliberal age in the mid-1970s with the rise of the religious right. (In fact, Frank reminds us that there's an interesting parallel between the Saudis using their new-found oil wealth to spread their conservative and intolerant Wahhabi version of Islam throughout the Muslim world, and the role played by American oil barons like the Koch family from Kansas, who at around the same time became among the biggest funders of the religious right.)[93] Over the next two decades this dynamic helped turn the US into what millions of Muslims, increasing numbers of Europeans, and even American critics call a "crusader state," whose self-proclaimed mission of spreading the American way of life has "invite[d] endless war and the ever-deepening militarization of US policy."[94] This dynamic is an important reason why, as the Egyptian paper *Al-Ahram Weekly* put it, so many people believe that "the US has turned the world into a battlefield."[95]

From this perspective we can see how economic considerations, such as controlling access to, and profits from, oil and other resources, have increasingly replaced ideologically motivated policies (e.g. confronting the Soviet Union during the Cold War) as the defining issues of American security policy. This is at the very moment that culture has become a defining force in politics in the global era. Together they have fed a perception of and (increasingly) longing for an apocalyptic "culture war" among both radical Christians and Muslims.[96]

What has made the culture war possible is that during the same period that neoliberal globalization spread across the globe, a particularly toxic form of religious belief and practice emerged that has become especially "aggressive, triumphalist, and thriv[es] on conflict."[97] Whether it's Abu Musab al-Zarqawi's psychotic executioners sawing off the heads of helpless victims in front of a worldwide internet TV audience – in what Thomas Friedman describes as "a mutant combination of Walmart and Wahhabism"[98]; American soldiers flattening parts of Iraqi cities with uncounted civilians buried under the rubble; young Israeli settler-soldiers shooting at Palestinian farmers from their hilltop "outposts"; or any one of a dozen other examples, the role of religion and/or ethnic hatred in the violence of the last two decades is impossible to ignore. This is why, as Moroccan progressive Islamist politician Nadia Yassine reminds us, it is crucial for progressives worldwide to meet this dynamic head on.[99]

From Kings to Contractors

The gruesome violence in Iraq reminds me of the way European monarchs used to display their kingly power by staging equally gruesome executions of anyone who challenged their authority.[100] As the leading French philosopher Michel Foucault described them in his seminal *Discipline and Punish*, in medieval and early modern Europe grisly executions were staged to reinforce the public's experience and acceptance of the absolute power of the king (or in rare cases, the people against the king) and the terrible price to be paid for violating it. For those who crossed the king, the punishments ranged from beheadings for nobles to the French public spectacle known as the *amends honorable*, which involved elaborate, lengthy, and horrifically painful executions by torture.[101]

Contemporary war, whatever the hype about precision munitions and smart bombs, remains equally gruesome. While Americans may see little of the carnage it wreaks, the rest of the world, especially the Muslim world, views it nightly around the same time "we" watch *Wheel of Fortune* or *Entertainment Tonight*. The intended message couldn't be any clearer: "Obey or face a horrible death" (in Iraq as of the time of writing, it would be "obey or face 100,000 horrible deaths and counting"). This slogan echoes – even louder than the original – the "dominate or die" mentality of the neoliberal "lite" 1990s; and indeed, in a militarized global system the best way to dominate is to make people so scared of you they accept your dictates no matter how much it goes against their economic, political or cultural interests.[102]

From a Muslim and even larger third-world perspective, we can understand the beheadings in Iraq (and copy-catted elsewhere)[103] as being perpetrated by people who are actually quite weak, whose public displays of gruesome murder are a vain attempt to demonstrate power they don't in fact possess. (Or perhaps the hope is that such grisly acts will scare people enough to give them power they don't currently have.)[104] But this explanation doesn't tell us why some militants suddenly feel compelled to butcher people on television or its internet equivalent when previously shootings or suicide bombings sufficed.

Perhaps it reflects a desire to get in on the action of the "pay-per-view globalization" Subcommandante Marcos described in the last chapter.[105] In the global era even terrorists realize that to get media attention you need a hook, and sadly, they've found one in beheading helpless captives, although how long people will be transfixed by the image remains to be seen. (I'm sure video-game programmers are already digitizing the gruesome videos to make "more realistic" murder scenes for their games, which will then desensitize people to the real thing.)

Here we should recall that at the start of the book I defined culture specifically as culture-in-performance rather than as a set of traditions or beliefs. If we agree with the consensus among scholars that cyberspace has become a virtual yet powerful public sphere, then these horrific videos can be seen as "political public performances," ritual-like extraordinary actions whose brutal aesthetic dimension helps them make the point that no one wants to hear. To Americans: "Despite your advanced weapons and disproportionate power, we can hurt you like you hurt us. We can't always kill 3,000 of you in one shot, but we can make the death of one of you gruesome enough to have a powerful psychological impact." To Iraqis and other Muslims who might work for the occupation: "Your fate will be no better than our enemies."[106]

But as horrible as the killings by militants and terrorists are, it is crucial to realize that the psychological and cultural illness in the Muslim world they represent has clear parallels in American culture. As several colleagues of mine suggested after the beheadings of September 2004 in Iraq, it is likely not a coincidence that the same year Mel Gibson had a hit movie that revolved around every gory detail of the execution of Christ, terrorists decided to start regularly beheading captives for a worldwide TV audience.

Without in any way equating Gibson's movie gore with the reality of the beheadings (although Gibson did in fact set out to make the film so realistic that it would evoke an effect similar to what witnesses of the actual crucifixion would have experienced), the popular reception and commercial success of *The Passion* brings to the fore just how strongly violence-laden Christian images, along with notions of martyrdom and victimization, resonate with large segments of the American public. Indeed, I would argue that the new, "cool" and muscular kind of Christianity that's sweeping across America – which often depicts a Schwarzenegger-like muscle-bound Christ waging brutal war on infidels upon his return to Earth – is inseparable from the larger fixation on fantastic violence in American culture. This problem in turn can't be understood outside the context of the "fetishization" of corporate brands that has become crucial to the success of the globalized economy, especially in the United States.

Fetishization is an off-putting word, as it raises the specter of intro-ductory anthropology classes dropped about two to three weeks into the semester precisely because of words like fetishization (at least that's what I did), or equally tortuous attempts to understand the imposing arguments of Volume One of Karl Marx's *Capital*. But fetishization is an important concept for us, because it links the economic processes and rationales of contemporary consumer capitalism with religious needs that remain a core need for the majority of the people on the planet.

Specifically, when we speak of the fetishization of brand names we mean a process in which people bestow a value – known in business-speak as "brand value" – on brand names and logos. In so doing the products that feature them are imbued with a value that far exceeds both the cost of producing them and the value that identical products without the brand name would have. How does this occur? By brand managers creating such a strong and positive identity around the brand that the target audience feels that buying the products helps them partake in the brand's supposed identity (smart, sexy, adventurous, rich, etc.). Think of how Virgin Atlantic airlines came to embody the rock-star adventurer image of Richard Branson to the extent that Branson got his own Fox television series (*The Rebel Billionaire*) where he bestows his brand identity on any contestant crazy enough to keep up with him for a few weeks.

Of course, branding is essentially a psychological sleight of hand. The manufactured image and magnetism of the brand helps the consumer to forget (if s/he ever realized) that it's merely a symbol with no intrinsic value of its own. Yet however fictitious, branding has strong religious parallels. Indeed, Marx borrowed the term "fetishization" from the study of so-called primitive religions, where it was used to describe the creation of an object ("fetish") that was endowed with powers and/or a spiritual essence such that believers supposedly forgot it was made by human beings and had no independent existence or powers.[107]

This phenomenon, which not surprisingly has been described as "brand imperialism," has clearly been crucial to the cultural economy of neoliberal globalization. Indeed, as we've already seen, it led the advertising agency Young & Rubicam to issue a 2001 report that argued that "brands are the new religion" based on the belief (according to the agency) that consumer brands have replaced religious faith as the provider of purpose to people's lives. Indeed, the report even argued that today's brand builders can be compared to the missionaries who spread Christianity and Islam around the world.[108]

In fact, as we've already seen, September 11 radically altered the brand equation. As I've already argued, to the extent that Christ has replaced Coke as an object of youthful desire this has occurred precisely through the kinds of aggressive marketing normally used to support secular brands.[109] And so as Americans desire their brands to function as forms of their innermost self-expression, an aggressive –

and because of this, in American culture, seductive – form of conservative religious expression, particularly within Christianity, has gained significant market share and become immensely profitable even as global brands from Coke to Microsfot have lost brand value during the last four years.

The problem is, if Christianity is cool precisely because it provides meaning to people's lives in an era of cultural vacuity, that's because, like Islam throughout much of the Muslim world, Christianity in the United States has been conquered by capital.[110] But it's worth repeating here that we're not talking about the 1960s capital of hip, shaggy-haired admen, or their yuppy counterparts of the 1990s. Rather, like American culture at large, Christianity has been conquered by the militarized capital of post-September 11 globalization.[111] This dynamic has unfolded because popular Evangelical culture in the US constantly offers images of suffering and apocalyptic atonement that support a "culture of righteousness and martyrdom" among tens of millions of Americans (including many American Jews, who excuse almost any action by the Israeli Government if taken in the name of "security").[112]

Such a culture is a major reason why there's been little outcry against the actions of the US military in Iraq, Afghanistan or Guantánamo Bay. Why, in fact, 100,000 dead Iraqis don't seem to faze the average American voter, soldier or presidential candidate. Whatever the particular reason for any American voter, the belief system underlying these feelings is in fact frightening; as one scholar who's investigated this brand of evangelical culture at length warns, "If the *Left Behind* series is any indication, millions of Americans are reading about and perhaps even praying for... a holy war" against Islam.[113] It's so powerful that as American soldiers prepare for battle by "swaying to Christian rock music ... M-16 assault rifles beside them, chant[ing] heavy metal-flavoured lyrics in praise of Christ," their compatriots on the home front are content to sacrifice them (never mind tens of thousands of dead, displaced, and tortured Iraqis) to the cause – and the soldiers content to be sacrificed – to further the utopian, even apocalyptic vision of a triumphant President redeeming the world for God's glory.[114]

We're All Israelis Now, or, Bush's Dreams of Apocalypse

Such sentiments, sadly, remind me of life in Israel. Three years ago, as the pungent odor of what was left of the World Trade Center slowly pervaded my neighborhood, I wrote a piece called "We're all Israelis Now." I didn't invent the idea; in the hours since the attacks I had heard several commentators say essentially the same thing, although our meanings were in fact diametrically opposed. For them, the September 11 attacks had constituted a tragic wake-up call to America about the mortal threat posed by Muslim terrorism, which Israel had been living through for decades and whose methods the US would now have to copy if it wanted to "win the war on terror."

For me, however, the attacks suggested a more troubling scenario: that like Israelis, Americans would never face the causes of the extreme violence perpetrated against us by those whose oppression we have supported and even enforced, nor engage in the honest introspection of what America's role has been in generating the kind of hatred that turns commuter jets into cruise missiles. Instead, my gut told me that Americans acquiesce to President Bush's use of the war to realize the long-held imperial, even apocalyptic, visions of the neoliberal Right, ones that find great sympathy with its Israeli counterpart.

As I watched George W. Bush celebrate his 2004 re-election I realized I never could have imagined just how much like Israelis Americans would become (and here I'm referring to a much broader social phenomenon than what Naomi Klein has rightly described as the "Likudinization" of American politics).[115] In Israel, the majority of Jewish citizens support the policies of Ariel Sharon despite the large-scale, systematic (and, according to international law, criminal) violence his government deploys against Palestinian society, despite the worsening economic situation for the lower-middle-class religious voters who constitute his main base of support, and despite rising international opprobrium and isolation. Sound familiar?

As for the country's "liberal" opposition, it's in a shambles, politically and morally bankrupt because in fact it was a willing participant in creating and preserving the system that is now eating away at the heart of Israeli society. Aside from occasional plaintive Op/Ed pieces by members of its progressive wing, the Labor Party can and will do nothing fundamentally to challenge Sharon's policies. Why? Because they reflect an impulse, nurtured by the Labor movement during its decades in power, that is buried deep in the heart of Zionism: to build an exclusively Jewish society on as much of the ancient homeland as possible, with little regard for the fate of the country's native inhabitants.

As any Native American will remind us, America was built on a similar holy quest. So it shouldn't surprise us that the parallels between Israel's mini-empire and America's Iraq adventure are striking. It's not just that America's occupation is faring as terribly as Israel's. As I alluded to above, in the week before the 2004 presidential election doctors from several of America's leading research hospitals published a study demonstrating that US forces have killed upwards of 100,000 Iraqis, the majority of them women and children killed by American bombs. In the context of the slow destructuring of the Iraqi state and the sowing of chaos across the country, this death toll comes perilously close to meeting the legal definition of genocide, which includes the intent to destroy a national group (in this case, a nation-state) coupled with activities that include killing, causing mental harm, and creating conditions bad enough to cause destruction of part of the nation. That certainly describes the situation I saw in my visit to the country in the spring of 2004, and the condition most Iraqi friends describe in my frequent emails and phone conversations with them.

In Israel most citizens know full well the realities of their occupation; even right-wing newspapers routinely publish articles that describe its details with enough clarity to make any ignorance willful. This dynamic is in fact why Israeli society has responded to the civil war with Palestinians by increasing the dehumanization of the occupation, accompanied by a fervent practice of getting on with life no matter what's happening ten or fifteen miles away in "the Territories." The alternative, actually working to stop the insanity of the occupation, would lead to much more hatred and violence within Israel and between Jews than Palestinians could ever hope to inflict on Israeli society from the outside.

The situation is almost identical vis-à-vis the American perspective on Iraq. Americans long to see Muslims display the courage of former Kuwaiti information minister Sad bin Tefla, who wrote an article in 2004 titled "We Are All Bin Laden."[116] But when will Americans look in the mirror? Abu Ghraib? Mass civilian casualties caused by a war launched on demonstrably false pretenses? The erosion of civil liberties? The transfer of hundreds of billions of dollars of tax payers' money (not to mention Iraqi resources and capital) by the US Government to its corporate allies? To more than 70 percent of America's eligible voters – that is, the approximately 30 percent that voted for Bush and the 40 percent that didn't feel this situation was compelling enough to warrant their taking the time to vote – none of this really matters. America is great and strong and can do what it wants, and to hell with anyone who gets in our way, especially if they fight back.

The numbing acceptance of large-scale and systematic violence perpetrated by the state as a normal part of its exercise of power, and the willingness of a plurality of the electorate to support parties and policies which are manifestly against their economic and social interests (as demonstrated by the increase in poverty and economic insecurity across most social classes in Israel and the US produced by the last two decades of neoliberalism), sadly characterize both societies today. This is why I never shared the optimism of friends who thought this situation would help elect Kerry in the 2004 election. Like Israel's Barak or Peres, in the context of post-September 11 militant globalization, John Kerry offered Americans little more than Bush lite on the most crucial issue of the day. With an increasingly obese culture, is there any wonder Americans chose SuperSize over Nutrasweet?

So here we are, three years after the tragic day of September 11. The smell of charred metal, fuel, and flesh no longer pervades the five boroughs of New York; instead it wafts across the major cities of Iraq (where most Americans don't have to smell it, but I can attest from personal experience that the odor in Baghdad is as pungent as in Queens). The Bush Administration is free to proceed with a violently imperialist foreign policy with little fear of repercussion or political cost at home – who cares about abroad? The Left is stupefied at its own political and moral incompetence, and the people at large are increasingly split between a fundamentalist religious-nationalist camp and a yuppie-liberal camp that has no real legs to stand on and has little hope of engaging the millions of poor and working class who have moved to the right because of "social issues."

This situation reveals something dark, even frightening, about America's collective character (although no darker than Russia's, China's or most other countries' characters, we must remember). But making the situation worse are the reasons why people voted for President Bush in 2004: the belief that he better represented America's "moral values," along with the faith that he, not Kerry, would fight a "better and more efficient war on terror." What kind of moral values the occupation of Iraq represents no one dares say. What kind of terror the US military has wrought in Iraq most Americans don't want to know. How come a Left whose roots lie with Gandhi and King couldn't figure out how to turn the values of war towards the most basic biblical values of peace and justice no one can figure out. Until they do, however, great damage will be done to the world and America's standing in it.

Anarchy in a Time of Chaos: Does Culture Jamming Stand a Chance against the Chaos of Corporate Capital?

Dinner Along the Tigris

This is a depressing situation, to be sure. But definitely not a hopeless one. On the last night of my trip to Iraq, I had dinner with Simona Torretta, along with other Italian, French, and Filipino researchers and activists who for a year had been resisting the occupation as best they could, by building bridges with Iraqis on the grass-roots level, risking their lives to find out the myriad ugly truths about the occupation, and bringing that information to the international public.[117] Our Chinese feast – surprisingly, the food in war-torn Baghdad was better than most Chinese meals I've had in the US or Europe – was one of the best examples of what I have called "culture jamming," as it brought together twenty-something French, Italian, and Filipino activists with thirty-something American and Iraqi intellectuals and journalists, and fifty-something Iraqi women, all in the common cause of building an alternative to imperialism, occupation, intolerance, and violence.

As we compared notes on the violence we'd all witnessed in the past few days, one of the participants, the Italian activist Paola Gasparoli of the group Ponte per... (with whom Simona Torretta also worked) explained: "This is what Iraqis live with every day." This comment sadly summed up life in Iraq one year into the occupation. Since most of us believed that the situation "would get worse before it gets better," the idea of bringing in more foreign activists to Iraq made little sense in the near future, even though up to that point none of us had been targeted for being foreigners (insurgents were still discriminating between people working for and against the occupation). But such was the impact of the chaos of post-Saddam Iraq that what was most needed – a strong international peace presence that could help lead the fight against the occupation through non-violence and supporting the emergence of a strong and pluralistic civil society and public sphere – had quickly become impractical and even impossible to achieve.

And so the peace caravan we all had expected to join us stayed home in Europe, watching from the sidelines as Iraq simultaneously exploded and imploded. But in a sense, the caravan was already a year too late. As a senior activist with the group United for Peace and Justice put it soon after the invasion, "What could be better than a thousand college students – not just Americans, but Arabs, Europeans too – going to Iraq, witnessing what is going on, and returning to tell their fellow citizens what they've experienced."[118] Witnessing would have been good; but helping to shape a different outcome was even more urgent. Yet if there had ever been a moment when this would have been possible, by the first anniversary the chaos and violence enveloping Iraq meant it was long gone. And the global peace and justice movement will have to live with the fact that they were not prepared for the small window of opportunity that opened after the invasion to "send in the troops" and help build an alternative to what everyone knew was soon to come.

Despite the deteriorating situation, my dinner companions were still hopeful that important work could be done. Simona discussed building ties to local communities by passing out flyers explaining the work of her organization, Bridge to Baghdad, on issues that mattered to Iraqis. Not surprisingly, these included people jailed indefinitely without charge and tortured in Abu Ghraib and other prisons (everyone in Iraq knew what was going on there long before the story "broke" in the United States), and the high civilian casualties and disastrous medical and water systems that have only grown more desperate in the months since our conversation. The Iraqi activists talked about the need to dig deep into the nuts and bolts of the occupation, into the problems of the Draft Constitution, and figure out ways to stop the everyday violence plaguing the country.

But in the context of an unending occupation the most important issue was to "think long term and build bridges between the global peace and justice movement and society here. We need concrete solidarity," is how one French activist, Thomas Sommer, put it. "But you need to know who the political forces are and how to work with them." Needless to say, the growing chaos made such knowledge impossible to obtain; and so Simona was kidnapped several months after he made this suggestion. But in fact she knew the answer even then: "There need to be two speeds – much faster outside Iraq but much slower inside because of the need to build trust... We wanted to have a demonstration with Iraqis for the anniversary of the invasion. Have you seen today any kind of demonstration against the occupation? This is my question! Have you seen any people around? Even the Iraqi Communist Party cancelled for security reasons!"

Eman Ahmed Khammas, then director of the occupation-monitoring organization Occupation Watch, explained in a similar vein that "trust is the key to building ties, but of course chaos makes trust much harder to build." In agreement, Simona argued that "it's good to have solidarity demonstrations, but you need a counterpart that understands and wants these kinds of activities... So we must first find some kind of synergy inside, and then build. It's a process."[119]

So what strategy could the global peace and justice movement adopt for Iraq? As Thomas explained, it would have to be based on a recognition that "It will take time. Iraq just ended a dictatorship where even three people meeting together were considered dangerous. They must reclaim thirty plus years of history to do this. But what we can do is try to bring support from outside to make connections between here and outside and give what help we can. But we can't change the situation essentially; Iraqis must do that."

Here's where what I have described as culture jamming meets what Iranian sociologist Asef Bayat eloquently describes as the "art of presence" to indicate a way forward to a different future. In Bayat's words, against the cultures of victimization and martyrdom now battling it out on the world stage,

> it is... extremely challenging to be heavily *present* at the heart of society, to struggle for liberation, and yet maintain one's integrity; to be effective but also principled. More precisely, I am referring to that delicate *art of presence* in harsh circumstances, the ability to create social space within which those individuals who refuse to exist, can advance three causes of human rights, equality and justice, and do so under formidable political conditions.[120]

Bayat feels that such a difficult strategy demands sharp vision, honesty, and above all endurance and energy. If these can be achieved and held on to, "meaningful change in the Muslim Middle East may well benefit."

This is certainly among the most important definitions of the task before the global peace and justice movement, not just in the Muslim majority world but in the West as well. As important, for Bayat the art of presence revolves around "active citizenship" by ordinary people, whose collective efforts have the power to challenge and even slowly transform the political and economic culture of their societies. Earlier I mentioned the Elastic Sheikh and his struggles to build an open and positive future for Iraqi society that clearly matches the kind of active citizenship and positive outlook envisioned by Bayat. After dropping off the radar for almost six months Sheikh Anwar suddenly turned up. He hadn't been in hiding, or jail, nor was he dead. He had been running medicines and injured people in and out of towns like Najaf and Falluja, trying to get sewerage and electricity into his neighborhood, and beginning to organize his "flock" for the January 2005 elections. Despite all the death and destruction he had seen, including that of his wife and numerous friends, he was as committed as ever to working through non-violence and bridge-building to repair his country and build a new future. He explained that this attitude is common among the hundreds of his (mostly younger) colleagues who have combined secular and religious educations, and who draw both from Western and Muslim sources to solve the myriad problems facing their communities.

As he explained to me, his kind of flexible view towards religion and culture is both natural and necessary. "The real Islam is not violence; it's peace and knowledge. Only if I can bring my people both will we win against occupation and extremism," the Scylla and Charybdis between which he constantly navigates. "I'm not an idiot," he was quick to point out. "I know the US is here for power and oil. It will try to engineer the elections to make sure its people win. But violence is not the solution. Remember, if the US controlled everything after the invasion, with Allawi – however problematic he is – we gained about 30 percent of the power; with the elections we'll have perhaps 50 percent, and within a few years we will control our country, regardless of Bush's dreams. But we have to be patient and willing to negotiate."

If Anwar was repeatedly shot at by American soldiers as he smuggled medicine and water into Najaf during the spring 2004 siege of the city, "now the terrorists are working to destroy me, because I have a peace message. But I won't give up. I can't give up. If we believe in God we can say God is with us, not with terrorists; God is with peace, He's the biggest power in the universe. You can't say you're scared if you're Muslim because God said He will protect those fighting for justice or reward them if they die." This sounds like the discourse of jihad, I suggested. "Yes, but the good jihad! Even after my wife died, within a week I was rebuilding my area, cleaning my neighborhood of cluster bombs with my own hands, because if I didn't, the children would find and play with them. This is jihad."

The problem is that the greater and more sustained the violence, the less the chance that the kind of peaceful jihad advocated by Sheikh Anwar will take root in Iraq. In that context, he explained, the main issue facing Iraqis in their relations between each other and with the outside world involves trust. "We need to find strategies to build trust between Iraqis, and with international civil society, against occupation and extremism." But violence and chaos makes trust – without which political, religious or cultural moderation and compromise are impossible – that much harder to develop. And in this situation, for peace and trust to overcome violence and chaos, Sheikh Anwar and his fellow citizens across the MENA need allies from cultures across the globe who will offer what Bayat describes as the "courage, solidarity ... and recognition" so needed by those risking their everything to struggle for peace, democracy, and sustainable development in their societies. How to find these allies and what strategies can they adopt to achieve what until now has been a dream?

The Sonny Boy Williamson and 'Um Kalthoum Axis meets the NWA and Moqtada al-Sadr Axis

At the beginning of this book, I mentioned what seemed to be a strange similarity in the performances of Led Zeppelin frontman Robert Plant and Lebanese diva Najwa Karam. I knew there was a connection between the two of them when I saw the footage of her concert in my Marrakesh hotel, and sure enough from discussions with both it is clear that their influences overlapped and that Karam was clearly familiar with Led Zeppelin.

The connection leading from Plant to Karam is deeper than this, however. It travels along the "gypsy route"[121] that took the music and cultures of the Middle East to Africa, then across the ocean to the Americas with the slave trade, and on to the birth of the blues (and bluegrass and country music as well, although I'm not sure how many country music fans would be happy to know their music wouldn't exist without the influence of Islam), to the birth of rock 'n' roll, to British blues bands like Zeppelin, and then back to the Middle East as Plant and his bandmates fell in love with Arab music.

This may sound like a circuitous route, but it exists just the same. In fact, there's a wonderful CD called *Music on the Gypsy Route*,[122] featuring gypsy music across the belt of the world from China to Appalachia. If you listen to it, the through line, the sound and feel that make the music inescapably gypsy and thus in a real sense, the blues, is crystal clear: it is the strong presence of Muslim inflections and tonality throughout. This is not surprising; as we now know, the blues, both in its instrumentation (especially guitar and the bending of strings to create "blue notes" – the equivalent of the Arab ruba', or quarter tone) and in its vocalization (especially the constant quarter tone modulation of pitches and the nasal style of singing), was derived in good measure from the Arabic call to prayer and other Muslim religious music, which was carried to the Americas by Muslim African slaves.[123]

So it's no surprise that many blues lovers find Arab/Muslim music so appealing, and therefore for a British blues band like Led Zeppelin to be influenced by both 'Um Kalthoum and Sonny Boy Williamson together.[124] And if an earlier generation of black singers and musicians was inspired by Muslim rhythms, instruments, and chants to use the blues to critique and even challenge their society, it should also not surprise us that a younger generation of artists would use a dissonant and sometimes dangerous music – hiphop – as a contemporary vehicle to politicize their own reading of Islam. (Plus we must remember that many gangsta rappers were strongly influenced by the Nation of Islam and other Muslim movements in the US that had strong ties to Wahhabi Islam.)

So it appears that Islam has been inspiring resistance cultures in the US for well over a century. Perhaps this is why hiphop and even heavy metal – which is ultimately derived from the blues – have in turn inspired Arab/Muslim artists to take on the dominant and usually repressive cultures in their societies, as we saw in Chapter Six.

The story I've just recounted helps us understand why culture jamming, the through line connecting the various subjects and issues discussed in this book, is such an important strategy for building bridges and even solidarities across the *barzakh* separating Western and Muslim cultures. We can think of the artists, intellectuals, and activists who are breaking new sonic and social boundaries and some-times even risking their lives to mend the "tear" between cultures, as the cultural equivalent of Romani,[125] or as Breyten Breytenbach calls them, "global village vagabonds," who refuse to fall into the categories set up for them by global capital or Islam.[126] Whether it's American hiphoppers like Common or Arrested Development or Muslim artists like Algerian Rai star Rachid Taha or Lebanese rapper Clotaire-K or the Iranian professor-turned-rapper Shahkar Binesh-Pajouh; all use the sonic and political inspiration of the blues, hiphop, and Islam to target unemployment, poverty, and other issues.

As important, at the same time – consciously or not – these artists push a multicultural vision that "doesn't argue for a future state of affairs... [that] owns up to its rich and creolized practice"; and they do this, in the words of Binesh-Pajouh, using music "as a medium to chal-lenge opinions" (which in Iran, means challenging a society where more than 70 percent of its 66 million people are under thirty years old).[127]

It seems then that the circle of culture jamming is a continuous and ever enlarging one, where politics and art intermix seamlessly. If we can recall Oday Rasheed's political-cultural critique of the US when he lamented that he knows John Coltrane but few Americans know of any Iraqi artists, poets or musicians, we could point out that Coltrane, at least, knew his culture too: a listen to the master recordings of his seminal "A Love Supreme" reveals that he chanted "Allah Supreme" along with the song's title in various sections.[128] In a sense, Rasheed loved a music that was in some sense already his own.

You might be asking what all this fascinating discussion of Iranian rappers and southern blues artists has to do with militarized globalization in the MENA today. A good many things, it turns out. It might be a cliché in the United States to talk about the importance of youth pop culture in shaping the consumption habits of most Americans. But the percentage of Americans under twenty is under 30 percent, and the figure is even lower in Europe. In Iraq, as in Iran, it's as much as 65 percent of the population (a number that is not that different from the statistics for other Arab and Muslim countries).

What these numbers mean is that if we want to talk about religious belief and culture in the MENA, and especially Islam, we have to start by recognizing that they are inextricably tied to youth culture. Even if the most powerful religious figures in the Muslim world today remain older men, they are inexorably giving way to a new generation of men, and increasingly women as well. And in this generation the relationship between pop culture and religion is key.

This dynamic suggests that it's a big mistake to look at the Muslim world only through the lens of religion and the "civilizations" it defines (as do most mainstream and conservative discussions of Islam and the MENA). For example, is the best way to view the phenomenon of the radical Shi'i preacher Moqtada al-Sadr in Iraq through the lens of religion? We could understand him as much as a phenomenon of popular youth culture – he's young, charismatic, with his ear to the street, spewing out tirades against the powers that be in a way that reminds me of the original gangsta rappers like NWA or Public Enemy. Of course his guns are real, and his people have killed and died in far greater numbers than young African Americans were in the 1980s, but this dynamic only increases the power of a religiously informed popular culture.

Moreover, as the French Orientalist Gilles Kepel points out in his seminal *Allah in the West*, there is a direct genealogy from Islamist trends in the MENA and Europe to hiphop in the US; and the reason for this can be traced to the same socio-economic and psychological forces of neoliberalism that have disproportionately affected the poor and the young around the world. Indeed there are strong similarities in the dynamics of the popular culture behind the rise of gangsta rap in the US and al-Sadr's in Iraq.[129]

Beyond the defining experience of economic marginalization, in both cultures youth culture has become dominated by figures willing to express the feelings of anger and alienation produced by this marginalization. And whether it's Ice Cube (at least in his early days) or Moqtada, the worldview offered by these cultural leaders is based on intolerance, misogyny, and violence; not surprising, given that the two primary groundings for this culture are patriarchy and religion (which are themselves inseparable in the Abrahamic religions).

So whether it's young black Americans or young Muslims in the MENA or Europe, during the last two generations marginalized young people have laid claim to separatist communal identities, especially one tinged by religion, that have in turn been used to

> mak[e] a deliberate cultural break with the dominant values of coun-
> tries of which they are for the most part citizens in law, but which in
> their view exclude them in fact. This separatism is as much a means of
> defense against dehumanized or hostile social environment as a way
> of mobilizing "brothers" and negotiating collectively in their name
> with the authorities.[130]

Of course, the anti-corporate globalization movement that emerged in the 1990s was precisely a positive and holistic attempt to create the kind of brother- or sisterhood described above; one that wouldn't wind up branded, as the hippies, punks or hiphoppers before them, as the next "cool," "hip," "dangerous," or "street" fashion and attitude for bored, trendy suburban kids to emulate. And perhaps the most important reason that the movement had achieved a good measure of success in creating such an identity has been the great energy spent on building trust and solidarity between members of the movement. This was achieved specifically through the use of strategies of cooperation drawn from the experience of the Direct Action Networks, the anarchists, the Zapatistas, and on a mass scale, the World Social Forums, which is why their ideas and strategies are so important for us to understand.

More specifically, the slow, methodical attempts by activists to build trust between sometimes radically different communities – a process that is at once extremely difficult, frustrating, and easy to destroy – is believed by philosophers Habermas and Derrida to be the key to repairing the separation or "tear" between cultures that is the spark for so much suspicion and violence between them. Habermas in particular argues for the importance of building trust to forging a common language between participants in a dialogue. Such a shared language is crucial because, as he explains, the violence at the core of the fundamentalisms and terrorism that define the post-September 11 relationship between the Muslim world and the West is at base the result of a "communicative pathology ... the spiral of violence begins as a spiral of distorted communication that leads through the spiral or uncontrolled reciprocal mistrusts, to the breakdown of communication."[131]

I would argue that not just terrorism but neoliberal globalization as well are communicative pathologies. And the best way to overcome the systematic distortions of communication that lead to cross-cultural violence is through the use of culture to (re)build the fundamental link of trust and solidarity between people. This is precisely the strategy behind and goal of culture jamming, which must build trust and fight fear and oppression at the same time if it is to succeed.

But how to get the various people/cultures on the same stage at the same time playing something that even slightly resembles the same tune? Mainstream liberals, and even scholars like Habermas, would say greater *tolerance* for others – moving from "terrorism to tolerance" as one columnist put it – is the first step in forging a common field of interaction.[132] Yet tolerance always has its limits, enforced by whoever has the power to decide what "alien" or foreign cultural practices will be tolerated. Or tolerance becomes counterproductive when "we" decide to tolerate cultural practices that are in fact repressive of various social groups (women, minorities, the poor) within the other culture.[133]

In reality, something much more radical is needed than tolerance. For Derrida, building on the work of his mentor Emanuel Levinas' call for "absolute respect" for the other, what is needed is "hospitality," in the time-honored Arab sense of the word. As he explains it,

> Pure or unconditional hospitality does not consist in an *invitation* ("I invite you, I welcome you into my home, on the condition that you adapt to the laws and norms of my territory, according to my language, tradition, memory, and so on"). Pure and unconditional hospitality, hospitality *itself*, opens or is in advance open to someone who is neither expected nor invited, to whomever arrives as an absolutely foreign *visitor*, as a new *arrival*, nonidentifiable and unforeseeable, in short, wholly other.[134]

This view has clear musical resonances. We've already seen that artists like Carlos Santana have little tolerance for sub-standard musicianship. Yet at the same time he, like other true artists, shows great hospitality to almost any new (to them) musical forms, styles, or instruments that come into earshot. As long as the level of musicianship is high, they'll bring in even the most dissonant voices to create a new sonic tapestry. (Of course, this can sometimes produce boring and/or self-indulgent albums, but no process is perfect.)

Perhaps what is needed is true hospitality and absolute respect coupled with strong *in*tolerance for any kind of repression (sexual, economic, cultural, etc.) that might be justified by the dominant ideology of any societies attempting to converse – in our language, jam – together. Such a strategy would seem to be the only guiding principle that could challenge the conflict between "barbarism and barbarism" that the US–al-Qa'eda world war has forced on the rest of us.[135]

In Conclusion: Building an Axis of Empathy

How Scholars, Activists, and Artists – Religious and Secular Together – Must Lead the Way

In Chapters Seven and Eight I offered a critique of the strategies and rhetoric of the global peace and justice movement as it strove unsuccessfully to stop the invasion of Iraq. One of my main criticisms was that its inability to take a holistic view of the problems in the MENA, to broaden the debate to acknowledge the horrendous nature of the Hussein regime, or to come down decisively against any form of violence made it harder for its arguments to reach the so-called "mainstream" public. This failure, I believe, is one reason why the invasion of Iraq wasn't prevented or the occupation brought to a swift conclusion.

One reason for the problematic strategies and rhetoric of the movement was that its leaders rarely sought the advice of scholars and other specialists on the MENA region and Islam to help develop their critiques of and alternatives to the policies of the Bush Administration.[136] Indeed, if we look at the three main participants in what I have described as culture jamming – scholars, activists, and artists – we can see that each of them has failed to learn from and work closely with the others, despite the reality that combining their talents, knowledge, and experience would be the surest way to advance toward their common goals.

For its part, the anti-war movement badly underutilized the talents of the people who had the most knowledge and experience of the region on which they were focusing – that is, the scholars of the Middle East and Islam who had long experience in the region and understood the complexities of American and European Middle East policy (not to mention the realities of the Hussein regime). Because of this, they could not develop ideological depth, nor could they provide alternative ideas about "what to do about Saddam," or how to build a very different Middle Eastern order based on real peace and democracy.[137]

Sadly, few lessons were learned by the movement since the invasion. And so a 2004 meeting in Beirut of 300 activists from 43 countries wound up sponsored (in part) by Hizbollah and the Popular Front for the Liberation of Palestine – two groups not exactly well-known for taking "anti-war" positions – and saw keynote speakers actually "salute the Lebanese resistance which has inspired us the world over," and offer it as a model for Palestine and Iraq. In essence, then, at the same time President Bush was touting his "Greater Middle East" initiative of "democracy and elections" and even organizing "forums of the future" to bring together MENA states and their G-8 counterparts in order to realize it, the Beirut participants saw little need to focus on democracy, corruption, and violence, refused to denounce publicly the Sudan or talk about Chechnya. They also largely ignored the oppression of women, and refused to condemn strongly and publicly the use of terrorism against civilians. This despite the fact that four of their comrades – the two Italian and two Iraqi Bridge for Baghdad employees we've discussed several times in this chapter – were then still in captivity and being threatened with imminent decapitation.

As a senior Iraqi activist explained to me with regard to movements who throw around slogans "supporting the Iraqi resistance": "I appreciate their work but I would like them to make a distinction between real patriots, millions of Iraqis, trying to build a democratic society, and those so-called resistance activists, using terrorism and sabotage against Iraqis. However legitimate our right to resist the occupation, the primary means have to be through politics and peaceful means, not violence: 'No to war, no to dictatorship' is the key slogan, but you must have both parts, because the road to our liberation must be through democracy and peace." Moreover, she continued, "the continued dictatorships in the Arab world make the occupation of Iraq and Palestine possible." Sadly, the organizers of the Beirut gathering did not heed her words. Instead they basically endorsed violent resistance against the "real" terrorists (naturally limited to the United States) without taking into account the horrible toll such resistance can take on civilians of the occupied country who have neither the voice nor power to define an alternative way of struggling for freedom.[138]

There were many reasons for this myopia; one of the most important for our purposes was that the organizers froze out the local, young and progressive Lebanese groups from the meeting; they would have brought a much broader, cosmopolitan yet more nuanced and grounded vision to the discussion. As I learned when I arrived in Beirut a few weeks afterwards, these groups have exactly the kind of vision that the global peace and justice movement needs to follow. Sadly, the importance of such a vision and cultural presence seems lost on many leaders of the movement, who would rather fetishize this generation's versions of Che Guevara, whose biopic, *The Motorcycle Diaries*, not so coincidentally opened around this time. But in their quest for "the broadest possible unity" and their desire for a "unified global resistance" based on the military model of Hizbollah, the global peace and justice movement leaders most involved in Iraq wound up endorsing the very violence, intolerance, and corruption the movement is fighting to defeat.[139]

At this point in our discussion it shouldn't surprise anyone if I argue that artists are among the most crucial voices in achieving the kind of structural, society-wide (today, humanity-wide) social transformation that is required to build the "other world" imagined by the many activists and intellectuals whose struggles and ideas we've discussed in the book.[140] Yet since September 11 they similarly failed to take advantage of the possibilities offered by working in a coordinated fashion with activists and scholars. Whether Michael Moore or Bruce Springsteen, all but the most politically radical refused to acknowledge just how little the policies of the Democratic Party have differed from those of Republicans, and so wound up simplistically blaming Iraq on an evil Republican cabal, or offering tepid public support for John Kerry that couldn't inspire a real movement for change (which would have to recognize the deep similarities in foreign and economic policy between the two parties).[141]

For such clear-eyed honesty we need to go back to John Lennon's 1971 anti-war tour, which featured a far more radical line-up: not just Stevie Wonder, but Bobby Seale of the Black Panther Party and the Yippie leader Jerry Rubin, who explained (in one of the first descriptions of what I would call culture jamming), "What we are doing here is uniting music and revolutionary politics to build a revolution around the country!"[142] In comparison to the truly radical politics of Lennon's gathering, it's not hard to figure out why the much publicized political tour of artists like Springsteen, Dave Matthews, REM and even the Dixie Chicks, couldn't win the country over to John Kerry.

Unfortunately, Lennon's innovative early incarnation of culture jamming didn't last long. The Nixon Administration began deportation proceedings against him soon after the first concert, causing the rest of the tour to be canceled (a generation later, country music stations "deported" the Dixie Chicks because they dared to criticize the President). Today the US Government rarely goes after rock stars; academics are much better prey. For this reason alone we might think that progressive scholars would have made the greatest effort to become a serious part of the public debate after the invasion. And indeed, some did step into a role of "public intellectual" that even decades of scholarship can't prepare one for – especially when it means taking on the likes of Daniel Pipes and Bill O'Reilly and the full weight of a conservative establishment that will stop at nothing to destroy an academic's career.[143]

But many scholars I was in touch with admitted that they didn't exactly go out of their way to influence the rhetoric and strategies of the anti-war movement, which led to at least one leader arguing derisively that rather than complaining after the fact "they should have invited themselves in."[144] This is certainly a valid criticism, as by remaining on the sidelines of the national debate in the year leading up to the invasion, it was too late to claim the public sphere to articulate a thorough critique of the Iraqi occupation until the situation got so bad it could no longer be ignored (and could no longer be solved without even more bloodshed).

As the occupation ground on, however, the increasingly negative news from Iraq forced the mainstream media to give voice to previously marginalized scholars, which allowed people like me to appear on shows like *The O'Reilly Factor* and even the *News Hour with Jim Lehrer*. (When long-haired progressive academics start appearing regularly on national television, you know things have gone from bad to worse in Iraq and the war on terror.) But even as events force open the media sphere, without activists and artists to help translate their knowledge and experience into usable cultural and political products, scholars will remain marginalized from the mainstream political debates, and the global peace and justice movement will be poorer for it.

So How Do We Get There from Here? Creating an Axis of Empathy through Culture Jamming

One of the main premises of this book has been that if people want to repair the "tear" that has for so long separated "Muslim" and "Western" cultures, artists, activists, and scholars need to blaze new trails through fear and violence in order to build hope and solidarity.

The question is, of course, how do you build the proverbial bridge across the *barzakh* and establish a common meeting place that can be the start of a shared future?[145] Only such a bridge can open the way to the kind of "active citizenship" that is as sorely needed in the US as it is in the MENA if a different globalization, and another world, is to be possible.

The global peace and justice movement has, it seems to me, only two choices: to brand itself in order to compete with the two dominant logos, or to work to deconstruct the entire brand-based political, economic, and cultural system. Either choice would be a formidable project.[146] Sadly, it seems in some ways that the movement has taken the first path even as it is ideologically committed to the second. The problem is that however powerful the brand allure (and the movement certainly has a strong attraction for young people and progressives of all ages and classes worldwide), a brand has to deliver the goods successfully and repeatedly to succeed. Sadly, as of the time of writing, the global peace and justice movement has failed to bring much peace or justice anywhere, especially in places like Iraq or Palestine where it has put so much of its focus.[147]

As I've argued above, the most viable way to pursue the second strategy would be through the kind of cross-cultural jamming that brings artists, scholars, and activists together to nurture the environments in which radically holistic social change can become possible. But this is never going to happen if the artists, activists, and scholars are limited to extremely cosmopolitan, largely secular people. For all their good work, Dave Matthews, the leadership of MoveOn.org, and the academic enemies list of Campus Watch are almost uniformly secular and have few of the cultural skills necessary to reach out to religious people, whether in the United States or the MENA.

What the global peace and justice movement needs to develop is a religious, or at least deeply spiritual, foundation that welcomes the kind of people for whom religious faith is the most basic parameter of their lives. And those who aren't personally religious need to "get religion," in the sense that they need to become as familiar with the religious texts and narratives as their counterparts are with secular popular culture.[148] To achieve this progressives – even those who are personally agnostic or even atheist – need to become as at home in the church, mosque or synagogue as are George Bush, Moqtada al-Sadr or Ariel Sharon. They need the Western equivalent of the Elastic Sheikh.

In short, they must make a welcoming and expansive space, not just for the kinds of progressive Muslim religious voices I've discussed many times in this book, but also for their counterparts in American and European culture. Voices from the Evangelical Left – yes, there is an Evangelical Left – and the Jewish religious Left; the experiences and powerful inspiration of Christian liberation theology, from the Zapatistas to Rete Lilliput, all need to take a much greater role in a global peace and justice movement that would not exist today without their predecessors having taken the lead in previous generations.

Only with such a spiritual maturity can the global peace and justice movement envision and popularize a desperately needed new – or rather, renewed – conception of who God is and how S/He works in the world. This strategy is vital; as Thomas Frank explained to me as we wondered how the Left could recover from Bush's re-election, "The Left can win the battle of theology. The conservative and fundamentalist vision of the Bible is easily punctured by a progressive reading of scripture. The problem is that 'we' can't convince the Americans represented by Kansas ourselves, and we can't do it unless a commitment for real progressive populist politics is joined with an absolute respect [as Derrida would say, hospitality] for their profound religious convictions... but remember, the slogan 'What would Jesus do' comes from a preacher in Topeka, Kansas. There is hope, especially if the Left readopts the social gospel that brought it victories in civil rights and the war on poverty."[149]

What Frank is saying is that if the Left want to win over – rather than ignore, which is stupid, or defeat, which is impossible – the tens of millions of conservative religious Americans (or their Muslim counterparts worldwide) to something resembling a progressive politics, then progressives need to learn the Qur'an, the Bible, and other religious texts well enough at least to understand the discourse of conservative religious people and begin to engage them on their own turf. Only when progressives can discuss religious themes and concepts with something approaching the conservatives' ability to manipulate the supposedly dominant secular culture will they have a shot at changing the political balance of power in the United States or the MENA. And this will only happen when the movement stops ignoring or reacting with arrogance and contempt (or at best, condescension) towards people of faith, and accepts that religion is one of the profoundest human needs and expressions that isn't going to fade away or be "secularized" anytime soon.[150]

Such a process would involve much more than reading *The Idiot's Guide to Radical Islam* or its Jewish or Christian equivalent between affinity group or MoveOn meetings. Progressives need to engage religion with the same fervor they once engaged Marx or Marcos, Che or Derrida. They need to get degrees in it, do anthropological fieldwork on it, actually go out and make friends with the creationist Christians or (if they happen to be studying in Lebanon or Egypt, the Hizbollah or Muslim Brother members) living down the block. They need to permeate faith-based religious culture with the same depth and alacrity as Evangelical Christians (and their Muslim counterparts) have permeated mainstream cultures even as they excoriate them for being the antithesis of everything truly "Christian" or "Muslim."

Once the global peace and justice movement can build up a sufficient baseline of knowledge to engage mainstream and conservative religious people it can develop a very specific kind of religious vision that is the only hope against right-wing Christians, Muslims or Jews. The good news is that it is a vision that progressives are uniquely positioned to offer: what the British theologian John Macquarrie calls the "humility of God" against the arrogance of man. Such a view of divinity is important because God's humility – God's earthliness, involvement in human affairs and love – transcends precisely the kind of arrogant, triumphalist, war-like religions that Christianity, Judaism, and Islam have increasingly become. As Macquarrie explains, "hope is humble, trustful, vulnerable. Optimism [one of President Bush's favorite words] is arrogant, brash, complacent. Hope has known the pang of suffering and has perhaps even felt the chill of despair … optimism has not faced the enormity of evil or the results of the fall of man and disfiguring sin that affects all human life, both personal and social."[151] Only by helping people to hear God's voice – even if they personally don't hear it – as "still, quiet and humble rather than loud and strident" can Christians transcend Bush and his dreams of apocalyptic rapture, Jews transcend Sharon and his "settler Judaism," Muslims transcend bin Laden and his nihilistic utopianism, and so on. Only with such a vision – advanced by secular as much as religious people – can the movement help all three religions transcend "the siege mentality and supremacist Puritanism" and the "nationalist religions" that increasingly grip them.[152]

But who in the movement of movements today is capable of even having this conversation? At least in the United States, aside from a few explicitly religious leaders like Michael Lerner, Jim Wallis and their comrades at the National Council of Churches, clearly not many. (And of those who can speak the language fluently, most are at least a generation removed from the majority of younger activists involved in the movement today. This is why figures like Reverend Dollar, mentioned at the start of this chapter as a counterpart to Egypt's Amr Khaled, have become hiphop icons and are filling a void left by the fading away of civil rights era leaders.)

What I would argue is necessary is for the global peace and justice movement to mature to a level already reached by "progressive Muslims" (as a recent pathbreaking book describes them) and their believing Jewish and Christian counterparts; to mature to a level that moves beyond the largely negative focus of what the movement opposes to a much more holistic and positive identity, strategy, and vision.[153] Such a strategy is the foundation upon which the "best practices" of the Zapatistas, anarchists, social-forumists, and related groups we've met throughout the book can be combined with the knowledge, inspiration, local knowledge, and connectivity of religious faith and practice to offer a radical yet powerful challenge to neoliberal fundamentalism.[154]

The Way Forward: A Truce, a Plan, and Action

So far I have only discussed the larger cultural, philosophical, and ideological moves that the global peace and justice movement has to make if it is going to grow into a truly mass movement that achieves fundamental social change worldwide. Here I'd like to offer a specific program that would be the *sine qua non* for implementing such a vision on the ground. What follows is not a detailed discussion of the mechanics of changing the world economy from neoliberal capitalism to a more humane system. Numerous writers, from David Korten, Susan George, and Michael Lerner to the members of the International Forum on Globalization, to the Earth Charter or politics of meaning movements, have laid out the specifics in great detail and with great clarity.[155] Rather, I want to highlight the most important issues that the movement needs to address specifically vis-à-vis the MENA in order to change the political dynamics in the region.

First and foremost, the global peace and justice movement must announce a truce with the Muslim world, and radical Islam in particular. It must do so by making the concept of a truce, and even the signing of actual "truces," the foundation of their strategies for future activities concerning the MENA and larger Muslim world. This may sound like a naïve, even defeatist statement in the context of America's obsessions with "Islamist terrorism" (as the *9/11 Commission Report* describes it). Yet a truce – in Arabic, *hudna* – rather than an increasingly dangerous "clash of civilizations" is the only way to avoid a long, ultimately catastrophic conflict.

There are many kinds of truces, most not relevant to the situation facing the United States today.[156] The kind of truce I am envisioning is one that signals the first step in a genuine reappraisal of US (and to a lesser extent European) core positions and interests as well as those of Muslims, so that genuine peace and reconciliation become conceivable. There is some historical precedent for this kind of truce in Islam. The Prophet Mohammed agreed to the first Muslim truce in 628. Known as the Treaty of Hudaybiyah, it was between the nascent Muslim community and the Meccan pagans, and lasted for two years before the Meccans broke it by attacking Muslim Bedouin tribes. During the truce, however, the Muslims respected its terms, even though many of them felt it to be unfair.

More important, during the past three decades an increasingly permanent Muslim presence in Europe has gradually led most Muslims to consider that region not *dar al-harb* (the Abode of War, the traditional Muslim categorization of all non-Muslim lands), but *dar al-hudna* – a land of truce between Muslims and non-Muslims – or even *dar al-Islam*, a land of peace where Muslims can feel at home. This same process is now happening in the United States, despite the war on terror and the occupation of Iraq. But especially in Europe, however dangerous the presence of a few thousand extremists out of a European Muslim population more than 10 million strong, Muslims increasingly think of Europe as a *terre de mediation* (land of mediation) between Muslims and the larger world. The global peace and justice movement needs to assure that this process of "enculturalization" continues across the Global North, on the grass-roots as much as the political level.[157]

What would a truce offer consist of? It must begin with an admission that the policies of Western governments – in the past, more Europe, today, predominantly the United States – have consistently violated the founding principles of Enlightenment and democracy that they have long boasted of bringing to the Muslim world, and that in the process significant pain has been caused to millions of Muslims worldwide. With the American and European peace and justice movements leading the way, a "searching and fearless moral inventory" must be undertaken based on "complete honesty" about America's past and present actions around the world.

If this reads like the Alcoholics Anonymous 12-step program, that's because America's addiction to oil and military might, coupled with its delusions of impeachable moral certitude, strongly resemble an alcoholic who refuses to own up to the impact of his abusive addiction. From this perspective, the increasing number of Muslims who support or engage in violent responses to US or other Western policies resemble victims of abuse who have lost the ability to find a healthy way either to resist or leave (the second option being impossible in the age of globalization). Instead, their attempts to match the abuser's destructiveness are helping to send both parties spiraling towards disaster.

In this context, a public acknowledgment of the damage done to the Muslim world by Europe and the United States and a pledge to redress it – and until there's such a move on the official level, the words must become the clarion call of the global peace and justice movement – would have a huge psychological impact on Muslims who feel humiliated and abused by centuries of Western imperialism, capitalism, and modernity. It would certainly do more to win hearts and minds than either the US military's much-vaunted "full spectrum dominance" or a spectrum's worth of American-sponsored radio and TV stations such as the overhyped and underperforming Radio Sawa' or al-Hurra TV.

Substantively, with a strong sense of the kind of humility advocated by John Macquarrie above, a meaningful *hudna* with Islam would include (but not be limited to) the following steps:

1. Just as many mainstream Muslim personalities have condemned their own religious extremism, the global peace and justice movement must urge American and European leaders to take the important psychological step of admitting their responsibility for the harm decades of support for dictatorship, corruption, and war have caused ordinary Muslims, especially in the Middle East. A similar admission vis-à-vis the costs of terrorism should be made by Muslims signing on to the truce document.
2. The movement must call on the US, the EU, and the North Atlantic Treaty Organization to halt all offensive military actions in the Muslim world and outline a serious plan for the removal of troops from Muslim countries, including Afghanistan and Iraq. (These could be replaced, where necessary, by robust United Nations peacekeeping forces or UN-assisted transitional administrations.)
3. The hunt for Osama bin Laden, al-Qa'eda, and related terror networks must be transformed from a war of vengeance into what it always should have been: a vigorous international effort led by the US, the UN and, where relevant, European and other governments to apprehend, prosecute, and punish people and groups involved in the September 11, 2001 assaults and similar attacks.
4. All military and diplomatic agreements and aid to Middle Eastern countries (in fact, to all countries) that are not democratic or don't

respect the rights of communities under their control should be suspended. Yes, this means Israel; but also Egypt, Jordan, Pakistan, Saudi Arabia, and other American "allies" and "partners." Such a step is crucial to stopping the regional arms race and cycle of violence that make peace and democratic reform impossible.

5. Finally, the movement needs to offer a detailed plan for how the hundreds of billions of dollars that would have been devoted to the "war on terror" should be redirected toward the kind of infrastructural, educational, and social projects the *9/11 Commission Report* argues are key to winning the "war on terror."

A truce does not equal capitulation to terrorists or letting Muslims off the hook for crimes committed in the name of their religion. Certainly, European leaders were right to reject the "truce offer" purportedly made by Osama bin Laden in April, 2004 on the condition that European countries remove their troops from Muslim lands and refuse to support the United States. Criminals can't offer truces, and bin Laden and other groups that use terrorist violence are indeed international criminals whom the world community has an obligation to bring to justice.

But states as well as communities and cultures can make truces. And in so doing they can also make demands of the "other" side. In this case a primary demand would be that Middle Eastern political leaders open their political and social systems and and hold internationally monitored elections within specified (short) time periods, or risk their regimes facing censure and sanctions by the international community. Such a uniform policy is the surest way to build a foundation for defeating terrorism.

Of course I have no illusions that the Bush Administration could be convinced to adopt such a plan of action. But here, as elsewhere, an EU in which most member states don't have the deep ties with either Israel or the oil princedoms of the Persian Gulf that anchor the 2005 US administration, is poised to lead the way. Indeed, I would argue that the international community, especially the EU, must assert a defiant tone against the imperial hubris of the US and take on the difficult but fundamental role of acting as a counterweight and alternative to America's imperial vision. But this will not happen on its own; it's up to citizens across the continent to ensure that their governments don't take the easy road of adopting a pragmatic approach of supporting the status quo and "working" with the Bush administration, while waiting for America to bleed itself dry in Iraq and other imperial adventures.[158]

Why is a truce a good strategy for the global peace and justice movement to pursue? Because of three inescapable realities: first, from an external perspective, no matter how "smarter and more effectively" Bush may fight the war on terror in his second Administration, it will be no more winnable than Vietnam, or the war on drugs, with far higher losses likely in the near future. From a moral as well as pragmatic point of view, such a stalemate demands that anyone who can – and in the West, this means each citizen – must take the lead in bringing hostilities to a close. Second, in the context of a political-military stalemate, a truce at the grass-roots level would have a significant impact on politics, especially if enough people become involved and refuse to participate in its violation by their governments (here's where the non-violent civil disobedience I'll discuss below becomes crucial in the United States and Western countries).

Third, however nostalgic some movement leaders might be for the good old days of the Cuban, Vietnamese or Nicaraguan revolutions, the reality is that President Bush and his millennarian policies will not be defeated by the kind of violence and hatred that guides his worldview. As Antonio Gramsci warned us seventy years ago, a "war of maneuver" or frontal assault on an advanced capitalist state by the Left cannot be won. Instead we need to dust off our copies of Gramsci's *Prison Notebooks* and buy a copy of Subcommandante Marcos's dispatches from the Lacandon jungle. Then perhaps we can find clues on how to fight a better and more efficient "war of position" against the terrifying prospect of four more years of George W. Bush.

While the Left has often turned to Gramsci for guidance, most commentators have ignored one of his chief insights: that however negative a role religion played in Italian society, it constituted the most important social force in the struggle against capitalism and fascism, without which the Left could never hope to achieve social hegemony against the bourgeoisie. This is because religion contains the kernel of "common sense" of the masses whose natural instinct is to rebel against the domination of the capitalist elite.[159] But because it is largely unformed or articulated, it is easily manipulated by that elite – as Thomas Frank has so eloquently shown in *What's the Matter with Kansas* – and needs to be joined to the "good sense" of radically progressive intellectuals in order to shape the kind of ideology and political program that could attract the majority of the poor and middle classes.

But in this dialogue the secular intellectuals would be transformed as much as the religious masses (both in fact would see their common sense transformed into a truly common good sense), creating the kind of organic unity that helped propel the religious Right from the margins of their party to the center of power. Indeed, as we saw in the last two chapters, a combination of religious motivations and innovative progressive political strategy was crucial to propelling the Zapatistas from the jungle to the world stage.

It's sad but telling that a sickly political prisoner in fascist Italy writing from memory on scraps of paper could anticipate the struggle facing America today better than most contemporary leaders of the so-called Left. Progressives need to do better; with a transformed culture that brings together the energy, spirituality, and radically holistic vision of the many movements and ideas we've discussed in this book, they at least have the tools to do so. At the very least they'd be wise to take the advice of Pierre Bourdieu, who called on the movement to "invent new forms of communication" between artists, academics, and activists, who together would "play a unique role by helping to create the social conditions for the collective production of *realistic utopias*."[160]

To lay the foundation for such a utopia the world needs both a hope that another world is possible and a plan to achieve it. The global peace and justice movement and its allies around the world are uniquely placed to offer both, but will foster neither until they embody the best ideals of America, Islam, and all the world's cultures. With gratitude to Gramsci and Subcommandante Marcos, here are some of the demands members of the global peace and justice movement worldwide could make in order to lay the foundation of a truly liberatory future. While for the sake of space I'm not including the kinds of environmental and health-related demands (such as honoring Kyoto or spending more on AIDS or other medical research, which are clearly vital concerns), they remain absolutely crucial to improving the lives of most citizens of the MENA:

The global peace and justice movement must unconditionally and without exception reject:

- all forms of occupation
- all forms of ethnic cleansing
- all settlement on conquered land
- all stationing of foreign troops in the countries of the region
- the use of violence to achieve political or economic ends by any government or group
- all preemptive war
- any denial of full democratic, political, social, and economic rights to individuals or groups because of religion, ethnicity, nationality, gender, sexuality or other social categories

- any presence of weapons of mass destruction in a country of the region, regardless of who else might have them
- all forms of non-democratic government
- all teaching of hatred and intolerance in secular or religious institutions or schools, or in government or organizations' propaganda
- all use of torture, cruel, inhuman, and degrading treatment, administrative detention, detention without trial, and other violations of human and political rights as protected by the Universal Declaration of Human Rights
- the death penalty

The global peace and justice movement must demand:

- the revocation of the right of veto for permanent members of the Security Council along with the expansion of the number of permanent members to include several countries of the Global South, including India, Brazil, and potentially South Africa, Indonesia or Turkey
- immediate debt forgiveness for all non-OECD countries
- a moratorium on all IMF/World Bank-sponsored structural adjustment programs
- the creation of a special fund derived from taxes on petroleum sales and profits to be directed towards sustainable development projects in the MENA and the development of alternative sources of energy
- an immediate reduction in defense spending in the region by a percentage of GDP that would increase yearly, as well as a reduction in arms sales and the production and stockpiling of nuclear weapons by the major nuclear powers
- the Tobin Tax on all currency trades across international borders at a rate of one tenth to two-and-a-half tenths of a percent
- the establishment of a permanent truth commission under UN auspices, with subpoena power, to investigate the root causes of continuing conflicts such as Israel/Palestine, Kashmir, the Sudan, Tibet, the plight of indigenous communities in Latin America and across the Global South, and to recommend fair and just solutions that would have some binding force
- the creation of a special UN commission that would report to the General Assembly and Security Council on how to integrate insights and best practices related to health and the environment into all future international rule- and treaty-making
- the creation of a special commission to investigate how to bring a more sustainable form of economic globalization – that is, one

based on holistic and environmental rather than neoliberal principles – to the MENA and other marginalized regions (most important among them being Africa)

- an end to all thefts or expropriation or appropriation of natural resources – oil, water, timber, etc. – by anyone other than the legitimate democratically elected government of the country
- that international labor, environmental, and human rights standards become part of the charter of the WTO and other international organizations and treaties
- the immediate adherence by all countries to the principles of the International Criminal Court
- that one set of political, legal, and moral standards be applied to *all* countries in the region

Most of these demands are no doubt familiar to readers (and many others, which I did not have space to include, would also be important). But if left on paper, no matter how many signatures were collected, such demands would ultimately remain just words. In order to realize them – and they will be opposed by American and regional political leaders with all their might – the global peace and justice movement must devote significant energy and resources to training its leaders and footsoldiers. They need to be trained to win what Gramsci describes as the long haul of a "war of position" against the state – that is, a war for social and political hegemony – whether in the public sphere or on the ground when the next resource-rich Southern country is invaded, or is driven or falls into chaos.

Such training would involve several areas. As we've already seen, for many it would mean becoming much more knowledgeable about the MENA through intensive study and/or work in the region. Just as tens of thousands of Muslims study in the West, a new generation of experts, who have established organic connections with their counterparts in the MENA *and* in so doing would have included many more people from the region among their numbers, must take the lead in coordinating the activities of the global peace and justice movement in the Muslim world.

Other members of the global peace and justice movement must focus on constantly improving the tactics of non-violent resistance to empire in all its forms. The techniques of the Ruckus Society or the Disobbedienti (and to the extent they adhere to non-violence, the Zapatistas or anarchists) must be learned by activists in the movement in the same way that soldiers go through basic training. And funds need to be raised to make such training much more readily available.

The movement must give tens of thousands of activists all over the world the training necessary to confront the full force of oppressive and even imperial states with the power of disciplined, positive, militant non-violence. (Remember, Rosa Parks didn't just decide one day not to give her seat up to a white man. It took great preparation and discipline to pull that off.) Moreover, these "soldiers" must have the language and cultural training to be mobilized quickly to countries that are being threatened with invasion or other forms of political violence, and be equipped with media technologies that are small, fast, yet inexpensive enough for activists to inexpensively and easily send live video reports on their activities to the world via the internet; no one must be allowed to be beaten or killed in the shadows again.[161]

Of course, all this needs to happen with almost no money, particularly when compared with the hundreds of billions spent on violence and war. (Although it would sure help if all the rich Hollywood supporters of Kerry and Clinton would stop wasting their money and give it to groups who are really trying to transform the system.) And this is another reason why the global peace and justice movement will only survive to the extent that it is in fundamental ways a religious movement – although not religious in the narrow theological sense, but rather in the manner the Protestant theologian Paul Tillich defines religion: as whatever activity or ideology is of "ultimate concern" to a person or group. If global peace and justice can become part of the religious/spiritual core of enough people (especially young people) worldwide, neither jihad nor McWorld stand a chance against it.[162]

The World We Want, or, Where to Find the "Other America" in which We'd All Like to Live

At the beginning of this book I argued that most Muslims don't hate America in and of itself, and that contrary to popular political belief, neither do most "old Europeans." What people across the globe are scared to death of, as University of Toronto philosopher Mark Kingwell so aptly describes it, is the "global virus" being spread by a consumption-crazy culture, one which "colonizes individuals around the world one by one until they are assimilated into the smoothly functioning logic of production."[163]

Against this vision of America as virus and the "inhuman globalization" it has spread, what kind of world do people want? At the dawn of the twenty-first century, millions of people are still fighting, killing, and dying to answer this question. Yet however deep the anger and intense the violence, millions of Muslims, Europeans, and people everywhere yearn for the kind of "human nationalism" that once symbolized America (even if it was often little more than a symbol) as a beacon of freedom to the world.

This vision is still redolent across the world in 2005, even as President Bush celebrates his re-election and American soldiers and their Iraqi adversaries compete to see who can most completely "liberate" Iraq. Whether it's the directors of Iraq's only think tank, Beyt al-Hikmah, asking their American guests where the ideals of Jefferson and Franklin have gone, Chilean author Isabel Allende sorting through the confusion over American fundamentalism in the German newspaper *Frankfurter Rundschau* or the editorial board of *Le Monde* trying to make sense of the Presidential elections: finding that "other" America is considered an urgent quest across the globe.[164]

For the intellectuals of Beyt al-Hikmah, returning America to its other and better self is an urgent task in which they feel powerless to participate; for Allende, nostalgia for the Clinton years – when globalization "lite" at least seemed reformable from below – is a counterweight to the reality of today; for *Le Monde*, the ideals that once guided America have been spotted in the rising socialist (and hopefully, social-democratic) political tide in Latin American countries such as Uruguay, Brazil, Argentina, and even Venezuela. No one really has the answer to the question of where to find the other America, but few people I've met, even those whom many would term terrorists, hate the United States of America per se, and many speak wistfully of it as an ideal, as a haven for the world's oppressed, hungry, and helpless. What they hate is the global virus that has not only infected the United States, but of which it's become a primary vector and carrier, spreading a sickness that increasingly afflicts their cultures and personalities and against which few people have the fortitude to resist: a sickness whose symptoms can be as violent as they are aggressive.

As I close this book the virus that is neoliberal globalization is becoming more virulent each day. Yet for every bombing in Baghdad or arms deal in Warsaw there is news of a successful protest in Buenos Aires, Cairo or Beirut. Just maybe, if those of us with a measure of immunity band together across the divide of cultures, the world can be healed before anger, hatred, and violence reach pandemic proportions.

Notes

Introduction

1. I am focusing on the MENA region because Central and Southeast Asia, and Africa, include cultures which, while in many ways similar and connected to those of the MENA, are historically distinct enough that including them in our discussion would make it impossible to engage in a comparative analysis.

2. More than one person has said it would have been a great cover, and I did get accused of being a spy more than once.

3. When I was in grammar school I remember being yelled at for using a word to define itself. But I guess things are different on the web.

4. This is not surprising when we realize who was actually at the gathering: a fair number of fairly reactionary elements from the Arab world (if they were truly progressive, the Government wouldn't have let the meeting occur) and uncritical far Left Western groups like the British Socialist Workers Party and ANSWER. The journal *New Politics* did an excellent critique of this and similar gatherings in its Summer 2003 (Vol. 9, No. 3) issue (Alan Johnson, "Iraq and the Third Camp," available at http://www.wpunj. edu/icip/newpol/issue35/Johnson35. htm, and Stan Crooke, "The Politics of

the Cairo Declaration," same issue, but not online).

5. For President Bush's use of said illegal right hook, see Jim Sleeper, "He's Got the Bad-Boy Vote Sewed Up," *LA Times*, August 9, 2004.

6. This is clearly nonsense, as there are innumerable contemporary events that never become Googleable "facts" because the people involved have neither the access to official "recorders of history" (such as reporters, activists or scholars) nor the technology to put it on the web themselves. Or the information could be on the web, but in Arabic, French, Japanese or a hundred other languages Prager doesn't know, or at least doesn't have the software to decipher. Indeed, at the beginning of the show, Prager claimed, based on another web search, that I have never written anything critical of Palestinian violence. But, as I then informed him, I had in fact written an article in *Le Monde* after the outbreak of the intifada in September 2000. Perhaps if he'd used google.fr, he would have found it.

7. Indeed, after the show – too late for the speed of talk radio – I remembered that I published an Op/Ed piece for the *Christian Science Monitor* in the wake of the 1996 wave of Palestinian terrorism. But since this was before the *Monitor*

created an online archive, Prager's Google search didn't find the article. And while Prager also accused me of never having written anything condemning Palestinian violence, only days before our interview, I wrote an article for *TIKKUN* magazine (which was on its website) criticizing continued violence by – and, as important, against – Palestinians. I still don't know why that didn't turn up on his Google search.

8. For a good example of this argument, see Said Aburish, *Saddam Hussein: The Politics of Revenge.*

9. For the documents and an article about them, see http://www.nytimes.com/library/world/mideast/041600iran-cia-index.html.

10. In the first coup, the CIA literally broadcast the names of suspected communists from a clandestine radio station in Kuwait, thousands of whom were summarily murdered by the new regime. The second coup brought to the center of power a young but equally ruthless Saddam Hussein.

11. But it's not just the lack of crucial information at the disposal of teachers that's a problem. Many parents are even worse. Whenever I meet with high school teachers I hear the same story: every time they teach or talk about Islam they're besieged by calls from furious parents literally screaming that the idea of teaching their children about Islam is "liberal," even "un-American." As one teacher explained to me, "even if we have good material, we have to toe the company line. If we present an accurate history of Iraq or Israel/Palestine, we risk being fired." These words were spoken by an Orange County, California high school teacher at a seminar I was giving on teaching Middle Eastern history in the spring of 2004 and was seconded by almost every other teacher in the room.

12. I use the terms together because they are analytically inseparable. Colonialism is a specific type of imperialism in which one political–territorial authority achieves direct control of, and/or sponsors, settlement in another, often conquered, territory.

Part I
Chapter 1

1. In this book I will usually use the term "Global South" to refer to countries outside the "advanced industrial" or G-8 economies that include the United States, Japan, Germany, France, the UK, Italy, Canada, and Russia (in fact, China would have been a more appropriate choice if the political need to incorporate Russia into this group wasn't so important). The countries of the Global South are often referred to as the "third world," which is a term that meant something when there was still a Cold War and a first (the West) and second (the Soviet bloc) world but is meaningless today; or the equally problematic "developing world," a term that suggests that there are already countries that have finished developing or reached the final stage of human history. This view, which is at the heart of the neoliberal self-imagination, is clearly nonsense from an empirical and historical perspective. The problems with these two terms have led increasing numbers of scholars to use the division "Global North" to refer to the richest countries of the world, which are largely located above the Tropic of Cancer in North America, Europe and Northern Asia, and the "Global South," which includes the rest of the world that is located geographically to the south of these countries.

2. This includes migration and unregulated labor markets, in this case closures by Israel and the replacement of Palestinian workers by more compliant and less "dangerous" Romanians, Thais or Nigerians.

3. Interview with ER doctor at Baghdad's Qadamiyyah Hospital,

March 21, 2004. For discussion of the situation in Iraq, see my "Who's Chaos is it Anyway?" Tomdispatch.com, April 2004, at www.nationinstitute.org/ tomdispatch/index.mhtml?pid=1396, and "Cash for Chaos," OC Weekly, April 2004, at www.ocweekly.com/ink/04/ 32/news-levine.php. I would argue, however, that a year after the invasion the larger argument I made that day still stands – while "No to the War" made for a nice chant, the movement for global peace and justice badly needed to shout what it was saying Yes, and not just No to, if it wanted to stop the war. As I will argue in Part Three, basing one's public program on No may work for the Right because Republicans appeal to people's most primitive and negative instincts. But it can't work for the global peace and justice movement, which needs to develop a much more positive yet realizable vision and set of strategies if it wants to be taken seriously by the mainstream public, let alone offer sufficient hope that "another world is possible" to motivate it to join the struggle.

4. See Mark LeVine, "'Human Nationalisms' versus 'Inhuman Globalisms.'"

5. See President Bush's speeches and public comments from the immediate aftermath of September 11, 2001 until his State of the Union address the following winter for variations on these statements.

6. Robert Frank, "A Merger's Message: Dominate or Die."

7. As *US News and World Report* described him.

8. Bernard Lewis, *What Went Wrong?*

9. As Nobel laureate and former World Bank chief economist Joseph Stiglitz calls them.

10. Even as he has criticized the US invasion of Iraq, pointing out, in seeming contrast to his position in *The*

End of History, that the US system is "not the only option" available to Muslims struggling for democracy. For the former belief, see Francis Fukuyama, *The End of History and the Last Man*. For an interesting interview in which Fukuyama comes off as much more open than either Friedman or Huntington (both of whom, for example, supported the invasion and occupation of Iraq), see his interview with Ezzat Ibraham in *Al-Ahram Weekly*, April 29–May 5, 2004, at http://weekly. ahram.org.eg/2004/688/intrvw.htm.

11. As he wrote in a column just before the book was released ("Time of the Turtles," New York *Times*, August 15, 1998, p. A13). Friedman attacks sixties radicals (and, ironically if implicitly, Huntington) for having believed that people around the world would desire something other than his vision of the American dream. He does point out that the wretched of the Earth will "eat up their rainforests if their governments can't provide them with the earning potential to go to Orlando, Los Angeles or Paris," although he doesn't explain how the Government can provide them with such earnings *without* eating up the rainforest.

12. Perhaps he hasn't visited Euro-Disney. Either way, unfortunately, any government or society that can't find the wherewithal to stomach and adapt to the strict regimens necessary to build the neoliberal theme park future are doomed to remain, literally, wireless in their olive groves – which sooner or later will no doubt be rendered obsolete by Monsanto-engineered super-olives that contain a full day's supply of twelve essential vitamins, and grow hair (and who knows what else) too.

13. Jeffrey Sachs, "Don't Know, Should Care," *Los Angeles Times*, Op/Ed, June 5, 2004.

14. For the older use of creative destruction see David Harvey, *The Condition of Postmodernity*; for the

more recent and celebratory use see Tyler Cowen, *Creative Destruction.*

15. Although her suggested reading list includes arch-conservative Daniel Pipes (see Irshad Manji, *The Trouble with Islam*).

16. Frank's analysis explores how "cultural anger is marshaled to achieve economic ends" by conservative politicians and the corporate elite they ultimately serve (Thomas Frank, *What's the Matter with Kansas*, p. 5).

17. Ibid.

18. Ibid, p. 6.

19. Ibid., pp. 27, 68–9.

20. Ibid., pp. 125, 159, 163. Both radical conservatives and radical Muslims have a penchant for conspiracy theories: Conservative listserves abound with stories of the Liberal elite seeking to outlaw professional sports, forbid red meat, decree that only gay couples can adopt children, etc., while radical Muslims believe the CIA and Israelis were behind September 11, and that the goal of the United States is to destroy Islam.

21. Ibid., p. 183.

22. Ibid., pp. 68–9.

23. See ibid., pp. 136–7. Moreover, both worldviews are particularly "attractive and even seductive way[s] to deal with an unfair universe," especially when both Kansans and Muslims "watch their culture, beamed in from the coasts, grow coarser every year" (ibid., pp. 157, 249). The political implications of both groups' beliefs are also profoundly similar. At the most basic level, members of both groups want to be identified with a winner. And so Midwesterners and their geographic compatriots across America identify culturally with the corporate and conservative elites whose policies in fact are increasing their economic woes because they identify vicariously with their celebrity and lifestyle, while many Muslims identify and even support Osama bin Laden even if his policies have led to US invasions of several countries and greater oppression in almost all MENA countries. This reasoning is very similar to that of many Muslims – for example, Palestinians or Iraqis – who support terrorist violence. Hamas or al-Qa'eda have brought their supporters nothing but more blood, violence, and economic hardship: intensified Israeli occupation, US occupations of at least two Muslim countries. Yet support only grows as the conflict widens and escalates. Why? Because whether it's Osama bin Laden or George Bush, fundamentalist leaders are adept at getting ordinary people who are suffering economically, politically, culturally, or all three, to sacrifice even more for the greater "good" of the mythological values and purity of the imagined community of the nation and/or religion.

24. Ibid., pp. 95–6. This latter point is crucial, because if material goals – that is, increasing their standard of living, bringing real economic development and justice to their communities – did matter, they wouldn't be supporting George W. Bush or Osama bin Laden, both of whom can offer only more economic hardship for all but the true economic and cultural elite.

25. Ibid., pp. 8, 76, 80.

26. Ibid., p. 92.

27. Ibid., p. 249.

28. "We have to cast off once and for all the 1970s cynicism that sneered from the back of the classroom at the joiner and the volunteer," the authors argue, before directing their fury almost as much at America's internal enemies as its external ones (David Frum and Richard Perle, *An End to Evil*, p. 78).

29. And so they describe the Middle East as a "fetid swamp" filled with "venomous vermin" (ibid., p. 161): "If our Muslim adversaries are not to destroy Western civilization, we must

gird for more battles," they tell us, advising the Government to topple more regimes in the Middle East, treating the French and Saudis as "the enemies they are," squeezing China, and launching an air and naval blockade against North Korea (ibid., p. 103). As for Americans, we are told "a free society is not an un-policed society. A free society is a self-policed society" (ibid., p. 77). Michel Foucault couldn't have said it any better, and to the extent that millions of Americans agree with them (and judging by its place on numerous best-seller lists they do), we have clear evidence of what I described earlier as the role of self-policing – in academic jargon, "disciplining" – in the early twenty-first-century war culture of America. In addition to the book, I owe these comments to the insightful reviews by Lewis Lapham ("Dar al-Harb") and Joshua Micah Marshall ("Power Rangers: Did the Bush Administration Create a New American Empire – or Weaken the Old One?".

And it's not just famous (former) Bush Administration insiders that are spewing venom against the majority of the peoples of the MENA. Whenever I'm asked to debate conservative professors in the US the same frightening, intellectually dishonest, and immoral discourse is repeated with various degrees of subtlety. It can get so absurd that I wind up having to spend most of my time correcting one inaccuracy after another, including claims that "the region has become more democratic since the invasion of Iraq."

30. Feldman begins by quoting two hadiths – sayings of the Prophet Mohammed recorded by his followers – about the so-called "greater" versus "lesser" jihad (that is, the "spiritual" struggle for inner purification and piety and the outward war to defend or expand the faith). He does this in order to demonstrate that jihad doesn't have to define Islam; but what he doesn't inform the reader is that neither hadith is considered reliable or even attributable to the Prophet Mohammed by authoritative Muslim sources (Noah Feldman, *After Jihad*, front matter). Indeed, Muslim conservatives and extremists have long delegitimized Muslim moderates and modernists for their use of these "unreliable" hadiths to downplay the importance of war and violence in Islamic theology and practice. You don't do anyone any favors, including Muslims, by rewriting its history or theology to downplay the violence that has been central to its – and to almost every world religion's – success. Cf. especially p. 206.

The larger problem is that in a book that is supposed to be about America's potential to nourish Islamic democracy, Feldman (like the *Arab Human Development Report* we discussed several times and the *9/11 Commission Report* discussed later in the text) spends no time discussing the role of the world political economy and American policy in particular in frustrating autonomous attempts to build democratic institutions or cultures in the Muslim world. The most he can say is that "certain expressions of Islam and Democracy are compatible in theory," while arguing for an interventionist US foreign policy, where trade and more aid would go to democracies, with autocracies receiving neither. Such policies "would be meddling, true, but meddling of a sort that one could hardly imagine the Egyptian public resenting" (ibid., pp. 212–13).

How could someone with his training not realize how the billions in aid that flow to MENA countries each year are tied to a much larger system – the weapons/petrodollar system – that makes any kind of change in US foreign aid policy, or foreign policy more generally, impossible without a radical restructuring of America's political and economic systems? Indeed, in tones of almost striking naïveté Feldman argues that "the promise of greater influence in Washington can also be used in concert with economic incentives to convince Muslim governments that democracy would serve their interests, while explaining that Palestinians in particular 'must be made to see' that one step toward improving their ties to Washington is to become more democratic." Aside from the imperial arrogance of "making" a colonized culture "see" that one's policies are the best for them, such advice betrays an utter lack of knowledge of the decade-long US role in destroying Palestinian civil and political institutions through the CIA's work with Israeli and Palestinian security services to stifle any democratic dissent to the Oslo process (ibid., pp. 218–19). Feldman also argues that "Israel, for its part, knows that a functioning democracy in Palestine would be the best guarantor of its own security," while "Palestinians who want democracy have three hurdles to overcome: Arafat's now entrenched [corrupt] Administration ... the conditions of occupation, and ongoing bombings of Israeli civilians." As if the occupation isn't profoundly the source of these other problems.

31. The professor/intelligence advisor frankly acknowledged that his phrase alluded to the goal of breaking the occupied population, in the manner of Israel's tactics in Palestine, and was little concerned by the fact that Israel's policies have failed miserably and at the cost of much blood during the past thirty-five years (see Jodie Evans, "Baghdad Diary," in Mark LeVine, Pilar Perez, and Viggo Mortensen, eds., *Twilight of Empire*). On the other hand, there is the example of Hoover Institution Senior Fellow Larry Diamond, who joined the CPA as a senior advisor on democratization but retained a critical distance from US policy goals even while working in Iraq.

32. Needless to say, like the California teaching materials described in the Introduction, his analysis is completely devoid of any discussion of the negative impact of European imperialism on colonized societies around the world. See Niall Ferguson, *Colossus: The Price of America's Empire*. And so, Ferguson, amazingly, describes the United States as having "difficulty imposing its will on other nations because it is uncomfortable with imperialism," as if the dozens of invasions of foreign countries across the globe never happened. For a similar critique, see Greg Grandin, "The Right Quagmire," *Harper's Magazine*, December 2004.

33. And so the report argues that the US is an innocent bystander to a conflict "*within* a civilization" which can only be solved by "Muslims themselves," pp. 262–4.

34. See John Esposito, *Unholy War: Terror in the Name of Islam*.

35. For a copy of the report, see Mark LeVine, "The Arab Human Development Report: A Critique."

36. To emphasize the report's radical credentials, one of its lead authors explained to the *Washington Post* that while the *AHDR* aims to start a dialogue in the Arab world, "it won't make many friends there."

37. As described in Chapter Six of the report (online version).

38. Source: World Bank estimates, http://www.worldbank.org/prospects/gdf2002/vol1-pdf/pdfcharts/ch1charts.pdf.

39. Cf. Tim Mitchell, "America's Egypt."

40. See Fareed Zakaria, *The Future of Freedom*.

41. This is made possible by "the virtual outlawing of history by the dominant culture" that is reflected in the Axis of Arrogance and Ignorance, and by a militant political and social utopianism that inspired Islamists and neoliberals much as it did their revolu-

tionary forefathers in France during the reign of the first Terror after 1789. See S.N. Eisenstadt, Jeffrey C. Alexander, and Steven Seidman, eds., *Fundamentalism, Sectarianism and Revolution: The Jacobin Dimension of Modernity*, Cambridge: Cambridge University Press, 2000.

42. Thus, for example, the best-selling books of Klein and Frank, which enjoy canonical status among progressive members of today's 15–40s generation, don't deal with the MENA (although Klein did spend a month in Iraq in the spring of 2004 and has been writing about it since), while Tariq Ali cannot engage most citizens of his own country (Pakistan) or culture (Islam at large) because he admittedly distrusts religion. But if progressives don't engage religious Muslims, what hope is there for dialogue, solidarity, and social change?

43. For an interesting take on this issue, see Galal Amin's discussion of "shishk-bishk" music in his *Whatever Happened to the Egyptians?*

44. Naomi Klein, *No Logo*, p. 114.

45. Despite the age difference, my conjecture is at least plausible since music and art have always traveled with incredible speed across the divide of cultures and geography; witness the fact that by the early 1920s country music had spread deep into the heart of Africa through records brought there by American visitors, and was already reshaping the local music in profound ways. In so doing it was completing a circle that began when the African slaves provided crucial melodic and harmonic input to what would become country, blues, and jazz.

46. Such a response may seem "traditional" or "atavistic," but in fact the ideas, ideologies, and actions are quite modern, revealing the anti-liberal, violent soul that has always fueled (and often consumed) enlightened liberal modernity.

47. And just so we don't think that it's all about hybridity and funky music, the largely moderate and geriatric leaders of the increasingly powerful *wasatiyya* movement within Islam are offering much the same challenge with their revolutionary fatwas, or religious rulings, that open new means of interpreting core Muslim texts for contemporary Muslim women and men. Their inspiration is both Islam itself and their interaction with Western legal and social traditions.

48. Friedman might want to argue that the fact that much of the interaction seems originally inspired by American artists supports his argument that globalization is ultimately the universalization of Western-style cultural, economic, and political systems. But my examples show the much more equal back and forth between the artists, with MENA and other "world music" artists profoundly shaping the way music and art more broadly are being produced in and by the West, even if there are far fewer Western teenagers blasting Egyptian pop singer Hani Shaker from their computer speakers than Middle Eastern teenagers listening to the latest Western hiphop.

49. Tariq Ramadan, "Conversations within Islam: Culture, Politics and Religion in the Global Public Sphere," Budapest, May 25, 2003. Transcript available at http://www. humamities. uci.edu/history/levineconference/ MLbudapesttranscriptedit2.pdf.

Chapter 2

1. Coefficient is the mathematical term for the components of the matrix, which works quite well here because of its suggestion of increased efficiency and power when all four are brought together.

2. This shouldn't be confused with Christian doctrine of the end of times

or the Jewish doctrine of the Messiah, which are focused on some future time that has yet to arrive, or with the cyclical and repetitive view of history that characterizes Hinduism and many tribal religions.

3. The most important signs of modernity have always been considered the secularization, rationalization, and bureaucratization of societies, accompanied by the dominance of capitalism in the economy. What is important about this belief is that most scholars studying modernity – and through them, politicians and other elites who used the work of scholars to make public policy – felt that the combination of events and processes they understood to be modern occurred only in Western, Christian Europe, taking root there specifically because of cultural traits its societies, and only they, possessed. This sentiment, famously represented by Max Weber's *The Protestant Ethic and the Spirit of Capitalism*, was and remains central to the ideological component of modernity, and profoundly impacted the way Europeans and later the United States confronted and justified their rule of the various "backward" peoples they colonized. For a detailed discussion of the debates over modernity, see the first three chapters of Mark LeVine, *Overthrowing Geography*.

4. For such an argument, see Charles Issawi, *The Middle East Economy*.

5. See Samir Amin, "The Ancient World Systems Versus the Modern Capitalist World System." Also see Samir Amin, "Imperialism and Globalization."

6. See LeVine, *Overthrowing Geography*, Introduction. These others were not just located outside the boundaries of the nation-state, but also included those within the nation and/or state whose identities in any way challenged or diverged from the official ideology.

7. See Samir Amin, *Eurocentrism*, pp. 72–3.

8. Karl Polanyi, *The Great Transformation*, p. 157.

9. Albert Memmi, *The Colonizer and the Colonized*; Aimé Césaire, *Discourse on Colonialism*; Frantz Fanon, *Dying Colonialism* and *The Wretched of the Earth*.

10. Polanyi, *The Great Transformation*, p. 130.

11. Olusegun Obasanjo, "Democracy and Development in Africa," speech, Kennedy School of Government, Harvard University, October 30, 1999.

12. A continent that is second in size and population, and arguably the richest of all in terms of natural resources, is home to a disproportionate number of the poorest people in the world, and has an average per capita income well less than 2 percent of that of the United States.

13. For a discussion of the implications of these figures, see David Clingingsmith and Jeffrey G. Williamson, "India's De-Industrialization under British Rule: New Ideas, New Evidence," NBER Working Paper Series No. 10586, June 2004.

14. Josiah Strong, *Our Country: Its Possible Future and its Present Crisis*, web version.

15. US Space Command, *Vision 2020*.

16. Quoted by Richard T. Cooper, "General Casts War in Religious Terms," *LA Times*, October 16, 2003.

17. Frank, "A Merger's Message."

18. For this analysis, see the World Bank, *Will Arab Workers Prosper or Be Left Out in the Twenty-first Century?*

19. For discussions pro and con of hybridity as a basic element of globalization see, among others, Taylor Cowen, *Creative Destruction*; Nestor Garcia Canclini, *Hybrid Cultures*; and Arjun Appadurai, *Modernity at Large*. One could argue that people intuitively know what it means to be "Egyptian" or

"French," but how is one supposed to be a "citizen of the world" or a member of the "Pepsi nation"?

20. This discussion of the history and political economy of modernity is drawn from the following works: Kenneth Pomeranz, *The Great Divergence*; André Gunder Frank, *ReOrient: Global Economy in the Asia Age*; Janet Abu-Lughod, *Before European Hegemony*; and Peter Gran, *Beyond Eurocentrism*. The history recounted here answers the kinds of leading questions offered by conservatives such as Bernard Lewis, who in his recent book, *What Went Wrong?*, asked: "Why did the discoverers of America sail from Spain rather than from a Muslim Atlantic port? Why did the great scientific breakthrough occur in Europe and not, as one might reasonably have expected, in the richer, more advanced, and in most respects more enlightened realm of Islam?" The exhaustion of Europe's resources, Asia's riches, and a drive to colonize are all factors Lewis and his colleagues neglect to consider.

21. The Ottoman Empire was founded at the turn of the fourteenth century by 'Uthman I and ruled until it was officially abolished by the Turkish Republic in 1923.

22. In fact, Columbus learned how to navigate the Atlantic in the waters off Madeira.

23. The central African "kingdoms" had centuries of experience capturing, selling, and owning slaves themselves and for the Muslim/Ottoman markets.

24. This is especially the case after the indigenous Amerindians were largely killed off.

25. Sources include: Joseph Inikori, *Africa and the Industrial Revolution in England: A Study in International Trade and Economic Development*, Cambridge: Cambridge University Press, 2002; Dharma Kumar, *The Cambridge Economic History of India*, Cambridge: Cambridge University

Press, 1981; Ann Ramenofsky, *Vectors of Death: The Archaeology of European Contact*, Albuquerque: University of New Mexico Press, 1998; Henry Dobyns, *Their Number Become Thinned: Native American Population Dynamics in Eastern North America*, Knoxville: University of Tennessee, 1983; Mike Davis, *Late Victorian Holocausts: El Niño Famines and the Making of the Third World*, London: Verso, 2001; Jared Diamond, *Guns, Gems and Steel: The Fate of Human Societies*, New York: W.W. Norton, 1999. Conversations from my own calculations and from http://www.eh.net/ehresources/howmuch/poundq.php.

26. Pomeranz, *The Great Divergence*, Introduction.

27. By this I mean that it has been dominated by an ideological belief, no longer supported by scholarship, that the empire, and indeed the entire Orient stretching to China, was backward, stagnant, and in need of European tutelage and development in order to "modernize."

28. This is one reason why trade within the borders of the empire was more valuable than trade with Europe until the nineteenth century (for relevant statistics, see Şevket Pamuk, *The Ottoman Empire and European Capitalism, 1820–1913*. Also, his *İstanbul ve Diğer Kentlerde: 500 yıllık Fiyatlar ve Ücretler, 1469–1998 (500 Years of Prices and Wages in Istanbul and Other Cities)*; and his edited volume with Jeffrey Williamson, *The Mediterranean Response to Globalization Before 1950*.

29. Polanyi, *The Great Transformation*, pp. 3–4.

30. See Butrus Abu-Manneh, "The Islamic Roots of the Gülhane Rescript."

31. Selim Deringil, *The Well-Protected Domains*, pp. 136–7, 148, 154, quoting Ottoman official correspondence.

32. This was nowhere more so than in its Anatolian heartland, where a

Turkish rather than cosmopolitan Ottoman perspective increasingly held sway even among the state elite after the turn of the twentieth century. The growing "Turkish" identity that was increasingly adopted by the Ottoman elite specifically alienated the Arab provinces, and prevented the formation of a powerful Arab Ottoman identity in favor of more specifically Arab national identities. The economic policies of the Ottoman state were also important. In order to earn the vast sums of hard currency needed to modernize – and in particular, to pay off the increasing debts to Europe – the Ottomans radically changed the legal categorizations of land so that more and more land could be sold. This would have a profound effect on the history of Palestine, in particular, as it made possible the purchase of huge tracts of land by Jews even when the official policy of the empire was opposed to Zionism. Of course, the spread of capitalism everywhere depended on the creation of a readily available labor force – more or less "free" in Europe, more or less enslaved in the colonies – drawn from people forced off their land.

33. I should point out that the following summaries can only touch the surface of the complex histories of these countries; and given our focus on the impact of the modernity matrix, they will be largely negative in tone because of the negative impact of the experiences of its component parts. This shouldn't obscure the many accomplishments of these and other MENA countries in building vibrant, if often deeply troubled, societies. But such accomplishments, I would argue, have mostly been in spite, not because, of the impact of modernity, colonialism, capitalism, and nationalism.

34. Khedive was the title given to Muhammad Ali and his successors when they were declared the hereditary rulers of the country.

35. Earl of Cromer, "Why Britain Acquired Egypt in 1882" (1908), available online at http://www.fordham.edu/halsall/mod/1908cromer.html.

36. Felix Frankfurter, "The Palestine Situation Restated," *Foreign Affairs*, April, 1931, p. 18.

37. See Gershon Shafir, *Land, Labor, and the Origins of the Israeli–Palestinian Conflict, 1882–1914*; and Derick Penslar, *Zionism and Technocracy*.

38. Mark LeVine, "The Discourse of Development in Mandate Palestine."

39. Ibid. and LeVine, *Overthrowing Geography*.

40. LeVine, "The Discourse of Development in Mandate Palestine."

41. For a detailed discussion of this see LeVine, *Overthrowing Geography*, especially the Introduction through Chapter 3.

42. The "conquest" of Palestinian jobs and land naturally exacerbated the conflict between the two communities; but such strategies reveal the role capitalism (and the divisions between workers it inevitably brings about) plays in shaping the other "coefficients" of the modernity matrix. See Shafir, *Land, Labor, and the Origins of the Israeli–Palestinian Conflict*, pp. 81, 89.

43. For a discussion of Nablus, see Beshara Doumani, *Rediscovering Palestine*.

44. Cf. ibid.; LeVine, *Overthrowing Geography*; Roger Owen, ed., *Studies in the Economic and Social History of Palestine in the Nineteenth and Twentieth Centuries*; Alexander Scholch, *Palestine in Transformation, 1856–1882*.

45. Cf. the discussion in LeVine, *Overthrowing Geography*, Introduction through Chapter 3.

46. See Jonathan Nitzan and Shimshon Bichler, *The Global Political Economy of Israel*.

47. For a good description of Iraq's history, see Geoff Simons, *Iraq: From Sumer to Saddam*.

48. Although the greater power of Europe helped convince Istanbul to depose the local governor before he became too independent. Once the Ottomans imposed more direct rule in the late 1860s the new governor modernized Baghdad with tramways, public parks, a water system, banks, paved and lighted streets, and the printing of modern textbooks, regular steamer service, and irrigation improvements to increase trade. Telegraph, ports, railroads, and postal services were all developed between the 1860s and World War I.

49. Winston Churchill, quoted in Simons, *Iraq: From Sumer to Saddam*, p. 213.

50. Aburish, *Saddam Hussein: The Politics of Revenge.*

51. For a good series of articles on how this played out in Iraq, see LeVine, Perez, and Mortensen, eds., *Twilight of Empire.*

52. The brutality and racism of the British policies in Iraq are well recounted in Simons, *Iraq: From Sumer to Saddam*, Chapter 5.

53. During World War II pro-Nazi factions in the Iraqi Government tried unsuccessfully to rebel against the British and join the Axis in response to the corruption and repression of the Nuri al-Said Government.

54. The Baghdad Pact was a military alliance formed in 1955 by Britain that included Iraq, Turkey, Iran, and Pakistan, and whose goal was to counter Nasserism, Arab nationalism, and Soviet influence in the Middle East. For a good summary of the rule of Abdul Karim Kassem, his relationship with Iraqi communists, and the rivalry that developed between him and Egypt's Gemal Abdel Nasser, see Simons, *Iraq: From Sumer to Saddam*, Chapter 6.

55. For analyses of the CIA's role in bringing the Ba'ath Party to power, see interview with Said Aburish on PBS's "Frontline," at http://www.pbs.org/wgbh/pages/frontline/shows/saddam/interviews/aburish.html, and interview with former CIA operative James Critchfield, at http://www.pbs.org/wgbh/pages/frontline/shows/saddam/interviews/critchfield.html, and United Press International report based on interviews with almost a dozen former US and British diplomats about the coups (Richard Sale, "Saddam Key in Early CIA Plot," UPI, April 10, 2003, http://www.globalpolicy.org/security/issues/iraq/history/2003/0410saddam.htm). Also see Roger Morris, "A Tyrant 40 Years in the Making," New York Times, Op/Ed, March 14, 2003 and Andrew and Patrick Cockburn's discussion of these events in their book *Out of the Ashes: The Resurrection of Saddam Hussein.*

56. Some scholars argue that Hussein actually played into a trap laid by the US, as by invading Kuwait he gave the US the pretext for a politically useful and incredibly profitable war to occur. Specifically, before the invasion the US State Department informed Hussein that the US had "no special defense or security commitments to Kuwait," which was followed by then US Ambassador April Glaspie's declaration to him that "we have no opinion on the Arab–Arab conflicts, like your border disagreement with Kuwait." And so *Foreign Policy* magazine observed, "the United States may not have intended to give Iraq a green light, but that is effectively what it did" (*Foreign Policy*, January–February 2003).

57. See Amine Thami, "Ta'addudiyya and Islamism: Lessons from Algeria," quote on p. 154.

58. Ibid., p. 151. Also, see Mark LeVine, "A Comparative Analysis of the Political Economies and Ideologies Underlying the Emergence of the Palestinian Hamas and the Algerian FIS."

59. For a good account of America's imperial adventures during the nine-

teenth and twentieth centuries, see Howard Zinn, *A People's History of the United States*; and Chalmers Johnson, *The Sorrows of Empire*.

60. As the philosopher Michel Foucault described it during a visit to Iran in 1978.

61. Bob Woodward, *Plan of Attack*, pp. 56–7. For the torture techniques, see the *Newsweek* story, "The Roots of Torture," by John Barry, Michael Hirsh, and Michael Isikoff, May 2004, http://msnbc.msn.com/ id/4989438/.

62. For a discussion of Boykin's role in the Abu Ghraib torture scandal in the spring of 2004, see Sidney Blumenthal, "The Religious Warrior of Abu Ghraib," *The Guardian*, May 20, 2004, http://www.guardian.co.uk/comment/story/0,3604,1220622,00.html.

63. Arianna Huffington, *Pigs at the Trough: How Corporate Greed and Political Corruption are Undermining America*, p. 104.

64. Ibid., pp. 111, 119.

65. Henri Lefebvre, *The Production of Space*, trans. Donald Nicholson-Smith, Cambridge: Blackwell, 1991, p. 68.

Part II
Chapter 3

1. If we look at the work of Jeffrey Williamson and Kevin O'Rourke, it is clear that between 1880 and 1939 a small number of European countries controlled the economies and politics of almost the entire world apart from the Americas and East Asia (Kevin O'Rourke and Jeffrey Williamson, *Globalization and History: The Evolution of a Nineteenth-Century Atlantic Economy*, Cambridge, Mass.: MIT Press, 1999; Williamson, "Globalization, Convergence, and History."

2. Niall Ferguson's discussion is worth quoting at length given his otherwise hostile position towards the idea of a link between imperialism and globalization. He explains, "That empires did not (and do not) matter in globalization seems implausible. Perhaps the most striking political fact about the period from around 1880 until 1939 was that a small number of European countries governed an inordinately large amount of the rest of the world (remarks at panel on "Globalization in Interdisciplinary Perspective," May 4–5, 2001, sponsored by the NBER, http://www.nber.org/books/global/). For the importance of migration to the late-nineteenth-century phase of globalization, see Philippe Aghion and Jeffrey C. Williamson, *Growth, Inequality and Globalization: Theory, History and Policy*, Cambridge: Cambridge University Press, 1999.

3. Thanks to Professor Joel Beinin of Stanford University for insightful comments on an earlier draft of this table which helped me broaden its coverage to focus on the impact of the nineteenth-century Great Depression and subsequent "new imperialism."

4. Taylorism is a group of principles of scientific management invented by Frederick Taylor in 1911 for use in modern factories to ensure maximum efficiency based on latest scientific discoveries and principles and the careful selection and training of workers. Keynesianism is based on the successful model employed by John Maynard Keynes during the Great Depression. It is an approach to economics which emphasizes responsible public management of economic problems in a world-system context based primarily on regulating aggregate demand in order to keep production levels – and thus employment – high. The Bretton Woods agreements of 1944 and 1945, which were in large part designed by Keynes, established the World Bank and IMF, and was the architecture of the post-World War II

international financial system, primarily through regulating exchange rates between currencies.

5. Thanks to Ken Pomeranz for suggesting the notion of "social empire" to me in comments on an earlier draft of this chapter.

6. These terms are defined in notes 1 and 7.

7. We can define post-Fordism as emerging out of the disintegration of the previous balance between the mass production and consumption of standardized goods, and towards a consumption-based economy in which flexible labor and production markets become crucial to driving down production, communication, and transportation costs, satisfying rapidly changing consumer demand, and in so doing increasing the profits of successful firms. The previous system was made possible by the tacit agreements between labor and capital, of which Ford was pioneer, in which workers were paid decent wages (in order to afford to purchase the goods they produced) in return for improved productivity and higher profits for corporations. This balance was supported by the Government-sponsored welfare state that guaranteed a decent wage for the working class and subsidies to industrial and productive sectors. Post-Fordism is a crucial dynamic underlying the six core processes that define contemporary economic globalization: 1. The effects of collapse of the Bretton Woods system and the OPEC oil crisis; 2. Financial institutions and manufacturers in this period of turbulence and inflation looked to compensate for domestic uncertainty by seeking wider outlets for investments and additional markets. This in turn led to widespread bank lending in the third world, and the growth of the Eurodollar market; 3. The abandonment of exchange controls and the spread of other kinds of market deregulation; 4. The tendency towards de-industrialization in Britain and the US and the growth of long-term unemployment in Europe; 5. The relatively rapid development of Newly Industrialized Countries; 6. A shift from standardized mass production to more flexible production methods. See Paul Hirst and Grahame Thompson, *Globalization in Question: The International Economy and the Possibilities of Convergence*, London: Polity Press, 1996, pp. 5–6.

8. The (in)famous phrase "Washington Consensus" was coined by economist John Williamson in 1990 to refer to the lowest common denominator of policy advice being addressed by the Washington-based institutions like the IMF to Latin American countries, including trade liberalization, fiscal austerity, deregulation, securing property rights, tax reform, competitive exchange rates, and a redirection of public expenditure toward primary health and education systems at the same time as it focuses on high-income-generating activities. John Williamson, "Did the Washington Consensus Fail?" Outline of remarks at CSIS. Washington, D.C.: Inst. for International Economics, November 6, 2002.

9. For the strategies through which this power is amassed, see Johnson, *The Sorrows of Empire*.

10. As Chalmers Johnson explains, there have seen several major buildups of defense spending: during the Korean war, the Vietnam War, the Reagan years, and the post-September 11 war on terror, all of which saw averages at or higher than $400 billion in 2002 dollars (ibid., p. 55).

11. Ibid., p. 56.

12. A brief but illuminating discussion of the militarization of police forces before September 11, 2001 is by George J. Bryjak, "The Militarization of Police Forces," San

Diego *Union Tribune*, September 4, 2000.

13. David Harvey, "The 'New' Imperialism: On Spatio-temporal Fixes and Accumulation by Dispossession." Available at http://titanus.roma1.infn.it/sito_pol/Global_emp/Harvey.htm. In fact, just as massive transnational corporations have distorted Adam Smith's original vision of free markets comprising individuals and small firms operating in local contexts, so today militarized capitalism distorts the potential for increased freedom, solidarity, and justice that could be realized through a (very different kind of) globalization of the world's economies, cultures, and politics.

14. Michael D. Bordo et al., *Globalization in Historical Perspective*.

15. For coverage of Wolfensohn's speech about Cuba, see http://www.oneworld.org/ips2/apr01/00_21_003.html. Two years earlier the United Nations Development Program (UNDP) argued much the same thing about the social welfare systems of former Eastern Bloc countries, explaining that they constituted a "contract between generations" that had ensured a decent standard of living and welfare for all citizens (David Gordon and Peter Townsend, eds., *Breadline Europe: The Measurement of Poverty*, Introduction).

16. Lindert and Williamson also argue that the incomes of various liberalizing countries are "converging" under globalization; but this is an almost meaningless claim, since those making up the increase in a country's GDP per capita could be a very small elite while the rest of the population struggles to maintain their already low living standards.

17. IMF, "Factors Driving Global Integration," August 2000, (http://www.imf.org/external/np/speeches/2000/082500.htm).

18. Information from Gordon and Townsend, eds., *Breadline Europe*.

19. Andrew Hurrel and Ngaire Woods, eds., *Inequality, Globalization, and World Politics*.

20. See the Economic Commission for Latin America and the Caribbean, *Globalization and Development*, LC/G.2157 (SES.29/3)/I, April 2002, available at http://www.eclac.cl/cgi-bin/getProd.asp?xml=/publicaciones/xml/0/10030/P10030.xml&xsl=/tpl-i/p9f.xsl&base=/tpl-i/top-bottom.xsl.

21. January 2002.

22. This quotation is from an untitled article on a Turkish Foreign Ministry website, with the author listed as Hakan Kamel and the journal *Milli Gazete*, May 1997. However, this citation seems to be incorrect as this issue does not contain an article by the author cited.

23. However powerful the critiques in this quote, we need to point out that while it most likely reflects the feelings of the majority of the world's Muslims it's quite likely a minority view among Turkey's seventy million citizens, whose historical tradition of small-scale entrepreneurism and industry was severely hampered by seventy years of a state-led economic system, and because of this, believe the liberalization of their economy and the weakening of state control are vehicles for winning greater freedom and prosperity for themselves. That Islam is having to be re-imagined as part of this process doesn't seem to bother most Turkish Muslims, much to the consternation of the writer quoted above.

24. This equation is followed by the argument for connecting the phenomenon of third world debt to a transformation of Islam from a religion into a commodity, something that Muslims would sell to one another like so many head-scarves or rain coats.

25. Thomas Friedman, *The Lexus and the Olive Tree*, pp. 7–8.

26. Ibid., pp. xv–xvi.

27. Writing in the *Financial Times* in May 1997.

28. Political scientist Timothy Mitchell explains that the very notion of an objective and independently existing realm of human relations called the "economy" only came into being during the Great Depression with the need for massive state intervention into capitalist relations of production and exchange in order to keep the system from collapsing. To this day there is no agreement on just what the nature and boundaries of the economy are (see Timothy Mitchell, *Rule of Experts: Egypt, Techno-politics, Modernity*, Berkeley: UC Press, 2002).

29. Neil Fligstein, *The Architecture of Markets*. At the very least, as Yahya Sadowski argues, the end of the Cold War changed the world less than either optimists or the pessimists imagined (*The Myth of Global Chaos*).

30. Instead, as the UN's Economic Commission for Latin America and the Caribbean put it in its 2002 Report *Globalization and Development*, "trade protectionism was the norm or, more specifically, the rule prevailing in all nations" that could maintain economic autonomy during the last two centuries, while one of the main functions of European imperialism was to do away with just such autonomy so as to make it easier to export their products.

31. José Antonio Ocampo and Juan Martin, eds., *Globalization and Development*.

32. As the World Bank admits, "The growth in international financial markets throughout the 1990s was enormous. International lending in the new medium- and long-term bonds and bank loans reached US$1.2 trillion in 1997, up from US$0.5 trillion in 1988. World trade in goods and services, though growing significantly since the early 1970s, is now dwarfed by international financial transactions of more than five times the value of world trade" (Vinod Thomas et al., "The Quality of Growth: Useful Facts," World Bank, official website, http://www.worldbank.org/wbi/qualityofgrowth/facts.htm, current as of August 2004).

33. Eswar S. Prasad, Kenneth Rogoff, Shang-Jin Wei, and M. Ayan Kose, "Effects of Financial Globalization on Developing Countries: Some Empirical Evidence," 2003 International Monetary Fund, September 9, 2003, http://www.imf.org/external/pubs/nft/op/220/index.htm.

34. Neil Fligstein, "Is Globalization the Cause of the Crises of Welfare States?"; Paul Pierson, "Post-Industrial Pressures on the Mature Welfare State"; and Richard Breen and Daniel Verdier, "Globalisation and Inequality." For a detailed examination of why economic globalization is not occurring as billed, see Robert Gilpin, *Global Political Economy: Understanding the International Economic Order*, Princeton: Princeton University Press, 2001. For example, Fligstein argues that the worldwide organization of production by multinationals has its roots in the middle of the nineteenth century, while the argument that technology drives globalization can be stood on its head – that is, we could just as easily claim that it is the need by corporations to search for more efficient means of production that has driven technological innovation (with railroads and steam ships the first examples of this). On the basis of a detailed statistical analysis he argues that there is "no systematic evidence to show that informationalism has produced a qualitative change in the organization of firms that has caused multinationals to change in form … Globalization is more gradual over time, less revolutionary in its impacts on economies and firms, and more uneven in its economic effects on the organization of firms and societies than the thesis implies."

Because of these dynamics, Fligstein and Pierson both conclude that even if there is a temporal coincidence between processes of transformation in the developed countries and increasing pressures on welfare states around the world, there is little concrete evidence to say that globalization *caused* – rather than coincided with – problems such as deindustrialization, increasing inequality, or the dismantling of welfare states. Their arguments are based on the fact that while world trade grew significantly during the 1990s, it still constituted only 15 percent of world economic activity: trade "has hardly overwhelmed the world economy" in the global era, while the so-called boom in the information technology and telecommunications industries only accounts for 10 percent of world exports and 1.5 percent of world GDP. Moreover, from the 1950s through 1990s the percentage of world trade between developed countries remained within a narrow range between 60 and 70 percent. As we will see in the next chapter, the percentage of the Middle East in world trade actually decreased significantly.

35. Ignazio Visco, "Global Economic Integration: Opportunities and Challenges," comments on Obstfeld and Rogoff's "Perspectives on OECD Economic Integration: Implications for US Current Account Adjustment," Jackson Hole Symposium, August 24–26, 2000.

36. David Korten, *When Corporations Rule the World*.

37. However corrupt their leaders might have been (especially in the third world), they usually had to retain a measure of legitimacy by maintaining or increasing standards of living.

38. That is, one no longer based on the practices of standardization and traditional assembly-line mass production, or the economic philosophy of paying workers enough to be able to afford the products they're producing that together

comprised the "grand bargain" between labor and capital in the US during much of the twentieth century.

39. As the buyer of a new giant SUV explained when interviewed on ABC News about its gas-guzzling, environmentally harmful engine and dangerous size.

40. For a detailed discussion of these issues, see Mark LeVine, "Globalization in the Middle East and North Africa."

41. Pierre-Richard Agénor and Peter J. Montiel, *Development Macroeconomics*, Princeton: Princeton University Press, 1999, pp. 19–20.

42. For example, since the mid-1970s poverty levels have risen from about 23 to over 36 million people, even as the percentage of Americans living below the poverty line has remained between 12 and 16 percent. See US Census Bureau, 2003 statistics; Edward Wolff, *Top Heavy: The Increasing Inequality in Wealth in America and What Can Be Done About It*, New York: New Press, 2002; and Lisa A. Keister and Stephanie Moller, "Wealth Inequality in the United States," *Annual Review of Sociology*, 26 (2000), pp. 63–81.

43. Claude Grasland and Malika Madelin, "The Unequal Distribution of Population and Wealth in the World," *Population & Sociétés*, 368, May 2001, web version. For a comprehensive list of relevant statistics, see the UN's Statistical Division, at http://unstats. un.org/unsd/mi/mi_goals.asp and also http://unstats.un.org/unsd/mi/mi_ series_results.asp?rowID=580&fID= r15&cgID= and http://unstats.un.org/ unsd/default.htm.

44. And in fact, the only way the economist Jeffrey Williamson could show that globalization had a positive impact on the convergence of incomes between countries was specifically to limit the countries looked at to Western/Northern Europe and North America. If he included the third – that

is, colonized – world, he admitted, such convergence in incomes would "immediately evaporate" (Williamson, "Globalization, Convergence and History").

45. Copenhagen Declaration on Social Development, 1995 World Summit for Social Development, Copenhagen, April 19, 1995, UN Doc. # A/CONF.166/9, http://www.un.org/documents/ga/conf166/aconf 166–9.html.

46. See Desmond Cohen, "Poverty and HIV/AIDS in Southern Africa," UNESCO, The International Institute for Capacity Building in Africa, Issue Paper No. 27, undated.

47. Source: "New Study Shows Over One Billion Children Severely Deprived in the Developing World," http://www.bris.ac.uk/Publications/TPP/rp052pr.htm.

48. Judith Melby, Christian Aid spokeswoman, quoted in *The Independent* (UK), "Global Trade Keeps a Billion Children in Poverty, Says Unicef," 22 October, 2003. The report defines children who lack one basic human need – food, safe drinking water, sanitation, health, shelter or education – as living in severe deprivation, while those deprived of two of these are in absolute poverty.

49. Mark Weisbrot, Dean Baker, Egor Kraev, and Judy Chen, "The Scorecard on Globalization 1980–2000: Twenty Years of Diminished Progress," Center for Economic and Policy Research, July 11, 2001, http://www.cepr.net/globalization/scorecard_on_globalization.htm.

50. Ronald Labonte, "Health, Globalization and Sustainable Development," paper presented at WHO meeting, Oslo, November, 2001.

51. See J. M. Rao, "Openness, Poverty and Inequality," in *Background Papers Human Development Report 1999*, Volume 1. New York: UNDP, 1999.

52. And here it would be useful to remember that neoliberal structural adjustment policies were imposed on workers in the UK and US at the same time, and even before they were imposed on workers and the poor of the developing world.

53. Information from Gordon and Townsend, eds., *Breadline Europe*.

54. All told, fully one out of six children in Europe, North America, and Japan live in poverty – 47 million in all (source: US Census Bureau data for 2002).

55. ECLAC, "Globalization and Development Summary: Twenty-Ninth Session," Brasilia, Brazil, May, 2002, UN Doc. # LC/G.2157(SES.29/3), http://www.eclac.cl/publicaciones/Secretaria Ejecutiva/7/LCG2176SES2917/summary INGLES.pdf.

56. Source: Mike Morris, "Changing Patterns of Global Competition," using data from the 1999 *Human Development Report*; article at http://www.nu.ac.za/csds/Publications/App-article-Morris.pdf.

57. From government statistics we know that the income of the poorest 20 percent of households has declined steadily since the early 1970s, while that of the richest 20 percent has increased by 15 percent and that of the top 1 percent by more than 100 percent (Nancy Birdsall, "Life Is Unfair: Inequality in the World," *Foreign Policy*, Summer 1998).

58. Ibid., web version.

59. Ibid.

60. Branki Milanovic, "World Apart: International and World Inequality, 1950–2000," paper presented to the Brookings Institution Globalization and Inequality Group, June 17, 2002, http://www.brookings.edu/gs/research/projects/glig/TransBrook.pdf. The workshop home page, with other papers, is at http://www.brookings.edu/gs/research/projects/glig/ glig_hp.htm.

61. The seventy-three countries are home to over four-fifths of the world's population.

62. Additionally, as the WTO's own statistics inform us, during the late 1980s and early 1990s world inequality increased from an already high Gini coefficient (which uses a scale that goes from zero, meaning perfect equality, to one, meaning one person owns everything) of .64 to .66, where anything above 0.4 is considered high. World Trade Organization, *Statistics on Globalization*, pp. 35–36. Cf. Giovanni Andrea Cornia and Julius Court, "Inequality, Growth and Poverty in the Era of Liberalization and Globalization," UNU/WIDER, 2001, p. 23, http://www.wider.unu.edu/publications/pb4.pdf; Giovanni Andrea Cornia and Sampsa Kiiski, "Trends in Income Distribution in the Post-World War II Period: Evidence and Interpretation," United Nations University, WIDER, Discussion Paper No. 2001/89, pp. 1, 37.

63. George Monbiot, "Goodbye, Kind World," *The Guardian*, August 10, 2004.

64. Jeffrey Williamson and Matthew Higgins, "Assessing the Effects of Population Change, Economic Growth and Globalization on Income Inequality," East–West Center: Population and Health Studies, July 2003, No. 66, http://www.eastwestcenter.org/stored/pdfs/p&p066.pdf, p. 1.

65. What's most fascinating is that one of the biggest contributors to income inequality is age – the greater the percentage of workers in a 40–59 age group, the less the inequality. But the MENA has among the youngest workforces in the world, so it will take them decades to join the ranks of the prosperous middle-aged, middle-class countries (which is perhaps one reason that as in so many other studies we've looked at, one dealing with the age question discussed every region in the world but the MENA), ibid.

66. EP Resolution on Financing of Development Aid, April 18, 2002, http://europa-eu-un.org/article.asp?id=1327.

67. Nicholas Eberstadt, "Four Suprises in Global Demography," *Watch on the West: A Newsletter of FPRI's Center for the Study of America and the West*, Volume 5, July 2004, web version.

68. T.N. Srinivasan, "China and India: Growth and Poverty, 1980–2000," Working Paper No. 182, Stanford Center for International Development, September, 2003.

69. Chakravarthi Raghavan, "Juggling of Poverty Statistics," *Third World Network Features*, http://csf.colorado.edu/mail/homeless/2001/msg00289.html. Conceived of another way, you could have two Chinese women doing their own household work who would not be considered "economically active," but if they did the same work at each other's houses and paid each other $100 a month, they would have a per capita income of $1,200 a year and the national GDP would increase by $2,400.

70. The gains were preconditions because they legitimized the regime and made it easier to accept wrenching changes, they created a lot of "human capital," and they probably have a fair amount to do with the success of the birth control policy, female literacy being one of the strongest indicators of the prospects for lowering the birth rate. Most of these increases have leveled off since then.

71. Interview with Pomeranz, May 2004.

72. Sanjay G. Reddy and Thomas W. Pogge, "How *Not* to Count the Poor," unpublished but widely circulated paper, author's copy. World Bank global income poverty estimates "do not stand up to serious scrutiny" because they use an ill-defined poverty line, a misleading and inaccurate measure of Purchase Power Parity, and a false sense of

accuracy that together lead to "a large understatement of the extent of global income poverty and to an incorrect inference that it has declined." And they are not the only ones to contest the Bank's methods, as we can see at "Counting the Poor: Do the Poor Count?" http://www.brettonwoods project.org/article.shtml?cmd%5B126 %5D=x-126–16224. Further, Peter Nunnenkamp, Research Division head at the Kiel Institute of World Economics, contests the World Bank's claims that its aid goes to countries with "good" policies and institutions. He condemns the Bank for producing "strongly misleading" figures on "aid effectiveness" for the Monterrey summit. He concludes that "little has changed in targeting aid at poor countries with good policies. In the longer run, the World Bank, by playing statistical tricks, may have weakened, rather than strengthened the case for more aid" ("Shooting the Messenger of Good News: A Critical Look at the World Bank's Success Story of Effective Aid," Kiel: Kiel Institute for World Economics, Working Paper No. 1103, April, 2002).

73. Perhaps part of the problem with the Bank's prescriptions is that it relies on what it terms "empirical *simulations*," rather than on hard empirical evidence to make its arguments. Through its virtual theories it can construct virtual realities with virtual poverty levels and virtual jobs and virtual systems of accountability, and when reality doesn't match up the Bank (or the IMF) can just blame the countries for not behaving as the models say they should (World Bank, "Overview: Creating 100 Million Jobs for a Fast-Growing Work Force," http://lnweb18. worldbank.org/mna/mena.nsf/ Attachments/Employment Overview/ $File/Employment-overview.pdf, p. 7). Thomas W. Pogge and Sanjay G. Reddy, "Unknown: The Extent, Distribution,

and Trend of Global Income Poverty." For Reddy and Pogge's paper, the World Bank's reply, and their counter-critique, see http://blog.ctrlbreak.co.uk/archives/ 000035.html. For the World Bank's view see "Dramatic Decline In Global Poverty, But Progress Uneven," The World Bank http://www.worldrevo-lution.org/article/1306, and especially http://web.worldbank.org/WEBSITE/ EXTERNAL/NEWS/0,,content MDK: 20194973~menuPK: 34463~pagePK: 64003015~piPK: 64003012~theSitePK: 4607,00.html, where there are several tables presenting the disputed World Bank data.

74. Pogge and Reddy, "Unknown: The Extent, Distribution, and Trend of Global Poverty," p. 9. They conclude that "it is very likely that the Bank, were it to use PPPs more closely related to the needs of the poor, would translate its $1/day standard into substantially higher national poverty lines for most poor countries," and double the amount of money it takes to feed a family of four in the US as well.

75. Martin Ravallion, "The Debate on Globalization, Poverty and Inequality: Why Measurement Matters," http://poverty.worldbank. org/files/13871_Why_measurement_m atters.pdf. My italics. His argument is supported by the fact that the latest poverty data from the Chinese Government reveals poverty to be increasing, Reuters News Service, "Abject Poverty in China Rises After a Long Decline," *Taipei Times*, July 20, 2004, p. 1. It should also be pointed out that in China differences in geography or location account for as much as 50 percent of the difference in poverty levels in the country, as opposed to a figure of about 3 percent in the United States. What is also not accounted for in most discussions of China is the fact that if everyone in a region is fairly poor, they don't individually feel as poor compared to a situation when there are

people with greatly divergent incomes living in closer proximity to each other. Now, however, with the spread of mass media and satellite television, poor people in rural China know that other Chinese are much better off than they are – a crucial impact of globalization – where a century ago they wouldn't know this firsthand.

A final problem with the way growth is discussed vis-à-vis China is that villages in prosperous parts of the country often forbid their factories to hire migrants from other regions until all local people have jobs – this perpetuates regional inequality but at the same time is done out of locally based egalitarianism. Such practices are linked to the fact that a huge percentage of local industry is either owned by local government or leased from them. So the idea of massive privatization in China is just plain wrong, as even if managers are hired private contractors, village governments still act as boards of directors and impose various conditions that range from corruption – kickbacks and crony hiring – to socially responsible efforts to limit the profits and/or incomes of managers to twenty times the earnings of the worker. Ultimately, if China is no longer socialist, it is clearly not a classical capitalist society either.

76. Pogge and Reddy, "Unknown," p. 9.

77. That is, free trade could only be achieved if massive subsidies to European and American farmers as well as defense companies were ended, and a radical change in American energy policies and consumption patterns occurred.

78. Thomas Friedman, "Think Global, Act Local," New York *Times*, June 6, 2004 Op/Ed page, where he cites a *Wall Street Journal* article from June 3, 2004 arguing the same thing.

79. In the June 2004 G-8 meeting in Georgia the Government prohibited all public gatherings.

80. But here again we need to point out that we're not talking about focusing more on culture as propaganda – such as the American-run Arab language Radio Sawa' or al-Hurra TV – to convince people that the United States Government is something that it's not (like interested in peace and democracy), but rather establishing the dialogues and coalitions to build peace, democracy, and development from the ground up by using culture to transform politics and the economy.

81. But the reality that the globalization debate is steeped as much in ideology as in hard facts demonstrates the centrality of culture to it. This is because an ideology arises precisely in the enmeshing of power relations with cultural symbols in order to convince people of, and get them to act based on, policies or doctrines that aren't supported by factual evidence.

82. Raymond Williams, *Keywords*.

83. Western, Latin American, Confucian, Japanese, Islamic, Hindu and Slavic-Orthodox (Huntington, *Clash of Civilizations*, pp. 22, 26; an online version of this article is available at http://www.alamut.com/subj/economics/misc/clash.html).

84. See Williams, *Keywords*.

85. Mahmood Mamdani, *Good Muslim, Bad Muslim*, pp. 22–5.

86. For an in-depth exploration of the role of Islam and the surrounding Muslim world in the construction of modern European identities, see Michael Frassetto and David R. Blanks, eds., *Western Views of Islam in Medieval and Early Modern Europe*.

87. The best German version can be found in *Johann Gottfried Herder Werke*, in B. Suphan et al., eds., Berlin: n.p., 1887. English excerpts can be found in F. M. Barnard, *J. G. Herder on Social and Political Culture*, London: Cambridge University Press, 1969.

88. Most importantly, culture always includes both material production – the

things that culture produces (art, architecture, books, roads) – and the symbolic systems by which people communicate. These two senses, needless to say, link the economic and the more purely symbolic/cultural inextricably together.

89. Cf. Michael Denning, *Culture in the Age of Three Worlds*, p. 92.

90. *The Economist*, special issue on globalization, September 23, 2000.

91. This should not suggest, as the famous Frankfurt School philosophers Adorno and Horkheimer assumed, that "the whole world is made to pass through the filter of the culture industry," since there is significant resistance to the industrialization of culture among culture creators and producers, even with the so-called "culture industries."

92. Here we can think of the adoption of certain fashion, musical, artistic, architectural, and other styles and conventions across cultures in ways that don't destroy the existing, indigenous versions of such cultural products. Similar to the problems accounting for economic globalization, the problem here is that too often we assume cultural penetration without searching for real evidence of it, or assume that the distribution of similar cultural products around the world signifies the Americanization or Cocacolonization of the world, when in reality it points only to the power of some corporations to command large markets and brand loyalty. As I explain in Chapter Four with regard to the amount of Coke consumed in India vis-à-vis Brazil, the sheer presence of American goods in a country is not in itself a token of converging toward capitalist monoculture or American-dominated globalization, while cultural transmission always travels in several directions and in a way that gives all participants at least some agency to determine the course.

93. Like the Ladakhi people of "Little Tibet" in northern India, who in the last few decades have gone from a relatively self-sufficient people with a wonderfully rich and successful culture, to a society embarrassed by their seeming inadequacies and desperate to modernize.

94. Ulf Hannerz, "Cosmopolitans and Locals in World Culture."

95. For a fascinating discussion of this issue see Gilles Kepel, *Allah in the West* and Michael Eric Dyson, *Between God and Gangsta Rap*.

96. Barber, *Jihad vs. McWorld*, p. 97.

97. Along with the tendency toward either market or religious fanaticism, however, is an even more dangerous long-term change, in which the emancipatory potential of modernity – however much it has been tied to and frustrated by its potential for violence and conquest – is rapidly fading away and more and more people are forced to "meekly acquiesce" to the commodification of everything (Zygmunt Bauman, *Liquid Modernity*) including, if we can recall the quote by Hakan Kamel earlier in the chapter, their most sacred religious beliefs and identities.

98. These terms are used by scholars such as John Tomlinson, David Harvey, and Anthony Giddens.

99. Malcom Waters, *Globalization*. For a critique of this argument, see Tomlinson, *Globalization and Culture*, pp. 23–4.

100. Tomlinson, *Globalization and Culture*, p. 104.

101. UNESCO, *The Futures of Cultures*, p. 10; this is the most relevant for our purposes, and has been the motivating force for the global peace and justice movement's annual gatherings at the world and European Social forums as much as for al-Qa'eda (Denis Goulet, "Inequalities in the Light of Globalization," Krok Institute Occasional Paper No. 22: OP: 2, 2002, p. 3). That is, culture becomes a way of

resisting modern institutions and the more destructive forces of the dominant society.

102. UNESCO, *Our Creative Diversity*, pp. 13, 16, 22, http://firewall. unesco.org/culture/development/wccd /summary/html_eng/index_en.htm, which argues that as a collective freedom, cultural freedom "guarantees freedom" for the whole society."

103. Comment on draft of this chapter, June 2004.

Chapter 4

1. For an example of articles that describe terrorism in this way, see Jonathan Stevenson, "The Two Terrorisms," New York *Times*, Op/Ed, December 2, 2003.

2. For an important article on the impact of this militarization, see Kevin Baker, "We're in the Army Now." For a more detailed analysis, see Johnson, *The Sorrows of Empire*; for a good example of the dynamics of the process, see "The Boeing Corporation and Military-Industrial Corruption," http://www. corporateswine.net/boeing.html.

3. For a good discussion of the ideology underlying this process vis-à-vis the construction of Islam as the new enemy, see Emran Qureshi and Michael A. Sells, eds., *The New Crusades*.

4. Paul Masson, "Globalization: Facts and Figures."

5. We could also discuss the tone of this passage, especially its reference to the IMF's supposed focus on poverty, as it bears little resemblance either to the Fund's founding mission or to its current ideological leaning (as Joseph Stiglitz makes clear in his *Globalization and its Discontents*).

6. For a detailed discussion of how the global financial institutions have pursued this policy, see Stiglitz, *Globalization and its Discontents*.

7. Hurrel and Woods, eds., *Inequality, Globalization, and World Politics*.

8. These include Paul Kingsnorth's *One No, Many Yeses: A Journey to the Heart of the Global Resistance Movement*, London: Free Press, 2003, or Andrew Stern in Notes from Nowhere, eds., *We Are Everywhere: The Irresistible Rise of Global Anticapitalism*.

9. See http://www.worldbank.org/ mdf/mdf4/papers/johntable.pdf for the tables from which this data is cited. These tables are clearly adapted from several studies by the World Bank up to the year 2000.

10. Ishac Diwan and Lyn Squire, "Economic Development and Cooperation in the Middle East and North Africa," World Bank Discussion Paper Series, MENA Division, No. 9, November 1993, http://lnweb18.world bank.org/mna/mena.nsf/Attachments/ WP+3/$File/12738.pdf, p. 37.

11. World Bank, "Overview: Creating 100 Million Jobs for a Fast-Growing Work Force," p. 5.

12. If the World Bank and the *AHDR* argue that the region is not sufficiently integrated into the world economy, let alone world community, they don't engage in any discussion of how Arab states are to secure the massive amounts of money needed to pay for all of the programs and policies it advocates that would lead to greater integration.

13. World Bank, "Overview," p. 2.

14. Even after oil prices – and because of this, growth – dropped significantly, governments of the region collectively spent significantly on social services, especially on health and education, and have invested heavily in modernizing infrastructure. Thanks to Chris Toensing of *Middle East Report* for his comments as to the uniqueness of the region's economic and political histories vis-à-vis discussions of globalization.

15. A similar assessment would seem to come from another 2003 World Bank report, this one on governance in

the MENA, in which the Bank assessed the efforts of regional governments to address core needs of their peoples (World Bank, "Overview," p. 2).

16. Statement by Dr. Salaam Fayyad, Minister of Finance, Palestinian National Authority, Fundraising dinner for Children of Palestine, London, October 4, 2003. And the continued low level of non-oil exports is also a serious problem, as "Although, at first glance, the region's export performance may not look that bad, a closer look reveals otherwise. With about 3.3 percent of the world's GDP, MENA accounts for 2.8 percent of world exports. However, over the period 1995–1999, non-oil Arab countries accounted for only 0.37 percent of world exports, compared to about 18 percent for Asia and 5 percent for Latin America. Indeed, at about US$ 130 per capita, MENA's non-oil exports are lower than in any other region around the world."

17. Indeed, in the wake of Seattle and then September 11, the World Bank has been at pains to emphasize that "development is ultimately about human development." (Human development is defined here as "the quality of material living, wider choices and opportunities for people to realize their potential, the guarantee of those intangible qualities that characterize all more-developed societies: equality of treatment, freedom to choose, greater voice, and opportunities to participate in the process by which they are governed" [World Bank, "Overview of governance in the MENA, Inclusiveness and Accountability," http://lnweb18.worldbank.org/MNA/mena.nsf/Attachments/govreport-eng/$File/GOVoverview-eng.pdf].) For the Bank human development is suffering in the region precisely because of the problems of governance in MENA countries. "Compared with countries that have similar incomes and characteristics – the main

competitors in the global marketplace – the MENA region ranks at the bottom on the index of overall governance quality" (ibid., p. 6).

18. A main proponent of this view is the World Bank report, *Globalization, Growth, and Poverty*. Cf. UNESCO, *The Futures of Cultures*, p. 10. A similar view of the "accelerated integration of the world economy" is found in UNRISD's *States of Disarray*, pp. 7, 26. Patricia Alonso-Gamo, Annalisa Fedelino, Sebastian Paris Horvitz, "Globalization and Growth Prospects in Arab Countries," IMF Working Paper WP/97/125, 1997, International Monetary Fund, p. 5; Ali Al-Shamali and John Denton, *Arab Business: The Globalization Imperative*, Kuwait: Arab Research Center, 2000.

19. Page and van Gelder, "Globalization, Growth, and Poverty Reduction in the Middle East and North Africa," p. 7.

20. See http://www.undp.org/rbas/AHDR/. Thus the MENA's export volumes are at 3.9 percent, well below the worldwide average annual growth rate of 5.9 percent, with a similar figure for imports. And from the perspective of the Washington Consensus, if globalization is naturally spreading throughout the world, then its absence in the MENA must be because the region suffers from low levels of both growth and trade integration, according to Mustapha Nabli, regional chief economist and Director of the Social and Economist Development Group in the World Bank MENA region (Mustapha Nabli, remarks at "The Challenges of Globalization in the Arab World" conference, cosponsored by the Middle East Institute and the World Bank, May 3, 2000, www.mideasti.org/html/wb050300-b.html). Or as another report described it, "MENA real GDP per capita growth has not kept pace with other developing countries ..." (IMF Survey, Supplement, No. 32, 2003, pp. 1,

4–6; http://www.imf.org/External/Pubs/ FT/SURVEY/2003/091503.pdf).

According to the World Bank, the "MENA remains one of the least integrated regions, having failed to take advantage of the expansion in world trade and foreign direct investment in the past two decades." "In the MENA, despite large hydrocarbon exports, trade declined from about 100 percent of GDP in the mid-1970s to 60 percent in the mid-1980s and has stagnated since" (World Bank, "Overview," p. 9). Similarly, the 2002 *Arab Human Development Report* informs us that growth in per capita income was the lowest in the world except for sub-Saharan Africa, at a measly 0.5 percent annually. Labor productivity and real wages have also been low and declining, and "it is evident that in both quantitative and qualitative terms, Arab countries have not developed as quickly or as fully as other comparable regions. From a human development perspective, the state of human development in the Arab world is a cause for concern."

Thus the report equates globalization with "integration," which can be expected to reduce poverty "because more integrated economies tend to grow faster and this growth is usually widely diffused," although it does admit that "within countries, globalization has not, on average, affected inequality ..." (see World Bank, *Globalization, Growth and Poverty*, pp. 1–2; World Bank, "Benefiting from Globalization," Mediterranean Development Forum II, Marrakech, Morocco, September 3–6, 1998, www.worldbank.org/mdf/mdf2/ global. htm).

21. He also admitted that in hindsight, by not explaining their rationale for an exclusively internal focus, they wound up playing into the hands of what I call the Axis of Arrogance and Ignorance.

22. World Trade Association Annual Report, 1995, tables III.1 and III.2,

reprinted in Fligstein, "Is Globalization the Cause of the Crises of Welfare States?," p. 15, and 2003, tables III.1 and III.2, online version. Also see Dani Rodrik, "Feasible Globalizations," Harvard University, May 2002, pp. 15, 17, www.ksghome.harvard.edu/~. rodrik.academic.ksg/feasible.pdf).

23. World Bank, *Globalization, Growth and Poverty*, p. x.

24. See http://www.dnb.com/UK/ communities/intlbusiness/resource_ center/middle_east/sep_2002.asp.

25. Here I am considering the Israeli–Palestinian conflict as an internal conflict, not an external one.

26. World Bank, "Overview," p. 11.

27. And as for public accountability, any government that was accountable to its public would have a radically different relationship with the United States Government than do the current regimes in Egypt, Turkey, Jordan, Morocco, Pakistan or many other MENA nations.

28. Eswar S. Prasad, Kenneth Rogoff, Shang-Jin Wei, and M. Ayan Kose, "Effects of Financial Globalization on Developing Countries: Some Empirical Evidence," Washington, D.C.: IMF, September 9, 2003, http://www.imf.org/external/ pubs/nft/op/ 220/index.htm.

29. Such policies are understood to have been crucial to the East Asian miracle (Dani Rodrik and Francisco Rodriquez, "Trade Policy and Economic Growth: A Skeptic's Guide to the Cross-National Evidence," Harvard University, May 2000, http://www.ksg.harvard.edu/ rodrik/tp1.pdf; K.S. Jomo, "Growth After the Asian Crisis: What Remains of the East Asian Model?" UN and Center for International Development, Harvard University, *G-24 Discussion Paper Series*, No. 10, March 2001, p. 43, http:// www.ksghome.harvard.edu/~.drodrik. academic.ksg/g24-jomo.pdf). Also see John Page, "Costs and Benefits of the European-Mediterranean Agreements,"

World Bank, Mediterranean Development Forum I: Towards Competitive and Caring Societies in the Middle East and North Africa, Marrakech, Morocco, May 12–17, 1997, http://www.worldbank.org/mdf/mdf1/ costs. htm; M. Shafik Gabr, "Globalization of the Arab Middle East and Maghreb Economies," paper presented at the Emerging Economies of the Arab World Euromoney Conference, September 15–17, 1998, p. 3, http:// www.artoc.com.eg/Document/artglob. doc; Ravi Kanbur, "Conceptual Challenges in Poverty and Inequality: One Development Economist's Perspective," Cornell University, April 2002, http://www.people.cornell.edu/ pages/sk145).

30. World Bank, "Sharp Slowdown in World GDP Growth," slide 5, http://www.worldbank.org/prospects/ gdf2001/slides/ppt/main_present.html. Also See World Trade Organization, *Statistics on Globalization.*

31. This is because growth-oriented policies push the countries of the MENA to "restructure [their] priorities with the objective of reducing overall expenditures ... and review the role of the public sector in the economy ... [increase] flexibility of the labor market ... and the level and quality of labor skills" (Mustapha Nabli, "The Fiscal Dimension of the European-Mediterranean Challenge"). To cite just one example here, the ability to provide increasing levels of health care, education, and training is hampered when states are being forced to reduce revenues through reduced tariffs, which in the MENA account for as much as 40–45 percent of state revenue (George Abed, "The European Union Agreement and Tax Reform in the Middle East and Mediterranean Region," World Bank, Mediterranean Development Forum I: Towards Competitive and Caring Societies in the Middle East and North Africa, Marrakech, Morocco, May

12–17, 1997, http://www.worldbank. org/mdf/ mdf1/tax.htm).

32. "International experience shows that rapid economic expansion remains the most powerful instrument for reducing poverty, especially in a region such as MENA where growth has an above-average impact on reducing the number of poor due to, *inter alia,* the lower the depth of poverty as measured by the poverty gap index" (Willem van Eeghen and Kouassi Soman, "Poverty in the Middle East and North Africa," World Bank, Mediterranean Development Forum I: Towards Competitive and Caring Societies in the Middle East and North Africa, Marrakech, Morocco, May 12–17, 1997, http://www.worldbank. org/wbi/mdf/mdf1/mena poor.htm).

33. The economists were Mattias Lundberg and Lyn Squire. The study, titled "The Simultaneous Evolution of Growth and Inequality," argues that: that is, if one actually looks simultaneously at growth and inequality in a non-mechanistic manner the data "strongly indicate" that more equitable distribution drives down growth, while "openness" to growth – the integration/ globalization and liberalization the World Bank report calls for – can increase poverty and inequality in income distribution to the point that "the negative effects outweigh the positive." Most importantly, "The costs of adjusting to greater openness are borne exclusively by the poor, regardless of how long the adjustment takes ... The poor are far more vulnerable to shifts in relative international prices, and this vulnerability is magnified by the country's openness to trade" (Mattias Lundberg and Lyn Squire, "The Simultaneous Evolution of Growth and Inequality," pp. 18–19, 26 29–31, http:// www.worldbank.org/research/growth/ pdfiles/squire.pdf/). The authors further add that "more equitable land distribution increases equality at the cost of

slower growth ... faster growth among the poor may indeed be obtained at the expense of slower growth among the rich." Ultimately, in fact, there is "no evidence ... of mutually beneficial policies ... Growth varies substantially from period to period, while inequality is much more persistent ... At least in the short run, globalization appears to increase poverty and inequality" (ibid., pp. 29–31).

34. Cf. John Madeley, "World Bank Edits Out Penalty on the Poor," *The Observer*, December 3, 2000, http://www.observer.co.uk/business/ story/0,6903,405969,00.html. And another report sponsored by the World Bank, "Globalization, Growth, and Poverty Reduction in the Middle East and North Africa, 1970–1999," similarly highlights the relatively good statistics on poverty, and admits that import-substitution development – placing high tariffs on certain imports in order to give local companies the time to become competitive at manufacturing them – which is completely at odds with Washington Consensus – was an important factor in keeping the statistics low. Page and van Gelder, "Globalization, Growth, and Poverty Reduction in the Middle East and North Africa, 1970–1999," p. 1, http://www. worldbank.org/mdf/mdf4/papers/page-vangelder.pdf. Also see World Bank, *World Development Report 2000/2001*, pp. 21, 23, Table 1.1, http://www.world bank.org/poverty/wdrpoverty/, Dani Rodrik, "Globalization, Social Conflict and Economic Growth," p. 2, http:// www.ksg.harvard.edu/rodrik/global. pdf). Thus the MENA grew at 2.3 percent during the 1960–73 period, compared with 1.3 percent for East Asia.

35. As argued by Samer Shehata of Georgetown University (personal communication, July 2004).

36. Ultimately, even if differences on the relationship between trade, growth, and poverty can be understood in terms of differences in perspective and framework, with the two main perspectives being one that tends to view the consequences of economic policy in much more aggregative terms than the latter, which is preoccupied with both shorter and longer time horizons (Ravi Kanbur, "Economic Policy, Distribution and Poverty: The Nature of the Disagreements," paper presented at the Swedish Parliamentary Commission on Global Development, September 22, 2000, http://www. people.cornell.edu/pages/sk145). Page and van Gelder, "Globalization, Growth, and Poverty Reduction in the Middle East and North Africa," p. 5. In fact it is only one of two regions, the other being South Asia, that recorded *any* reduction in income inequality over time. See Table 1 on p. 24 for a worldwide comparison of poverty figures from 1987 through 1998.

37. Page and van Gelder, "Globalization, Growth, and Poverty Reduction in the Middle East and North Africa, 1970–1999," p. 1, http://www.worldbank.org/mdf/mdf4/ papers/page-vangelder.pdf. Cf. ibid., p. 8.

38. Especially as remittances earned and sent home by workers laboring abroad, along with oil and geostrategic "rents," continue to stagnate or even decline. Thus Page and van Gelder argue that "where poverty has increased ... the poverty dynamics have been primarily driven by macroeconomic adjustments and changes in migration and remittances ..." (ibid., p. 24; cf. Ishac Diwan, "Global Changes and What they Mean for the Development Strategies of the Middle East and North Africa," World Bank, Mediterranean Development Forum I: Towards Competitive and Caring Societies in the Middle East and North Africa, Marrakech, Morocco, May 12–17, 1997, http://www.worldbank.org/mdf/mdf1/ changes.htm).

39. As a World Bank report explains, "Starting in the late 1980s several countries in the region – Morocco, Tunisia, and soon after, Jordan, embarked on far-reaching programs of macroeconomic stabilization and policy reform. By the 1990s nearly all of the non-GCC countries of the region followed suit, as did several of the Gulf countries ... The overall change in policy throughout the region would seem to be a significant step forward in creating an environment in which the private sector could emerge and become an engine for higher and sustainable growth" (Dasgupta et al., "Reform and Elusive Growth," p. 16).

40. The larger rubric of the reform process is "macroeconomic prudence, outward orientation and domestic liberalization." For the Bank, these indicators include measures of fiscal discipline, public expenditure quality, tax reform, interest rate liberalization, competitive real exchange rate, freer trade, fostering FDI, privatization, deregulation, and property rights.

41. For a detailed analysis of the effects of Walmart on workers' wages and working conditions in the US and around the world, see the series of articles on Walmart in the *LA Times* in November 2003. Also see the series on Chinese labor practices in the New York *Times* in December 2003, http://www.nytimes.com/pages/world/worldspecial4/.

42. Should Middle Eastern countries lower tariffs on imported products (as recommended by the report) when doing so will wipe out many domestic industries? Can we blame the region for "bearing the rear guard" in privatization among developing regions? And what if the liberalization/privatization of the economy – which means privatizing formerly public services such as health care, water, and the like – leads to a worsening of the living conditions for millions of inhabitants of a country, which is in fact what's happening almost everywhere liberalization is occurring?

43. Dasgupta et al., "Reform and Elusive Growth," p. 2.

44. Ibid., p. 12.

45. World Bank, MENA division, "Overview," undated assessment on the Bank's MENA website, http://lnweb18.worldbank.org/mna/mena.nsf/Attachments/Trade+Report/$File/trade-overview. pdf, p. 5. What's most interesting here is that one of the reasons the international financial community "recommends" liberal growth strategies and reform programs to these countries is that they are relatively "resource-poor," and thus can't rely on oil sales to prop up an otherwise inefficient economy.

46. As Joseph Stiglitz points out over and over again in his *Globalization and its Discontents*.

47. Thanks to *Middle East Report* editor Chris Toensing for this insight (personal communication, June 2004).

48. See http://www.worldbank.org/mdf/mdf4/papers/johntable.pdf for the tables from which this data is cited. These tables are clearly adapted from several studies by the Bank up to the year 2000.

49. The issue of workers' remittances cannot be an important factor lowering growth or increasing poverty in each of the countries because the statistics provided in the survey show that it increased for all of them.

50. Source: Mennonite Central Committee (MCC), "Facts About Global Poverty," http://www.mcc.org/us/globalization/GEJ%20Facts.pdf; OECD numbers: http://www.oecd.org/dataoecd/48/46/1960936.pdf.

51. Source: EU statistics on trade: http://trade-info.cec.eu.int/doclib/docs/2003/july/tradoc_113483.pdf.

52. For a discussion of the role of longer working hours on increased productivity, see Steven Roach, "The Productivity Paradox," New York *Times*, November 30, 2003, Op/Ed.

53. Clement M. Henry and Robert Springborg, *Globalization and the*

Politics of Development in the Middle East, see in particular pp. 15, 20, 41, and 66. They conclude that "the rate of economic growth and integration into the world capitalist economy depends primarily upon any given country's political capacities [most importantly involving the ability to tax adequately the population]. In the MENA region such capacities are heavily indebted to the country's colonial legacy, yet they remain the main determinants of the structural power of capital in these states" (p. 63).

54. Source for both tables: World Bank, "Countries at a Glance" Series, 2003 data, UNDP, Human Development Report, 2003, statistical indicators, http://www.undp.org/hdr2003/indicator/pdf/hdr03_indicators.pdf.

55. From 12 percent in Jordan to 50 percent in Egypt, with most countries in the teens or twenties (UNDP, Human Development Report, 2003, statistical indicators, http://www.undp.org/hdr2003/indicator/pdf/hdr03_indicators.pdf). The average HDI for Arab states is .622, for Latin America and the Caribbean is .777, and for the world the average is .722.

56. Dina Ezzat, "Worlds Apart," *Al-Ahram*, June 27, 2002, citing ILO ESCWA statistics. For an extensive country by country review, see the 2002 and 2003 *Arab Human Development Reports*, and the UNDP statistics yearbooks.

57. World Bank, 2003 Annual Report for MENA Region, http://www.worldbank.org/annualreport/2003/middle_east.html.

58. The three biggest problems with Middle Eastern governments are a lack of "inclusiveness," "accountability," and "transparency" (World Bank, "Improved Public Governance in Middle East Could Boost Economic Growth by One Percentage Point a Year," Report released in Dubai, September 8, 2003, http://web.worldbank.org/WBSITE/EXTERNAL/NEWS/0,,

content MDK: 20127106~menuPK: 34464~pagePK: 64003015~piPK: 64003012~theSitePK: 4607,00,html).

59. Ibid. Italics in the original.

60. World Bank, MENA division, "Overview," undated assessment on Bank's MENA website, http://lnweb18.worldbank.org/mna/mena.nsf/Attachments/Trade+Report/$File/trade-overview.pdf, p. 1.

61. Ibid., p. 2.

62. And so when the Bank argues that private investment will "improve female participation in labor markets as has been the case elsewhere around the world" (ibid., p. 4) do they really want Arab/Muslim women to work in the same circumstances as their sisters in Indonesia, China or El Salvador? Is that the best the world and its bank can do? Indeed, if we look at how workers have fared over the last two decades in terms of their wages, the evidence shows that real wages in the manufacturing sector declined throughout the region, particularly in Algeria, Egypt, and Jordan, especially in the 1990s (Edward Gardner, "Creating Employment in the Middle East and North Africa," IMF Policy Paper, 2003, http://www.imf.org/external/pubs/ft/med/2003/eng/gardner/). More broadly, wages have stagnated or declined since the mid-1980s while unemployment has increased, making it increasingly difficult even for people with jobs to continue to raise living standards for their families. One of the only things stopping a further slide is, not surprisingly, the "continued strength of government job creation," which of course is an anathema to the policy-makers at the IMF. As important – and absolutely crucial for any discussion of work in the MENA region – is that the public sector, which is the biggest employer, has also been the main vehicle for ensuring greater and more equal participation of women in the labor force. In contrast, "In the

private sector … women have faced significant disadvantages, often working in jobs with low wages and little potential for growth" (World Bank, "Overview: Gender and Development in the Middle East and North Africa: Women and the Public Sphere," 2003, http://lnweb18.world bank.org/mna/mena.nsf/Attachments/ Gender Report-overview/$File/ GENDER-REPORToverview.pdf).

63. Nehemia Strasler, "Growth Versus Poverty," *Ha'aretz*, December 4, 2003, http://www.haaretz.com/hasen/ spages/368182.html. Also see *Ha'aretz*, December 28, 2004.

64. The then US-owned company, formed in 1944 and bought out by the Saudis from Standard Oil/Exxon in 1980.

65. CRS Issue Brief for Congress, 1/25/02, http://fpc.state.gov/documents/ organization/7966.pdf. The UK was actually a bigger supplier of weapons than the US thanks to Israeli pressure on various US administrations not to sell the Kingdom too many advanced US systems (source: Anthony Cordesman, "Saudi Arabia Enters the 21st Century: The Military Dimension," p. 33, http:// www.csis.org/burke/saudi21/SaudiMil Book_03.pdf).

66. See Cordesman, ibid., p. 7.

67. See Anthony Cordesman, "Stability and Instability in the Gulf," Washington: CSIS, 1999, tables on pp. 22 and 51.

68. The UK spent 2.5 percent; France, 2.5 percent; Hungary, 1.8 percent; the Czech Republic, 2.0 percent; the "miraculous" Irish economy, 0.7 percent; Korea, 2.8 percent; even India and Pakistan only spent 2.5 percent and 4.5 percent respectively.

69. See "Continuing Storm: The US Role in the Middle East," in *Foreign Policy in Focus*, http://www.foreignpolicy-infocus.org/papers/mideast/democracy. html#Figure%208.

70. It should be pointed out that Saudi military expenditures decreased in the mid-1990s because of the fall in oil revenues, but picked up and stabilized by the latter half of the decade at between 13 and 15 percent of per capita GDP and between US$17 and 20 billion per year (see Anthony Cordesman, "Saudi Arabia: The Broader Factors Driving the Need for Foreign Investment and Economic Diversity," Center for Strategic and International Studies paper, April 2002, http://www.csis.org/burke/saudi21/ saudi_broaderneed.pdf).

71. As Chalmers Johnson points out, the top thirty-five private military companies are among the most profitable businesses in the country today – that is, not the biggest or having the highest revenue, but the most profitable to their managers and, usually, shareholders (*Sorrows of Empire*, p. 140).

72. Nitzan and Bichler, *The Global Political Economy of Israel*, pp. 201–2.

73. Ibid., p. 202.

74. See their discussion of "breadth" versus "depth" capitalist accumulation in Chapter Two of their book. As important, Nitzan and Bichler confirm the argument, first made by John Hobson in his classic 1902 study of imperialism, that what's crucial for the success of imperialism is not that it bring wide benefits to the home society as a whole, or even to the majority of the capitalist class; rather it needs only to be very profitable for particular sectors within the dominant class – precisely those who control the state. Well, who's running Washington these days, the boys (and one lady) from the military, oil, and heavy engineering companies?

75. John Perkins, *Confessions of an Economic Hit Man*, San Francisco: Berrett-Koehler Publishers, 2004, front matter.

Chapter 5

1. Ronald Inglehart, Pippa Norris, and Christian Welzel, "Gender Equality and

Democracy," in Inglehart, ed., *Human Values and Social Change*, pp. 91–115, p. 110.

2. Middle Eastern Christians are another matter, because since the imperial era they have been much closer to European political ideologies and also because their economic position is usually that of business people, merchants or others in the professional classes, which means they would benefit disproportionately from neoliberal reforms. For Israel, we can see this in the vehement denunciations of secular culture, equality for women in prayer, and even Shas spiritual leader Rabbi Ovadaiah Yosef's remarks that he "has more in common with the Ayatollah Khomeini than with the dominant Israeli culture." For more on this issue, see the work of Shlomo Swirsky, Sami Shalom Chetrit, Ilan Peled, Sara Helman, and a conference I organized titled "Socio-Religious Movements and the Transformation of Political Community: Israel, Palestine and Beyond," at http://www.humanities. edu/history/levineconference, currently being organized into an edited volume by Armando Salvatore and myself.

3. Mansoor Moaddel and Taqhi Azadarmaki, "The Worldviews of Islamic Publics: The Cases of Egypt, Iran and Jordan," in Inglehart, ed., *Human Values and Social Change*, pp. 69–89.

4. Before neoliberals celebrate this view as proving their point about the laudable ends of their project, it should be pointed out that the kind and scope of liberalization imagined by most Iranians or Turks is nothing like the laissez-faire Hobbesian world imagined by its American backers.

5. For a discussion of the impact of soap operas in Egypt, see Lila Abu-Lughod, *Dramas of Nationhood: The Politics of Television in Egypt*, Chicago: University of Chicago Press, 2004.

6. Quoted in Lawrence Wright, "The Kingdom of Silence," p. 63.

7. As my old guitar teachers, the late great Ted Dunbar and *Tonight Show* bandleader Kevin Eubanks, used to warn me as a student at Mason Gross Jazz Conservatory, "When you hit that bandstand you better be ready; 'cause if you're not they'll throw you right off." In the much-needed global jam session, everyone needs to know the head (the main melody of the song) and leave their fears and prejudices off the stage. We can't afford to tolerate anything less.

8. George al-Rasi, interview in *al-Nahar*, December 13, 1999, p. 14. In fact, the New World Order spreads its hegemony by spreading its ideology (Asamah Abdul-Rahman, ed., *Tanmiyyah al-Takhalaf wa-idarah al-Tanmiyyah*, p. 118; Lamchichi, *Islam-Occident*, Ch. 1). Abbas criticizes Huntington because Islam is the only civilization that is defined by a religion, as well as because he defines civilization in terms of "cultural identity" which allows him to claim that there is no shared community between the West and Islamic culture. Abbas believes that such a claim is the whole point of Huntington's definition (Qassem Khadir Abbas, *Masdaqiyyah al-Nitham Dawli al-Jadid*, pp. 101–4).

9. Ibid., pp. 30, 73.

10. Also described as "disharmony" (*tafawutt*) (Muhammad 'Abed al-Jabari, *Qadaya fi al-fikr al-mu'asir*, pp. 139–40). Moreover, an inhuman globalization that separates and segments humanity (*yafraduha*) is a major reason why Arabs have yet to achieve the potential of national independence (interview with Farida al-Niqash, *al-Nahar*, December 4, 1999, p. 11); cf. Homi Bhabha, *The Location of Culture*, p. 34.

11. Pippa Norris and Ronald Inglehart, "Islamic Culture and Democracy: Testing the 'Clash of Civilizations' Thesis," in Inglehart, ed., *Human Values and Social Change*, pp. 5–34, pp. 7, 21, emphasis in the original.

And indeed, key values associated with the so-called "Protestant Ethic" such as hard work, thrift, and determination, or issues like interpersonal trust and respect for others show Muslims to have similar and in some cases stronger levels of "faith" in these values than people in Protestant or Catholic countries (Yilmaz Esmer, "Is There an Islamic Civilization?" in Inglehart, ed., *Human Values and Social Change*, pp. 36–68).

12. What's most important to keep in mind here is that in many ways nineteenth-century European women were little more liberated than their Muslim sisters. Moreover, the kind of liberation Europeans – and their Arab/Muslim protégées – were talking about was very much a Victorian-era liberation: enough education and freedom to be "modern" mothers who could raise properly educated modern sons to administer their peoples according to Western/European values and norms and in a manner that would preserve Western economic interests, if not control. But the focus on women as a primary target for "liberation" led Arab/Muslim religious and nationalist movements to see the preservation of a rapidly invented conservative "traditional role" of women in their societies – with issues such as the veil being the greatest symbol to this day – as paramount in the struggles for autonomy and independence.

13. See Margot Badran, *Feminists, Islam and the Nation: Gender and the Making of Modern Egypt*, Princeton: Princeton University Press, 1995; Leila Ahmed, *Women and Gender in Islam*, New Haven: Yale University Press, 1992; Deniz Kandyoti, *Woman, Islam and the State*, London: Macmillan Press, 1991; and Ziba Mir-Hosseini, *Islam and Gender: The Religious Debate in Contemporary Iran*.

14. How this would compare with the percentage of Americans who support a traditional role for women the survey authors don't tell us.

15. Musa al-Darir, "al-'Awlamah: Mafhumuha-ba'ada al-Malamih," p. 6.

16. al-Jabari, *Qadaya fi al-fikr al-mu'asir*, p. 149. Moreover, such a global village inevitably stunts the drive by the Arab world and the rest of the third world to achieve any kind of renaissance. In fact, intolerance in turn is seen as a major cause of continuing hostility between the two civilizations; thus the fight against Westernization is understood not as a "clash," but as the continuation of struggles for independence begun decades earlier. And today more than ever, only democracy and Arab unity are powerful enough to help "the weaker peoples" fight globalization and achieve a real measure of autonomous development (Abdul-Rahman, ed., *Tanmiyyah al-Takhalaf wa-idarah al-Tanmiyyah*, pp. 114, 156, 170).

17. Donald Heisel, ed., *The Middle East and Development in a Changing World* (Cairo: Cairo Papers in Social Science, Vol. 20, No. 2, May 1999), p. 1; Khalal Amin, *al-'Awlamah*, p. 5; al-Said Yassin, *al-'Awlamah wa-al-tariq al-thalathah*, p. 5; Hans-Peter Martin and Harald Schumann, *Die Globalisierungsfalle: Der Angriff auf Demokratie und Wohlstand*, trans. into Arabic as *Fakh al-'awlama: al-i'tida' 'ala al-dimoqratiyyah wa al-rifahiyyah*), Kuwait: Silsilah 'alim al-mu'arifah, 1998).

18. Al-Darir, "al-'Awlamah: Mafhumuha ...," p. 16.

19. As Bishara points out, it is important to be careful to separate the "new-fangled ideology" from the long-running historical process ("Jedaliya al-'awlama Isra'ilia," in Osama Amin al-Khawli, ed., *al-'Arab wal-al-'awlama*, Beirut: Center for Arab Unity Studies, 1997, pp. 281–96). Depending on the writer, its origins lay as far back as (what for them is) the foundational event of modernity, the 1492 expulsion of Muslims from Spain, while special emphasis is placed on Napoleon and the era of European imperialism/

colonialism in the Middle East that he inaugurated (al-Khawli, ed., *al-'Arab wal-al-'awlama*, p. 8; Yassin, *al-'Awlamah wa-al-tariq al-thalathah*, pp. 23–4); al-Jabari, *Qadaya fi al-fikr al-mu'asir,* pp. 135, 137, 153.

20. Abdul-Rahman, ed., *Tanmiyyah al-Takhalaf wa-idarah al-Tanmiyyah* pp. 115, 150.

21. Abbas, *Masdaqiyyah al-Nitham Dawli al-Jadid*, p. 26.

22. Yassin, *al-'Awlamah wa-al-tariq al-thalathah*, p. 65; al-Khawli, ed., *al-'Arab wal-al-'awlama*, p. 9. The "global village" is in fact a "new imperialism" (Abu Za'rur, *al-'Awlamah,* p. 14). As the martyred leader of the Muslim Brotherhood Sayyid Qutb argued, "There is a natural alliance (*halfan*) between colonialism and dictatorship of governance and capital, each of them supports the other, and shares [lit.: exchange] interests" (Sayyid Qutb, *Ma'araka al-Islam*, p. 102).

It should be pointed out that a similar view exists in West Africa, where "two antagonistic systems, the market and the nation-state," are seen as competing for economic and cultural capital (cf. Manthia Diawara, "Toward a Regional Imaginary in Africa," pp. 103–24, p. 117; al-Jabari, *Qadaya fi al-fikr al-mu'asir,* pp. 139–46; cf. Abu Za'rur, *al-'Awlamah,* p. 14; al-Jabari, *Qadaya fi al-fikr al-mu'asir …*, pp. 139–40; Abdul-Rahman, ed., *Tanmiyyah al-Takhalaf wa-idarah al-Tanmiyyah*, pp. 76, 81.

23. Al-Jabari, *Qadaya fi al-fikr al-mu'asir,* pp. 140–6; cf. Abu Za'rur, *al-'Awlamah*, p. 14; Abdul-Rahman, ed., *Tanmiyyah al-Takhalaf wa-idarah al-Tanmiyyah*, pp. 76, 81.

24. Muhammad 'Abed al-Jabari, "al-'Awlamah," p. 300; 'Abdalila Balqziz, "al-'Awlamah wa-al-huwiyyah al-thaqafiyyah: 'awlama al-thaqafiyyah am thaqafa al-'awlamah," in al-Khawli, ed., *al-'Arab wal-al-'awlama*, p. 317; Amin, *al-'Awlamah*, pp. 51, 66. Cf. Abu Za'rur, *al-'Awlamah*, p. 7.

25. Haider, "Mafhum al-siadah ba'ada al-harb al-baderah …," p. 56. Cf. Pierre Bourdieu and Loïc Wacquant, "The New Global Vulgate," *The Baffler* 12, 1999, pp. 69–78. Cf. Ihsan Hindi, "al-'Awlaman wa-Aharua al-silbi 'ala siasah al-duwal" ("Globalization and its Negative Influence on the Sovereignty of States") *Mu'alumat Dawliyyah* (*International Information*), 58, Autumn, 1998, pp. 61–68; Fuwad Nahra, "al-Watan al-'arabi wa-tahadiyat al-'awlamah: beina waqa' al-taghi'yah wa-darurah al-wihdah" ("The Arab Nation and the Challenges of Globalization: Between Fragmentation/Partition and the Necessity of Unity") *Mu'alumat Dawliyyah* (*International Information*), 58, Autumn, 1998, pp. 69–82. 'Atrisi, "al-Huwiyyah al-thaqafiyyah fi muawijah al-'awlamah."

26. The most outrageous recent example of this is Frum and Perle, *An End to Evil.*

27. Virginie Coulloudon, "World: Interview With Olivier Roy: The 'Illusions' Of 11 September," http://www.rferl.org/nca/features/2002/09/10092002170333.asp.

28. "For the reality is the opposite of the rhetoric" (Amin, *al-'Awlamah*, pp. 31–2). In fact, this critique is shared outside the Muslim majority world. Thus the liberal Moscow newspaper *Nezavisimaya Gazeta* editorialized that no matter how influential the most powerful countries and the MNCs become, nation-states will not die away, but rather will strengthen themselves and seek to democratize the global economic environment (Oleg Bogomolov, *Nezavisimaya Gazeta*, January 27, 2000, reprinted in *World Press Review*, April 2000, p. 8).

29. Thus in line with the historical view of globalization, some writers use the term "new globalization," which is epitomized by the culture and policies of privatization that bring about the "destruction of the customs house walls

and the usurpation of the political and economic hegemony of the national state by new global system of exchange" (Amin, *al-'Awlamah*, pp. 27–9; Yassin, *al-'Awlamah wa-al-tariq al-thalathah*, p. 21; al-Jabari, *Qadaya fi al-fikr al-mu'asir*, p. 147). There is thus a perceived connection from the beginning between globalization and privatization (because of the weakening of the state) (al-Jabari, *Qadaya fi al-fikr al-mu'asir*, p. 135).

30. Al-Jabari, *Qadaya fi al-fikr al-mu'asir*, p. 143.

31. Ibid., pp. 140–6. Another author describes it more strongly as "galloping penetration" (Noureddine Afaya, *L'Occident dans l'imaginaire Arabo-Musulman*, pp. 87, 95, 116).

32. Timothy Mitchell, *Colonising Egypt*, Berkeley: University of California Press, 1991, p. 126; emphasis mine.

33. Sheik al-Jabarti, *Napoleon in Egypt: Al-Jabarti's Chronicle of the French Occupation, 1798*, trans. Shmuel Moreh, Berlin: Markus Wienner, 1993. He also criticized the establishment of French "diwans," which divided the law into religious and secular categories.

34. Al-Afghani believed that in the end it was science, and not the French and British imperialists, which was responsible for "conquest, usurpation and aggression," to which we might add that one cannot separate the history and use of science from that of capitalism, for as Nietzsche argued in the *Will to Power*, the "drive to knowledge always goes back to desire to conquer and appropriate." Such a framework opens up new ways to understand the impact of the "knowledge economy" on the third world (Jamal ad-Din al-Afghani, *An Islamic Response to Imperialism*, pp. 131–73). See in particular his discussion of the etiology of the contemporary materialist philosophy from Greek philosophy (p. 139, note 6), p. 151 for his discussion of egoism, and p. 169, where he

discusses, in almost identical language to contemporary writers, the "firm and sure foundation" of Islam to grapple with the challenges of modernity.

35. Hassan al-Banna, *Between Yesterday and Today*, trans. and published on the web by Prelude Company at http://www.prelude.co.uk/mb/banna/today.htm.

36. Some, including Mawdudi, saw even then the model of the European Community as an example for the Muslim world to follow. Mawdudi argued simultaneously for the supremacy of Islam over capitalism and socialism (a frequent theme during this period) and the necessity of creating an Islamic state, "A purely ideological state … [devoid of] the element of nationalism … which can be managed and administered by any one who believes in the principles laid down by Islam for running it" (Maulana Sayyid Abul 'Ala Maudoodi, *Islamic State: Political Writings of Maulana Sayyid Abul 'Ala Maudoodi*, compiled and trans. Mazheruddin Siddiqi, Karachi: Islamic Research Academy, 1986, ch. 1). Cf. Syed Abul Ala Maudoodi, *Capitalism, Socialism and Islam*, Kuwait: Islamic Book Publishers, 1977.

37. Cf. Bryan Turner, *Orientalism, Postmodernism and Globalism*, New York: Routledge, 1994.

38. Jalal al-e Ahmad, *Gharbzadegi*. It should be pointed out that the feeling of "rootlessness" this condition produces is one of the defining psychological states of both the colonial and globalizing moments (cf. Mehrzad Boroujerdi, *Iranian Intellectuals and the West*. The Sorbonne-trained Ali Shariati, who has been called the "idealogue of the Islamic Revolution," emphasized the responsibility of the masses – even more than the Prophet Mohammed – in liberating Islam from this "disease." Shariati hoped that the development of an "Islamic humanism" would lead to the creation

of a new *Gemeinschaft*, or community, free of both unthinking clericism and Western rationalism, that would have the power to "eradicat[e] capitalism" (Cf. 'Ali Shariati, *On The Sociology of Islam*); Ervand Abrahamian, "Ali Shariati: Ideologue of the Iranian Revolution," *MERIP Reports*, 102, 1992, pp. 24–8). In sum, the alliance of *ulama*, intellectuals, and clergy that made the Islamic Revolution would likely have been impossible without the unifying critique of the market that helped mobilize the country against the modernizing regime of the Shah and its close alliance with the West.

39. Sayyid Qutb, *Ma'araka al-Islam.*

40. Ibid., p. 25. For a discussion of the effect of Qutb's stay in the United States on his perception of the country and his subsequent thinking, see John Calvert, "'The World is an Undutiful Boy!': Sayyid Qutb's American Experience," *Islam and Christian–Muslim Relations*, 11, 1, 2000, pp. 87–103. Qutb was also critical of the Nasserist, state-centered model of development; in his view "the state cannot do its job because [it] is sympathetic to needs of capitalists, is in the hands of the capitalists, who are like the state" (Qutb, *Ma'araka al-Islam*, pp. 8–9). It should be pointed out that liberal critics of Arab étatism have reached a similar conclusion, believing that "economic policies of the patron state increased its dependency on the advanced industrial world," although they would argue that it was because of problems internal to the regime and its macro-economic policies (import substitution, nationalization) that was solely responsible, withholding any blame from Western financial and regulatory institutions or the strateigc policies of Western governments (cf. Iliya Harik and Denis Sullivan, eds., *Privatization and Liberalization in the Middle East*, Bloomington: Indiana University Press, 1992, p. 2).

41. Paul Berman, "The Philosopher of Islamic Terror," *NY Times Magazine*, March 23, 2003.

42. Gilles Deleuze and Felix Guattari, *Anti-Oedipus: Capitalism and Schizophrenia*, trans. Robert Hurley, Mark Seem, and Helen R. Lane, Minneapolis: University of Minnesota Press, 1983 [1972]; and *A Thousand Plateaus*, trans. Brian Massumi, Minneapolis: University of Minnesota Press, 1987 [1980].

43. Qutb, *Ma'araka al-Islam.* More recently, according to the director of the Ministry of Awqaf in Egypt, the difference between "Islamic globalization" and the "new globalization" is exploitation and subjugation of people that the latter is based on, which also preaches the freedom of the individual to the level that the individual is freed from all social and moral constraints. And this very reality obligates Muslims to actively participate in the new globalization to stop the headlong rush to self-destruction and help shape it along more Islamic – that is, truly "human" – principles (cf. Mahmud Hamdi Zaqzuq, *Islam fi 'Asr al-'Awlamah*, p. 22).

44. Qutb, *Ma'araka al-Islam*, pp. 57–61.

45. These include issues such as excessive and destructive materialism, oppression masked by a "rational–scientific" worldview promoting objectivity and progress (one of the basic ideologies of imperialism), deep social, economic, and racial injustices masked by formal democracy, the failure of the nation-state to bring freedom, progress, security or prosperity to much of the world's population, the desirability of a supra-national government to attend to the needs of most human beings, and the need for an alternative system to both Communism and runaway capitalism that is not centered egoistically on "man."

46. Jamal al-Din al-Afghani, "An Islamic Response to Imperialism," in John Donohue and John Esposito, eds., *Islam in Transition: Muslim Perspectives*, Oxford: Oxford University Press, 1982, pp. 16–19.

47. Their research includes the problem of modernizing agriculture, increasing literacy, or the increasingly problematic *"zones urbaines clandestines"* – that is the shantytowns on the edges of the major Arab cities where the hundreds of thousands of people pushed out of agriculture and into the cities (in many cases specifically as a result of structural adjustment programs demanded/imposed by the World Bank and IMF) eke out marginal livings through the unofficial economy – that is, the breeding ground of al-Qa'eda.

48. This powerful quote comes from Habib Benrahhal Serghini, "Culture and Development," in Taieb Belghazi and Lahcen Haddad, eds., *Global/Local Cultures and Sustainable Development*, pp. 203–6, p. 204. I have paraphrased the quote a bit, as the original is much more jargony and difficult to follow.

49. Noam Chomsky, September 21, 2001 interview, http://www.productof mexico.com/war_updates/Noam%20 Chomsky% 209-21-01.htm.

50. *Retrospective: A bin Laden Special on al-Jazeera Two Months Before September 11*, transcript at http://www.uebersetzungen_analysen/themen/islamistische _ideologie/isl_binladen_21_12_01.pdf. The show was from July 10, 2001, on the talk show *Opposite Direction*, with a show titled *Bin Laden – The Arab Despair and American Fear*.

51. Ron Moreau, Sami Yousafzai, and Zahid Hussain, "Holy War 101," *Newsweek*, December 1, 2003, p. 28.

52. Quoted in Anonymous, *Through Our Enemies' Eyes*, p. 31.

53. And so Sheikh Yasin, the spiritual leader of Hamas, explained that deportation and exile from the homeland – and, one can imagine, living in Europe and the US while planning terrorist attacks – is "tourism for the sake of God," a clearly cultural description of politically, strategically and/or economically necessitated migration (quoted in ibid., p. 63).

54. Ibid., pp. 16–25.

55. Wright, "The Kingdom of Silence," p. 64.

56. "In a country where discontent with the ruling family is widespread but rarely expressed directly, where resentment against the power and influence of the West is nearly universal, and where unemployment is creating a class of well-educated but idle young men, bin Laden's words resonated so strongly in part because no one else would say them" (ibid.).

57. For such an argument, see Austin Bay, "McDonalds: the Best Weapon Against Terrorism," http://www. strategypage.com/onpoint/articles/ 20021211.asp.

58. *Retrospective: A bin Laden Special on al-Jazeera Two Months Before September 11*. See note 50 above.

59. Ibid.

60. For a documentary about this street theater see the PBS Frontline episode, *India: Starring Osama bin Laden*, aired in June 2003, http://www.pbs. org/frontlineworld/stories/india205/. It would very likely be inaccurate to generalize that most of India's nearly one billion people share similar sentiments to the audience of the Jatra, but it is clear that even if only 10 percent of people feel similarly, that's one hundred million people.

61. John Gray, *Al Qaeda and What it Means to be Modern*.

62. For a discussion of the modern roots and dynamics of religious fundamentalism of various stripes, see S.N. Eisenstadt, *Multiple Modernities*, Somerset, N.J.: Transaction Publishers, 2002; and Bruce Lawrence, *Defenders of*

God: The Fundamentalist Revolt Against the Modern Age, Columbia, S.C.: University of South Carolina Press, 1995.

63. Charles Kurzman, "Bin Laden and Other Thoroughly Modern Muslims," *Context*, fall–winter 2002, http://www.asanet.org/pubs/kurzman.pdf.

64. John O. Voll, "Bin Laden and the Logic of Power," CIAO Responds to the Terrorist Attacks against the United States: A Recruiting Tape of Osama bin Laden: Excerpts and Analyses. http://www.ciaonet.org/cbr/cbr00/video/cbr_v/cbr_v_2c.html.

65. Ibid.

66. Remember, it's the logo that counts, not the sweatshop where the garment was made.

67. And moreover, Voll is wrong to assume that "the very format of a contemporary, well-produced video argues against seeing the movement that the video represents as 'anti-modern.'"

68. Ibid.

69. 'Ali Harb, interview in *al-Nahar* 9/xii, December, 1999, p. 20; Interview with Mudthir Abdulrahim al-Tib, in *al-Nahar* 9/xii, December, 1999, p. 20. A similar view is held in Africa (cf. Diawara, "Toward a Regional Imaginary in Africa," p. 111).

70. Ibid., p. 20; interview with Adnan Abu-'Audih, *al-Nahar*, December 16, 1999, p. 13.

71. 'Amr Muqdad, "al-Sir'a beina al-'awlamah wa-al-huwiyyah" ("The Conflict between Globalization and Identity") *Mu'alumat Dawliyyah* (*International Information*) 58, Autumn, 1998, pp. 97–107.

72. Abdul Satar Fath Allah Sa'id, *al-Ghazu al-fikri wa al-tayarat almu'asara l-il-Islam*, pp. 10–11; cf. 'Atrisi, "al-Huwiyyah al-thaqafiyyah fi muawijah al-'awlamah"; al-Khawli, ed., *al-'Arab wal-al-'awlama*, p. 28; Kemal al-Din 'Abd al-Ghana al-Musari, *al-'Almaniyyah wa-al-'awlamah wa-al-Azhar*, p. 99; Amin, *al-'Awlamah*, p. 51,

where he points out that Napoleon invaded Egypt in the name of "culture." Other analyses discussing its long history go back to the expulsion from Spain and/or the fifteenth century (al-Khawli, ed., *al-'Arab wal-al-'awlama*, p. 8; Yassin, *al-'Awlamah wa-al-tariq al-thalathah*, pp. 23–4). Globalization is also described as the stage after colonial modernity (al-Jabari, *Qadaya fi al-fikr al-mu'asir*, p. 135).

73. During a March 2004 visit to Iraq most religious leaders with whom I spoke talked in these terms.

74. Instead of the borders of nation and the national state, we have the new, "unhealthy" global borders which facilitate and ultimately enforce a system of global hegemony of economy, tastes, and sensibilities (*al-ath[zz]waq*), and cultures (al-Jabari, *Qadaya fi al-fikr al-mu'asir*, pp. 140–6).

75. Ibid., p. 148.

76. Amin, *al-'Awlamah*, pp. 45–50. Cf. Yassin, *al-'Awlamah wa-al-tariq al-thalathah*, p. 10.

77. Allah Sa'id, *al-Ghazu al-fikri wa al-tayarat almu'asara l-il-Islam*, pp. 76, 152. Cf. note 32.

78. Abdallah 'Abd al-Da'im, *al-Qawmiyyah al-'Arabiyyah wa-al-nitham al-'alami al-jadid*, pp. 70–3. The cultural situation facing the third world "is seen to be facing the Arab world even more so" (p. 73). This leads to the contradictory assessment that "because of our spiritual and psychological bankruptcy and inferiority we must submit to whatever the United States wants," yet criticizes "all the social maladies faced by Western society, which suffers from fragmentation, where individual doubt [is pressed] to the edge of an abyss" (Abbas, *Masdaqiyyah al-Nitham Dawli al-Jadid*, pp. 187, 192).

79. Al-Khawli, ed., *al-'Arab wal-al-'awlama*, p. 9; al-Da'im, *al-Qawmiyyah al-'Arabiyyah wa-l-nitham al-'alami al-jadid*, p. 5. This issue is given greater

salience since the Arab world has yet to produce its own modernity, that is, its own cultural revolution (Yassin, *al-'Awlamah wa-al-tariq al-thalathah*, pp. 83–4). Thus a major concern is how to adopt modern technology when there is such an abyss between "intellectuals and the street" (al-Musari, *al-'Almaniyyah wa-al-'awlamah wa-'l-Azhar*, p. 117), and when technology itself is the "negation of culture" (Amin, *al-'Awlamah*, pp. 51, 66).

80. Abdulrahim al-Tib, interview in *al-Nahar*, December 13, p. 14. In fact, "democracy is the only way that the weaker peoples can fight against globalization" (Abdul-Rahman, ed., *Tanmiyyah al-Takhalaf wa-idarah al-Tanmiyyah*, p. 114).

81. George al-Rasi, interview in *al-Nahar*, December 13, 1999, p. 14.

82. For an interesting discussion of this trend in Egypt see Husam Tammam and Patrick Haenni, "Egypt's Air-Conditioned Islam," *Le Monde Diplomatique*, March 9, 2003, online at http://mondediplo.com/2003/09/03 egyptislam.

83. For English versions of Yassine's books, see Abdessalem Yassine, *Winning the Modern World for Islam*, n.p.: Justice and Spirituality Publications, 2000, and *The Muslim Mind on Trial: Divine Revelation Versus Secular Rationalism*, n.p.: Justice and Spirituality Publications, 2003.

84. As she argued in a forum of leading younger Islamist intellectuals I organized in Budapest, May 25, 2003, transcript available at http://www.humanities.uci.edu/history/levine conference/mlbudapesttranscriptedit.pdf.

85. The fact that one can find verses in the Qur'an that support misogyny or that the search for more acceptable "origins" of various ideas or concepts within Islam is a theoretically problematic endeavor should not detract from the power and importance of the kind of exercises in which Yassine, Ramadan, and others are engaged.

86. The Barcelona Process is a program of economic integration between the European Union and various MENA countries, initiated in 1995, whose goal is "establish a common Euro-Mediterranean area of peace and stability based on fundamental principles including respect for human rights and democracy (political and security partnership)," and "shared prosperity through the establishment of a free-trade area" (for the official EU description, see http://europa.eu.int/comm/external_ relations/euromed/.

87. Qur'an, al-Furqan: 53, al-Kahfi: 60–82.

88. See Taieb Belghazi, "The Mediterranean(s), Barzakh, Event," in Belghazi and Haddad, eds., *Global/Local Cultures and Sustainable Development*, pp. 217–36.

89. See http://www.barzakh.net/barzakhe.htm/.

90. That is, it was viewed as something specifically defined against the "Turk" who was perceived as the antithesis of everything Europeans imagined themselves to be.

91. For more on the influence of the gangs, see Hakan Yavuz, "The Search for a New Social Contract in Turkey: Fethullah Gülen, the Virtue Party and the Kurds," note 3. Even the Interior Ministry admitted that "terror gangs and drug traffickers are dominating the state's political, economic and security spheres."

92. Although we should remember that the re-Islamization in fact involved mostly politicians, as the majority of the population never stopped practicing some form of Islam.

93. The quotes from Bulaç are drawn from his books *Islam ve Fundamentalizm*; *Din, Devlet ve Demokrasi*; *Nuh'un Gemisine Binmek*; and *Bir Aydin Sapmasi*.

94. Ali Bulaç, "Moronization Project," *Zaman*, September 10, 2003.

95. Ali Bulaç, "Iraq the Pilot Region," *Zaman*, February 22, 2003. http://www.zaman.org/default.php?kn=749&bl= commentary.

96. The general focus on the relationship between globalization and democratic crises, and the role of religion in the dynamic between globalization versus localization, are quite important; particularly when we add the European dimension to the discussion (which we'll do in the next chapter). Several important recent books in Turkish dealing with these subjects include Ali Eren, *Küreselleşme İslam Dünyası ve Türkiye*, Istanbul: ISAV, 2002; and Taner Timur, *Küreselleşme ve Demokrasi Krizi*, Ankara: IMGE Kitabevi, 1996.

97. The economic and political benefits are just too great to allow ideological considerations or fear of Western "cultural invasion" to override them. Moreover, Turkey's position as the only non-major oil-producing Muslim country that is part of the OECD (the Organization for Economic Cooperation and Development, the club of the world's "advanced" or "developed" economies) makes it harder to popularize an anti-Western and anti-liberal ideology.

98. Hakan Yavuz, *Islamic Political Identity in Turkey*.

99. Hakan Yavuz and John Esposito, *Turkish Islam and the Secular State: The Gulen Movement*, Syracuse: Syracuse University Press, 2003.

100. The Association of Independent Industrialists and Businessmen. The membership of MUSIAD happens to be much larger, younger, and comprised of small and medium-sized businesses compared with the older secular and state-aligned TUSIAD (Turkish Industrialists' and Businessmen's Association, which represents the large-scale companies).

101. In fact, with an eye toward emulating East Asian capitalism (which itself – in some ways inaccurately – is lauded by Western commentators for possessing a Protestant-like "capitalist spirit"), the Islamist business community and the Gülen movement have worked with, and to a certain degree penetrated, the Government and state apparatus. One reason for doing so has been to ensure that their interests have been protected when more uncompromising religious voices have been silenced – something their Arab counterparts could only dream of.

102. In the 1990s Erdogan was jailed by the military for his supposedly extremist views. For a good early analysis of this phenomenon, see Ziya Onis, "The Political Economy of the Islamic Resurgence in Turkey: The Rise of the Welfare Party in Perspective," *Third World Quarterly* 18, 1997, pp. 743–73. Also see Yavuz, "The Search for a New Social Contract in Turkey."

103. Ian Lesser and F. Stephen Larrabee, *Turkish Foreign Policy in an Age of Uncertainty*, Santa Monica, Calif.: RAND, 2003.

104. Deputy prime minister and the leader of the Nationalist Movement Party (MHP), Devlet Bahceli, as quoted in the *Turkish Daily News*, April 3, 2002.

105. Cf. Azadeh Kian, "L'invasion culturelle occidentale: mythe ou realité."

106. For an important mid-1990s assessment of this trend, see ibid.

107. Ibid.

108. This process can neither be separated from the impact of the larger forces of globalization on Iran, nor can it be assumed to be only the result of foreign influence rather than the natural tendency within Islam and Iranian society to adapt to changing political, economic, and cultural circumstances.

109. Yet he also criticizes "communities like Iran, which were once the centers and creators of science and knowledge for many years, [which] are

suffering now from backwardness and depression," and need to "wake up and redress the shortcomings and deficiencies" ("Khatemi Criticizes 'Misuse' of Globalization," Iranmania.com, February 4, 2003, http://www.iranmania.com/News/ArticleView/Default.asp?NewsCode=14143&NewsKind=CurrentAffairs&ArchiveNews=Yes).

110. Not surprisingly, then, in conferences organized by the Iranian Government related to the Dialogue of Civilizations project, speakers specifically criticize the clash of civilizations thesis as the enemy of peace and dialogue, and call for better use of new media technologies, as well as the news media more broadly, by the Global South – and here it is key that Iran is trying to place itself in a larger context – to combat it and to make the West realize that "imagining different civilizations as a disintegrated phenomena is simple-mindedness and an oversimplification of universal matters" ("Clash of Civilizations condemned at Tehran peace conference," *Tehran*, October 5, 2002).

111. In fact, in Iran one can criticize neoliberal development practices without being against privatization or increased efficiency per se. (For an interesting critique of Iranian Government development theory see the article in honor of the death of a well-known Iranian economist, "Dr. Hussein Azimi: Always Envisaging Iran's Globalization," *Iran International Magazine*, May 2003, No. 23, http://www.iraninternational-magazine.com/issue_23/text/dr.%azimi.htm). Indeed, one economic official said that "although globalization creates opportunities for countries, it also brings forth challenges for the national economies," which require Iran to "tread the path of reforms" that in some ways agree with structural adjustment programs in order to rehabilitate the economy ("Globalization Brings

Challenges," Iranmania.com, September 22, 2003).

112. Text of the Statement by His Excellency, Seyyed Mohammad Khatami, President of the Islamic Republic of Iran, at The United Nations Millennium Summit, New York, September 6, 2000. http://www.un.org/millennium/webcast/statements/iran.htm.

113. And while Khatemi and other senior religious figures are able both to critique the existing state of affairs in Iran and propose grand solutions involving globalization, other figures, such as former revolutionary-turned-journalist Akbar Ganji, have been jailed for "insulting Islamic sanctities" because they criticize the "religious fascism" of conservative officials. A good elaboration of much of this discussion can be found in the writings of Afshin Molavi, particularly his 2002 book *Persian Pilgrimages*, and several online articles at The Globalist, e.g., http://www.theglobalist.com/DBWeb/StoryId.aspx?StoryId=2839, http://www.theglobalist.com/DBWeb/StoryId.aspx?StoryId=2837.

114. In the 2004 elections the conservatives won back a majority of the Parliament after rigging it so that many more progressive candidates, including sitting parliamentarians, were disqualified.

115. As of early 2005, one can see that very few Iranians are voting in municipal elections, which is a damning indictment of Khatemi, who pushed them as a way to strengthen the forces of democratization in the country.

116. Cf. Asef Bayat, *Street Politics*.

117. Even more radical younger jurists like Ayatollah Sa'dzadeh reconstruct Islam so that "Islam is what the Prophet brought the people from God. This is all I recognize as Islam" (quoted in Mir-Hosseini, *Islam and Gender*, p. 253). Such challenges to the existing religious system in Iran help re-imagine Shar'ia in such a way that women are

understood to be legally equal to men, and find whenever possible ethical rather than legal solutions to social problems. For what is undoubtedly the best treatment of the subject of reforming Islamic law and attitudes towards women in Iran, see Mir-Hosseini, *Islam and Gender*.

118. Soroush seeks, in a manner that challenges the religious hierarchy in Iran, to realize the validity of all truths – especially those of science – and pursuing an orientation toward development that does not try to "arrest development, attack science or glorify poverty" but rather seeks to mature and build a world where the values of religion and tolerance can guide development along a better path than it's generally traveled. For an English collection of Soroush's writings see *Reason, Freedom, and Democracy in Islam*.

119. Student Movement Coordinating Committee for Democracy in Iraq, "Who we are," http://www.daneshjoo.org/article/publish/article_2566.shtml.

Chapter 6

1. Omid Safi, ed., *Progressive Muslims: On Justice, Gender and Pluralism*.

2. Marc Schade-Poulsen, *Men and Popular Music in Algeria*, Austin: University of Texas Press, 1999.

3. In good measure because of the influence of the Nation of Islam, which gave a critical (if in some ways distorted) impetus to young black rappers as they sought to write about the world around them.

4. For a description of some of the arrested musicians and fans, see http://monsite.wanadoo.fr/marock/page6.html.

5. As reported by Reuters on March 7, 2003.

6. "Dans une époque où le doute flotte sur le ciel marocain, au lieu de s'occuper des problèmes alarmants que connaît le Maroc aujourd'hui, la misère, le chômage, l'impunité … etc et élargir le champs des libertés qui ont été arrachées au prix fort par nos aînés, le maklizeu invente une nouvelle façon pour intimider le peuple marocain en général et sa jeunesse en particulier" ("Communiqué de soutien aux 14 musiciens," March 7, 2003. http://membres.lycos.fr/cdmel/musiciens.html).

7. See the website in support of the jailed rockers, at http://monsite.wanadoo.fr/marock/; including the pages http://monsite.wanadoo.fr/marock/page8.html and http://monsite.wanadoo.fr/marock/page7.html.

8. A.R.B. [pseudonym], "Une seconde mascarade serait fatale," Tel-Quel online, March 14, 2003, reprinted at http://monsite.wanadoo.fr/marock/page1.html under the title "lettre ouverte a M6" (i.e., King Muhammed VI).

9. "Du sangs pour les vampires," at http://monsite.wanadoo.fr/marock/page6.html.

10. "La Guitare endiablée," http://monsite.wanadoo.fr/marock/page3.html.

11. Email communication, December, 2003.

12. Scott Peterson, "You Say You Want a Revolution? Iran Bands Rock On," *The Christian Science Monitor*, October 1, 2003. Metal bands even blend in choirs and string sections (also like Ozzy did in his more recent recordings), and play "deeply Persian and religious themes and rhythms." Such a fusion of styles exemplifies the attitudes of young Iranians, among whom perhaps more than their peers elsewhere in the Muslim majority world there is a feeling that the discourse of cultural aggression is overplayed. As one twenty-one-year-old Iranian described it, "Cultural aggression is harmful if it is aimed at our principles, but if it encourages us to learn more, I am all for it." Other young people worry that "in the past 20 years

our country's immune system has been weakened, so much so that I see the youngsters around me have become totally self-alienated and try to copy everything western, even when they speak. There should be moderation. If only we had not been limited so much."

13. As cited in "*Sesame Street* Breaks Iraqi POWs," BBC News, May 20, 2003.

14. Nilüfer Göle, "Snapshots of Islamic Modernities," pp. 93, 94, 113.

15. Al-Da'im, *al-Qawmiyyah al-'Arabiyyah wa-al-nitham al-'alami al-jadid*, pp. 75, 80. As Abu Za'rur argues, Islam is the only alternative to globalization, precisely because it offers the most radical solution – that is, the way of the Prophet (*al-'Awlamah*, pp. 60–62). Interview with Ibrahim Abu-Lughod, *al-Nahar*, December 4, 1999, p. 11.

16. More precisely, "the heart of Islam" (al-Musari, *al-'Almaniyyah wa-'l-'awlamah wa-'l-Azhar*, pp. 103–4, 168, 196; al-Khawli, ed., *al-'Arab wal-al-'awlama*, p. 11). Islam is elsewhere described as a new "global" culture, one with the ability to pursue the "unity of the human race" (Yassin, *al-'Awlamah wa-al-tariq al-thalathah*, p. 11). This call to equality does not mean isolation from the world, but rather free and autonomous Arab development with all classes participating together (Abdul-Rahman, ed., *Tanmiyyah al-Takhalaf wa-idarah al-Tanmiyyah*, p. 32) to respond to social needs, and to "re-organize our classes to our own vision, and not how others see us, to build a philosophy that has deep roots in our land" (Abbas, *Masdaqiyyah al-Nitham Dawli al-Jadid*, p. 194). Finally, as Abdallah al-Nafisi argues: "We live in a condition/time of cultural, moral, intellectual and spiritual void, and the Islamic movement comes to fill and take control of [it] ... The Islamic movement is fighting the trend in the Third World to follow the West" (Abdallah al-Nafisi, ed., *al-Haraka al-*

islamiyyah: ru'ya mustaqbiliyyah, awraq fi al-naqd al-thati [*The Islamic Movement: View Toward the Future*], Cairo: Madbouli Press, 1989, pp. 16, 36). This is understood as an effort that would have to include military and political leaders as well as intellectuals and religious figures, and from the Islamist perspective, one that would have to include a sharpening of the critical reasoning of the Islamic movement in order to succeed (ibid., pp. 154, 301).

17. Cf. UNESCO, *The Futures of Cultures*, pp. 13–14.

18. Here globalization is seen as a desire for hegemony and erasure of particularity, whose goal is to end the ideological struggle concerning interpretation of culture, the past, and the way toward the future (al-Jabari, "al-'Awlamah wa-al-huwiyyah al-thaqafiyyah," pp. 301, 303). In fact, at the very time when the Iron Curtain was falling throughout Europe many writers declared the need for the third world as a whole to create its own system. In this context, "what the Islamic movement needs is a legal and modern political logic in light of analys[e]s of the present conditions. [We] need a theory coming from religion, [but] cannot succeed without an organic intellectual effort" (al-Nafisi, *al-Haraka al-islamiyyah: ru'ya mustaqbiliyyah*, p. 18).

19. Kabir Helminski, "How is Dialogue Possible Between Islam and the West?" rough draft of a talk delivered at the Conference, Islam and World Peace, sponsored by The International Centre for the Dialogue Among Civilizations, Tehran, Iran. October 2002, available at http://www.sufism.org/society/articles/HowIsDialog Possible.htm.

20. Salman Rushdie, "More Fanaticism as Usual," New York *Times*, December 7, 2002.

21. Which if Muslims like Khomeini had bothered to read they would have

realized was one of the most searing indictments of the West and its modernity ever written, and certainly no insult to the Prophet Mohammed considering that the main character, Mahound, dies insane at the end.

Part III
Chapter 7

1. Tariq Ali, interviewed in the documentary *Preventive Warriors*, directed by Michael Burns, as heard on Democracy Now, May 28, 2004.

2. A "doppleganger" (a misspelling of the German word *doppelgänger*) is a ghostly or "evil" twin that has the ability to assume the form of its original, feed on its life-force, and in so doing steal and deform its identity in favor of its own more nefarious one.

3. The term "liberal Islam" has been used by scholars and policy-makers for the last two decades or more to refer to the potential emergence of a kind of Islamic theology, politics, and practice that can embrace the values of pluralistic democracy and free-market capitalism as epitomized by the United States and other Western countries.

4. Cf. Denning, *Culture in the Age of the Three Worlds*, p. 45, citing George Katsiaficas, *The Imagination of the New Left: A Global Analysis of 1968*, Boston: South End Press, 1987.

5. But it wasn't just the working class that was coopted by capital. The liberatory and progressive impulses of the 1960s movements were also coopted fairly successfully by corporate power. In fact, by the early 1970s business groups had realized the need for business to "explain itself better" to an increasingly "anticorporatist" movement (Amory Starr, *Naming the Enemy*).

6. Moreover, it failed to involve people from a wide range of social backgrounds or move beyond mostly symbolic confrontations with state power in the ensuing decade.

7. John Mattausch, "The Peace Movement: Retrospects and Prospects," in Robin Cohen and Shirin M. Rai, eds., *Global Social Movements*, pp. 184–95, pp. 190, 193.

8. Cohen and Rai, eds., *Global Social Movements*.

9. Cf. Jean-Pierre Le Goff, *Mai 68: L'héritage impossible*.

10. Ibid.

11. Christopher Chase-Dunn and Terry Boswell, "Transnational Social Movements and Democratic Socialist Parties in the Semiperiphery."

12. See Le Goff, *Mai 68: L'héritage Impossible*.

13. This strategy was made easier by the fact that the leadership of the May 1968 "revolution" quickly became arrogant in its self-celebration (Roland Hureaux, "Les trois ages de la gauche," *Le débat*, January–February 1999, 103, pp. 29–38).

14. As Michael Lerner has cogently argued Americans increasingly believed that anyone could become rich and powerful, and in fact *should want* to become rich and powerful. But if they didn't succeed in doing so, and in fact became economically more insecure (as happened to most of the middle class), this couldn't be because of the weakening of unions and the welfare state by the country's increasingly "rich and famous" elite, whose lifestyles everyone was busy trying to emulate (thus the sky-rocketing levels of personal debt beginning in this period). Nor was it their own fault, even though all the cultural signs said it was precisely a person's own fault if they didn't succeed, since everyone had the same opportunity to do so. Instead it was the fault of all those others – Japanese, gays, Arabs, Muslims, liberals, elitist tree-huggers, you name it – against whom the righteous Right was waging its "culture war" in defense of the values of the silent but moral majority (Lerner, *The Politics of Meaning*).

But as we saw in the Introduction in our comparison of Muslims and Kansans, it is important to stress that this dynamic is in no way unique to the US; around the world the negative effects of neoliberal globalization have led weaker groups within societies to reassert narrow and exclusivist national and/or religious identities, be it "America," "Israel," "Serbia," or "Islam" as a way of coping with their descending social status. For an important discussion of this dynamic in Israel, see Gershon Shafir and Yoav Peled's important book, *Being Israeli*. For a more general discussion see Peter Beyer, *Religion and Globalization*, London: Sage, 1994. Making this dynamic worse, especially in the US, is the "two-income trap" that has forced mothers and fathers to work long hours to maintain a standard of living earned by one parent a generation ago. This situation has left young people easier prey to television and the corporations who advertise through it than ever before, producing both the militarized, hyper-consumerist culture in which we're now living along with the chauvinism and resentment that such a culture inevitably produces.

15. In part through the first three dynamics, the dominant culture in the US, if not the West at large, has not just become dominated *by* brands, but is itself experienced *as* a brand. Specifically, twenty-five years ago, in his seminal *Orientalism*, Edward Said first told us about the power of European colonial discourses and institutions literally – physically as well as ideologically – to remake the world in the image of colonizer. Today Naomi Klein argues that branding has become a process through which, thanks to deregulation and privatization, corporations transform advertising from "mere representations" (which can be ignored if so desired) into a lived reality: "To transform culture into little more than a collection of brand-

extensions-in-waiting" (Klein, *No Logo*, p. 29). So today's Orientalism is then doubly powerful – the full weight of the colonial discourses of the US Empire in perfect synergy (at least as of early 2005) with the needs of major sectors of the business world.

16. Geoffrey Crossick and Serge Jaumain, *Cathedrals of Consumption: The European Department Store: 1850–1939*, London: Ashgate, 1999; George Ritzer, *Enchanting a Disenchanted World*. Ritzer similarly argues that "to many people throughout the world, McDonald's has become a sacred institution" (George Ritzer, *The McDonaldization of Society* [New Century Edition], Thousand Oaks, Calif.: Pine Forge Press, 2000, p. 7).

17. Ritzer, *Enchanting a Disenchanted World*, pp. 51, 193.

18. Upwards of 40 percent of American voters identify themselves as Evangelical Christians; no comparably sized base of support exists for the Democratic Party, let alone progressives.

19. Indeed, such games "anaesthetize" and even "lobotomize" the moral and aesthetic character of an entire generation. For the use of the word "anaesthetize," see *Le Monde*, horizons dossier, "L'autre monde de Porto Alegre," 27–28 Janvier 2002, supplement. For the use of the word "lobotomize," see Alessandro Baricco, *Next*.

20. Simon Penny, "Representation, Enaction, and the Ethics of Simulation," http://www.electronic-bookreview.com, June 26, 2004.

21. Baker, "We're in the Army Now."

22. One where a President has sought to identity himself so completely with the military – more than any other President before him – that a "huah-culture" is taking over the Government. Increasingly, through sports, SUVs, video games, and movies, it is dominating other arenas of popular culture as well.

384 | *Why They Don't Hate Us*

23. Even if the Democratic Party had managed to win back the presidency in 2004 it would not change the basic reality that the political, economic, and cultural "center" of the United States has moved steadily to the neoliberal Right in the last generation.

24. If the German of the last sentence sends a few shivers down your spine, it was meant to. I can't count how many elderly Germans (both Jews and Christians) have come up to me since the war on terror heated up and said that the United States today reminds them of Germany in the 1930s, particularly in the manner in which people are willingly handing away their most basic rights to an increasingly powerful, myth-making Big Brother state and its "info-tainment" complex, with no sign of an active and effective opposition in sight (of course, this hasn't stopped the police and FBI from engaging in surveillance of anti-war groups and even hiphop artists on the ludicrous premise that they might contain terrorists or even "anarchists").

25. The Jacobins were one of the two main revolutionary groups at the time of the French Revolution. Along with the Girondins they were liberal and bourgeois, but they sought a centralized government that they could control based on their belief that only a well-organized, disciplined, and ideologically strong group could save and direct the Revolution, and this sentiment won them the support of crucial sectors of the working class, including the *sans-culottes* (the poor but "useful" working man who "lived simply" and "always has his sabre sharp, to cut off the ears of all enemies of the Revolution" as one pamphlet of the period put it). In order to stem the civil war and threats of foreign invasion when the Revolution touched off they instituted a brutally repressive regime known as the "reign of terror" in 1793–4 to solidify their control over the new French republic, but ultimately the Jacobin ideology and ruthlessness proved too great and they were replaced by "moderates" who desired neither the old regime nor something approaching mass democracy.

26. The trick, of course, is that this is being accomplished in large part through the use of the rhetoric of "individualism" that has defined America's self-perception for two centuries, and the Republican Party's, at least since Reagan.

27. For a discussion of the report, see "Belief Brands ... Oh Really?," Editorial, *Christian Science Monitor*, March 1, 2001, at http://www.humphreys.co.uk/articles/intellectual_property_1.htm. The Young & Rubicam report picked up on a previous year's report from the London design consultancy Fitch that also deified brands. The Fitch report said many people flocked to Ikea instead of church on Sunday; Young & Rubicam says today's brand builders can be compared to the missionaries who spread Christianity and Islam aound the world: "The most successful brands today – 'belief brands' – are those that stand not just for quality and reliability but for a set of beliefs that they refuse to compromise." Calvin Klien, Gatorade, Ikea, Microsoft, MTV, Nike, Virgin, Sony Playstation and Yahoo! were all examples of uncompromising "belief brands." What is most interesting is that the Church of England explained that Y&R's findings were "good news" if they meant they'd be under more pressure to incorporate social responsibility into their brand values. Of course, it took the church 1,967 years to become similarly "responsible." And alerting us to the stakes involved in the deification of corporate brands, one column to the left of the article on Y&R was one titled "EU Must Take Lead on World Poverty," which quoted then UK Secretary of State Claire Short arguing that "economic growth w[ill] have a positive

impact on reducing poverty only if combined with declining inequality" (Judy Dempsey, "EU Must Take Lead on World Poverty," *Financial Times*, March 1, 2001).

28. Richard Tomkins, "Christ Replaces Coke as the Focus of Youthful Longing."

29. Hannah Arendt, *Imperialism*; Tariq Ali, *Clash of Fundamentalisms: Crusades, Jihads and Modernity*, London: Verso, 2003.

30. When that hegemony is challenged the CIA and/or 82nd Airborne, and now mercenaries, can be called in to "discipline" foreigners, while domestic troublemakers are confronted by the FBI, Patriot Acts, Fox News, and Campus Watch. At the same time, the US, Europe, and Japan retain the services of the IMF, WTO, World Bank, and other international financial institutions and regulations to act as the "disciplinarians" who enforce the kind of economic policies that were achieved more democratically by the Government and corporate elites at home.

31. As Simon Sebag Montefiore argues, Osama bin Laden has become a "brand name" ("Human Faces of our Favorite Evildoers," *LA Times*, Op/Ed, May 31, 2004).

32. See Olivier Roy, "al-Qaeda: label ou organization," *Le Monde Diplomatique*, Septembre, 2004. An English translation can be found on the English version of the website under the title "Al Qaeda Brand Name Ready for Franchise," although the French site contains a nice editorial comparing the worldviews of bin Laden and Bush warning readers not to fall into the trap of the clash of civilizations and the "thousand years war" both seem willing to fight for the glory of their God.

33. Noël Mamère and Olivier Warin, *Non merci, Oncle Sam!*, p. 71: "A South thus condemned to poverty will be the hostage of the strongest. And who is the strongest today: the United States."

34. And so today it is all too easy to "condense the target of globalization, the target of anti-American nationalism and the target of internationalization into one apparently unified super target" (Sidney Tarrow, "From Lumping to Splitting: Specifying Globalization and Resistance," in Smith and Johnston, eds., *Globalization and Resistance*, pp. 229–49, p. 244). But let's remember that this dynamic doesn't mean that the US is somehow uniquely responsible for the world's problems. If France or China were the dominant world power in the global era, the response to them would be similar. And the global system is in fact so complex that to blame the US alone for all the world's problems is simplistic and strategically disastrous – although this hasn't stopped many leaders of the global peace and justice movement from doing just that (Davide Demichelis, Angelo Ferrari, Raggaele Masto, Luciano Scalettari, *No Global: Gli inganni della globaizzazione sulla povertà sull'ambiente e sul debito*, Milan: Zelig editore, 2001, p. 14).

35. Roland Hureaux, "Les trois âges de la gauche," *Le débat*, January–February 1999, No. 103, pp. 29–38. For that promising, if violent, summer of 1968, the first thrusts of the neoliberal system against the welfare state order helped produce a common transnational response by activists in American and European youth-oriented Left movements (Jackie Smith and Frank Johnston, "Globalization and Resistance: An Introduction," in Smith and Johnston, eds., *Globalization and Resistance*, pp. 1–12, p. 3).

36. In the US, the larger movement for civil rights and then peace was really a "collaboration of differences" that were not controlled by political organizations or parties (Allen Smith, "Present at the Creation and Other Myths: The Port Huron Statement and

the Origins of the New Left," *Socialist Review*, 27, 1–2 January–February 1999, pp. 1–27).

37. For a good analysis of these dynamics, see Lerner, *The Politics of Meaning*.

38. João Pedro Destile, "Brasil's Landless Battalions," in Tom Mertes, ed., *A Movement of Movements*, p. 41.

39. Denning, *Culture in the Age of Three Worlds*, p. 45.

40. Food riots also occurred in Latin America in the Dominican Republic, Brazil, and dozens of other countries. Unfortunately, however, they've "been wiped from memory" (See James Davis and Paul Rowley, "Internationalism Against Globalization," pp. 24–8; George Katsiaficas, "Seattle Was Not the Beginning," p. 31).

41. Samir Amin, quoted by Terry Boswell and Christopher Chase-Dunn, *The Spiral of Capitalism and Socialism: Toward a Global Democracy*, Boulder: Lynne Reiner, 2000, p. 221.

42. Marco G. Giugni, "Explaining Cross-National Similarities Among Social Movements," in Smith and Johnston, eds., *Globalization and Resistance*, pp. 13–29, p. 25. In fact, the efforts in the 1980s of environmental and human rights groups to curb World Bank lending for projects that threatened peoples and ecosystems in the Global South drew the attention of Northern peace activists in the 1980s, and so the older activists at Seattle said they were first involved through the 1980s mobilizations around third world debt and its relationship to conflict and economic justice in Central American and other developing regions (Jackie Smith, "Globalizing Resistance: The Battle of Seattle and the Future of Social Movements," in Smith and Johnston, eds., *Globalization and Resistance*, pp. 207–27, pp. 208–12).

43. Sophie Style, "People's Global Action," *Z Magazine*, January 2002.

44. Patrick Grady and Kathleen Macmillan, *Seattle and Beyond: The WTO Millennium Round*, Ottawa: Global Economics Ltd., 1999.

45. "The Non-Governmental Order," *The Economist*, December 11, 1999.

46. There were also simultaneous major demonstrations in fourteen US cities (see Davis and Rowley, "Internationalism Against Globalization," pp. 24–8; Katsiaficas, "Seattle Was Not the Beginning," pp. 29–35).

47. James Mittelman, *The Globalization Syndrome: Transformation and Resistance*, Princeton: Princeton University Press, 2000, p. 176. The process of transnationalism at the heart of both economic globalization and of the resistance towards it "paved the way" for Seattle (Jeffrey M. Ayres, "Transnational Political Processes and Contention Against the Global Economy," in Smith and Johnston, eds., *Globalization and Resistance*, pp. 97–114).

48. One of the critiques of May 1968 was that we "wanted everything right away, not something more concrete" (Christian Losson and Paul Quinio, *Génération Seattle*, pp. 16–18, p. 18). Such tactics owed their origin to the British Reclaim the Streets movement and the European Autonomist Marxist groups of the 1970s, and had never before been seen in an urban context on such a large scale (Eddie Yuen, George Katsiaficas, and Daniel Burton Rose, eds., *The Battle of Seattle*, p. 10).

49. Robert Borosage, "The Battle in Seattle," *The Nation*, November 18, 1999.

50. On top of this, labor and progressive activists were those who had been blindsided by President Clinton during the NAFTA debates in 1993 (particularly through the White House's misleading arguments about the benefits of so-called "free trade")

and were not about to be made fools again in Seattle. In Europe, slow growth in the 1990s had left millions unemployed by decade's end, Japan was still mired in a decade of decline, and much of Asia (and in fact, the Global South) was just recovering from the financial meltdown of 1998 (William Greider, "The Battle Beyond Seattle," *The Nation*, December 27, 1999).

51. Michael Lerner, "Protests in Seattle: The Modern Maccabees," *TIKKUN*, January/February 2000.

52. Ibid.

53. Starhawk, *Webs of Power*, p. 96.

54. Cf. Denning, *Culture in the Age of Three Worlds*.

55. D.L.O. Mendis, ed., *WTO Globalization and Eppawala After Seattle*.

56. Losson and Quinio, *Génération Seattle*, pp. 16–18.

57. Aarrg!! was formed after the Nice Summit in December 2000, as a way of showing how individuals, particularly from minority communities in France, were crucial to the success of the movement.

58. This book is actually the second installment in a series titled The Specter of Globalization, Which Closed the Horizons of the Global South and MENA in Particular.

59. Moreover, the Arabic word for "disaster," *ghashiyyah*, also having the meanings of misfortune and calamity, and as interestingly, of stupor and servitude: all meanings that are quite relevant to the Arab view of globalization, as we discussed in the last chapter (Abdessaïd Cherkaoui, *al-'Awlamah – al-ghashiyya b-siyatel* [*Globalization – Disaster in Seattle*]).

60. Most important, as the title suggests, Cherkaoui sees the Seattle protests as illustrating a tremendous struggle within Western societies over the nature of globalization and its clear militarization, with an open question remaining as to whether it will lead to "the realization or destruction of peace?

[will there be] Freedom … or Shackles?" We can imagine how Iraq has impacted this calculus.

61. The most important French anti-corporate globalization movement organization (focused largely on advocating for the Tobin tax on international financial flows).

62. Susan George, "Another World is Possible," *Dissent*, Winter 2001, pp. 5–8.

63. *Le Monde*, January 5, 2001.

64. This is particularly true since the South has remained unable to get greater access to its products in the North while the anti-corporate globalization movement has failed either to gain better access to Northern markets or slow down global trade. It is no doubt for this or similar reasons that at the same time as George made her remarks in the American journal *Dissent*, *Le Monde* ran a headline that asked, "Can We Organize the Globalization of the Planet?" Especially when the job of organizing has traditionally been reserved to governments and nation-states ("Peut-on organizer la mondialisation de la planète?" *Le Monde*, January 22, 2001).

65. Kevin Groves, "Naomi Klein Speaks about the Future of Anti-Globalization."

66. Alexander Cockburn, Jeffrey St. Clair, and Allan Sekula, *5 Days That Shook the World: Seattle and Beyond*, London: Verso, 2000, p. 7.

67. Losson and Quinio, *Génération Seattle*, p. 151.

68. Even Czech President Havel found himself unable to stop the police from brutalizing protesters.

69. Bernard Cassen, "Inventing ATTAC," p. 170.

70. Christophe Aguiton, "A Strategy Appropriate to New Times," in Houtart and Polet, eds., *The Other Davos*, pp. 45–59, p. 45.

71. Starhawk, *Webs of Power*, pp. 51–5.

72. Also frightening the powers that be was the May 2000 "Joyous Disorder" in London, sponsored by Reclaim the Streets, that created "temporary autonomous zones" in the streets of the city's financial district (Losson and Quinio, *Génération Seattle*, p. 21).

73. Yuen et al., eds., *The Battle of Seattle*, pp. 3–4.

74. Ibid.

75. Starhawk, *Webs of Power*.

76. "Another World is Possible," *Utne Reader*, November/December 2001, pp. 64–78. The research and interviews for this section were conducted during the spring through fall of 2003, and were originally published by *Middle East Report* under the title "The Peace Movement Plans for the Future." See http://www.merip.org/mero/interventions/levine_interv.html.

77. Patrick Tyler, "The Second Superpower," New York *Times*, February 17, 2003.

78. Interview with author, spring 2003.

79. "At the World Social Forum in Brazil in 2003, it was clear that the [global justice] movement had totally embraced the peace movement. War sessions were the biggest ones, while the idea for the February 15 worldwide protest day was actually hatched at the European Social Forum in November [2002]."

80. Interview with author, April 2002.

81. Yet disagreements inside the movement about what the appropriate posture towards Hussein should be, especially compared with a more narrow focus on the US war plans, were also important. Progressive American religious magazines such as *Sojourners* and *Tikkun* did call for the removal, indictment, and trial of Hussein while simultaneously opposing a US invasion. Most organizers believed that focusing on Hussein "would have taken away from our argument and even supported people saying that his regime is the reason we needed to go to war to get rid of him," as Rami Elamine, an activist in Washington, described it (personal communication, spring 2003).

82. Indeed, when I suggested to a senior member of UFPJ that the movement focus equally on other situations of extreme oppression and violence such as the Sudan, he replied that he was scared that the Bush Administration would use such arguments as a pretext to invade those countries next. But I would argue that if the movement is scared of criticizing despotic regimes because it might give Bush the excuse to attack them, we've entered an era of Orwellian self-censorship that can only mean that George Bush and his Empire have already won. Few in the movement asked this question before the war. A review of the websites and literature of over three dozen organizations heavily involved in anti-war protests revealed almost nothing mentioning the realities of Ba'athist rule or the need to bring Hussein to justice, and still less addressing problems of autocracy and militarization in the Middle East. Instead, visitors could read "10 Things To Do To Stop the War" – none of which mentioned Hussein – and find out about the "catastrophic casualties predicted by a US invasion." If you clicked enough times, you might have reached a discussion of "Big Problems: Even Bigger Solutions: A More Humane Foreign Policy."

83. Sara Flounders, who was in Cairo, disagrees with this assessment, explaining that "the coalition at the meeting was composed of Nasserites, leftists, communists and Islamists, which acted as enormous restraint. At the same time, we felt that the best way to challenge the Egyptian government was to challenge the coming war,

because in challenging the US war and Israel, by subtext, we were attacking the government that supports both. So the meeting reflected a people's movement from below looking for ways to find political space to resist and to link up globally."

84. In Europe there's a similar situation. The supposedly pro-peace position of the conservative Chirac government gave little space for French intellectuals and academics to adopt an independently critical tone. And after the occupation France slowly worked to repair its rift with Washington, caving in on issues such as giving Security Council imprimatur to the CPA and forgiving Iraqi debt, while French activists have remained largely silent. In Britain, as one British activist-academic explained to me, "the lead-up to the war marked the first time in British history you had major Muslim and South Asian groups involved at the highest level, with significant crossover between the old British left and Muslim associations, against the wishes of many of the more conservative Muslim leaders. But a lot of this community building died the minute the war started. Once Stop the War failed to stop the war, what else was there for it to do?"

85. Tariq Ramadan, *Globalization: Muslim Resistances.*

86. Such movements included Win Without War and MoveOn.

87. Interviews with lead organizers of two major coalition members of UFPJ and ANSWER, May 2003.

88. Interview with Naomi Klein, spring 2004.

89. I put the term anti-Semitism in quotes because in fact it is a very problematic term. This is because technically the term "Semite" refers to a linguistic and ethnic group. In this sense not only are Ashkenazi Jews not "Semites" but Arab Muslims would be Semites too. A better term is "anti-Jewish" or "anti-

Muslim," but since anti-Semitism still has the generally accepted meaning of anti-Jewish sentiments I'm using the term here to call to mind this larger discourse.

90. Along with the prevention of figures such as *TIKKUN* magazine editor Michael Lerner from speaking at anti-war rallies before the war.

91. As one Jewish and self-described anti-Zionist participant in a post-Occupation meeting of movement organizers explained, "While the leadership is trying to be strategic and inclusive, on the grass-roots level if you compare the discourse to the language of the ANC, with its calls for a multiracial society in South Africa, it's just absent here. The Left is doing the same thing as the US Government – going around and attacking certain regimes as illegitimate and unworthy of existence (Israel and in some ways the US), and giving a pass to others, like Sudan or Saudi Arabia. Nor was there a willingness to address issues of violence and terrorism, which is surprising from a group that is vocally committed to non-violence."

92. Indeed, at the UFPJ meeting in July 2003 an overwhelming majority of participants voted down a call to join a march commemorating the outbreak of the second intifada because it fell on Rosh Hashanah (ANSWER and al-'Awda ultimately changed the date too). The managing editor of *TIKKUN* was elected to the steering committee. It is true, as a few people complained, that no members of self-identified Jewish organizations were invited to the meeting of the Palestine Caucus, but Mitchell Plitnick, co-director of A Jewish Voice for Peace, counters that "Jews were part of it. The US Campaign to End the Israeli Occupation wasn't invited, and they have Arab members. I don't think it was about excluding Jews per se, but rather about bringing together people who had more radical views of the conflict. Ultimately,

while there is a tendency toward insensi-
tivity and perhaps even anti-Semitism
among a few people, as an organization
UFPJ clearly respected Jews and desired
Jewish participation."

93. UFPJ leaders are aware of these
issues. As Khalil explains, "Important
concerns were raised by some Jewish
participants. However, Israel is engaged
in a brutal occupation that must be challenged on its own terms. The problem is
that some Jewish participants seemed to
want to make a moral critique of the
occupation without actually calling for
changes in US policies to combat it. But
yes, we should expand our critique to be
more systematic, and it is true that as
long as every regime in the region is in
some way working with the US, its
military and economic aid to these
regimes is part and parcel of maintaining regimes that are not acting in the
interests of their peoples." For a broader
Muslim critique of Arafat's actions and
policies, see Eqbal Ahmed, *Confronting
Empire*.

94. Interview with Sara Flounders,
spring 2003.

95. No author, "Silencing the Voice
on the Streets," *Index for Free
Expression*, February 19, 2003.

96. This and other quotations in this
section have been personal communications with the author, fall 2003
through spring 2004.

Chapter 8

1. Klein argues that "We have to show
them that there is no fence big enough to
contain the kind of grass roots mobilizing that we're all seeing … It's a
demand for self determination, a
knowledge that we actually have the
ability and the skills to solve our own
problems if we are given the resources
and the power to do so" (Groves,
"Naomi Klein Speaks").

2. There are in fact at least five
different types of movements which

have emerged during the last decade
that have some bearing on the way
Muslims are responding to the
common threat faced by the Global
South in the post-September 11 era. In
some ways these responses correspond
to at least five threads of contemporary
globalization: the market/economic
thread, the globalization of communications, and the cultural, ideological,
and political trends (Zaki Laïdi,
Malaise dans le mondialisation, p. 28).

3. Specifically, the WTO's plan to
"save capitalism" (Bernard Cassen, "Un
'plan de sauvetage' du captialisme," *Le
Monde diplomatique*, Décembre 1999,
p. 19). See Walden Bellow, "The Global
South," in Mertes, ed., *A Movement of
Movements*, p. 60. A good synopsis of
this view is Institute for Agriculture and
Trade Policy director Mark Ritchie's
belief that "global cooperation rather
than globalization" is what's needed
today. Indeed, for many activists it is the
local revitalization of landscapes, environments, businesses, and communities that is "the strength of the
movement, more than the protests"
(quoted in "Another World is Possible,"
Utne Reader, November/December
2001, pp. 64–78).

More specifically, we can distinguish
between several trends in the anti-
corporate globalization movement:
first, "contestation and reform" movements, which are critical of but don't
seek the total dismantling of the capitalist system (pursuing corrective
measures such as the Tobin tax on
currency transfers; the idea behind the
founding of ATTAC); second, antisys-
temic movements that seek to democratize global governance by means of
globalization from below (often
through imposing regulatory limitations on corporations through
increased state interference in the
market); third, movements of "deglobalization," or delinking and relocalization of sovereignty through the

voluntary cutting off of communities from the global market; and finally, anti-globalization movements that attack the powers that be in order to revitalize so-called traditional non-democratic civilizational values (that is, "fundamentalist" religious or nationalist movements (Starr, *Naming the Enemy* p. 9; Chase-Dunn and Boswell, "Transnational Social Movements and Democratic Socialist Parties in the Semiperiphery"). Starr further explains that contestation and reform movements fight structural adjustment and pro-growth policies, and for corporate welfare reform, peace, and human rights, or land reform, anti-growth; the globalization from below movement focuses on the environment, labor, socialism, anti-Free Trade Agreements, and Zapatismo; and the delinking/ relocalization tendency includes movements motivated by ideologies of anarchy, sustainable development, small-business sovereignty, and religious nationalism. It should be noted that there is great disagreement among leading theoreticians and activists over the possibility, stressed by ATTAC, of "reclaiming sovereignty" for states (Toni Negri, quoted in *Le Monde*, horizons dossier, "L'autre monde de Porto Alegre, 27–28 Janvier 2002, supplement, p. 10).

4. Starr, *Naming the Enemy*, pp. 44, 55, 65, 78; Simon Tormey, *Anti-Capitalism: A Beginner's Guide*, Oxford: Oneworld Publications, 2004; Alex Callinicos, *An Anti-Capitalism Manifesto*, Cambridge: Polity Press, 2003.

5. There are two kinds of anarchism involved in the anti-corporate globalization movement: on the one hand, anarchism is often used to describe the fact that the movement lacks an overall ideological goal or set of strategies for achieving it; on the other, the ideologies and practices of people and groups calling themselves or called "anarchists" have exerted an important influence on the movement as a whole.

6. This and similar phrases are the stock in trade of most anarchist materials I have seen, either in print or on the web. See, for example, "The Anarchist Platform," at http://flag.blackened.net/revolt/anarchism/platform.html.

7. David Graeber, "The New Anarchists." Yet even radicals usually have a "transitional" program that includes focusing on reforming global institutions to have greater representation of the South and civil society organizations, deglobalizing global trade, broad debt relief if not cancellation, fairer international trade agreements, an end to subsidized agricultural dumping from North to South, sustainable development policies, global treaties to secure better working conditions for all, and greater control of the arms trade.

8. Naomi Klein, "Rebels in Search of Rules," New York *Times*, December 2, 1999, p. A35.

9. It is for this reason that anarchists historically, and especially today, have distinguished themselves from traditional working-class trade unions, because the hierarchical union structure made it much easier for them to be coopted by the US, European, and Japanese states. Against a labor movement that seeks to carve out a bigger slice of the pie for its members, the amorphous collection of people working within the rubric of anarchism seek ultimately to "reinvent daily life as a whole" from an explicitly anti-capitalist perspective (Graeber, "The New Anarchists").

10. People engaging in black bloc activities stress, in good anarchist fashion, that the black bloc is a "tactic, not a group or organization" that seeks physically and visually to ratchet up protests beyond mere reformism and appeals to the state. And so black was chosen as the color scheme in order to gain visibility: "The black bloc as gay pride march," as one website describes it

(see black bloc *for Dummies*, at http://www.infoshop.org/blackbloc.html).

11. Among the issues the DAN sought to highlight in Seattle were "war, low wages, deforestation, gentrification, gridlocked cities, genetic engineering, the rich getting richer, cuts in social services, increasing poverty, meaningless jobs, global warming, more prisons, and sweatshops."

12. After Seattle, the Direct Action Network became a loose continental network with locals in at least a dozen cities. Many of its actions and activities are announced on its website. At the top of one web page DAN proclaims its mission: "We are a continental network committed to overcoming corporate globalization and all forms of oppression. We are part of a growing movement united in common concern for justice, freedom, peace, and sustainability of all life, and in a commitment to take direct action to realize radical visionary change."

13. Every affinity group must decide for itself how it will make decisions and what it wants to do, and within the groups strong consensus, rather than majority decision making, is demanded. This is, of course, the epitome of anarchistic practice.

14. Starhawk, *Webs of Power*, p. 96. Indeed, some would argue that most of the creative energy for radical politics is coming from anarchist-inspired groups and collectives, whether in the US or Europe.

15. Graeber, "The New Anarchists."

16. The choice at this level affects whether anarchist groupings can inspire a broad ideological transformation in American/Western culture, or will only be able to play the more limited role of shocking people out of their complacency.

17. Yuen et al., eds., *The Battle of Seattle*, p. 14.

18. In the northwest in the 1990s anarchists also attacked police with bottles and even vomited on a mayor. Most significant, more prominent advocates of black bloc tactics have gone on record advocating, if the conditions were right, armed resistance against the state: in the post-September 11 environment, one explained, merely "breaking windows [à la Seattle] is, like, so '99" (David Samuels, "Notes from the Underground: Among the Radicals of the Pacific Northwest," *Harper's Magazine*, May 2000, pp. 35–47; interview with black bloc member Bobo, Hans Bennett, "The black bloc," http://www.altpr.org/apr16/blackbloc.html).

19. John Sellers, "Raising a Ruckus," in Mertes, ed. *A Movement of Movements*, pp. 187–8. Although we should recall, as Bové describes in great detail in his book, that when the dismantling first happened the French media totally bought into the official labeling of it as "destruction" and looting. But we must also realize that the public perceives his activism and that of "a few black clad kids breaking windows" (as one critic within the movement categorized it) quite differently, although the negative perception of the black bloc is not always warranted, as in the case of Seattle, for example, the property destruction was carefully planned and coordinated by the DAN so that only major corporate entities were attacked (they attacked Starbucks, but protesters lined up for coffee from a locally owned café across the street) while people and personal (as opposed to "private") property were, as a matter of policy, not put in harm's way (Bové and Dufour, *The World is Not for Sale*).

20. Instead, as happened in Najaf, older religious leaders turned on Moqtada al-Sadr and sided with the occupation forces, in large part because of the violence his rebellion unleashed.

21. As one abused Arab/Muslim proverb goes, "better sixty years of tyranny than one day of anarchy."

22. "The Hourglass of the Zapatistas," interview with Subcommandante Marcos and guerrilla Commandante Marquez Roberto Pombo, in Mertes, ed., *A Movement of Movements*, pp. 3–12, p. 6.

23. Justin Paulson, "Peasant Struggles and International Solidarity: The Case of Chiapas," *Socialist Register*, 2001.

24. Juana Ponce de León, ed., *Our Word is Our Weapon*, pp. 13, 17.

25. Starr, *Naming the Enemy*.

26. Ponce de León, ed., *Our Word is Our Weapon*.

27. The focus on autonomy rather than seizing state power is the reason for Marcos's oft-quoted comments that the insurgency was "born to fail," and that they wanted the "world to watch over our battles." Most important, rather than advocating a grand strategy the Zapatistas from the start pushed to open an inclusionary arena, and to activate a mass movement throughout civil society in Mexico that would ultimately have implications for linking local and global struggles. And at perhaps the most basic level the Zapatista movement from the start has sought to create an ethics of mutual understanding as exhibited by the development of a global moral community through their struggle (Adam David Morton, "Mexico, Neoliberal Restructuring and the EZLN: A Neo-Gramscian Analysis," in Barry Gills, ed., *Globalization and the Politics of Resistance*, pp. 255–79). It was, perhaps ironically, Marcos's and the Zapatistas' leadership's humility, their admission that "We have not come to lead you, to tell you what to do, but to ask for your help," that gave the movement such international resonance and influence as the anti-corporate globalization movement began to develop, to the point of inspiring the Ya Basta! movement in Italy and Spain particularly (we'll look at the activities of the Italian movements below).

28. Marco Revelli, "Aquel primero de enero," *Perfil de la Jornada*, December 30, 2003, http://www.jornada.unam.mx/2003/dic03/031230/per-1.html.

29. The *caracol*, which also means sea-shell, is also used as a Mayan metaphor in relationship to the spiral nature of the shell (thanks to film maker and critic Mariana Botey for providing me with the insights surrounding the *caracoles* issue). *Caracoles* has actually taken on a practical political meaning for the Zapatistas, as it is the name of the new autonomous governments and municipal councils (or *juntas del buen gobierno*) established in December 2003 as a new stage of Zapatista organization.

30. Some critics believe that the social and economic marginalization of the Zapatistas that has been so important to their "brand consciousness" will prevent the movement from "having universal value," since such marginalization is deemed to be "incomprehensible" to a wealthy West (Revelli, "Aquel primero de enero").

31. Chittaroopa Palit, "Monsoons Rising," in Mertes, ed., *A Movement of Movements*, p. 81.

32. Many people argue that Subcommandante Marcos's mask serves as a mirror for the larger movement – "He is simply us: we are the leader we've been looking for" – he reflects the intellectual and moral courage of so many Islamist activists today who are working, often at personal peril, to reconstruct a more humane and progressive Muslim theology, law, and culture in their societies (Naomi Klein, "Farewell to the 'End of History': Organization and Vision in Anti-Corporate Movements," *The Socialist Register*, 2002, pp. 1–14).

33. Editorial, Subcommandante Marcos, "Naissance d'une nouvelle droite: Le fascisme liberal," *Le Monde Diplomatique*, August 2000, pp. 1, 14–15.

34. Ibid.

35. While the anti-corporate globalization movement looks toward the Zapatistas with an almost mythical (and perhaps even mystical) vision, there has been significant criticism of their initial limited call for autonomy (although their end goal was clearly a much broader democratization of Mexico), precisely because it cost the Mexican Government nothing to let the indigenous peoples "close in on themselves" and absolve it of the need to redistribute significantly the nation's resources and put greater state investment and presence in the largely destitute state of Chiapas. And just as the larger anti-corporate globalization movement has yet to win a significant permanent shift in the architecture of global economic and political governance, in Mexico while the famous 1996 San Andrés Accords signed by the representatives of the EZLN and the Mexican state called for "the recognition of the right of indigenous people to self-determination within a context of autonomy, the expansion of their participation and political representation, the guarantee of their access to justice, and the promotion of their cultural, educational and economic activities," these goals have not been met by the state, which as of early 2004 had just invaded an "autonomous" region to dismantle its locally elected council. For more on these criticisms see Judith Adler Hellman, "Real and Virtual Chiapas: Magic Realism and the Left," *Socialist Register*, 2000. In fact, however inspiring for worldwide anti-corporate globalization movement activists it was that the Zapatistas focused explicitly on neoliberalism as the major world threat to grass-roots democracy and justice, the dynamics of Chiapas complex history, like that of so many other locales around the world, can't be reduced purely to neoliberalism and its discontents.

36. Marcos, quoted in Ponce de León, *Our Word is our Weapon*, p. 47.

37. Ibid., p. 49.

38. Ibid., pp. 17–9.

39. Ibid., p. 63.

40. Ibid., p. 46.

41. Ibid., p. 126.

42. When Starr maps the relationships between various types of movements today, it is clear that the anti-corporate and anti-free trade area movements are the core of the larger "movement of movements." After them, the movements fighting structural adjustment and for sustainable development are the next best connected, followed by indigenous sovereignty movements (Starr, *Naming the Enemy*, p. 126).

43. More specifically, we can create the table below from her information:

Issue: Does the movement criticize:	Religious Nationalists	Zapatistas
Capitalism	No*	Yes
Neoliberalism	No*	Yes
Globalization	No*	Yes
Growth	No*	Yes
Consumption	Yes	No
Dependency	Yes	Yes
Does it see corporations as colonial?	Yes	Yes
Use an alternative epistemology?	Yes	Yes
Is the "street" a major site of action?	Yes	Yes
Does it involve a struggle for ideological hegemony?	Yes	Yes
Is the movement interested in a transformative dialogue with the enemy?	No*	No
Does it focus on legislative and/or judicial reforms?	Yes	No
Does it advocate direct pressure on corporations?	Yes	No
Does it engage in party politics?	Yes	No
Does it see popular culture as a means of struggle?	No*	No
Does it see everyday life as a medium of struggle?	Yes	Yes
Does it create alternative spaces?	Yes	Yes

Issue: Does the movement criticize:	Religious Nationalists	Zapatistas
Does it see traditional culture as a critical lens for engaging in resistance?	Yes	Yes
Does it seek "progress" or industrial-style development?	No*	No
Does it presume ecological limits?	No*	Yes

*indicates where the answer for the MENA is the opposite of what Starr presents in her table for the Zapatistas, providing evidence of where non-extremist Islamist movements would differ from the Zapatistas

44. This and following quotes, personal communications, fall 2003 through spring 2004.

45. Jagdish Bhagwati, "Globalization in Your Face: A New Book Humanizes Global Capitalism," *Foreign Affairs*, July/August 2000.

46. Bernard Cassen, "Dove arrivera Porto Alegre?" *Il manifesto*, 10/02, No. 32, http://www. larivistadel manifesto. it/archivio/32/32A20021013.html. Larry Elliott, "Silence of the Cardigan Capitalists," *The Guardian*, January 23, 2004.

47. As we saw Bernard Cassen explain, "The Left wants to ask 'what kind of organization do we need' and then 'what kind of ideas do we need,' as if you can ask them in that order" (Cassen, "Inventing ATTAC," pp. 170–4).

48. Ibid. He continues, "What we are seeing today is a movement that, for the first time, is hitting the same targets and developing all over the world, linking local struggles to global objectives."

49. See the website for the 2001 meeting: http://www.forumsocial-mundial.org.br. It is worth noting how the language of the first forum's website is a quaint broken English – obviously translated from Portuguese – that would not be seen in future years as the event became more English- if not Anglo-centered.

50. François Houtart, "Preface: From Davos to Porto Alegre," in Houtart and Polet, eds., *The Other Davos*, pp. vi–viii.

51. Sader, "Beyond Civil Society."

52. This included a four-level focus on issues related to wealth and civil society. According to organizers, the WSF needed to "open space" in order to search for the alternatives to the dominant model. "Truly the WSF will be the first step, but a step really new, which it's winning the repercussions over and over the whole world" (website for the 2001 meeting: www.forum socialmundial.org.br). The text continues, "The WSF will be a new international arena for the creation and exchange of social justice and sustainable development. The WSF will provide a space for building economic alternatives, for exchanging experiences and for strengthening – South–North alliances betwen NGOs, unions and social movements. It will also be an opportunity for developing concrete projects to educate the public and to mobalize civil society internationally."

53. Gilles Luneau, "A Porto Alegre, pour une mondialisation différente," *Le Monde diplomatique*, Janvier 2002, pp. 20–1.

54. Ibid.

55. Ibid.

56. For 2004 there were panels dealing with "Kurds, Palestinians, Tibetans: Peoples under Occupation or Foreign Domination," "Religious Communities, Response to Globalisation and Terrorism," "US occupation of Iraq and the problem of Palestine and Afghanistan," "Spiritualities and Identities in the Dialogue of Civilizations," "Imperialism and Liberation: Iraq, Palestine, Kashmir," "The Apartheid Wall," "Religious, Ethnic, and Linguistic, Exclusion and Oppression," "Development in the Arab World," "Wild West in the Middle East? Iraq, Palestine and the Region after the War – Risks and Options," "US Hegemony and the Arab Street," a "Presentation of the situation in Palestine," and "the Rise of Religious Fundamentalism in India."

57. "Eighty thousand unite against globalization," 17 January 2004, http://www.nu.ac.za/ccs/default.asp?2, 27,3,340.

58. Even al-Jazeera and other news media from the Global South reported growing concern among some circles within the WSF movement that it remained focused too much on talk and too little on action, especially in light of the stated desire to build "an alliance against Bush" (Al-Jazeera arts on Mumbai: WSF seeks alliance against Bush, http://www.aljazeera.net, Sunday January 18, 2004).

59. Sader, "Beyond Civil Society."

60. Cf. Nezar Al-Sayyad and Manuel Castells, eds., *Muslim Europe or Euro-Islam*, p. 1. There is also the similarity of perceptions and strategies between both state–corporate elites and protesters on both sides of the Atlantic. That is, despite the traditional power of the European welfare states, governments and economic elites across the EU view globalization in manner not that different from their American counterparts: as a "purposeful project to stabilize contemporary capitalism" administered by a transnational class of corporate/state managers whose interests are increasingly separate from those of the citizens they used to represent much more closely (cf. Axtmann, *Globalization and Europe*).

61. Giuliano Amato, Mireille Delmas-Marty, David Marquand, and Sergio Romano, *What Future for Europe?* Florence: Robert Schuman Center for Advanced Studies, 1999.

62. Philippe Frémeaux, *Sortir du piège: la gauche face à la mondialisation*, Paris: Éditions La Découverte et Syros, 1998.

63. Suzanne Daley, "More Vehemently than Ever, Europe is Scorning the US," New York *Times*, April 9, 2000. Cf. John Vinocur, "Jospin Envisions an Alternative EU," *IHT*, May 29, 2001, web edition, which describes Jospin as offering "no place for collabo-

ration with the United States." Also see Flora Lewis, "Soured Allied Relations Under Bush Need Fixing," *IHT*, September 25, 2001, p. 9; William Pfaff, "America and Europe: A New World Order Will Have to Wait," *IHT*, May 17, 2001, web edition; Martin Kettle, "The New Anti-Americanism," *Wall Street Journal* Online, January 10, 2001; and "Roger Cohen, Arrogant or Humble? Bush Encounters Europeans' Hostility," *IHT*, May 8, 2001, p. 1.

64. The "unprecedented level of anger towards the US in Europe" was based on the shared belief that its economic power will ultimately force social as well as economic changes on European countries that will threaten welfare states and protected national cultures.

65. The shared anger at and fear of the United States has led to greater emphasis on building a successful "Euro-mediterranean partnership" that would benefit both sides of the Mediterranean *barzakh* (Lamchichi, *Islam-Occident*, p. 19).

66. Tariq Ramadan and Alain Gresh, *L'Islam en questions*, p. 2.

67. Peter Mandaville, *Transnational Muslim Politics: Reimagining the Umma*, London, Routledge, 2003, pp. 132–3, quoting Zaki Badawi.

68. Jamie Dowand and Gabi Hinsliff, "British Hostility Towards Muslims Could Trigger Riots," *The Observer*, May 30, 2004, http://www.guardian.co.uk/race/story/0,11374,1227977,00.html.

69. For a detailed discussion of Islam and Europe, including an extensive bibliography as of 2002, see LeVine, "'Human Nationalisms' versus 'Inhuman Globalisms'".

70. Carla Power and Christopher Dickey, "Generation M," *Newsweek International*, December 1, 2003, http://msnbc.msn.com/id/ 3540615/; Catherine Withol de Wenden and Rémy Léveau, *La bourgeoisie: le trois*

âges de la vie associative issue de l'immi-gration, Paris: CNRS, 2001.

71. Charles Pellegrini, *Le FIS en France: Mythe ou réalité,* Paris: Édition 1, 1992, p. 60. These dynamics also underlie the turn toward Islam by disadvantaged communities in the United States such as African Americans, who have taken the full force of postindustrial economic restructuring from the late 1970s onwards (Kepel, *Allah in the West,* p. 84).

72. Cf. Kepel, *Allah in the West,* p. 206.

73. Such as ATTAC and Bové's CNSTP (Confédération Nationale des Syndicats de Travailleurs Paysans, the National Confederation of Unions of Farm Workers).

74. While Bové and his farmers' movement are among the most important activist forces in Europe, their focus is largely within the French context. For Cassen and ATTAC, formed in 1998 as an "action oriented movement of popular education," the imposition of the Tobin tax on currency transfers is the paradigm for greater national controls on the market. For the farmer Bové the issues involved are literally much more grass roots – biodiversity, protecting and even encouraging the consumption of locally produced agricultural products that use no hormones, no antibiotics, and no genetically modified organisms, and a campaign against *malboufe,* or all the junk food snacks and assembly-line processed foods that are symbolized by the McDonald's he so famously "disas-sembled." For a discussion of the philosophy behind ATTAC, see Cassen, "Inventing ATTAC." For a detailed discussion of Bové's philosophy, see Bové and Dufour, *The World is Not For Sale.*

75. Losson and Quinio, *Génération Seattle,* pp. 42–5.

76. Of course, like France, Italy has some of the most important journals and newspapers in the worldwide movement including *Derive Approdi, Carta,* and the communist newspaper *Il Manifesto,* and the more centrist *La Repubblica* daily. In fact, it was the Italian daily *Corriere della Sera,* and not one of its French counterparts, that had the foresight to commission none other than Michel Foucault to go to Iran to cover the 1978–9 Islamic Revolution, which produced some of Foucault's most important yet least discussed (since they were available only in Italian or French until recently) political writings. And today some of the most insightful columns in Europe on issues related to globalization are to be found in the "idée" column of *La Repubblica.* For a full discussion of Foucault's trip to Iran, his writings, and the debates they sparked in France, see Mark LeVine and Armando Salvatore, "Socio-Religious Movements and the Transformation of 'Common Sense' into a Politics of 'Common Good'," in LeVine and Salvatore, eds., *Religion, Social Practice, and Contested Hegemonies.*

77. This is achieved by enlarging the public forum of debate on issues ranging from global matters such as environmental conservation and the growing disparities between the Global North and South, to local-national ones such as the case for protecting the last remnants of the pre-globalized industrial/welfare-state economy.

78. We can see how Ya Basta! would challenge the neoliberal paradigm, as its vision calls for universally guar-anteed basic income, global citizenship, free movement of people across borders, and free access to new tech-nologies made possible by strong limits on patent rights. Indeed, one of its projects is the "No Border Network" whose slogan, "no one is illegal," is clearly attractive to the millions of Muslim immigrants on the continent. "More specifically, the Ya Basta! associ-ation is a network of many groups across many Italian cities. It was formed

after Italian militants participated in the first Encuentro in Chiapas in 1996. It has the dual purpose of supporting the Zapatista struggle and of spreading the deep meaning of the struggles against neo-liberalism in Europe. For details on Ya Basta! visit their website, at http://www.yabasta.it. In 1998, most Ya Basta! militants also joined the emerging movement called the Tute Bianche (white overalls). This comprises young people from the social centres, unemployed and casual workers, people searching for their first job, all united against the pressure of neo-liberalism, asking for a universal basic income, but also asking for better conditions of life for everybody. White overalls were chosen as a strong image to symbolize the condition of invisibility imposed upon all those people forced to live without guarantees, without social security, on the margins of a normal life.

79. As a parish priest, part of the Ya Basta! contingent with whom I marched in Prague in September 2000, declared as the group faced off against the police: "With our bodies, with what we are, we came to defend the rights of millions, dignity and justice. Even with our lives. In the face of the total control of the world which the owners of money are exercising, we have only our bodies for protesting and rebelling against injustice" (Jess Ramrez Cuevas, "The Body as a Weapon for Civil Disobedience," *La Jornada*, October 15, 2000, http://www.nadir.org/nadir/initiativ/agp/s26/praga/bianche.htm).

80. And indeed, the more anarchistic wing of the Italian movement promotes "the abolishment of international institutions and the introduction of a comprehensive social wage" to be achieved through non-violent "civil disobedience" (Donatella Della Porta and Lorenzo Mosca, eds., *Globalizzazioue e movimenti Sociali*, Rome: Manifestolibri, 2003, p. 36).

81. The even more militant black bloc, however, has engaged in more direct violence against "private property" such as corporate headquarters and stores, but not direct attacks on people unless attacked first. As Rete Lilliput explains, "The concept of solidarity is extended from the relationship between man and society to the one between man and nature, and it is subsequently integrated with a discourse of biodiversity that analyses the relationship between men and women." For a good discussion of the Lilliput strategy see Jeremy Brecher and Tim Costello, *Global Village or Global Pillage: Economic Reconstruction from the Bottom Up*, Boston: South End Press, 1994.

82. Jacopo Moroni, "Global or No-Global? Drawing a few lines on the meaning of global and Italian dissent," unpublished research paper, January 2004.

83. Email correspondence between author and Jacopo Moroni, January 2004.

84. "Cos'è il forum sociale europeo?" on website for the ESF: http://www.fse-esf.org/article717.html?var_recherche=firenze. Like its global predecessor, the gathering attempted to be "a space open to all the protagonists in civil society … without negating divergences of opinion."

85. This level of organization allowed the organizers to focus on creating "a continental space of meeting of organizations and individuals from the countries of Western, Central and Eastern Europe as well as organizations from other continents … all with the goal of affirming not only the necessity of another Europe at the service of its citizens and people, but also to demonstrate the real possibility of finding the means for its realization." The plenaries and break-outs of the Forum dealt in great detail with issues such as the pending invasion of Iraq

and moving from an "EU of liberal globalization to an alternative EU," to more mundane but equally important discussions of food safety, gender, and labor relations, and fighting social exclusion. Other panels dealt with financial liberalization, or with titles such as "Europe is not for Sale," "Against the Privatization of Sanity ...," "Missing Links: Feminism and Globalized resistance", and "To Melt Down the Patriarchal Iceberg."

86. These included panels such as "Christianity, Islam, Hebraism in Europe," "Cultural Identities in Europe," "The Place of Islam in Europe," and "Islamophobia – The Respectable Face of the European Racism."

87. The Florence plenaries and workshops are archived on the ESF website at http://www.fse-esf.org/rubrique63.html. The seminars are not available on the ESF website, but were archived at http://www.carta.org/agenzia/ForumEuropeo/021015seminars.htm.

88. Among the issues related to Islam that the Paris ESF dealt with were "Racism, anti-Semitism and Islamophobia" (at which Ramadan spoke), "Islam in Europe: Stakes and Challenges," "What Future for Eastern Europe and Turkey?," "Europe, Vector for Imposing Liberal Globalisation in the Mediterranean Region," "Spiritual Resistance to Neoliberal Globalization: Christianity, Islam, Judaism, and Buddhism," "Human Liberation and Religion," "The Clash of Civilizations of Dialogue of Cultures and Peoples," "Public Space in the Maghreb," and several panels dealing with human rights in general and Berbers and Palestinians in particular. The program for the 2003 Paris ESF is at http://www.fse-esf.org/validation/plenieres.php; http://www.fse-esf.org/validation/seminaires.php; http://www.fse-esf.org/validation/ ateliers.php.

89. *Luoghid comuni: il movimento globale come spazivo di polticizzazionel* (*Common Places: The Global Movement as an Open Space for Politicization*, Derive Approdi, Rome: 2003.

90. Ibid., pp. 22–3.

91. Ibid., p. 23. It continues, "Having easily registered the crisis of representative democracy, the global movement has not yet found new organizational alchemies capable of overcoming it" (ibid., p. 24).

92. Ibid., p. 25.

93. As important, however, the authors warn against "transferring ... these aspirations from the national to the continental level, pointing to Europe as the strong subject of a renewed anti-Americanism" (ibid., pp. 25–6).

94. Ramadan, *Globalization*, p. 3.

95. Ibid., p. 4.

96. He continues, "The absence of dialogue between the leaders of the resistance movements and the repetition of old ideological arguments to the point of overdose is preventing the evolution and renewal of critical thought in the Arab and Muslim world. Political projects are sadly lacking, strategies for resistance are lacking" (ibid., p. 20). This is why it's so important for the Arab world to interact continuously with the global peace and justice movement, in particular because "if one listens in on the dominant views of Arab society, one thing becomes immediately clear: the cause of all woes is 'Israel'" (ibid.). For Ramadan it's crucial for the Arab world and the larger Muslim world to move far beyond such simplistic formulas; indeed, he argues that "one can only note the failure of the Muslim resistance movements to take into account the international dynamics of the global justice movement." To which we should note that such a task is made all the more difficult when the global peace and justice movement itself is based in good measure on simplistic critiques of the US and Israel.

97. Ibid., p. 6, his emphasis. At the same time he acknowledges, quoting Susan George, that the world economic system was structured in such a way as to leave the Muslim world with little means to propose "something else."

98. For a chilling discussion of just how serious the terror threat in Europe is becoming, see Antony Barnett, Jason Burke, and Zoe Smith, "Terror Cells Regroup – and Now their Target is Europe," *The Observer*, Sunday, January 11, 2004, http://observer.guardian.co.uk/waronterrorism/story/0,1373,1120658,00.html.

99. Ramadan, *Globalization*, p. 8.

100. Ibid., p. 11.

101. Ibid., p. 14.

102. Ibid., p. 15.

103. Ibid., p. 25.

104. Ibid., pp. 26–7.

105. "There are no leaders, nor a unified structure ... the movement, they say, is open to individuals as much as to ideas ... This remains to be seen. Very quickly at the heart of the dynamic, one perceives the old complicities, common interests, unspoken but recognized all the same ... The populations most affected are virtually absent from the numerous forums where one thinks for them, without them. If they do come along, they are questioned, suspected" (ibid., p. 28).

106. In fact, as *Ha'aretz* reported, Ramadan publicly argued "To my regret, anti-Semitic utterances have been heard not only from frustrated and confused young Muslims, but also from certain Muslim intellectuals and imams ... who in every crisis or political backsliding see the hand of the 'Jewish lobby.' There is nothing in Islam that gives legitimization to Judeophobia, xenophobia and the rejection of any human being because of his religion or the group to which he belongs. Anti-Semitism has no justification in Islam, the message of which demands respect for the Jewish religion and spirit, which

is considered a noble expression of the People of the Book" (as reported by David Bloo, in *Ha'aretz*, May 26, 2003).

107. Tariq Ramadan, "Critique des (nouveaux) intellectuels communautaires," October 3, 2003, published on his website, http://oumma.com/article.php3?id_article=719.

108. His larger point was that uncritical support of Israel, and of the US when it engages in actions which – arguably at best, in the case of invading Iraq – support Israel's interests, only serve to make it harder for Jews to work with other communities against prejudice and oppression and to forge a common progressive identity. And so most important, "Whether its about the interior plan (the struggle against anti-Semitism) or on the international scene (defending Zionism), one can see the emergence of a new attitude among certain intellectuals who are omnipresent in the media scene [in France]. Is it legitimate to ask what those principles are and which interests they defend first? We can perceive clearly that their political position responds to a communitarian logic" (ibid.).

109. In May 2003 he published a call with Jewish and Christian leaders in the French media decrying the growing anti-Semitism in France.

110. Tariq Ramadan, "Ce que j'ai toujours dit: Réponse à Bernard-Henri Lévy," November 5, 2003, http://oumma.com/article.php3?id_article=783.

111. More broadly, the accusations generally revolved around saying different things to different audiences, that he couldn't be trusted because he speaks "passionately" to his largely young (and, one is led to assume, impressionable) audiences, or (without anyone ever giving a shred of evidence as far as I can tell) that he is much more militant when he speaks to Muslims than when he speaks to European or

American academic audiences. As he explained about the reaction he received at the 2003 ESF, it was such that "my 12 minutes speaking at the ESF has surprisingly convinced them that I wasn't an intellectual, but a preacher!" (Tariq Ramadan, "Mon but est de faire évoluer les mentalités," November 21, 2003, http://oumma.com/article.php3?id_article=783). See Dimitri Friedman, "Tariq Ramadan: Le Forum Social Européen a choisi son camp," http://www.col.fr/article-350.html.

112. The last argument led Bernard Cassen, for example, to disassociate himself from Ramadan; but if we look at what Ramadan has actually said on the subject the accusations are not borne out. One could say that the accusation that he hasn't condemned Islam's condemnation of homosexuality is ostensibly true in that Ramadan argues that "The [Qur'an] commands and the Qur'an condemns," but the accusation falls apart with the next sentence: "But we shouldn't reprimand ... people who don't pray or act a certain way" ("Mon but est de faire").

113. Caroline Monnot and Xavier Ternisien, "Tariq Ramadan accusé d'antisémitisme," *Le Monde*, October 10, 2003, http://www.lemonde.fr/web/imprimer_article/0,1-0@2-3226, 36-337508,0.html.

114. They go on to say that the very idea that Ramadan would mention the religion of a French person as being relevant to critiqueing them is so appalling that it can only mean that he's not really French (in fact, he's Swiss). In the words of Jean-Luc Mélenchon, Vincent Peillon, and Manuel Vallis, "Ramadan, pretends to be our friend. He inscribes his denunciation of Jews in a progressive cadre in the name of defending Palestine, the values of humanity, he does it in the cadre of the preparation of the Social Forum. This manipulation is quite odious ... To

reduce them to an origin is an infamy" (Jean-Luc Mélenchon, Vincent Peillon, and Manuel Vallis, "Monsieur Ramadan ne peut pas être des nôtres," *Nouvel Observateur Hebdo* N.2033 – 23/10/2003, http://archives.nouvelobs.com/recherche/article.cfm?id=124234&).

115. Khalfa "defended" him by arguing that "Ramadan's essay is not anti-Semitic. It is dangerous to wave the red flag of anti-Semitism at any moment. However, it is a text marked partly by Ramadan's communitarian thought and which communicates his view of the world to others." Even the movement's star, José Bové, chimed in, arguing that "the anti-globalization movement defends universalist points of view which are therefore necessarily secular in their political expression ... That there should be people of different cultures and religions is only natural. The whole effort is to escape such determinisms," Mohamed Sid-Ahmed, "The Furor over Tariq Ramadan," *Al-Ahram Weekly*, January 1–7, 2004.

116. Shammar Fishman, "Some notes on Arabic terminology as a link between Tariq Ramadan and Sheikh Dr Taha Jabir al-Alwari," PRISM, no date.

117. "Pro-Israel" only if you consider supporting a brutal occupation that is destroying Zionism and even Judaism as "supportive" of Israel's present and future interests.

118. For a discussion of the barring of Ramadan from entering the US as of late August 2004, see Mark LeVine, "Why is this Man Banned," *LA Times*, December 12, 2004.

119. What's most disturbing are not the attacks by the Right, or even by the intellectuals Ramadan critiqued. It's that the progressives in the ESF by and large did not come to his defense. This led him to argue that "the ESF must refuse to be a platform or where Judeophobia or Islamophobia can be expressed, it can't be, itself, either pro-Palestinian or anti-

Israeli ... The ESF must refuse the expressions of racisms and be a space where all the injustices are denounced: from Russia to China, Saudi Arabia to Israel, the ghettos (bideonvilles) to poor suburbs (banlieues). Without distinction. What's important is to come as individuals, to bring their culture and their religion, yes, in their communal desire to change the world, to refuse any differentiating the victims and distinguishing the executioners (Tariq Ramadan, "Antisémitisme et communautarisme: des abcès à crever," October, 29, 2003, http://oumma.com/article.php3? id_article=749, published in *Le Monde*, October 28, 2003). Later on in the interview he explains that "historically immigrant communities functioned thus: they began by coming together based on nationalist ... second through religious regrouping. I am trying to help to bring to pass a third phase, where one acts in the name of principles that one defends and not based on the identity one carries."

120. Mendis, *WTO Globalization and Eppawala After Seattle.*

Chapter 9

1. Interview with Ayatollah Baghdadi, March 22, 2004, Najaf. Of course, any attempt to bring Western-style democracy to Iraq would do little more than "make the un-Islamic halal and what's halal illegal."

2. As interesting as the motivations for her presentation was the reaction of the various participants. The other Muslim scholars present, including some who were quite religious, didn't voice much opposition to her talk. But the European ones criticized her harshly for being so clearly "biased" against religious expression. One colleague said later that her montage looked like it was made by a right-wing Christian to show that all Muslims are terrorists.

3. Kelefa Sanneh, "Creflo Dollar's Ministry of Money," *The New Yorker*, October 11, 2004.

4. See Vincent Giret, "En Egypte, un drôle d'élite islamo-capitaliste," *L'Expansion*, No. 690, October, 2004, pp. 68–72.

5. Many activists associated with the IndyMedia movement in Beirut complained, both in emails and in interviews, of being ignored by the organizers of the meeting, in favor of Hizbollah and other organizations which they describe as regressive, patriarchal, oppressive of women, gays and lesbians, and minority populations, and otherwise not representative of the highest ideals of the World Social Forum movement.

6. Tom Peters, *Thriving on Chaos*, pp. xi–xii.

7. This view was most strongly endorsed early on by Naomi Klein in a series of articles and public talks in the wake of the successful anti-WTO protests in Seattle. Also see Wat Tyler, "Dancing on the Edge of Chaos: A Spanner in the Works of Global Capitalism," in Notes from Nowhere, eds., *We Are Everywhere: The Irresistible Rise of Global Anticapitalism*, pp. 189–95, and "Organizing Chaos," ibid., pp. 214–15.

8. Cf. Chalmers Johnson, *The Sorrows of Empire*, Chapter 6.

9. Douglas Jehl and David Sanger, "Prewar Assessment on Iraq Saw Chance of Strong Divisions," New York *Times*, September 28, 2004. More recently, Vice President Cheney has publicly supported a "Lebanese model" for Iraq, which is explained as supporting a pluralist republic but as likely hints at (or less likely but much worse, forgets) the fifteen-year disintegration of the state and civil war it took to build the current fragile model (see Charles Tripp, "Iraq as Lebanon: Fears for the Future," *ISIM Newsletter*, No. 14, June, 2004, p. 12).

10. Even before the invasion Iraq was viewed as "a huge pot of honey that's attracting a lot of flies" (Senator John McCaine, quoted in Thomas B. Edsall and Juliet Eilperin, "Lobbyists Set Sights on Money-Making Opportunities in Iraq," *Washington Post*, October 2, 2003).

11. We now know that former CPA Administrator Paul Bremer was repeatedly told that firing the army and the larger program of de-Ba'athification would lead precisely to the insurgency that erupted across the country in 2004, yet refused to even discuss changing his decision (see John Lee Anderson, "Letter from Iraq," *The New Yorker,* November 15, 2004).

12. Peters, *Thriving on Chaos*, p. 38.

13. As we know from Bob Woodward's detailed chronology in *Plan of Attack*, and other reporting on the timeline to war.

14. Cf. Johnson, *Sorrows of Empire* for this argument. For a good description of the politics of privatization in Iraq, see Philip Mattera, "Postwar Iraq: A Showcase for Privatization?" Corporate Research E-Letter EXTRA, April 3 2003, http:// www.corpresearch.org/extra_ 040303. htm. For a good analysis of the dynamics in Latin America, see Fernando Arellano Ortiz, "El Alca Imposición económica y militarización de América Latina," EcoNoticias April 24, 2003, http://www.iepe.org/ econoticias/042003/23042003alatin_ adolfo_perez_esquivel.htm.

15. Fadel Gheit, oil analyst for Oppenheimer & Co, quoted in Linda McQuaig, "Crude Dudes."

16. See Antonia Juhasz, "A Nice Little War to Fill the Coffers," *LA Times*, October 14, 2004, Op/ Ed.

17. Johnson, *The Sorrows of Empire*, pp. 255–7.

18. As Eqbal Ahmed explains it (*Confronting Empire*).

19. Bryan Mealer, "Dying for Dollars: Are you Ready for the Iraqi Gold Rush?"

20. Naomi Klein, "Baghdad Year Zero."

21. Quoted in Giovanna Borradori, *Philosophy in a Time of Terror*, p. 123. Pierre Bourdieu similarly describes globalization as a "myth" (Pierre Bourdieu, *Acts of Resistance*, p. 34).

22. Afghanistan has too many unique dynamics to be easily situated into any particular category – the length of the Soviet occupation, the brutality of the war, the presence of foreign fighters, Afghanistan's drug-based economy, the roots and success of the Taliban. All these have contributed to the chaos that is choking the attempt to build a positive future.

23. In Palestine in particular, I remember watching the euphoria of the 1996 Palestinian elections – likely the freest and fairest elections in the history of the Middle East – being systematically undermined by the semi-weekly "coordinating" meetings between the Palestinian security services, Israeli intelligence, and CIA personnel, which were always announced with some urgency in the Israeli press. These meetings were ostensibly to help coordinate the fight against Palestinian terror, but what they wound up doing was solidifying Arafat's corrupt and autocratic rule while emasculating a Legislative Assembly that was seriously trying to build a democratic base in the government.

24. Patrick Chabal and Jean-Pascal Daloz, *Africa Works*, p. 47.

25. Scholars call these processes the "instrumentalization of disorder." See ibid., p. xviii. They continue, African "individuals, groups and communities [have sought] to instrumentalize the resources which they command within th[e] general political economy of disorder"; a condition that should not be confused with irrationality specifically because it offers significant opportunities for those on all sides who

"know how to play the system" (ibid., pp. xix–xx; see also Paul Tiyambe Zeleza, *Rethinking Africa's Globalization*, Vol. 1, Trenton, N.J.. Africa World Press, 2003).

26. See Joel Migdal, *Strong Societies and Weak States: State–Society Relations and State Capabilities in the Third World*, Princeton: Princeton University Press, 1988.

27. Sub-Saharan Africa supplies the United States with 16 percent of its oil supplies. Through International Military Education and Training, government-to-government weapons deliveries, and commercial arms sales the US has increasingly fueled the violence on the continent, although nothing compares to the negative impact of US farm subsidies on African farmers. For arms sales, see William D. Hartung and Bridget Moix, "Deadly Legacy: US Arms to Africa and the Congo War," *Arms Trade Resource Center, Weapons at War*, January, 2000. See *Arms Sales Monitor*, No. 45, May, 2001 for a discussion of US military aid to Africa pre-September 11.

28. Chabal and Daloz, *Africa Works*, p. 81. And just as in Africa, in the MENA the position of civil societies has been challenged not just by chaos or war and greater political repression but also by the very NGO process that was supposed to support them.

29. Ibid., pp. 94, 123.

30. Joma Nazpary, *Post-Soviet Chaos*, especially p. 4. People use the term *bardok* even though the word *kaos* exists in Russian. The former term is much stronger and implies total social disorder coupled by rampant immorality that together are quite paralyzing to the social body, especially to groups attempting to reform their societies.

31. Similarly, Vadim Volkov's *Violent Entrepreneurs* explores how the chaos of the post-Soviet era enabled a "counter-revolution" in Russia and other former Soviet republics, as networks of groups, from criminal gangs and political parties to families and friends, all competed for resources in the decidedly one-sided contest for power and wealth that is the globalized market economy. Violence has played a crucial role in creating the institutions of the new market economy through these networks – which, as in Africa, are a direct result of the "liberal reforms" of the early 1990s. This is important for us because Iraq is clearly following this trend.

32. This was clearly an important development compared with the much more (ostensibly) communist system of the Soviet era. In Iraq, everyone knew that Hussein and the Ba'athist regime were horrifically corrupt, but the new situation has produced a small comprador elite whose power is dependent specifically on an outside power rather than the national Government. A similar situation exists in Palestine, as anyone knows who has driven past the ugly "palaces" of Palestinian government officials on roads into and out of Ramallah and other major cities.

33. Like economic globalization in so many other countries of the developing world, the experience of Iraq is an unmitigated disaster. My visits to hospitals, schools, think tanks, political party headquarters, art galleries, and refugee camps reveal conditions clearly as bad, and often worse, than on the eve of the US invasion. That is the main reason why, outside the Kurdish north, there has been almost universal antipathy for the occupation at the time of writing. This antipathy is born of a year of distrust of the CPA and of what Iraqis derisively referred to as the "Governed Council," and of a draft constitution that analysts in Iraq felt had enough holes to ensure continued repression and corruption, however appealing the veneer of democracy.

34. For some articles of mine on the role of chaos in Iraq, see "Whose Chaos

is it Anyway?"; "Cash for Chaos: Mark LeVine's Spring Break in Falluja"; "The Chaos Theory in Action," *Asia Times*, April 6, 2004; and "Seeing Iraq through the Globalization Lens."

35. For example, the CPA budgeted only $10,000 to "rehabilitate" schools where UNICEF allocated $40,000, and then most received little more than a paint job by CPA-hired contractors. Iraqi principals complained that they could do the job for $1,000, and wondered where the other $9,000 was going. Then there's the social rights granted to women by an otherwise oppressive Ba'athist system, which are being eroded in the new Iraq. The plight of women is being compounded by growing religious conservatism, massive unemployment, and lack of education and health care. What does chaos mean? Four to six hours without electricity in Baghdad out of each twenty-four. It means having to travel with a satellite phone, a regular Iraqi cellphone ("Iraqnafone"), and a special CPA phone with a 914 (Westchester, NY) area code just to stay in touch with people. Even then, most of the time you can't call one type of phone from the others. Chaos also means desperately underequipped hospitals, bullet-ridden ambulances, and millions of dollars earmarked for rehabilitation siphoned into the pockets of US contractors and their Iraqi middle-men.

36. Mohammad Hassan al-Balwa, quoted in Rory McCarthy, "US Denies Need for Falluja Aid Convoy," *The Guardian*, November 15, 2004.

37. As one press review put it just after my trip: "US Seen Fuelling Anarchy to Entrench its Foothold," IslamOnline.net, April 12, 2004.

38. Giovanni Maria Bellu, "Rete no global sotto shock: È strategia della tensione," *La Repubblica*, September 11, 2004.

39. Or as one Washington insider put it, "pure stupidity" (interview with Washington-based columnist and editor of a major weekly magazine, July 2004). Kennedy quoted by Richard Cohen, "Dear Ted: I'm Sorry I Ignored You," *Washington Post*, September 15, 2004.

40. As late one night he and another friend, Isam, both now working for an international NGO as translators and drivers, plied me with arak, the national drink of Iraq, they recounted life under, and after, Saddam Hussein. Isam explained how, having escaped a death sentence personally signed by Saddam, he'd become a Buddhist and lived for a time in Thailand and the Philippines. Yet, as we spoke of peace, Maher and Isam drilled me on how to disassemble and reassemble one of the three AK-47s in their 200 square-foot apartment.

41. I don't want to romanticize Gandhi's famed aggressive non-violent resistance, as its successes cannot mask significant problems. For example, the act of refusing to purchase British goods and burning British products in markets and shops by poor Hindus hurt the Muslim middle class in India and helped cause the very separatism and animosity between Hindus and Muslims that Gandhi was striving to overcome (see Ahmed, *Confronting Empire*, pp. 4–6).

42. Yet chaos and incompetence should not be understood as mutually exclusive, and in fact can come together in synergistic ways, as in the person of a USAID official I sat next to on the plane out of Baghdad. She had spent the last year "reforming" Iraqi hospitals without ever visiting one. Safe in the completely unverified belief that her tireless efforts to "decentralize the system and make it more efficient" were actually making things better, she could remain in her office in the Green Zone oblivious to the chaos outside. Such cluelessness would seem to be an almost necessary qualification for the planning they're engaged in.

Otherwise, they would have to quit their jobs or do them very differently. If chaos and privatization thrive on ignorance, it's a willful and purposeful ignorance. Maybe my companion on that plane thought she was doing a good job. Whatever her true feelings, ignorance, chaos, privatization, and planning have come together in powerful ways in Iraq.

43. Specifically, Kaplan prophesied a coming anarchy in which the world would be dominated not by stable capitalist states but rather by the "shadowy tentacles... of drug cartels, mafias and private security agencies." He even called for the creation of new kinds of maps that could more accurately capture the "ever mutating representation of chaos" that resulted from the growing power of transnational identities (see Robert Kaplan, "The Coming Anarchy," *Atlantic Monthly*, 273, No. 2, February, 1994, pp. 44–76; G.M. Tamás and Samuel Huntington, "Identity and Conflict," US Institute of Peace, *Peaceworks*, 4, 1994; and Robert Kaplan and Jessica Tuchman Matthews, "'The Coming Anarchy' and the Nation-State under Siege," in *Sources of Conflict: Highlights of the Managing Chaos Conflict*, US Institute of Peace, *Peaceworks* 4, 1995). Thanks to Martin Lewis and Kären Wigen's *The Myth of Continents: A Critique of Metageography*, Berkeley: UC Press, 1997, p. xi, for alerting me to these writings.

44. As I was finishing this chapter, on the same day (November 14, 2004), the LA and New York *Times* each published articles based on this discourse. The *LA Times* published "Bush is No Emperor," by Anthony Pagden, which ludicrously argued that the US is not an empire because it's never had colonies (he seems to have forgotten about the Philippines, Puerto Rico, Hawaii, and the entire forty-eight contiguous states, which were all "colonized" and saw their native populations decimated by war, disease, and ethnic cleansing) and because – according to him – the worst critics of Iraq can say is that Bush is imposing our democratic ideals on a hopelessly authoritarian region (as if the whole anti-war discourse didn't exist). The New York *Times* published Kaplan's "Barren Ground for Democracy," which argued like his earlier work and that of Huntington that because the Middle East was once part of the "poorer and more chaotic Ottoman Empire" it had no "exposure to Enlightenment ideas," an utterly false representation of the history of the empire, as the discussion in Chapter Two has demonstrated. More astonishingly, Kaplan hopes for the US to follow what he describes as the "calmer, more pragmatic [British] empire" of the mid-nineteenth century onwards, completely ignoring the millions of Africans and others killed by the British in the advancement of their colonial/imperial interests during the empire's last century.

45. *L'Expansion*, October, 2004, No. 690.

46. For an analysis of the global terror myth, see Andy Beckett, "The Making of the Terror Myth," *The Guardian*, October 15, 2004, a discussion of the BBC 2 documentary *The Power of Nightmares: The Rise of the Politics of Fear*, that aired that month.

47. Donald Rumsfeld, "Iraq on a Bicycle," *LA Times*, October 8, 2004; excerpted comments from a news conference published on the paper's opinion page.

48. Sadowski, *The Myth of Global Chaos*. He also castigated their belief in a supposedly unalterable difference in "values" between Muslims and Westerners, a difference which would produce a "reaction of irrational violence" when Muslims experienced globalization (of course, our discussion in Chapter Five of the Ronald Inglehart *Human Values and Social Change*

survey shows how off the mark such an argument is).

49. Catherine Besteman and Hugh Gusterson, eds., *Why America's Top Pundits Are Wrong*, Berkeley: UC Press, 2005.

50. World Bank, *Will Arab Workers Prosper or Be Left Out in the Twenty-first Century?*

51. United States Space Command, *Vision 2020*.

52. Michael Ledeen, *The War Against the Terror Masters*, New York: St Martin's Press, 2003, elaborating on an article he wrote in the *Wall Street Journal*, November 14, 2001. Also see Jeet Heer and Dave Wagner, "Man of the World: Michael Ledeen's Adventures in History," *Boston Globe*, October 10, 2004, where Ledeen explains that the iron will of the American political Right is crucial to "root out the corruption and establish a virtuous state, or to institute a new one" – *in America*. Ledeen's foreign-policy line had two things going for it: the fear of such a machinery of chaos and massive violence heading one's way can often compel local leaders to fall into line and pressure rebels to stop fighting (as has happened in Falluja and Najaf at different times); but if it doesn't, the resulting chaos and violence can in turn be used to further the program. In the US, as we've seen, such chaos and the acts that go with it only inflame people, convincing many Americans that what's happening in Iraq is anything but our fault, and that the only option is to "stay the course," whatever that is. Moreover, generating such chaos and misery also means that any fall-off in the same, any move toward political or economic normalcy, however modest, can be touted as proof of the "success" of the US-sponsored "reconstruction" of the country.

53. Jacques Derrida, quoted in Borradori, *Philosophy in a Time of Terror*, p. 110.

54. Julian Borger, "Pentagon Blamed for Abu Ghraib 'Chaos,'" *The Guardian*, August 25, 2004. The supposed chaos at play in the prison, coupled with the seemingly thoughtless actions of the US military elsewhere in the country, confused many Iraqi politicians. A former US ally among the Iraqi Governing Council, Muhammad Bahr al-Ulum, admitted, "I do not understand why America craves crisis. A peaceful solution to the confrontation with Muqtada [al-Sadr] could have been reached. We were hoping that Prime Minister Iyad Allawi would lead the way, but he sided with oppression" ("Najaf Assault Turns Allies Against US," *al-Jazeera*, August 13, 2004).

55. For a report on this issue see André Verlöy and Daniel Politi, "Contracting Intelligence: Department of Interior Releases Abu Ghraib contract," Center for Public Integrity, Windfalls of War Project, http://www.publicintegrity.org/wow/bio.aspx?act=pro&ddlC=5.

56. An August 2004 audit by the CPA's own Inspector General said at least $8.8 billion of the Development Fund for Iraq (made up of proceeds from Iraqi oil sales, frozen assets from foreign governments, and surplus from the UN Oil for Food Programme) went "unaccounted for" and was likely lost to "fraud, waste or corruption," leading Senators Ron Wyden of Oregon, Tom Harkin from Iowa, and Byron Dorgan of North Dakota to demand an accounting from the Defense Department (as first reported by *al-Jazeera*, August 20, 2004).

57. Many workers are desperate enough to become regular users of meta-amphetamines in order to work the long hours and hold down the two or even three jobs necessary to buy the American dream in the new economy.

58. Naomi Klein, "Baghdad Year Zero," my italics. Of course, in response, we can see both in the intense and

violent national–religious resistance in Iraq, and in the non-violent but strategically crucial return to "national projects" by Germany, Russia, Japan or China, a response to the US's drive for world military and economic domination (Pepe Escobar, "The South Strikes Back," *Asia Times*, June 12, 2003).

59. Anonymous, *Imperial Hubris: Why the West is Losing the War on Terror*, Dulles, Va.: Brassey's Inc., 2004. As Derrida reminds us, "Many Islamic cultures flourished in soil rich in natural resources like oil," which he describes as the last "nonvirtualizable and non-deterritorializable" resource. This situation makes Muslim societies more vulnerable to the "savage modernization" brought about by globalized markets and dominated by a small number of states and international corporations, with the disappearing act – whether of money, resources or people – being at the hearty of the savagery (Borradori, *Philosophy in a Time of Terror*, p. 22).

60. Mealer, "Dying for Dollars."

61. The researcher continued, "At the same time, it might be useful to think while some sectors profit from sponsored chaos, others can't stand it. I'm sure the oil companies wouldn't mind if bombs keep exploding all over Iraq – as long as they have control over the pipes and the reserves. So do all those who keep having to repair the roads and bridges that get blown up and keep getting paid every time" (interview, April 2004.)

62. These were books that I was allowed to examine in Baghdadi's study, but for which I did not have the time to obtain a full citation.

63. See Mansur Abdal-Hakim, *Nihayat wa-damar Amrika wa-Isra'il*, n.p.: al-Maktabah al-Tawfikiyyah, 1999. I don't want to suggest that most recent books in Iraq are about globalization and against the US or Israel. In fact,

many of the biggest sellers have been translations of famous novels, books by exiled Iraqi writers, or memoirs of life under Saddam. But the best-selling books across the board are religious books that deal with theological/moral issues and politics and economics from a Muslim perspective. And most of these are extremely hostile to the US and its policies in the MENA, never mind in Iraq itself (interviews with booksellers in Iraq, Najaf and other towns, spring and summer 2004). Given this context, Ayatollah Baghdadi is a good person to look at because he is two generations removed from Moqtada al-Sadr or Abu Musab al-Zarqawi, yet his writings clearly foreshadow much of their rhetoric regarding the West and the US in particular.

64. Interview with Sheikh al-Dhari, Baghdad, March 19, 2004. He stressed in our meeting, and after the two Simonas and their Iraqi comrades were kidnapped, that foreign anti-occupation aid workers should not be touched. The problem is, you can't split hairs like this, as we'll discuss below. We can only imagine that his opinion didn't improve after American forces burst into his house and threatened him and his family for supporting the insurgents during the battle of Falluja of November 2004.

65. This became clear in meetings with professors from several universities, retired politicians, and think tank officials like the famed Beyt al-Hikmah in Baghdad. And the issue of globalization is a common theme in the magazines, newspapers, journals, sermons, and video CDs of both the Sunni and Shi'i mainstream in Iraq, as the primary tool by which the evil twins – the Americans and the Jews – would conquer Iraq and the rest of the Muslim world, wiping out Islam and replacing it with Judaism or Christianity, and introduce corruptions such as pornography and alcohol use by Muslims to

weaken society. About the only people I could find who didn't oppose this system out of hand were, ironically, members of the Iraqi Communist Party who, after decades of brutal repression by the Ba'athists, decided it was better to participate in the interim government and forsake their socialist ideology than to remain in the wilderness with their ideological virtue (but little else) still intact.

66. Moreover, the Iraqi situation is hardly unique. In the *bardok* of Kazakhstan and rest of the former USSR, for instance, the Western-promoted "shock therapy" of the early 1990s impoverished whole populations but successfully brought their resources (oil, gold, forest products, labor, intellectual capital) onto the global market in a major way. And just as in Russia, sexual exploitation as both imagery and reality is not far from the surface of the increasing chaos in Iraq. During the first year of occupation increasing numbers of Iranians have been bringing in women and setting up bordellos in parts of the country so that Shi'i Iraqi men could obtain "temporary marriages" in order to have sex with women who are clearly prostitutes (a practice that, while sanctioned in Shi'i Islam and widespread in Iran, was frowned upon in Iraq before the occupation).

67. Jonathan Steele, "US Creating its Own Gaza," *The Guardian*, April 2, 2004.

68. See Mark LeVine, "Four Times Falluja Equals?" originally published on tomdispatch.com, November 11, 2004 with an excellent introductory essay by Tom Engelhardt, and republished on ZNet, in *Asia Times* and many other media outlets as a stand-alone piece with slightly modified titles.

69. Here I am referring to the fact, as I mentioned at the beginning of the chapter, that there were comparatively few activists in the country to meet the

challenge of the hundreds if not thousands of American civilians who were there in support of the occupation. I tried to organize several large-scale missions of activists and scholars and artists to Iraq during the first year, but to little avail. Activists seemed more interested in combating US imperialism from New York or Washington, while most scholars I contacted about coming to Iraq had one or more reasons for not doing so. Similarly, most artists I know didn't want to take the risk to go to Iraq and create something new with their Iraqi counterparts. Some of the few people who did go – people like Naomi Klein, Michael Franti of the hiphop group Spearhead, Chris Toensing of *Middle East Report*, the poet and radio host Jerry Quickley, International Solidarity Movement founder Adam Shapiro, Georgetown University Professor Samer Shehata, Georgetown graduate student Bassen Haddad, and the many wonderful independent journalists from the US, blazed a trail that was sadly left to lie fallow by most of their colleagues.

70. George Monbiot, "An Answer in Somerset: The Age of Entropy is Here," *The Guardian*, August 24, 2004. Also see his "Break out the Bicycles," *The Guardian*, June 8, 2004.

71. For an important discussion of this argument, see George Caffentzis, "Oil, Globalization, and Islamic Fundamentalism," in David Solnit, ed., *Globalize Liberation: How to Uproot the System and Build a Better World*, San Francisco: City Lights Books, 2004, pp. 97–110. Caffentzis argues that in 1998 the Saudi Government decided to go for broke and completely open up to globalization by changing the foreign investment laws and allowing new types of bids for exploration in the kingdom which allowed foreigners much greater access, control over, and even ownership of, land and resources in the kingdom. This would naturally

have infuriated bin Laden and those with similar worldviews and religious sensibilities in particular.

72. Kevin Morrison, "Wuild to Become More Dependent on Mideast Oil," *Financial Times*, October 27, 2004, p. 6.

73. William Engdahl, "Iraq and the Problem of Peak Oil," *Current Concerns*, No. 1, 2004, http://globalresearch.ca/articles/ENG408A.html. Two other good non-expert discussions on peak oil and its implications (which offer slightly rosier estimates for when peak oil production will be reached) are Paul Roberts, "Over a Barrel," *Mother Jones*, November/December 2004, and Nonna Gorilovskaya, "The End of Oil," MotherJones.com, June 8, 2004. One of the most important impacts for our discussion is related to the growing competition between the US and China in the context of diminishing world oil supplies at the same time that China's ravenous energy needs continue to grow. Some Left scholars have argued that this situation explains the shift of US foreign policy in the direction of a more militarized globalization – in one writer's words, "a crude neo-imperial military presence globally, from Kosovo to Afghanistan, from West Africa to Baghdad and beyond" (Engdahl, "Iraq and the Problem of Peak Oil"). Such a policy could then be seen as a likely cause for the invasion of Iraq – the country with the second biggest proven reserves in the world with 90 percent of the country still to be explored – especially in the context of major disappointments with other potential major oil suppliers (the failed promise of the Caspian basin, for example) and the potential "loss" of Saudi Arabia.

74. Quoted in Monbiot, "The Age of Entropy is Here." For the overstating of oil reserves see Adam Porter, "Elusive Truth about Oil Figures," *al-Jazeera*, August 12, 2004. To cite one example, Kuwait has used the same figure of 94 billion barrels in reserves since 1992, despite the millions of barrels pumped daily since then with no major new finds. The oil problem is compounded by the gradual move (led by Iran and Saddam Hussein in 1999 and 2000 respectively) to base their pricing of oil in Euros rather than dollars, which would disastrously impact the ability for the US to use world trade to finance its skyrocketing deficits (see John Chapman, "The Real Reasons Bush Went to War," *The Guardian*, July 28, 2004). It should be mentioned that many mainstream papers, including the New York *Times*, have yet to give this issue much attention; compare Jad Mouawad, "Irrelevant? OPEC is Sitting Pretty," which does not mention any of these issues directly, with McQuaig, "Crude Dudes," which not only discusses them, but links them directly to the work of Cheney's Energy Task Force.

75. For a discussion of the connection between oil and conflict in Central Africa, see Michael Peel, "Why Africa Keeps Fighting Over Oil," *Christian Science Monitor*, October 1, 2004, and Mouawad, "Irrelevant? OPEC is Sitting Pretty."

76. See Michael Klare, *Resource Wars*.

77. This priority replaced the Cold War focus on maintaining alliances and large-scale military capability specifically designed to counter a no longer existing Soviet threat (ibid.).

78. But it's very hard for governments to sell empire and war to citizens in the West on purely economic terms. Culture is a much easier marketing tool, which accounts for the re-demonization of the culture that just happens to hold most of the world's petroleum resources, the Muslim world (a process made easier, of course, by the dynamic of Muslim terrorism around the world).

79. For the most recent figures on the mass labor migration of Muslims,

see Giovanna Tattolo, "Arab Labour Migration to the GCC States," Jean Monnet Working Paper on Trans-Mediterranean Relations, undated, but probably 2003.

80. Fatima Mernissi reminds us that in the US, "liberals" supported the Saudis as far back as the 1940s and never met a Muslim fundamentalist figure or group they didn't like – from Pakistan's Zia to Osama bin Laden – as long as they helped us fight the Soviets (Fatima Mernissi, "Palace Fundamentalism and Liberal Democracy," in Qureshi and Sells, eds., *The New Crusades*, pp. 51–67). As Klare puts it, "American leaders would like to reduce America's dependence on Saudi Arabia. But there is only ONE way to permanently reduce America's reliance on Saudi Arabia: by taking over Iraq and using it as an alternative source of petroleum … By occupying Iraq and controlling its government, the United States will solve its long-term oil-dependency dilemma for a decade or more." He continues, "Iraq is the ONLY country in the world with sufficient reserves to balance Saudi Arabia: at least 112 billion barrels in proven reserves, and as much as 200–300 billion barrels of potential reserves … And this, I believe, is a major consideration in the administration's decisionmaking about Iraq" (Michael Klare, "The Coming War with Iraq; Deciphering the Bush Administration's Motives," *Foreign Policy in Focus*, January 16, 2003, http://www.fpif.org/commentary/2003/0301warreasons_body. html).

81. See Maps and Charts of Iraqi Oil Fields, Cheney Energy Task Force, obtained by court order, posted on the website of Judicial Watch, http://www.judicialwatch.org/071703.c_.shtml.

82. This is no doubt why the staff of the National Security Council was ordered to cooperate fully with the work of the task force (McQuaig, "Crude Dudes." Also see her book, *It's*

the Crude, Dude: War, Big Oil, and the Fight for the Planet, Toronto: Doubleday Canada, 2004).

83. See Maps and Charts cited in note 81 above. Not to mention the fact that controlling Iraq would mean creating the world's biggest "military base with a very large oil reserve underneath," one located smack in the middle of the first- and fourth-largest oil-producing countries in the world – Saudi Arabia and Iran (McQuaig, "Crude Dudes.").

84. Here I don't want to accuse the entire USAID system of doing little of value, but in Iraq and the MENA region more broadly, the agency has long been linked to CIA and other intelligence activity, and more importantly, has been at the forefront of changing economies such as Egypt from being self-sufficient producers of primary agricultural foodstuffs for human consumption, to being producers of animal feed, cattle, and other export products. This then forces the countries to import grains and other foods from the US (involving subsidies to US agricultural companies). For a seminal discussion of this issue, see Mitchell, "America's Egypt."

85. In fact Habermas links globalization in the post-September 11 period closely to August 1914, the onset of World War I, rather than to Pearl Harbor, i.e., to the beginning of an era of pronounced instability not only with regard to the relations between East and West, but also, and perhaps even more unsettling, between the United States and Europe (quoted in Borradori, *Philosophy in a Time of Terror*, p. 50). If the chaos of the Great War and the ensuing twenty years created the stage for an even bigger and more destructive war in 1939, what does that mean for today?

86. Indeed, Russia is increasingly dependent upon high oil prices to support its otherwise moribund economy, and chaos is one of the best ways to ensure that prices remain high.

87. Thanks to University of Michigan Professor Juan Cole for explaining the argument to me in a convincing manner (personal interview, November 2004). Larry Diamond in his new book presents a similarly compelling argument for the chaos being the result of incompetence, although I would argue that the incompetence he describes in no way forecloses the possibility that there was a larger policy of "sponsored chaos" which nurtured the levels of incompetence he describes (Diamond, *Squandered Victory*).

88. For China's burgeoning oil needs, see Don Lee, "China Barrels Ahead in Oil Market," *LA Times*, November 14, 2004. For a discussion of the relationship between the Sudan and China, see John Laughland, "The Mask of Altruism Disguising a Colonial War: Oil will be the Driving Factor for Military Intervention in Sudan," *The Guardian*, August 2, 2004. It is in this context that we can understand the call by the Heritage Foundation half a year before the invasion of Iraq that "to rehabilitate and modernize its economy, a post-Saddam government will need to move simultaneously on a number of economic policy fronts, utilizing the experience of privatization campaigns and structural reforms in other countries ... rule No. 1 'Privatization Worlds Everywhere'" (Ariel Cohen and Gerald O'Driscoll, paper presented at Heritage Foundation conference, http://www.heritage.org/Research/MiddleEast/bg1633_cfm).

89. We can see evidence of this strategy in the attempts to woo hi-tech computer design to China, as described in John Markoff, "Have Supercomputer, Will Travel," New York *Times*, November 1, 2004.

90. As a UN report explains, "At a time when global poverty-eradication and development goals are not being met due to a shortfall of necessary funds, rising global military expenditure is a disturbing trend" ("The Relationship between Disarmament and Development in the Current International Context." Report to the 59th Session of the General Assembly, as cited by Thalif Deen, "Military spending nears $1 trillion," *Asia Times*, August 19, 2004).

91. See Lockheed Martin Overseas Corporation, sponsor, "Globalization of the Defense Industry: NIDA Conference," March 28, 2001, which demonstrates the pre-September 11 strategy already in place for focusing on civil defense and other commercial and non-high-end military users that would spread US arms sales across the world rather than being heavily invested in the domestic market.

92. Andrew Bacevich, *The New American Militarism*, front matter.

93. Interview with author, October 2004.

94. "The upshot, acutely evident in the aftermath of 9/11, has been a revival of vast ambitions and certainty, this time married to a pronounced affinity for the sword." Bacevich urges us to restore a sense of realism and a sense of proportion to US policy. He proposes, in short, to bring American purposes and American methods – especially with regard to the role of the military – back into harmony with the nation's founding ideals. For a discussion of the "new crusades" see Qureshi and Sells, eds., *The New Crusades*.

95. "A Lawless World," *Al-Ahram Weekly*, September 16–22, 2004, editorial.

96. Michael Klare describes this phenomenon as the "economization of security affairs." At the same time, militarization abroad is tied to increasing civil hostility at home, as the religious conservative Right in the United States openly "covets 'culture wars' and goes out of its way to force the kind of black

and white scenario of good versus evil on the rest of the United States," as we saw in the discussion of Thomas Frank's *What's the Matter with Kansas* in Chapter One. This leaves their fellow citizens too scared to choose anything but more war and hostility towards anyone who doesn't share their ideological and economic vision. For a discussion of how important the strategy of culture wars has become to the Republican Party, see James Rainey, "Christians Back Bush and Covet 'Culture Wars,'" *LA Times*, September 3, 2004; and Martin Kettle, "Despite the Double Speak, Bush's Message is Clear," *The Guardian*, September 4, 2004.

97. As quoted by Tony Bayfield, "Religion is a Bloody Disgrace," *The Guardian*, September 11, 2004.

98. This is how Friedman accounted for the hundreds of willing "human missiles" in Iraq ("The Suicide Supply Chain," New York *Times*, December 9, 2004).

99. Nadia Yassine, quoted in the Budapest Forum of younger Islamist scholars, transcript, May 29, 2003.

100. Michel Foucault, *Discipline and Punish: The Birth of the Prison*, New York: Vintage Books, 1979.

101. Thus King Henry VIII beheaded Sir Thomas More in recognition of his high rank. In more extreme cases, punishment could include having one's flesh torn out, boiling potions poured all over one's body, being drawn and quartered, and then burned at the stake.

102. Frank, "A Merger's Message." In a sad twist, as Naomi Klein puts it, in Iraq the slogan has become "Die, Then Vote" (*The Guardian*, November 13, 2004).

103. Beheading has become a common means of executing captured Russian soldiers, first in Afghanistan and now in Chechnya, and was first brought to the attention of post-

September 11 America with the beheading and dismemberment of *Wall Street Journal* reporter Daniel Pearl. In Haiti, beheadings of police officers were called "Operations Baghdad" (see Louis Meixler, "Beheadings on the Rise Around the World," *LA Times*, November 5, 2004).

104. For this view, see Michael Keane, "The Enemy's Shock and Awe," *LA Times*, Op/Ed, September 28, 2004.

105. If so, let's hope it doesn't become as popular a "weapon of the weak" as professional wrestling and other PPV stalwarts.

106. That is, the videos have a kind of theatrical quality in which the terrorists would seem to be trying to show the world that they in fact have power too, and the more violent the occupation is, the more they will use their own spectacular terroristic violence as a counterpunch to feeling "impotent and humiliated" (Jonathan Steele, "Humiliated and Impotent, Every Iraqi is a Hostage Now," *The Guardian*, September 24, 2004). While the beheadings and other murders have had mixed success in forcing foreign contractors and "coalition" forces out of the country as of early 2005, they do seem to be making some Iraqis feel empowered, as video CD compilations of the executions sell briskly for about fifty US cents in the markets of Baghdad and other Iraqi cities. But lest we assume that this is just another example of the pathological tendency in Islam, we should remember that violent ritual-like political performances with strong aesthetic dimensions have long been part of human cultural–political expression. Whether it's been pre-Columbian Mesoamerican human sacrifices (beheadings and cutting out the hearts of living victims); the assembly-line beheadings of the French Terror; American lynchings with the audience in their Sunday best, posing for the camera; or

the snuff pictures of Abu Ghraib, humans have long had a penchant for engaging in and (even more) watching other people die in the worst possible ways. Thanks to Manouchehr Shiva for the insights discussed in these last paragraphs.

107. See Marx, *Capital*, Volume 1, Chapter 3.

108. For a discussion of the report, see "Belief Brands ... Oh Really?," editorial, *Christian Science Monitor*, March 1, 2001, http://www. humphreys.co.uk/articles/intellectual_ property_1.htm. The Young & Rubicam report picked up on a previous year's report from the London design consultancy Fitch, which also deified brands. The Fitch report said many people flocked to Ikea instead of church on Sunday; Young & Rubicam says today's brand builders can be compared to the missionaries who spread Christianity and Islam around the world: "The most successful brands today – 'belief brands' – are those that stand not just for quality and reliability but for a set of beliefs that they refuse to compromise." For the term "brand imperialism" see "Five Minutes with Naomi Klein," *The Guardian*, December 5, 2000.

109. Tomkins, "Christ Replaces Coke."

110. That is, in the case of Islam, there would have been no spread of Wahhabi Islam to every poor neighborhood in the Muslim world without the unprecedented oil wealth brought to the Saudis and other Gulf sheikhdoms by their incorporation into the world capitalist system.

111. It is this feeling that similarly enables Israelis to excuse their soldiers for killing thousands of Palestinian civilians, demolishing homes, uprooting olive groves, and innumerable other acts of violence. It seems that just as in the witch hunts of the Middle Ages, and anti-communist witch hunts of a generation ago, if you're accused of something, at the very least you're probably a little guilty and deserve a little punishment.

112. Which shouldn't be thought of as the only type of Evangelical culture, as there is a significant if still small progressive Evangelical culture too. Cf. Dock Douwes and Linda Herrera, Editorial, *ISIM Newsletter*, No. 14, June, 2004, p. 4 for a discussion of the ideological and political motivations underlying the rhetoric of security in Zionism during the last century. See also Mark LeVine, "At What Cost? The Rhetoric of Security in Zionist and Israeli Political Discourse."

113. Elliot Colla, "A Culture of Righteousness and Martyrdom," *ISIM Newsletter*, No. 14, June, 2004, pp. 6–7.

114 Agence France Press, "Holy War: Evangelical Marines Prepare to Battle Barbarians," November 7, 2004. It is also clear that Americans are becoming increasingly inured to the violence – no doubt in part because of the violence of video games and movies – and so quickly get used to the idea of their countrymen (as of writing this, it's only been men) being beheaded for the cause of freedom. We can recall that when Nicholas Berg was decapitated the idea was so shocking that a host of conspiracy theories popped up immediately to say that the beheading was fake or that Berg was dead before he was decapitated. (In fact, there is, strangely, hardly any blood in the video of his execution when compared with subsequent videos, which lends some credence to this hypothesis.) No one says the later crop of videos are fake.

115. Naomi Klein, "The Likud Doctrine," *The Guardian*, September 10, 2004.

116. In the article he lamented that few if any Muslim religious figures issued fatwas condemning Osama bin Laden for his actions ("We Are All Bin Laden, *al-Sharq al-Awsat*, August 30,

2004; also see his interview on Jordanian TV, June 8, 2004).

117. The increase in chaos had been increasingly palpable even during my almost two weeks there in the latter half of March, with suicide bombings (including the big one at the Jebal Lubnan Hotel that blew out the first three storys' windows), not to speak of the nightly missile/RPG strikes and battles with US troops on the city's streets.

118. See Hany Khalil of United for Peace and Justice, quoted in Mark LeVine, "The Peace Movement Plans for the Future."

119. Of course, making that process harder was that the perception held by many Iraqis of foreigners was increasingly distorted – a mirror image of the distorted view Americans have of Muslims. As Simona continued, "I'd like to have an answer, but I still don't have an answer, though I try to work on it day by day. To understand the feeling of the people, their perception about us is crucial, and we need to have better information. But it seems for many Iraqis that they increasingly know only two categories of people in the world: Americans and Jews. They don't take into consideration that there are Europeans. And so it's becoming more untenable to be here."

120. Asef Bayat, "The Art of Presence," *ISIM Newsletter*, No. 14, June, 2004, p. 5, his emphasis.

121. Here I use the term gypsy, which is felt by many Romani people to be a derogatory term, because this is the term used by musicians and even many Romani artists to describe themselves.

122. Paris: Fremeaux & Associes, 1997.

123. Jonathan Curiel, "Muslim Roots of the Blues."

124. Plant discovered 'Um Kalthoum early on in his career, while Jimmy Page played with Sonny Boy Williamson (not the original Chicago harmonica player,

but Sonny Boy II, aka Aleck Ford Rice Miller, who took the name in order to attract listeners to his radio show). Page played with Williamson on his final album, the 1964 *It's a Bloody Life*. Personally, this dynamic also explains why I moved from working with Texas blues guitarists like Johnny Copeland and Albert Collins to Arab artists like Hassan Hakmoun and getting a Ph.D. in Middle Eastern histories and cultures.

125. A more common term would be "gypsies," as discussed in note 121, in its vernacular usage of signifying people with nomadic or vagabond personalities or lives.

126. Breyten Breytenbach, "Notes from the Middle World," in Heide Ziegler, ed., *The Translatability of Cultures: Proceedings of the Fifth Stuttgart Seminar in Cultural Studies, 3/8–14/8/1998*, Stuttgart: Verlag J.B. Metzler, 1998, pp. 47–64.

127. Binesh-Pajouh is a poet and professor with a doctorate in urban planning. "I chose rap because I can say many things with it, not because I live like a rapper," said Binesh-Pajouh in his affluent north Tehran apartment. "No one is born a thief, but you cannot find a loaf of bread at night … Have you ever seen your child biting a watermelon skin from hunger in a slum?" ("Dapper Rapper Stirs Iran," *al-Jazeera*, September 3, 2004). Also see Megan Stack, "Lost Generation of Iran Seeks Escape," *LA Times*, December 25, 2004. For the discussion of multiculturalism and hiphop, see Eric Dyson, *Between God and Gangsta Rap*, pp. 125–7.

128. As recounted by Professor Mustafa Bayoumi of Brooklyn College in Curiel, "Muslim Roots of the Blues."

129. See Kepel, *Allah in the West*.

130. Ibid., pp. 2, 54–67.

131. Quoted in Borradori, *Philosophy in a Time of Terror*, p. 19.

132. See Jim Hoagland, "From Terrorism to Tolerance," *Washington Post*, October 6, 2004.

133. If, as Habermas argues, "Tolerance is crucial for us because it is true that globalization opens up new avenues of participation," why does the threshold of tolerance seem to recede, spreading "more the illusion than the reality of universal participation" (Borradori, *Philosophy in a Time of Terror*, pp. 18–19)? Yet ultimately tolerance involves specific power relations where a group with power in a society will "tolerate" other groups within its borders or even as legitimate members of the society, but only on the condition that they conform to specific norms and practices of that group. In other words, tolerance has its limits, beyond which people or groups will be ostracized.

134. Quoted in ibid., pp. 17, 129. Also see Emmanuel Levinas, *Outside the Subject*, Stanford: Stanford University Press, 1993.

135. For Habermas and Derrida the protests of February 15, 2003 were the most important events in Europe since the end of World War II and if developed correctly will be known as the harbinger of a "European public forum" (Jürgen Habermas and Jacques Derrida, "After the War, the Rebirth of Europe," *Frankfurter Allgemeine Zeitung*, May 31, 2003; and the French version of the same article, published the same day, in *Libération*, titled "A Plea for a Common Foreign Policy"). Indeed, the demonstrations of February 15 against the war in Iraq designed a new European public space." See Pepe Escobar, "Europe's 3D Vision," *Asia Times*, June 13, 2003.

136. LeVine, "The Peace Movement Plans for the Future."

137. As a past president of the Middle East Studies Association put it, "The anti-war coalition, the left and Arab intellectuals have not come to grips with the problem of the lack of democracy and development in the Arab world. Period. They have thus left

this issue to Fox and the neo-cons." The absence of progressive scholars of the MENA and Islam seems particularly odd when the Bush Administration early on forged strong ties with scholars on the Right, which should have signaled the activist community of the need to build similar bridges to natural allies in academia. Middle East expert Phyllis Bennis, quoted in ibid.

138. As Chris Nineham of the Stop the War Coalition explained about the conference, "We will not allow the resistance to be trivialized as some Terrorist movement ... it is a popular insurrection resistance occupation. We see the real terrorists as the one with the B-52 bombers" (quoted in Sanjay Suri, "'Resistance' Call at Anti-War Rally," Interpress Service News Agency, October 17, 2004). And so the movement offered support for the Iraqi insurgents, who weeks later engaged in a brutal fight against the Americans in Falluja that sent hundreds of fighters and likely thousands of civilians to their deaths, and destroyed large sections of the city, in a battle they had no chance of winning. But few members of the anti-war movement ask, given the balance of power and the clear willing of the US and Allawi Government to kill large numbers of civilians, whether violent resistance at that moment was a morally correct choice. For a similar critique to mine, see the *Beirut Daily Star* editorial for November 11, 2004, titled "Iraq Beyond Tragedy: A Country Gripped in the Twin Jaws of Absurdity."

139. These dynamics raise the issue of how the movement is ever going to compete with either neoliberal globalization or, even more urgently, al-Qa'eda, at a time when it is perceived by many in the Global South as having "join[ed] the vanguard of movements contesting established order and US domination" (Olivier Roy, "The

Business of Terror: Al-Qa'eda Brand Name Ready for Franchise," *Le Monde Diplomatique*, September, 2004). Here it should be pointed out that we need to draw a clear line between Hizbollah's military strategies and activities, which clearly include violence and even terrorism as defined by international law, and its social/political activities, which are among the least corrupt and most responsive to constituents in all of Lebanon, and which have empowered many more women and working-class people than have most members of the global peace and justice movement.

140. As one critic describes it, "Music is prophecy: its styles and economic organizations are ahead of the rest of society because it explores, much faster than material reality can, the entire range of possibilities in a given code" (Jacques Attali, *Noise*, p. 11).

141. And so Moore's narrow focus on Bush and the Republicans completely missed the point that it has been the whole foreign-policy establishment, Republican and Democrat alike going back decades (as we saw in Chapters Two and Three), that produced the political and economic dynamics so well documented in the movie.

142. Jon Wiener, "Rocking the Youth Vote – From 1972 to 2004," *The Nation*, October 7, 2004.

143. The fear and loathing of the likes of O'Reilly among my friends and colleagues was so great that when I was invited to appear on his show people at the most senior level of the academic profession urged me not to do it. Why? Because they feared that he'd use every trick of the dirty journalist to discredit my arguments, while afterwards I'd be bombarded by hate email; both of these did occur.

144. Middle East expert Phyllis Bennis, quoted in Le Vine, "The Peace Movement Plans for the Future."

145. For a specifically Mediterranean view of this perspective, see the chapters in Thierry Fabre, ed., *Rencontres d'Averroès: La Méditerranée, frontières et passages*, Paris: Actes Sud, 1999.

146. We could argue, of course, that the anti-war movement is already a brand. Have millions of people ever hit the streets to support McDonald's or Disney, or even Michael Jordan and Nike? But of course, they do spend billions buying those brands, so who needs public displays of support?

147. If successful brands "change the lifestyle of larger culture," the anti-war movement has yet to do that to any significant degree. Until it does, Empire and Terror will remain the only two choices for too many people around the world.

148. For a similar argument that was published at the same time I wrote this chapter see Gary Younge, "Convert or be Damned," *The Guardian*, November 15, 2004. Whether in the MENA or Midwest, if the Left remains unable to engage the core supporters of Bush or bin Laden – the lower- and middle-class people who are actively Christian or Muslim and socially conservative, but whose faith can in fact be the source of new alliances precisely because of the inherently radical and progressive message of Christianity, Islam or Judaism) – it will continue to be a marginal political and cultural force. Some might hope that when the overextension of US resources to the military finally crushes the rest of the economy beneath it, progressives (or at least New Democrats) will be positioned to reclaim public power. But Baker argues convincingly that a more likely scenario is that the Left has become so discredited that Americans won't turn to it for an alternative. Instead, "we'll practically beg for the coup" (to quote the last sentence of the story), since only the military can be trusted to have the integrity to lead the country out of this morass. What this frightening scenario reminds us is that if we want to understand how the

Middle East has become so militarized and undemocratic, we need to understand how the US has become increasingly militarized and pseudodemocratic at best, in direct proportion to the level of denial experienced by most Americans about just what's happening to their country. Put simply, we're more alike than we imagine. Yet how many of the supposedly tens of thousands of Americans who've bought a copy of the Qur'an since September 11, most of them in order to better understand their new enemy, were members of the peace movement?

149. Interview with author, October, 2004.

150. For an important post-2004 election critique of how the Left condescended towards people of faith, see Michael Lerner, "Overcoming Liberal Arrogance and Contempt for Americans who Voted for Bush," TIKKUN online (www.tikkun.org), November 8, 2004. A view of religion that accepts its permanent place in the public sphere on its own terms seems to be opposed to commentators like Olivier Roy or Nicolas Sarkozy, who want to give Islam "a helping hand," but who still argue that Islam will be ultimately "secularized" by the (sometimes bloody) march of Westernization (Nicolas Sarkozy, *La République, les religions, l'ésperance*; for Roy's argument, see his new book, *Globalized Islam: The Search for a New Ummah*, London: Hurst, 2004). While Roy does an admirable job of explaining that Islam is not the problem in Muslim societies, that's because he blames the MENA's political backwardness on Arab nationalism.

151. John Macquarrie, *The Humility of God*, Philadelphia: The Westminster Press, 1978, pp. 13, 15.

152. Khaled Abou El Fadl, "The Ugly Modern and the Modern Ugly," in Safi, ed., *Progressive Muslims*, pp. 33–77; Jim Wallis, "Bush's Theology of Empire," *Sojourner's*, September/October 2003.

Indeed, what Abou El Fadl says about Islam is equally true for American, Christian, Jewish or any other culture: "Confronted by extreme acts of ugliness, there is no alternative for a Muslim who is interested in reclaiming the moral authority of Islam but to confront the quintessential questions of: Is this Islam? Can this be Islam? And, should this be Islam? It is far too easy for contemporary Muslims to avoid taking responsibility for the extreme acts of ugliness committed by zealots in our midst and instead cast all the blame upon Western imperialism and colonialism" ("The Ugly Modern," p. 42).

153. For a description of the emergence of a specifically "progressive Muslim" intellectual discourse, see Farid Esack, "In Search of Progressive Islam Beyond 9/11," in Safi, ed., *Progressive Muslims*, pp. 79–97. For progressive Jewish voices see TIKKUN and *Sojourner's* magazines and the writings of Michael Lerner and Jim Wallis respectively.

154. Here we need to remember, as Tomlinson explained in Chapter Three, that globalization is best defined as "complex connectivity." But as Thomas Sommer explained at our Baghdad dinner, "We can't arrive in Iraq and say, 'Look, there was a struggle in Palestine and they did this, the Zapatistas did this, etc.' We can speak and suggest certain strategies, but even to ask people to speak outside is difficult or to ask organizations to sign something for the outside takes so much time, because they're afraid, first of Saddam, now Americans. This is a problem for people fighting the occupation."

155. See David Korten, *When Corporations Rule the World* and *The Post-Corporate World: Life After Capitalism*, San Francisco: Berrett-Koehler Publishers, 2000; Susan George, *Another World is Possible If?* London: Verso, 2004. Also see Michael

Lerner, *The Politics of Meaning* and *Spirit Matters*; Jim Wallis, *Faith Works: Lessons from the Life of an Activist Preacher*, New York: Random House, 2000; and Diane Sterling, *The Soul of Politics: Beyond "Religious Right" and "Secular Left,"* Fort Washington, Pa.: Harvest Books, 1995. For the Earth Charter, see www.earthcharter.org; for the International Forum on Globalization and its various publications, see www.ifg.org; for a detailed list of books and a discussion of the politics of meaning, see www.meaning.org and www.tikkun.org.

156. Some of the earliest truces, such as the (aborted) Thirty Years' Treaty during the Peloponnesian War of the fifth century BCE, were made only out of tactical necessity and collapsed as soon as the balance of forces changed. Such a truce – during which both sides would attempt to gain an advantage before re-igniting hostilities – would surely be a disaster in our world. Other truces, such as those that ended the Korean War in 1953 or the 1973 Arab–Israeli war, became by default unsatisfactory political resolutions to otherwise insoluble conflicts. A truce like this almost certainly will end in renewed violence because the roots of the war on terror go to the core values underlying US/Western policies in the Middle East and Muslim responses to it.

157. For the use of "enculturalization" see Lars Pedersen, *Newer Islamic Movement in Western Europe*, Brookfield, Vt.: Ashgate Publishing, 1999.

158. Fortunately, the EU established the "Euro-Med" area as of 1995, whose viability depends on expansive economic and political development, and so on increasing interchange with the Muslim world.

159. For Gramsci's writings dealing with religion, see: *Selections from the Prison Notebooks*, ed. and trans. Quitin Hoare and Geoffrey Nowell Smith,

N.Y.: International Publishers, 1971; *La religione come senso comune*, ed. Tommaso La Rocca, Milan: EST, 1993; and for the complete text of all his writings on religion, see his *Quaderni del carcere*, 4 volumes, Rome and Trento: Istituto Gramsci/Einaudi, 2001. See also Roberto Vinco, *Una fede senza futuro? Religione e mondo cattolico in Gramsci*, Verona: Mazziana, 1983. For a detailed analysis of Gramsci and Foucault's dialogues with religion see Mark LeVine and Armando Salvatore, eds., *Religion, Social Practice, and Contested Hegemonies*.

160. Bourdieu, *Acts of Resistance*, p. 57. He repeats the theme, this time arguing for the importance of American scholars and activists to join their European counterparts against neoliberal globalization, in *Firing Back*, pp. 8–10. See also Bourdieu, *Firing Back*, p. 23 and pp. 46–7 for a discussion on how to bring intellectuals and activists together again, which is done precisely by combining cutting-edge research and equally cutting-edge art with innovative forms of progressive social activism.

161. Here it's important to note that the movement must be very careful about where it dispatches its "troops." While non-violent protests that include significant numbers of Americans or Europeans would likely have a powerful impact against American or European troops, their ability to stop violence in conflicts such as the Sudan, Colombia, or other regions would likely be significantly constrained and their lives put in much greater peril.

162. This may seem like a grandiose and unrealistic plan of counter-attack against American empire, the Axis of Arrogance and Ignorance, and their doppelgangers in the Muslim world. But even in the absence of a huge groundswell of participation worldwide, for people in the MENA the opportunity for the kind of training and

interaction discussed here would provide an important alternative to other, more violent forms of training in how to resist neoliberal globalization in all its forms. It would give the burgeoning youth movements of the region vital tools to engage in their own struggles for freedom and democracy against repressive regimes; most importantly, in a manner that encourages project rather than resistance identities.

163. Kingwell, *The World We Want*, New York: Penguin, 2000, p. 60.

164. *Le Monde* editorial, "L'autre Amérique," November 3, 2004; Isabel Allende, "Ich stehe fur das andere Amerika," *Frankfurter Rundschau*, November 5, 2004; author interviews with board members of Beyt al-Hikmah, Baghdad, March, 2004.

Bibliography

This bibliography contains works cited multiple times in the endnotes, as well as a number of books and articles that were drawn on for the discussions in the book. This should not be considered a comprehensive or complete bibliography; readers are urged to see the endnotes for a complete list of references on topics related to each chapter.

Abbas, Qassem Khadir (ed.) (1996) *Masdaqiyyah al-Nitham Dawli al-Jadid (Righting the New International System)*. Beirut: Dar al-Adwa'.

Abdul-Rahman, Asamah (ed.) (1999) *Tanmiyyah al-Takhalaf wa-idarah al-Tanmiyyah...: Idara al-Tanmiyyah fi al-watan al-'Arabi wa al-Nitham al-'Alami al-Jadid (Development of Backwardness and the Management of Development: Managing Development in the Arab Nation and the New World Order)*. Beirut: Merkaz al-Dirasat al-Wahda al-'Arabiyya.

Abu-Lughod, Janet (1991) *Before European Hegemony: The World System AD 1250–1350*. Oxford: Oxford University Press.

Abu-Manneh, Butrus (1994) "The Islamic Roots of the Gülhane Rescript." *Die Welt des Islams*, 34, pp. 173–203.

Aburish, Said (1999) *Saddam Hussein: The Politics of Revenge*. New York: Bloomsbury.

Abu Za'rur, Muhammad Said Bin Sahu (1998) *al-'Awlamah: Ma hayatuha–nash'atuha–ahdafuha–al-khiyar al-badil*. Amman: Dar al-Bayaraq.

Afaya, Noureddine (1997) *L'Occident dans l'imaginaire Arabo-Musulman (The Occident in the Arab-Muslim Imagination)*. Casablanca: Les Editions Toubka.

al-Afghani, Jamal ad-Din (1983) *An Islamic Response to Imperialism: Political and Religious Writings of Sayyid Jmamal ad-Din "al-Afghani."* Trans. Nikki Keddie. Berkeley: University of California Press.

Ahmad, Jalal al-e (1962) *Gharbzadegi (Weststruckness)*. Tehran: Ravaq.

Ahmed, Eqbal (2000) *Confronting Empire: Interviews with David Bersamian*, Cambridge, Mass.: South End Press.

Allah Sa'id, Abdul Satar Fath (1989) *al-Ghazu al-fikri wa al-tayarat almu'asara l-il-Islam (The Intellectual Invasion and the Contemporary Streams in Islam)*. Cairo: Dar al-Wafa'.

Al-Sayyad, Nezar and Manuel Castells (eds.) (2002) *Muslim Europe or Euro-Islam: Politics, Culture and Citizenship in the Age of Globalization*. New York: Lexington Books.

Amin, Galal (1997) *Whatever Happened to the Egyptians? Changes in Egyptian Society from 1950 to the Present*. Cairo: American University of Cairo Press.

Amin, Khalal (1998) *al-'Awlamah (Globalization)*. Beirut: Dar al-Ma'arafa.

Amin, Samir (1989) *Eurocentrism*. New York: Monthly Review Press.

—— (1993) "The Ancient World Systems Versus the Modern Capitalist World System," in André Gunder Frank and Barry K. Gills (eds.) *The World System: Five Hundred Years or Five Thousand*. London: Routledge, pp. 247–77.

—— (2001) "Imperialism and Globalization," presentation at the first annual World Social Forum, Porto Alegre, Brazil, January.

Anonymous (2002) *Through Our Enemies' Eyes: Osama bin Laden, Radical Islam, and the Future of America*. Washington, D.C.: Brassey's, Inc.

Appadurai, Arjun (1996) *Modernity at Large: Cultural Dimensions of Globalization*. Minneapolis: University of Minnesota Press.

Arendt, Hannah (1968) *Imperialism*. Boston: Harvest Books.

'Atrisi, Talal (1998) "al-Huwiyyah al-thaqafiyyah fi muawihah al-'awlamah" ("Cultural Identity in the Face of Globalization"), *Mu'alumat Dawliyyah (International Information)* 58, Autumn, 1998, pp. 83–8.

Attali, Jacques (1985) *Noise: The Political Economy of Music*. Minneapolis: University of Minnesota Press.

Axtmann, Roland (1998) *Globalization and Europe: Theoretical and Empirical Investigations*. London: Pinter Publishers.

Bacevich, Andrew (2005) *The New American Militarism: How Americans are Seduced by War*. Oxford: Oxford University Press.

Baker, Kevin (2003) "We're in the Army Now." *Harper's Magazine*, October.

Barber, Benjamin (1995) *Jihad vs. McWorld*. New York: Times Books.

Baricco, Alessandro (2002) *Next: Piccolo libro sulla globalizzazione e sul mondo che verrà (Next: A Little Book on Globalization and the World that will Come)*. Milan: Feltrinelli.

Bauman, Zygmunt (2000) *Liquid Modernity*. Cambridge: Polity Press.

Bayat, Asef (1997) *Street Politics*. New York: Columbia University Press.

Belghazi, Taieb and Lahcen Haddad (eds.) (2001) *Global/Local Cultures and Sustainable Development*. Rabat, Faculty of Letters and Human Sciences, Mohammed V University, Conferences and Colloquia Series No. 91, 2001.

Bhabha, Homi (1994) *The Location of Culture*. New York: Routledge.

Bordo, Michael D. et al. (2003) *Globalization in Historical Perspective*. Chicago: University of Chicago Press.

Boroujerdi, Mehrzad (1996) *Iranian Intellectuals and the West: The Tormented Triumph of Nativism*. Syracuse: Syracuse University Press.

Borradori, Giovanna (2003) *Philosophy in a Time of Terror: Dialogues with Jürgen Habermas and Jacques Derrida*. Chicago: University of Chicago Press.

Bourdieu, Pierre (1998) *Acts of Resistance: Against the New Myths of our Time*. Cambridge: Polity Press.

—— (2003) *Firing Back: Against the Tyranny of the Market 2*. London: Verso.

Bové, José and François Dufour (2002) *The World is Not For Sale: Farmers Against Junk Food*. Trans. Anna de Casparis. London: Verso.

Breen, Richard and Daniel Verdier (1999) "Globalisation and Inequality," in *Globalization, European Economic Integration and Social Protection*. Conference held at the European University Institute, March 11–12.

Bulaç, Ali (1997) *Islam ve Fundamentalizm* (*Islam and Fundamentalism*). Istanbul: Iz Yayıncılık.

—— (2001) *Din, Devlet ve Demokrasi* (*Religion, State, and Democracy*). Istanbul: Zama cep kitplari.

Cassen, Bernard (2004) "Inventing ATTAC," in Mertes, ed., *A Movement of Movements*, pp. 170–4.

Césaire, Aimé (2000) *Discourse on Colonialism*. New York: New York University Press.

Chabal, Patrick and Jean-Pascal Daloz (1999) *Africa Works: Disorder as Political Instrument*. Bloomington: Indiana University Press.

Chase-Dunn, Christopher and Terry Boswell (2002) "Transnational Social Movements and Democratic Socialist Parties in the Semiperiphery," paper presented at the Annual Conference of the California Sociological Association, Riverside, Calif., October 19, 2002, http://www.irows.ucr.edu/papers/csa02/csa02.htm.

Cherkaoui, Abdessaïd (2002) *al-'Awlamah – al-ghashiyya b-siyatel: harb al-suq wa suq al-harb beina al-gharb wa-l-gharb* (*Globalization – Disaster: in Seattle: War of the Market and Market of War between the West and the West*). Rabat: n.p.

Cockburn, Andrew and Patrick (2000) *Out of the Ashes: The Resurrection of Saddam Hussein*. London: Verso.

Cohen, Robin and Shirin M. Rai (eds.) (2000) *Global Social Movements*. London: Athlone Press.

Cordesman, Anthony (2002) "Saudi Arabia Enters the 21ˢᵗ Century: The Military Dimension." Washington, D.C.: Center for Strategic and International Studies, October 30.

Cowen, Tyler (2002) *Creative Destruction: How Globalization is Changing the World's Cultures*. Princeton: Princeton University Press.

Curiel, Jonathan (2004) "Muslim Roots of the Blues: The Music of Famous American Blues Singers Reaches Back Through the South to the Culture of West Africa," *San Francisco Chronicle*, August 15.

al-Da'im, Abdallah 'Abd (1994) *al-Qawmiyyah al-'arabiyyah wa-al-nitham al-'alami al-jadid*. Beirut: Dar al-Adab.

al-Darir, Musa (1998) "al-'Awlamah: Mafhumuha-ba'ada al-Malamih" ("Globalization: Its Meaning [and] Some Features") *Mu'alumat Dawliyyah* (*International Information*), 58, Autumn, pp. 6–18.

Dasgupta, Dipak, Jennifer Keller, and T.G. Srinivasan (2001) "Reform and Elusive Growth in the Middle-East – What has Happened in the 1990s?" Paper for MEEA Conference on Global Change and Regional Integration: The Redrawing of the Economic Boundaries in the Middle East and North Africa, London, July 20–22.

Davis, James and Paul Rowley (2001) "Internationalism Against Globalization: A Map of Resistance," in Yuen et al. (eds.), *The Battle of Seattle*, pp. 24–8.

Denning, Michael (2004) *Culture in the Age of Three Worlds*. London: Verso.

Deringil, Selim (1998) *The Well-Protected Domains: Ideology and the Legitimation of Power in the Ottoman Empire, 1876–1909*. London: I.B. Tauris.

Derive Approdi (eds.) (2003) *Luoghi comuni: il movimento globale come spazivo di polticizzazione* (*Common Places: The Global Movement as an Open Space for Politicization*). Rome: Derive Approdi.

Diamond, Larry (2005) *Squandered Victory: The American Occupation and the Bungled Effort to Bring Democracy in Iraq*. New York: Times Books.

Diawara, Manthia (1998) "Toward a Regional Imaginary in Africa," in Jameson and Miyoshi (eds.), *The Cultures of Globalization*, pp. 103–24.

Doumani, Beshara (1995) *Rediscovering Palestine: Merchants and Peasants in Jabal Nablus, 1700–1900*. Berkeley: University of California Press.

Dyson, Michael Eric (1996) *Between God and Gangsta Rap: Bearing Witness to Black Culture*. New York: Oxford University Press.

Esposito, John (1999) *The Islamic Threat: Myth or Reality*. Oxford: Oxford University Press.

—— (2003) *Unholy War: Terror in the Name of Islam*. Oxford: Oxford University Press.

Fanon, Frantz (1965) *Dying Colonialism*. Boston: Grove Press.

—— (1965) *The Wretched of the Earth*. Boston: Grove Press.

Feldman, Noah (2003) *After Jihad: America and the Struggle for Islamic Democracy*. New York: Farrar, Straus, and Giroux.

Ferguson, Niall (2003) *Colossus: The Price of America's Empire*, New York: The Penguin Press.

Fligstein, Neil (1999) "Is Globalization the Cause of the Crises of Welfare States?" *Globalization, European Economic Integration and Social Protection*. Conference held at the European University Institute, March 11–12.

—— (2001) *The Architecture of Markets: An Economic Sociology of Twenty-First-Century Capitalist Societies*. Princeton: Princeton University Press.

Frank, Robert (2000) "A Merger's Message: Dominate or Die," *New York Times*, January 11, Opinion Page.

Frank, Thomas (1997) *The Conquest of Cool: Business Culture, Counterculture, and the Rise of Hip Consumerism*. Chicago: University of Chicago Press.

—— (2000) *One Market Under God: Extreme Capitalism, Market Populism, and the End of Economic Democracy*. New York: Doubleday.

—— (2004) *What's the Matter with Kansas: How Conservatives Won the Heart of America*. New York: Metropolitan Books.

Frassetto, Michael and David R. Blanks (eds.) (1999) *Western Views of Islam in Medieval and Early Modern Europe: Perception of Other*. London: Palgrave.

Friedman, Thomas (1998) "Time of the Turtles," New York *Times*, August 15, p. A13.

—— (1999) *The Lexus and the Olive Tree*. New York: Farrar, Straus, and Giroux.

Frith, Simon (2000) "The Discourse of World Music," in Georgina Born and David Hesmondhalgh (eds.), *Western Music and its Others: Difference, Representation, and Appropriation in Music*. Berkeley: University of California Press, pp. 305–22.

Frum, David and Richard Perle (2003) *An End to Evil: How to Win the War on Terror*. New York: Random House.

Fukuyama, Francis (1992) *The End of History and the Last Man*, New York: Free Press.

—— (2004) interview with Ezzat Ibraham in *Al-Ahram Weekly*, April 29–May 5.

Garcia Canclini, Nestor (1995) *Hybrid Cultures: Strategies for Entering and Leaving Modernity*. Minneapolis: University of Minnesota Press.

Gills, Barry (ed.) (2002) *Globalization and the Politics of Resistance*. New York: Palgrave.

Göle, Nilüfer (2000) "Snapshots of Islamic Modernities," *Daedalus*, "Multiple Modernities" issue, 129, 1: 91–118.

Gordon, David and Peter Townsend (eds.) (2001) *Breadline Europe: The Measurement of Poverty*. London: Policy Press.

Graeber, David (2002) "The New Anarchists," *New Left Review*, 13, January–February.

Gran, Peter (1996) *Beyond Eurocentrism: A New View of Modern*

World History. Syracuse: Syracuse University Press.

Gray, John (2003) *Al Qaeda and What it Means to be Modern*. New York: New Press.

Groves, Kevin (n.d.) "Naomi Klein Speaks about the Future of Anti-Globalization: Urges Movement to Re-examine Goals and Successes," *CUP*, http://www.trentu.ca/arthur/archive/37/04/canada.shtml.

Gunder Frank, André (1998) *ReOrient: Global Economy in the Asia Age*. Berkeley: University of California Press.

Haider, Mahmud (1998) "Mafhum al-siadah ba'ada al-harb al-baderah…: Dawla al-ma'ulamah" ("Understanding Sovereignty After the Cold War: The Globalization State") *Mu'alumat Dawliyyah* (*International Information*), 58, Autumn, pp. 43–60.

Hannerz, Ulf (1990) "Cosmopolitans and Locals in World Culture," in Mike Featherstone (ed.), *Global Culture: Nationalism, Globalization and Modernity*, London: Sage, pp. 237–51.

Hardt, Michael and Antonio Negri (2001) *Empire*. Cambridge, Mass.: Harvard University Press.

Harvey, David (1989) *The Condition of Postmodernity*. London: Blackwell.

Henry, Clement M. and Robert Springborg (2001) *Globalization and the Politics of Development in the Middle East*. New York: Cambridge University Press.

Houtart, François and François Polet (eds.) (2001) *The Other Davos: The Globalization of Resistance to the World Economic System*. New York: Zed Books.

Huffington, Arianna (2003) *Pigs at the Trough: How Corporate Greed and Political Corruption are Undermining America*. New York: Crown Publishers.

Huntington, Samuel (1996) *The Clash of Civilizations and the Remaking of the World Order*. New York: Simon and Schuster.

Hurrel, Andrew and Ngaire Woods (eds.) (1999) *Inequality, Globalization, and World Politics*. Oxford: Oxford University Press.

Inglehart, Ronald (ed.) (2003) *Human Values and Social Change: Findings from the Values Surveys*. Leiden: Brill.

Issawi, Charles (1995) *The Middle East Economy: Decline and Recovery: Selected Essays*. Princeton: Princeton University Press.

al-Jabari, Muhammad 'Abed (1997) *Qadaya fi al-fikr al-mu'asir* (*Issues in Contemporary Thought*). Beirut: Center for the Study of Arab Unity.

—— (1998) "al-'Awlamah wa-al-huwiyyah al-thaqafiyyah: 'Ashara Atruhat," in al-Khawli (ed.), *al-'Arab wal-al-'awlama*.

Jameson, Frederic and Masao Miyoshi (eds.) (1998) *The Cultures of Globalization*. Durham, N.C.: Duke University Press.

Johnson, Chalmers (2004) *The Sorrows of Empire: Militarism, Secrecy and the End of the Republic*. New York: Metropolitan Books.

Katsiaficas, George (2001) "Seattle Was Not the Beginning," in Yuen et al. (eds.), *The Battle of Seattle*, pp. 29–35.

Kepel, Gilles (1997) *Allah in the West: Islamic Movements in America and Western Europe*. Trans. Susan Milner. Cambridge and New York: Polity Press.

al-Khawli, Usana Amin (ed.) (1998) *al-'Arab wal-al-'awlama*. Beirut: Markaz al-Dirasat al-Wahda al-'Arabiyya.

Kian, Azadeh (1995) "L'invasion culturelle occidentale: mythe ou realité." *Cahiers d'études sur al Méditerranée orientale e le monde turco-iranien*, 20, July–December, pp. 72–90.

Klare, Michael (2001) *Resource Wars: The New Landscape of Global Conflict*. New York: Metropolitan Books.

Klein, Naomi (1999) *No Logo: Taking Aim at the Brand Bullies*. New York: Picador Press.

—— (2004) "Baghdad Year Zero." *Harper's Magazine*, September.

Korten, David (1995) *When Corporations Rule the World*. West Hartford, Conn.: Kumarian Press.

Laïdi, Zaki (1997) *Malaise dans le mondialisation*. Paris: Les Éditions Textuel.

Lamchichi, Abderrahim (2000) *Islam-Occident, Islam-Europe: choc des civilisations ou coexistence des cultures*. Paris: L'Harmattan.

Lapham, Lewis (2004) "Dar al-Harb." *Harper's Magazine*, March.

Lasn, Kalle (1999) *Culture Jam: How to Reverse America's Suicidal Consumer Binge – And Why we Must*. New York: Eagle Brook.

Le Goff, Jean-Pierre (1998) *Mai 68: L'héritage impossible*. Paris: Éditions La Decouverte.

Lerner, Michael (1996) *The Politics of Meaning: Restoring Hope in an Age of Cynicism*. New York: Addison Wesley.

—— (2002) *Spirit Matters*. Charlottesville, N.C.: Hamptons Road.

LeVine, Mark (1995a) "At What Cost? The Rhetoric of Security in Zionist and Israeli Political Discourse," MA thesis, Dept. of Near Eastern Studies, NYU.

—— (1995b) "The Discourse of Development in Mandate Palestine." *Arab Studies Quarterly*, Winter, pp. 95–120.

—— (2002a) "The Arab Human Development Report: A Critique." *MERIP Press Information Note*, No. 10, 2002, http://merip.org/pins/pin101.html.

—— (2002b) "A Comparative Analysis of the Political Economies and Ideologies Underlying the Emergence of the Palestinian Hamas and the Algerian FIS," Workshop on Socio-Religious Movements and the Transformation of Political Community: Israel, Palestine, & Beyond, UCI, October 2002.

—— (2002c) "Globalization in the Middle East and North Africa: Conflicting Narratives of Growth, Inequality and Integration." Robert Schuman Centre for Advanced Studies, European University Institute, Florence, Italy, Working Paper series.

—— (2003a) "'Human Nationalisms' versus 'Inhuman Globalisms': Cultural Economies of Globalization and the Re-Imagining of Muslim Identities in Europe and the Middle East" in Stefano Allievi and Jorgen Nielsen (eds.), *Muslim Networks and Transnational Communities in and Across Europe*, Leiden: Brill.

—— (2003b) "The Peace Movement Plans for the Future." *MERIP Online*, July 2003, http://www.merip.org/mero/interventions/levine_interv.html.

—— (2004a) "Cash for Chaos: Mark LeVine's Spring Break in Falluja." *OC Weekly*, April, 16–22.

—— (2004b) "Seeing Iraq Through the Globalization Lens." *Christian Science Monitor*, April 5.

—— (2004c) "Whose Chaos is it Anyway?" Nation Institute/Tomdispatch.com, April.

—— (2005) *Overthrowing Geography: Jaffa, Tel Aviv and the Struggle for Palestine, 1880–1948*. Berkeley: University of California Press.

LeVine, Mark, Pilar Perez and Viggo Mortensen (eds.) (2003) *Twilight of Empire: Responses to Occupation*, Los Angeles: Perceval Press.

LeVine, Mark and Armando Salvatore (eds.) (2005) *Religion, Social Practice, and Contested Hegemonies: Reconstructing Muslim Public Spheres*. Oxford: Palgrave.

Lewis, Bernard (2003) *What Went Wrong? The Clash Between Islam and Modernity in the Middle East*. New York: Perennial Books.

Losson, Christian and Paul Quinio (2002) *Génération Seattle: Les rebels de la mondialisation*. Paris: Éditions Grasset.

Lundberg, Mattias and Lyn Squire (1999) "The Simultaneous Evolution of Growth and Inequality." World Bank, Research Report, December.

Mamdani, Mahmood (2004) *Good Muslim, Bad Muslim: America, the Cold War and the Roots of Terror*. New York: Pantheon Books.

Mamère, Noël and Olivier Warin (1999) *Non merci, Oncle Sam! (No thanks, Uncle Sam!)*. Paris: Éditions Ramsay.

Manji, Irshad (2004) *The Trouble with Islam: A Muslim's Call for Reform of Her Faith*. New York: St. Martin's Press.

Marshall, Joshua Micah (2004) "Power Rangers: Did the Bush Administration Create a New American Empire – or Weaken the Old One?" *The New Yorker*, February 2.

Masson, Paul (2001) "Globalization: Facts and Figures," IMF Policy Discussion Paper, 10/01, PDP 01/4, http://www.imf.org/external/pubs/ft/pdp/2001/pdp04.pdf.

McQuaig, Linda (2004) "Crude Dudes," *Toronto Star*, September 20.

Mealer, Bryan (2004) "Dying for Dollars: Are You Ready for the Iraqi Gold Rush?" *Harper's Magazine*, October, pp. 62–70.

Memmi, Albert (1991) [1965] *The Colonizer and the Colonized*. Boston: Beacon Press.

Mendis, D.L.O. (ed.) (2000) *WTO Globalization and Eppawala After Seattle: A Collection of Essays*. Kandy and Colombo, Sri Lanka: Sri Lanka Pugwash Group.

Mertes, Tom (ed.) (2004) *A Movement of Movements: Is Another World Really Possible?* London: Verso.

Mir-Hosseini, Ziba (1999) *Islam and Gender: The Religious Debate in Contemporary Iran*. Princeton: Princeton University Press.

Mitchell, Tim (1991) "America's Egypt," *MERIP*, 169.

Monbiot, George (2004) "An Answer in Somerset: The Age of Entropy is Here. We Should All Now be Learning How to Live Without Oil." *The Guardian*, August 24.

Mouawad, Jad (2004) "Irrelevant? OPEC is Sitting Pretty," New York *Times*, Week in Review, October 3.

Müller, Manfred Julius (2002) *Anti-Globalisierung. Zurück zur Vernunft! Das Ende eines Irrweges (Anti-Globalization: Back to Reason! The End of Daring)*. Norderstedt: BoD GmbH.

al-Musari, Kemal al-Din 'Abd al-Ghana (1999) *al-'Almaniyyah wa-'l-'awlamah wa-'l-Azhar*. Cairo: Dar al-Mu'rifa al-jana'iyyah.

Nabli, Mustapha (1997) "The Fiscal Dimension of the European-Mediterranean Challenge." World Bank, Mediterranean Development Forum I: Towards Competitive and Caring Societies in the Middle East and North Africa, Marrakech, Morocco, May 12–17.

National Commission on Terrorist Attacks Upon the United States (2004) *The 911 Commission Report*. New York: W.W. Norton and Co.

Nazpary, Joma (2002) *Post-Soviet Chaos: Violence and Dispossession in Kazakhstan*. London: Pluto Press.

Nitzan, Jonathan and Shimshon Bichler (2003) *The Global Political Economy of Israel*. London: Pluto Press.

Notes from Nowhere (eds.) (2003) *We Are Everywhere: The Irresistible Rise of Global Anticapitalism*, London: Verso.

Ocampo, José Antonio and Juan Martin (eds.) (2002) *Globalization and Development*. New York: World Bank.

Osterhammel, Jürgen and Niels P. Petersson (2003) *Geschichte der Globalisierung (The History of Globalization)*. Berlin: 128 Seiten.

Owen, Roger (ed.) (1982) *Studies in the Economic and Social History of*

Palestine in the Nineteenth and Twentieth Centuries. Oxford: Oxford University Press.

Page, John and Linda van Gelder (2002) "Globalization, Growth, and Poverty Reduction in the Middle East and North Africa, 1970–1999." The World Bank, March 15.

Pamuk, Şevket (1987) *The Ottoman Empire and European Capitalism, 1820–1913.* Cambridge: Cambridge University Press.

—— (2000) *Istanbul ve Diger Kentlerde: 500 yillik Fiyatlar ve ücretler, 1469–1998 (500 Years of Prices and Wages in Istanbul and Other Cities).* Ankara: State Institute of Statistics.

Pamuk, Şevket and Jeffrey Williamson (eds.) (2000) *The Mediterranean Response to Globalization Before 1950.* London: Routledge.

Penslar, Derick (1991) *Zionism and Technocracy: The Engineering of Jewish Settlement in Palestine, 1870–1918.* Bloomington: Indiana University Press.

Peters, Tom (1998) *Thriving on Chaos: Handbook for a Management Revolution.* New York: Knopf.

Pierson, Paul (1999) "Post-Industrial Pressures on the Mature Welfare State," *Globalization, European Economic Integration and Social Protection.* Conference held at the European University Institute, March 11–12.

Pogge, Thomas W. and Sanjay G. Reddy (2003) "Unknown: The Extent, Distribution, and Trend of Global Income Poverty," Version 3.4, July 26, http://blog.ctrlbreak.co.uk/archives/000035.html.

Polanyi, Karl (1947) *The Great Transformation.* Boston: Beacon Press.

Pomeranz, Kenneth (2000) *The Great Divergence: China, Europe, and the Making of the Modern World Economy.* Princeton: Princeton University Press.

Ponce de León, Juana (ed.) (2001) *Our Word is our Weapon: Selected Writings of Subcommandante Insurgente Marcos.* New York: Seven Stories Press.

Qureshi, Emran and Michael A. Sells (eds.) (2003) *The New Crusades: Constructing the Muslim Enemy.* New York: Columbia University Press.

Qutb, Sayyid (1993) *Ma'araka al-Islam wa-al-Rasma'liyyah (The Battle between Islam and Capitalism).* Cairo: Dar al-Shuruq.

Ramadan, Tariq (1999) *To Be a European Muslim.* Leicester: UK Islamic Foundation.

—— (2003) *Globalization: Muslim Resistances.* Paris: Tawhid.

Ramadan, Tariq and Alain Gresh (2002) *L'Islam en questions (Islam in Question).* Paris: Actes Sud.

Ritzer, George (1999) *Enchanting a Disenchanted World: Revolutionizing the Means of Consumption.* Thousand Oaks: Pine Forge Press.

Rodrik, Dani (1997) "Globalization, Social Conflict and Economic Growth." Unpublished article. December 11, 1997, www.ksg.harvard.edu/rodrik/global.pdf.

Sachs, Jeffrey (2004) "Don't Know, Should Care," *Los Angeles Times,* Op/Ed, June 5.

Sader, Emir (2002) "Beyond Civil Society: the Left after Porto Alegre," *New Left Review,* 17, September/October.

Sadowski, Yahya (1998) *The Myth of Global Chaos.* Washington, D.C.: Brookings Institution.

Safi, Omid (ed.) (2003) *Progressive Muslims: On Justice, Gender and Pluralism.* Oxford: Oneworld Publications.

Sarkozy, Nicolas (2004) *La République, les religions, l'espérance.* Paris: Cerf.

Schmidt, Helmut (1999) *Globalisierung (Globalization).* Berlin: Goldmann.

Scholch, Alexander (1993) *Palestine in Transformation, 1856–1882: Studies* in Social, Economic and Political Development. Trans. William C. Young and Michael C. Gerrity. Washington: Institute for Palestine Studies.

Shafir, Gershon (1995) *Land, Labor, and the Origins of the Israeli–Palestinian Conflict, 1882–1914*. New York: Cambridge University Press.

Shafir, Gershon and Yoav Peled (2003) *Being Israeli: The Dynamics of Multiple Citizenship*. Cambridge: Cambridge University Press.

Shariati, ʿAli (1979) *On the Sociology of Islam*. Trans. Hamid Algar. Berkeley: Mizan Press.

Simons, Geoff (1994) *Iraq: From Sumer to Saddam*. London: Macmillan.

Smith, Jackie and Frank Johnston (eds.) (2002) *Globalization and Resistance: Transnational Dimensions of Social Movements*. New York: Rowman and Littlefield.

Soroush, Abdel Karim (2000) *Reason, Freedom, and Democracy in Islam*. Trans. Mahmoud and Ahmad Sadri. Oxford: Oxford University Press.

Starhawk (2002) *Webs of Power: Notes from the Global Uprising*. Gabriola Island, BC: New Society Publishers.

Starr, Amory (2000) *Naming the Enemy: Anti-Corporate Movements Confront Globalization*. London: Zed Books.

Stiglitz, Joseph (2002) *Globalization and its Discontents*. New York: W.W. Norton.

Strong, Josiah (1885) *Our Country: Its Possible Future and its Present Crisis*. New York: The American Home Missionary Society.

Thami, Amine (1998) "Taʿaddudiyya and Islamism: Lessons from Algeria," in May Jayyusi (ed.), *Liberation, Democratization, and Transitions to Statehood in the Third World*. Ramallah: Muwatin Press, pp. 143–69.

Tomkins, Richard (2004) "Christ Replaces Coke as the Focus of Youthful Longing," *Financial Times*, July 30.

Tomlinson, John (1999) *Globalization and Culture*. Chicago: University of Chicago Press.

UNDP (2002) *Arab Human Development Report*. New York: United Nations Development Program.

—— (2004) *Human Development Report, 2004: Cultural Liberty in Today's Diverse World*, New York: UNDP.

UNESCO (1994) *The Futures of Cultures*. Paris: United Nations Educational, Scientific and Cultural Organization.

—— (1995) *Our Creative Diversity: Report of the World Commission on Culture and Development*. Paris: United Nations Educational, Scientific and Cultural Organization.

United States Space Command (n.d.) *Vision 2020*, http://www.fas/org/spp/ military/docops/usspac/visbook.pdf.

UNRISD (1995) *States of Disarray: The Social Effects of Globalization*. Geneva: United Nations Research Institute for Social Development.

Volkov, Vadim (2002) *Violent Entrepreneurs: The Use of Force in the Making of Russian Capitalism*. Ithaca: Cornell University Press.

Waters, Malcolm (1995) *Globalization*. New York: Routledge.

Williams, Raymond (1985) *Keywords: A Vocabulary of Culture and Society*. New York: Oxford University Press.

Williamson, Jeffrey (1996) "Globalization, Convergence, and History," *Journal of Economic History*, 56, 2, pp. 277–306.

Woodward, Bob (2004) *Plan of Attack*. New York: Simon and Schuster.

World Bank (1995) *Will Arab Workers Prosper or Be Left Out in the Twenty-first Century?* Washington, D.C.: The World Bank.

—— (1997) "Global Changes and What They Mean for the Development Strategies of the Middle East and

North Africa." Mediterranean Development Forum I: Towards Competitive and Caring Societies in the Middle East and North Africa. Marrakech, Morocco, May 12–17.

—— (2001) *World Development Report 2000/2001: Attacking Poverty*. New York: Oxford University Press.

—— (2002) *Globalization, Growth, and Poverty*. Washington, D.C.: World Bank.

—— (Various years) *Annual Reports for Middle East and North Africa*.

—— (n.d.) "Overview: Creating 100 Million Jobs for a Fast-Growing Work Force," http://lnweb18.worldbank.org/mna/mena.nsf/Attachments/EmploymentOverview/$File/ Employment-overview.pdf.

World Trade Organization (2001) *Statistics on Globalization*. Washington, D.C.: WTO, 2001.

Wright, Lawrence (2004) "The Kingdom of Silence," *The New Yorker*, January 5.

Yassin, al-Said (1999) *al-'Awlamah wa-al-tariq al-thalathah* (*Globalization and the Third Way*). Cairo: Mirit lil-nashar wa-al-mu'alumat.

Yavuz, Hakan (1999) "The Search for a New Social Contract in Turkey: Fethullah Gülen, the Virtue Party and the Kurds." *SAIS Review*, 19.1, pp. 114–143.

—— (2003) *Islamic Political Identity in Turkey*. Oxford: Oxford University Press.

Yuen, Eddie, George Katsiaficas, and Daniel Burton Rose (eds.) (2001) *The Battle of Seattle: The New Challenge to Capitalist Globalization*. New York: Soft Skull Press.

Zakaria, Fareed (2003) *The Future of Freedom: Illiberal Democracy and Home and Abroad*. New York: W.W. Norton.

Zaqzuq, Mahmud Hamdi (2001) *Islam fi 'asr al-'awlamah* (*Islam in the Age of Globalization*). Cairo: Maktab al-Sharuq.

Zinn, Howard (1980) *A People's History of the United States*. New York: Harper and Row.

Index